PHILIP'S

STREET ATLAS
North
Yorkshire

First published in 2002 by

Philip's, a division of
Octopus Publishing Group Ltd
2-4 Heron Quays, London E14 4JP

Second edition 2005
First impression 2005
NYOBA

ISBN-10   0-540-08765-3 (pocket)
ISBN-13   978-0-540-08765-5 (pocket)

© Philip's 2005

OS Ordnance Survey®

This product includes mapping data licensed from
Ordnance Survey® with the permission of the
Controller of Her Majesty's Stationery Office.
© Crown copyright 2005. All rights reserved.
Licence number 100011710.

Contents

III	**Key to map symbols**
IV	**Key to map pages**
VI	**Route planning**
X	**Administrative and Postcode boundaries**
1	**Street maps** at 1⅓ inches to 1 mile
208	**Street maps** at 2⅔ inches to 1 mile
233	**Street map of York city centre** at 5⅓ inches to 1 mile
234	**Index** of towns and villages
238	**Index** of streets, hospitals, industrial estates, railway stations, schools, shopping centres, universities and places of interest

y mapping found in this atlas is available as digital data in TIFF
tible to other bitmapped (raster) image formats.

digital form as a standard database table. It contains all the details
ther with the National Grid reference for the map square in which

iscuss your requirements, please contact Philip's on
n@philips-maps.co.uk

D1464995

Symbol	Description
(22a)	**Motorway** with junction number
	Primary route – dual/single carriageway
	A road – dual/single carriageway
	B road – dual/single carriageway
	Minor road – dual/single carriageway
	Other minor road – dual/single carriageway
	Road under construction
	Tunnel, covered road
	Rural track, private road or narrow road in urban area
	Gate or obstruction to traffic (restrictions may not apply at all times or to all vehicles)
	Path, bridleway, byway open to all traffic, road used as a public path
	Pedestrianised area
DY7	**Postcode boundaries**
	County and unitary authority boundaries
	Railway, tunnel, railway under construction
	Tramway, tramway under construction
	Miniature railway
Walsall	**Railway station**
	Private railway station
South Shields	**Metro station**
	Tram stop, tram stop under construction
	Bus, coach station

Symbol	Description
◆	**Ambulance station**
◆	**Coastguard station**
◆	**Fire station**
◆	**Police station**
✚	**Accident and Emergency entrance to hospital**
H	**Hospital**
✛	**Place of worship**
i	**Information Centre** (open all year)
🛒	**Shopping Centre**
P P&R	**Parking, Park and Ride**
PO	**Post Office**
△ ⌂	**Camping site, caravan site**
►	**Golf course**
✕	**Picnic site**
Prim Sch	**Important buildings, schools, colleges, universities and hospitals**
	Built up area
	Woods
River Ouse	**Tidal water, water name**
	Non-tidal water – lake, river, canal or stream
‹ ▷ ⊃ ⊂	**Lock, weir, tunnel**
Church	**Non-Roman antiquity**
ROMAN FORT	**Roman antiquity**
87	**Adjoining page indicators and overlap bands**
246	The colour of the arrow and the band indicates the scale of the adjoining or overlapping page (see scales below)

Enlarged mapping only

Symbol	Description
	Railway or bus station building
	Place of interest
	Parkland

Acad	**Academy**	Inst	**Institute**	Recn Gd	**Recreation Ground**
Allot Gdns	**Allotments**	Ct	**Law Court**		
Cemy	**Cemetery**	L Ctr	**Leisure Centre**	Resr	**Reservoir**
C Ctr	**Civic Centre**	LC	**Level Crossing**	Ret Pk	**Retail Park**
CH	**Club House**	Liby	**Library**	Sch	**School**
Coll	**College**	Mkt	**Market**	Sh Ctr	**Shopping Centre**
Crem	**Crematorium**	Meml	**Memorial**	TH	**Town Hall/House**
Ent	**Enterprise**	Mon	**Monument**	Trad Est	**Trading Estate**
Ex H	**Exhibition Hall**	Mus	**Museum**	Univ	**University**
Ind Est	**Industrial Estate**	Obsy	**Observatory**	W Twr	**Water Tower**
IRB Sta	**Inshore Rescue Boat Station**	Pal	**Royal Palace**	Wks	**Works**
		PH	**Public House**	YH	**Youth Hostel**

■ The small numbers around the edges of the maps identify the 1 kilometre National Grid lines
■ The dark grey border on the inside edge of some pages indicates that the mapping does not continue onto the adjacent page

The scale of the maps on the pages numbered in blue is 4.2 cm to 1 km • 2⅔ inches to 1 mile • 1: 23810

0   ¼   ½   ¾   1 mile
0   250m   500m   750m   1 kilometre

The scale of the maps on pages numbered in green is 2.1 cm to 1 km • 1⅓ inches to 1 mile • 1: 47620

0   ¼   ½   ¾   1 mile
0   250m 500m 750m 1 kilometre

The scale of the maps on pages numbered in red is 8.4 cm to 1 km • 5⅓ inches to 1 mile • 1: 11900

0   220 yards   440 yards   660 yards   ½ mile
0   125m   250m   375m   ½ kilometre

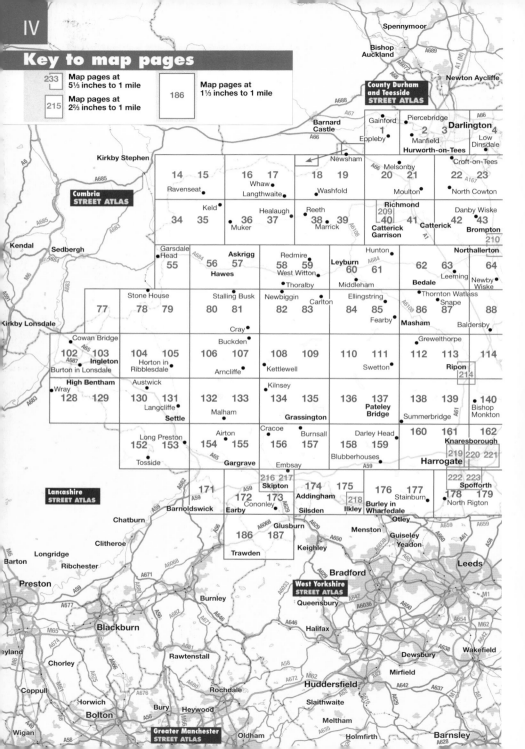

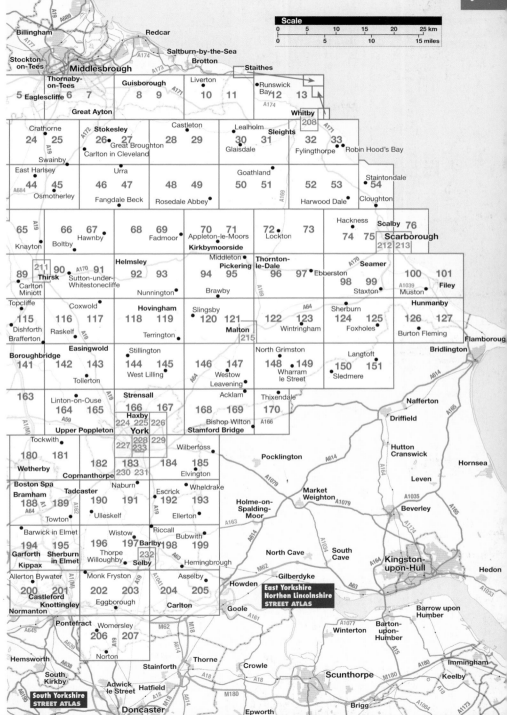

Route Planning

Scale

0	5	10	15 km
0		5	10 miles

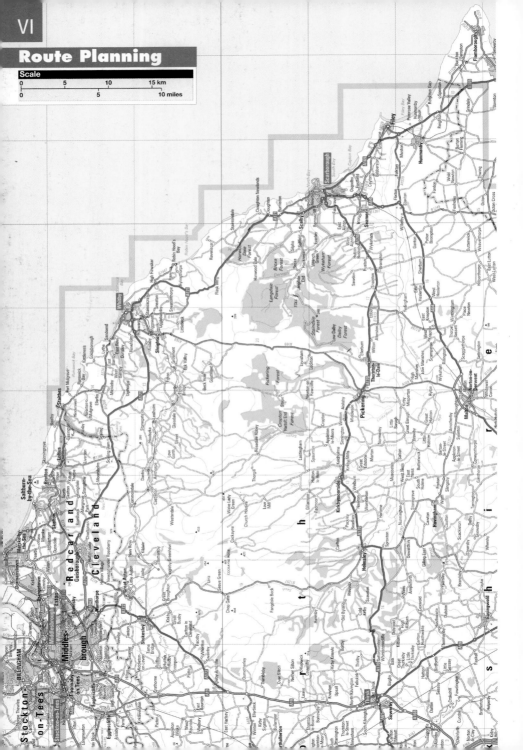

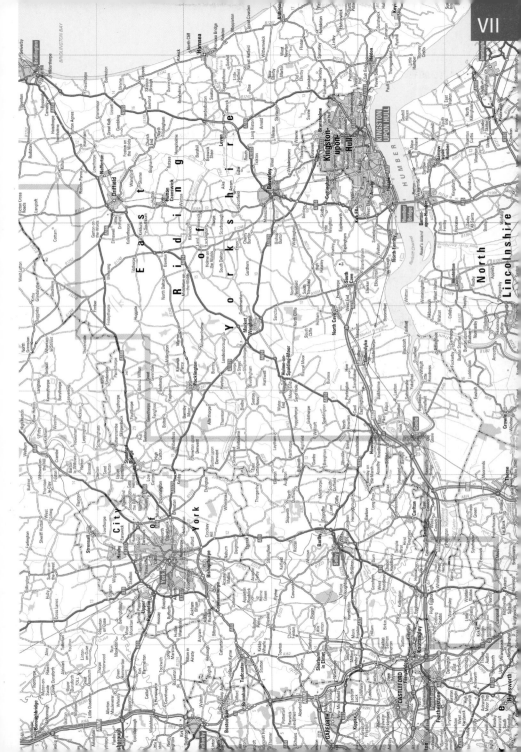

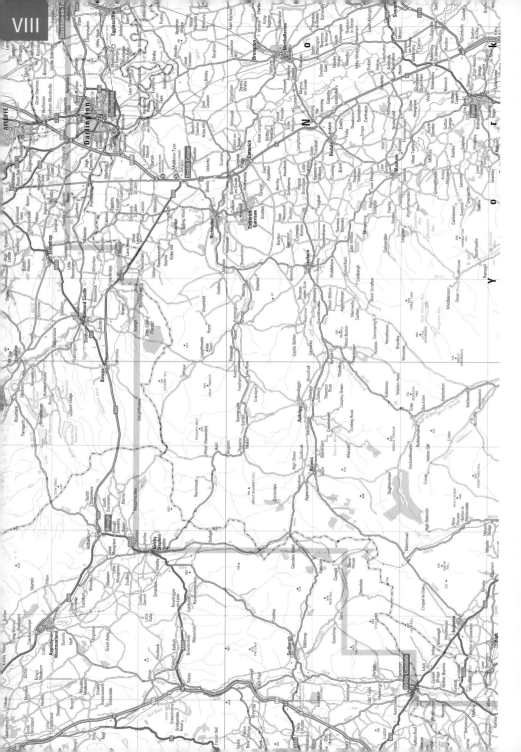

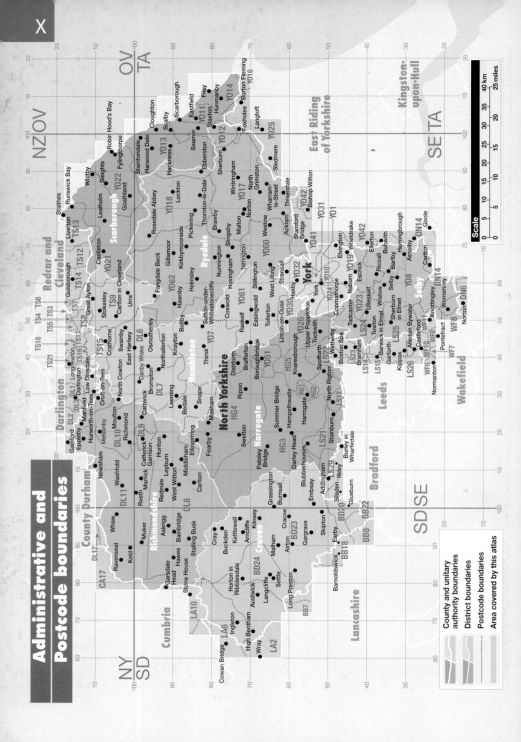

Administrative and Postcode boundaries

Scale

0	5	10	15	20	25	30	35	40 km
0	5	10	15	20	25 miles			

County and unitary authority boundaries

District boundaries

Postcode boundaries

Area covered by this atlas

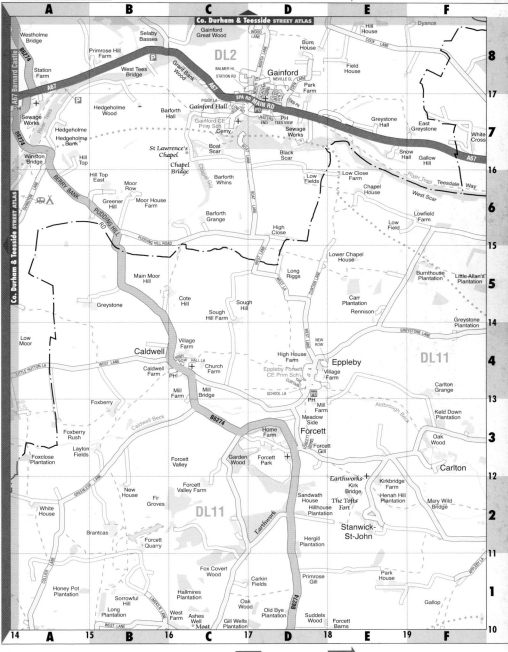

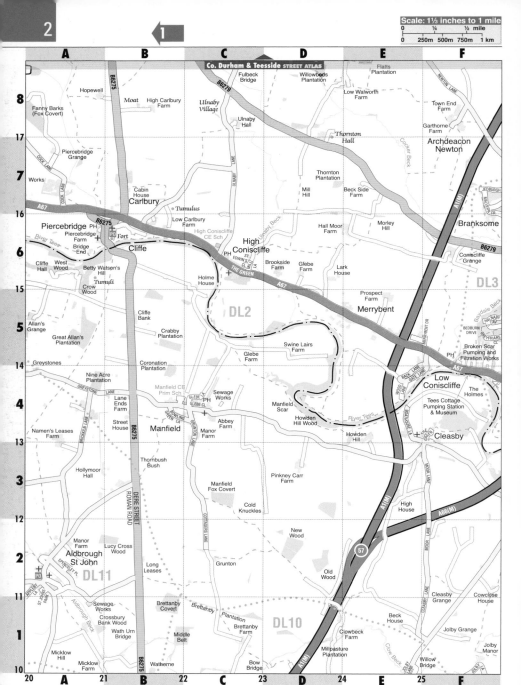

Scale: 1⅓ inches to 1 mile

0   ¼   ½ mile
0   250m 500m 750m 1 km

Co. Durham & Teesside STREET ATLAS

A **B** **C** **D** **E** **F**

8
Hopewell
Moat
High Carlbury Farm
Ulnaby Village
Fulbeck Bridge
Willowbeds Plantation
Flatts Plantation
Low Walworth Farm
Town End Farm
Fanny Barks (Fox Covert)
Ulnaby Hall
Garthorne Farm

17
Piercebridge Grange
Thornton Hall
Cocker Beck
Archdeacon Newton

7
Works
Cabin House
Thornton Plantation
Mill Hill
Beck Side Farm
JEDBURGH
MALVERN CR

16
A67
B6275
Carlbury
Tumulus
Low Carlbury Farm
High Coniscliffe CE Sch
Hall Moor Farm
Morley Hill
Branksome
B6279

Piercebridge PH
B6275
Fort
High Coniscliffe
Conscliffe Grange

6
Piercebridge Farm
Bridge End
Cliffe
PH
ST EDWIN'S
MILL LA
THE GREEN
Brookside Farm
Glebe Farm
Lark House
DL3

Cliffe Hall
West Wood
Betty Watson's Hill
Holme House
A67
Prospect Farm
Baydale Beck

15
Crow Wood
Tumuli
Merrybent
HALNABY AV

5
Allan's Grange
Cliffe Bank
Crabby Plantation
Swine Lairs Farm
DL2
BEDBURN DRIVE
CYFRIARS

Great Allan's Plantation
Coronation Plantation
Glebe Farm
PH
Broken Scar Pumping and Filtration Works

14
Greystones
Nine Acre Plantation
Manfield CE Prim Sch
Sewage Works
BACK LANE
GATE LANE
Low Coniscliffe

4
GREYSTONE LANE
Lane Ends Farm
GLEBE GLEBE CL
PH
Manfield Scar
Howden Hill Wood
WOOL LANE
Tees Cottage Pumping Station & Museum
The Holmes

Namen's Leases Farm
Street House
B6275
GREEN LA
BRUNTON LANE
Manfield
Abbey Farm
Manor Farm
Howden Hill
River Tees
BLACKWELL CX
Cleasby

13
Hollymoor Hall
Thornbush Bush

3
ROMAN ROAD
DERE STREET
Manfield Fox Covert
Pinkney Carr Farm
MOOR LANE

12
Manor Farm
Lucy Cross Wood
Cold Knuckles
New Wood
High House
A66(M)
A1(M)

2
Aldbrough St John
DL11
Long Leases
Grunton
57
Old Wood
Cleasby Grange
Cowclose House

11
PO
ST JOHNS PARK
Sewage Works
Brettanby Covert
Brettanby
Plantation
Beck House
Jolby Grange

Crossbury Bank Wood
Brettanby Farm
DL10

1
Micklow Hill
Wath Urn Bridge
Middle Belt
Clowbeck Farm
Willow Bridge
Jolby Manor

Aldbrough Beck
Millpasture Plantation

10
Micklow Farm
Watherne
Bow Bridge
A1(M)
Clow Beck

20 **A** **21** **B** **22** **C** **23** **D** **24** **E** **25** **F**

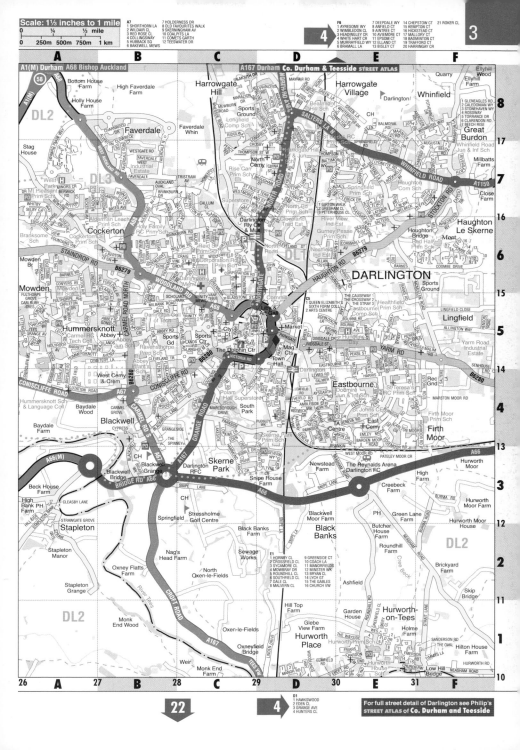

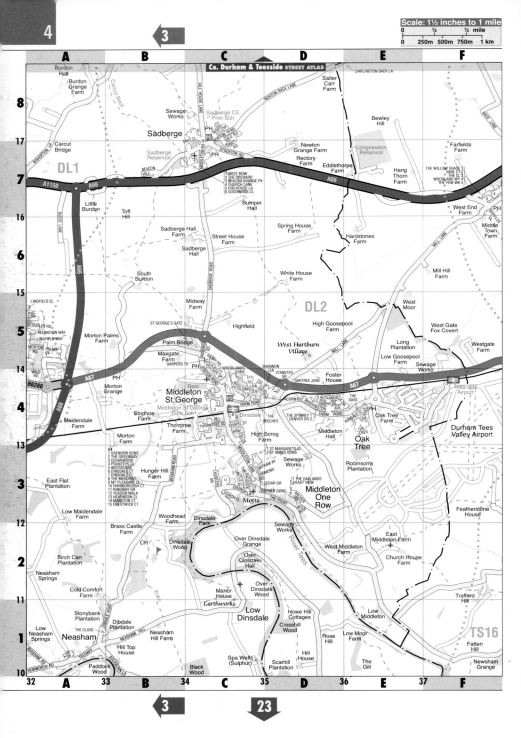

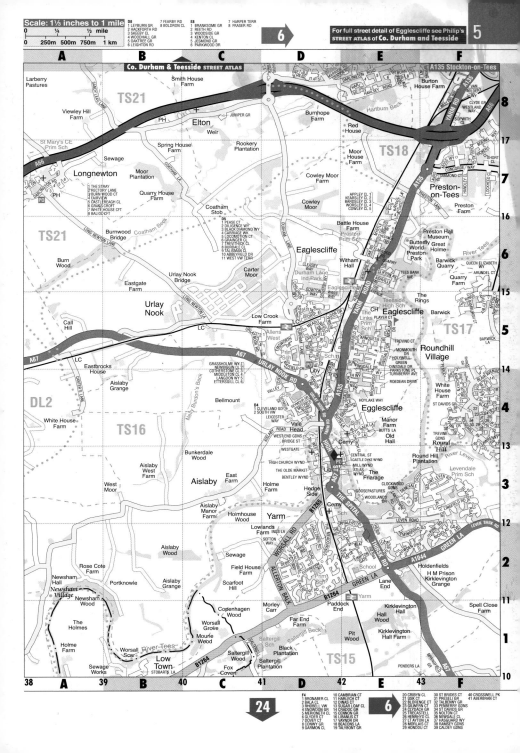

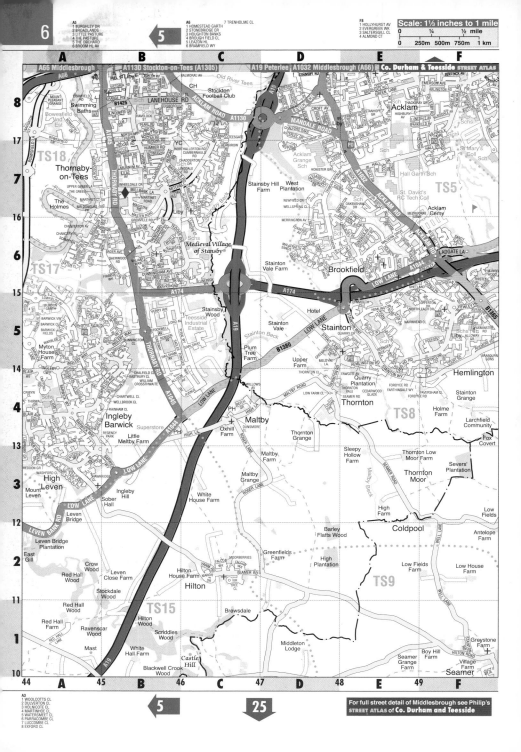

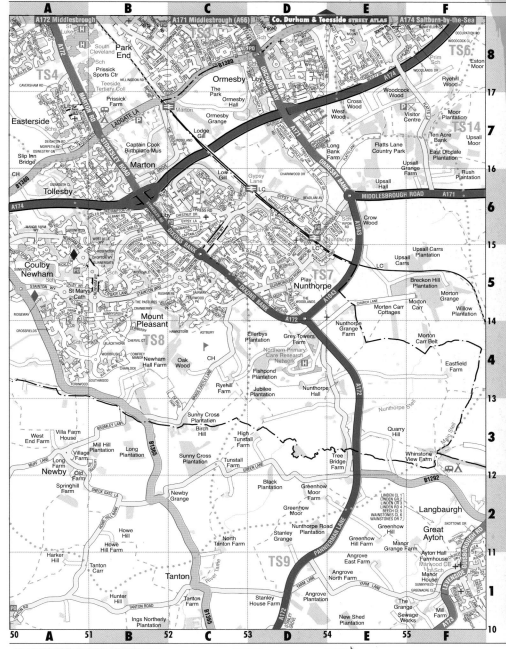

Scale: 1⅓ inches to 1 mile

0   ¼   ½ mile

0   250m   500m   750m   1 km

B6
1 THE WICKETS
2 MEMORIAL DR
3 CLEVELAND DR

7

A172 Middlesbrough   A171 Middlesbrough (A66)   Co. Durham & Teesside STREET ATLAS   A174 Saltburn-by-the-Sea

A B C D E F

8

St Lukes
Park End
South Cleveland Sch
Prissick Sports Ctr
Teeside Tertiary Coll
TS4
Easterside
Caversham Rd
Prissick Farm
TS3
Ormesby
The Park
Ormesby Hall
Ormesby Grange
Lodge Gill
Low Gill
Roseland Dr
Marton
TS6
Eston Moor
Ryehill Wood
Cross Wood
West Wood
Woodcock Wood
Visitor Centre
Moor Plantation
Ten Acre Bank
Upsall Moor
TS14

17

Captain Cook Birthplace Mus
Slip Inn Bridge
Deighton Rd
Morpeth Av
Oswestry Gn
Marton
The Grove
Long Bank Farm
Flatts Lane Country Park
Upsall Grange Farm
East Dibdale Plantation

7

Tollesby
A174
Sidmouth Cl
B1380
Dixons Bank
Gypsy Lane
Charnwood Dr
Beadlam Av
Ormesby Bank
Middlesbrough Road   A171
Upsall Hall
Rush Plantation

16

Cypress Rd
Chestnut Dr
Ripon Rd
A1043
Crow Wood
Nunthorpe

6

Coulby Newham
Sunnyside
St Marys Cath
Gate Lane
The Pastures
Cranberry
TS7
Play Nunthorpe
The Woodlands
Upsall Carrs Plantation
Upsall Carrs
Breckon Hill Plantation
Morton Grange
Willow Plantation

15

Mount Pleasant
TS8
Hawkstone
Astbury
Ellerbys Plantation
Grey Towers Farm
Morton Carr Cottages
Church Lane
Morton Carr
Morton Carr Belt

5

Newham Hall Farm
Oak Wood
CH
Fishpond Plantation
Northern Primary Care Research Network
H
Nunthorpe Hall
Nunthorpe Grange Farm
Eastfield Farm

14

Ryehill Farm
Jubilee Plantation
A172

4

Sunny Cross Plantation
Birch Hill
High Tunstall Farm
Nunthorpe Hall
Quarry Hill
Whinstone View Farm

13

West End Farm
Villa Farm House
Bromley Lane
Mill Hill Plantation
Long Plantation
B1365
Sunny Cross Plantation
Tunstall Farm
Green Lane
Black Plantation
Tree Bridge Farm
B1292

3

Newby
Springhill Farm
Village Farm
Old Farm
Long Farm
Sneck Gate La
Newby Grange
Greenhow Moor Farm
Greenhow Moor
Nunthorpe Road Plantation
Greenhow Hill
LINDEN CL 1
LINDEN GR 2
LINDEN DR 3
LINDEN RD 4
BEECH CL 5
WAINSTONES CL 6
WAINSTONES DR 7
Langbaurgh
Great Ayton
Skottowe Dr

12

Harker Hill
Howe Hill
Howe Hill Farm
North Tanton Farm
Stanley Grange
Greenhow Hill Farm
Manor Grange Farm
Angrove East Farm
Ayton Hall Farmhouse
Marwood CE Inf Sch
Manor House
Sunnyfield
Greenacre Cl

2

Tanton Carr
Tanton
TS9
Pannierman Lane
River Tame
Angrove North Farm
Yarm Lane
Angrove Plantation
The Grange
Mill Farm
A173

11

Hunter Hill
Tanton Road
Tanton Farm
Ings Northerly Plantation
B1365
Stanley House Farm
Stanley Grove
A172
New Shed Plantation
Sewage Works

10

50 A 51 B 52 C 53 D 54 E 55 F 10

For full street detail of Middlesbrough see Philip's STREET ATLAS of Co. Durham and Teesside

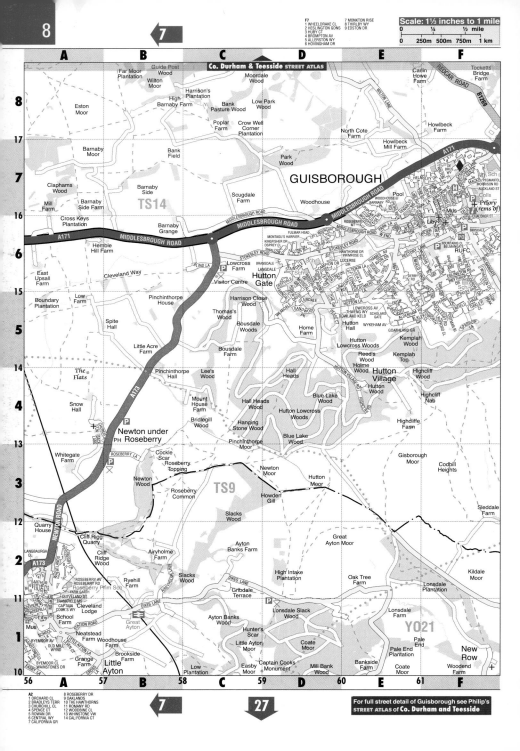

Scale: 1⅓ inches to 1 mile

0 ¼ ½ mile
0 250m 500m 750m 1 km

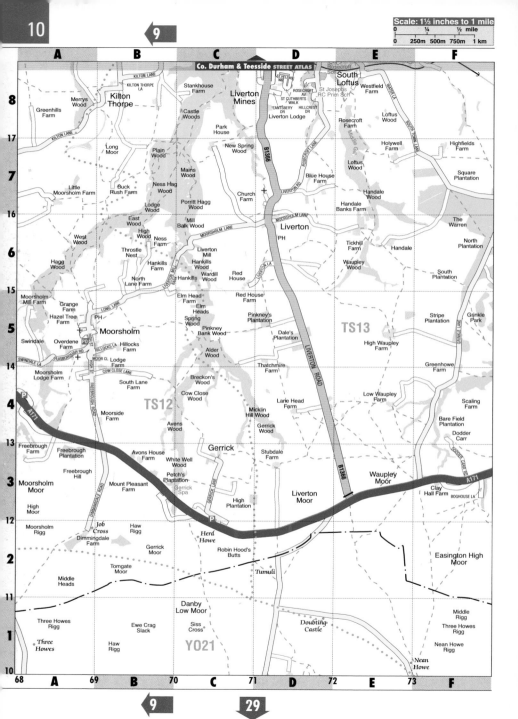

Co. Durham & Teesside STREET ATLAS

Kilton Lane
Kilton Thorpe La

Merrys Wood
Greenhills Farm
Kilton Thorpe
Stankhouse Farm
Castle Woods
Park House

8

Liverton Mines
St Helens
Rosecroft AV
St Cuthberts Walk
Cantsbery DR
Liverton Lodge
Hillcrest DR
South Loftus
Rosecroft
St Josephs RC Prim Sch
Westfield Farm
Loftus Wood

17

Kilton Lane
Long Moor
Plain Wood
New Spring Wood
B1366
Rosecroft Road
Rosecroft Wood
Holywell Farm
Highfields Farm

7

Little Moorsholm Farm
Buck Rush Farm
Mains Wood
Ness Hag Wood
Church Farm
Liverton Rd
Blue House Farm
Loftus Wood
Handale Wood
Square Plantation

Lodge Wood
Porritt Hagg Wood
Handale Banks Farm

16

East Wood
High Wood
Mill Balk Wood
Moorsholm Lane
Liverton
The Warren

West Wood
Ness Farm
Moorsholm Lane
PH
Tickhill Farm
Handale
North Plantation

6

Hagg Wood
Throstle Nest
Liverton Mill
Hankills Wood
Liverton La
Waupley Wood
South Plantation

North Lane Farm
Hankills Farm
Liverton Mill Rd
Hankills Wood
Wardill Wood
Red House

15

Moorsholm Mill Farm
Grange Farm
Hazel Tree Farm
Long Lane
Elm Head Farm
Elm Heads
Red House Farm

Swindale
Overdene Farm
PH
Moorsholm
Hillocks La
Hillocks Farm
Spring Wood
Pinkney Bank Wood
Pinkney's Plantation
Dale's Plantation
TS13
Stripe Plantation
Grinkle Park

5

Guisborough Rd
Moor Cl
Lodge Farm
Cow Close Lane
Alder Wood
High Waupley Farm
Greenhowe Farm

14

Swindale La
Moorsholm Lodge Farm
South Lane Farm
Breckon's Wood
Thatchmire Farm
Grinkle Lane

P
A171
TS12
Freebrough Road
Moorside Farm
Cow Close Wood
Liverton Road
Lane Head Farm
Low Waupley Farm
Scaling Dam
Bare Field Plantation

4

Avens Wood
Micklin Hill Wood
Gerrick Wood
Dodder Carr

Freebrough Farm
Freebrough Plantation
Avons House Farm
Gerrick
Stubdale Farm
Waupley Moor
Dodder Carr Rd

13

Freebrough Hill
White Well Wood
Petch's Plantation
B1366
Clay Hall Farm
A171
Boghouse La

3

Moorsholm Moor
Mount Pleasant Farm
Gerrick Spa
Liverton Moor

High Moor
Berrick Lane
High Plantation
P

12

Moorsholm Rigg
Job Cross
Dimmingdale Farm
Haw Rigg
Herd Howe

Gerrick Moor
Robin Hood's Butts
Easington High Moor

2

Middle Heads
Tomgate Moor
Tumuli

11

Three Howes Rigg
Ewe Crag Slack
Danby Low Moor
Siss Cross
Doubting Castle
Middle Rigg
Three Howes Rigg

1

Three Howes
Haw Rigg
Y021
Nean Howe Rigg
Nean Howe

10

68 A 69 B 70 C 71 D 72 E 73 F

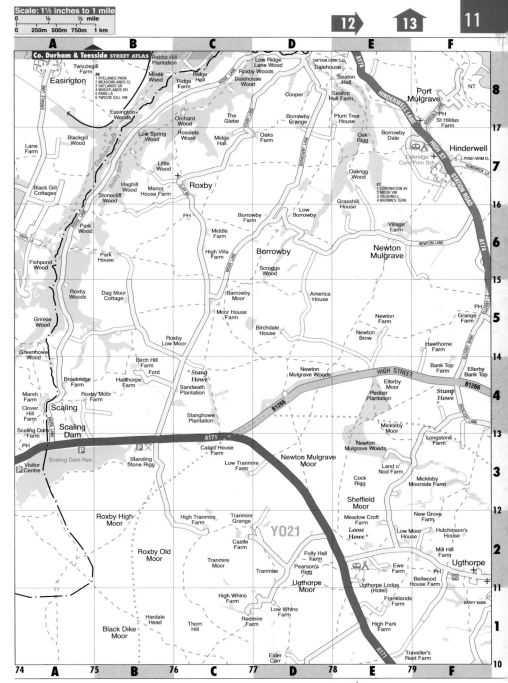

Co. Durham & Teesside STREET ATLAS

A B C D E F

8 17 **7** 16 **6** 15 **5** 14 **4** 13 **3** 12 **2** 11 **1** 10

Rabbit Hill Plantation

Twizziegill Farm

Easington

A8
1 RYELANDS PARK
2 MEADOWLANDS CL
3 OATLANDS GR
4 WHEATLANDS DR
5 PARK LA
6 TWIZZIE GILL VW

Mines Wood

Ridge Farm

Ridge Hall

Low Ridge Lane Wood

Roxby Woods

Dalehouse Wood

Dalehouse

CAPTAIN COOK'S CL

Seaton Hall

Cooper

Seaton Hall Farm

Plum Tree House

Port Mulgrave

NT

St Hildas Farm

PH

Easington Woods

Orchard Wood

The Glebe

Borrowby Grange

Oak Rigg

Borrowby Dale

Hinderwell

Blackgill Wood

Low Spring Wood

Rosslets Wood

Midge Hall

Oaks Farm

Oakridge Com Prim Sch

Pond Farm CL

RUNSWICK LA

Lane Farm

Little Wood

Oakrigg Wood

Village Farm

F7
1 CORONATION AV
2 MOOR VW
3 HILDEWELL TERR
4 BROWN'S TERR

Black Gill Cottages

Haghill Wood

Manor House Farm

Roxby

Grasshill House

Stonecliff Wood

PH

Borrowby Farm

Low Borrowby

Park Wood

Middle Farm

Village Farm

Newton Mulgrave

NEWTON LANE

Fishpond Wood

Park House

High Villa Farm

Borrowby

Scroggs Wood

Grinkle Wood

Roxby Woods

Dag Moor Cottage

Barrowby Moor

America House

Newton Farm

Grange Farm

PH

Moor House Farm

Newton Brow

Hawthorne Farm

Greenhowe Wood

Roxby Low Moor

Birchdale House

Bank Top Farm

Ellerby Bank Top

B1266

Birch Hill Farm

Ford

Stang Howe

Newton Mulgrave Woods

HIGH STREET

Stump Howe

Marsh Farm

Hailthorpe Farm

Roxby Moor Farm

Sandwath Plantation

Ellerby Moor

Pedoar Plantation

B1266

Clover Hill Farm

Scaling

Stanghowe Plantation

Mickleby Moor

Longstone Farm

Scaling Dam Farm

Scaling Dam

PH

A171

Calais House Farm

Standing Stone Rigg

Newton Mulgrave Moor

Newton Mulgrave Woods

Land o' Nod Farm

Mickleby Moorside Farm

Visitor Centre

Scaling Dam Res

Low Tranmire Farm

Cock Rigg

Sheffield Moor

Roxby High Moor

High Tranmire Farm

Tranmire Grange

Y021

Meadow Croft Farm

Loose Howe

New Grove Farm

Low Moor House

Hutchinson's House

Roxby Old Moor

Castle Farm

Tranmire Moor

Tranmire

Folly Hall Farm

Pearson's Rigg

Mill Hill Farm

Ugthorpe

PH

Hardale Head

High Whins Farm

Ugthorpe Moor

Ewe Farm

Bellwood House Farm

BARRY BANK

Black Dike Moor

Thorn Hill

Redmire Farm

Low Whins Farm

Ugthorpe Lodge (Hotel)

Franklands Farm

High Park Farm

Elder Carr

Traveller's Rest Farm

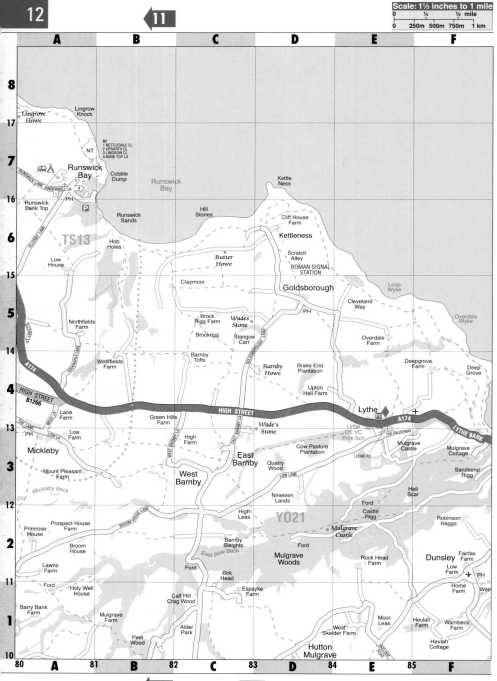

A7
1 NETTLEDALE CL
2 UPGARTH CL
3 LINGROW CL
4 BANK TOP LA

Lingrove Howe

Lingrow Knock

NT

Runswick Bay

Cobble Dump

Runswick Bay

Kettle Ness

RUNSWICK LANE
HINDERWELL LA

PH

P

Runswick Bank Top

Runswick Sands

Hill Stones

Cliff House Farm

Kettleness

TS13

ELLERBY LANE

Hob Holes

Scratch Alley

ROMAN SIGNAL STATION

Low House

Butter Howe

Claymoor

Goldsborough

Loop Wyke

Cleveland Way

Overdale Wyke

Northfields Farm

Brock Rigg Farm

Wades Stone

Brockrigg

Stangoe Carr

PH

Overdale Farm

ELLERBY LA

GOLDSBOROUGH LANE

Westfields Farm

Barnby Totts

Barnby Howe

Brake End Plantation

Deepgrove Farm

Deep Grove

A174

HIGH STREET
B1266

Lane Farm

Green Hills Farm

High Farm

Upton Hall Farm

Lythe

PO

A174

Deepgrove Farm

THE CAUSEWAY

LYTHE BANK

HIGH STREET

Wade's Stone

Lythe CE VC Prim Sch

WESTLA
THE LANE

PH

Low Farm

EAST BARNBY LA

WEST BARNBY LA

Mickleby

Mount Pleasant Farm

Mickleby Beck

Green Hills Farm

East Barnby

West Barnby

Cow Pasture Plantation

Quarry Wood

LOW LANE

Mulgrave Castle

LODGE RD

Mulgrave Cottage

Hell Scar

Sandsend Rigg

Prospect House Farm

Primrose House

Broom House

BROOM HOUSE LANE

High Leas

Barnby Sleights

East Row Beck

Nineteen Lands

YO21

Mulgrave Woods

Ford

Mulgrave Castle

Castle Rigg

Ford

Rock Head Farm

Robinson Haggs

Dunsley

Fairfax Farm

Low Farm

PH

Lawns Farm

Ford

Holy Well House

Calf Hill Crag Wood

Ford

Birk Head

Espsyke Farm

Home Farm

Weir

Barry Bank Farm

Mulgrave Farm

Peel Wood

Alder Park

West Skelder Farm

Moor Leas

SKELDER ROAD

Heulah Farm

Warnbeck Farm

Heulah Cottage

Hutton Mulgrave

80   81   82   83   84   85

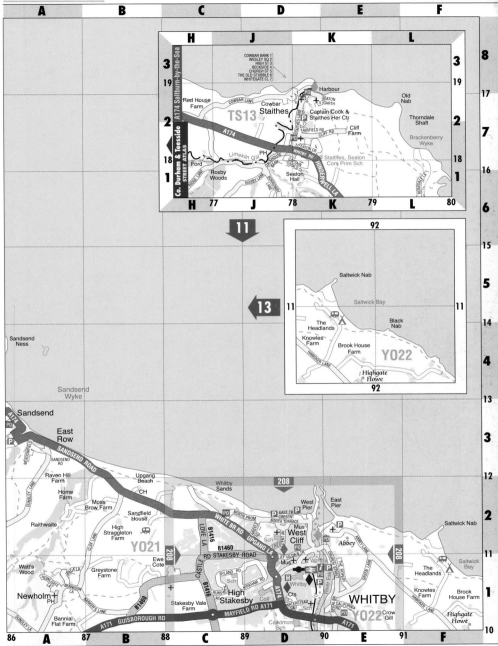

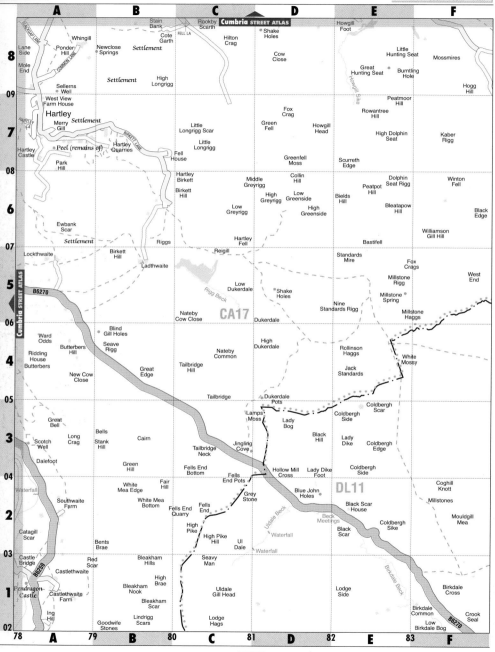

Cumbria STREET ATLAS

8

Whinghill
Lane Side
Ponder Hill
Newclose Springs
Settlement
Stain Bank
Cote Garth
Rookby Scarth
FELL LA
Hilton Crag
Shake Holes
Howgill Foot
Little Hunting Seat
Mossmires
Mole End
Great Hunting Seat
Burntling Hole

09

Sellerns Well
Settlement
High Longrigg
Hogg Hill
West View Farm House
Hartley
Merry Gill
Settlement
Peatmoor Hill

7

HARTLEY LA
Peel (remains of)
Hartley Quarries
BIRKETT LANE
Little Longrigg Scar
Little Longrigg
Fox Crag
Green Fell
Howgill Head
Rowantree Hill
High Dolphin Seat
Kaber Rigg
Hartley Castle
Fell House

08

Park Hill
Hartley Birkett
Birkett Hill
Middle Greyrigg
Collin Hill
Greenfell Moss
Scurreth Edge
Dolphin Seat Rigg
Winton Fell
Ewbank Scar
High Greyrigg
Low Greenside
Peatpot Hill
Bleatapow Hill

6

Low Greyrigg
High Greenside
Bields Hill
Black Edge
Settlement
Riggs
Hartley Fell
Williamson Gill Hill

07

Lockthwaite
Birkett Hill
Ladthwaite
Reigill
Bastifell
Standards Mire
Fox Crags
B6270
Millstone Rigg
West End

5

Rigg Beck
CA17
Low Dukerdale
Shake Holes
Nine Standards Rigg
Millstone Spring
Millstone Haggs

06

Nateby Cow Close
Dukerdale
Blind Gill Holes
Seave Rigg
High Dukerdale
Rollinson Haggs
White Mossy

4

Ward Odds
Butterbers Hill
Ridding House Butterbers
New Cow Close
Great Edge
Nateby Common
Tailbridge Hill
Jack Standards

05

Tailbridge
Dukerdale Pots
Coldbergh Scar
Lamps Moss
Lady Bog
Coldbergh Side

3

Great Bell
Scotch Well
Long Crag
Bells
Stank Hill
Cairn
Tailbridge Neck
Jingling Cove
Black Hill
Lady Dike
Coldbergh Edge

04

Dalefoot
Green Hill
Fells End Bottom
Fells End Pots
Hollow Mill Cross
Lady Dike Foot
Coldbergh Side

White Mea Edge
Fair Hill
Blue John Holes
DL11
Coghill Knott

2

Southwaite Farm
White Mea Bottom
Fells End Quarry
Fells End
Grey Stone
Black Scar House
Millstones
Mouldgill Mea
Catagill Scar
Bents Brae
High Pike
High Pike Hill
Ul Dale
Black Scar
Beck Meetings
Coldbergh Sike

03

Castle Bridge
Red Scar
Bleakham Hills
Seavy Man
Waterfall
B6259

1

Pendragon Castle
Castlethwaite
Castlethwaite Farm
Bleakham Nook
High Brae
Bleakham Scar
Uldale Gill Head
Lodge Side
Birkdale Cross
Birkdale Common
Crook Seal

02

Ing Hill
Goodwife Stones
Lindrigg Scars
Lodge Hags
Birkdale Beck
Low Birkdale Bog
B6270

Waterfall
Uldale Beck
Waterfall

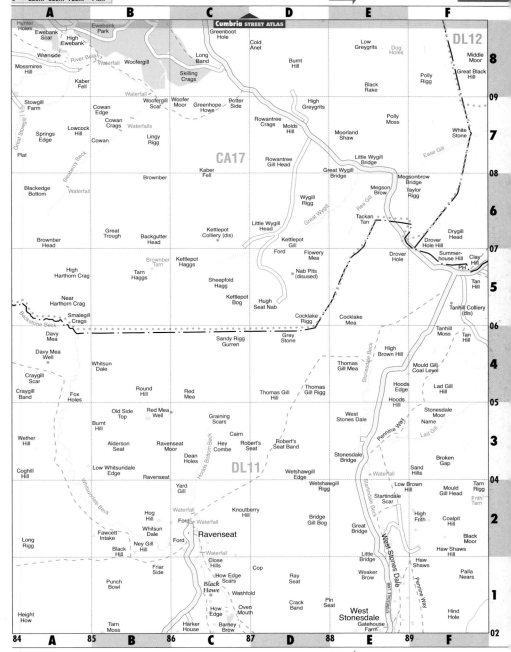

Cumbria STREET ATLAS

DL12

CA17

DL11

A — **B** — **C** — **D** — **E** — **F**

Hunter Holes
Ewebank Scar
High Ewebank
Ewebank Park
Greenboot Hole
Cold Anet
Low Greygrits
Dog Holes
Middle Moor

Wrenside
River Belah
Waterfall
Woofergill
Long Band
Burnt Hill
Black Rake
Polly Rigg
Great Black Hill

Mossmires Hill
Kaber Fell
Waterfall
Skilling Crags

Stowgill Farm
Cowan Edge
Woofergill Scar
Woofer Moor
Greenhope Howe
Potter Side
Rowantree Crags
Molds Hill
High Greygrits
Polly Moss
White Stone

Springs Edge
Lowcock Hill
Cowan Crags
Lingy Rigg
Waterfalls
Rowantree Gill Head
Little Wygill Bridge
Great Wygill Bridge
Moorland Shaw
Ease Gill

Plat
Cowan
Kaber Fell
Brownber
Wygill Rigg
Great Wygill
Megson Brow
Megsonbrow Bridge
Taylor Rigg

Blackedge Bottom
Waterfall
Great Trough
Backgutter Head
Kettlepot Colliery (dis)
Little Wygill Head
Rea Gill
Tackan Tan
Drover Hole Hill
Drygill Head

Brownber Head
Brownber Tarn
Kettlepot Haggs
Kettlepot Gill
Ford
Flowery Mea
Drover Hole
Summerhouse Hill
PH
Clay Hill

High Harthorn Crag
Tarn Haggs
Sheepfold Hagg
Nab Pits (disused)
Tan Hill

Near Harthorn Crag
Smalegill Crags
Kettlepot Bog
Hugh Seat Nab
Cocklake Rigg
Cocklake Mea
Tanhill Colliery (dis)

Backstone Beck
Davy Mea
Sandy Rigg Gurren
Grey Stone
Tanhill Moss
Tan Hill

Davy Mea Well
Whitsun Dale
Thomas Gill Mea
High Brown Hill
Mould Gill Coal Level

Craygill Scar
Round Mea
Red Mea
Thomas Gill Rigg
Hoods Edge
Lad Gill Hill

Craygill Band
Fox Holes
Thomas Gill Hill
Hoods Hill
Stonesdale Moor
Name

Wether Hill
Old Side Top
Red Mea Well
Graining Scars
West Stones Dale
Lad Gill

Burnt Hill
Cairn
Robert's Seat
Robert's Seat Band

Coghill Hill
Alderson Seat
Ravenseat Moor
Hey Combe
Dean Holes
Wetshawgill Edge
Stonesdale Bridge
Broken Gap

Low Whitsundale Edge
Ravenseat
Yard Gill
Wetshawgill Rigg
Wetshawgill Edge
Low Brown Hill
Mould Gill Head
Tarn Rigg
Frith Tarn

Long Rigg
Hog Hill
Waterfall
Knoutberry Hill
Bridge Gill Bog
Startindale Scar
High Frith
Coalpit Hill

Fawcett Intake
Whitsun Dale
Ford
Waterfall
Ravenseat
Great Bridge
Black Moor

Black Hill
Ney Gill Hill
Ford
Little Bridge
Haw Shaws Hill

Height How
Punch Bowl
Friar Side
Close Hills
How Edge Scars
Cop
Weaker Brow
Haw Shaws
Palla Nears

Black Howe
Washfold
Ray Seat
West Stonesdale
Pennine Way

Tarn Moss
Harker House
How Edge
Oven Mouth
Barney Brow
Crack Band
Pin Seat
Gatehouse Farm
Hind Hole

Pennine Way
Stonesdale Beck
Startindale Beck
West Stones Dale

	A	B	C	D	E	F

8

Bog Moss

Bowes Moor

Pennine Way

Malice End

DL12

09

Dry Gill

Washfold Rigg

Rushy Moor Bottom

Coney Seat Hill

7

Frumming Beck

SLEIGHTHOLME MOOR ROAD

Rushy Moor End

Rushy Moor

08

Rushy Moor End

West Moor

6

Pennine Way

Sleightholme Moor

Cocker Top

LONG CAUSEWAY

Cocker

The Disputes

Mudbeck

Washfold Rigg

Beck Crooks Bridge

Ford

Leading Stead Bottom

07

Broadshaw Bottom

Mirk Fell End

Mirk Fell Side

Annaside Rigg

Foster Well (spring)

White Springs

5

Mirk Fell

Annaside Beck

Ford

Leading Stead

Mirk Fell Edge

Scollit Side

DL11

Annaside

06

William Gill Houses

Arkengarthdale Moor

Roe Beck

4

Stonesdale Moor

Annaside Head

Swanasit

05

Lad Gill Head

William Gill Colliery (dis)

Ford

West Moor

3

Water Crag

Roe Beck Head

Routh

Standard Man

04

East Gill Head

Punchard Coal Level Mine (dis)

2

East Gill

Little Water Crag

Wham Bottom

Little Punchard Head

Punchard Moor

Waterfall

Long Rigg

03

High Moor

Rogan's Seat

Blakethwaite

Blakethwaite Lead Mines (dis)

1

Hall Moor

Gunnerside Moor

Friarfold Moss

Little Punchard Gill Head Moss

East Stonesdale

Blakethwaite Moss

Waterfall

02

90	A	91	B	92	C	93	D	94	E	95	F

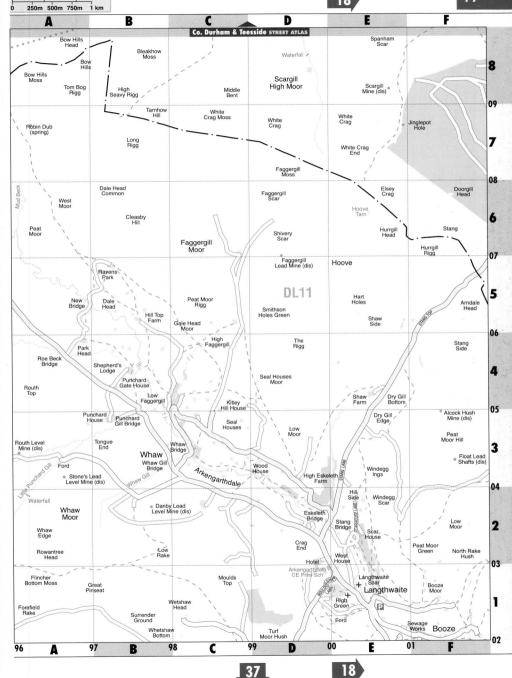

A B C D E F

8

Bow Hills Head
Bleakhow Moss
Waterfall
Spanham Scar

Bow Hills
Bow Hills Moss
High Seavy Rigg
Scargill High Moor
Scargill Mine (dis)

Tom Bog Rigg

09

Tarnhow Hill
Middle Bent
White Crag Moss
White Crag
White Crag
Jinglepot Hole

Robin Dub (spring)
Long Rigg

7

White Crag End

08

Faggergill Moss

Mud Beck

Dale Head Common
Faggergill Scar
Elsey Crag
Doorgill Head

West Moor
Cleasby Hill
Hoove Tarn

6

Peat Moor
Faggergill Moor
Shivery Scar
Hurrgill Head
Stang

Hurrgill Rigg

07

Faggergill Lead Mine (dis)
Hoove

Ravens Park

DL11

5

New Bridge
Dale Head
Peat Moor Rigg
Smithson Holes Green
Hart Holes
Arndale Head

Hill Top Farm
Gale Head Moor
Shaw Side

06

Park Head
High Faggergill
The Rigg
Stang Side

STANG TOP

Roe Beck Bridge
Shepherd's Lodge

4

Routh Top
Punchard Gate House
Seal Houses Moor
Shaw Farm
Dry Gill Bottom

05

Punchard House
Punchard Gill Bridge
Low Faggergill
Kitley Hill House
Dry Gill Edge
Alcock Hush Mine (dis)

Seal Houses
Low Moor
Peat Moor Hill

Routh Level Mine (dis)
Tongue End
Whaw Bridge

3

Float Lead Shafts (dis)

Little Punchard Gill

Ford
Stone's Lead Level Mine (dis)
Whaw
Whaw Gill Bridge
Wood House
Windegg Ings

04

Waterfall
Whaw Gill
Arkengarthdale
High Eskeleth Farm
Hill Side
Windegg Scar

STANG LANE

Whaw Moor
Danby Lead Level Mine (dis)
Eskeleth Bridge
Stang Bridge
Scar House

2

Low Moor

Whaw Edge
Crag End
West House
Peat Moor Green
North Rake Hush

03

Rowantree Head
Low Rake
Hotel
Arkengarthdale CE Prim Sch
Langthwaite Scar
Booze Moor

Flincher Bottom Moss
Great Pinseat
Moulds Top
Langthwaite

1

SLEI GILL LANE

Forefield Rake
Wetshaw Head
High Green
Sewage Works
Booze

Surrender Ground
Ford

02

Whetshaw Bottom
Turf Moor Hush

96 A 97 B 98 C 99 D 00 E 01 F 02

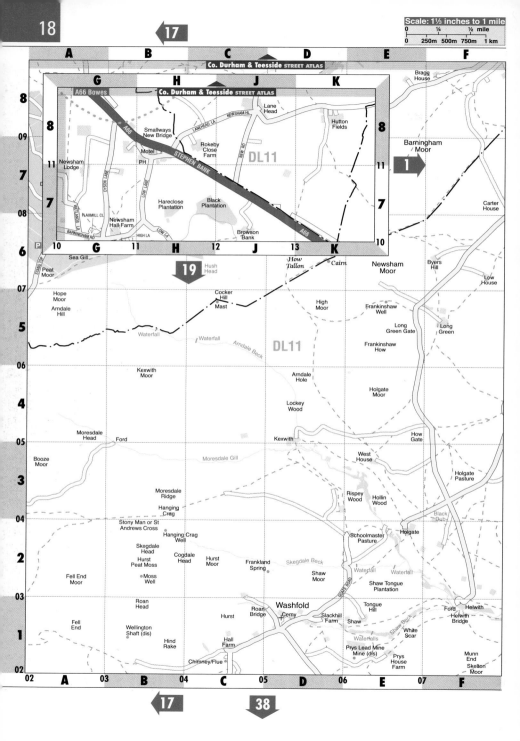

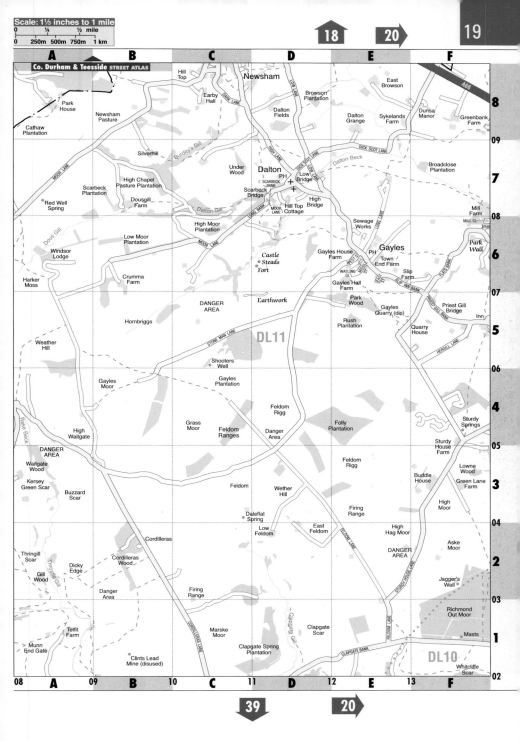

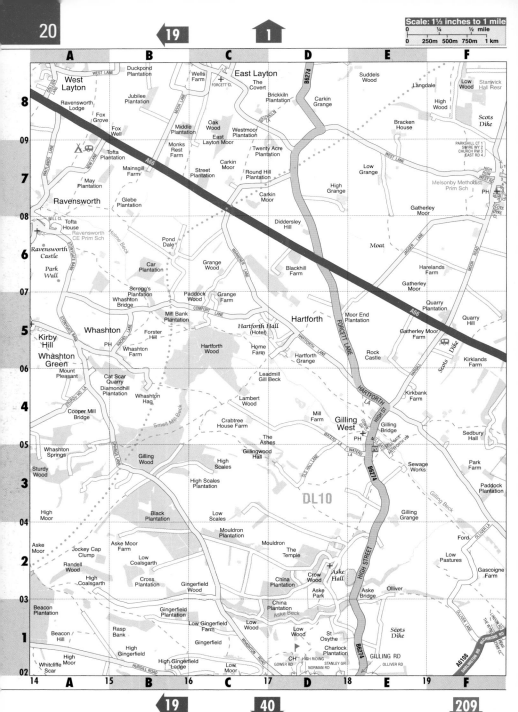

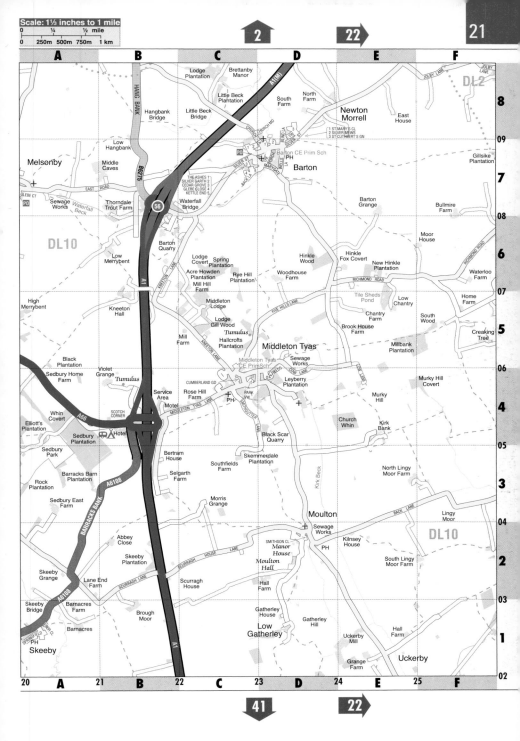

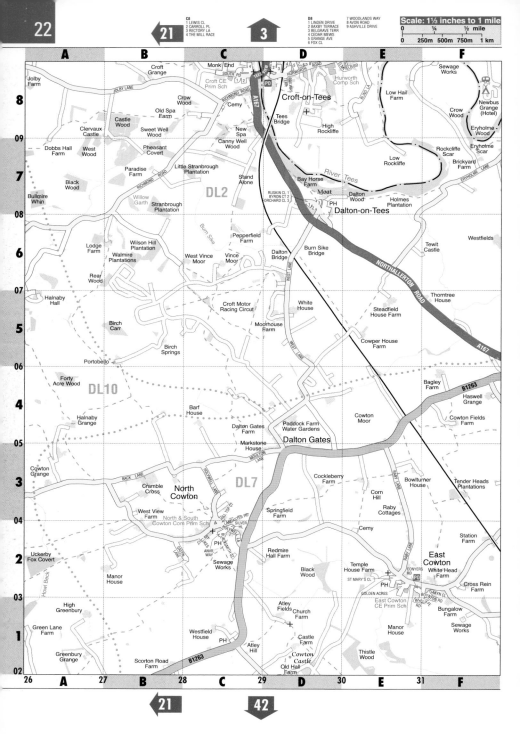

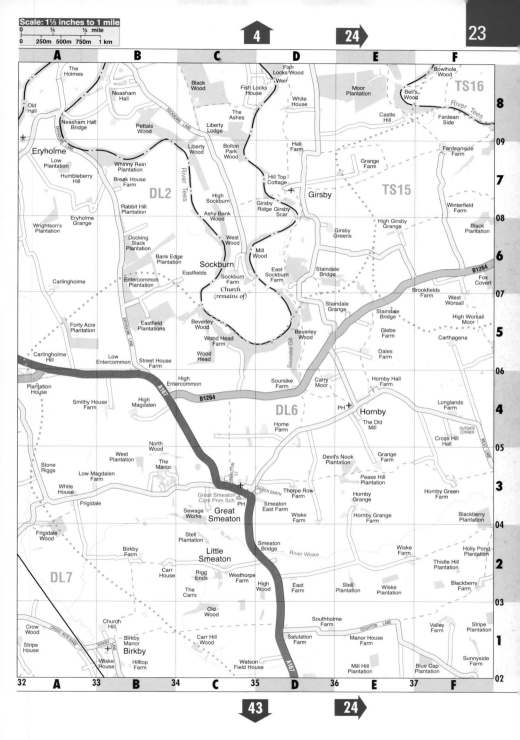

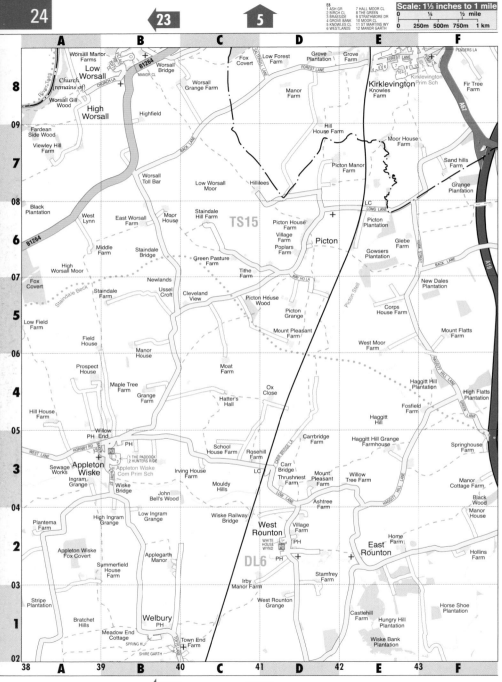

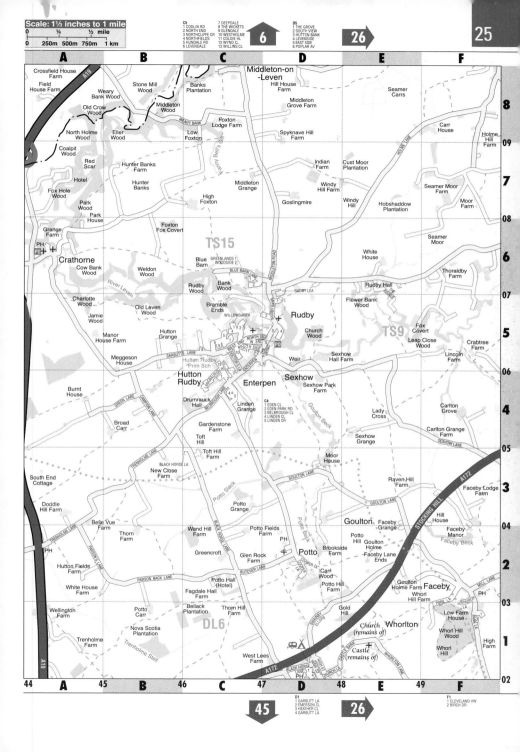

Scale: 1⅓ inches to 1 mile

0   ¼   ½ mile
0   250m 500m 750m 1 km

CS
1 CODLIN RD
2 NORTH END
3 NORTHCLIFFE CR
4 NORTHFIELDS
5 HUNDALE RD
6 LEVENDALE

7 DEEPDALE
8 THE WICKETS
9 GLENDALE
10 WESTHOLME
11 COLDIE HL
12 WYND CL.
13 WILLINS CL.

6

D5
1 THE GROVE
2 SOUTH VIEW
3 HUTTON BANK
4 LEVENSIDE
5 EAST SIDE
6 POPLAR AV

26

25

A   B   C   D   E   F

Crossfield House Farm
Field House Farm
Weary Bank Wood
Stone Mill Wood
Banks Plantation
Middleton-on-Leven
Hill House Farm
Seamer Carrs
8

Old Crow Wood
Middleton Wood
Foxton Lodge Farm
Middleton Grove Farm
Carr House
Holme Hill Farm
09

North Holme Wood
Eller Wood
Low Foxton
Spyknave Hill Farm

Coalpit Wood
Red Scar
Hunter Banks Wood
Indian Farm
Cust Moor Plantation
Seamer Moor Farm
7

Hotel
Hunter Banks
Middleton Grange
Windy Hill Farm
Goslingmire
Windy Hill
Hobshaddow Plantation
Moor Farm
08

Fox Hole Wood
Park Wood
High Foxton

Park House
Grange Farm
PH PO
Foxton Fox Covert
Seamer Moor
6

Crathorne
Cow Bank Wood
Weldon Wood
Blue Barn
GREENLANDS 1 WOODSIDE 2
White House
Thoraldby Farm

TS15

Charlotte Wood
Old Leven Wood
Rudby Wood
Bank Wood
BLUE BARN LANE
RUDBY LEA
Rudby Hall
07

River Leven
Bramble Ends
Flower Bank Wood
5

Jamie Wood
WILLOWGARTH
Rudby
TS9
Fox Covert
Leap Close Wood
Crabtree Farm

Manor House Farm
Hutton Grange
NORTH SIDE
WEST END
SOUTH SIDE
PO
Church Wood
Lincoln Farm
06

Meggeson House
GARBUTTS LANE
Hutton Rudby Prim Sch
ENTERPEN
Weir
Sexhow Hall Farm

Hutton Rudby
Enterpen
Sexhow
Sexhow Park Farm

Burnt House
GREEN LANE
CAMPION LANE
Drumrauck Hall
Linden Grange
C4
1 EDEN CL
2 EDEN PARK RD
3 BELBROUGH CL
4 LINDEN CL
5 LINDEN CR
Lady Cross
Carlton Grove
4

Broad Carr
Gardenstone Farm
Toft Hill
Goulton Beck
Sexhow Grange
Carlton Grange Farm
SEXHOW LANE

TRENHOLME LANE
Toft Hill Farm
Moor House
05

South End Cottage
BLACK HORSE LA
New Close Farm
GOULTON LANE
Raven Hill Farm
A172
Faceby Lodge Farm
3

Doddle Hill Farm
Potto Slack
Potto Grange
GOULTON LANE
Goulton
Faceby Grange
Hill House
STOCKING HILL
04

Belle Vue Farm
Thorn Farm
Wand Hill Farm
Potto Fields Farm
PH
Potto Hill
Goulton Holme
Faceby Manor
Faceby Beck

PH
TRENHOLME LANE
PARSONS LANE
Greencroft
Glen Rock Farm
Potto
Brookside Farm
Faceby Lane Ends
Goulton Holme Farm
Faceby
MILL LANE
2

Hutton Fields Farm
PARSON BACK LANE
Potto Hall (Hotel)
BUTCHER LANE
COOPER DR
Cart Wood
Potto Hill Farm
Whorl Hill Farm
FORE LA
CHURCH
PH
03

White House Farm
Fagdale Hall Farm
Thorn Hill Farm
Gold Hill
Low Farm House
BIRK LA

Wellington Farm
Potto Carr
Beliack Plantation
SMABY ELLENS
Church (remains of)
Whorlton
Whorl Hill Wood
High Farm
1

Nova Scotia Plantation
DL6
CASTLE WALK
Castle (remains of)
Whorl Hill

Trenholme Farm
Trenholme Stell
West Lees Farm
A172
BLACK HORSE LANE 1 2 3
PH
WHORLTON LANE
02

A19

44   A   45   B   46   C   47   D   48   E   49   F   02

45

D1
1 GARBUTT LA
2 EMERSON CL
3 HEATHER CL
4 GARBUTT LA

26

F1
1 CLEVELAND VW
2 BIRCH DR

26

25

7

1 CEDARWOOD AV
2 BEECHWOOD AV
3 DALEWOOD WK
4 CHERRYWOOD AV
5 COPSEWOOD WK
6 ELMWOOD CL

7 PINEWOOD WK
8 MEADOWFIELD
9 QUEENS DR

Scale: 1⅓ inches to 1 mile

¼   ½ mile
250m 500m 750m 1 km

A B C D E F

Norman's Wood
Tanton Dykes
WOODLANDS WK
Quakers Grove Farm
Winley Hill Farm
Angrove Shed Plantation
East Angrove
Ayton Firs

Seamer Hill
Daleview Farm
JACKSON DR
HILDYARD CL
NEASHAM CT
Angrove West Farm
ROSEBERRY AV
River Leven
Applebridge Farm
Harland Hill Farm
Harland Hill

Oneholmes
Apple Grove Farm
GRANGE DR
THE STRIPE
NORTHFIELD CL
FAIRFIELD RD
Stokesley
Stokesley Com Prim Sch
Kirby School Farm
Halfway House Plantation
Primrose Hill Farm

Crabtree Farm
HIGH ST
Liby
Leisure Centre
Prospect House Farm
Broughton Bridge
Mill Vale Farm
Crow Wood Farm Covert

Seamer Moor
Tame Bridge
White House Farm
NORTH END
Stokesley Sch
B1257
Broughton Bridge
Castle House Farm

Tame Bridge
Tame Bridge Farm
HAMBLETON GATE
Kirby Bridge
Stokesley Ind Park
Broughton Bridge Farm
Field House Farm
Lockey's Covert
Whitehouse Farm

South Lund Farm
Brawith
C7
1 SPRINGFIELD GDNS
2 WESTFIELD RD
3 WEAVERS CT
4 THE GARTH
5 MANOR CL
6 THE STRIPE
7 THREE TUNS WYND
8 ANGEL CT
9 LEVEN WYND
10 BRIDGE RD
11 THE BEECHES
12 LADY HULLOCKS CT
13 ROSE HL DR
14 ST MARYS CL
Sewage Works
Field House
Kirby Bridge Farm
Creyke Nest Farm
Ings Farm

Bense Bridge Farm
Dromonby Grange Farm
Railway Bridge Farm
Manor Farm
Glebe Farm
Stanison Villa Farm
Chapelgarth

Thorn Tree Farm
Chesnut Farm
Fir Tree Farm
TS9
West Beck
Kirby Lane Farm
Great Broughton
Grove Hill Farm
Well Farm

Parish Crayke Farm
Busby House
The Grange
Kirkby
Oxford House
THE DORKINGS
LOWCROSS DR
INGLEBY RD

Dromonby Hall Farm
Dromonby House
Kirby House Farm
THE HOLME
Annaclay Farm
Broughton Grange

Low House Farm
Brass Sykes Farm
Viewley Hill
South View Farm
Great Busby
Dromonby Grange Farm
Dromonby Farm
Kirby House Farm
Kirkby & Great Broughton CE VA Prim Sch
CRINGLE MOOR CHASE
White Post Farm

Town End Plantations
Long Plantation
Nine Acre Plantation
Cote House
Manor Farm
Kirby Grange
Oxfield House
White House Farm

Church Farm
PH
Carlton & Faceby CE VA Prim Sch
Long Plantation
Bagdale Farm
Toft Hill Farm
Broughton Banks Farm
Hunters Folly Farm

Carlton in Cleveland
THE CRESCENT
Busby Hall
Manor Farm
Broughton Plantation

FACEBY ROAD
Busby Wood
Rice Road Side
Busby Moor
Cringle End
Viewpoint
Wain Stones

Butter Hill Plantation
Underhill Farm
Carlton Hall Wood
Cringle Moor
Cringle Moor Plantation
Drake Howe

Meeks Farm
Ash Tree Farm
Carlton Bank
Carlton Moor
Harry Wath Wood
Wath Wood
Whingroves

Plane Tree Farm
Long Wood
Cringle Moor Plantation
Beak Hills

Thwaites House
Beak Hill Farm
Cold Moor

The Gill
Great Bonny Cliff
Bilsdale West Moor

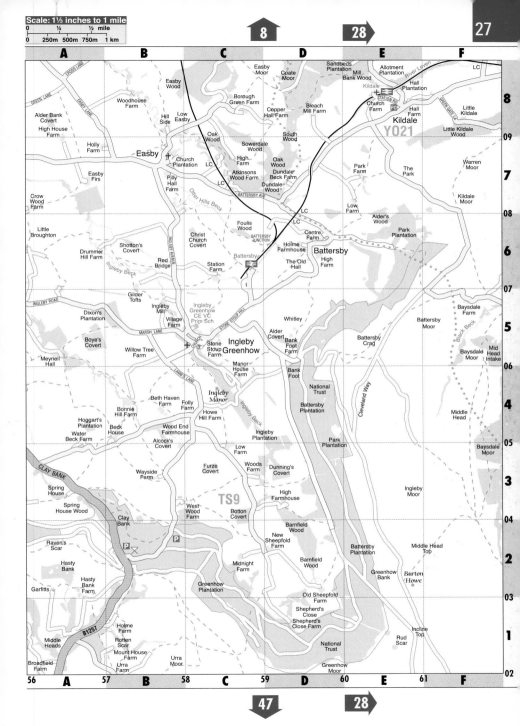

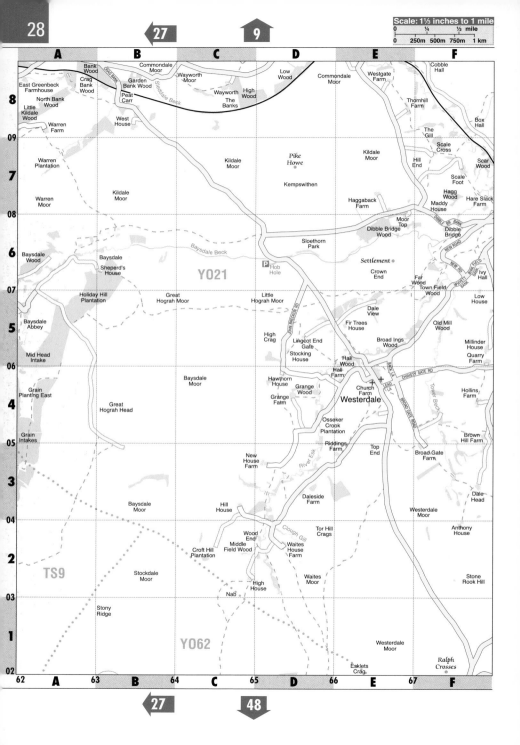

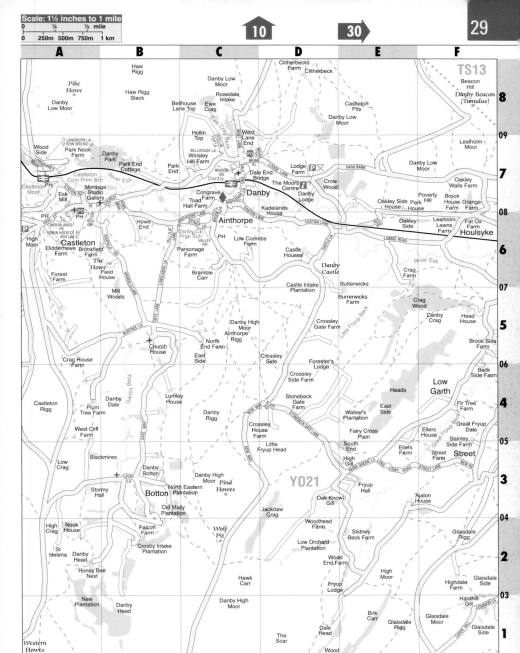

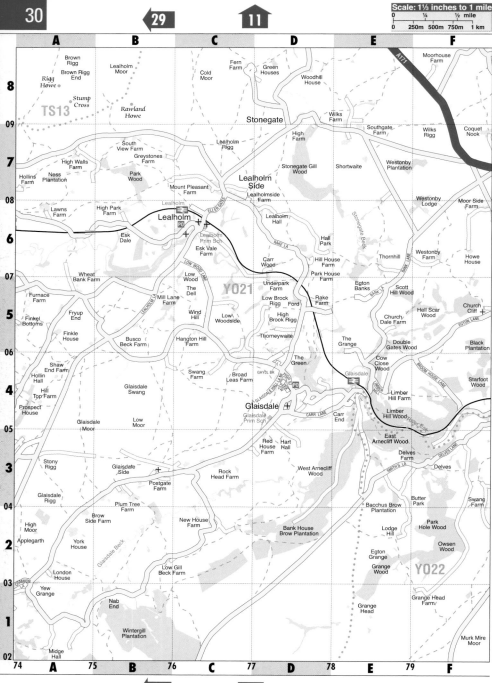

Scale: 1½ inches to 1 mile

0   ¼   ½ mile
0 250m 500m 750m 1 km

29   **11**

8
09
7
08
6
07
5
06
4
05
3
04
2
03
1
02

A   B   C   D   E   F

Brown Rigg
Brown Rigg End
Lealholm Moor
Cold Moor
Fern Farm
Green Houses
Woodhill House
Moorhouse Farm

Rigg Howe
Stump Cross
Rawland Howe

TS13

Stonegate

Wilks Farm
Southgate Farm
Wilks Rigg
Coquet Nook

South View Farm
Greystones Farm
Lealholm Rigg
High Farm
Westonby Plantation

High Walls Farm
Ness Plantation
Park Wood
Lealholm Side
Stonegate Gill Wood
Shortwaite

Hollins Farm
Mount Pleasant Farm
Lealholmside Farm
Westonby Lodge
Moor Side Farm

Lawns Farm
High Park Farm
Lealholm
Lealholm
PO
Lealholm Hall
Stonegate Beck

Esk Dale
Lealholm Prim Sch
Esk Vale Farm
Carr Wood
Hall Park
Hill House Farm
Thornhill
Westonby Farm
Howe House

Wheat Bank Farm
Low Wood
The Dell
YO21
Underpark Farm
Park House Farm
Egton Banks
Scott Hill Wood

Furnace Farm
Mill Lane Farm
Wind Hill
Low Brock Rigg
Rake Farm
Church Dale Farm
Hell Scar Wood
Church Cliff

Fryup End
Low Woodside
High Brook Rigg
Double Gates Wood
Black Plantation

Finkel Bottoms
Finkle House
Busco Beck Farm
Hangton Hill Farm
Thorneywaite
The Grange
Cow Close Wood
Starfoot Wood

Shaw End Farm
Swang Farm
Broad Leas Farm
The Green
GHYLL BR
Glaisdale
Limber Hill Farm

Hollin Hall
Glaisdale Swang
Limber Hill Wood

Hill Top Farm
Low Moor
Glaisdale
Carr End
East Arncliff Wood
Delves Farm
Delves

Prospect House
Glaisdale Moor
Glaisdale Prim Sch
Red House Farm
Hart Hall

Stony Rigg
Glaisdale Side
Rock Head Farm
West Arncliff Wood
Butter Park
Swang Farm

Glaisdale Rigg
Postgate Farm
Bacchus Brow Plantation
Park Hole Wood

High Moor
Brow Side Farm
Plum Tree Farm
New House Farm
Bank House Brow Plantation
Lodge Hill
Owsen Wood

Applegarth
York House
Egton Grange
Grange Wood
YO22

London House
Low Gill Beck Farm
Grange Head Farm

Yew Grange
Glaisdale Beck
Grange Head

Nab End
Midge Hall
Wintergill Plantation
Murk Mire Moor

74   75   76   77   78   79

A   B   C   D   E   F

29   **50**

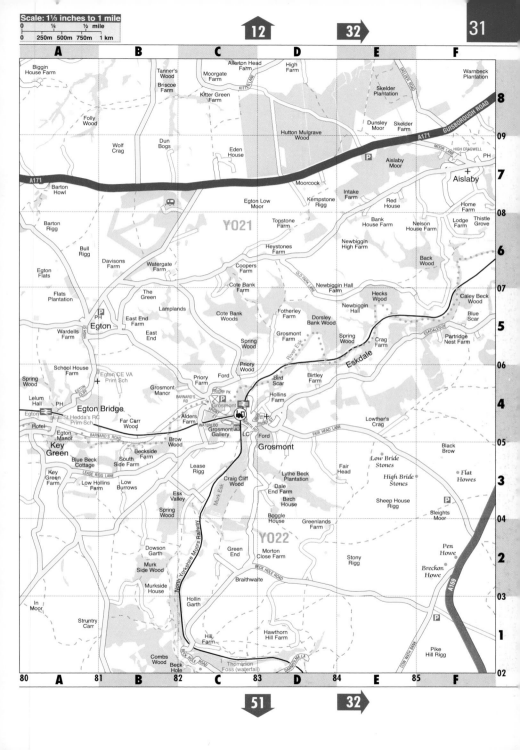

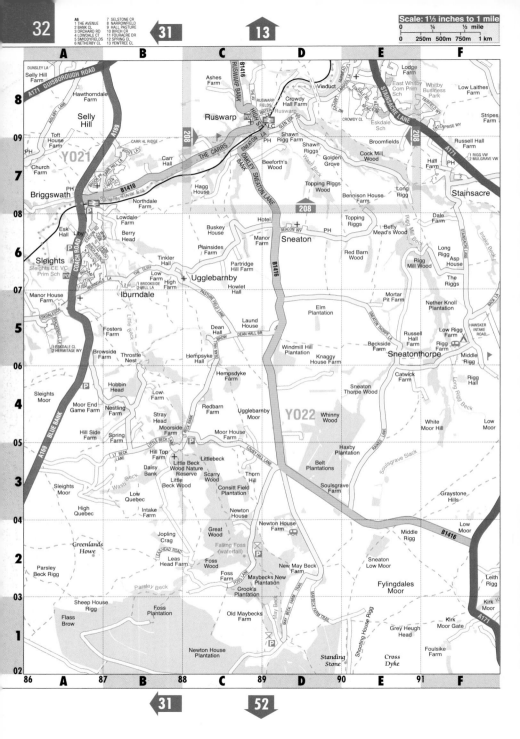

Scale: 1½ inches to 1 mile

| 0 | ¼ | ½ | mile |
| 0 | 250m | 500m | 750m | 1 km |

C3
1 THORPE GN BANK
2 KINGSTON GARTH
3 MIDDLEWOOD CL
4 MIDDLEWOOD GARTH
5 MIDDLEWOOD CR

D4
1 MOUNT PLEASANT N
2 MOUNT PLEASANT E
3 MOUNT PLEASANT S
4 THE CLOSE
5 PROSPECT FIELD

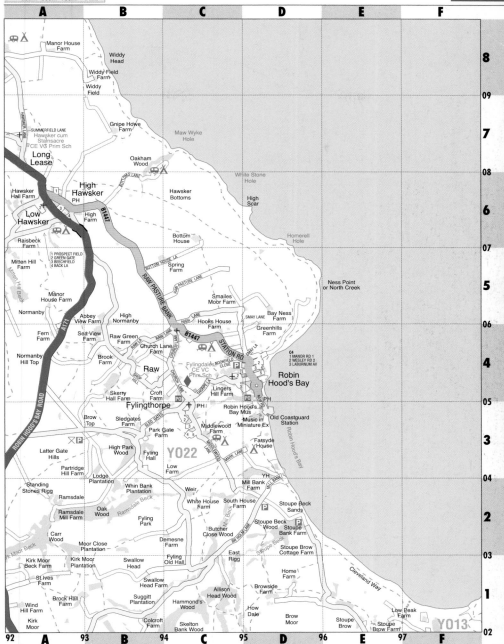

Manor House Farm
Widdy Head
Widdy Field Farm
Widdy Field
Gnipe Howe Farm
Maw Wyke Hole
SUMMERFIELD LANE
Hawsker cum Stainsacre CE VC Prim Sch
Long Lease
Oakham Wood
White Stone Hole
Hawsker Hall Farm
High Hawsker
PH
Hawsker Bottoms
High Scar
Low Hawsker
B1447
High Farm
Bottom House
Homerell Hole
Raisbeck Farm
Mitten Hill Farm
1 PROSPECT FIELD
2 GREEN GATE
3 BEECHFIELD
4 BACK LA
Spring Farm
Manor House Farm
Smailes Moor Farm
Ness Point or North Creek
Normanby
Abbey View Farm
High Normanby
Hooks House Farm
SMAY LANE
Bay Ness Farm
Fern Farm
Sea View Farm
Raw Green Farm
Church Lane Farm
B1447
Greenhills Farm
Normanby Hill Top
Brook Farm
Raw
STATION RD
C4
1 MANOR RD 1
2 WESLEY RD 2
3 LABURNUM AV
Fylingdales CE VC Prim Sch
NOOKFIELD CLOSE
Robin Hood's Bay
Skerry Hall Farm
Croft Farm
Lingers Hill Farm
Fylingthorpe
PH
Robin Hood's Bay Mus
Music in Miniature Ex
Old Coastguard Station
Brow Top
Sledgates Farm
Park Gate Farm
Middlewood Farm
Latter Gate Hills
High Park Wood
Fyling Hall
Low Farm
Farsyde House
Partridge Hill Farm
Lodge Plantation
YH
Mill Bank Farm
Standing Stones Rigg
Ramsdale
Whin Bank Plantation
Weir
White House Farm
South House Farm
Stoupe Beck Sands
Ramsdale Mill Farm
Oak Wood
Fyling Park
Stoupe Beck Wood
Stoupe Bank Farm
Carr Wood
Moor Close Plantation
Demesne Farm
Butcher Close Wood
Stoupe Brow Cottage Farm
Kirk Moor Beck Farm
Kirk Moor Plantation
Swallow Head
Fyling Old Hall
East Rigg
Home Farm
Browside Farm
Cleveland Way
St Ives Farm
Swallow Head Farm
Allison Head Wood
Low Peak Farm
Wind Hill Farm
Brock Hall Farm
Suggitt Plantation
Hammond's Wood
How Dale
Brow Moor
Stoupe Brow
Stoupe Brow Farm
Kirk Moor
Colcroft Farm
Skelton Bank Wood

YO22
YO13

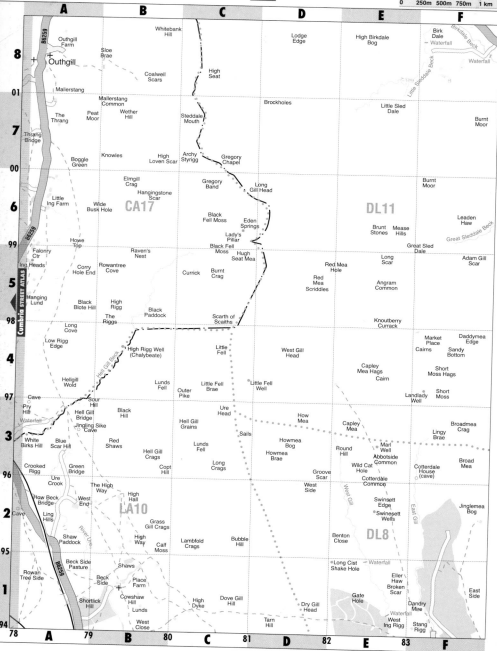

Scale: 1⅓ inches to 1 mile

0   ¼   ½ mile
0 250m 500m 750m 1 km

8

01

7

00

6

99

5

98

4

97

3

96

2

95

1

94

Outhgill Farm
Outhgill
Sloe Brae
Whitebank Hill
Coalwell Scars
High Seat
Lodge Edge
High Birkdale Bog
Birk Dale
Waterfall
Birkdale Beck
Waterfall

Mallerstang
Mallerstang Common
The Thrang
Peat Moor
Wether Hill
Steddale Mouth
Brockholes
Little Sled Dale
Burnt Moor
Little Sleddale Beck

Thrang Bridge
Boggle Green
Knowles
High Loven Scar
Archy Styrigg
Gregory Chapel

Elmgill Crag
Gregory Band
Long Gill Head
Burnt Moor

Little Ing Farm
Hangingstone Scar
Wide Busk Hole
CA17
Black Fell Moss
Eden Springs
DL11
Leaden Haw
Great Sleddale Beck

Howe Top
Raven's Nest
Lady's Pillar
Black Fell Moss
Hugh Seat Mea
Brunt Stones
Mease Hills
Great Sled Dale
Adam Gill Scar

Falonry Ctr
Ing.Heads
B6259
Corry Hole End
Rowantree Cove
Currick
Burnt Crag
Red Mea Hole
Red Mea Scriddles
Long Scar
Angram Common

Hanging Lund
Black Blote Hill
High Rigg
The Riggs
Black Paddock
Scarth of Scaiths
Knoutberry Currack

Long Cove
Low Rigg Edge
High Rigg Well (Chalybeate)
Little Fell
West Gill Head
Market Place Cairns
Daddymea Edge
Sandy Bottom

Hellgill Wold
Hell Gill Beck
Lunds Fell
Little Fell Brae
Little Fell Well
Capley Mea Hags
Cairn
Short Moss Hags

Cave
Pry Hill
Sour Hill
Outer Pike
Ure Head
Landlady Well
Short Moss

Waterfall
Hell Gill Bridge
Jingling Sike
Cave
Black Hill
Hell Gill Grains
Sails
How Mea
Capley Mea
Broadmea Crag

White Birks Hill
Blue Scar Hill
Red Shaws
Lunds Fell
Howmea Bog
Round Hill
Marl Well
Lingy Brae
Abbotside Common
Broad Mea

Crooked Rigg
Ure Crook
Green Bridge
Hell Gill Crags
Copt Hill
Long Crags
Howmea Brae
Groove Scar
Wild Cat Hole
Cotterdale Common
Cotterdale House (cave)

How Beck Bridge
River Ure
West End
The High Way
High Hall
LA10
West Side
West Gill
Swinsett Edge
Jinglemea Bog

Cave
Ling Hills
Grass Gill Crags
Swinesett Wells
East Gill

Shaw Paddock
High Way
Calf Moss
Lambfold Crags
Bubble Hill
Benton Close
DL8

Beck Side Pasture
Shaws
Long Cist Shake Hole
Waterfall
Eller Haw
Broken Scar

Rowan Tree Side
B6259
Beck Side
Place Farm
Cowshaw Hill
High Dyke
Dove Gill Hill
Gate Hole
Dandry Mire
East Side

Shortlick Hill
Lunds
West Close
Tarn Hill
Dry Gill Head
Waterfall
West Ing Rigg
Stang Rigg

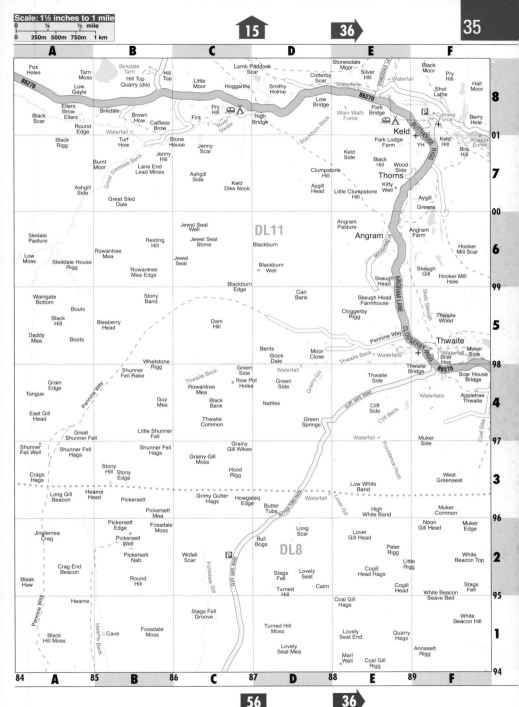

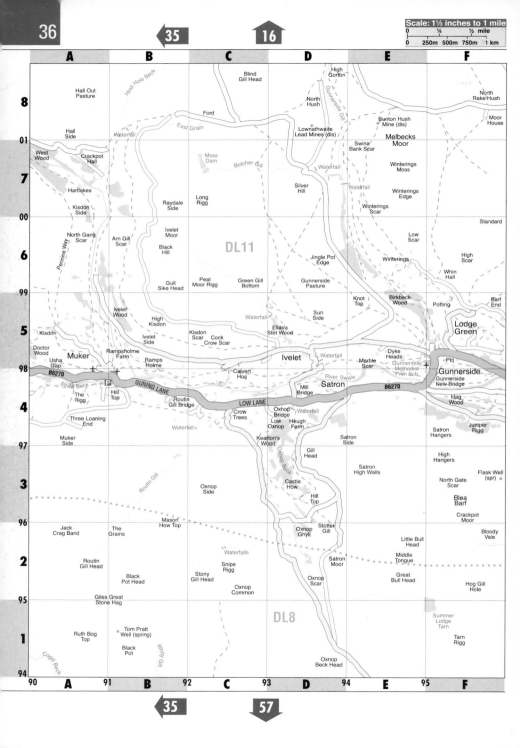

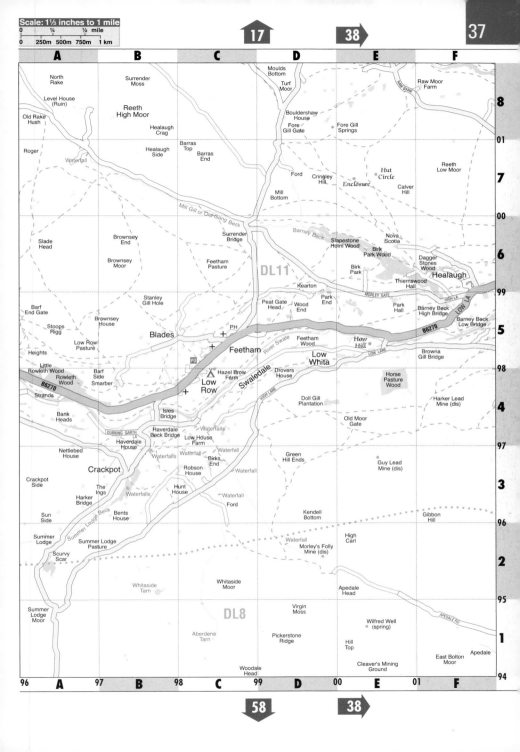

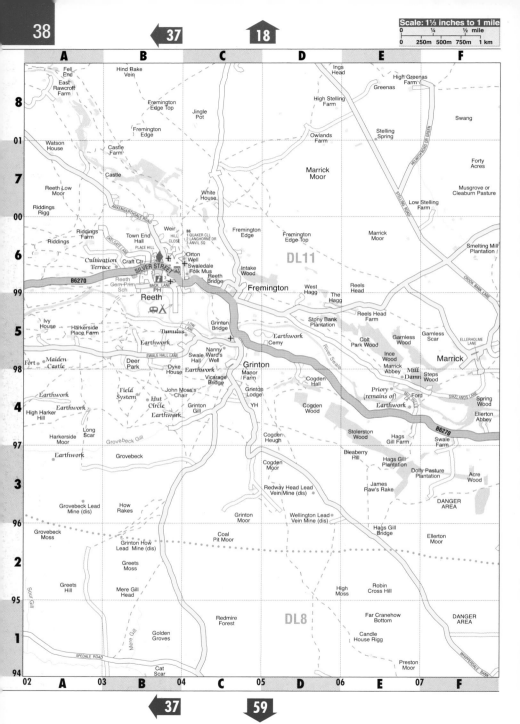

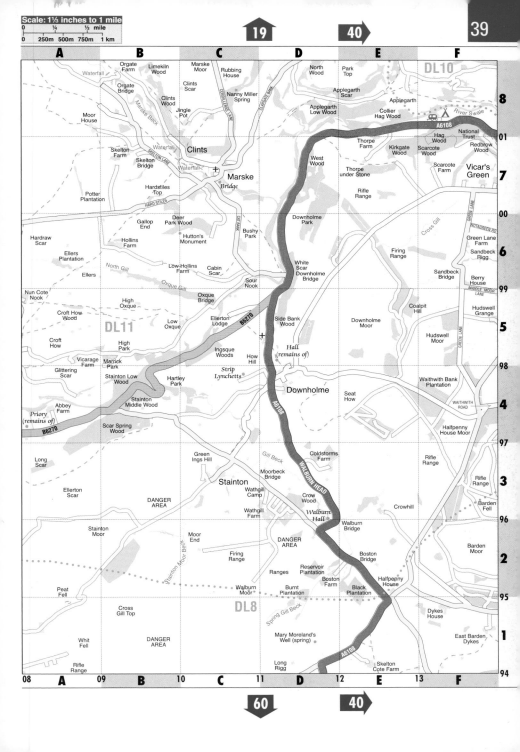

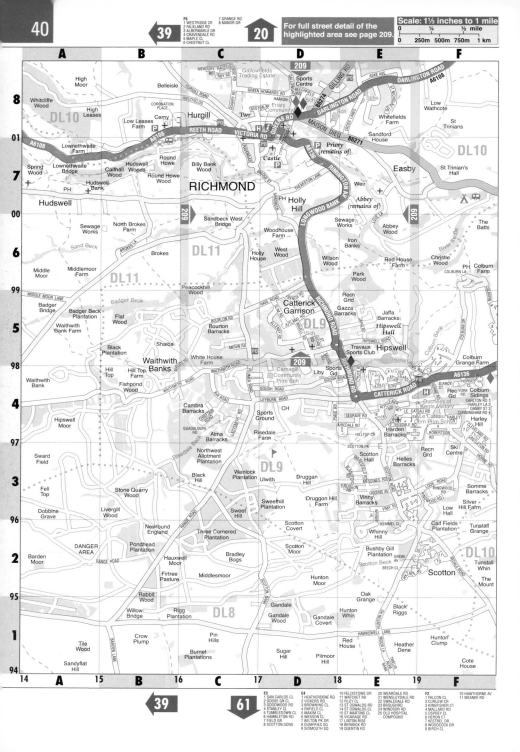

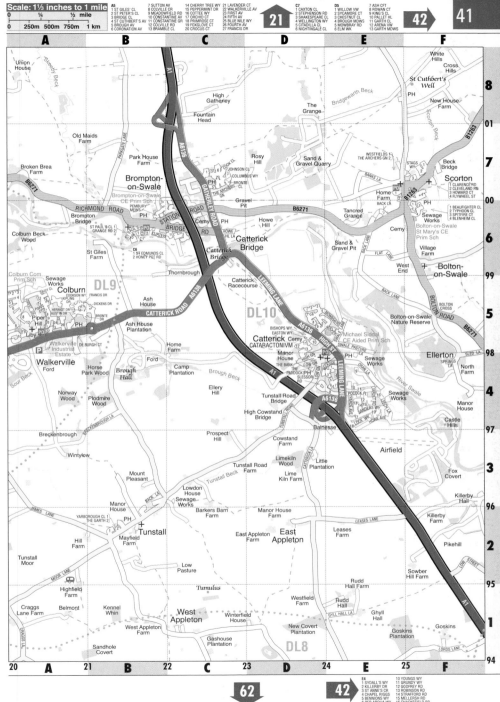

Scale: 1⅓ inches to 1 mile

0 ¼ ½ mile
0 250m 500m 750m 1 km

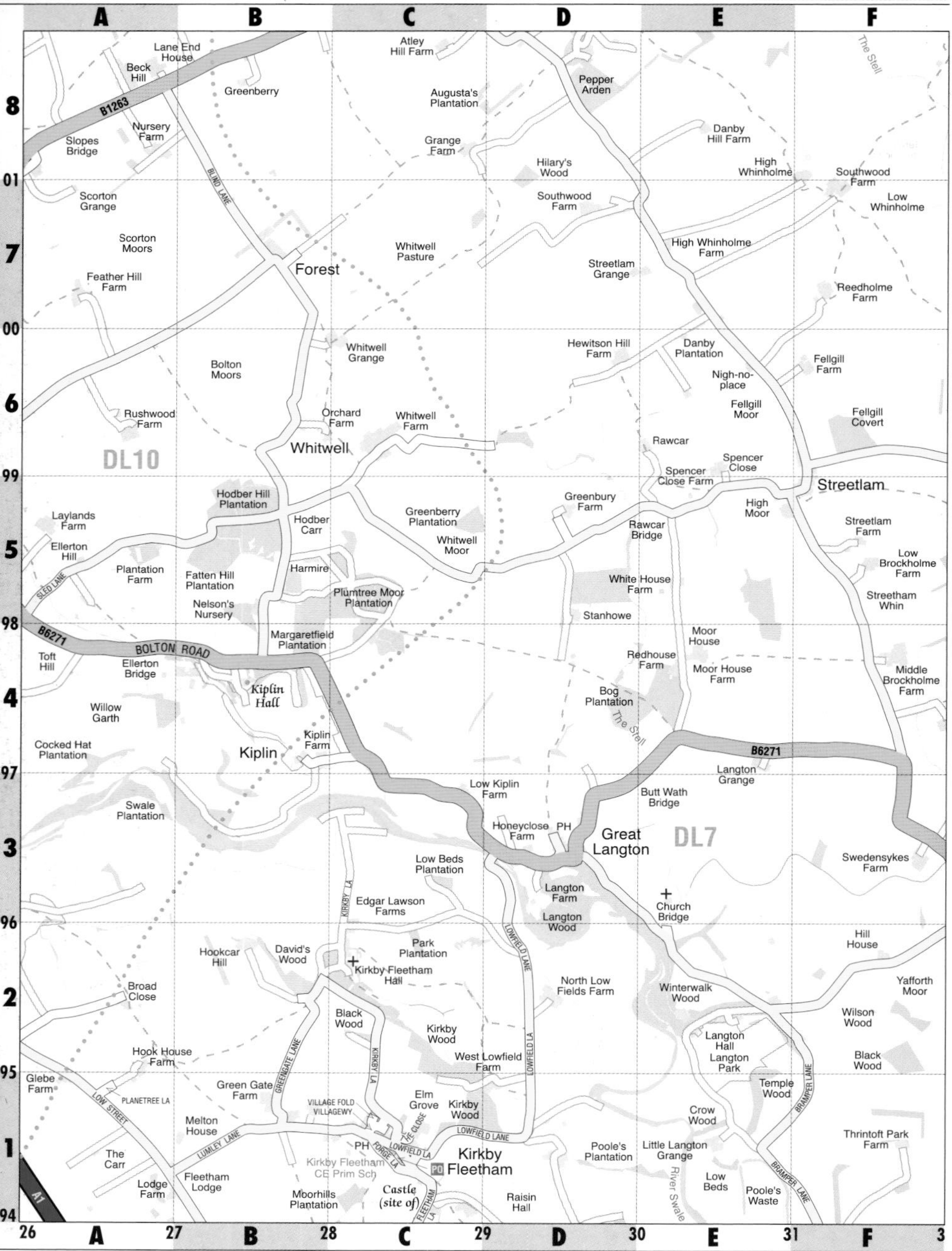

Grid columns: A B C D E F

The Stell

Lane End House
Beck Hill
B1263
Atley Hill Farm
Greenberry
Augusta's Plantation
Pepper Arden
Danby Hill Farm
High Whinholme
Southwood Farm
Nursery Farm
Slopes Bridge
Grange Farm
Hilary's Wood
Low Whinholme

8

01

Scorton Grange
Scorton Moors
Forest
Whitwell Pasture
Southwood Farm
High Whinholme Farm
Reedholme Farm

7

Feather Hill Farm
Streetlam Grange
Danby Plantation
Fellgill Farm

00

Rushwood Farm
Bolton Moors
Whitwell Grange
Hewitson Hill Farm
Nigh-no-place
Fellgill Moor
Fellgill Covert

6

DL10
Orchard Farm
Whitwell
Whitwell Farm
Rawcar
Spencer Close
Streetlam

99

Laylands Farm
Hodber Hill Plantation
Greenberry Plantation
Greenbury Farm
Rawcar Bridge
Spencer Close Farm
High Moor
Streetlam Farm

Ellerton Hill
Hodber Carr
Whitwell Moor
Low Brockholme Farm

5

SEED LANE
Plantation Farm
Fatten Hill Plantation
Harmire
Plumtree Moor Plantation
White House Farm
Streetham Whin

Nelson's Nursery
Stanhowe

98

B6271
Toft Hill
BOLTON ROAD
Ellerton Bridge
Margaretfield Plantation
Redhouse Farm
Moor House
Moor House Farm
Middle Brockholme Farm

4

Willow Garth
Kiplin Hall
Bog Plantation
The Stell

Cocked Hat Plantation
Kiplin
Kiplin Farm
B6271
Langton Grange

97

Swale Plantation
Low Kiplin Farm
Butt Wath Bridge

3

Low Beds Plantation
Honeyclose Farm
PH
Great Langton
DL7
Swedensykes Farm

Edgar Lawson Farms
Langton Wood
Church Bridge

96

Hookcar Hill
David's Wood
Park Plantation
Langton Wood
North Low Fields Farm
Hill House

2

Broad Close
Kirkby Fleetham Hall
Black Wood
Kirkby Wood
Winterwalk Wood
Wilson Wood
Yafforth Moor

Black Wood

95

Hook House Farm
Green Gate Farm
West Lowfield Farm
Langton Hall
Langton Park
Temple Wood

Glebe Farm
PLANETREE LA
Melton House
VILLAGE FOLD VILLAGEWY
Elm Grove
Kirkby Wood
Crow Wood
Thrintoft Park Farm

1

The Carr
LUMLEY LANE
Kirkby Fleetham CE Prim Sch
PH
Kirkby Fleetham
Poole's Plantation
Little Langton Grange
Low Beds
Poole's Waste

Lodge Farm
Fleetham Lodge
Moorhills Plantation
Castle (site of)
Raisin Hall
River Swale

94

A1

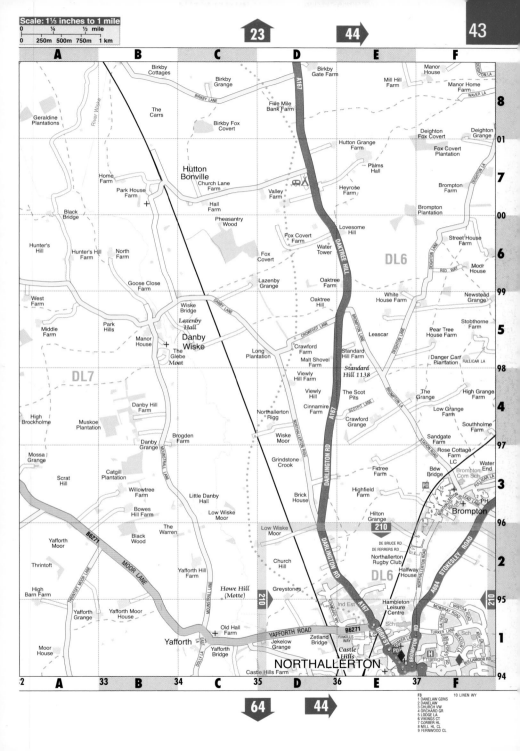

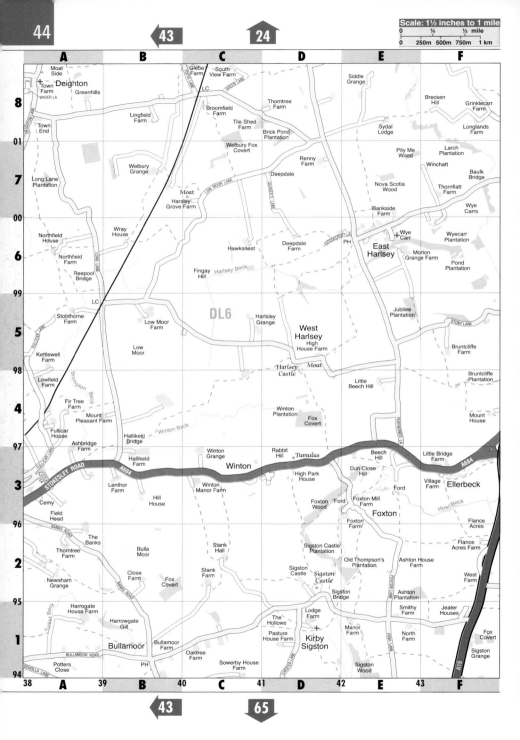

Scale: 1⅓ inches to 1 mile

0   ¼   ½   mile
0   250m 500m 750m 1 km

A7
1 THE PARKLANDS
2 COOKS CL
3 HILLSIDE
4 PRIORY WY

25   46   **45**

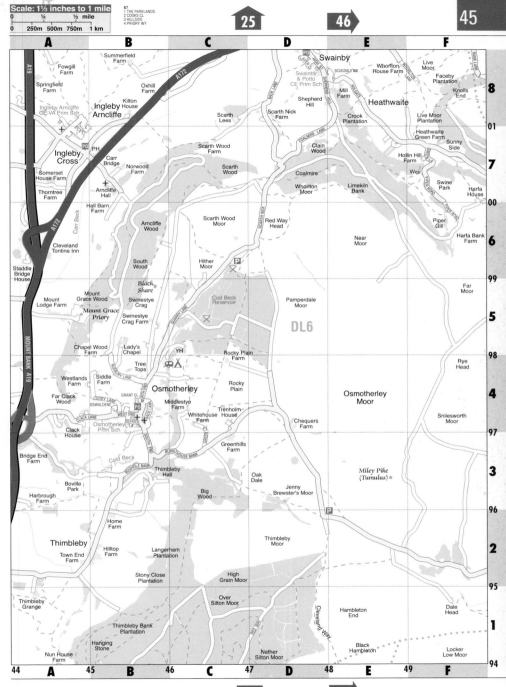

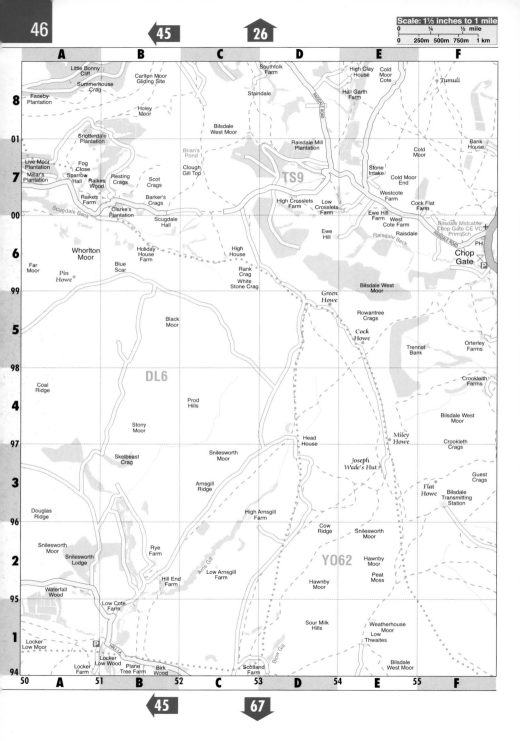

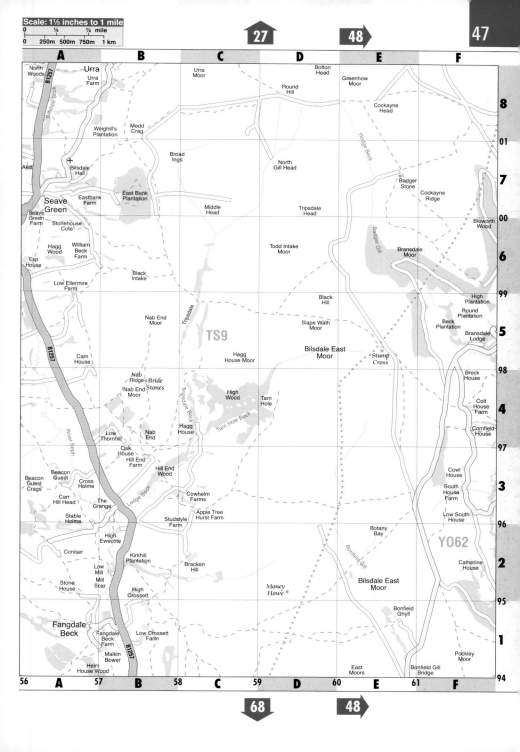

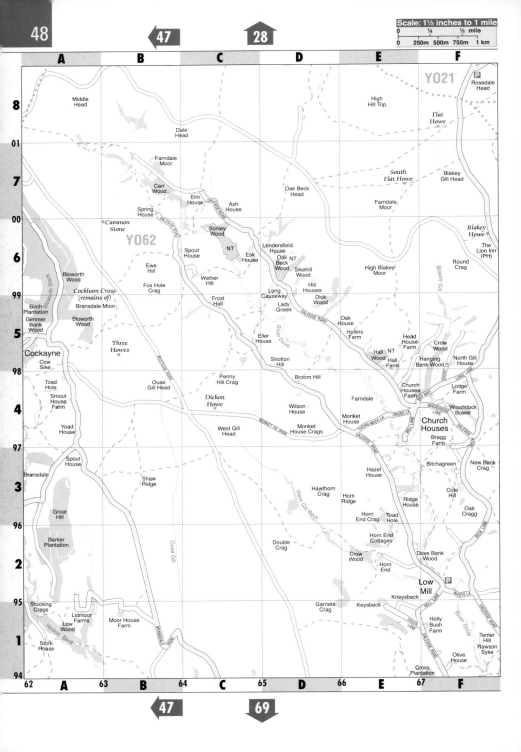

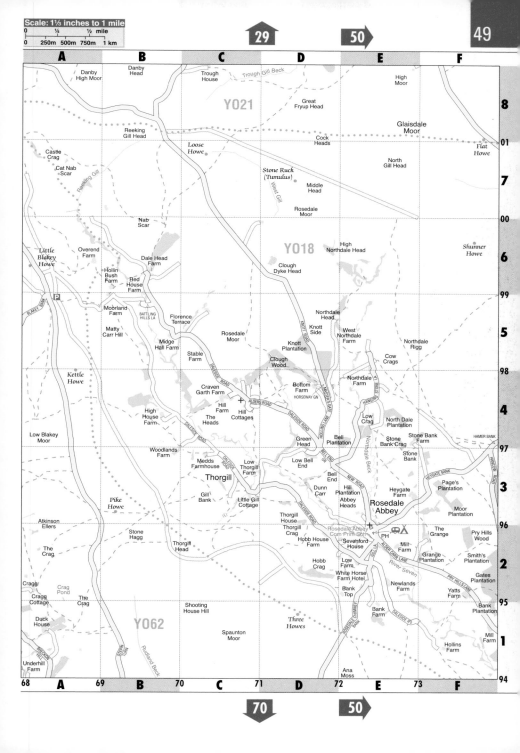

A   B   C   D   E   F

Danby
High Moor
Danby
Head
Trough
House
Trough Gill Beck
High
Moor

8

YO21

Great
Fryup Head

Glaisdale
Moor

Reeking
Gill Head
Loose
Howe
Cock
Heads
Flat
Howe

01

Castle
Crag
Cat Nab
Scar
North
Gill Head
Shunner
Howe

7

Reeking Gill

Stone Ruck
(Tumulus)
West Gill
Middle
Head

Nab
Scar
Rosedale
Moor

00

Little
Blakey
Howe
Overend
Farm
Dale Head
Farm
Clough
Dyke Head

YO18
High
Northdale Head

6

Hollin
Bush
Farm
Red
House
Farm

Moorland
Farm
BATTLING
HILLS LA
Florence
Terrace
Northdale
Head
Knott
Side
West
Northdale
Farm
Northdale
Rigg

5

Matty
Carr Hill
Midge
Hall Farm
Rosedale
Moor
Knott
Plantation
Cow
Crags

BLAKEY BANK

Stable
Farm
Clough
Wood
Northdale
Farm

98

Kettle
Howe
Craven
Garth Farm
Bottom
Farm
HORSEWAY GN
Low
Crag
North Dale
Plantation

KNOTT ROAD

ALDERS ROAD

DALESIDE ROAD

MASTERS LANE

MILL LANE

BELL END

DALESIDE ROAD

HAMER ROAD

HANGING STONE

4

High
House
Farm
Hill
Farm
Hill
Cottages
Northdale
Farm
Stone
Bank
Farm
HAMER BANK

The
Heads
Green
Head
Bell
Plantation
Stone
Bank Crag
Stone
Bank

97

Low Blakey
Moor
Woodlands
Farm
Low Bell
End
Heygate
Farm
Page's
Plantation

HEYGATE BANK

Medds
Farmhouse
Low
Thorgill
Farm
Bell
End
Bell
Plantation
New Road
Moor
Plantation

3

Thorgill
Gill
Bank
Dunn
Carr
Hill
Plantation
Abbey
Heads
Rosedale
Abbey
The
Grange
Pry Hills
Wood

Pike
Howe
Little Gill
Cottage
Thorgill
House
Rosedale Abbey
Com Prim Schl
Sevenford
Grange
Plantation
Smith's
Plantation

2

Atkinson
Ellers
Stone
Hagg
Thorgill
Crag
Hobb House
Farm
Sevenford
House
Mill
Farm
Gates
Plantation

The
Crag
Thorgill
Head
Hobb
Crag
Low
Farm
White Horse
Farm Hotel
Newlands
Farm
Yatts
Farm

Cragg
Bank
Top
Bank
Plantation

Cragg
Cottage
Crag
Pond
The
Crag
Shooting
House Hill
Bank
Farm
Mill
Farm

1

Duck
House
YO62
Three
Howes
Hollins
Farm

Underhill
Farm
Spaunton
Moor
Ana
Moss

49
30

Scale: 1⅓ inches to 1 mile

0   ¼   ½ mile
0   250m 500m 750m 1 km

A · **B** · **C** · **D** · **E** · **F**

Murk Mire
Moor

Glaisdale
Head

Nab
Rigg

Middle
Heads

Brown
Hill

8

Traverse
Moor

YO21

Egton High
Moor

YO22

Three
Howes

Pike Hill
Moss

01

Yarlsey
Moss

Peat
Moss

Winter Gill

7

Upper
Heads

Wheeldale Gill

00

Wheeldale
Plantation

Cottergill

Bluewath Beck

6

White
Moor

Wheeldale
Howe

Blue Man-
i'-th'-Moss

Wheeldale Gill

99

Turnhill
Rigg

Black
Moor Rigg

Rutmoor
Head

Raven
Stones

Scar
End

5

Hamer
Moor

98

Crook Beck
Rigg

Owlet
Moor

YO18

Wheeldale
Moor

Hamer
Bridge

Row Mires
Rigg

4

Low
Hamer

Higher Row
Mires

Howth
Rigg

Hutts Bank

97

Lower Row
Mires

Black Rigg Beck

Middle
Rigg

Hartoft
Moor

Black
Rigg

3

Dukes Lea
Farm

White
House

Middleton
Moor

Rutmoor Beck

Russell's
Wood

Ford

96

Hartoft
Rigg

High Wind
Hill

Low Wind
Hill

Ramsden
Head

Keys Beck Road

2

Allotment
Plantation

Low Wind Hill
Farm

Ford

Leaf Howe
Hill

Allotment
Farm

95

Rock House
Farm

Heads House
Farm

St James
Farm

Cropton
Forest

1

Craven
Farm

Dyke House
Farm

Rock House
Wood

Head House
Wood

Ford

Wrelton
Moor

Leaf
Howe

Low Leaf
Howe House

Mauley
Cross
Old Wive's
Well

Low
Muffles

Dragory Road

Pry Hills Lane

94

74 · **A** · 75 · **B** · 76 · **C** · 77 · **D** · 78 · **E** · 79 · **F**

49
71

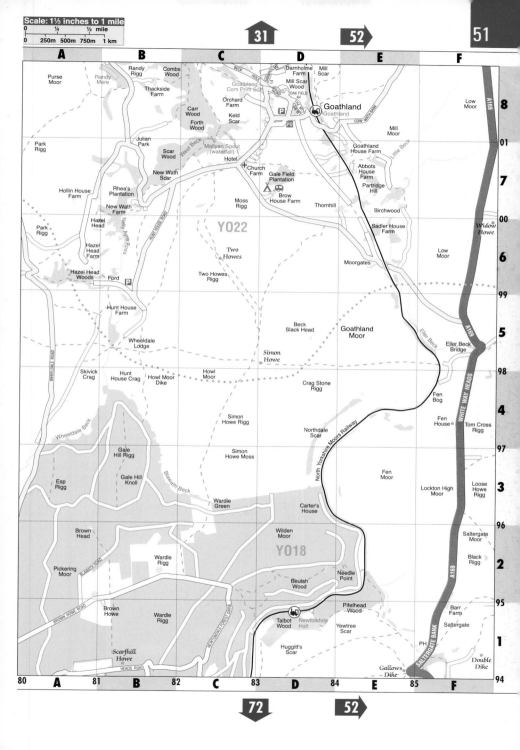

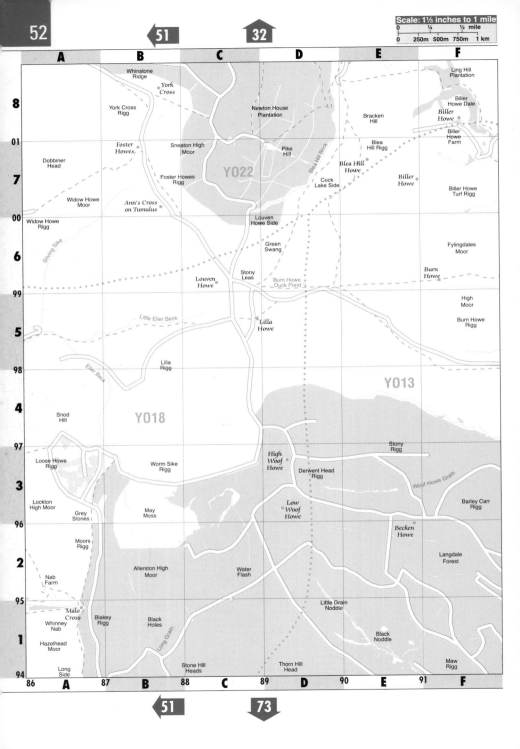

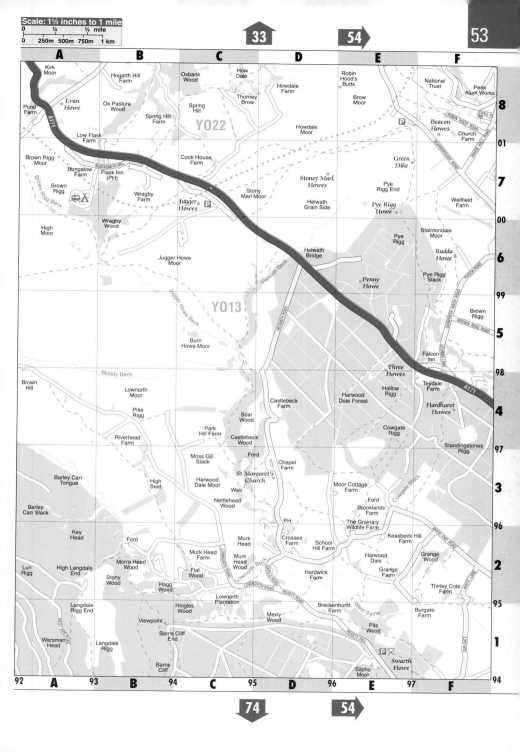

Scale: 1½ inches to 1 mile

0   ¼   ½ mile
0   250m   500m   750m   1 km

A   B   C   D   E   F

Old Peak or
South Cheek

02

Ravenscar

8

Blea Wyke
Point

P

Church Rd
Farm

P

CLIFF RD

STATION RD

01

Common
Cliff

CHURCH ROAD

7

Bent Rigg
Farm

Bent
Rigg

00

Danesdale
Farm

BENT RIGG LANE

Bell Hill
Farm

6

Grange
Farm

Rudda

RUDDA RD

Sandybed
Wood

WAR DIKE LANE

Prospect
House Farm

99

Church
Farm

Meeting
House Farm

Petard
Point

Cleveland Way

Wellington Lodge Llamas

PRIOR WATH ROAD

Bees
Nest Farm

White
Hall Farm

Plane
Tree Farm

Tofta
Farm

TOFTA ROAD

Staintondale
Shire Horse
Farm

Rigg
Hall

5

Island
Farm

BOWEN RIGG RD

PRIOR WATH RD

Staintondale

Rigg Hall
Farm

Shirehorse
Centre

PRIOR
WATH RD

PH

98

Crowdon

Quarry
Farm

North Bridge
End

White House
Farm

Bridge
Farm

DOWNDALE ROAD

4

Hunter
Howe

Wyke
Lodge

Whitestone
Farm

Redhouse
Farm

A171

Cloughton
Moor House

Hayburn Beck
Farm

HODGSON HILL

Nab
End

Hayburn
Wyke

RINGING KELD HILL

Standingstones
Rigg

97

Hayburn
Wyke Hotel

NT

Hodgson Moor
Plantation

Cloughton
Moor

YO13

CRAVEN'S HILL

3

Linglands
Farm

Cloughton
Woods

Rockwood
Farm

The
Hulleys

Newlands
Farm

Caywood
Plantation

Rodger
Trod

96

Tongue Field
Plantation

Gowland
Farm

Cloughton
Newlands

PH

Sycarham
Wood

Cloughton
Plantations

Stone Dale
Plantation

RATTLE HILL

MOOR END RD

2

Spring
House
Farm

Little
Moor Road

Greystone
Farm

Sycarham
Farm

HOOD LANE

Middle /
Part Farm

GOWLAND LANE

Cloughton
Woods

Little
Moor

SALT PANS ROAD

Cloughton
Wyke

95

Ellis
Close
Farm

Moorside
Farm

Court Green
Farm

HOLM HL

WHITE WY

WEST LA

NEWLANDS LA

Hundale
Point

Thirley Beck
Farm

Ripley's
Farm

Cloughton

PO

1 COURT GREEN CL
2 LOCKWOOD CHASE

HAGWOOD DALE ROAD

RIPLEY'S
RD

Green
Farming

PH

Cleveland Way

EGGE SYKE

1

Surgate Brow
Plantation

RIPLEY'S ROAD

LITTLE MOOR CL 1
MOOR LA 2
BECK LA 3

A171

STATION LA

Cloughton
Fields Farm

Long
Nab

94

LINTON CL

98   A   99   B   00   C   01   D   02   E   03   F

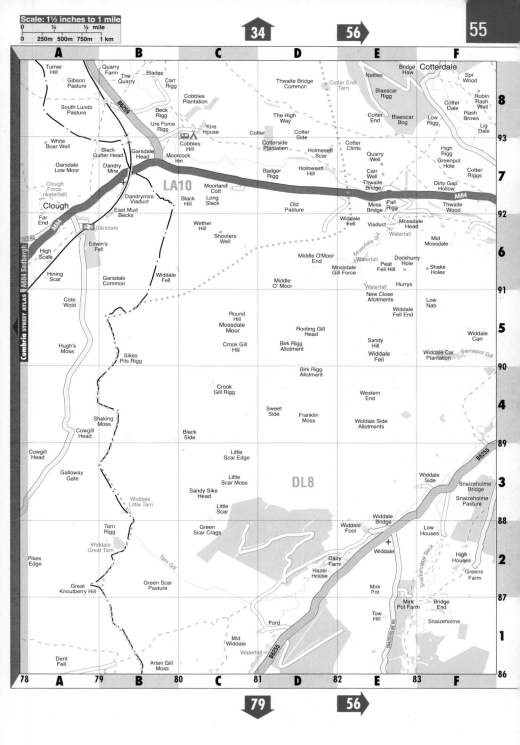

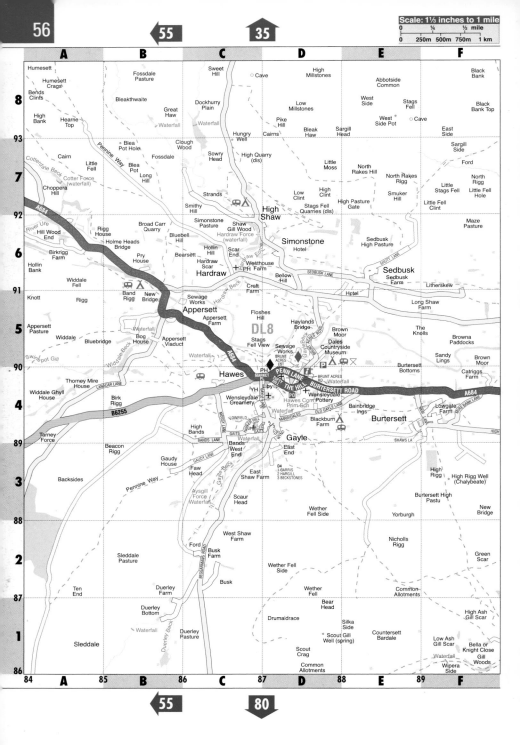

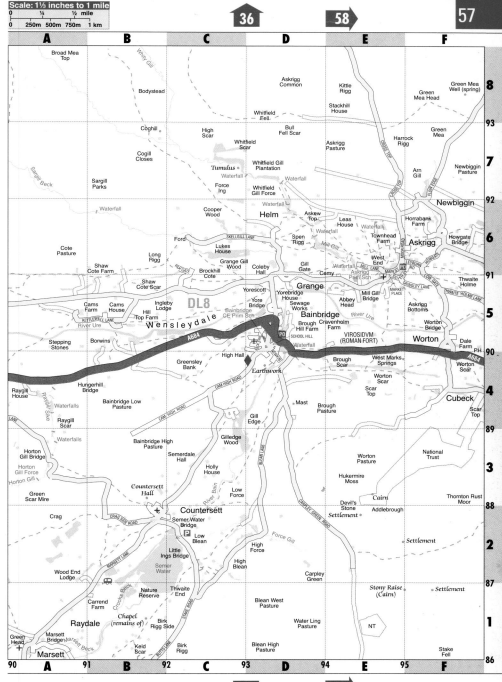

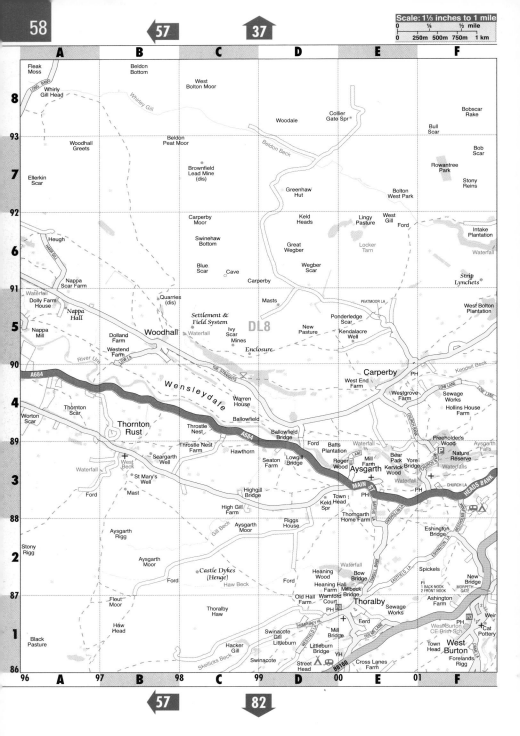

Scale: 1⅓ inches to 1 mile

0   ¼   ½ mile
0   250m 500m 750m 1 km

8

Fleak
Moss

Beldon
Bottom

West
Bolton Moor

Whirly
Gill Head

Whirley Gill

Woodale

Collier
Gate Spr

Bobscar
Rake

Bull
Scar

93

Woodhall
Greets

Beldon
Peat Moor

Beldon Beck

Bob
Scar

Rowantree
Park

7

Ellerkin
Scar

Brownfield
Lead Mine
(dis)

Greenhaw
Hut

Bolton
West Park

Stony
Reins

92

Heugh

Carperby
Moor

Keld
Heads

Lingy
Pasture

West
Gill
Ford

Intake
Plantation

6

Nappa
Scar Farm

Swinehaw
Bottom

Great
Wegber

Locker
Tarn

Waterfall

Waterfall

Dolly Farm
House

Nappa
Hall

Blue
Scar

Cave

Carperby

Wegber
Scar

Strip
Lynchets

91

Nappa
Mill

Dolland
Farm

Quarries
(dis)

Settlement &
Field System

Masts

Ponderledge
Scar

PEATMOOR LA

West Bolton
Plantation

5

Woodhall

Waterfall

Ivy
Scar
Mines

DL8

New
Pasture

Kendalacre
Well

Westend
Farm

Enclosure

Nappa
Mill

LOW LA

River Ure

THE STRAIGHTS

Carperby

Kendell Beck

90

A684

Wensleydale

West End
Farm

PH

LOW LANE

LOW LANE

Worton
Scar

Thornton
Scar

Warren
House

Westgrove
Farm

Sewage
Works

Hollins House
Farm

4

Thornton
Rust

Throstle
Nest

Ballowfield

Ballowfield
Bridge

Batts
Plantation

Waterfall

Freeholder's
Wood

Aysgarth
Falls

West
Beck

Throstle Nest
Farm

Hawthorn

Ford

Bear
Park

Yore
Bridge

P

Nature
Reserve

89

Seaton
Farm

Lowgill
Bridge

Roger
Wood

Mill
Farm

Kervick
Wood

Waterfalls

Scargarth
Well

CHURCH LANE

St Mary's
Well

Aysgarth

GRIFFS

Waterfall

PH

3

Waterfall

Ford

Mast

Highgill
Bridge

Town
Keld Head
Spr

MAIN ST

PH

CHURCH LA

HEADS BANK

High Gill
Farm

Thorgarth
Home Farm

88

Aysgarth
Rigg

Aysgarth
Moor

Riggs
House

Eshington
Bridge

Stony
Rigg

Gill Beck

Spickels

New
Bridge

MORPETH
GATE

2

Aysgarth
Moor

Castle Dykes
(Henge)

Ford

Heaning
Wood

Waterfall

Bow
Bridge

Ashington
Farm

Flout
Moor

Ford

Haw Beck

Heaning Hall
Farm

Millbeck

Sewage
Works

87

Thoralby
Haw

Old Hall
Farm

Warnford
Court

Thoralby

Ford

West Burton
CE Prim Sch

Hôw
Head

PH

HUMPHREY HL

Cat
Pottery

1

Black
Pasture

Hacker
Gill

Swinacote
Gill
Littleburn

Mill
Bridge

HOLME LANE

Town
Head

West
Burton

Forelands
Rigg

86

Swinacote

Skellicks Beck

Littleburn
Bridge

YH

Street
Head

B6160

Cross Lanes
Farm

| 96 | A | 97 | B | 98 | C | 99 | D | 00 | E | 01 | F |

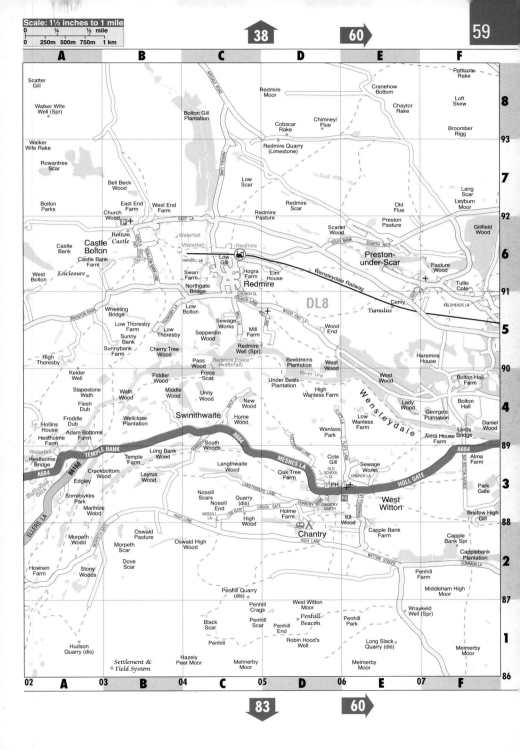

Scale: 1⅓ inches to 1 mile

0   ¼   ½ mile
0   250m 500m 750m 1 km

A B C D E F

Scatter Gill

Petticote Rake

Loft Skew

Walker Wife Well (Spr)

Redmire Moor

Cranehow Bottom

Chaytor Rake

Broomber Rigg

Bolton Gill Plantation

Cobscar Rake

Chimney/ Flue

Walker Wife Rake

Redmire Quarry (Limestone)

Rowantree Scar

Low Scar

Lang Scar

Leyburn Moor

Bell Beck Wood

Gillfield Wood

Bolton Parks

East End Farm

West End Farm

Redmire Scar

Old Flue

Church Wood

Redmire Pasture

Preston Pasture

EAST LA

Castle Bank

Castle Bolton

Bolton Castle

Waterfall

Redmire

Scarlet Wood

Preston-under-Scar

Pasture Wood

Castle Bank Farm

Waterfall

CISSY BANK

SCARTH NICK

Enclosure

Low Gill

Hogra Farm

Elm House

Tullis Cote

West Bolton

Swan Farm

Redmire

Wensleydale Railway

Cerny

KELDHEADS LA

Northgate Bridge

Church CL

DL8

Tumulus

BRUNTON BANK

Wheeling Bridge

Low Bolton

CHURCH LANE

WOOD END LA

Low Thoreshy Farm

Low Thoreshy

Sewage Works

Mill Farm

Wood End

High Thoreshy

Sunny Bank

Sepperdin Wood

Redmire Well (Spr)

Beeldreins Plantation

Haremire House

Sunnybank Farm

Cherry Tree Wood

Pass Wood

Redmire Force (waterfall)

River Ure

West Wood

Kelder Well

Fiddler Wood

Force Scar

Unity Wood

Under Beals Plantation

High Wanless Farm

West Wood

Lady Wood

Bolton Hall Farm

Slapestone Wath

Wath Wood

Middle Wood

New Wood

Wensleydale

George's Plantation

Bolton Hall

Flesh Dub

Swinithwaite

Home Wood

Low Wanless Farm

Daniel Wood

Hollins House

Froddle Dub

Wellclose Plantation

Wanless Park

Alma House Farm

Lords Bridge

Hestholme Farm

Adam Bottoms Farm

South Woods

Pattenham Lane

Cote Gill

Sewage Works

Alma Farm

Waterfall

TEMPLE BANK

Long Bank Wood

Langthwaite Wood

OLD SCHOOL CL

HOLL GATE

Park Gate

Hestholme Bridge

Temple Farm

CHURCH LA

PH

West Witton

A684

BLATFORD BECK

A684

B6160

Crookbottom Wood

Layrus Wood

LANGTHWAITE LANE

PO

Bristow High Gill

Edgley

MOOR LANE

Sorrelsykes Park

Nossill Scars

Quarry (dis)

CHANTRY BANK

Chantry Garth

Kit Wood

Capple Bank Spr

Marlhobe Wood

Nossill End

GREEN GATE

Cappelbank Plantation

ELLERS LA

Morpeth Wood

Oswald Pasture

NOSSILL LA

ON GATE

High Wood

Holme Farm

Capple Bank Farm

COMMON LA

Morpeth Scar

Dove Scar

Oswald High Wood

Chantry

HIGH LANE

Penhill Farm

Howrein Farm

Stony Woods

HIGH LANE

WITTON STEEPS

Middleham High Moor

Penhill Quarry (dis)

West Witton Moor

Hudson Quarry (dis)

Settlement & Field System

Hazely Peat Moor

Black Scar

Penhill Crags

Penhill Scar

Penhill End

West Witton

Penhill Beacon

Penhill Park

Wraykeld Well (Spr)

Melmerby Moor

Penhill

Robin Hood's Well

Melmerby Moor

Long Slack Quarry (dis)

Melmerby Moor

8 93 7 92 6 91 5 90 4 89 3 88 2 87 1 86

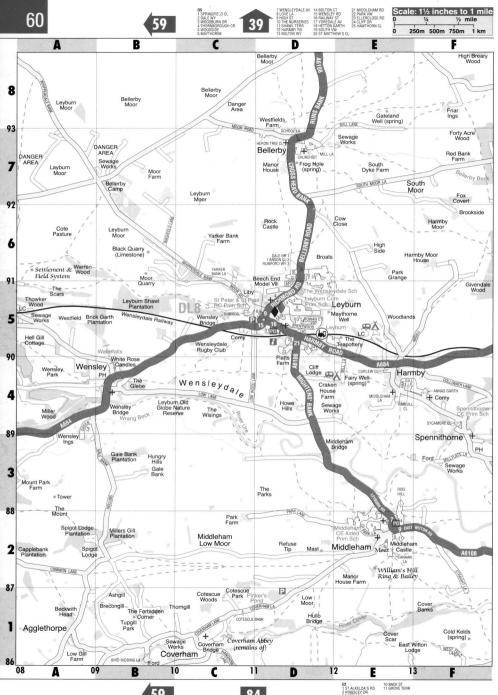

D5
1 SPRINGFIELD CL
2 DALE WY
3 WOODBURN DR
4 THORNBROUGH CR
5 WOODSIDE
6 MAYTHORNE

7 WENSLEYDALE AV
8 LOVE LA
9 HIGH ST
10 THE NURSERIES
11 SHAWL TERR
12 HARMBY RD
13 BOLTON WY

14 BOLTON CT
15 WENSLEY RD
16 RAILWAY ST
17 YOREDALE AV
18 HETTON GARTH
19 SOUTH VW
20 ST MATTHEW'S CL

21 MIDDLEHAM CL
22 PARK VW
23 ELLERCLOSE RD
24 CLYF DR
25 HAWTHORN CL

Scale: 1⅓ inches to 1 mile
0   ¼   ½ mile
0 250m 500m 750m 1 km

8
High Breary Wood
Bellerby Moor
Leyburn Moor
Bellerby Moor
Bellerby Moor
Danger Area
Friar Ings
Westfields Farm
Gateland Well (spring)

93
MOOR ROAD
SCHOOL LA
Forty Acre Wood
Red Bank Farm
Sewage Works
MILL LANE
DANGER AREA
Sewage Works
Layburn Moor
Moor Farm
HERON TREE CL
Bellerby
MILL LA
CHURCHST
Frog Hole (spring)
Manor House
South Dyke Farm
Bellerby Beck

7
DANGER AREA
Layburn Moor
Bellerby Camp
CROSS HEAD BANK
SOUTH MOOR LA
South Moor
Fox Covert

92
Leyburn Moor
Leyburn Moor
Cow Close
Harmby Moor
Brookside

6
Cote Pasture
Black Quarry (Limestone)
Yarker Bank Farm
Rock Castle
RUMFORO WY 3
High Side
Harmby Moor House
Park Grange
Givendale Wood

WHIPPERDALE BANK
SWASSEDALE LANE
Settlement & Field System
Warren Wood
Moor Quarry
YARKER BANK LA
DALE GR 1
I'ANSON CL 2
Broats
BELLERBY ROAD
RICHMOND RD

91
The Scars
Thowker Wood
LC
Leyburn Shawl Plantation
Beech End Model Vill
Liby
St Peter & St Paul RC Prim Sch
The Wensleydale Sch
Leyburn Com Prim Sch
Leyburn
Maythorne Well
Woodlands

5
Sewage Works
Westfield
Brick Garth Plantation
Wensleydale Railway
Wensley Bridge
RISEBER
PO
BRENTWOOD
ROWAN CT
LC
The Teapottery
DL8

90
Hell Gill Cottage
Waterfalls
Wensleydale Rugby Club
Cemy
Flatts Farm
HARMBY ROAD
A684
Fairy Well (spring)
CURLEW CL
Woodlands

White Rose Candles
The Glebe
Leyburn Old Globe Nature Reserve
Cliff Lodge
Craken House Farm
MIDDLEHAM LA
Annas Garth
RARGILL CL
Cemy
COLLIWATH LANE

4
Wensley Park
PH
Wensley
Wensleydale
Howe Hills
Sewage Works
Harmby
GILL LA
SYCAMORE LA
Spennithorne CE Prim Sch

Miller Wood
A684
Wensley Bridge
Wrang Beck
The Wisings
Middleham Bridge
Spennithorne
PH

89
Wensley Ings
GREEN LA
GALE BANK
Gale Bank Plantation
Hungry Hills
Gale Bank
River Ure
LOW LANE
Ford
MILLFLATS LA
Sewage Works

3
Mount Park Farm
Tower
The Parks
DOG HILL
LEYBURN RD

88
The Mount
Spigot Lodge Plantation
Millers Gill Plantation
Park Farm
PARK LANE
Refuse Tip
Mast
Middleham CE Aided Prim Sch
EAST WITTON RD
PARK LA

2
Capplebank Plantation
Spigot Lodge
Middleham Low Moor
Middleham
Moat
Middleham Castle
CANAAN LA
A6108
COMMON LANE
William's Hill Ring & Bailey
STRAIGHT LA

87
Ashgill
Brecongill
Thorngill
Cotescue Woods
Cotescue Park
P
Pinker's Pond
Low Moor
Manor House Farm
Cover Banks

1
Agglethorpe
Beckwith Head
The Forbidden Corner
Tupgill Park
COVERHAM LANE
COTESCUE BANK
Hullo Bridge
Cover Scar
East Witton Lodge
Cold Kelds (spring)
WEST LA

Low Gill Farm
Sewage Works
Coverham Bridge
BIRD RIDDING LA
Coverham
Ford
Coverham Abbey (remains of)
River Cover
HARMBY LANE

86

E2
1 ST ALKELDA'S RD
2 KINGSLEY DR
3 NORTH RD
4 THE SPRINGS
5 PARK LA
6 CHURCH ST
7 KIRKGATE
8 BACK LA
9 MARKET PL
10 BACK ST
11 GROVE TERR

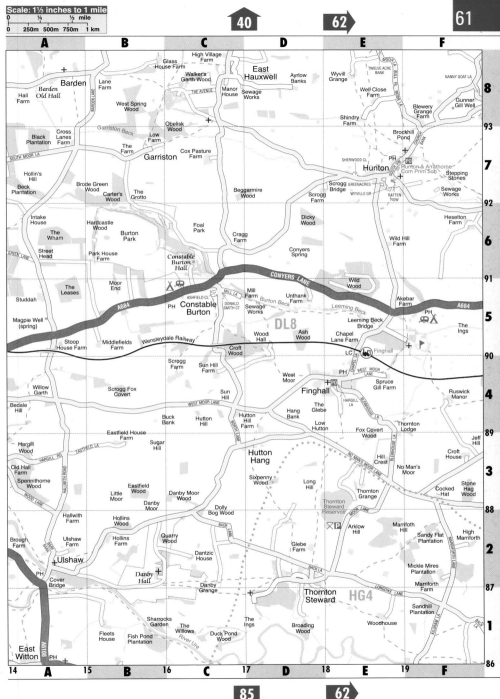

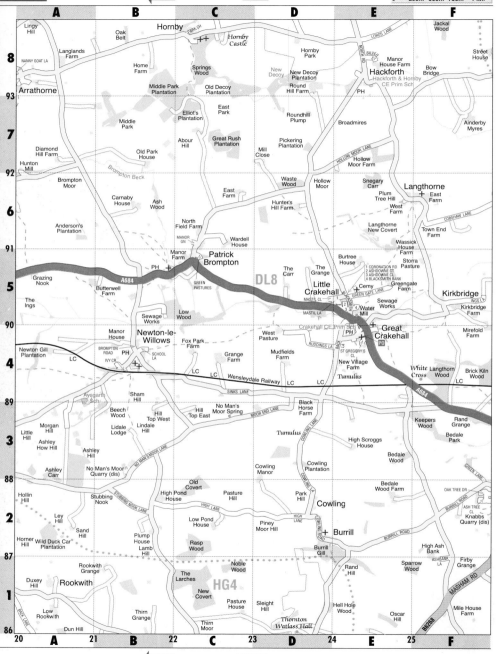

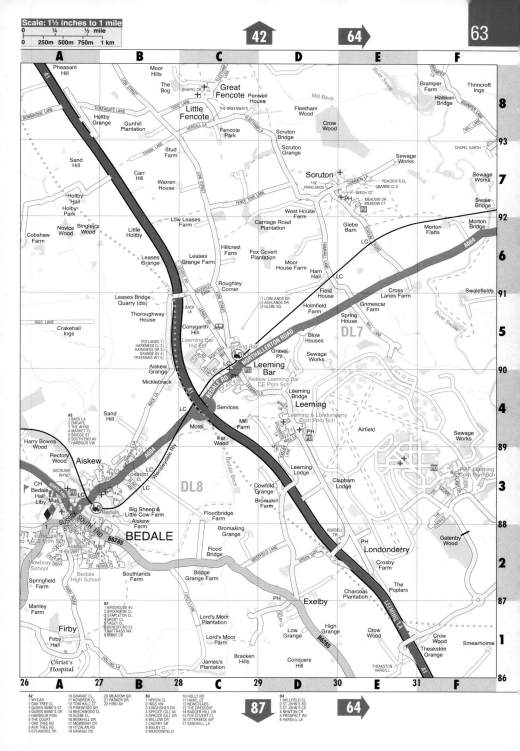

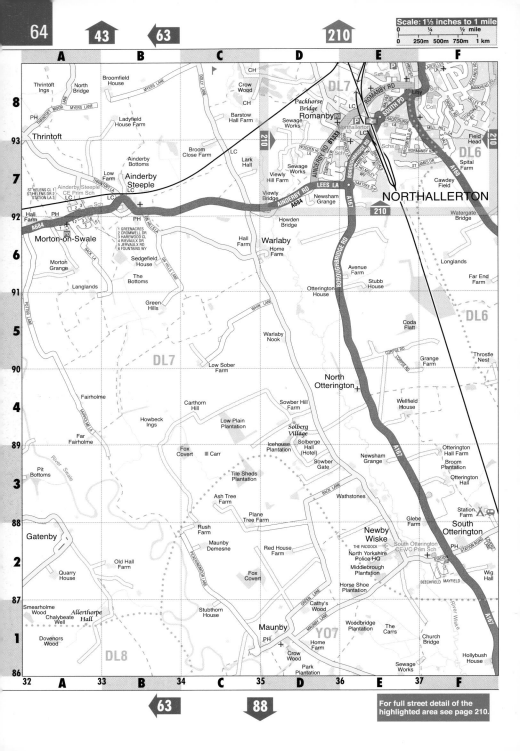

For full street detail of the highlighted area see page 210.

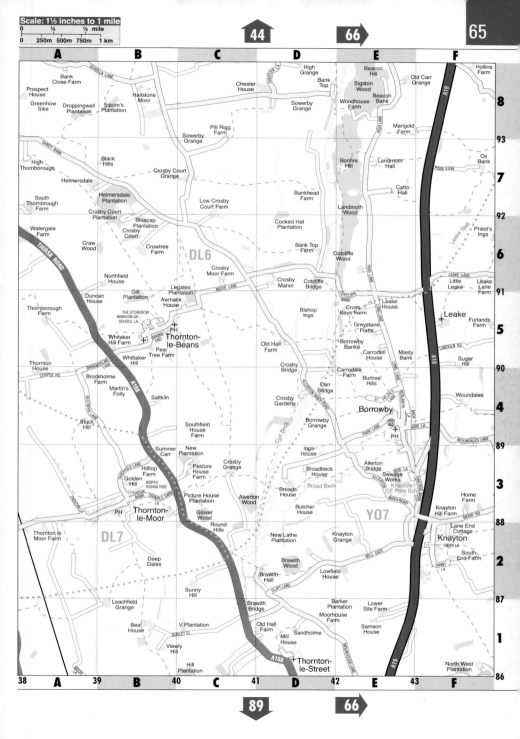

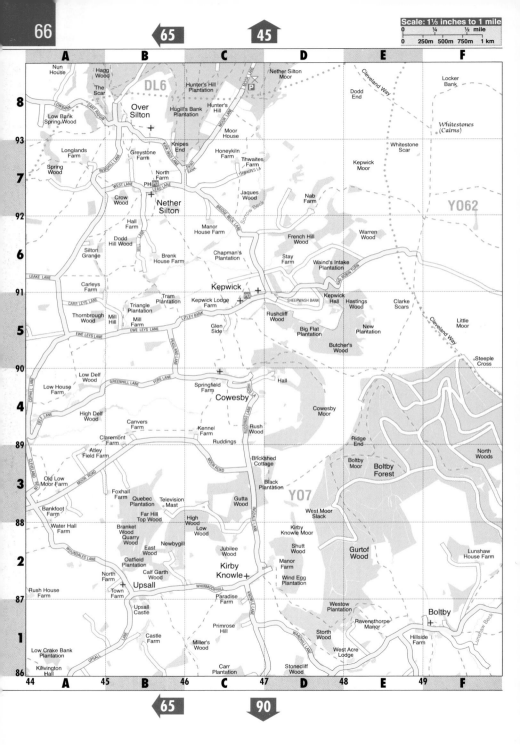

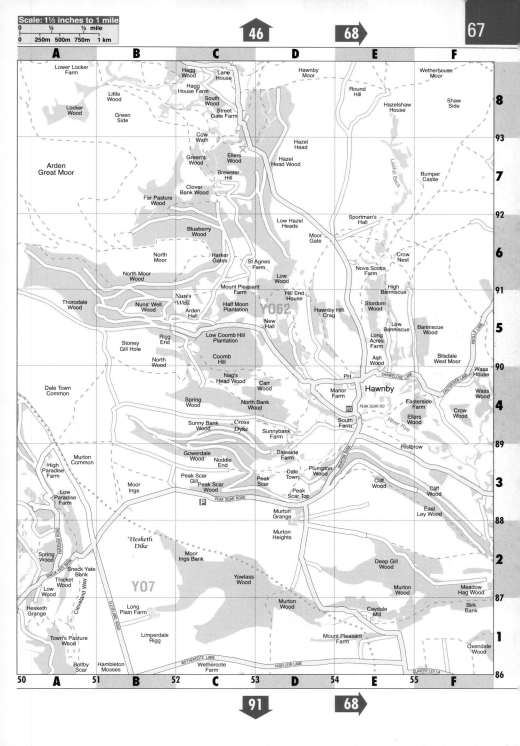

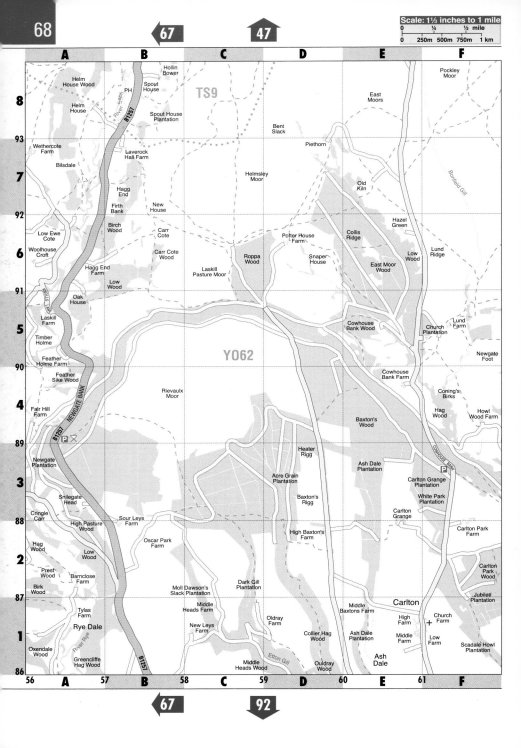

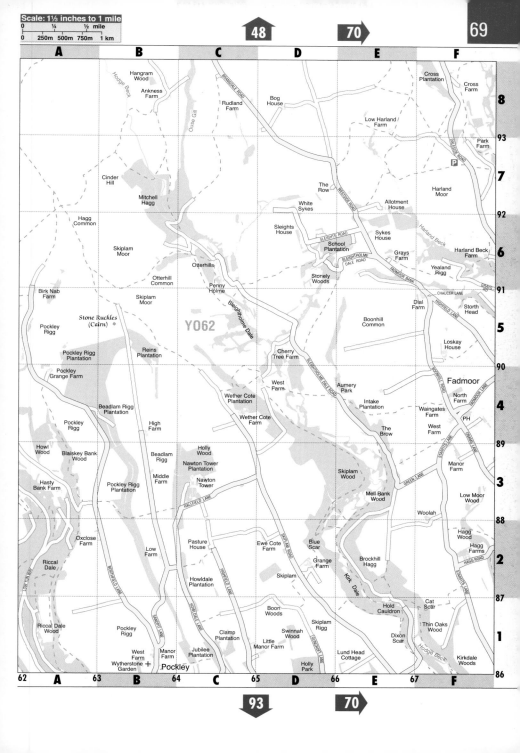

Scale: 1½ inches to 1 mile

0   ¼   ½   mile
0   250m 500m 750m   1 km

8
93
7
92
6
91
5
90
4
89
3
88
2
87
1
86

Hangram Wood
Hodge Beck
Ankness Farm
Ouse Gill
Bransdale Road
Rudland Farm
Bog House
Cross Plantation
Cross Farm
Low Harland Farm
Park Farm
Dalesend Road
P
The Row
Harland Moor
Cinder Hill
Mitchell Hagg
White Sykes
Westside Road
Allotment House
Hagg Common
Sleights House
Sleights Road
Sykes House
Harland Beck
Skiplam Moor
School Plantation
Grays Farm
Harland Beck Farm
Otterhills
Bleightholme Dale Road
Stonely Woods
Moneor Bank
Yealand Rigg
Birk Nab Farm
Otterhill Common
Penny Holme
Chaucer Lane
Grays Rd
Skiplam Moor
Dial Farm
Highfield Lane
Storth Head
Stone Ruckles (Cairn)
YO62
Boonhill Common
Loskay House
Pockley Rigg
Bleightholme Dale
Reins Plantation
Cherry Tree Farm
Fadmoor
Pockley Rigg Plantation
West Farm
Aumery Park
Moneor Road
North Farm
Pockley Grange Farm
Wether Cote Plantation
Intake Plantation
Waingates Farm
PH
Sturdy Lane
Oakley Lane
Beadlam Rigg Plantation
Wether Cote Farm
The Brow
West Farm
Pockley Rigg
High Farm
Holly Wood
Skiplam Wood
Green Lane
Manor Farm
Howl Wood
Blaiskey Bank Wood
Beadlam Rigg
Nawton Tower Plantation
Mell Bank Wood
Low Moor Wood
Hasty Bank Farm
Middle Farm
Nawton Tower
Woolah
Pockley Rigg Plantation
Tallfield Lane
Skiplam Road
Hagg Wood
Oxclose Farm
Pasture House
Ewe Cote Farm
Blue Scar
Brockhill Hagg
Hagg Farms
Hagg Road
Low Farm
Grange Farm
Riccal Dale
Northfield Lane
Howldale Plantation
Highfield Lane
Skiplam
Kirk Dale
Cat Scar
Riccal Dale Wood
Low Ickk Way
Boon Woods
Swinnah Wood
Skiplam Rigg
Hold Cauldron
Thin Oaks Wood
Stardy Lane
Pockley Rigg
Bansdy Lane
Clamp Plantation
Little Manor Farm
Longster Lane
Lund Head Cottage
Dixon Scar
Hodge Beck
Kirkdale Woods
West Farm Wytherstone Garden
Manor Farm
Jubilee Plantation
Pockley
Holly Park

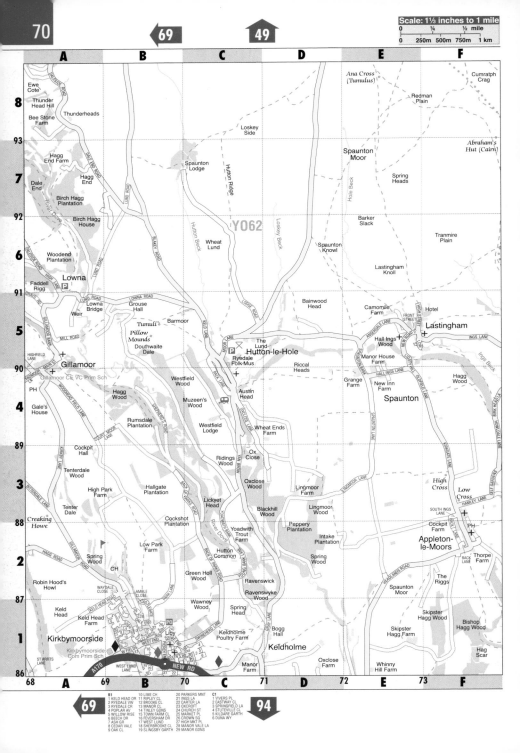

Scale: 1½ inches to 1 mile

0   ¼   ½ mile
0   250m 500m 750m 1 km

A   B   C   D   E   F

8

93

7

92

6

91

5

90

4

89

3

88

2

87

1

86

Ewe Cote
Thunder Head Hill
Bee Stone Farm
Thunderheads
DALESIDE ROAD
Hagg End Farm
Hagg End
Dale End
Birch Hagg Plantation
Birch Hagg House
LUND ROAD
DALE END ROAD
River Dove
Woodend Plantation
DALESIDE ROAD
Lowna
Faddell Rigg
GILLAMOOR ROAD
HIGH LANE
MILL ROAD
Weir
Lowna Bridge
LUND ROAD
LOWNA ROAD
Grouse Hall
Barmoor
BLAKEY ROAD
Tumuli
Pillow Mounds
Douthwaite Dale
HIGHFIELD LANE
MAIN ST
Gillamoor
Gillamoor CE VC Prim Sch
PH
WOODHEAD FIELD LANE
COURT MOOR LANE
KIRKBY LANE
Gale's House
Hagg Wood
Rumsdale Plantation
SHEPHERD'S ROAD
Cockpit Hall
Tenterdale Wood
High Park Farm
Hallgate Plantation
Tenter Dale
BUTTERDALE LANE
Creaking Howe
HAGG ROAD
GILLAMOOR ROAD
Cockshot Plantation
Low Park Farm
Spring Wood
CH
Robin Hood's Howl
WAYDALE CLOSE
AMBLE CLOSE
Keld Head
Keld Head Farm
WEST FIELD ROAD
Kirkbymoorside
Kirkbymoorside Com Prim Sch
ST AELRED'S LANE
WEST LUND LANE
A170
NEW RD

Loskey Side
Hutton Ridge
Hutton Beck
Spaunton Lodge
KELD LANE
Wheat Lund
YO62
Loskey Beck
LODGE ROAD
The Lund
Hutton-le-Hole
Ryedale Folk Mus
BACK LANE
Westfield Wood
Muzeen's Wood
Austin Head
Westfield Lodge
DALESIDE LANE
Riccal Heads
Wheat Ends Farm
Ridings Wood
Ox Close
Oxclose Wood
FOUNTAIN LANE
RIVER DOVE
Lickyet Head
Blackhill Wood
River Dove
Yoadwith Trout Farm
Hutton Common
Green Holl Wood
Ravenswick
Ravenswyke Wood
Spring Head
SWINEHERD LANE
Wawney Wood
Keldholme Poultry Farm
Bogg Hall
Manor Farm
Keldholme
Oxclose Farm

Ana Cross (Tumulus)
Redman Plain
Spaunton Moor
Hole Beck
Spring Heads
Barker Slack
Spaunton Knowl
Bainwood Head
Camomile Farm
ANESIDE LANE
Hall Ings Wood
GREEN LANE
SPAUNTON LANE
Manor House Farm
Grange Farm
New Inn Farm
HALL INGS LANE
Spaunton
LIDMOOR LANE
Lingmoor Farm
Lingmoor Wood
Peppery Plantation
Intake Plantation
MOORLANDS ROAD
Spring Wood
Spaunton Moor
Skipster Hagg Farm
Whinny Hill Farm

Cumraph Crag
Abraham's Hut (Cairn)
Tranmire Plain
Lastingham Knoll
Hotel
Lastingham
INGS LANE
Ings Beck
Hagg Wood
BIRK HEAD LANE
HAMLEY LANE
High Cross
Low Cross
SOUTH INGS LANE
Cockpit Farm
PH
Appleton-le-Moors
BACK LANE
Thorpe Farm
The Riggs
Skipster Hagg Wood
Bishop Hagg Wood
Hag Scar

B1
1 KELD HEAD DR
2 RYEDALE VW
3 RYEDALE CR
4 POPLAR AV
5 WILLOW RISE
6 BEECH DR
7 ASH GR
8 CEDAR VALE
9 OAK CL
10 LIME CH
11 RIPLEY CL
12 BROOKE CL
13 MANOR CL
14 TINLEY GDNS
15 TOWN FARM CL
16 FEVERSHAM DR
17 WEST LUND
18 SHERBROOKE CL
19 SLINGSBY GARTH
20 PARKERS MINT
21 INGS LA
22 CARTER LA
23 OXCROFT
24 CHURCH ST
25 MARKET PL
26 CROWN SQ
27 HIGH MKT PL
28 MANOR VALE LA
29 MANOR GDNS
C1
1 VIVERS PL
2 EASTWAY CL
3 SPRINGFIELD LA
4 STUTEVILLE CL
5 KILDARE GARTH
6 DUNA WY

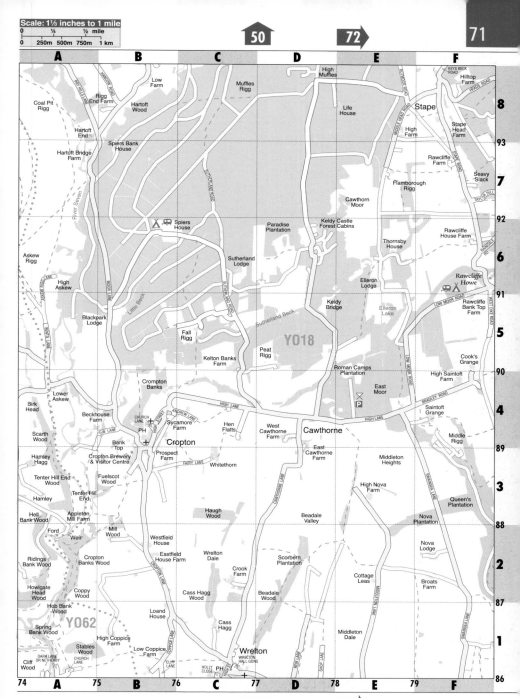

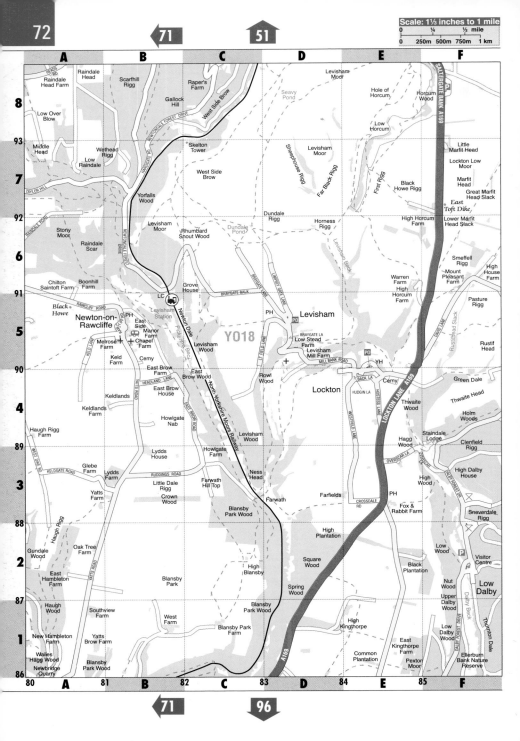

Scale: 1½ inches to 1 mile

0   ¼   ½ mile
0   250m 500m 750m 1 km

8

HEADS RD
Raindale
Head Farm

Raindale
Head

Scarfhill
Rigg

Raper's
Farm

West Side Brow

Gallock
Hill

Levisham
Moor

Hole of
Horcum

Horcum
Wood

P

Low Over
Blow

93

Middle
Head

Wethead
Rigg

Low
Raindale

Skelton
Tower

Seavy
Pond

Levisham
Moor

Low
Horcum

Little
Marflit Head

Lockton Low
Moor

7

TAYLOR HILL

West Side
Brow

Sheephouse Rigg

Far Black Rigg

First Rigg

Black
Howe Rigg

Marflit
Head

Great Marflit
Head Slack

East
Toft Dike

Yorfalls
Wood

Levisham
Moor

Rhumbard
Snout Wood

Dundale
Rigg

Horness
Rigg

High Horcum
Farm

Lower Marflit
Head Slack

92

RANDALE ROAD

Stony
Moor

Raindale
Scar

Levisham
Moor

Dundale
Pond

Levisham Beck

Smeffell
Rigg

Mount
Pleasant
Farm

High
House
Farm

6

Chilton
Saintoft Farm

Boonhill
Farm

Grove
House

BRAYGATE BALK

Warren
Farm

High
Horcum
Farm

Pasture
Rigg

91

RAWCLIFF ROAD

Black
Howe

LC

Levisham
Station

PH

Newton-on-
Rawcliffe

East
Side

Manor
Farm

Chapel
Farm

Newton Dale

Picks Beck

PH

Levisham

PH

P

Rustifhead Slack

SIDE LANE

Rustif
Head

5

KELD ROAD

Melrose
Farm

Keld
Farm

Cemy

Levisham
Wood

Y018

Braygate LA
Low Stead
Farm

Levisham
Mill Farm

P
YH

90

East Brow
Farm

East
Brow Wood

East Brow
House

HEADLAND LANE

Rowl
Wood

MILL BANK ROAD

Cemy

BACK LA

Lockton

Green Dale

4

Keldlands

Keldlands
Farm

YATTS ROAD

Howlgate
Nab

EAST BERN ROAD

Levisham
Wood

Mont Yorkshire Moors Railway

HUDGIN LA

LOCKTON LANE A169

Thwaite
Wood

Staindale
Lodge

Thwaite Head

Holm
Woods

Clenfield
Rigg

89

Haugh Rigg
Farm

WEST DIKE RD

KELDGATE ROAD

Glebe
Farm

Lydds
House

Lydds
Farm

RUDDINGS ROAD

Howlgate
Farm

Ness
Head

WESTFIELD LANE

Hagg
Wood

OVERSAR LA

High Dalby
House

3

Haugh Rigg

Yatts
Farm

Little Dale
Rigg

Crown
Wood

Farwath
Hill Top

Farwath

Farfields

CROSSDALE
RD

PH

Fox &
Rabbit Farm

High
Wood

DALBY FOREST DR

Sneverdale
Rigg

88

Gundale
Wood

Oak Tree
Farm

Blansby
Park Wood

High
Plantation

Black
Plantation

P

Visitor
Centre

2

East
Hambleton
Farm

YATTS ROAD

Blansby
Park

High
Blansby

Square
Wood

Nut
Wood

Upper
Dalby
Wood

**Low
Dalby**

87

Haugh
Wood

Southview
Farm

West
Farm

Blansby
Park Wood

Spring
Wood

High
Kingthorpe

Low
Dalby
Wood

DALBY BECK

Thornton Dale

1

New Hambleton
Farm

Wailes
Hagg Wood

Yatts
Brow Farm

Blansby Park
Farm

A169

Common
Plantation

East
Kingthorpe
Farm

Pexton
Moor

Ellerburn
Bank Nature
Reserve

86

Newbridge
Quarry

Blansby
Park Wood

80   **A**   **81**   **B**   **82**   **C**   **83**   **D**   **84**   **E**   **85**   **F**

SALTERGATE BANK A1169
A1169
NEWTONDALE FOREST DRIVE
HARGATE RD
NEWTONDALE FOREST DRIVE
TARGET GATE LANE
BRAYGATE LANE
HOSTESS LANE

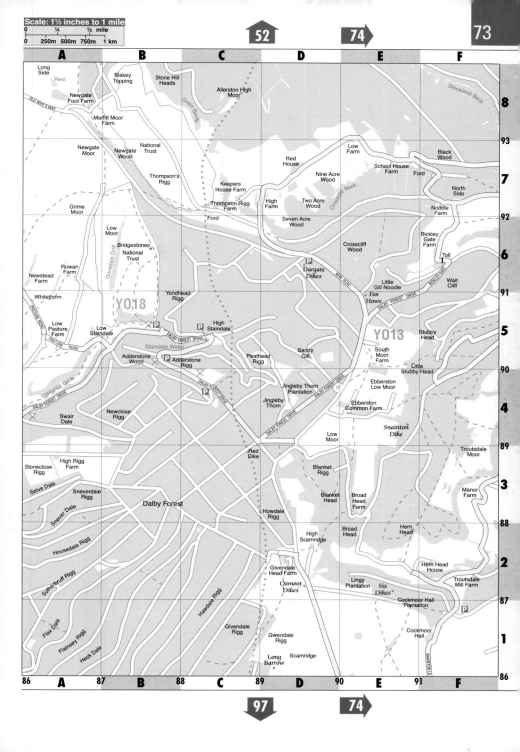

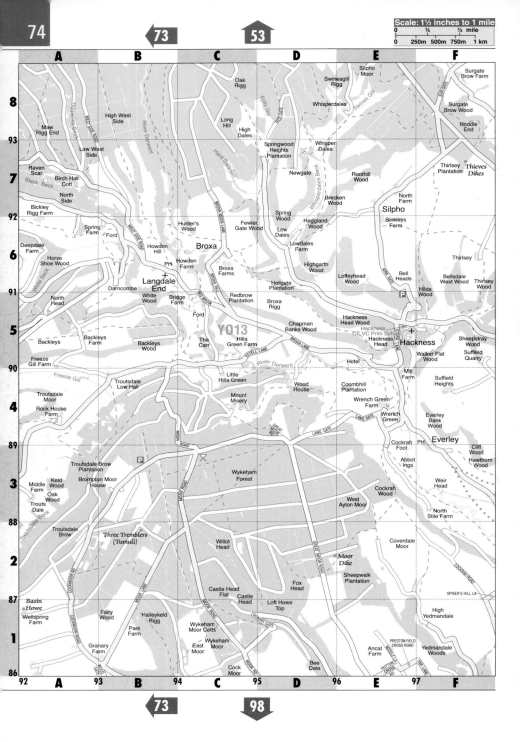

Scale: 1⅓ inches to 1 mile

A **B** **C** **D** **E** **F**

Maw Rigg End

High West Side

Oak Rigg

Long Hill

High Dales

Silpho Moor

Swinesgill Rigg

Whisperdales

Surgate Brow Farm

Surgate Brow Wood

Noddle End

Low West Side

Springwood Heights Plantation

Whisper Dales

Newgate

Roothill Wood

North Farm

Thirlsey Plantation

Thieves Dikes

Raven Scar

Birch Hall Cott

North Side

Black Beck

Bickley Rigg Farm

Spring Farm

Ford

Hunter's Wood

Fewler Gate Wood

Spring Wood

Low Dales

Haggland Wood

Brecken Wood

Silpho

Binkleys Farm

Thirlsey

Deepdale Farm

Horse Shoe Wood

White Beck

WEST SIDE ROAD

Howden Hill

Broxa

Howden Farm

Lowdales Farm

Highgarth Wood

Loffeyhead Wood

Bell Heads

Bellsdale West Wood

Thirlsey Wood

PH

Langdale End

Darncombe

White Wood

Bridge Farm

Broxa Farms

Holigate Plantation

Hilda Wood

North Head

Ford

Redbrow Plantation

Broxa Rigg

Hackness Head Wood

Hackness CE VC Prim Sch

Hackness Head

Hackness

Sheepstray Wood

Backleys

Backleys Farm

Backleys Wood

The Carr

Hilla Green Farm

Chapman Banks Wood

Walker Flat Wood

Suffield Quarry

Freeze Gill Farm

Freeze Gill

Troutsdale Low Hall

Little Hilla Green

River Derwent

Hotel

Wood House

Coombhill Plantation

Mill Farm

Suffield Heights

Troutsdale Moor

Rock House Farm

Mount Misery

Wrench Green Farm

Wrench Green

Lang Gate

Everley Bank Wood

Cockrah Foot

PH

Everley

Troutsdale Brow Plantation

Brompton Moor House

Wykeham Forest

MOOR ROAD

Abbot Ings

Cliff Wood

Hawthorn Wood

Middle Farm

Keld Wood

Oak Wood

Trouts Dale

West Ayton Moor

Cockrah Wood

Weir Head

North Stile Farm

Troutsdale Brow

Three Tremblers (Tumuli)

Willot Head

Moor Dike

Coverdale Moor

SPIKER'S HILL LA

Basin Howe

Wellspring Farm

Fairy Wood

Halleykeld Rigg

Park Farm

Castle Head Flat

Castle Head

Loft Howe Top

Fox Head

Sheepwalk Plantation

High Yedmandale

Granary Farm

Wykeham Moor Cotts

East Moor

Wykeham Moor

Bee Dale

Ancat Farm

PRESTON FIELD CROSS ROAD

Yedmandale Woods

Cock Moor

A **B** **C** **D** **E** **F**

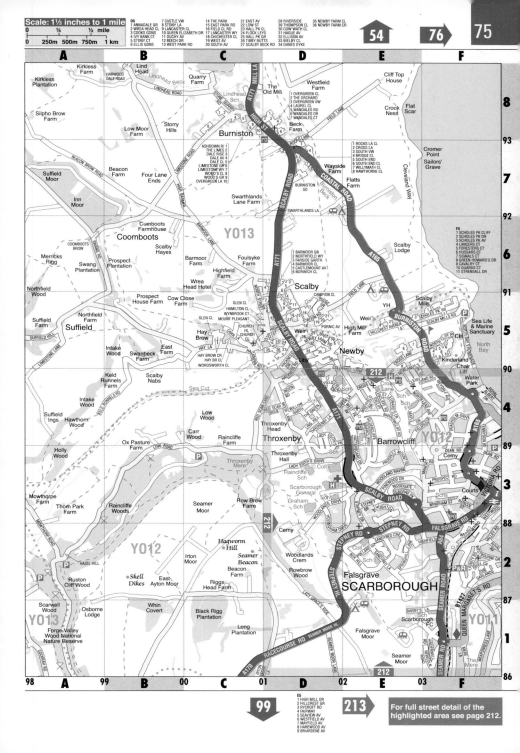

Scale: 1⅓ inches to 1 mile
0   ¼   ½ mile
0   250m 500m 750m 1 km

A B C D E F

8
93
7
92
6
91
5
90

213

North Bay
YO12
Castle Cliff
ROYAL ALBERT DRIVE
MARINE DRIVE
P
Castle
4
CASTLE RD
LONGWESTGATE
YO11
89
P
PO
ST THOMAS ST
Sch
SANDSIDE
3
Mus
Art Gall
SCARBOROUGH
South Sands
88
The Spa Complex
213
2
South Bay
PO
ESPLANADE
QU VICTORIA
87
Sch
Black Rocks
P
1
Sports Ctr
A165
Schs
White Nab
COLLEGE LA
FILEY RD
YO11
Raven Scar
CH
KNOX LA
Univ
Cornelian Bay
86
04   A   05   B   06   C   07   D   08   E   09   F

213

For full street detail of the highlighted area see page 213.

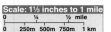

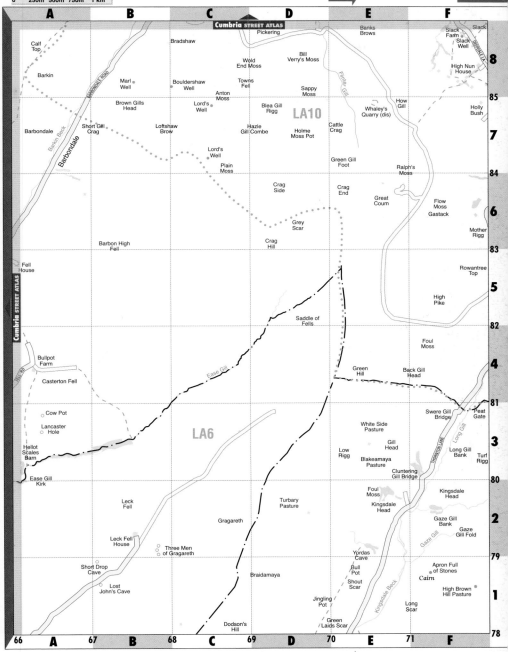

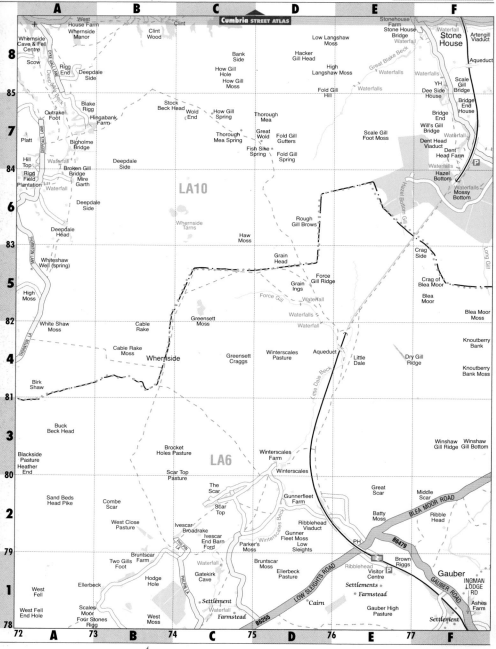

77

Scale: 1½ inches to 1 mile

Cumbria STREET ATLAS

West House Farm
Whernside Cave & Fell Centre
Scow
Whernside Manor
Clint Wood
Clint
Low Langshaw Moss
Stonehouse Farm
Stone House Bridge
Waterfall
Stone House
Artengill Viaduct

Rigg End
Deepdale Side
Bank Side
Hacker Gill Head
Aqueduct
Waterfalls
YH
Dee Side House
Scale Gill Bridge

Outrake Foot
Blake Rigg
Hingabank Farm
Stock Beck Head
Wold End
How Gill Hole
How Gill Moss
High Langshaw Moss
Fold Gill Hill
Waterfalls
Bridge End
Will's Gill Bridge
Bridge End House

Platt
Bigholme Bridge
Deepdale Side
Thorough Mea Spring
Great Wold
Thorough Mea
Fish Sike Spring
Fold Gill Gutters
Fold Gill Spring
Scale Gill Foot Moss
Dent Head Viaduct
Waterfall

Hill Top
Rigg Field Plantation
Broken Gill Bridge
Mire Garth
Waterfall
Deepdale Side
LA10
Dent Head Farm
Dent
Hazel Bottom
Waterfalls

Deepdale Side
Whernside Tarns
Haw Moss
Rough Gill Brows
Mossy Bottom
Waterfalls

Deepdale Head
Crag Side
Long Gill

Whiteshaw Well (spring)
Grain Head
Crag of Blea Moor

High Moss
Grain Ings
Force Gill Ridge
Blea Moor
Blea Moor Moss

White Shaw Moss
Cable Rake
Greensett Moss
Force Gill
Waterfall
Waterfalls
Knoutberry Bank

Cable Rake Moss
Whernside
Greensett Craggs
Winterscales Pasture
Aqueduct
Little Dale
Dry Gill Ridge
Knoutberry Bank Moss

Birk Shaw
Little Dale Beck

Buck Beck Head
Brocket Holes Pasture
LA6
Winterscales Farm
Winscar
Gill Ridge
Winshaw Gill Bottom

Blackside Pasture
Heather End
Scar Top Pasture
Winterscales
Great Scar
Middle Scar
Blea Moor Road

Sand Beds Head Pike
Combe Scar
The Scar
Gunnerfleet Farm
Batty Moss
Ribble Head

West Close Pasture
Scar Top
Ribblehead Viaduct
B6479

Ivescar
Broadrake
Ivescar End Barn
Gunner Fleet Moss
Low Sleights
PH
Gauber

Bruntscar Farm
Two Gills Foot
Hodge Hole
Ford
Parker's Moss
Winterscales Beck
Bruntscar Moss
Ribblehead Visitor Centre
Brown Riggs
Ingman Lodge RD

West Fell
Ellerbeck
Gatekirk Cave
Waterfall
Ellerbeck Pasture
Low Sleights Road
Settlements
Farmstead
Gauber High Pasture
Ashes Farm

West Fell End Hole
Scales Moor Four Stones Rigg
West Moss
Waterfall
Settlement
Farmstead
Cairn
B6255
Settlement

104

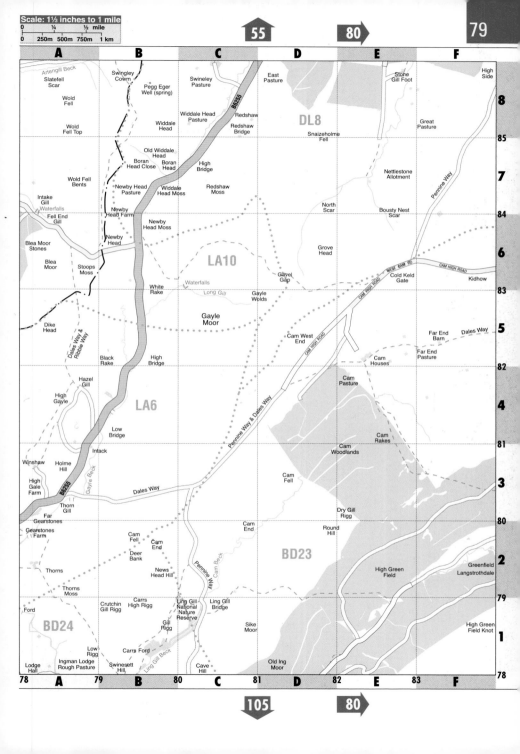

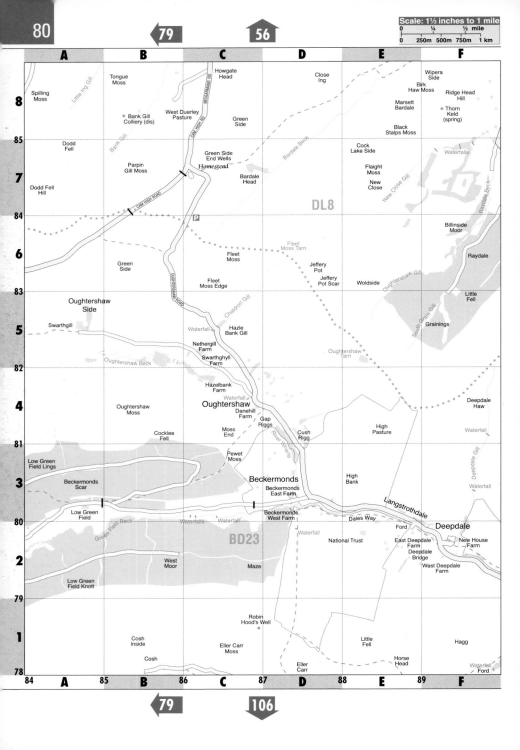

79
56

Scale: 1⅓ inches to 1 mile

| 0 | ¼ | ½ mile |
| 0 | 250m | 500m | 750m | 1 km |

A **B** **C** **D** **E** **F**

Spilling Moss

Little Ing Gill

Tongue Moss

Howgate Head

Close Ing

Wipera Side

Birk Haw Moss

Ridge Head Hill

8

Bank Gill Colliery (dis)

West Duerley Pasture

Green Side

Marsett Bardale

Thorn Keld (spring)

Dodd Fell

Bank Gill

Green Side End Wells

Black Stalps Moss

Waterfalls

85

Parpin Gill Moss

Homestead

Bardale Head

Bardale Beck

Cock Lake Side

7

Dodd Fell Hill

CAM HIGH ROAD

Flaight Moss

New Close

New Close Gill

Raydale Beck

CAM HIGH ROAD

DL8

84

P

Fleet Moss Tarn

Billinside Moor

6

Green Side

Fleet Moss

Jeffery Pot

Jeffery Pot Scar

Woldside

Oughtershaw Gill

Raydale

Fleet Moss Edge

83

Oughtershaw Side

OUGHTERSHAW ROAD

Chaldron Gill

South Gram Gill

Grainings

Little Fell

5

Swarthgill

Waterfall

Hazle Bank Gill

Oughtershaw Tarn

Nethergill Farm

82

Oughtershaw Beck

Swarthghyll Farm

Hazelbank Farm

4

Oughtershaw Moss

Waterfall

Oughtershaw

Danehill Farm

Gap Riggs

Cush Rigg

High Pasture

Deepdale Haw

Waterfall

81

Cocklee Fell

Moss End

River Wharfe

Deepdale Gill

Pewet Moss

Waterfall

3

Low Green Field Lings

Beckermonds Scar

Beckermonds

Beckermonds East Farm

High Bank

Langstrothdale

Waterfall

80

Low Green Field

Green Field Beck

Waterfalls

Waterfall

Beckermonds West Farm

Dales Way

Ford

Deepdale

East Deepdale Farm

New House Farm

2

BD23

West Moor

Maze

Waterfall

National Trust

Deepdale Bridge

West Deepdale Farm

Low Green Field Knott

79

1

Cosh Inside

Robin Hood's Well

Little Fell

Hagg

Eller Carr Moss

Horse Head

Cosh

Eller Carr

Waterfall Ford

78

84 **A** **85** **B** **86** **C** **87** **D** **88** **E** **89** **F**

79
106

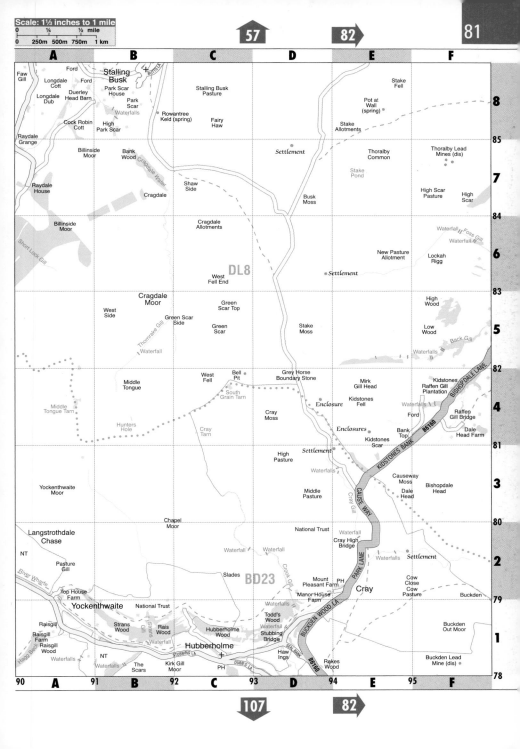

A **B** **C** **D** **E** **F**

Faw Gill
Ford
Longdale Cott
Ford
Longdale Dub
Duerley Head Barn
Stalling Busk
Park Scar House
Park Scar
Waterfalls
Stalling Busk Pasture
Stake Fell
Pot at Wall (spring)

8

Cock Robin Cott
High Park Scar
Rowantree Keld (spring)
Fairy Haw
Stake Allotments

Raydale Grange
Billinside Moor
Bank Wood
Settlement
Thoralby Common
Thoralby Lead Mines (dis)

85

Raydale House
Cragdale
Shaw Side
Busk Moss
High Scar Pasture
High Scar

7

Billinside Moor
Cragdale Allotments
Waterfall
Foss Gill
Waterfall

84

Short Lock Gill
West Fell End
Settlement
New Pasture Allotment
Lockah Rigg

6

DL8

Cragdale Moor
West Side
Green Scar Top
High Wood

83

Green Scar Side
Thornake Gill
Green Scar
Stake Moss
Low Wood
Back Gill

5

Waterfall
Waterfalls

82

Middle Tongue
West Fell
Bell Pit
Grey Horse Boundary Stone
Mirk Gill Head
Kidstones
Raffen Gill Plantation
Bishopdale Lane

Middle Tongue Tarn
South Grain Tarn
Cray Moss
Kidstones Fell
Waterfalls
Ford
Raffen Gill Bridge

4

Hunters Hole
Cray Tarn
Enclosure
Enclosures
Bank Top
Dale Head Farm
B6160

High Pasture
Settlement
Kidstones Scar
Kidstones Bank

81

Yockenthwaite Moor
Waterfalls
Causeway Moss
Bishopdale Head

3

Middle Pasture
Dale Head
Cray Gill

Chapel Moor
National Trust
Waterfall
Cray High Bridge
Settlement

80

Langstrothdale Chase
NT
Waterfall
Waterfall
Park Lane
Waterfalls

2

Pasture Gill
Slades
BD23
Mount Pleasant Farm
PH
Cray
Cow Close Cow Pasture
Buckden

River Wharfe
Top House Farm
Manor House Farm
Buckden Wood La.

79

Yockenthwaite
National Trust
Todd's Wood
Buckden Out Moor

1

Raisgill
Strans Wood
Rais Wood
Hubberholme Wood
Waterfall
Stubbing Bridge
Seat Bank

Raisgill Farm
Raisgill Wood
Strans Gill
Waterfall
Hubberholme
Haw Ings
Buckden Lead Mine (dis)

Haigh Beck
Waterfalls
NT
The Scars
Kirk Gill Moor
Stubbing La.
Dubb's La.
PH
Rakes Wood
B6160

78

A **B** **C** **D** **E** **F**
90   91   92   93   94   95

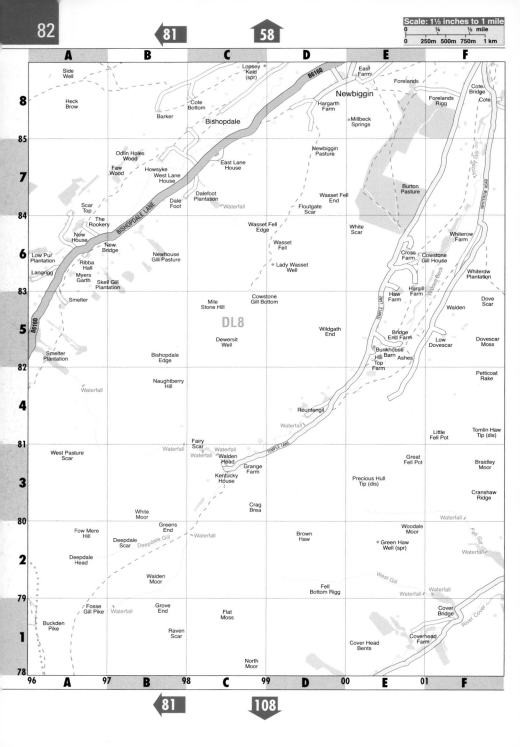

Scale: 1⅓ inches to 1 mile

0   ¼   ½ mile
0 250m 500m 750m 1 km

81
58
81
108

Side Well
Heck Brow
Cote Bottom
Barker
Lopsey Keld (spr)
Bishopdale
Hargarth Farm
Newbiggin
East Farm
Forelands
Forelands Rigg
Cote Bridge
Cote
Millbeck Springs

Odlin Holes Wood
Faw Wood
Howsyke West Lane House
East Lane House
Newbiggin Pasture
Burton Pasture

Scar Top
The Rookery
New House
New Bridge
Dale Foot
Dalefoot Plantation
Waterfall
Wasset Fell End
Floutgate Scar
Wasset Fell Edge
White Scar
Cross Farm
Cowstone Gill House
Whiterow Farm

Low Pur Plantation
Langrigg
Ribba Hall
Myers Garth
Skell Gill Plantation
Newhouse Gill Pasture
Wasset Fell
Lady Wasset Well
Haw Farm
Hargill Farm
Whiterow Plantation

Smelter
Mile Stone Hill
DL8
Cowstone Gill Bottom
Wildgath End
Bridge End Farm
Walden
Dove Scar

Smelter Plantation
Bishopdale Edge
Dewersit Well
Bunkhouse
Barn
Ashes
Hill Top Farm
Low Dovescar
Dovescar Moss

Naughtberry Hill
Petticoat Rake

Waterfall
Rountengil
Waterfall
Little Fell Pot
Tomlin Haw Tip (dis)

West Pasture Scar
Fairy Scar
Waterfall
Waterfall
Walden Head
Waterfall
Grange Farm
Great Fell Pot
Braidley Moor

Kentucky House
Precious Hull Tip (dis)
Cranshaw Ridge

White Moor
Crag Brea
Waterfall

Fow Mere Hill
Greens End
Waterfall
Brown Haw
Woodale Moor
Waterfall

Deepdale Scar
Deepdale Gill
Green Haw Well (spr)
Waterfall

Deepdale Head
Walden Moor
West Gill

Fell Bottom Rigg
Waterfall
Waterfall

Fosse Gill Pike
Waterfall
Grove End
Flat Moss
Cover Bridge
River Cover

Buckden Pike
Raven Scar
Coverhead Farm

North Moor
Cover Head Bents

B6160
WHITEROW ROAD
Tyrosy Gill
Walden Beck
TEMPLE LANE
BISHOPDALE LANE
Fall Gill

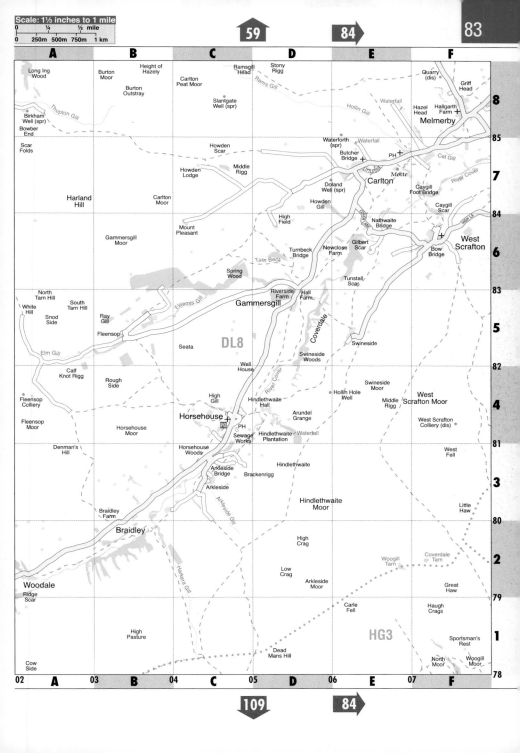

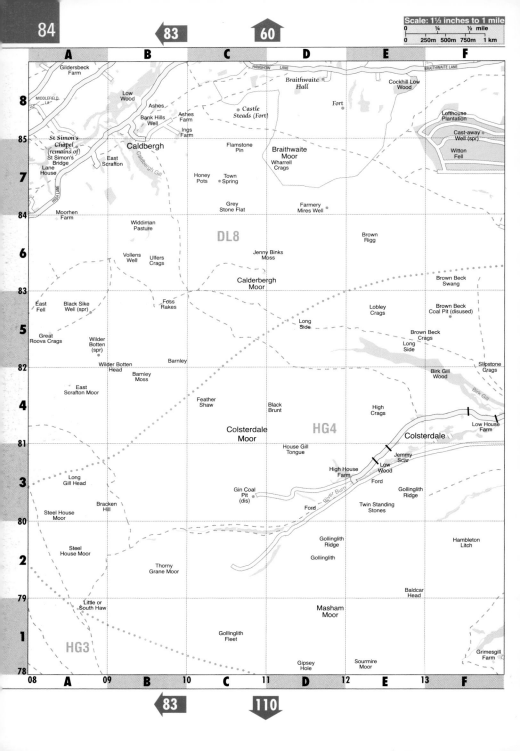

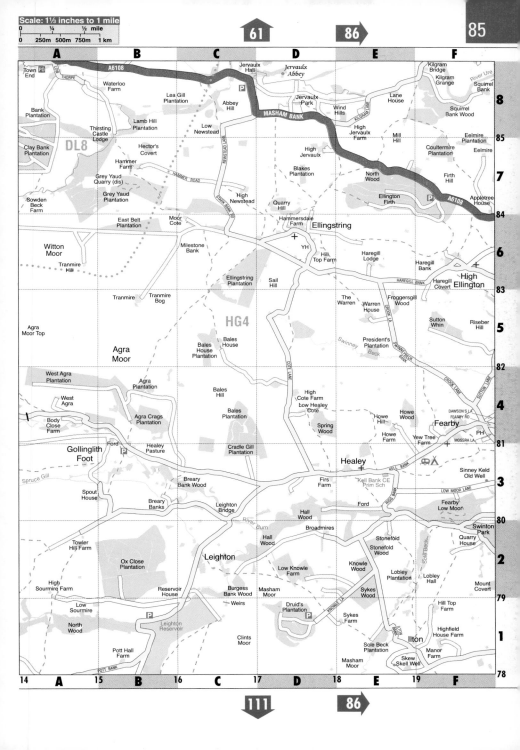

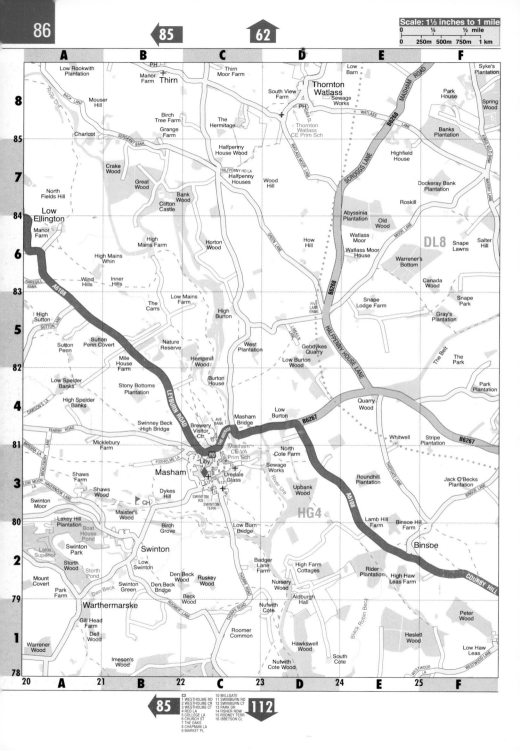

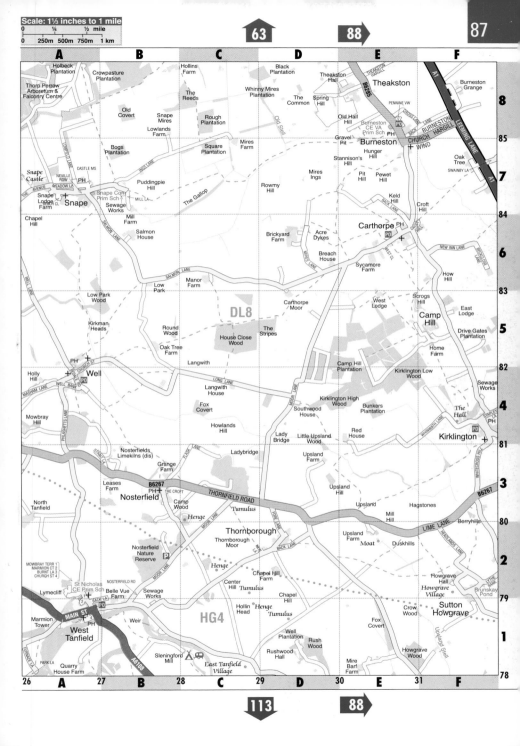

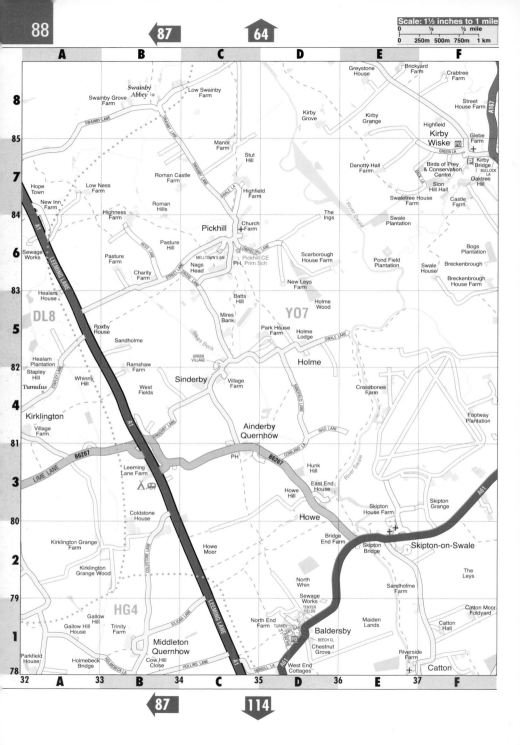

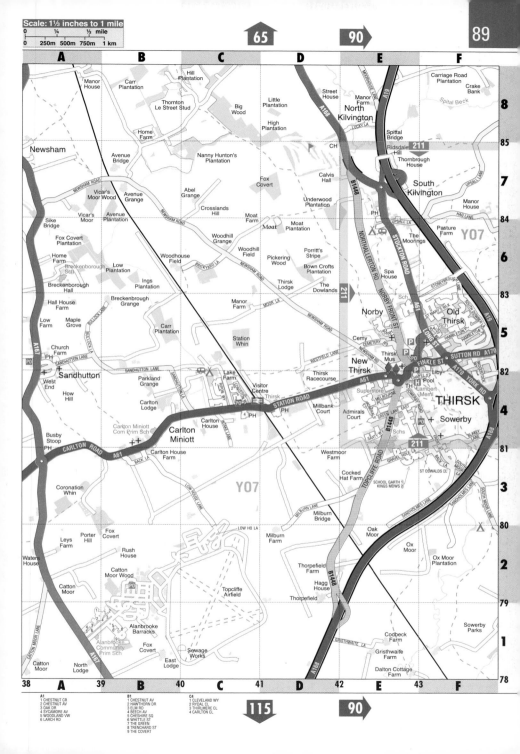

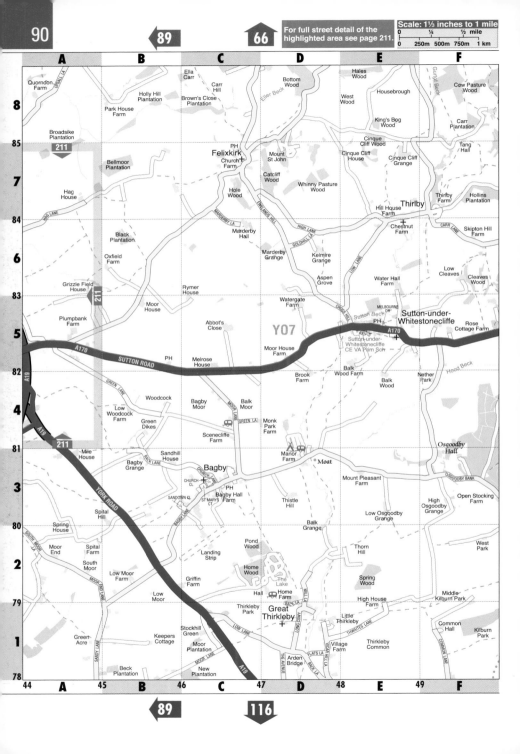

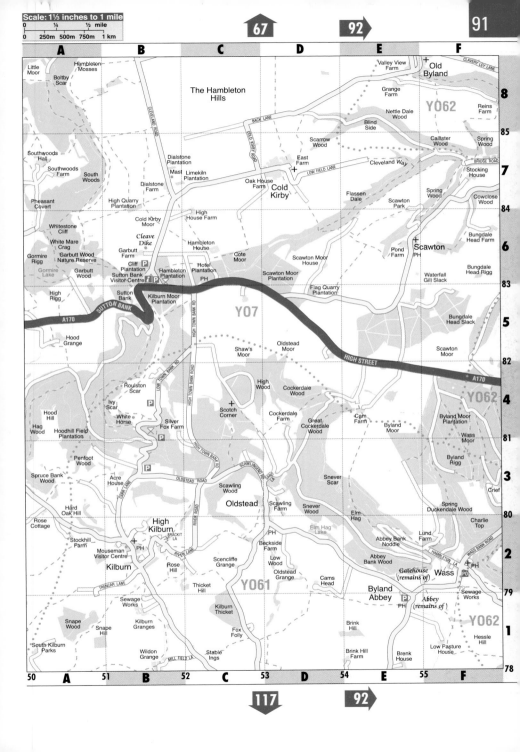

F6
1 ELMSLAC CL
2 CANONS GARTH LA
3 STONE GARTH
4 HIGH ST
5 CHURCH ST
6 CASTLEGATE

7 BUCKINGHAM SQ
8 BUCKINGHAM SQ
9 BOROGATE
10 MARKET PL
11 MARKET PL
12 BRIDGE ST
13 RYEGATE

14 POTTERGATE
15 BELL'S CT
16 EASTGATE
17 THE CRESCENT
18 SOUTH GATE
19 SOUTHLANDS
20 ALLENBY RD

21 CHAPEL CL
22 CROSLAND CL
23 CONOWL CL
24 ACRES CL
25 RICCAL DR
26 STOREY CL

Scale: 1⅓ inches to 1 mile

0   ¼   ½ mile
0 250m 500m 750m 1 km

F7
1 BAXTON'S SPRUNT
2 WARWICK PL
3 ELMSLAC PL
4 RUTLAND PL
5 ASHWOOD CL
6 WITHINGTON RD
7 ELM GN
8 VILLIERS CT
9 ELMSLAC CL

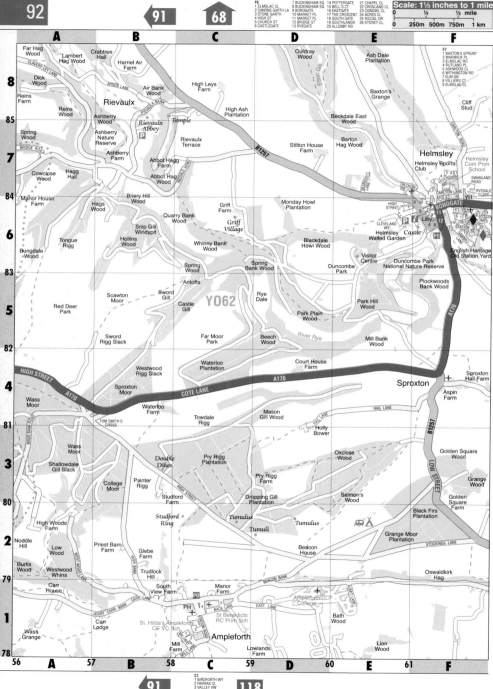

C1
1 BIRDFORTH WY
2 FAIRFAX CL
3 VALLEY VW
4 OLD STATION RD
5 THE ORCHARD
6 ST HILDA'S WK

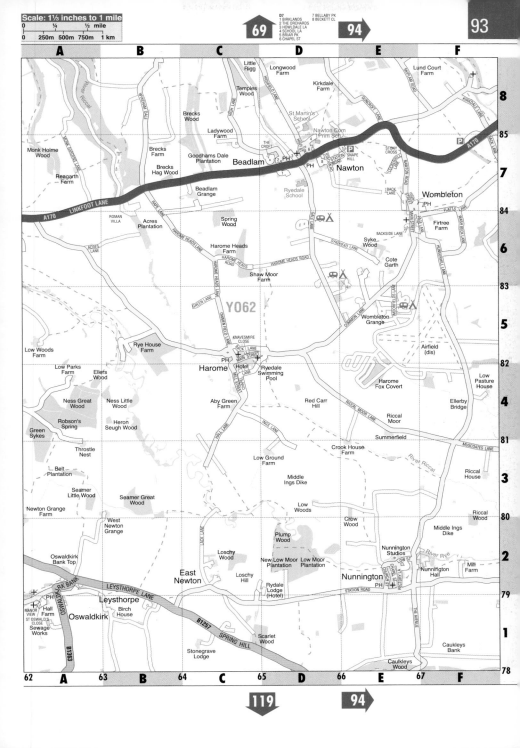

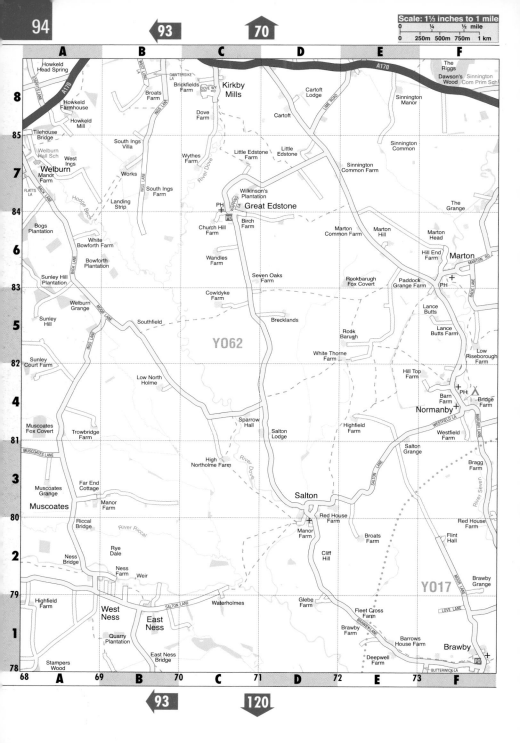

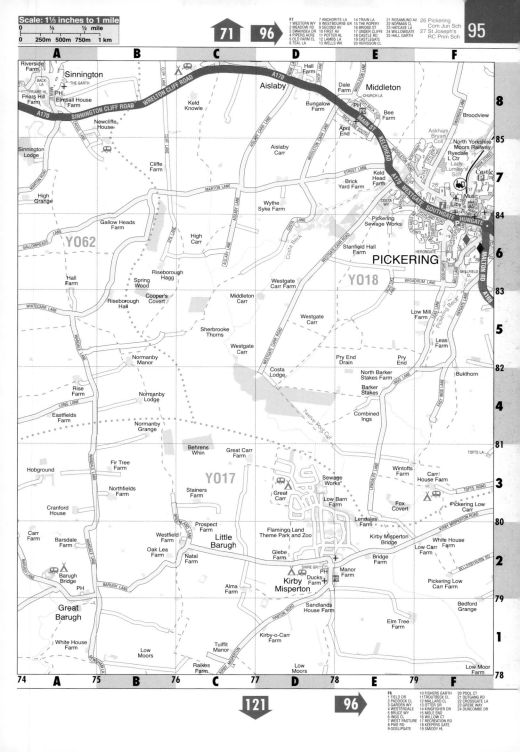

Scale: 1½ inches to 1 mile

0   ¼   ½ mile
0   250m 500m 750m 1 km

71   96

95

F7
1 WESTERN WY
2 MEADOW RD
3 SWAINSEA DR
4 PIPERS ACRE
5 OLD FARM CL
6 TEAL LA

7 ANCHORITE LA
8 WESTBOURNE GR
9 SECOND AV
10 FIRST AV
11 POTTER HL
12 LAMBS LA
13 WELLS WK

14 TRAIN LA
15 THE ROPERY
16 BRIDGE ST
17 UNDER CLIFFE
18 CASTLE RD
19 CASTLEGATE
20 HERISSON CL

21 ROSAMUND AV
22 NORMAN CL
23 HATGASE LA
24 WILLOWGATE
25 HALL GARTH

26 Pickering
   Com Jun Sch
27 St Joseph's
   RC Prim Sch

Riverside Farm
Sinnington
THE GARTH
BACK LA
Friars Hill Farm
PH
Elmsall House Farm
SINNINGTON CLIFF ROAD
WRELTON CLIFF ROAD
A170
Newcliffe House
Sinnington Lodge
MARTON ROAD
CROSS LANE
CLIFF LANE
Cliffe Farm
Keld Knowle
MIDDLETON CARR LANE
NEW LANE
SHOP LANE
MAIN ST
A170
Hall Farm
Aislaby
Dale Farm
Middleton
CHURCH LA
BACK ST SOUTH
PH
BACK ST
Bungalow Farm
April End
Bee Farm
Broodview
Askham Bryan Coll
North Yorkshire Moors Railway
Ryedale L Ctr
Lady Lumley's Sch
Castle
P
Mus
Lby
POL
A170 WESTGATE
SOUTHGATE
HUNGATE
MALTON RD
A169

High Grange
Y062
GALLOWHEADS
Gallow Heads Farm
Hall Farm
Spring Wood
Riseborough Hagg
Cooper's Covert
Riseborough Hall
WHITECARR LANE
ISLABY LANE
MARTON LANE
Aislaby Carr
High Carr
Wythe Syke Farm
Brick Yard Farm
Keld Head Farm
STREET LANE
COSTA LANE
Stanfield Hall Farm
PICKERING
Y018
Pickering Sewage Works
WESTGATE CARR ROAD
Westgate Carr Farm
BROADRUM LANE
Low Mill Farm
Pickering Beck

Middleton Carr
Sherbrooke Thorns
Westgate Carr
Westgate Carr
Costa Lodge
Pry End Drain
Pry End
North Barker Stakes Farm
Barker Stakes
Leas Farm
Bukthorn

Normanby Manor
Rise Farm
Eastfields Farm
Normanby Lodge
Normanby Grange
LONG LANE
WHIMWELL LANE
Combined Ings
Twelve Foot Cut
EAST INGS LANE
INGS LANE

Hobground
Behrens Whin
Great Carr Farm
Y017
Fir Tree Farm
Northfields Farm
Cranford House
Stainers Farm
Great Carr
Sewage Works
Low Barn Farm
Lendales Farm
Wintofts Farm
Fox Covert
Carr House Farm
Pickering Low Carr
TOFTS LA
TOFTS ROAD
KIRBY MISPERTON RD

Carr Farm
Barsdale Farm
Westfield Farm
Prospect Farm
Little Barugh
Oak Lea Farm
Natal Farm
Glebe Farm
Flamingo Land Theme Park and Zoo
Kirby Misperton Bridge
Bridge Farm
White House Low Carr Farm
Pickering Low Carr Farm
Bedford Grange
BELLERBYDOWNE RD
HIGHLAND LANE
SHIRE GR
BARUGH LANE
KIRBY MISPERTON
MALTON ROAD

Barugh Bridge
PH
Great Barugh
Alma Farm
Kirby Misperton
Ducks Farm
PH
Manor Farm
Sandlands House Farm
Elm Tree Farm

White House Farm
Low Moors
Tuiffit Manor
Kirby-o-Carr Farm
Raikes Farm
Low Moors
Low Moor Farm

74   A   75   B   76   C   77   D   78   E   79   F   78

121   96

F6
1 FIELD DR
2 PADDOCK CL
3 GARDEN WY
4 WESTERDALE
5 BRUCE WY
6 INGS CL
7 WEST PASTURE
8 PIKE RD
9 GOSLIPGATE

10 FISHERS GARTH
11 TROULBECK CL
12 MALLARD CL
13 OTTER DR
14 KINGFISHER DR
15 MOLE END
16 WILLOW CT
17 RECREATION RD
18 KEEPERS GATE
19 SMIDDY HL

20 POOL CT
21 OUTGANG RD
22 CROSSGATE LA
23 GREBE WAY
24 DUNCOMBE DR

8   85   7   84   6   83   5   82   4   81   3   80   2   79   1

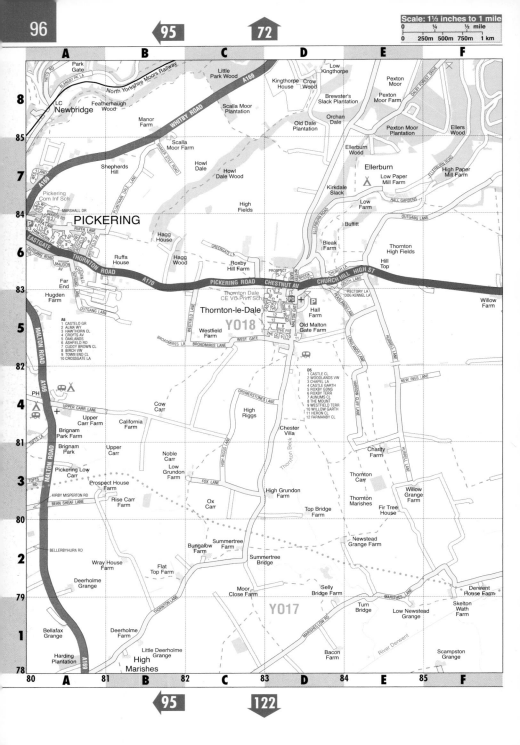

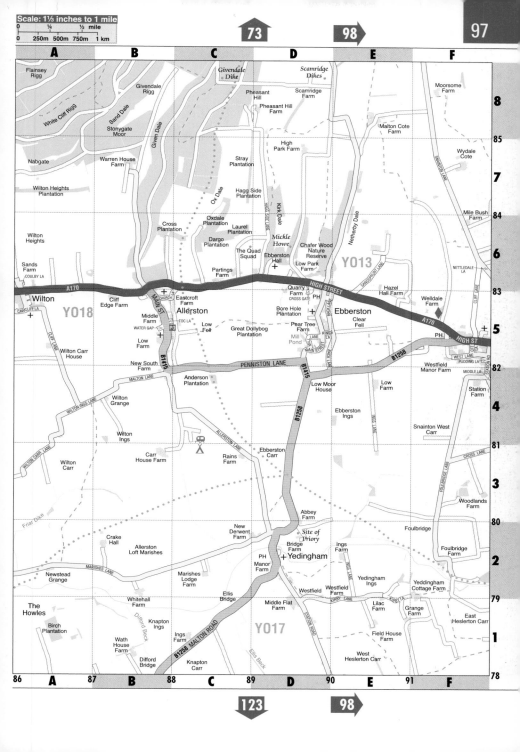

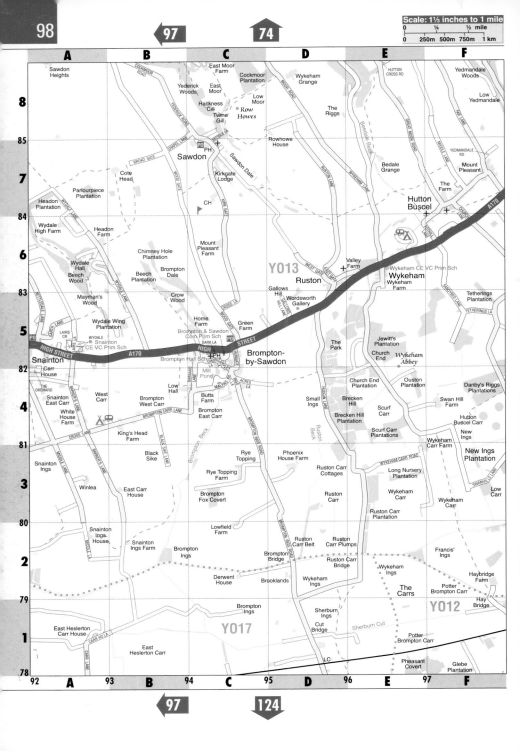

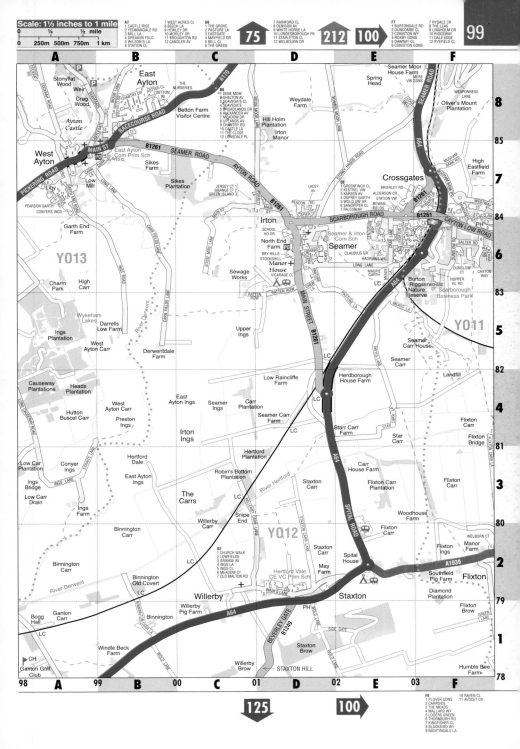

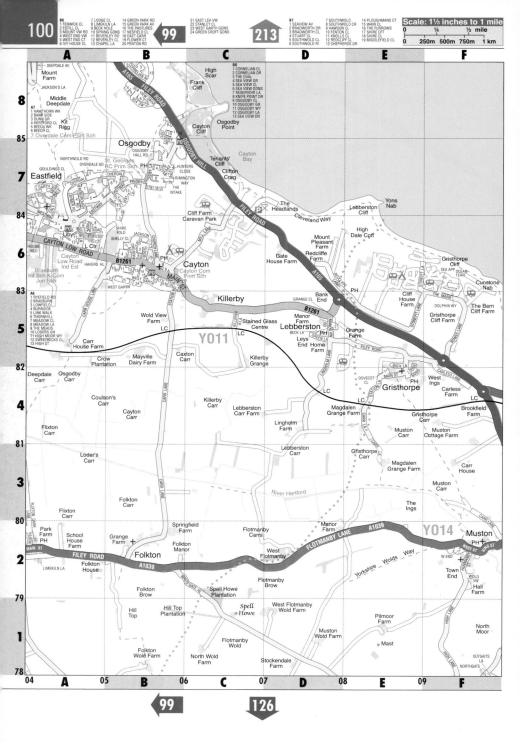

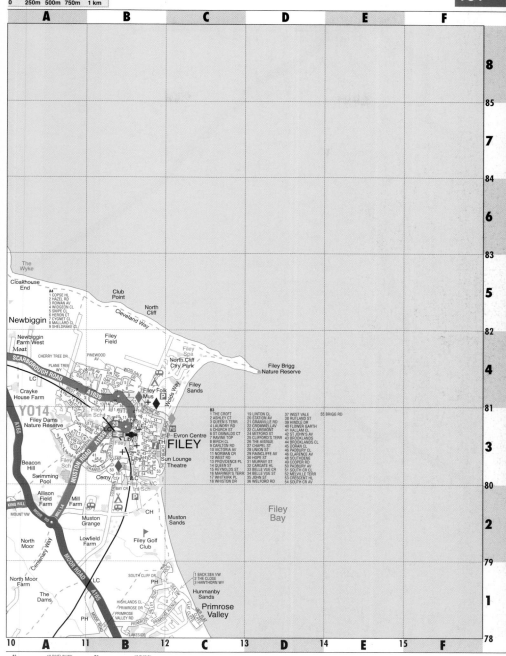

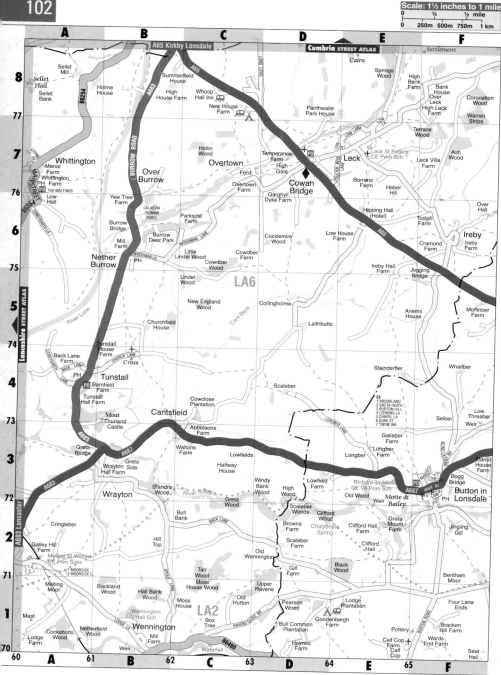

Scale: 1½ inches to 1 mile

0   ¼   ½ mile
0   250m 500m 750m 1 km

A B C D E F

8
Sellet Mill
Sellet Hall
Sellet Bank
Holme House
A65 Kirkby Lonsdale
Summerfield House
High House Farm
Whoop Hall Inn
New House Farm
Cairn
Settlement
Springs Wood
High Bank Farm
Bank House Over Leck
High Leck Farm
Coronation Wood
Warren Strips

77

7
Whittington
Manor Farm
Whittington
PH
The Maltings
Low Hall
Over Burrow
Hollin Wood
Overtown
Ford
Overtown Farm
Temperance Farm
High Gale
Leck
Leck St Peter's CE Prim Sch
Leck Villa Farm
Ash Wood

76
Yew Tree Farm
Burrow Bridge
CALACVM (ROMAN FORT)
Parkside Farm
Garghyll Dyke Farm
Cowan Bridge
Borrens Farm
Heber Hill
Over Hall

6
Burrow Bridge
Mill Farm
Burrow Deer Park
Little Lindel Wood
Cowdber Farm
Cocklemire Wood
Hipping Hall (Hotel)
Low House Farm
Todgill Farm
Ireby
Cramond Farm
Ireby Farm

75
Nether Burrow
PH
Lindel Wood
Cowdber Wood
LA6
Ireby Hall Farm
Jogging Bridge

5
River Lune
New England Wood
Cant Beck
Collingholme
Laithbutts
Anems House
Moffinber Farm

74
Churchfield House
Tunstall House Farm
Church Lane
Cross
Stainderber
Whaitber

4
Tunstall
Barnfield Farm
Tunstall Hall Farm
Cowclose Plantation
Scaleber
1 BROOKLAND
2 GRETA HEATH
3 BURTON HILL
4 LEEMING LA
5 CHAPEL LA
6 DUKE ST
7 TWINE WK
Low Threaber Weir

73
Moat
Thurland Castle
Cantsfield
Abbotsons Farm
Longber Lane
Gallaber Farm
Selber

3
Greta Bridge
A683
A687
Greta Side
Wrayton Hall Farm
Waltons Farm
Lowfields
Halfway House
Lowfield Farm
Longber
Longber Farm
Richard Taylor CE VA Prim Sch
Old Wood
Weir
Eldron House Farm
Bogg Bridge
Burton in Lonsdale

72
A683 Lancaster
Wrayton
Standra Wood
River Greta
Greta Wood
Windy Bank Wood
High Wood
Scaleber Woods
Clifford Wood
Motte & Bailey
Greta Mount Farm
Jingling Gill

2
Cringleber
Galley Hill Farm
Melling St Wilfred CE Prim Sch
Bull Bank
Back Lane
Browns Farm
Chalybeate Spring
Scaleber Farm
Clifford Hall Farm
Clifford Hall

71
1 MOORSIDE
2 MOORSIDE CL
Melling Moor
Backland Wood
Hill Top
Tarr Wood
Moss House Wood
Old Wennington
Upper Ravens
Gill Farm
Black Wood
Lodge Plantation
Bentham Moor
Four Lane Ends

1
Mast
Lodge Farm
Cockshotts Wood
Netherfield Wood
Wennington Hall Sch
Hall Bank Wood
Moss Wood
LA2
Box Tree
Old Hutton
Pearson Wood
Bull Common Plantation
Goodenbergh Farm
Holmes Farm
Pottery
Calf Cop
Calf Cop
Bracken Hill Farm
Wards End Farm
Seat Hall

70
Mill Farm
Weir
Waterfall
B6480

60 A 61 B 62 C 63 D 64 E 65 F

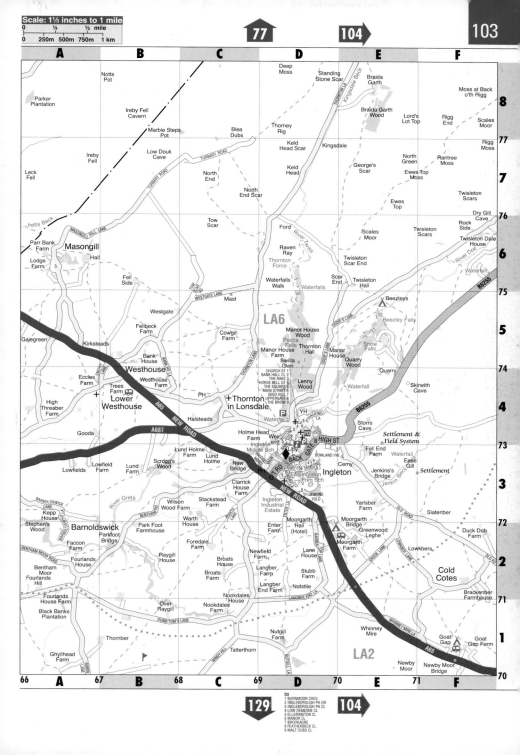

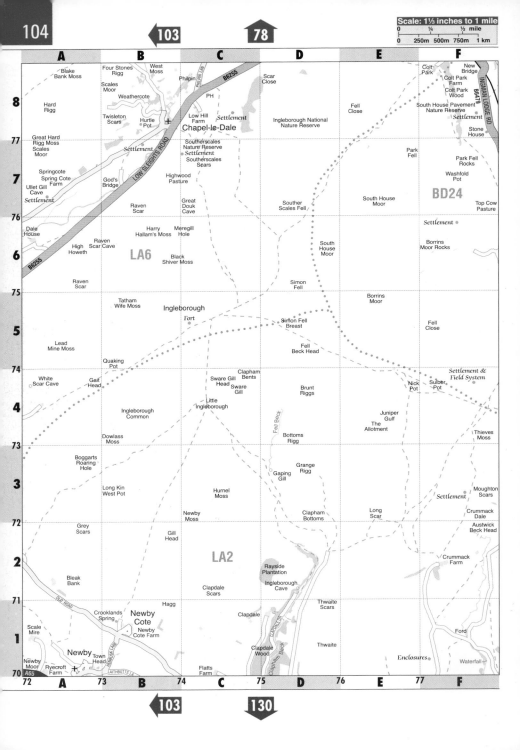

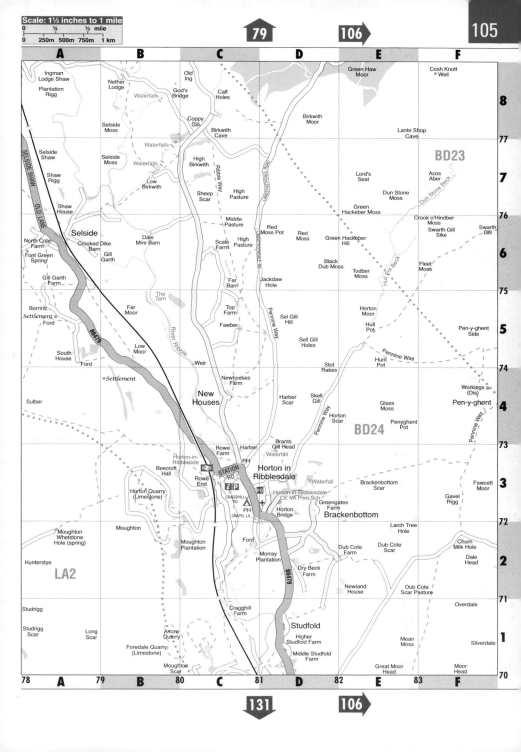

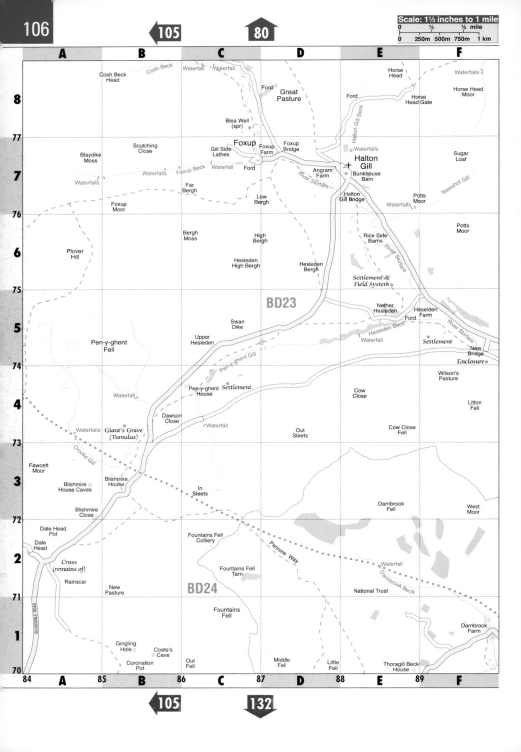

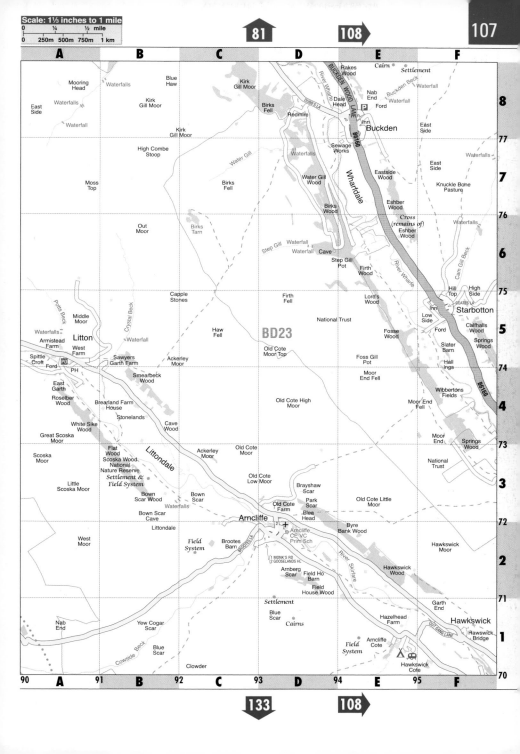

Scale: 1⅓ inches to 1 mile

0   ¼   ½   mile
0   250m   500m   750m   1 km

81   108

A   B   C   D   E   F

Mooring Head
Waterfalls
Blue Haw
Kirk Gill Moor
Rakes Wood
Cairn
Settlement
Buckden Beck
Waterfall

East Side
Waterfalls
Kirk Gill Moor
Kirk Gill Moor
Birks Fell
Gibbs La
River Wharfe
Buckden Wood Lane
Nab End
Dale Head
Ford
Waterfall
East Side

Waterfall
Redmire
Inn
Buckden
B6160

8

77

High Combe Stoop
Water Gill
Sewage Works
Eastside Wood
East Side
Waterfalls

Moss Top
Birks Fell
Water Gill Wood
Wharfedale
Esbher Wood
Knuckle Bone Pasture

7

Out Moor
Birks Tarn
Birks Wood
Cross (remains of) Eshber Wood
Waterfalls

76

Step Gill
Waterfall
Waterfall
Cave
Step Gill Pot
Firth Wood
River Wharfe
Hill Top
High Side

6

Capple Stones
Firth Fell
Lord's Wood
National Trust
Low Side
Inn
Starbotton
COATES LA

75

Haw Fell
BD23
Fosse Wood
Ford
Callfalls Wood
Springs Wood

Middle Moor
Waterfalls
Litton
Waterfall
Old Cote Moor Top
Foss Gill Pot
Slater Barn
Hall Ings

5

Armistead Farm
West Farm
Sawyers Garth Farm
Ackerley Moor
Moor End Fell
Wibbertons Fields

Spittle Croft
Ford
PH
PO
Smearbeck Wood
Old Cote High Moor
Moor End Fell
Moor End
B6160

74

East Garth
Roselber Wood
Brearland Farm House
Stonelands
Cave Wood
Moor End
Springs Wood

4

White Sike Wood
Great Scoska Moor
Ackerley Moor
Old Cote Moor
National Trust

73

Scoska Moor
Flat Wood
Scoska Wood. National Nature Reserve
Settlement & Field System
Old Cote Low Moor
Brayshaw Scar
Old Cote Little Moor

Little Scoska Moor
Bown Scar Wood
Bown Scar
Old Cote Farm
Park Scar
Blea Head

3

Littondale
Bown Scar Cave
Waterfalls
Arncliffe
Arncliffe CE VC Prim Sch
Byre Bank Wood

72

West Moor
Field System
Brootes Barn
Hawkswick Moor

2

1 MONK'S RD
2 GOOSELANDS HL
Arnberg Scar
Field Ho Barn
Field House Wood
Hawkswick Wood

Nab End
Yew Cogar Scar
Settlement
Blue Scar
Cairns
River Skirfare
Garth End
Hawkswick

1

Cowside Beck
Blue Scar
Field System
Arncliffe Cote
Hazelhead Farm
Out Gang Lane
Hawkswick Bridge

Clowder
Hawkswick Cote

90   A   91   B   92   C   93   D   94   E   95   F   70

133   108

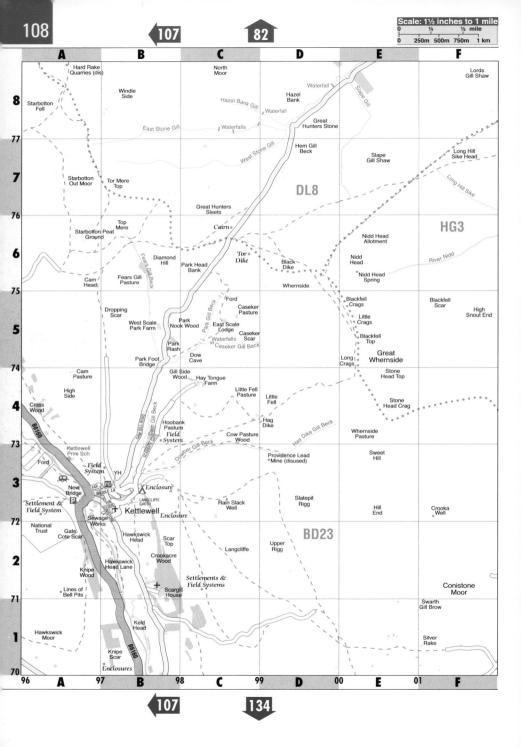

107

82

Scale: 1½ inches to 1 mile

0   ¼   ½   mile

0   250m   500m   750m   1 km

A   B   C   D   E   F

8

Hard Rake
Quarries (dis)

North
Moor

Lords
Gill Shaw

Windle
Side

Hazel
Bank

Waterfall

Slape Gill

Starbotton
Fell

Hazel Bank Gill

Waterfall

Great
Hunters Stone

77

East Stone Gill

Waterfalls

West Stone Gill

Hem Gill
Beck

Long Hill
Sike Head

7

Starbotton
Out Moor

Tor Mere
Top

DL8

Slape
Gill Shaw

Long Hill Sike

Great Hunters
Sleets

76

Top
Mere

Starbotton Peat
Ground

Cairn

Nidd Head
Allotment

HG3

6

Diamond
Hill

Park Head
Bank

Tor
Dike

Black
Dike

Nidd
Head

River Nidd

Cam
Head

Fears Gill
Pasture

Fears Gill Beck

Whernside

Nidd Head
Spring

75

Dropping
Scar

Park Gill Beck

Ford

Caseker
Pasture

Blackfell
Crags

Blackfell
Scar

High
Snout End

5

West Scale
Park Farm

Park
Nook Wood

East Scale
Lodge

Caseker
Scar

Little
Crags

Park
Rash

Waterfalls

Caseker Gill Beck

Blackfell
Top

Great
Whernside

Park Foot
Bridge

Dow
Cave

Long
Crags

Stone
Head Top

74

Cam
Pasture

Gill Side
Wood

Hay Tongue
Farm

Stone
Head Crag

High
Side

Little Fell
Pasture

Little
Fell

Whernside
Pasture

4

Cross
Wood

B6160

ONE ELM ROAD

Cam Gill Beck

Hoobank
Pasture
Field
System

Hag
Dike

Hay Dike Gill Beck

73

Kettlewell
Prim Sch

Field
System

YH

Cow Pasture
Wood

Providence Lead
Mine (disused)

Sweet
Hill

Ford

FAR LA

PO

MIDDLE LA

Enclosure

Dowber Gill Beck

3

New
Bridge

THE
SLIT

LANGCLIFFE
GARTH

Settlement &
Field System

Kettlewell

Enclosure

Rain Slack
Well

Slatepit
Rigg

Hill
End

Crooka
Well

72

National
Trust

Gate
Cote Scar

Sewage
Works

Hawkswick
Head

Scar
Top

Langcliffe

Upper
Rigg

BD23

2

Knipe
Wood

Hawkswick
Head Lane

Crookacre
Wood

Settlements &
Field Systems

Conistone
Moor

Lines of
Bell Pits

Scargill
House

71

Swarth
Gill Brow

Keld
Head

Silver
Rake

1

Hawkswick
Moor

B6160

Knipe
Scar

Enclosures

70

96   A   97   B   98   C   99   D   00   E   01   F

107

134

A B C D E F

DL8

Little Whernside

Lodge Pasture

How Gill

Edge Tops

Carle Fell Side

8

Raydale Knotts

High Pasture

High Woodale

Carle Side

Scar Plantation

77

Angram Pasture

Scar House Reservoir

Weirs

Woodale Scar

7

Weir

Tower

Angram Low Pasture

Angram Reservoir

Haden Carr Pasture

Brown Hill

Scar House Pasture

P ✕

Woodale Moss

Weir

Side Allotment

Scar House Moss

76

Weir

Waterfall

Wising Gill Crags

Maiden Gill Allotment

Kay Head Allotment

IN MOOR LANE

6

Cocklake

Stone Beck

Clack Gill Beck

75

Waterfall

Lodge Moor

Nab End

Maiden Gill Crags

Key Head

Moor Allotments

Armathwaite

5

Red Scar

East Gill Dike

Aygill Beck

High Riggs

Low Riggs

74

Low West Moor

Far Pasture

West End Lathe

West Gill Dike

Aygill Pike

How Stean Beck

West End

Hard Gap

4

HG3

Riggs Moor

Sandy Sikes Gill

Staining Gill Beck

Riggs Moor

Wising Gill

Blake Hill

High West Moor

Great Blowing Gill Beck

Staining Gill Intake

Flaystones

Whey Crags

73

Stott Crags

3

BD23

Waterfall

High West Moor

Stock Ridge

Black Hill Drive

72

White Stean Well

Great Scar

Stone Butts Drive

Stock Ridge Bottom

Mossdale Beck

Straight Stean Beck

Acoras Scar

Backstean Gill

Oliver Scar

Peat Moor Butts (Grouse)

2

Sandy Gate

Waterfall

Red Scars

Green Grooves Gill

Stean Moor

West Gill

Friar Hood Gill

71

Peat Moor Drive

Meugher

Great Stangate

Moss Drive

1

Mossdale

70

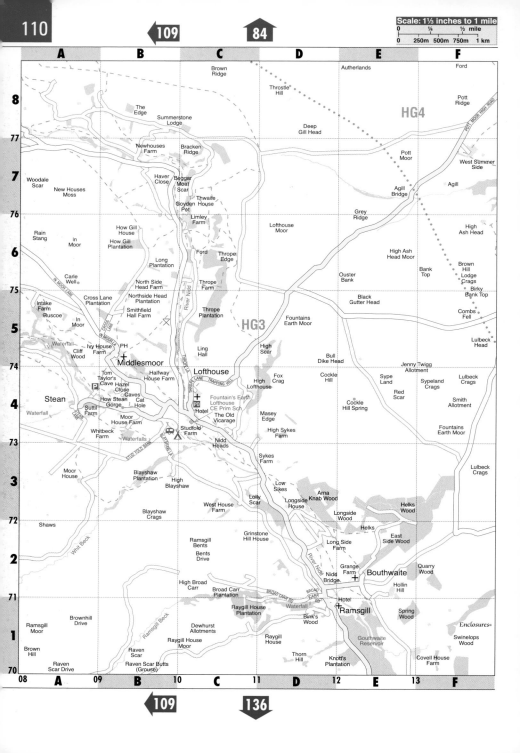

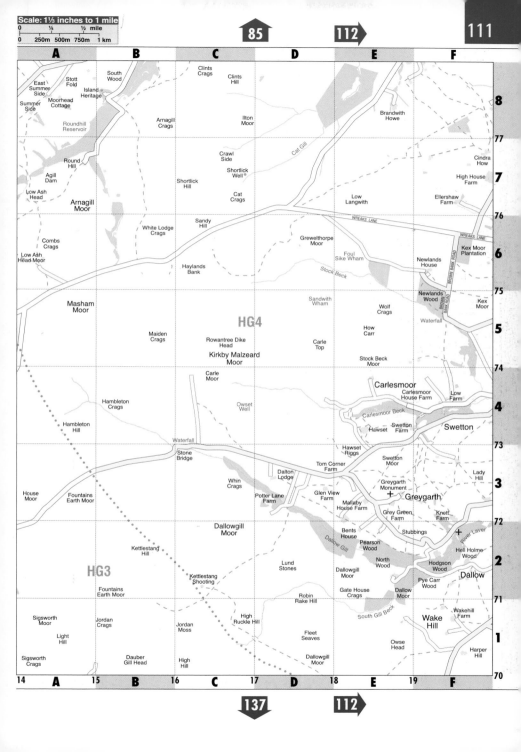

111
86

Scale: 1⅓ inches to 1 mile

0   ¼   ½ mile
0   250m   500m   750m   1 km

8

Nutwith Common
NUTWITH LANE
Hutts Wood
The Hutts Farm
High Bramley Grange
Lime Tree Farm
Glen Farm
Horsepasture Hill
Hill Top Farm
Camp Farm
Cote Wood
Limehouse Hill
Hack Fall
Stubbings
Westwood Farm
North Park Wood
Tanfield Hall Farm
South Park Wood
Ings Well

77

Avenue Farm
Blackhill House
Bramley Grange
Spring House Farm
Grewelthorpe Moor
Oak Stile Farm
HUTTS LA
Magdalen Wood
Common Wood
Tanfield Lodge
Weir
Mickley Wood
Manor Farm
Mickley

7

Low Bramley Grange
Fir Tree Farm
Plover Hall Farm
Foulgate Farm
Grewelthorpe CE Prim Sch
HUTTS LANE
PH
Grewelthorpe
HAZEL CL
HOLMFIELD
Sewage Works
Mowbray Hall
Black Plantation
Bush Farm
Tower Hill
Westfield

76

Bramley Wood
Wreaks Beck
FOULGATE NOOK LANE
Crimble Dale
Thorpe Grange
Holmes Farm
Newholme Farm
Mowbray View Farmhouse
Grove Dale
Spring Hall Farm
Spring Hall Wood
Frizer Hill Plantation

6

HG4

Middle Biggin
Biggin Wood
Biggin Grange
Wilson's Plantation
Moorland's Wood
Kex Beck
Highfield Farm
North Close Farm
Greenass Farm
Chasd

75

Kex Moor
KIRK BANK
Ash Tree Farm
Ringbeck
Sycamore Farm
Ringbeck Farm
Avenue Farm
Kirkby Malzeard CE Prim Sch
Mowbray Castle (site of)
Azerley Park
The Lake
Mill Farm

5

Thwaite Wood
Thwaite House
Paley's Plantation
Peacock's Plantation
Young Plantation
Dogell Top
GREYSTONE HEAD
BACK LANE
MAIN ST
BACK LA
Kirkby Malzeard
Lawnwith
East Plantation
Shellums Wood

74

Kirkby Malzeard Moor
Carr House
Meetings Plantation
High Intake
Low Intake
Jubilee Wood
High Keld
Sugar Hill
Thirkell's Plantation
Deep Gill Farm
Willow House Farm
1 RICHMOND GARTH
2 PINFOLD CT
3 MANOR CT
4 THE GREEN
5 MOWBRAY CR
6 ST ANDREWS GATE
7 CHURCH ST
8 ST ANDREWS MDWS
Oxley's Plantation
Hubber Wood
Hills Wood
Owster Wood

4

Swetton Bridge
Hedge Nook
GILLGATE ROAD
Buck House Farm
Beckmeeting Farm
River Laver
Low Intake
Laverton
West Leas
Braithwaite Hall
Warren House Farm
Owster Hill Plantation

73

Ford
Low Belford Farm
Mossie Mire
Carter Syke Farm
MISSIES LANE
Olive House Farm
Laver House
WARREN LANE
PH
Galphay

3

Belford
Hogerston Hill
Mount Pleasant
Hole Trough
Weir
High Missies Farm
The Watermill
Plover Hill Farm
West Farm
Skeaf House

72

High Ray Carr
PH
Castiles Farm
Cast Hills
Laverton Woods
Zanzibar Wood
Kooroomooroo Wood
Westowe Farm
Missise Farm
Gate Bridge
Five Gates Farm
GATE BRIDGE ROAD
WEST LANE
Skeaf Wood
Simfield

2

Bowes Farm
Cast Hills (Settlement)
Galphay Moor
West Hill Edge
Lumley Moor Plantation
West Hill Edge Plantation
Woodhouse Farm Caravan & Camping Park
Toldrum
Weir
Laver Bank Farm
Galphay Wood

71

Skelding Moor
Lumley Moor
Lumley Moor Farm
Holborn Bridge (upper)
Winksley Moor
Whin Covert
Hencliffe Cottage Farm
Winksley Bridge
GREEN LA
PH
Peacock Farm
Winksley
Winksley Plantation

1

Black Hill
Lumley Moor Resr
Ruddings Plantation
Hill Top
Holborn Bridge (lower)
Hencliffe Wood
Kendale Wood
River Laver
Ings Bridge

70

Heatherlands
Cornet Farm
Low Grantley
Sun Wood
North Wood

20 21 22 23 24 25

111
138

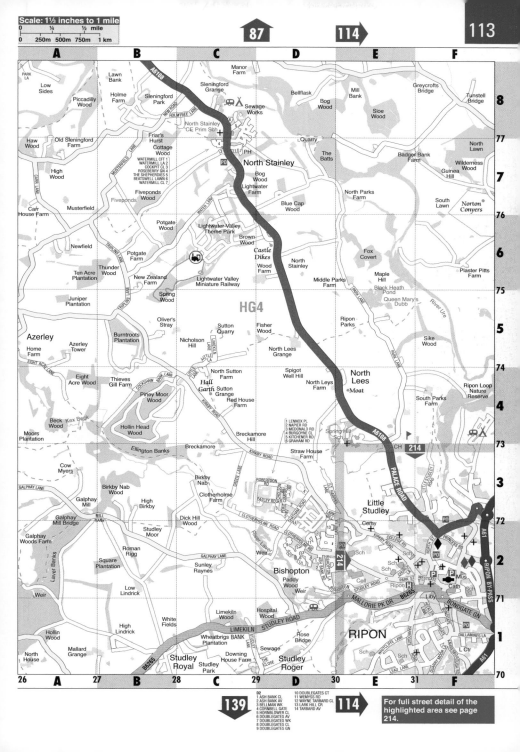

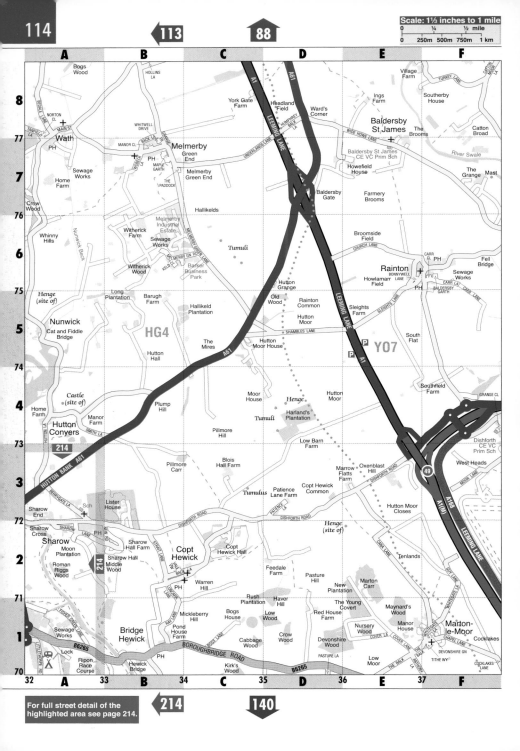

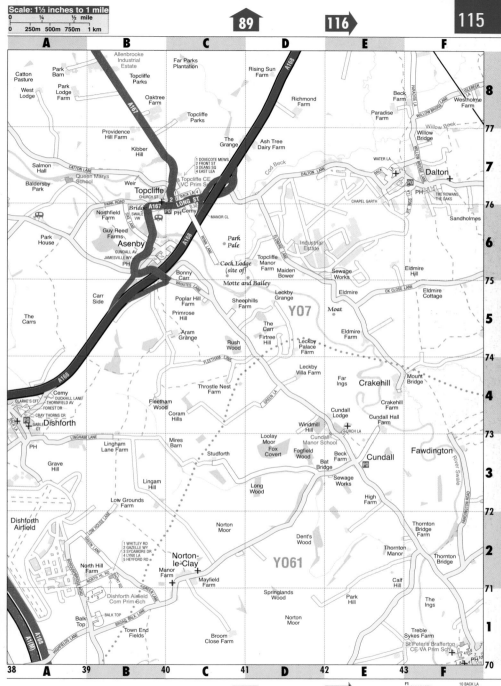

F1
1 HOLLY GARTH
2 MANOR DR
3 BAFFERTON HALL GARDENS
4 HALL LANE
5 FOX GARTH
6 THE ORCHARDS
7 RASKELF RD
8 THE MALTINGS
9 BRIDGE ST
10 BACK LA
11 THE LEAS

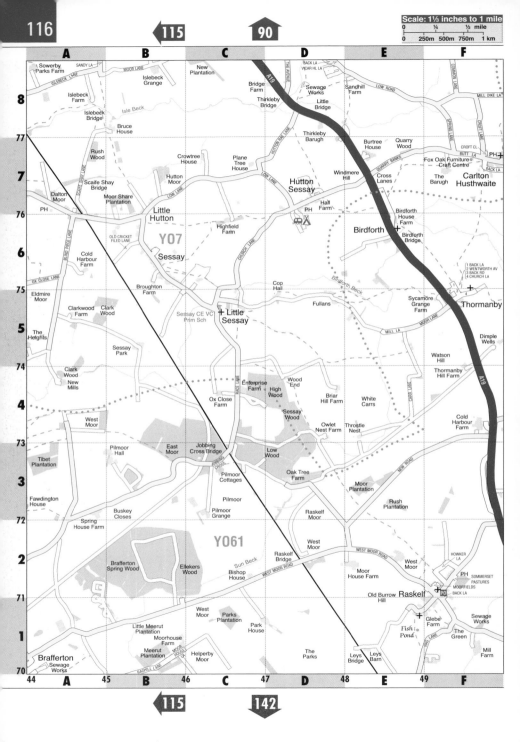

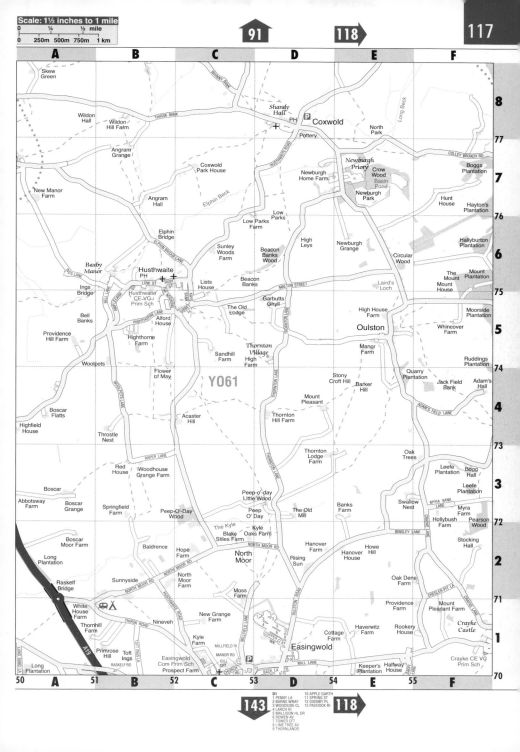

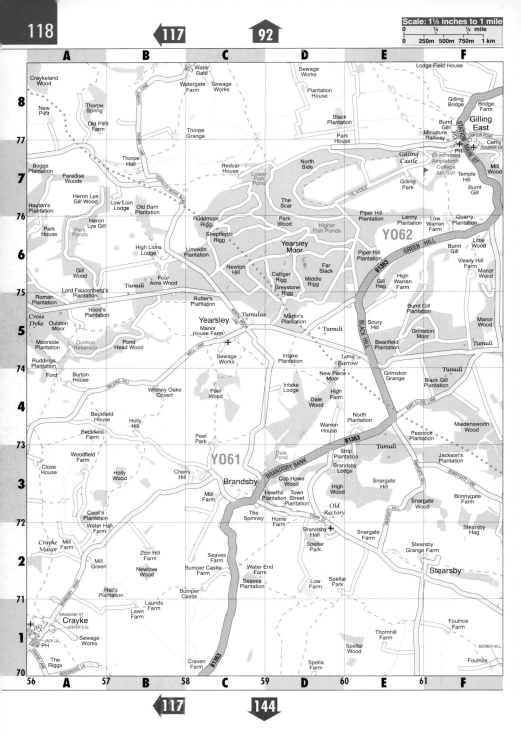

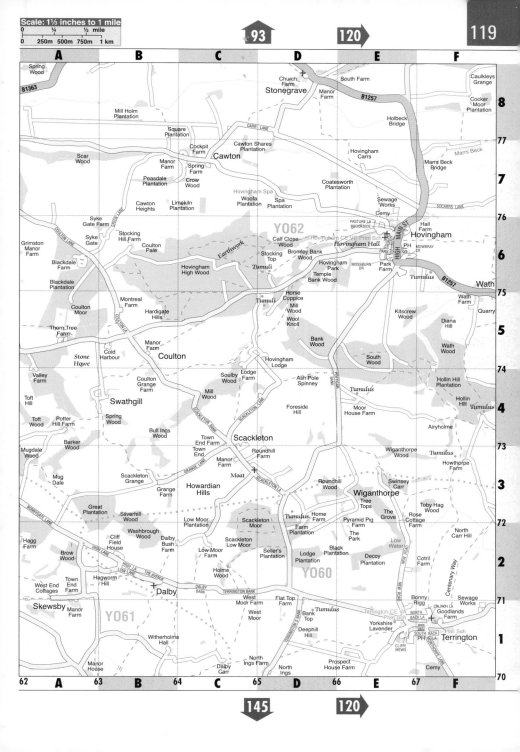

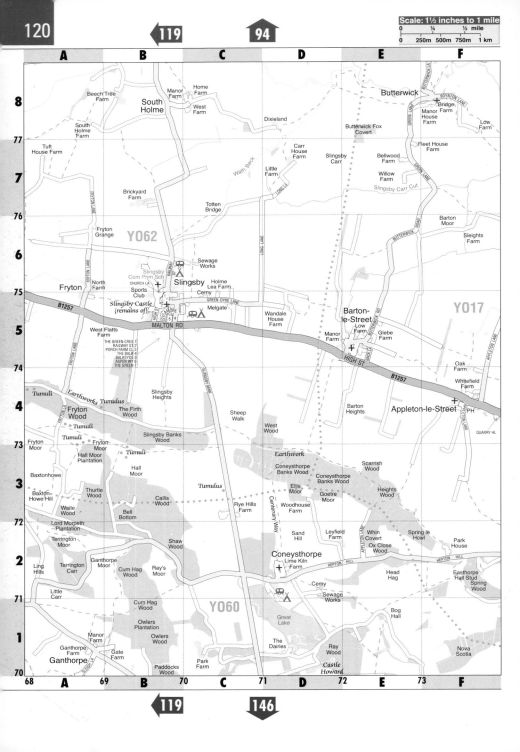

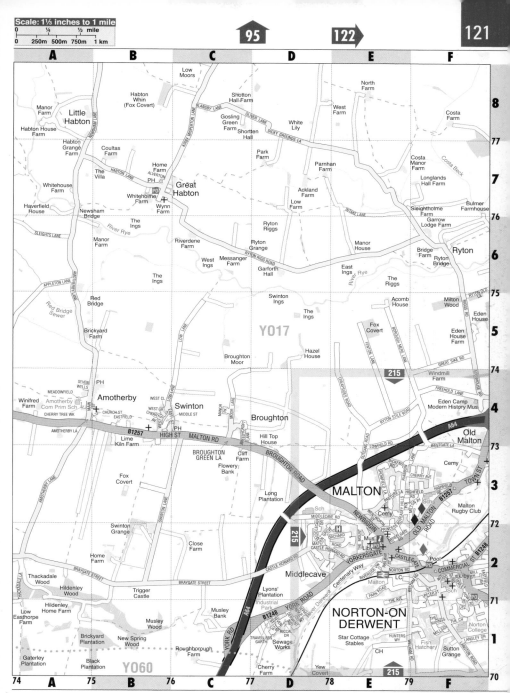

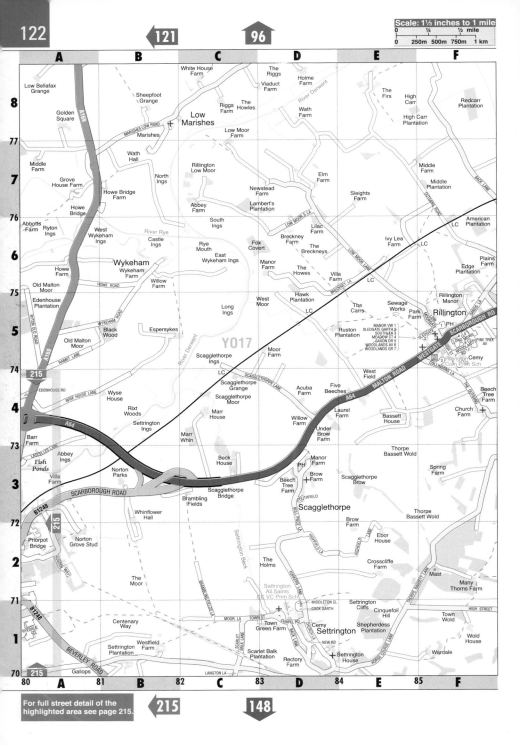

Scale: 1⅓ inches to 1 mile

0   ¼   ½ mile
0   250m 500m 750m 1 km

A · **B** · **C** · **D** · **E** · **F**

8

Low Bellafax Grange

Golden Square

Sheepfoot Grange

White House Farm

The Riggs

Viaduct Farm

Holme Farm

River Derwent

The Firs

High Carr

Redcarr Plantation

MARSHES LOW ROAD

Marishes

Riggs Farm

The Howles

Low Marishes

Low Moor Farm

Wath Farm

High Carr Plantation

77

Wath Hall

Middle Farm

Grove House Farm

North Ings

Rillington Low Moor

Newstead Farm

Lambert's Plantation

Elm Farm

Sleights Farm

Middle Farm

Middle Plantation

7

Howe Bridge Farm

Abbey Farm

South Ings

Low Moor S LA

Lilac Farm

76

Abbotts Farm

Ryton Ings

Howe Bridge

West Wykeham Ings

Castle Ings

Rye Mouth

East Wykeham Ings

Breckney Farm

The Breckneys

Fox Covert

American Plantation

River Rye

Ivy Lea Farm

LC

Plains Farm

6

Howe Farm

Wykeham

Wykeham Farm

Willow Farm

Manor Farm

The Howes

Villa Farm

BRECKNEY LA

LC

Edge Plantation

Old Malton Moor

HOWE ROAD

Rillington Manor

75

Edenhouse Plantation

Black Wood

Espersykes

Long Ings

West Moor

Hawk Plantation

LC

The Carrs

Sewage Works

Park Farm

Rillington

PH

SCARBOROUGH RD

5

Old Malton Moor

Rabbit Lane

Scagglethorpe Ings

Moor Farm

Ruston Plantation

MANOR VW 1
SLEDGATE GARTH 2
SOUTHLEA 3
MEADOW CT 4
SAXON DR 5
WOODLANDS DR 6
WOODLANDS GR 7

WESTGATE

PINE TREE AV

Rillington Com Prim Sch

Cemy

74

215

EDENHOUSE RD

WISE HOUSE LANE

Wyse House

SCAGGLETHORPE LANE

Scagglethorpe Grange

LC

Acuba Farm

Five Beeches

West Field

MALTON ROAD

Beech Tree Farm

Church Farm

4

A64

Barr Farm

Rixt Woods

Settrington Ings

Scagglethorpe Moor

Marr House

Willow Farm

Laurel Farm

Under Brow Farm

Bassett House

73

Fish Ponds

LASCELLES LANE

Abbey Ings

Villa Farm

Norton Parks

Marr Whin

Beck House

Manor Farm

PH

Brow Farm

Scagglethorpe Brow

Thorpe Bassett Wold

Spring Farm

3

SCARBOROUGH ROAD

B1248

Whinflower Hall

Scagglethorpe Bridge

Brambling Fields

Beech Tree Farm

SOUTHFIELD

Scagglethorpe

BILL FREE LA

Brow Farm

Thorpe Bassett Wold

72

Priorpot Bridge

215

Norton Grove Stud

Settrington Beck

The Holms

HOPGREEN LA

HIGHFIELD LA

Ebor House

Crosscliffe Farm

Mast

2

B1248

The Moor

Settrington All Saints CE VC Prim Sch

FOWGERS LANE

MIDDLETON CL

COOK GARTH

Settrington Cliffs

Cinquefoil Hill

Shepherdess Plantation

Many Thorns Farm

71

RYEDALE CL

Centenary Way

MOOR LA

TOWN ST

CHAPEL RD

BACK LANE

Cemy

HIGH STREET

Town Wold

Wold House

1

BEVERLEY ROAD

215

Gallops

Settrington Plantation

Westfield Farm

SCARLET BALK LANE

Town Green Farm

Settrington

NEW RD

Settrington House

HORSE PASTURE LANE

Wardale

70

215

LANGTON LA

Scarlet Balk Plantation

Rectory Farm

YO17

A · 81 · **B** · 82 · **C** · 83 · **D** · 84 · **E** · 85 · **F**

For full street detail of the highlighted area see page 215.
215
148

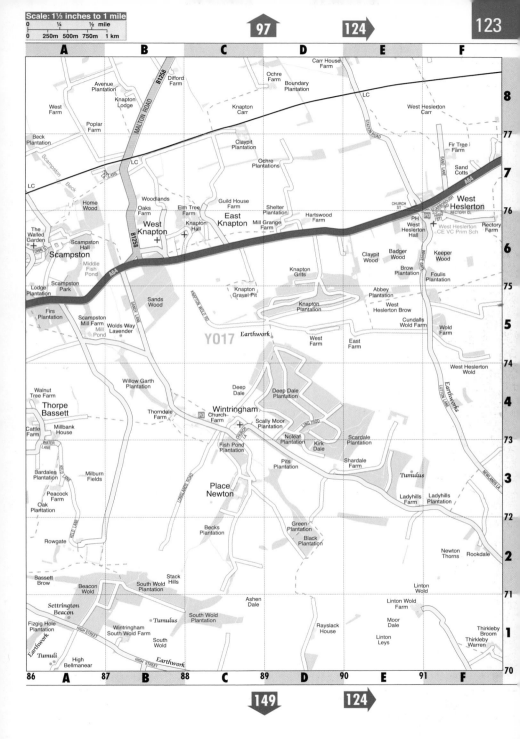

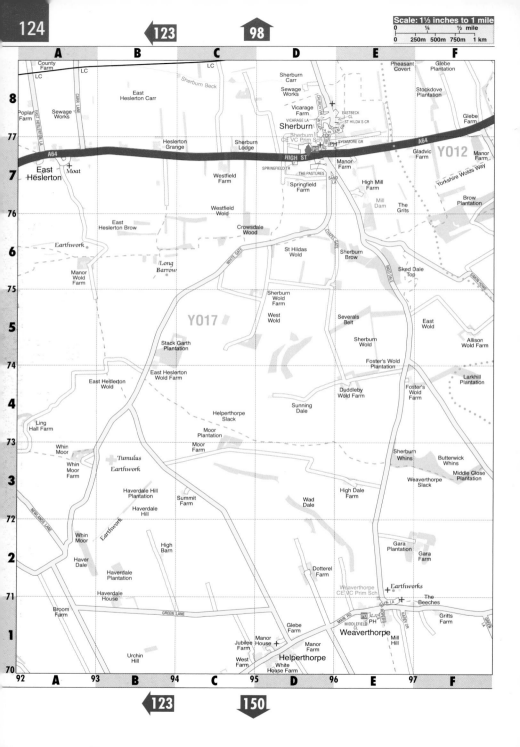

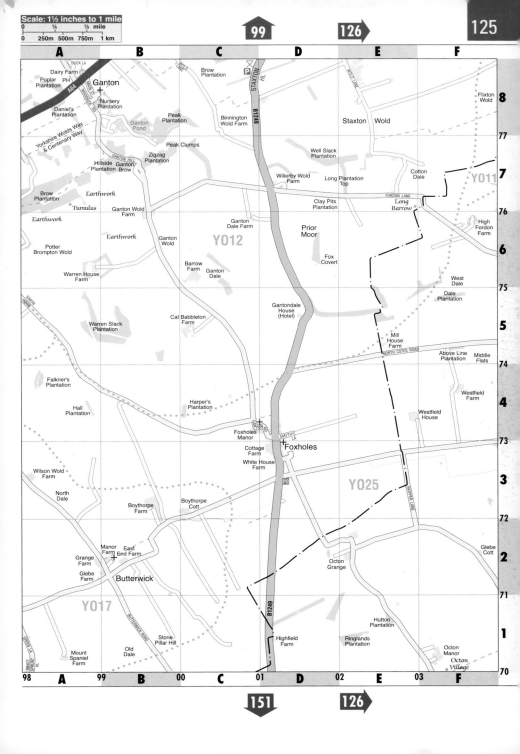

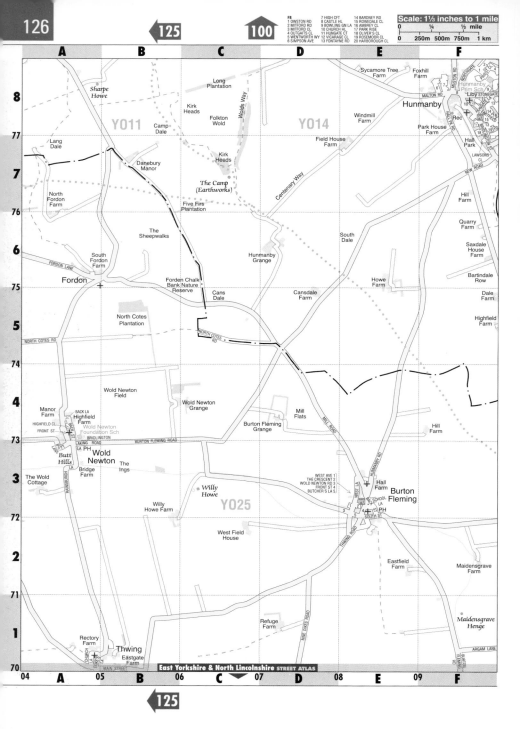

Scale: 1½ inches to 1 mile

0	¼	½ mile
0	250m	500m	750m	1 km

A8
1 WRANGHAM DR
2 LENNOX CL
3 BURLYN RD
4 CHERRY RD
5 HAWKE GARTH
6 MANOR GDNS
7 CECIL RD
8 HOWES RD
9 WATSON CL
10 HAMERTON RD
11 HAMERTON CL
12 GRIMSTON RD
13 STRICKLAND RD
14 PERCY RD
15 HAVERCROFT RD
16 COWLINGS CL

101

127

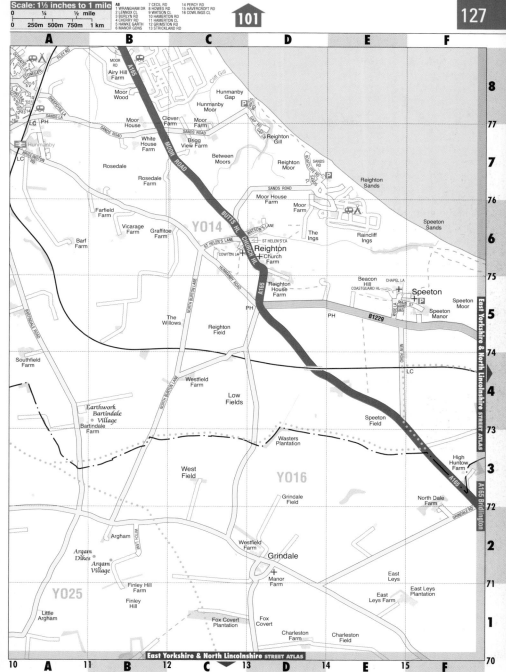

102

Scale: 1½ inches to 1 mile

0   ¼   ½   mile
0   250m 500m 750m 1 km

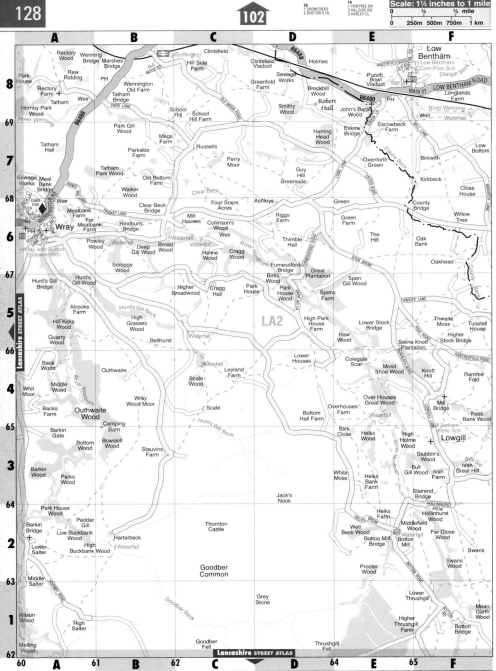

Low Bentham
Low Bentham
Com Prim Sch
Ellergill Beck

Rectory Wood
Wenning Bridge
Marshes Bridge
Wennington
Clintsfield
Clintsfield Viaduct
Holmes
B6480

Park House
Raw Ridding
PH
Hill Side Farm
Greenfold Farm
Sewage Works
Brockhill Wood
Punch Bowl Viaduct
Longlands Farm

Rectory Farm
Tatham
Wennington Old Farm
Tatham Bridge
Smithy Wood
Robert Hall
John's Bank
B6480
PH
Low Bentham Road

Hornby Park Wood
Weir
PARK LANE
School Hill
School Hill Farm
Herring Head Wood
Eskew Bridge
Escowbeck Farm
Weir
Waterfall
River Wenning

Tatham Hall
Park Gill Wood
Megs Farm
Russells
Perry Moor
Guy Hill Greenside
Oxenforth Green
Low Bottom

Parkside Farm
Tatham Park Wood
Old Bottom Farm
Clear Beck
Kirkbeck
Birkwith

Sewage Works
Meal Bank Bridge
Walker Wood
Clear Beck Bridge
Four Score Acres
Ashleys
Green
County Bridge
Close House

Weir
Mealbank Farm
Far Mealbank Farm
Hindburn Bridge
Mill Houses
Collinson's Wood
Weir
Riggs Farm
Green Farm
Willow Tree

Wray
Powley Wood
Deep Gill Wood
Broad Wood
Waterfall
Cragg Wood
Thimble Hall
The Hill
Oak Bank
Oakhead

Wray with Botton Endowed Sch
Scroggy Wood
Holme Wood
Furnesford Bridge
Birks Wood
Great Plantation
Spen Gill Wood
Spen Brow

Hunt's Gill Bridge
Hunt's Gill Wood
Higher Broadwood
Cragg Hall
Park House
Park House Wood
Spens Farm

Alcocks Farm
High Grasses Wood
Thwaite Lane

Hill Kirks Wood
Bellhurst
Waterfall
Leyland Farm
High Park House Farm
Lower Stock Bridge
Thwaite Moss
Tunstall House

Quarry Wood
Haw Wood
Swine Knott Plantation
Higher Stock Bridge

Back Wood
Outhwaite
Waterfall
Lower Houses
Colegate Scar
Mosit Shoe Wood
Knott Hill
Rantree Fold

Whit Moor
Middle Wood
Wray Wood Moor
Scale Wood
Over Houses Great Wood
Waterfall
Mill Bridge
Foss Bank Wood

Backs Farm
Camping Barn
Scale
Bottom Hall Farm
Overhouses Farm
High Holme Wood
Lowgill
Tatham Fells Sch

Barkin Gate
Bowskill Wood
Stauvins Farm
Stirk Close
Helks Wood
Stubbin's Wood
Ivah Great Hill

Barkin Wood
Bottom Wood
Parks Wood
White Moss
Helks Bank Farm
Bull Gill Wood
Ivah Farm

Park House Wood
Pedder Gill
Low Buckbank Wood
Jack's Nook
Stairend Bridge
Hollinhurst Brow

Barkin Bridge
High Buckbank Wood
Harterbeck
Waterfall
Thornton Castle
Helks Farm
Well Beck Wood
Middlefield Wood
Hollinhurst Wood
Far Close Wood

Lower Salter
Goodber Common
Botton Mill Bridge
Botton Mill
Swans

Middle Salter
Grey Stone
Procter Wood
Swans Wood

Wilson Wood
High Salter
Goodber Beck
Lower Thrushgill
Higher Thrushgill Farm
Mean Garth Wood

Melling Wood
Goodber Fell
Thrushgill Fell
Botton Bridge

LA2

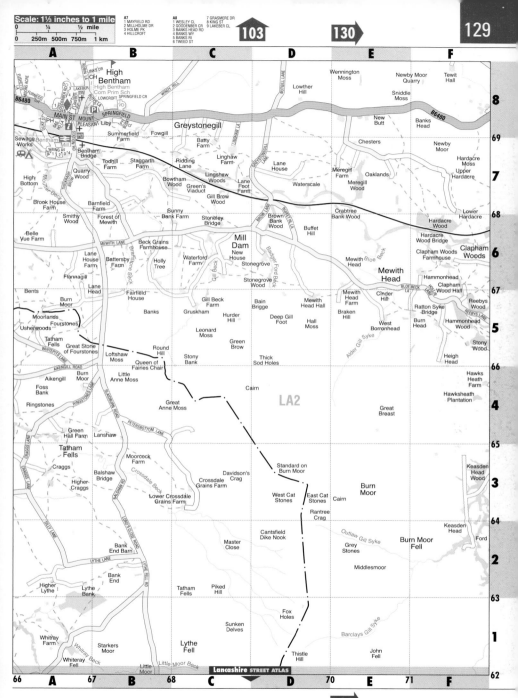

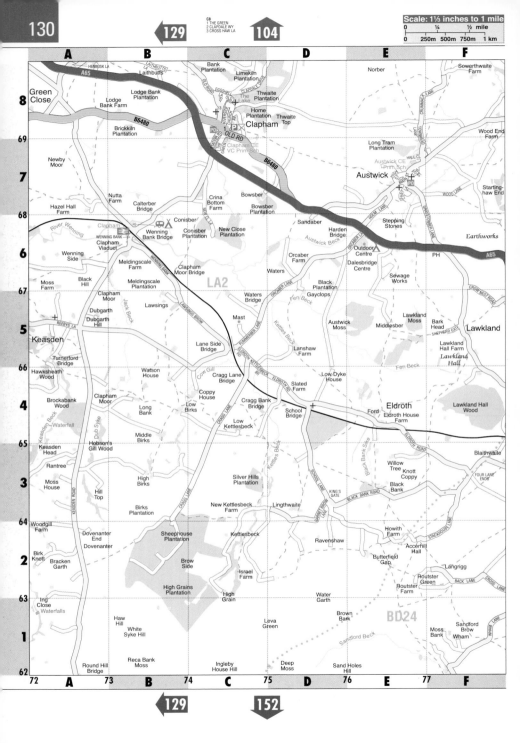

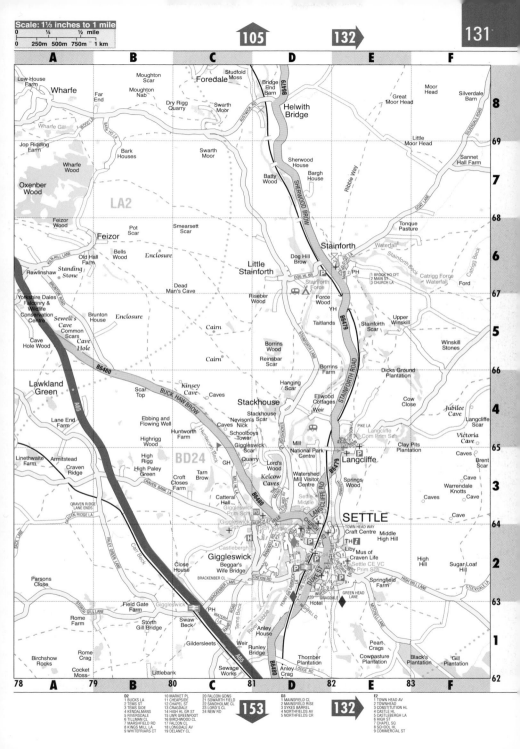

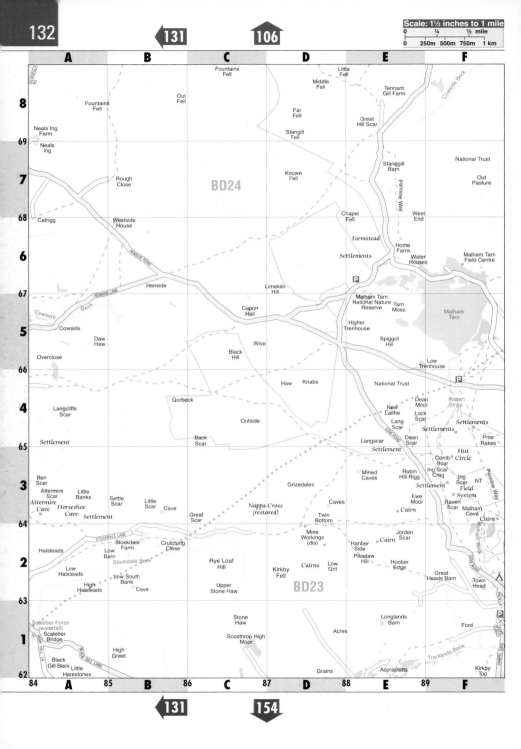

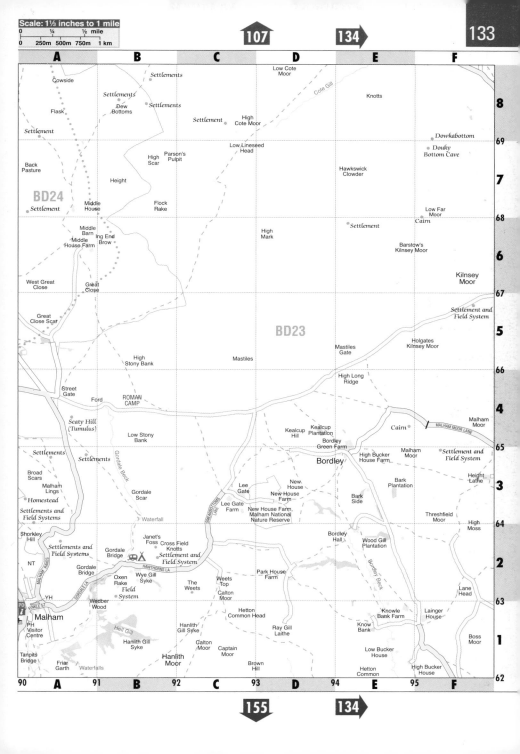

Scale: 1⅓ inches to 1 mile

| 0 | ¼ | ½ | mile |
| 0 | 250m | 500m | 750m | 1 km |

A   B   C   D   E   F

8

Cowside
Settlements
Knotts
Flask
Settlements
Dew Bottoms
Settlements
Low Cote Moor
Cote Gill
Settlement
Settlement
High Cote Moor
Dowkabottom
69
Low Lineseed Head
Douky Bottom Cave
High Scar
Parson's Pulpit
Hawkswick Clowder
7
Back Pasture
BD24
Height
Middle House
Flock Rake
Low Far Moor
Cairn
68
Middle Barn
Settlement
Middle House Farm
Ing End Brow
High Mark
Settlement
Barstow's Kilnsey Moor
6
West Great Close
Great Close
Kilnsey Moor
Great Close Scar
67
Settlement and Field System
BD23
5
High Stony Bank
Mastiles
Mastiles Gate
Holgates Kilnsey Moor
66
Street Gate
Ford
ROMAN CAMP
High Long Ridge
4
Seaty Hill (Tumulus)
Low Stony Bank
Kealcup Hill
Kealcup Plantation
Cairn
MALHAM MOOR LANE
Malham Moor
65
Settlements
Settlements
Gordale Beck
Bordley Green Farm
High Bucker House Farm
Malham Moor
Settlement and Field System
Broad Scars
Gordale Scar
Lee Gate
New House
Bordley
Bark Plantation
Height Lathe
3
Malham Lings
Lee Gate Farm
New House Farm
Bark Side
Threshfield Moor
Homestead
Waterfall
New House Farm, Malham National Nature Reserve
64
High Moss
Settlements and Field Systems
Janet's Foss
Cross Field Knotts
Bordley Hall
Wood Gill Plantation
Shorkley Hill
Gordale Bridge
Settlement and Field System
Bordley Beck
2
NT
Gordale Bridge
HAWTHORNS LA
Park House Farm
Lane Head
Oxen Rake Field System
Wye Gill Syke
The Weets
Weets Top
Calton Moor
YH
Wedber Wood
Knowle Bank Farm
Lainger House
63
Malham
Hetton Common Head
Ray Gill Laithe
Know Bank
Boss Moor
PH Visitor Centre
Hell Gill
Hanlith Gill Syke
Galton Moor
Captain Moor
Low Bucker House
1
Tarnpits Bridge
Friar Garth
Waterfalls
Hanlith Gill Syke
Hanlith Moor
Brown Hill
Hetton Common
High Bucker House
62

90   A   91   B   92   C   93   D   94   E   95   F

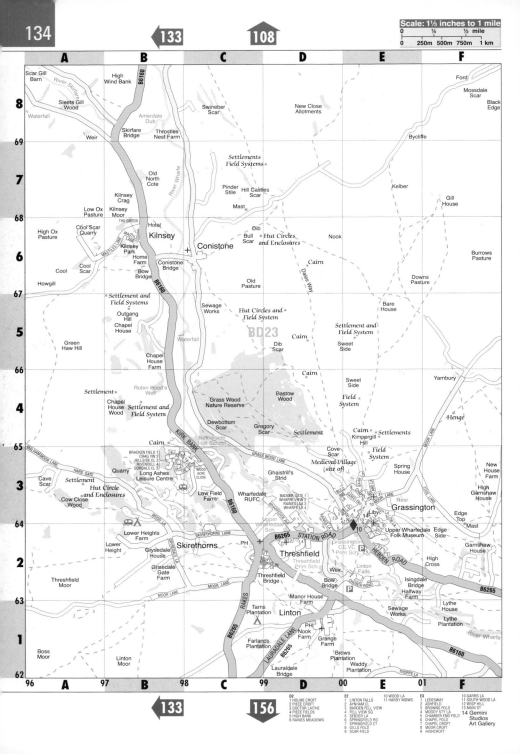

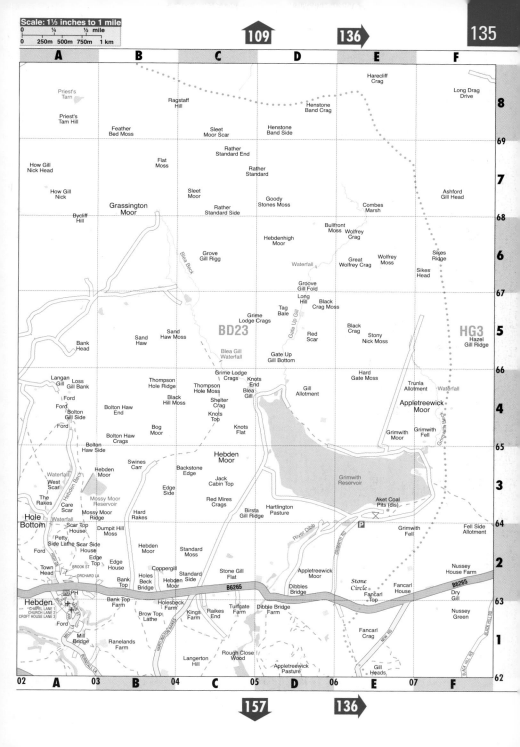

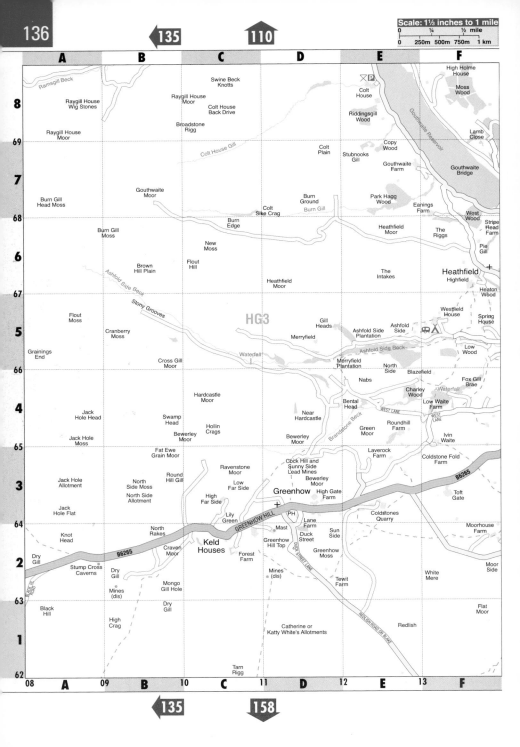

Scale: 1⅓ inches to 1 mile

0   ¼   ½ mile
0   250m 500m 750m 1 km

A   B   C   D   E   F

8

Ramsgill Beck

Raygill House
Wig Stones

Swine Beck
Knotts

Raygill House
Moor

Colt House
Back Drive

Colt
House

Riddingsgill
Wood

High Holme
House

Moss
Wood

Lamb
Close

Gouthwaite Reservoir

Gouthwaite
Bridge

Broadstone
Rigg

Raygill House
Moor

69

Colt House Gill

Colt
Plain

Copy
Wood

Gouthwaite
Farm

Stubnooks
Gill

7

Burn Gill
Head Moss

Gouthwaite
Moor

Burn
Ground

Burn Gill

Park Hagg
Wood

Eanings
Farm

West
Wood

Stripe
Head
Farm

68

Burn Gill
Moss

Burn
Edge

Colt
Sike Crag

Heathfield
Moor

The
Riggs

Pie
Gill

Brown
Hill Plain

New
Moss

Flout
Hill

6

The
Intakes

Heathfield

Highfield

Heaton
Wood

Heathfield
Moor

67

Ashfold Side Beck

Stony Grooves

Flout
Moss

Cranberry
Moss

Gill
Heads

Merryfield

Ashfold Side
Plantation

Ashfold
Side

Westfield
House

Spring
House

5

Grainings
End

Waterfall

Ashfold Side Beck

Low
Wood

Cross Gill
Moor

Merryfield
Plantation

North
Side

Blazefield

Fox Gill
Brae

66

Nabs

Charley
Wood

Waterfall

Low Waite
Farm

4

Hardcastle
Moor

Bental
Head

WEST LANE

WEST
LANE

Jack
Hole Head

Swamp
Head

Hollin
Crags

Near
Hardcastle

Green
Moor

Roundhill
Farm

Ivin
Waite

Jack Hole
Moss

Bewerley
Moor

Bewerley
Moor

Brandstone Beck

Laverock
Farm

Coldstone Fold
Farm

65

Fat Ewe
Grain Moor

Cock Hill and
Sunny Side
Lead Mines

Bewerley
Moor

B6265

Toft
Gate

3

Jack Hole
Allotment

North
Side Moss

Round
Hill Gill

Ravenstone
Moor

Low
Far Side

Greenhow

High Gate
Farm

North Side
Allotment

High
Far Side

Coldstones
Quarry

Moorhouse
Farm

Jack
Hole Flat

Lily
Green

PH

Lane
Farm

Sun
Side

64

Knot
Head

North
Rakes

GREENHOW HILL

Mast

Duck
Street

Greenhow
Moss

Moor
Side

Dry
Gill

B6265

Craven
Moor

Keld
Houses

Forest
Farm

Greenhow
Hill Top

Greenhow
Moss

White
Mere

2

Stump Cross
Caverns

Dry
Gill

Mines
(dis)

Tewit
Farm

63

Black
Hill

Mongo
Gill Hole

Dry
Gill

Redlish

Flat
Moor

High
Crag

Catherine or
Katty White's Allotments

1

Tarn
Rigg

62

08   A   09   B   10   C   11   D   12   E   13   F

HG3

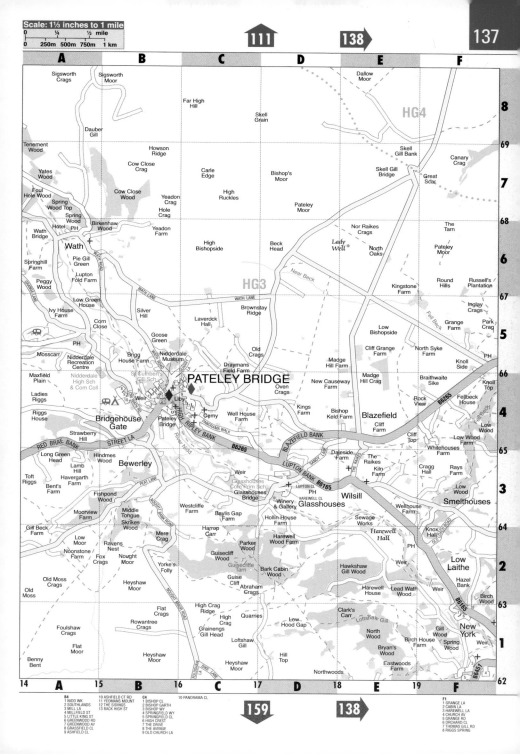

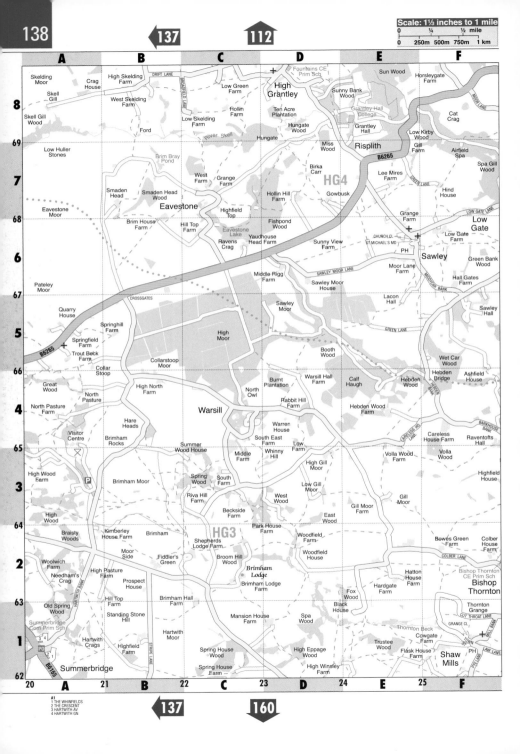

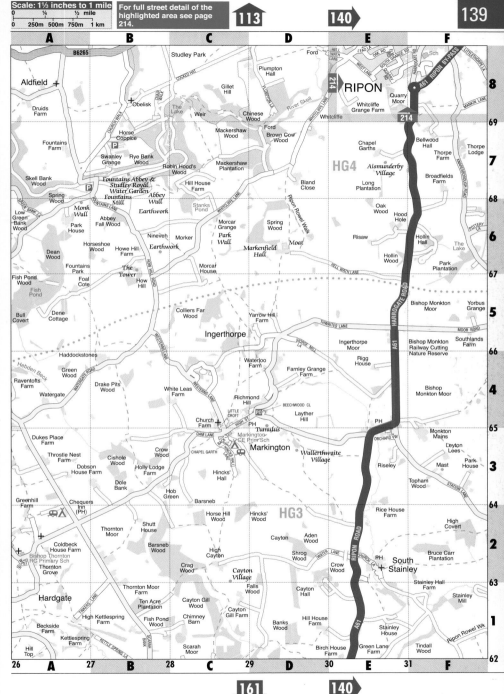

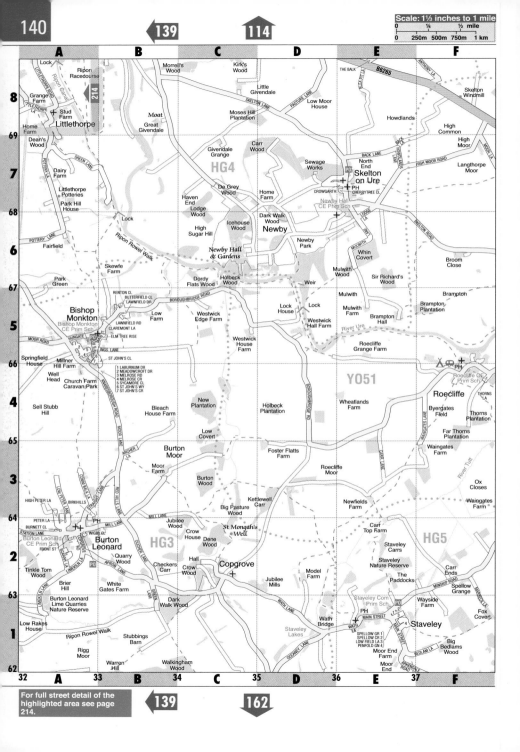

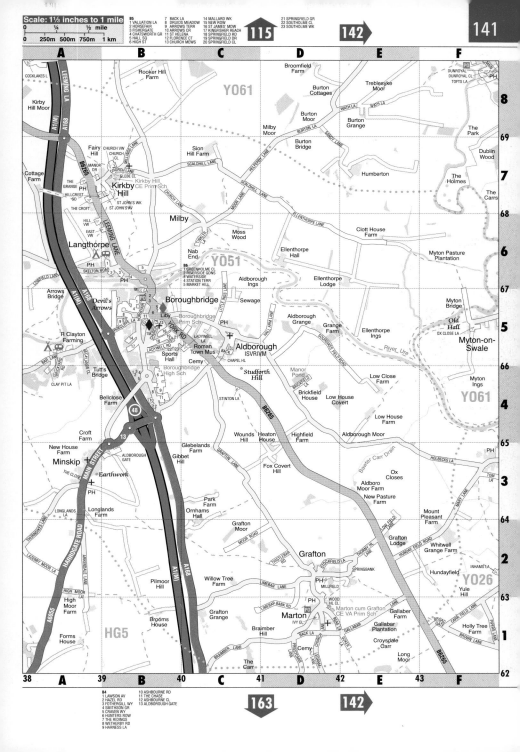

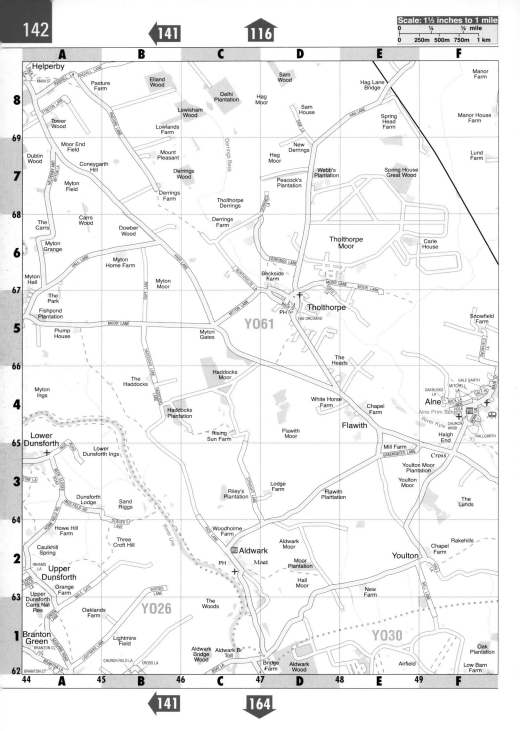

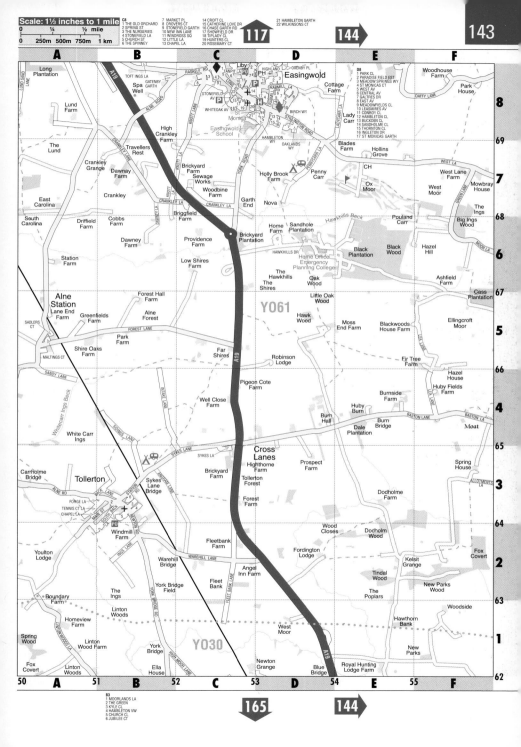

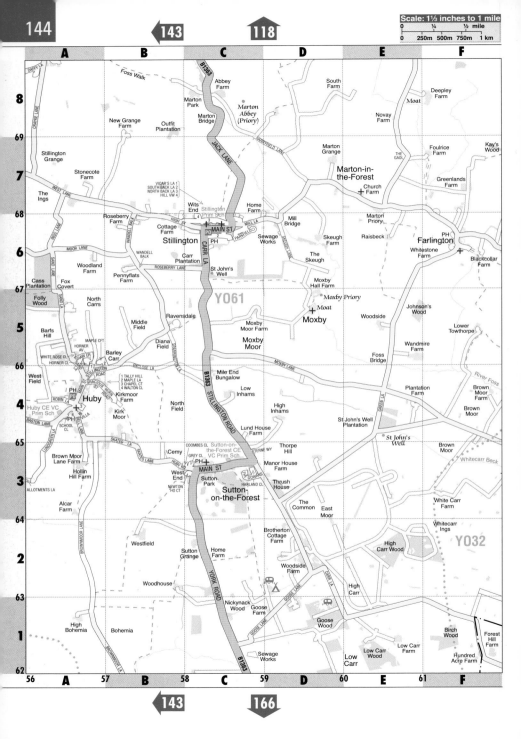

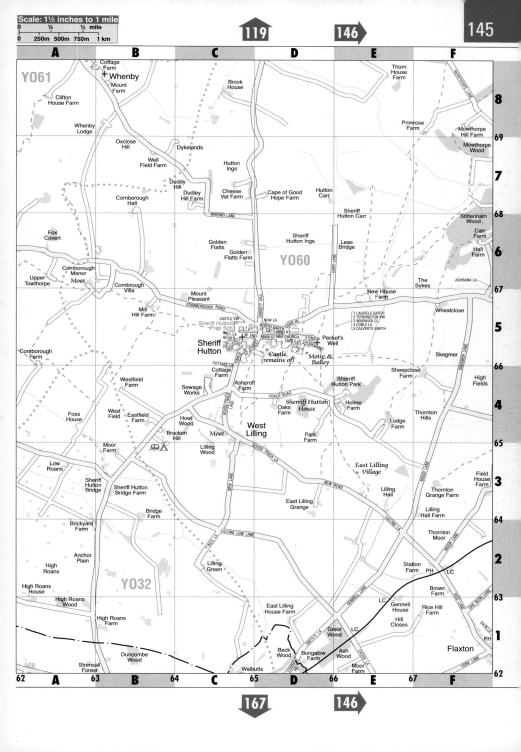

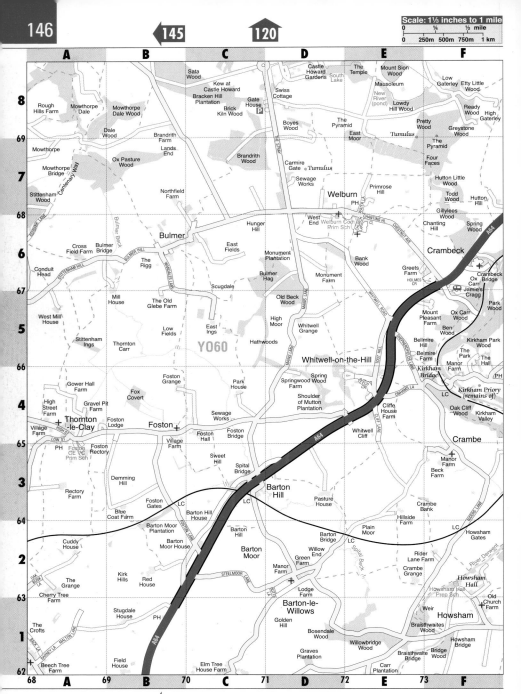

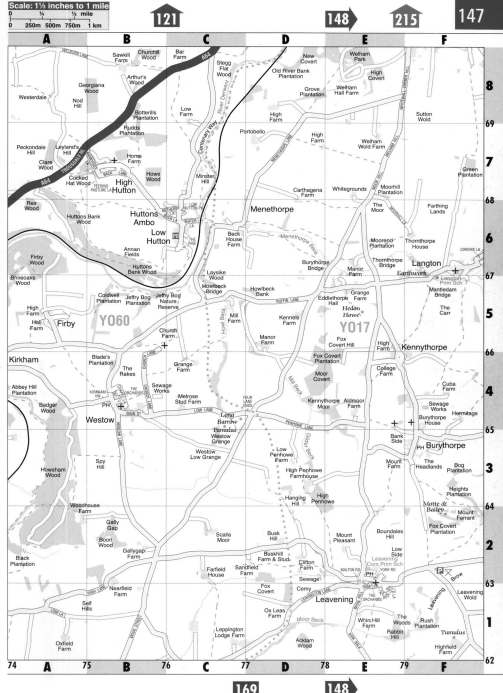

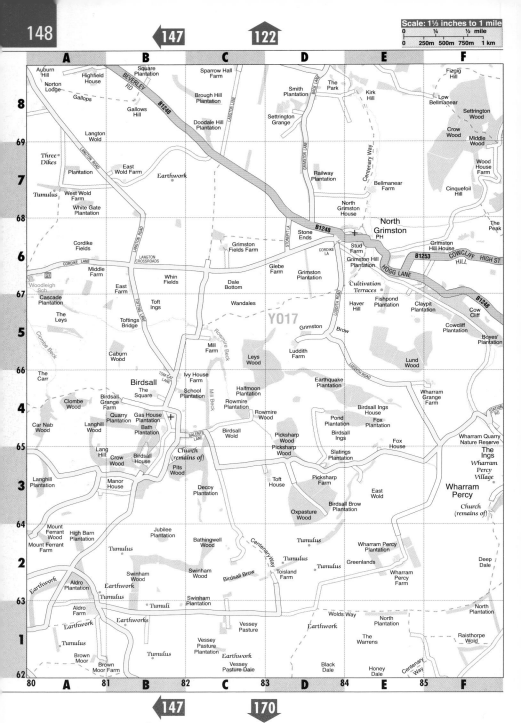

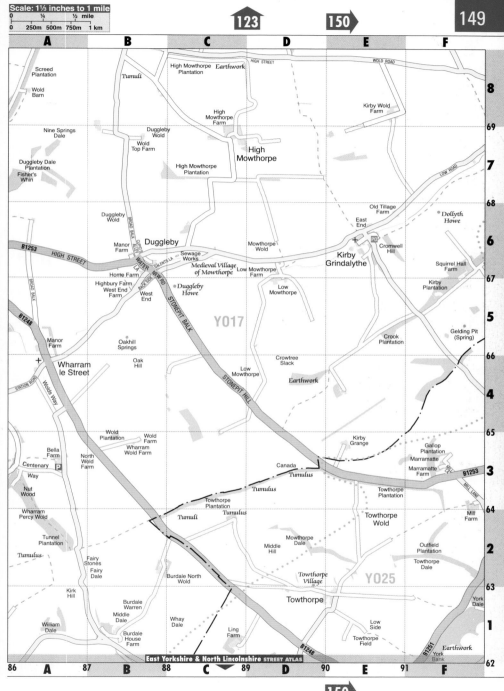

Scale: 1½ inches to 1 mile

0   ¼   ½   mile

0   250m   500m   750m   1 km

A   B   C   D   E   F

Screed
Plantation

Wold
Barn

Tumuli

High Mowthorpe
Plantation

Earthwork

HIGH STREET

WOLD ROAD

Kirby Wold
Farm

8

Nine Springs
Dale

Duggleby
Wold

High
Mowthorpe
Farm

69

Duggleby Dale
Plantation

Fisher's
Whin

Wold
Top Farm

High Mowthorpe
Plantation

High
Mowthorpe

LOW ROAD

7

Duggleby
Wold

Old Tillage
Farm

East
End

Dollyth
Howe

68

B1253   HIGH STREET

Manor
Farm

Duggleby

Mowthorpe
Wold

Kirby
Grindalythe

Cromwell
Hill

Squirrel Hall
Farm

6

Home Farm

BROAD BALK

WATER LA

GALENS LA

Sewage
Works

Medieval Village
of Mowthorpe

Low Mowthorpe
Farm

Kirby
Plantation

67

BROAD BALK

Highbury Farm
West End
Farm

West
End

BACK SIDE

NEW RD

Duggleby
Howe

Low
Mowthorpe

5

B1248

Manor
Farm

Oakhill
Springs

STONEPIT BALK

YO17

Crowtree
Slack

Crook
Plantation

Gelding Pit
(Spring)

66

Wharram
le Street

Oak
Hill

Low
Mowthorpe

Earthwork

4

STATION ROAD

WOLDS WAY

STONEPIT HILL

65

Wold
Plantation

Wold
Farm

Wharram
Wold Farm

Kirby
Grange

Gallop
Plantation

Marramatte

Marramatte
Farm

MILL LA

B1253

3

Bella
Farm

Centenary
Way

North
Wold
Farm

Canada

Tumulus

Tumulus

Towthorpe
Plantation

MILL LANE

Mill
Farm

64

Nut
Wood

Wharram
Percy Wold

Towthorpe
Plantation

Tumulus

Tumulus

Towthorpe
Wold

Outfield
Plantation

Towthorpe
Dale

2

Tunnel
Plantation

Tumulus

Fairy
Stones

Fairy
Dale

Tumuli

Middle
Hill

Mowthorpe
Dale

Towthorpe
Village

YO25

63

Kirk
Hill

Burdale
Warren

Burdale North
Wold

Towthorpe

York
Dale

William
Dale

Middle
Dale

Burdale
House
Farm

Whay
Dale

Ling
Farm

Low
Side

Towthorpe
Field

B1248

B1251

Earthwork

York
Bank

1

62

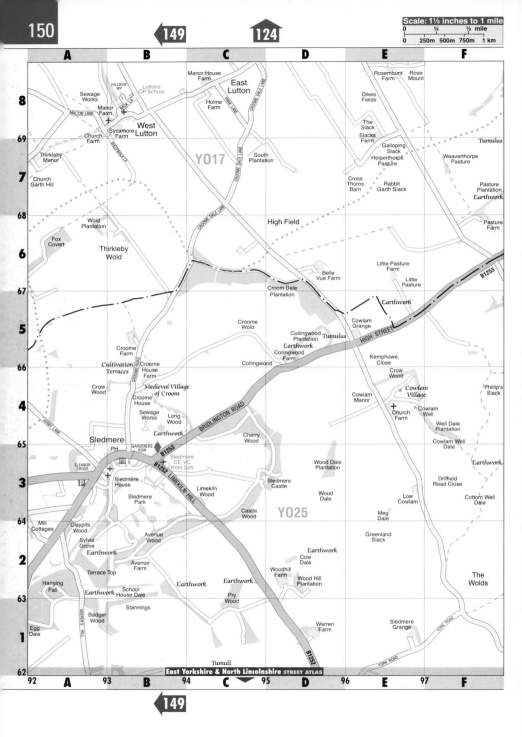

Scale: 1⅛ inches to 1 mile
0   ¼   ½ mile
0   250m 500m 750m 1 km

A   B   C   D   E   F

8

Sewage
Works
HILLSIDE
WY
Luttons
CP School
Manor House
Farm
East
Lutton
Rosemount
Farm
Rose
Mount

Manor
Farm
MALTON LANE
Holme
Farm
Dikes
Fields

69
Church
Farm
Sycamore
Farm
West
Lutton
SYCAMORE LA
The
Slack
Slacks
Farm
Tumulus

Thirkleby
Manor
Y017
South
Plantation
Galloping
Slack
Helperthorpe
Pasture
Weaverthorpe
Pasture

7
Church
Garth Hill
CROOME DALE LANE
Cross
Thorns
Barn
Rabbit
Garth Slack
Pasture
Plantation
Earthwork

68
Wold
Plantation
High Field
Pasture
Farm

Fox
Covert
Thirkleby
Wold
Little Pasture
Farm
B1253

6
Belle
Vue Farm
Little
Pasture

67
Croom Dale
Plantation
Earthwork
HIGH STREET

Croome
Wold
Cowlam
Grange

5
Croome
Farm
Collingwood
Plantation
Earthwork
Tumulus
Kemphowe
Close
Crow
Wood
Phillip's
Slack

66
Cultivation
Terraces
Croome
House
Farm
CROOME ROAD
Collingwood
Collingwood
Farm

Crow
Wood
Medieval Village
of Croom
Cowlam
Manor
Cowlam
Village

4
Croome
House
Long
Wood
BRIDLINGTON ROAD
Church
Farm
Cowlam
Well
Well Dale
Plantation

KIRBY LANE
Sewage
Works
Earthwork
Cowlam Well
Dale
Earthwork

65
Sledmere
PH
GARDENERS
ROW
B1253
Cherry
Wood
Wood Dale
Plantation
Driffield
Road Close

ELEANOR
CROSS
Sledmere
CE VC
Prim Sch
Sledmere
Castle
Cottom Well
Dale

3
P
Sledmere
House
B1252 LIMEKILN HILL
Limekiln
Wood
Wood
Dale
Low
Cowlam

64
Mill
Cottages
Claypits
Wood
Sledmere
Park
Castle
Wood
Y025
Meg
Dale

Sylvia
Grove
Earthwork
Avenue
Wood
Greenland
Slack

2
Terrace Top
Avenue
Farm
Earthwork
Earthwork
Earthwork
Cow
Dale
The
Wolds

Hanging
Fall
Earthwork
School
House Dale
Pry
Wood
Woodhill
Farm
Wood Hill
Plantation

63
Badger
Wood
Stannings
KEEPER'S HILL
Warren
Farm
Sledmere
Grange
YORK ROAD

1
Egg
Dale
B1252

62
Tumuli
East Yorkshire & North Lincolnshire STREET ATLAS
YORK ROAD

92   A   93   B   94   C   95   D   96   E   97   F

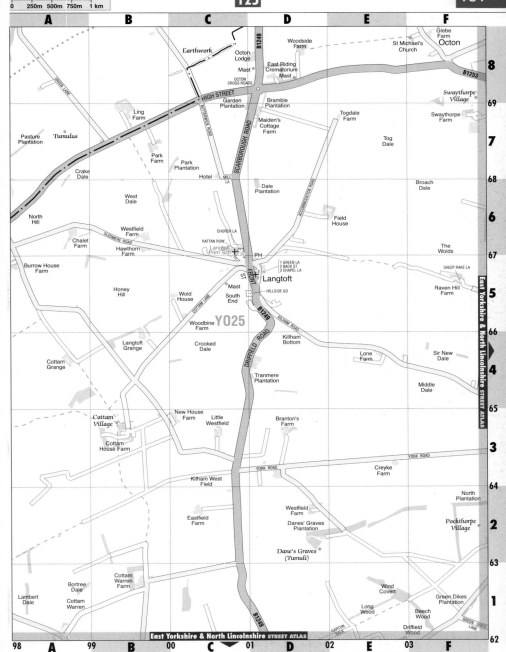

East Yorkshire & North Lincolnshire STREET ATLAS

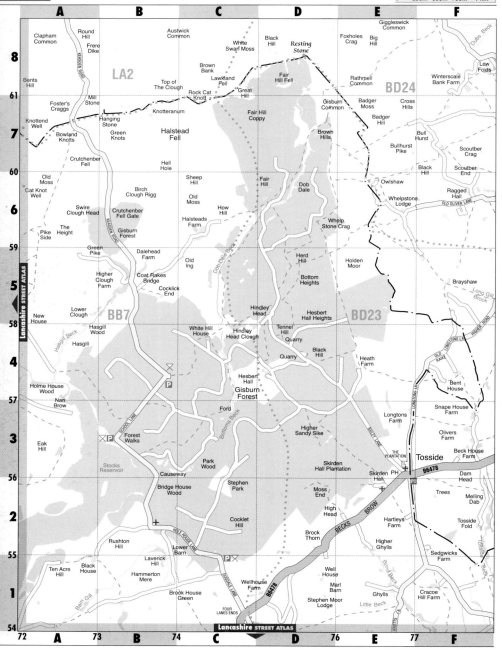

Scale: 1⅓ inches to 1 mile

0   ¼   ½ mile
0   250m 500m 750m 1 km

Clapham Common
Round Hill
Frere Dike
Austwick Common
White Swan Moss
Black Hill
Resting Stone
Foxholes Crag
Big Hill
Gigglesworth Common
Dubs Beck
Low Foids

Bents Hill
Brown Bank
Lawkland Fell
Fair Hill Fell
Rathrpell Common
Winterscale Bank Farm

LA2
Top of The Clough
Great Hill
Rock Cat Knott
Gisburn Common
Badger Moss
Cross Hills
BD24

Foster's Craggs
Mill Stone
Knotteranum
Fair Hill Coppy
Badger Hill
Bull Hurst

Knottend Well
Hanging Stone
Halstead Fell
Brown Hills
Bullhurst Pike
Scoutber Crag

Bowland Knotts
Green Knots
Hell Hole
Brown Hills
Owlshaw
Black Hill
Scoutber End

Crutchenber Fell
Sheep Hill
Fair Hill
Dob Dale
Whelpstone Lodge
Ragged Hall

Old Moss
Birch Clough Rigg
Old Moss
How Hill
Whelp Stone Crag
OLD OLIVER LANE

Cat Knot Well
Swire Clough Head
Crutchenber Fell Gate
Halsteads Farm
Herd Hill
Holden Moor
Brayshaw
Long Gill Brook

Pike Side
The Height
Gisburn Forest
Old Ing
Bottom Heights
Hesbert Hall Heights
BD23

Green Pike
Dalehead Farm
Hindley Head
Tennel Hill
Heath Farm

New House
Lower Clough
BB7
Coat Rakes Bridge
Cocklick End
Higher Clough Farm
White Hill House
Hindley Head Clough
Quarry
Black Hill
Quarry
Bent House

Hasgill Wood
Hasgill
Hesbert Hall
Gisburn Forest
Snape House Farm

Holme House Wood
Nan Brow
Forest Walks
Ford
Higher Sandy Sike
Longtons Farm
Olivers Farm
Beck House Farm

Eak Hill
Park Wood
Skirden Hall Plantation
THE PLANTATION
Tosside
B6478

Stocks Reservoir
Causeway
Bridge House Wood
Stephen Park
Moss End
Skirden Hall
PH
Dam Head
Trees
Melling Dab

Rushton Hill
Cocklet Hill
High Head
Hartleys Farm
Tosside Fold

Ten Acre Hill
Black House
Lower Barn
Laverick Hill
Hammerton Mere
Brock Thorn
Higher Ghylls
Sedgwicks Farm

Barn Gill
Brook House Green
Wellhouse Farm
BRIDGE LANE
Well House
Marl Barn
Ghylls
Little Beck
Cracoe Hill Farm

HOLE HOUSE LANE
FOUR LANES ENDS
Stephen Moor Lodge
Bond Beck
KNOTTS LANE

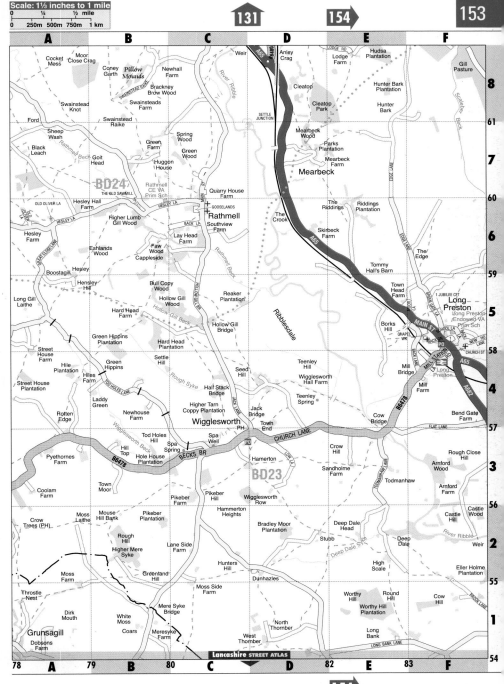

Cocket Moss
Moor Close Crag
Coney Garth
Pillow Mounds
Newhall Farm
Brackney Brow Wood
SWAINSTEAD PARK
Swainsteads Farm
Weir
River Ribble
Anley Crag
LODGE RD
Lodge Farm
Hudsa Plantation
Gill Pasture
Cleatop
Hunter Bark Plantation
Scaleber Beck

Swainstead Knot
Swainsteads Farm
Cleatop Park
Hunter Bark

Ford
Swainstead Raike
SETTLE JUNCTION

Sheep Wash
Spring Wood
Mearbeck Wood
Parks Plantation

Black Leach
RATHMELL BECK
Goit Head
Green Farm
Green Wood
Huggon House
Mearbeck
Mearbeck Farm
EDGE LANE

BD24
THE OLD SAWMILL
Rathmell CE VA Prim Sch
Quarry House Farm
The Riddings
Riddings Plantation

OLD OLIVER LA
Hesley Hall Farm
HESLEY LA
GOOSELANDS
BACK LA
Rathmell
Southview Farm
The Crook
Skirbeck Farm
The Edge

Hesley Farm
Higher Lumb Gill Wood
Lay Head Farm
Tommy Hall's Barn

GREAT CLOSE LANE
Eshlands Wood
Faw Wood
Cappleside
Reaker Plantation
Town Head Farm
Long Preston
1 JUBILEE COT
Long Preston /Endowed VA Prim Sch

Boostagill
Hesley
Hensley Hill
Bull Copy Wood
Hollow Gill Wood
Ribblesdale
MAIN ST
GREEN GATE LA
Borks Hill
CHAPEL WK
SCHOOL LA

Long Gill Laithe
Hard Head Farm
HOLLOW GILL BECK
HOLLOW MILL LA
Hollow Gill Bridge
Borks Hill
BACK LA
PO
CHURCH ST

Street House Farm
Green Hippins Plantation
Hard Head Plantation
Seed Hill
Teenley Hill
Mill Bridge
MILL STATION RD
A65

Hile Plantation
Green Hippins
Settle Hill
ROUGH SYKE
Wigglesworth Hall Farm
Long Preston
Mill Farm

Street House Plantation
Hiles Farm
TOD HOLES LANE
Half Stack Bridge
JACK LANE
Teenley Spring
Mill Farm

Laddy Green
Higher Tarn Coppy Plantation
Jack Bridge
Cow Bridge
Bend Gate Farm

Rotten Edge
Newhouse Farm
Tod Holes Hill
Wigglesworth
PH
Town End
CHURCH LANE
FLAT LANE

WIGGLESWORTH BECK
Spa Spring
Spa Well
PO
Crow Hill
Rough Close Hill

Pyethornes Farm
Hill Top
Hole House Plantation
BECKS BR
Hamerton
LOW LA
Sandholme Farm
Arnford Wood

B6478
BD23
Todmanhaw
Arnford Farm

Coolam Farm
Town Moor
Pikeber Farm
Pikeber Hill
Wigglesworth Row
Hammerton Heights
Deep Dale Head
Castle Hill
Castle Wood

Crow Trees (PH)
Moss Laithe
Mouse Hill Bank
Pikeber Plantation
Bradley Moor Plantation
Stubb
Deep Dale
River Ribble
Weir

Rough Hill
Higher Mere Syke
Lane Side Farm
High Scale
Eller Holme Plantation

Moss Farm
Greenland Hill
Hunters Hill
Dunhazles
DEEP DALE SYKE
Worthy Hill
Round Hill
Cow Hill
BROOK LANE

Throstle Nest
Dirk Mouth
White Moss
Mere Syke Bridge
Moss Side Farm
Worthy Hill Plantation

Grunsagill
Dobsons Farm
Coars
Meresyke Farm
West Thomber
North Thomber
Long Bank
LONG BANK LANE

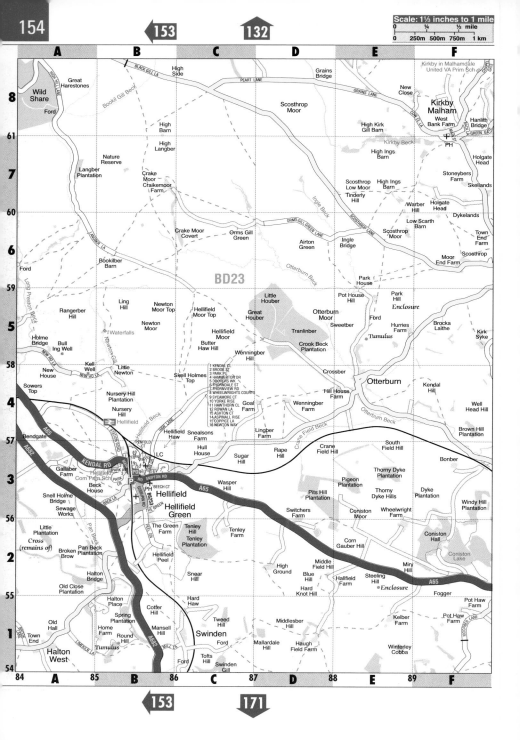

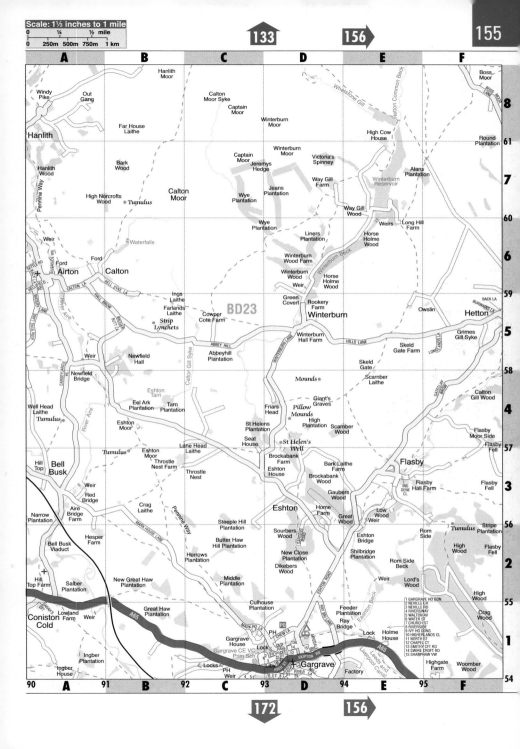

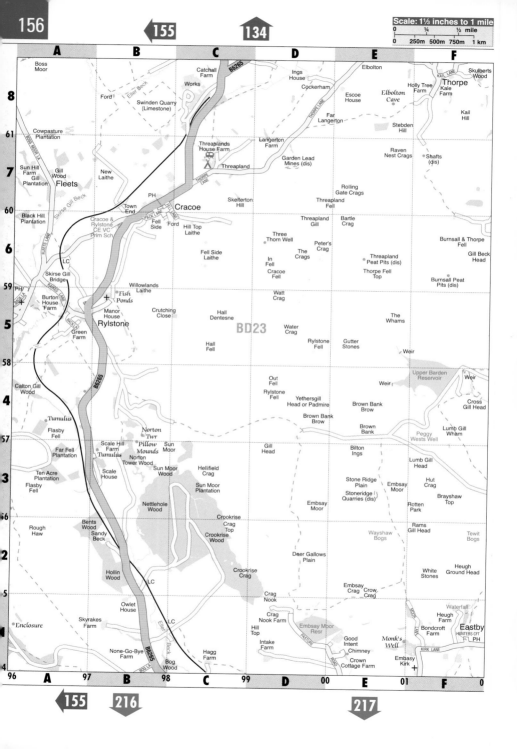

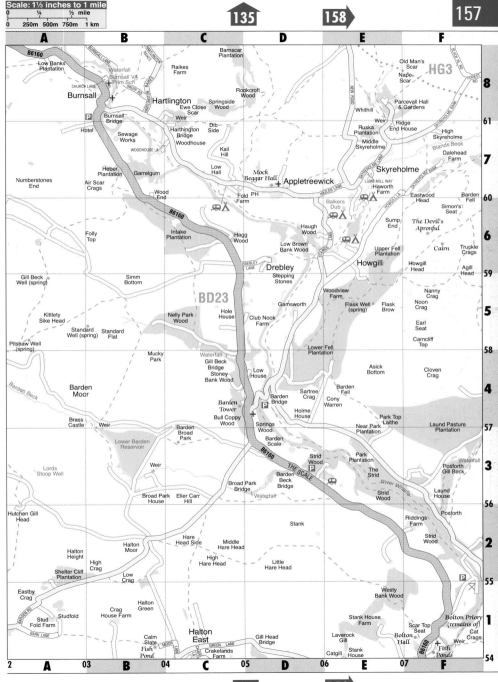

Scale: 1⅓ inches to 1 mile

0 ¼ ½ mile
0 250m 500m 750m 1 km

135
158
HG3

A

B6160
Low Banks Plantation
Church Lane
Burnsall
Burnsall Lane
Waterfall
Burnsall VA Prim Sch
Skue Rd
Martin Rd

B

Hartlington
Hartlington Lane
Burnsall Bridge
Hotel
Sewage Works
Woodhouse La
Heber Plantation
Garrelgum
Air Scar Crags
Wood End
B6160
Intake Plantation
Simm Bottom
Nelly Park Wood
Mucky Park
Waterfall
Gill Beck Bridge
Stoney Bank Wood
Barden Broad Park
Lower Barden Reservoir
Weir
Broad Park House
Eller Carr Hill
Hare Head Side
Halton Moor
Halton Height
High Crag
Low Crag
Halton Green
Crag House Farm
Calm Slate Fish Pond
Green Lane
Moor Lane

Numberstones End

C

Raikes Farm
Barnscar Plantation
Rookcroft Wood
Ewe Close Scar
Springside Wood
Weir
Harthington Bridge
Woodhouse
Dib Side
Kail Hill
Low Hall
Mock Beggar Hall
Fold Farm
Hagg Wood
Drebley Lane
Drebley
Hole House
Club Nook Farm
Low House
Barden Tower
Bull Coppy Wood
Barden Broad Park
Broad Park Bridge
Waterfall
Hare Head Side
Middle Hare Head
High Hare Head
Halton East
Crakelands Farm
Gill Head Bridge

BD23

D

Barnscar Plantation
Appletreewick
PH
Haugh Wood
Low Brown Bank Wood
Stepping Stones
Gamsworth
Lower Fell Plantation
Sartree Crag
Barden Bridge
Springs Wood
Barden Scale
B6160
The Scale
Barden Beck Bridge
Waterfall
Stank
Little Hare Head
Stank House
Catgill

E

New Road
Whithill
Weir
Ruska Plantation
Middle Skyreholme
Balkers Dub
Skyreholme Bank
Sump End
Woodview Farm
Flask Well (spring)
Flask Brow
Lumb Mill Way
Haworth Farm
Howgill
Howgill Head
Asick Bottom
Barden Fell
Cony Warren
Holme House
Near Park Plantation
Park Top Laithe
Park Plantation
The Strid
Strid Wood
P
Riddings Farm
Strid Wood
Stank House Farm
Laverock Gill
Westy Bank Wood
Bolton Hall

F

Old Man's Scar
Nape Scar
Black Hill Rd
Forest Rd
Parcevall Hall & Gardens
Ridge End House
High Skyreholme
Blands Beck
Dalehead Farm
Skyreholme Bank
Eastwood Head
Barden Fell
Simon's Seat
The Devil's Apronful
Cairn
Truckle Crags
Agill Head
Nanny Crag
Noon Crag
Earl Seat
Carncliff Top
Cloven Crag
Laund Pasture Plantation
Waterfall
Posforth Gill Beck
Laund House
Posforth
Strid Wood
P
Scar Top Seat
Bolton Priory (remains of)
Cat Crags
Bolton Hall
Weir
Fish Ponds
B6160

Barden Moor
Brass Castle
Weir
Lords Stoop Well
Hutchen Gill Head
Shelter Cliff Plantation
Eastby Crag
Studfold
Stud Fold Farm
Bark Lane
Baston Rd

Gill Beck Well (spring)
Kittlety Sike Head
Standard Well (spring)
Standard Flat
Pitshaw Well (spring)
Folly Top

River Wharfe

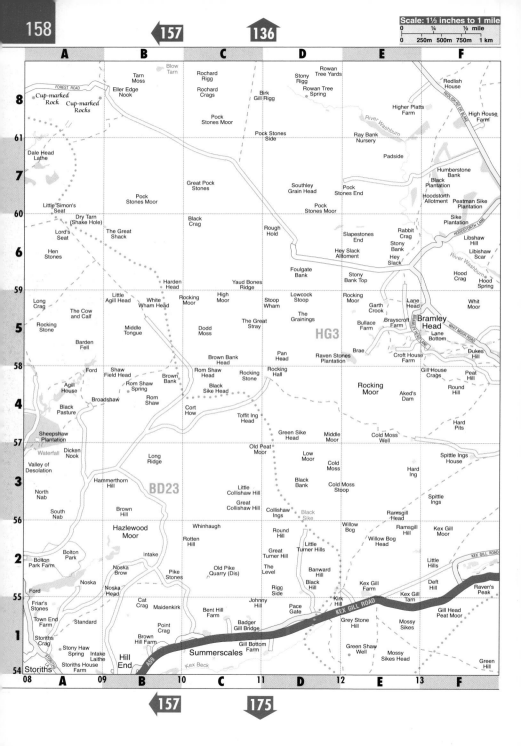

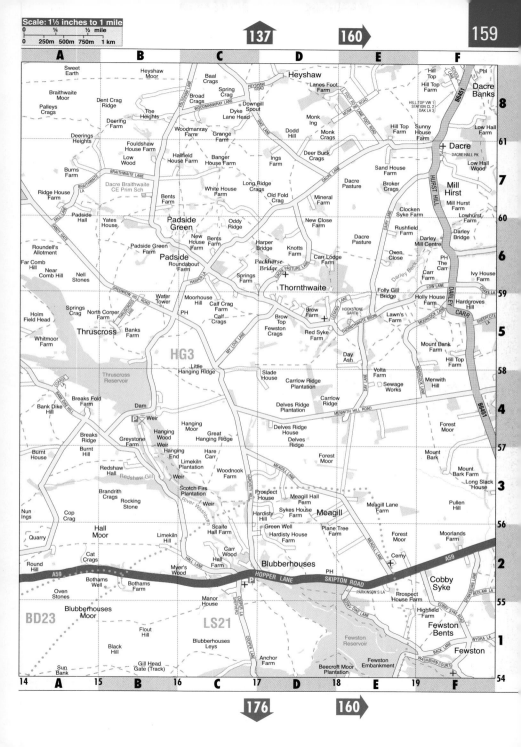

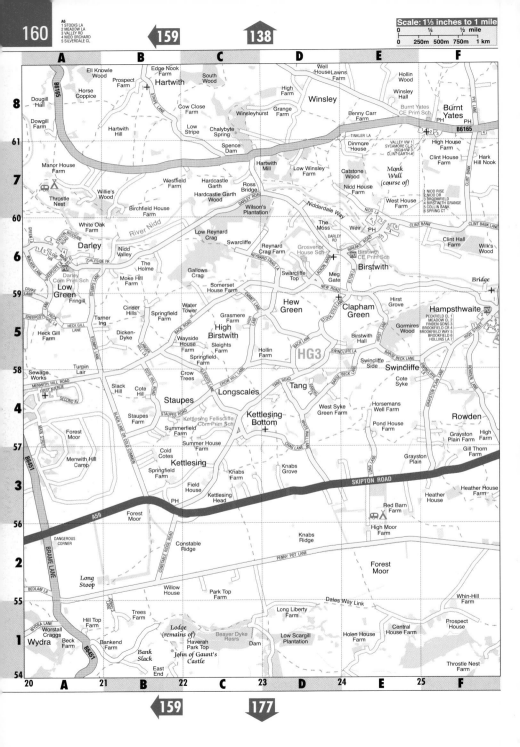

160

A6
1 STOCKS LA
2 MEADOW LA
3 VALLEY RD
4 NIDD ORCHARD
5 SILVERDALE CL

159   138

Scale: 1⅓ inches to 1 mile
0   ¼   ½   mile
0   250m 500m 750m 1 km

A   B   C   D   E   F

8

Ell Knowle Wood
Edge Nook Farm
Prospect Farm
Hartwith
South Wood
Well House Lawns Farm
Hollin Wood
Winsley Hall
Burnt Yates
CE Prim Sch

Dougill Hall
Horse Coppice
Cow Close Farm
Winsleyhurst
Grange Farm
Winsley
Benny Carr Farm
Burnt Yates
PH   PH

61

Dowgill Farm
Hartwith Hill
Low Stripe
Chalybate Spring
Spence Dam
High Farm
TINKLER LA
Dinmore House
VALLEY VW 2
SYCAMORE CL 2
HIGH VW 3
CLINT GARTH 4
High House Farm
Clint House Farm
Hark Hill Nook
B6165

7

Manor House Farm
Throstle Nest
Willie's Wood
Westfield Farm
Hardcastle Garth
Hardcastle Garth Wood
Ross Bridge
Hartwith Mill
Low Winsley Farm
Catstone Wood
Nidd House Farm
Monk Wall (course of)
West Home Farm

60

White Oak Farm
Birchfield House Farm
River Nidd
Wilson's Plantation
Nidderdale Way
The Moss
Weir
PH
Birstwith
CE Prim Sch
Clint Hall Farm
Wilk's Wood

6

GREEN LA
Darley
Nidd Valley
DALESIDE PK
The Holme
Low Reynard Crag
Swarcliffe
Reynard Crag Farm
Grosvenor House Sch
DARLEY RD
BREAKS ROAD
CLINT BANK
CLINT BANK LANE
Bridge

59

Darley Com Prim Sch
Low Green
Fringill
Moke Hill Farm
Gallows Crag
Somerset House Farm
Swarcliffe Top
Meg Gate
NEW ROAD
Swincliffe Side
Swincliffe
Hampsthwaite

5

Heck Gill Farm
Turner Ing
Cinder Hills
Dicken-Dyke
Springfield Farm
Water Tower
Grasmere Farm
High Birstwith
Wayside House Farm
Sleights Farm
Springfield Farm
Hollin Farm
Hew Green
Clapham Green
Birstwith Hall
Hirst Grove
Gormires Wood
PECKFIELD CL 1
MEADOW CL 2
FINDEN GDNS 3
BROOKFIELD CR 4
BROOKFIELD WAY 5
BROOKFIELD 6
HOLLINS LA 7

58

Sewage Works
Turpin Lair
MENWITH HILL ROAD
FIRST AVENUE
Slack Hill
Cote Hill
Crow Trees
HG3
Swincliffe Side
Swincliffe
Cote Syke

4

SECOND AV
Forest Moor
Staupes Farm
Staupes
Staupes Road
Kettlesing Felliscliffe Com Prim Sch
Summerfield Farm
Longscales
Kettlesing Bottom
Tang
West Syke Green Farm
Horsemans Well Farm
Pond House Farm
Rowden
Grayston Plain Farm
High Farm

57

Menwith Hill Camp
Cold Cotes
Summer House Farm
Kettlesing
Springfield Farm
Field House
Knabs Farm
Knabs Grove
Grayston Plain
Gill Thorn Farm

3

A59
Forest Moor
PH
Kettlesing Head
SKIPTON ROAD
Red Barn Farm
Heather House
Heather House Farm

56

DANGEROUS CORNER
Forest Moor
Constable Ridge
Knabs Ridge
High Moor Farm

2

BRAME LANE
BEDLAM LA
Long Stoop
Willow House
Park Top Farm
PENNY POT LANE
Forest Moor
Whin-Hill Farm
Prospect House

55

WYDRA LANE
Hill Top Farm
Trees Farm
Long Liberty Farm
Dales Way Link
Central House Farm

1

Wydra
Worstall Craggs
Beck Farm
Bankend Farm
Bank Slack
East End
Lodge (remains of)
Haverah Park Top
John of Gaunt's Castle
Beaver Dyke Resrs
Dam
Low Scargill Plantation
Holen House Farm
Throstle Nest Farm

54

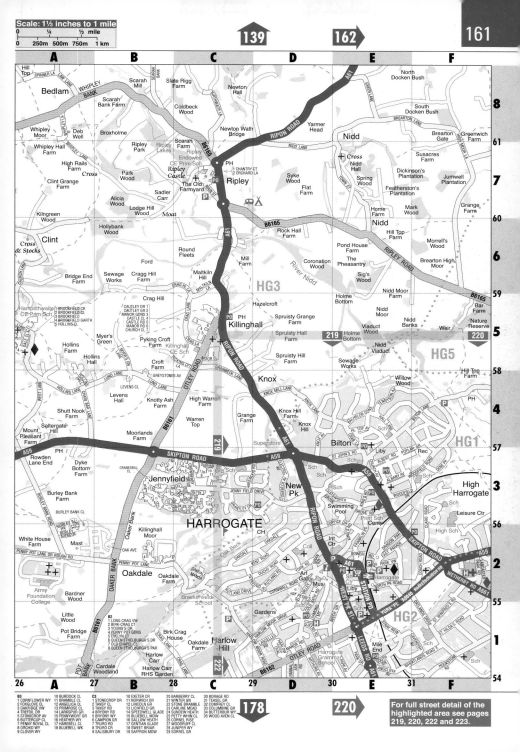

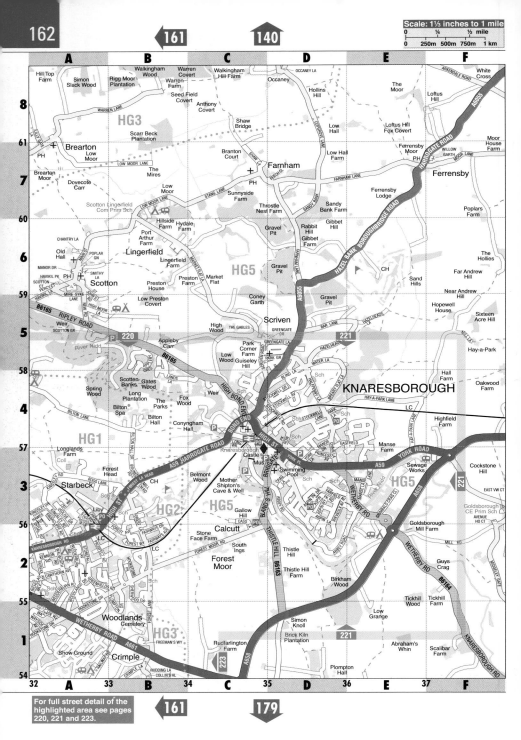

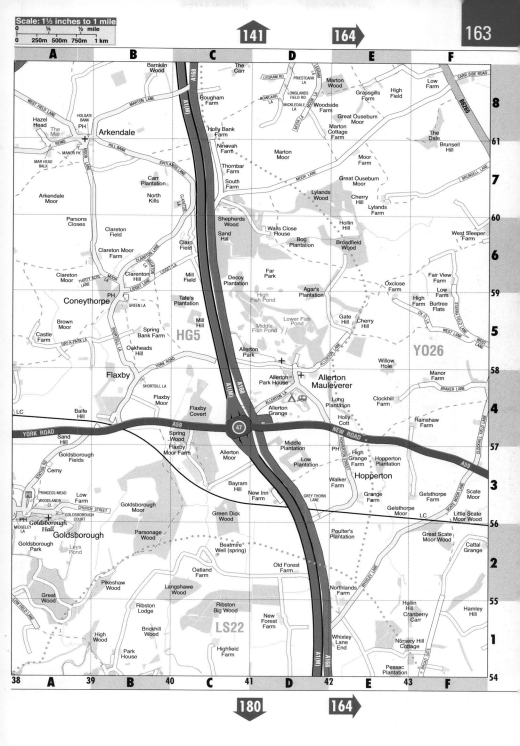

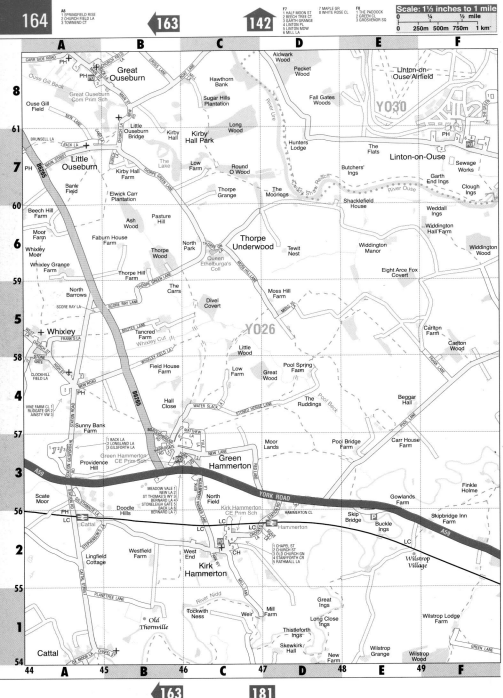

A8
1 SPRINGFIELD RISE
2 CHURCH FIELD LA
3 TOWNEND CT

163

142

F7
1 HALF MOON ST
2 BEECH TREE CT
3 GARTH GRANGE
4 LINTON PL
5 LINTON MDW
6 MILL LA

7 MAPLE GR
8 WHITE ROSE CL

F8
1 THE PADDOCK
2 GREEN CL
3 GROSVENOR SQ

Scale: 1⅓ inches to 1 mile

0   ¼   ½ mile
0   250m 500m 750m 1 km

Great Ouseburn

Great Ouseburn
Com Prim Sch

Little
Ouseburn
Bridge

Kirby
Hall

**Kirby
Hall Park**

Hawthorn
Bank

Sugar Hills
Plantation

Aldwark
Wood

Pecket
Wood

Fall Gates
Woods

**Linton-on-
Ouse Airfield**

YO30

Ouse Gill Beck

Ouse Gill
Field

NEW LANE

BRUNSELL LA

BACK LA

**Little
Ouseburn**

PH

Kirby Hall
Farm

The
Lake

Long
Wood

Low
Farm

Round
O Wood

Hunters
Lodge

The
Flats

Linton-on-Ouse

PH

Sewage
Works

Garth
End Ings

Clough
Ings

Bank
Field

Elwick Carr
Plantation

Thorpe
Grange

The
Moorings

Butchers'
Ings

River Ouse

Shacklefield
House

Weddall
Ings

Beech Hill
Farm

Moor
Farm

Ash
Wood

Pasture
Hill

Faburn House
Farm

North
Park

**Thorpe
Underwood**

Tewit
Nest

Widdington
Manor

Widdington
Hall Farm

Widdington
Wood

Whixley
Moor

Whixley Grange
Farm

Thorpe
Wood

Thorpe Hill
Farm

Queen
Ethelburga's
Coll

Eight Arce Fox
Covert

North
Barrows

The
Carrs

SCORE RAY LA

Divel
Covert

Moss Hill
Farm

YO26

Carlton
Farm

Carlton
Wood

Whixley

FRANK'S LA

Tancred
Farm

Whixley Cut

Little
Wood

Field House
Farm

Low
Farm

**Great
Wood**

Pool Spring
Farm

STONE
GATE

CLOCKHILL
FIELD LA

NEW ROAD

PH

Hall
Close

WATER SLACK

STONED HORSE LANE

The
Ruddings

Beggar
Hall

VINE FARM CL 1
RUDGATE GR 2
AINSTY VW 3

Sunny Bank
Farm

MATTHEW
LA

Moor
Lands

Pool Bridge
Farm

Carr House
Farm

1 BACK LA
2 LONGLAND LA
3 GILSFORTH LA

Providence
Hill

Green Hammerton
CE Prim Sch

**Green
Hammerton**

A59

Scate
Moor

PH

LC

Cattal

MEADOW VALE 1
NEW LA 2
ST THOMAS'S WY 3
BERNARD LA 4
STONELEIGH GATE 5
BACK LA 6
BERNARD LA 7

Doodle
Hills

North
Field

Kirk Hammerton
CE Prim Sch

YORK ROAD

Hammerton

Skip
Bridge

Buckle
Ings

Gowlands
Farm

Skipbridge Inn
Farm

Finkle
Holme

LC

HAMMERTON CL

LC

A59

Westfield
Farm

West
End

LC

1 CHAPEL ST
2 CHURCH ST
3 OLD CHURCH GN
4 STANYFORTH CR
5 RATHMALL LA

CH

Wilstrop
Village

Lingfield
Cottage

**Kirk
Hammerton**

CATTAL STREET

PLANETREE LANE

River Nidd

Tockwith
Ness

Old
Thornville

Weir

Mill
Farm

Great
Ings

Long Close
Ings

Wilstrop Lodge
Farm

Thistleforth
Ings

Skewkirk
Hall

New
Farm

Wilstrop
Grange

Wilstrop
Wood

GREEN LANE

Cattal

OX MOOR LA

CHAPEL ST

163

181

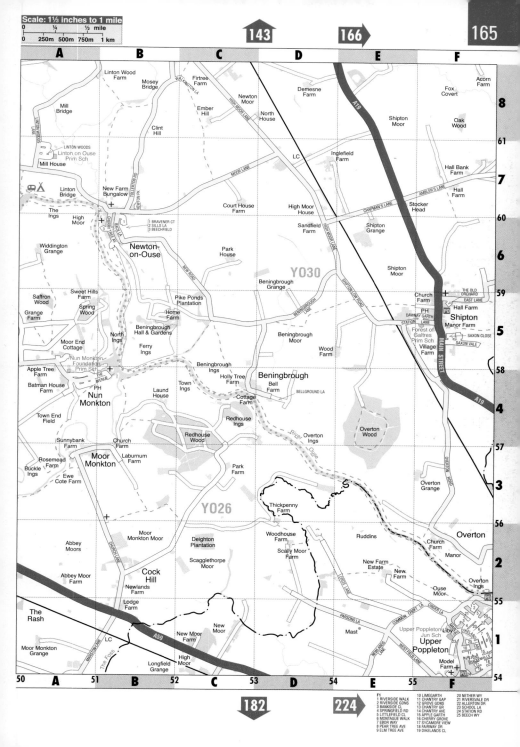

Scale: 1½ inches to 1 mile

0   ¼   ½ mile
0   250m   500m   750m   1 km

Linton Wood Farm
Mosey Bridge
Firtree Farm
Newton Moor
Demesne Farm
Fox Covert
Acorn Farm

Mill Bridge
Ember Hill
North House
Shipton Moor
Oak Wood

Clint Hill
Linton Woods
Linton on Ouse Prim Sch
LC
Ingfield Farm
Hall Bank Farm

Mill House
Widdington Grange
New Farm Bungalow
Court House Farm
High Moor House
Ambler's Lane
Chapman's Lane
Stocker Head
Hall Farm

The Ings
High Moor
1 BRAVENER CT
2 SILLS LA
3 BEECHFIELD
Newton-on-Ouse
Park House
Sandfield Farm
Shipton Grange
Church Farm
The Old Orchard
East Lane
PH
PO
Shipton

Saffron Wood
Sweet Hills Farm
Spring Wood
Pike Ponds Plantation
Beningbrough Grange
Shipton Moor
Dawnay Garth
Station Lane
Manor Farm
Forest of Galtres Prim Sch
Village Farm
Saxon Close
Saxon Vale

Grange Farm
Home Farm
Beningbrough Hall & Gardens
Ferry Ings
Beningbrough Moor
Wood Farm

Moor End Cottage
North Ings
Nun Monkton Foundation Prim Sch
Beningbrough Ings
Holly Tree Farm
Beningbrough
Bell Farm
Bellground La

Apple Tree Farm
The Avenue
PH
Town Ings
Cottage Farm

Batman House Farm
Nun Monkton
Laund House
Redhouse Ings
Overton Wood

Town End Field
Redhouse Wood
Overton Ings
River Ouse

Sunnybank Farm
Church Farm
Laburnum Farm
Park Farm
Overton Grange

Rosemead Farm
Moor Monkton
Overton Road
Church Farm
Overton
Manor

Buckle Ings
Ewe Cote Farm
Abbey Moors
Moor Monkton Moor
Thickpenny Farm
Woodhouse Farm
Ruddins
New Farm Estate

Abbey Moor Farm
Deighton Plantation
Scagglethorpe Moor
Scally Moor Farm
New Farm
New Farm

The Rash
Cock Hill
Newlands Farm
Lodge Farm
Long's Lane
Parsons La
Mast
Common
Croft La
Cinder La
Library
Overton Ings
Ouse Moor

Moor Monkton Grange
LC
New Moor Farm
New Moor
Upper Poppleton Jun Sch
Upper Poppleton
Model Farm

Longfield Grange
High Moor
Newlands Lane
West End Lane
PO

YO30
YO26

F1
1 RIVERSIDE WALK
2 RIVERSIDE GDNS
3 BANKSIDE CL
4 SPRINGFIELD RD
5 LITTLEFIELD CL
6 MONTAGUE WALK
7 EBOR WAY
8 PEAR TREE AVE
9 ELM TREE AVE
10 LIMEGARTH
11 CHANTRY GAP
12 GROVE GDNS
13 CHANTRY GR
14 CHANTRY AVE
15 APPLE GARTH
16 CHERRY GROVE
17 SYCAMORE VIEW
18 FAIRWAY DR
19 DIKELANDS CL
20 NETHER WY
21 RIVERVALE DR
22 ALLERTON DR
23 SCHOOL LA
24 STATION RD
25 BEECH WY

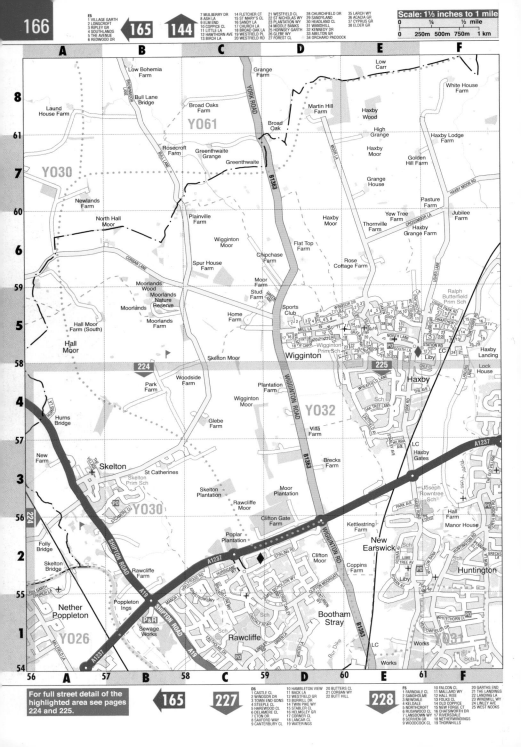

E5
1 VILLAGE GARTH
2 LONGCROFT
3 RIPLEY GR
4 SOUTHLANDS
5 THE AVENUE
6 REDWOOD DR

7 MULBERRY DR
8 ASH LA
9 ELM END
10 COPPICE CL
11 LITTLE LA
12 HAWTHORN AVE
13 BIRCH LA

14 FLETCHER CT
15 ST MARY'S CL
16 SANDY LA
17 CHURCH LA
18 BROAD OAK LA
19 WESTFIELD PL
20 WESTFIELD RD

21 WESTFIELD CL
22 ST NICHOLAS WY
23 PLANTATION WY
24 MIDDLE BANKS
25 HORNSEY GARTH
26 GLEBE WY
27 FOREST CL

28 CHURCHFIELD DR
29 SANDYLAND
30 HEADLAND CL
31 WANDHILL
32 KENNEDY DR
33 ABELTON GR
34 ORCHARD PADDOCK

35 LARCH WY
36 ACACIA GR
37 CYPRUS GR
38 ELDER GR

Scale: 1½ inches to 1 mile

0   ¼   ½ mile
0 250m 500m 750m 1 km

Map labels

YO61
YO30
Low Bohemia Farm
Laund House Farm
Bull Lane Bridge
Broad Oaks Farm
Grange Farm
Low Carr
White House Farm
Martin Hill Farm
Haxby Wood
High Grange
Haxby Lodge Farm
Rosecroft Farm
Greenthwaite Grange
Greenthwaite
Broad Oak
Haxby Moor
Golden Hill Farm
Newlands Farm
Plainville Farm
Haxby Moor
Thornville Farm
Haxby Grange Farm
Pasture Farm
Jubilee Farm
North Hall Moor
Wigginton Moor
Flat Top Farm
Yew Tree Farm
Grange House
Corban Lane
Spur House Farm
Chipchase Farm
Rose Cottage Farm
Moorlands Wood
Moorlands Nature Reserve
Moorlands
Moorlands Farm
Moor Farm
Stud Farm
Sports Club
Ralph Butterfield Prim Sch
Hall Moor Farm (South)
Home Farm
Wigginton Prim Sch
Hall Moor
Skelton Moor
Wigginton
Haxby
Haxby Landing
Lock House
Woodside Farm
Park Farm
Plantation Farm
Whitefield Lane
Skelton Moor
YO32
224
225
Hurns Bridge
Wigginton Moor
Glebe Farm
Villa Farm
Brecks Farm
Haxby Gates
New Farm
Skelton
St Catherines
Skelton Prim Sch
Skelton Plantation
Rawcliffe Moor
Moor Plantation
Joseph Rowntree Sch
Hall Farm
Manor House
YO30
224
Folly Bridge
Skelton Bridge
Rawcliffe Farm
Clifton Gate Farm
Kettlestring Farm
New Earswick
Huntington
Poppleton Ings
Poplar Plantation
Clifton Moor
Coppins Farm
Bootham Stray
Nether Poppleton
P&R
Sewage Works
YO26
Rawcliffe
Butt Hill
YO31
Works
Works

For full street detail of the highlighted area see pages 224 and 225.

165   227   228

D5
1 CASTLE CL
2 WINDSOR DR
3 TOWN END GDNS
4 STEEPLE CL
5 HAREWOOD CL
6 DELAMERE CL
7 ETON DR
8 SAXFORD WY
9 CANTERBURY CL

10 HAMBLETON VIEW
11 BACK LA
12 WESTFIELD GR
13 BURRILL DR
14 TWIN PIKE WY
15 STABLER CL
16 HELMSLEY GR
17 CORNER CL
18 LANCAR CL
19 WATERINGS

20 BLITTERS CL
21 CORBAN WY
22 BUTT HILL

F5
1 FARNDALE CL
2 SANDHOLME
3 NEWDALE
4 KELDALE
5 NORTHCROFT
6 RUSHWOOD CL
7 LANSDOWN WY
8 SCRIVEN GR
9 WOODCOCK CL

10 FALCON CL
11 MALLARD WY
12 HALL RISE
13 FOLKS CL
14 OLD COPPICE
15 NEW FORGE CT
16 CHATSWORTH DR
17 RIVERSDALE
18 NETHERWINDINGS
19 THORNHILLS

20 GARTHS END
21 THE LANDINGS
22 LANDING LA
23 WINDMILL WY
24 LINLEY AVE
25 WEST NOOKS

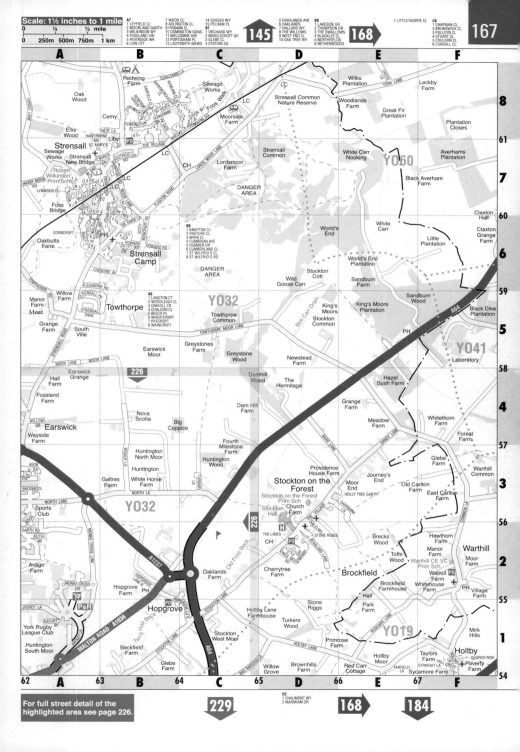

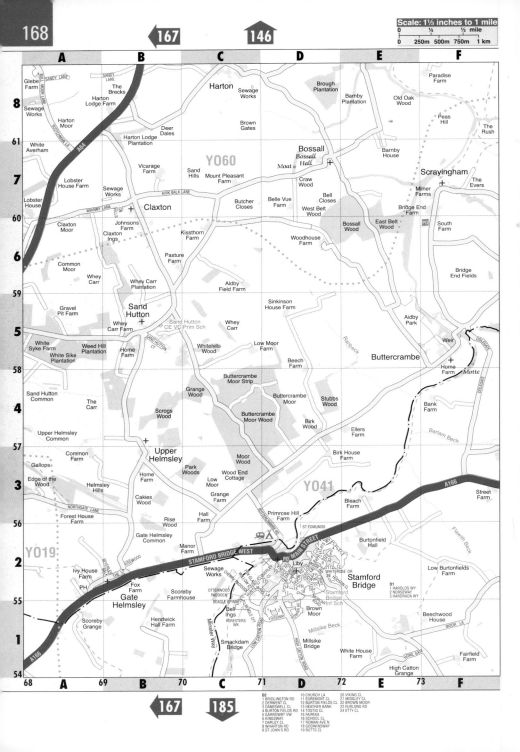

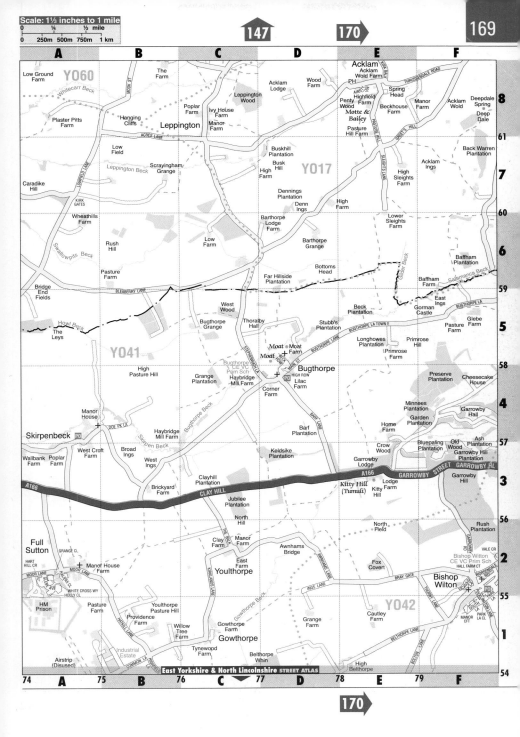

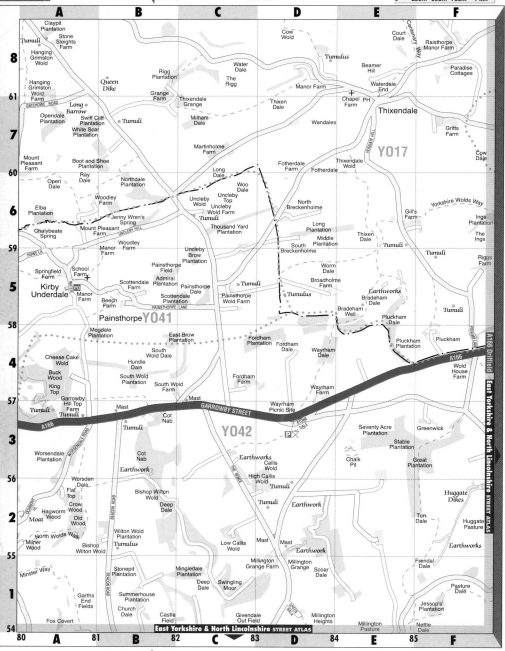

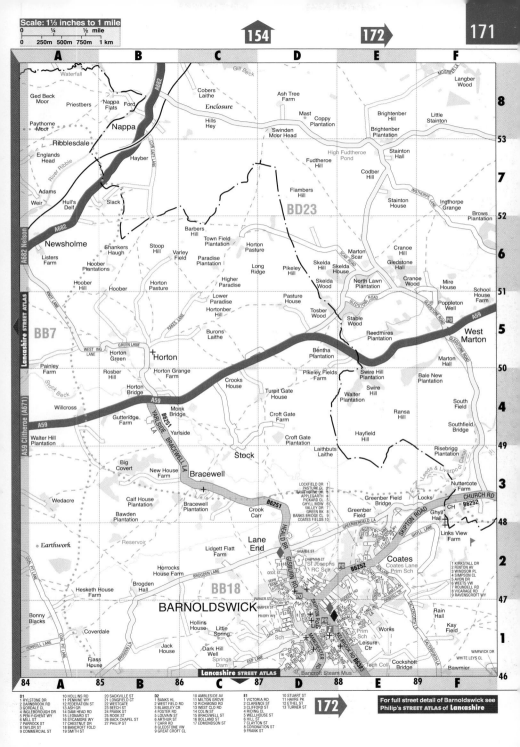

Scale: 1½ inches to 1 mile

| 0 | ¼ | ½ mile |
| 0 | 250m 500m 750m | 1 km |

A B C D E F

8

Viaduct
Weir Weir PH
MARTON ROAD
WALTON CL
CHURCH CFT
Gargrave
River Aire
Woomber Wood
Aqueduct
Moat
Gargrave
Weir
CHURCH LA
Highgate Bridge (swing)
Sulber Laithe
Priest Holme Bridge
Mosber La Bridge
Lobby Bridge
Kelber Hill Farm
Kirk Sink Farm
Sewage Works
A65

53

Newton Hall
Locks
Parkers Farm
Scaleber
Butter Haw Farm
Broughton Quarry
Robin Wood
Bank Newton
Lock
Copy Hill Plantation
Thorlby Bridge (swing)

7

Newton Bridge
Newton Grange Farm
Moorber Hill
CHURCH STREET
Smellows Quarry
Copy Hill
Pennine Way
River Aire
Small House

52

Pasture House
Oxen Close
Greenbank Farm
Turnbers Hill Plantation
Acliffe Hill Plantation
Oxenclose Farm
Hall Close Wood
Broughton Copy Farm

6

Brows Plantation
Green Bank
Langber Plantation
Trenet Laithe
Corringer Hill
Clints Delf (dis)
Skinnerground Wood
BD23
Skinner Ground Farm
Deer Haw Plantation
OLD LA
GARGRAVE ROAD
Broughton
A59
Heslaker Bridge

51

Tempest Farm
Williamson Bridge
HEBER DR
A59
Church Farm Barn
PH
East Marton
Micklethorne Farm
Mill Farm
Broughton Hall
Weir
The Grove Hall
Dancliff Plantation
CHURCH LA
PH
Home Farm
Denbers Plantation
Primrose Hill
OLD LA

5

Sewage Works
Crickle Farm
EDMONDSON LANE
A456
A59
Low Ground Farm
Pasture House Farm
Langber
Gubbs Hill Farm
PH Elslack Bridge
ELLER GILL LANE
CHURCH LANE
Croft Wood
Yellison House
Yellison Wood
Lower Scarcliffe Farm
Higher Scarcliff
Scarcliffe Farm
Lane Head Quarry

50

4

Far Fence End Farm
Johnsons Gate Farm
BURWEN CASTLE RD
White House Farm
Mitton House
Pennine Way
Fence End
Merlinwood
Elslack Hall
BURWEN CASTLE FARM (ROMAN FORT)
Smearber Farm
Old Cote Farm
A56
Thompson House Farm
Redfirth Gill Cote
Baxter House
Baxter House Farm
Gawthorpe House

49

Thornton-in-Craven Com Prim Sch
Rectory Farm
CHURCH RD
Earby Beck
OLD ROAD
Brown House Bridge
Brown House
Wood House
Park House Farm
MOOR LANE
Stories House Farm
Mill Fold
Standrise Plantation
Elslack Resr
Frozen Well

48

B6252
Hotel
1 THE FOLD
2 QUEENS GARTH
Pennine Way
Ransable Well
Clarke Moss Hill
Carleton Moor

3

PENDLE RD
Booth Bridge Farm
Little Moor
Oak Slack Farm
Elslack Moor
Broughton Hill

2

Grange Farm
PH
Pendle Way
Mine Mus
SCHOOL FIELDS
Sewage Works
Batty House
Cowgarth Farm
YH
Marl Field Farm
Thornton Moor
P
Pinhaw Moor
Pinhaw
Pennine Way
Kirk Sykes Farm

47

HILL TOP LA
PO
Mill Bridge
DARK LA
Wendcliff Brook
DODGSON RD
B81
Out Laithe Farm
Hill Top Farm
Calf Edge Farm
Sunny Side
Hewitts Farm
Knott Farm
WHITE HILL LA
Pennine Way

1

COLNE RD
A56
Raike Bank Farm
Springfield Prim Sch
Highbank Farm
Windle Field Farm
Lower Verjuice Farm
Dodgsons Farm
Harrow Ings Farm
MITTON LA
WINTER GAP LANE
CALF WOOD LANE
The Fold

46

EARBY
Bleara Moor
Mitton Moor

90 A 91 B 92 C 93 D 94 E 95 F

← **171**   **186** →

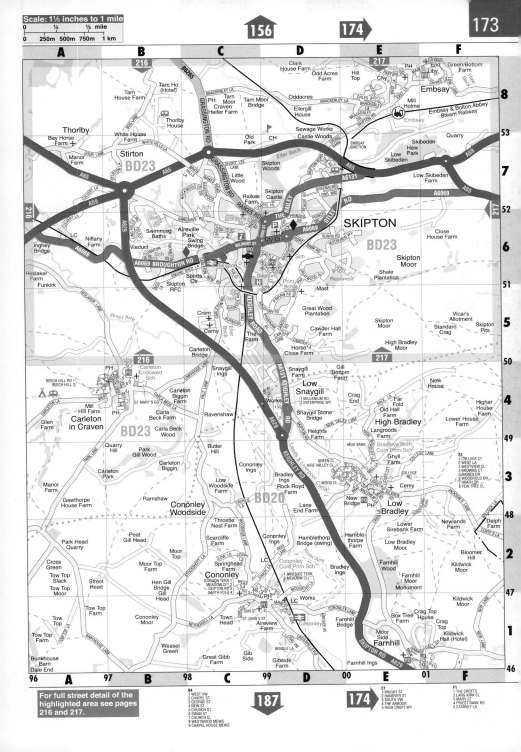

A   B   C   D   E   F

8
Clark
House Farm
Odd Acres
Farm
Hill
Top
Cross
End
Green Bottom
Farm
217   Sch
PH
Lby
Embsay
Tarn Ho
(Hotel)
Tarn
House Farm
PH
Tarn
Moor
Craven
Heifer Farm
Tarn Moor
Bridge
Oddacres
BRACKENLEY LA
Ellergill
House
Mill
Holme
Embsay & Bolton Abbey
Steam Railway
Thorlby
Bay Horse
Farm
White House
Farm
Thorlby
House
Old
Park
CH
Sewage Works
Castle Woods
Embsay
JUNCTION
Low
Skibeden
Skibeden
Haw
Park
Quarry   53
Manor
Farm
Stirton
BD23
Eller Beck
Skipton
Woods
Low Skibeden
Farm   7
Short Lee
Lane
Little
Wood
A6131
Low Skibeden
A59
52
216
Niffany
Farm
Raikes
Farm
Skipton
Castle
Chapel Hill
THE BAILEY
PRINCE'S
OTLEY RD
SKIPTON
A6069
Close
House Farm   6
Inghey
Bridge
LC
Swimming
Baths
Aireville
Park
Swing
Bridge
Viaduct
A6069   BROUGHTON RD
Sch
Skipton
City Ctr
BD23
Skipton
Moor
Heslaker
Farm
Funkirk
Sports
Ctr
Skipton
RFC
Shale
Plantation
Reservoir   51
River Aire
Crem
Cemy
Carleton
Bridge
Great Wood
Plantation
Mast
Cawder Hall
Farm
Skipton
Moor
Vicar's
Allotment
Standard
Crag
Skipton
Pits   5
Carleton
Endowed
Sch
216
PH
PO
Snaygill
Ings
Snaygill
Farm
Horse
Close Farm
High Bradley
Moor
217
50
BEECH HILL RD 1
BEECH HILL 2
Mill
Hill Farm
PH
Carleton
Biggin
Farm
Carla
Beck Farm
Ravenshaw
Low
Snaygill
Works
1 MILLENNIUM RD
2 ENTERPRISE WY
Snaygill Stone
Bridge
Crag
End
New
House
Back La
Far
Fold
Old Hall
Farm
Lower House
Farm
Higher
House
Farm   4
Glen
Farm
Carleton
in Craven
BD23
Carla Beck
Wood
Butler
Hill
Heights
Farm
HIGH BANK
Langroods
Farm
Bradleys Both
Com Prim Sch
Ghyll
Farm
COLLEGE LANE   49
Quarry
Hill
Park
Gill Wood
Cononley
Ings
GREEN CL
Aire Valley CL
Cemy
E3
1 COLLEGE CT
2 WEST LA
3 WESTVIEW CL
4 BROWNS CT
5 RAINES DR
6 WOODFIELD DR
7 HEATH DR
8 YEW TREE CL   3
Manor
Farm
Carleton
Park
Cononley
Woodside
BD20
Bradley
Ings
Rock Royd
Farm
Lane
End Farm
New
Bridge
PH
Low
Bradley
Gawthorpe
House Farm
Ramshaw
Throstle
Nest Farm
Scarcliffe
Farm
Cononley
Ings
Hamblethorp
Bridge (swing)
Hamble-
thorpe
Farm
Lower
Sirebank Farm
Low Bradley
Moor
Newlands
Farm
Delph
Farm   48
Park Head
Quarry
Peat
Gill Head
Moor
Top
Springhead
Farm
River Aire
Bradley
Ings
Farnhill
Wood
Bloomer
Hill
Kildwick
Moor   2
Cross
Green
Tow Top
Slack
Tow Top
Moor
Moor Top
Farm
Hen Gill
Bridge
Gill
Head
Cononley
Cononley
Com Prim Sch
1 AIRESIDE TERR
2 MEADOW CL
LC
Works
Farnhill
Moor
Monument
Kildwick
Moor   47
Street
Head
Tow Top
Farm
Cononley
Moor
Town
Head
Aireview
Farm
St John's St
Cononley
Bridge
Farnhill
Bridge
Box Tree
Farm
Moor
Side
Farm
Crag Top
House
Crag
Top
Kildwick
Hall (Hotel)   1
Tow
Top
Tow Top
Farm
Weasel
Green
Great Gibb
Farm
Gib
Side
Gibside
Farm
Farnhill
SKIPTON RD
A629
Farnhill Ings   46
Bunkhouse
Barn
Dale End

96   A   97   B   98   C   99   D   00   E   01   F

For full street detail of the
highlighted area see pages
216 and 217.

187   174

B4
1 WEST VW
2 CHAPEL ST
3 GEORGE ST
4 NEW ST
5 CHURCH ST
6 SWAN ST
7 CHURCH CL
8 WESTWOOD MEWS
9 CHAPEL HOUSE MEWS

E1
1 BRIGHT ST
2 HANOVER ST
3 SOUTH VW
4 THE ARBOUR
5 HIGH CROFT WY

F1
1 THE CROFTS
2 LANG KIRK CL
3 MARY ST
4 PRIEST BANK RD
5 STARKEY LA

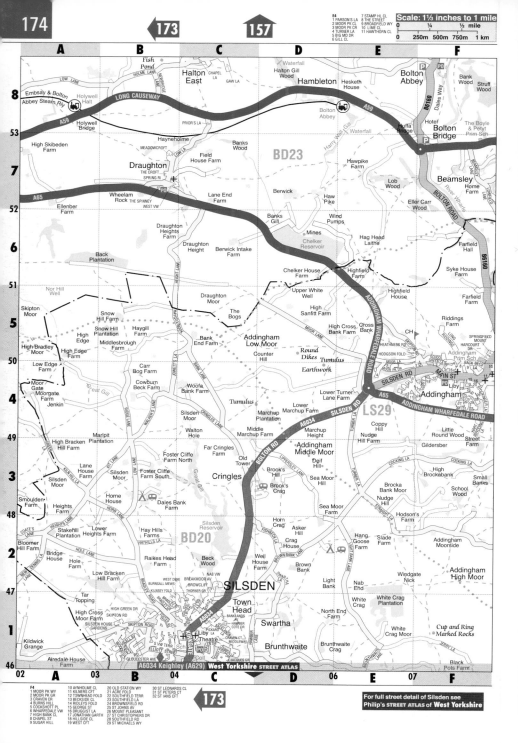

173
157

E4
1 PARSON'S LA
2 MOOR PK CL
3 MOOR PK GR
4 TURNER LA
5 BIG MD DR
6 GILL CL
7 STAMP HL CL
8 THE STREET
9 BROADFIELD WY
10 LIME CL
11 HAWTHORN CL

Scale: 1⅓ inches to 1 mile

0   ¼   ½ mile

0   250m 500m 750m   1 km

A B C D E F

Fish Pond
Halton East
Chapel LA
GAW LA
Waterfall
Halton Gill Wood
Hambleton
Hesketh House
Bolton Abbey
Bank Wood
Struff Wood

Low Lane
HOLME LANE
MEREBROOK LANE
LONG CAUSEWAY
A59
Dales Way
B6160

8
Embsay & Bolton Abbey Steam Rly
Holywell Halt
PRIOR'S LA
A59
Bolton Abbey
Hotel
Bolton Bridge
The Boyle & Petyt Prim Sch

53
Holywell Bridge
Hayneholme
MEADOWCROFT
Banks Wood
Waterfall
Huffa Bridge
Harry Wall Gill

High Skibeden Farm
Draughton
THE CROFT
SPRING RI
Field House Farm
BD23
Hawpike Farm
Beamsley
Home Farm

7
A65
Wheelam Rock
THE SPINNEY
WEST VW
Lane End Farm
Berwick
Haw Pike
Lob Wood
BOLTON ROAD
River Wharfe

52
Ellenber Farm
Banks Gill
Wind Pumps
Hag Head Laithe
Eller Carr Wood
Farfield Hall

Draughton Heights Farm
Draughton Height
Berwick Intake Farm
Mines
Chelker Reservoir
Highfield Farm
Syke House Farm

6
Back Plantation
Chelker House Farm
Upper White Well
Highfield House
Farfield Farm

51
Nor Hill Well
HIGH LANE
Draughton Moor
The Bogs
High Sanfitt Farm
High Cross Bank Farm
Cross Bank
CH
Riddings Farm
SPRINGFIELD MOUNT
HARCOURT
Addingham Prim Sch

5
Skipton Moor
Snow Hill Farm
Snow Hill Plantation
Haygill Farm
Bank End Farm
Addingham Low Moor
Counter Hill
MOOR LANE
ADDINGHAM WHARFEDALE ROAD
HODGSON FOLD
HEATHSIDE RD
SILSDEN RD
MAIN ST
Liby

High Edge
Middlesbrough Farm
Round Dikes
Tumulus
Earthwork
SKIPTON RD

High Bradley Moor
High Edge Farm
Carr Bog Farm
Woofa Bank Farm
Tumulus
LS29
Addingham

4
Low Edge Farm
Moor Gate
Moorgate Farm
Jenkin
Great Gill
WALKER'S LA
RIDGE LANE
JOWETT'S LA
BANK LANE
Silsden Moor
GRINGLES LANE
Lower Turner Lane Farm
SILSDEN RD
A65
ADDINGHAM WHARFEDALE ROAD

49
Marlpit Plantation
High Bracken Hill Farm
Walton Hole
Lower Marchup Farm
Marchup Plantation
Marchup Height
A6034
Coppy Hill
Nudge Hill Farm
Little Round Wood
Gildersber
Street Farm

3
Lane House Farm
KILN LANE
KIT LANE
Silsden Moor
Foster Cliffe Farm North
Far Cringles Farm
Old Tower
BOLTON RD
Addingham Middle Moor
Deif Hill
COCKING LA
High Brockabank
Small Banks

Silsden Moor
Foster Cliffe Farm South
Great Gill
Cringles
Brook's Hill
Brook's Crag
Sea Moor Hill
TURNER LA
Brocka Bank Moor
Nudge Hill
School Wood

48
Smoulden Farm
Heights Farm
Horne House
Dales Bank Farm
HORN LANE
Sea Moor Farm
LIPPERSLEY LANE
Hodson's Farm

2
Bloomer Hill Farm
COATE'S LANE
HEIGHTS LANE
Stakehill Plantation
Lower Heights Farm
Hay Hills Farms
HAYHILLS LA
Silsden Reservoir
BD20
Horn Crag
Asker Hill
Crag House
FISHER LANE
Hang Goose Farm
Slade Farm
Addingham Moorside

Bridge Farm
Hole Farm
HOLE LANE
Raikes Head Farm
Beck Wood
Well House Farm
Brown Bank
CRAG LANE
LIGHT BANK LANE
Windgate Nick
Addingham High Moor

47
NEW DENNIS LA
Tar Topping
Low Bracken Hill Farm
WEST DENE
BURNSALL MEWS
NAB VW
BREAKMOOR FM
BROWCLIFF
THORNER GR
Light Bank
Nab End
White Crag Plantation

1
Kildwick Grange
High Cross Moor Farm
SKIPTON RD
HIGH GREEN DR
SILSDEN HOUSE GARDENS
SKIPTON ROAD
A6034
SILSDEN
Town Head
BANKLANDS
HAWBER COTE DR
PICKARD LA
CRAVEN CT
MIDDLEWAY
Swartha
Brunthwaite
White Crag
North End Farm
White Crag Moor
Cup and Ring Marked Rocks

Bloomer Hill Farm
Airedale House Farm
Library
Theatre
Coll
ELLIOTT STREET
GLOUCESTER ST
JACQUES GR
Brunthwaite Crag
Black Pots Farm

46
A6034 Keighley (A629) **West Yorkshire** Street Atlas

173

For full street detail of Silsden see
Philip's **STREET ATLAS** of **West Yorkshire**

02 03 04 C D 06 E 07 F

F4
1 MOOR PK WY
2 MOOR PK GR
3 CRAVEN CR
4 BURNS HILL
5 COCKSHOTT PL
6 WHARFEDALE VW
7 HIGH BANK CL
8 CHAPEL ST
9 SUGAR HILL
10 AYNHOLME CL
11 KILNERS CFT
12 TOWNHEAD FOLD
13 BECKSIDE CL
14 RIDLEYS FOLD
15 GEORGE ST
16 DRUGGIST LA
17 JONATHAN GARTH
18 HILLSIDE CL
19 WEST CFT
20 OLD STATION WY
21 ACRE FOLD
22 SOUTHFIELD TERR
23 SOUTHFIELD LA
24 BROWNSFIELD RD
25 ST JOHNS AV
26 MOUNT PLEASANT
27 ST CHRISTOPHERS DR
28 SOUTHFIELD RD
29 ST MICHAELS WY
30 ST LEONARDS CL
31 ST PETERS CT
32 ST IANS CT

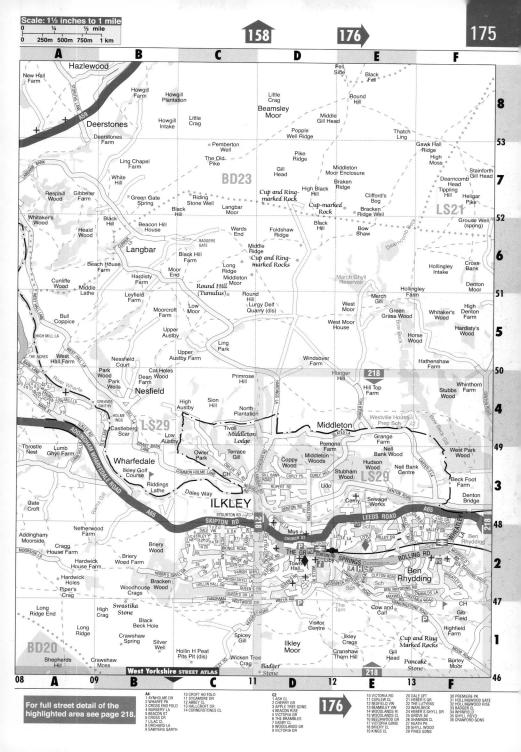

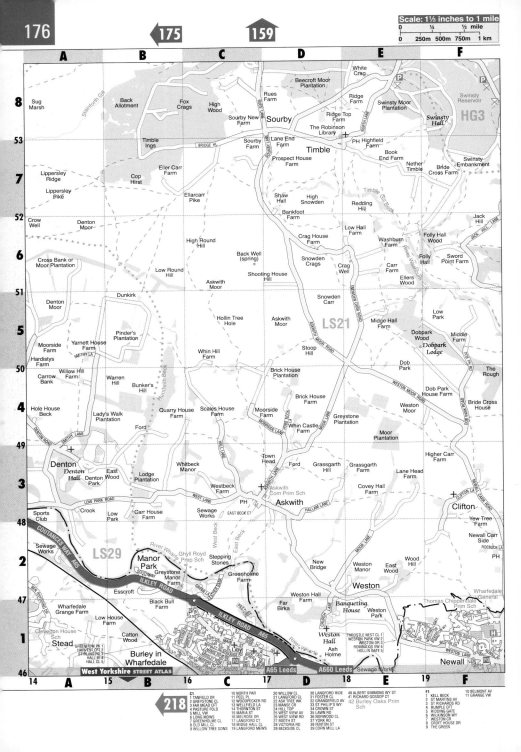

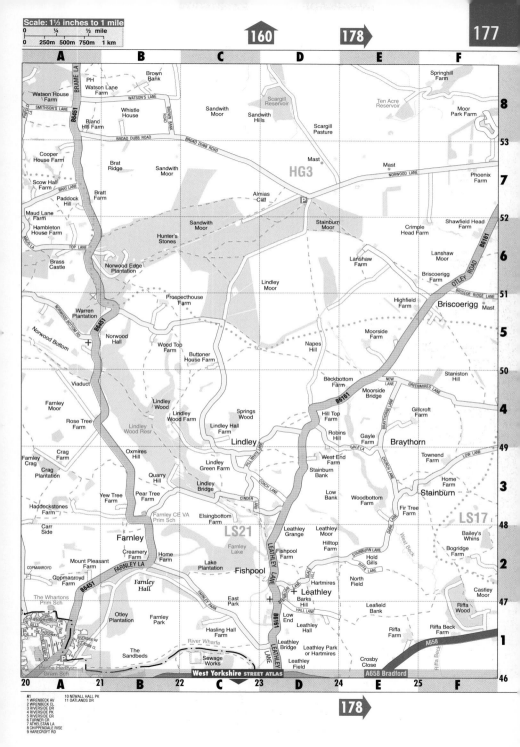

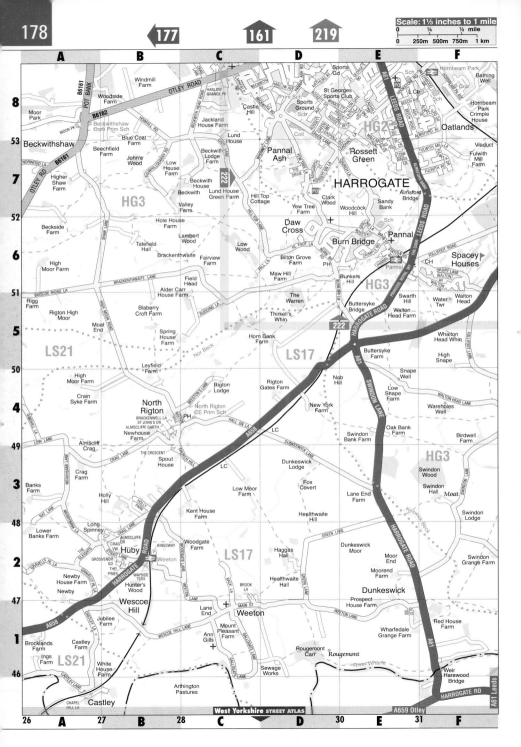

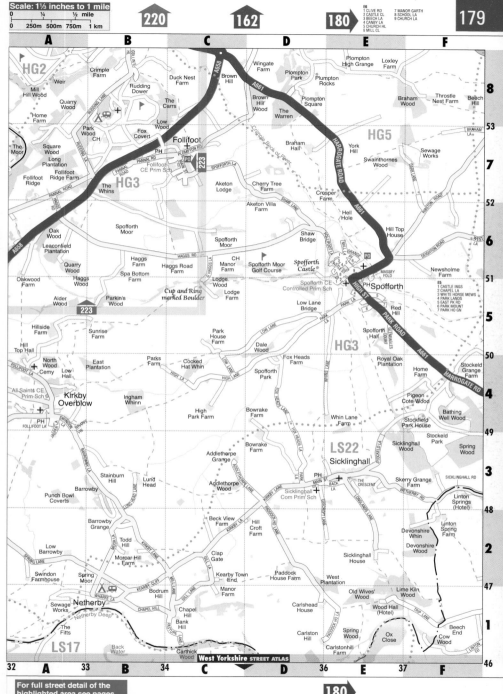

Scale: 1⅓ inches to 1 mile

| 0 | ¼ | ½ mile |
| 0 | 250m | 500m | 750m | 1 km |

220

162

180

E6
1 CLIVE RD
2 CASTLE CL
3 BEECH LA
4 CANBY LA
5 CHURCH HL
6 MILL CL

7 MANOR GARTH
8 SCHOOL LA
9 CHURCH LA

179

HG2

Crimple
Farm

Weir

Mill
Hill Wood

Quarry
Wood

Home
Farm

The
Moor

Square
Wood

Park
Wood

Long
Plantation

Follifoot
Ridge Farm

Follifoot
Ridge

Rudding
Dower

Duck Nest
Farm

The
Carrs

Low
Wood

Fox
Covert

Follifoot

PH

Follifoot
CE Prim Sch

223

HG3

The Whins

Oak
Wood

Leaconfield
Plantation

Quarry
Wood

Oakwood
Farm

Haggs
Wood

Alder
Wood

Parkin's
Wood

223

Hillside
Farm

Hill
Top Hall

North
Wood
Cemy

Low
Hall

All Saints CE
Prim Sch

Kirkby
Overblow

PH
FOLLIFOOT LA

Sunrise
Farm

East
Plantation

Ingham
Whinn

Parks
Farm

Cocked
Hat Whin

Spofforth
Park

High
Park Farm

Stainburn
Hill

Barrowby

Punch Bowl
Coverts

Barrowby
Grange

Low
Barrowby

Swindon
Farmhouse

Todd
Hill

Morcar Hill
Farm

Spring
Moor

Netherby

The
Fitts

LS17

Back
Water

Carthick
Wood

Brown
Hill

Wingate
Farm

Plompton
Park

Brown
Hill Wood

The
Warren

Plompton
Rocks

Plompton
Square

Braham
Hall

Cripple Beck or Fleet

Aketon
Lodge

Cherry Tree
Farm

Aketon Villa
Farm

Shaw
Bridge

Spofforth
Moor

Spofforth
Moor

CH

Manor
Farm

Haggs Road
Farm

Spa Bottom
Farm

HAGGS RD

Haggs
Farm

Lodge
Wood

Lodge
Farm

Cup and Ring
marked Boulder

Spofforth Moor
Golf Course

Spofforth
Castle

Low Lane
Bridge

Park House
Farm

Dale
Wood

Fox Heads
Farm

HG3

Bowrake
Farm

Whin Lane
Farm

Bowrake
Farm

Addlethorpe
Grange

Addlethorpe
Wood

Beck View
Farm

Hill
Croft
Farm

Clap
Gate

Kearby Town
End

Manor
Farm

Lund
Head

Barrowby
Hill

Bodrum
Hill

Chapel
Hill

Bank
Hill

Sicklinghall
Com Prim Sch

PH

Paddock
House Farm

West
Plantation

Sicklinghall
House

LS22

Sicklinghall

PH

The
Crescent

Skerry Grange
Farm

SICKLINGHALL RD

Sicklinghall
Wood

Stockeld
Park

Spring
Wood

Carlshead
House

Old Wives'
Wood

Carlston
Hill

Spring
Wood

Carlstonhill
Farm

Wood Hall
(Hotel)

Ox
Close

HG5

York
Hill

Braham
Hill

Swainthorpes
Wood

Crosper
Farm

Hell
Hole

Sewage
Works

Newsholme
Farm

Hill Top
House

Spofforth
Hall

Royal Oak
Plantation

Home
Farm

Pigeon
Cote Wood

Stockfield
Park House

Stockeld
Grange
Farm

Bathing
Well Wood

Spofforth CE
Controlled Prim Sch

Spofforth

PH

Red
Hill

Braham
Wood

Throstle
Nest Farm

Beech
Hill

Sewage
Works

Linton
Springs
(Hotel)

Devonshire
Whin

Linton
Spring
Farm

Devonshire
Wood

Lime Kiln
Wood

Beech
End

Cow
Wood

E5
1 CASTLE INGS
2 CHAPEL LA
3 WHITE HORSE MEWS
4 PARK LANDS
5 EAST PK RD
6 PARK MOUNT
7 PARK HO GN

For full street detail of the
highlighted area see pages
222 and 223.

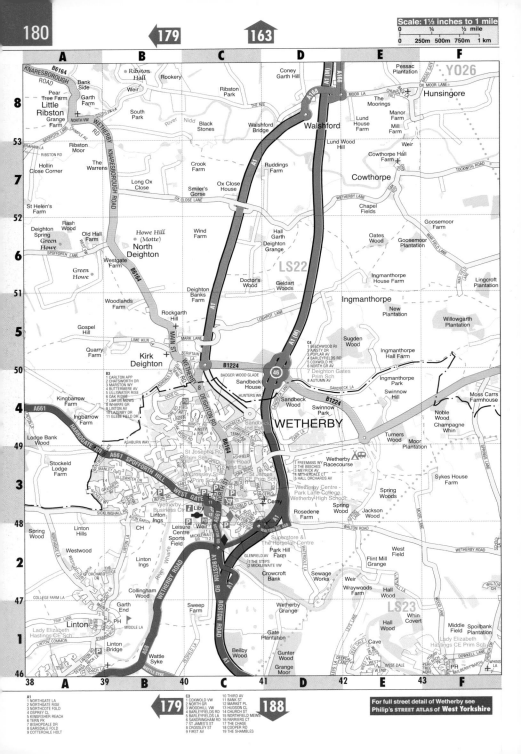

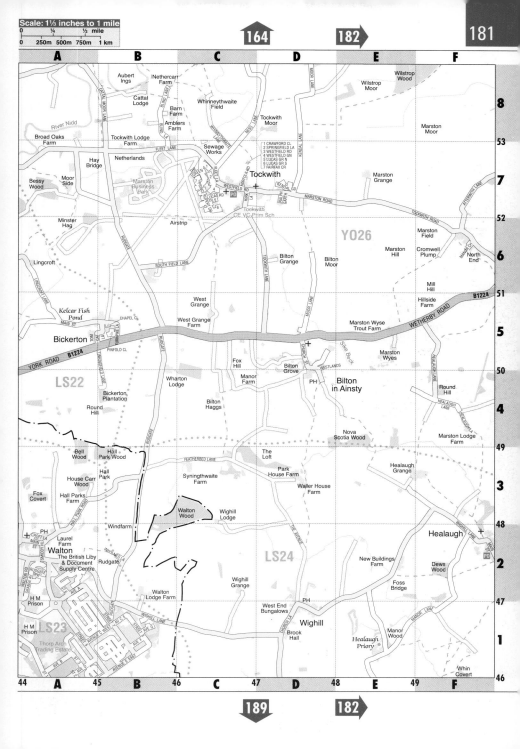

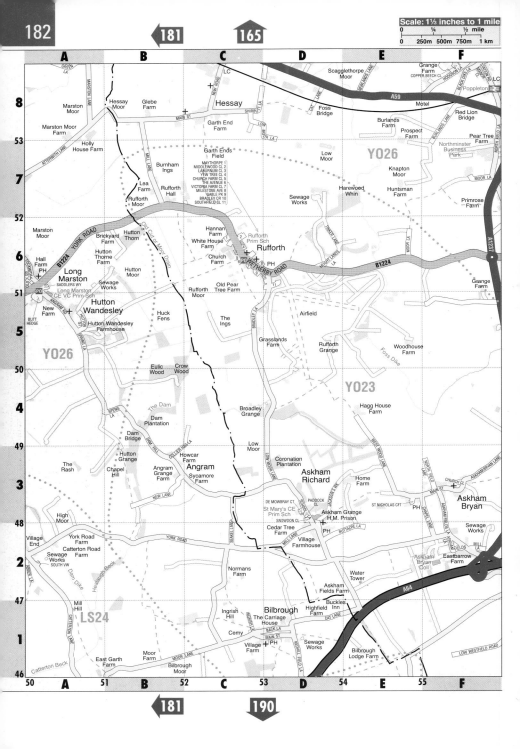

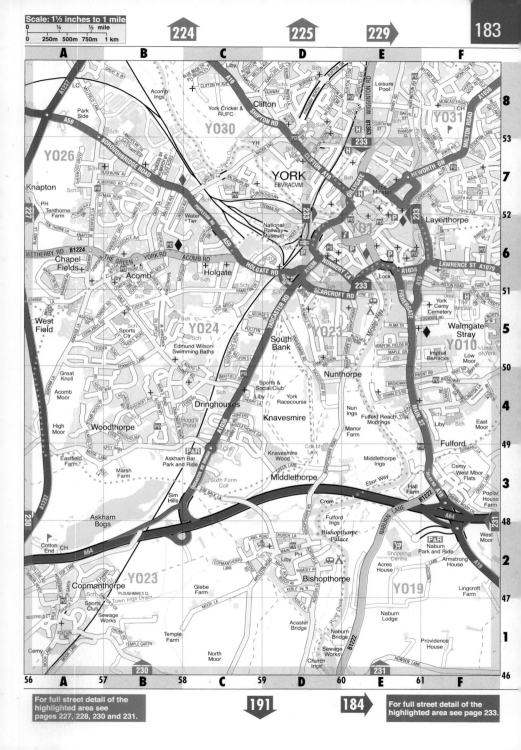

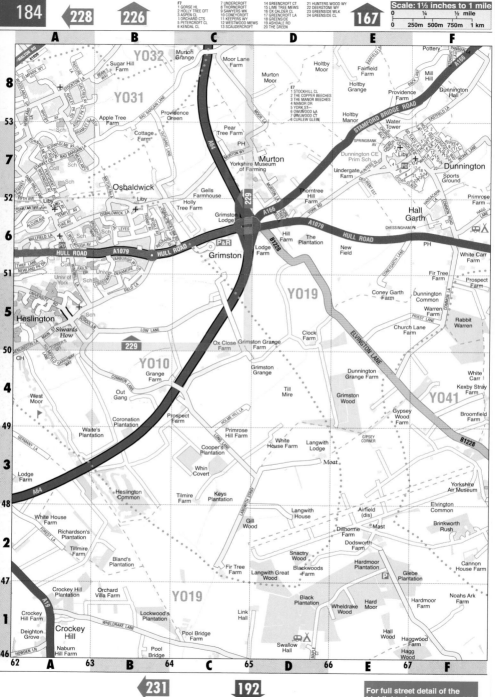

228
226
167

Scale: 1½ inches to 1 mile

F7	7 UNDERCROFT	14 GREENCROFT CT	21 HUNTERS WOOD WY
1 GORSE HL	8 THORNCROFT	15 LIME TREE MEWS	22 DEERSTONE WY
2 HOLLY TREE CFT	9 SAWYERS WK	16 OX CALDER CL	23 GREENSIDE WLK
3 ASPEN CL	10 CONEYCROFT	17 GREENCROFT LA	24 GREENSIDE CL
4 ORCHARD CTS	11 KEEPERS WY	18 GREENSIDE	
5 PETERCROFT CL	12 WESTWOOD MEWS	19 ASHDALE RD	
6 KENDAL CL	13 SCAUDERCROFT	20 THE GREEN	

For full street detail of the highlighted area see page 229.

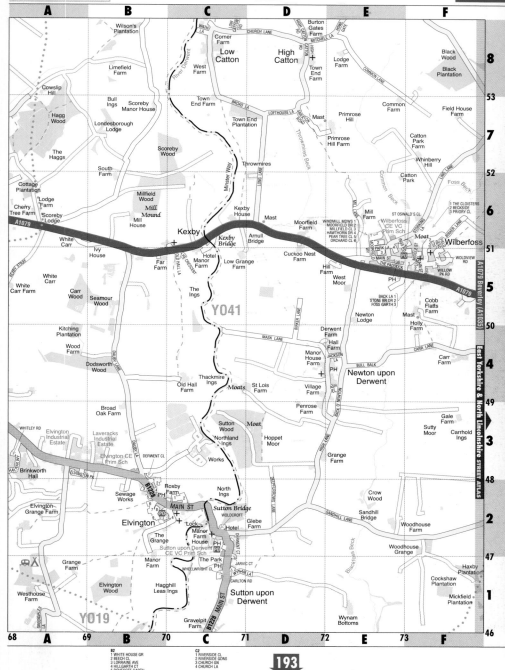

East Yorkshire & North Lincolnshire STREET ATLAS

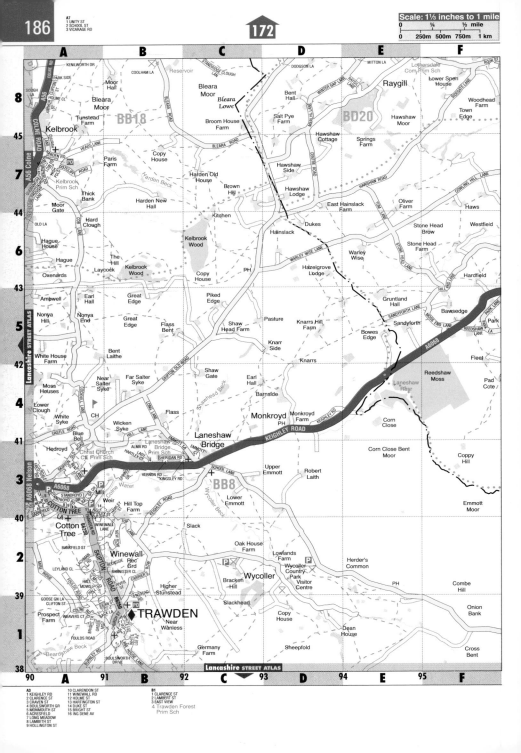

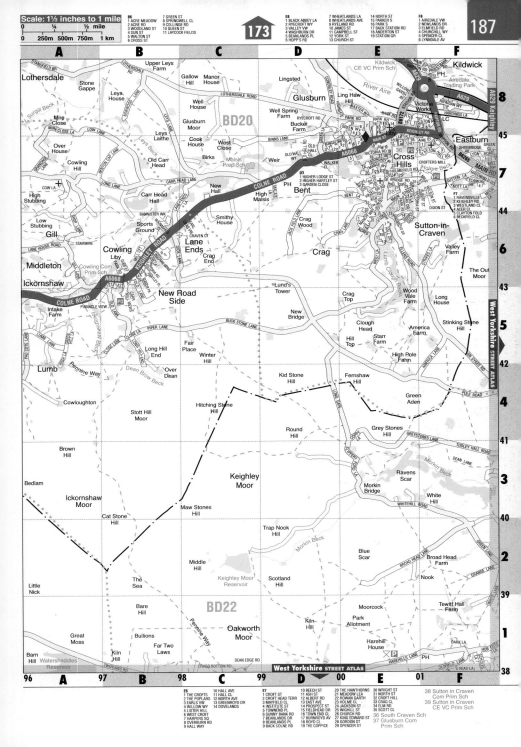

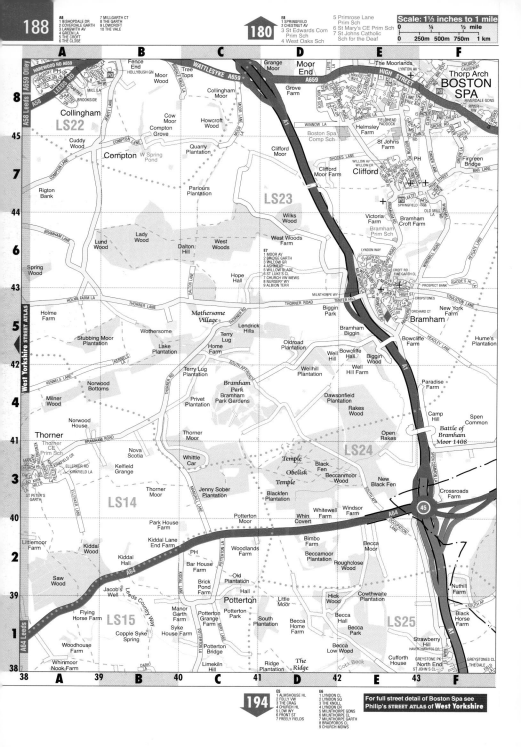

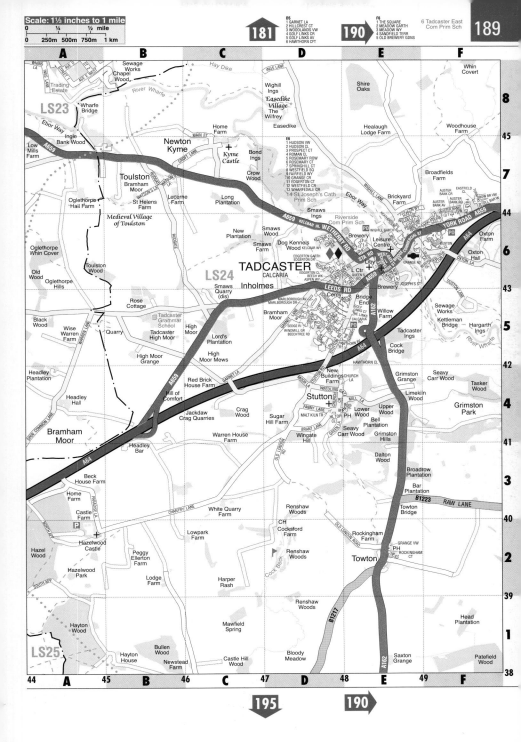

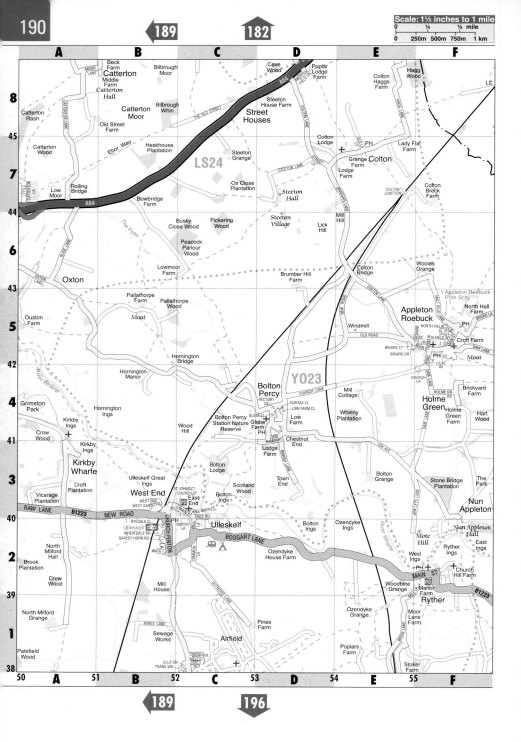

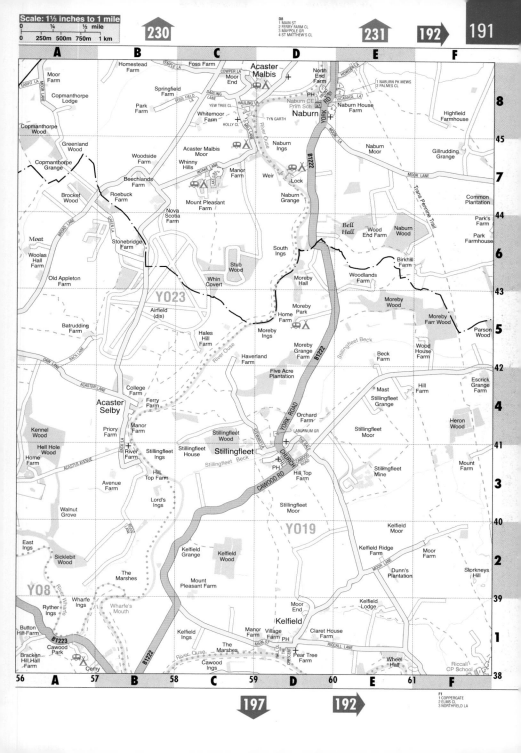

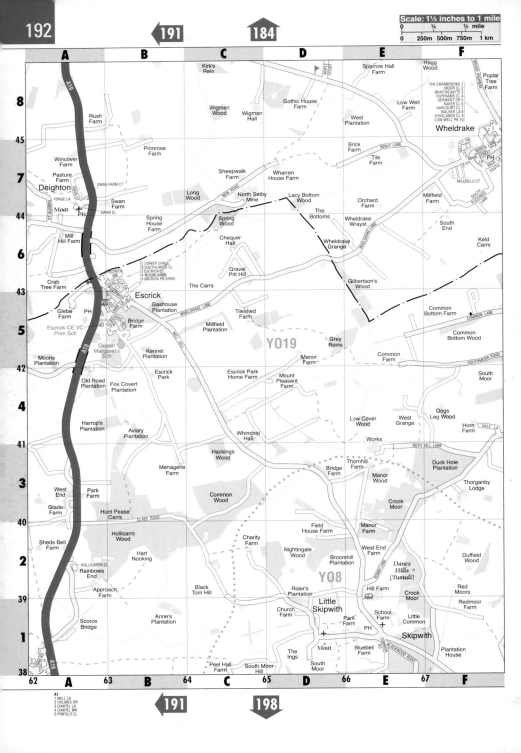

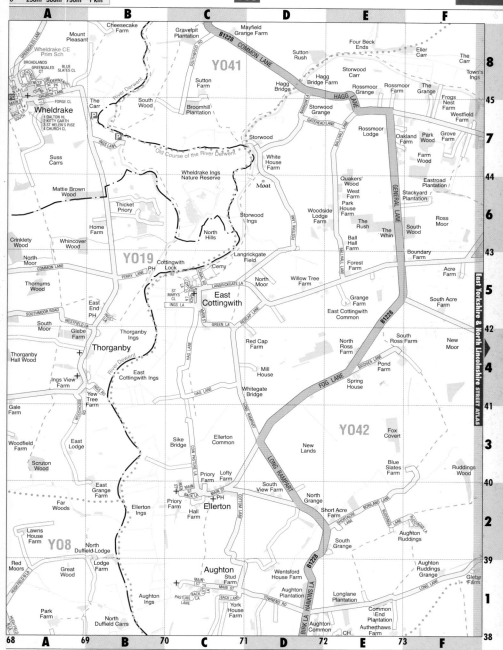

Mount
Pleasant
Cheesecake
Farm
Gravelpit
Plantation
Mayfield
Grange Farm
Four Beck
Ends
Eller
Carr
The
Carr
Town's
Ings
Wheldrake CE
Prim Sch
BROADLANDS
GREENGALES
CT
BLUE
SLATES CL
Y041
COMMON LANE
B1228
Sutton
Rush
Storwood
Carr
Hagg
Bridge Farm
Rossmoor
Grange
Rossmoor
Farm
The
Grange
Frogs
Nest
Farm
45
COURTNEYS
ELDERWALK
Sutton
Farm
Sutton
Hagg
Bridge
Westfield
Farm
The Carr
South
Wood
Broomhill
Plantation
HAGG LANE
Storwood
Grange
Storwood
HAGG LANE
GATEHEAD LANE
BALLHALL LANE
Oakland
Farm
Park
Wood
Grove
Farm
Wheldrake
1 DALTON HL
2 KITTY GARTH
3 ST HELEN'S RISE
4 CHURCH CL
INGS LANE
FORGE CL
White
House
Farm
Rossmoor
Lodge
Farm
Wood
7
Old Course of the River Derwent
Storwood
GENERAL LANE
Suss
Carrs
Wheldrake Ings
Nature Reserve
Moat
Quakers'
Wood
West
Farm
Eastroad
Plantation
Stackyard
Plantation
44
Mattie Brown
Wood
Park
House
Farm
Ross
Moor
6
Thicket
Priory
Storwood
Ings
Woodside
Lodge
Farm
The
Rush
The
Whin
South
Wood
Home
Farm
North Hills
POSTERN LANE
BALLHALL LANE
Ball
Hall
Farm
Boundary
Farm
43
Crinklety
Wood
Whincover
Wood
Y019
Langrickgate
Field
Forest
Farm
Acre
Farm
North
Moor
COMMON LANE
Cottingwith
Lock
Cemy
North
Moor
Willow Tree
Farm
Thornums
Wood
FERRY LANE
St Marys
Cl
CANAL LANE
Langrickgate La
Grange
Farm
South Acre
Farm
5
East
End
PH
INGS LA
East
Cottingwith
East Cottingwith
Common
B1228
42
SOUTHMOOR ROAD
WESTFIELD LA
GREEN LA
REDCAP LANE
Red Cap
Farm
South
Ross Farm
New
Moor
South
Moor
Glebe
Farm
Thorganby
Ings
North
Ross
Farm
Thorganby
Hall Wood
Thorganby
East
Cottingwith Ings
Mill
House
FOG LANE
South
Ross Farm
Pond
Farm
BRIDGES LANE
4
Ings View
Farm
Yew Tree
Farm
River Derwent
HAGG LANE
Whitegate
Bridge
Spring
House
41
Gale
Farm
WOODHOUSE
EDGE TRABANT
Fox
Covert
Woodfield
Farm
East
Lodge
Sike
Bridge
Ellerton
Common
New
Lands
Y042
Blue
Slates
Farm
Ruddings
Wood
3
Scruton
Wood
COW PASTURE LA
Priory
Farm
Lofty
Farm
LONG RAMPART
North
Grange
RUDDINGS LA
East
Grange
Farm
MAIN LA
BACK LA
Priory
Farm
Hall
Farm
Ellerton
PH
South
View Farm
Short Acre
Farm
SHORTACRE LANE
ROWLAND LANE
RUDDINGS
Aughton
Ruddings
2
Far
Woods
Ellerton
Ings
South
Grange
Aughton
Ruddings
Grange
Lawns
House
Farm
Y08
North
Duffield Lodge
Lodge
Farm
Aughton
MAIN ST
MAIN ST
Wentsford
House Farm
Longlane
Plantation
Glebe
Farm
39
Red
Moors
HIGHFIELD LA
Great
Wood
PASTURE
LANE
BACK LANE
Stud
Farm
York
House
Farm
TOWNEND RD
Aughton
Plantation
BIRK LA
HANKINS LA
Aughton
Common
Common
End
Plantation
LONG LANE
1
Park
Farm
HUDDLE LA
North
Duffield Carrs
Aughton
Ings
CH
Autherthaws
Farm
38
68   69   70   71   72   73
A   B   C   D   E   F

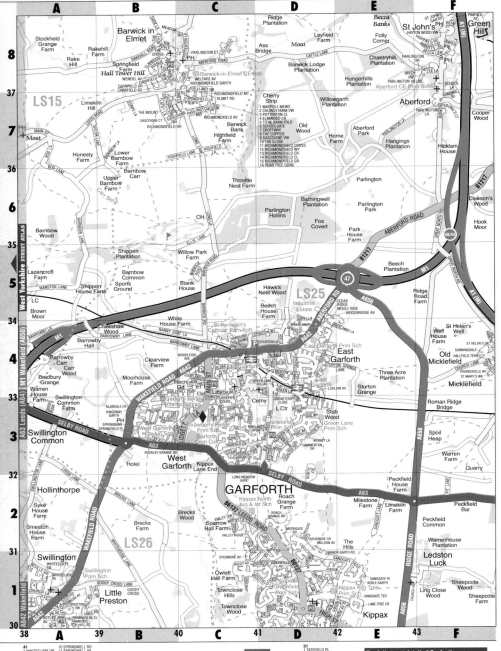

Scale: 1⅓ inches to 1 mile

A1
1 WHITECLIFFE DR
2 LOWTHER DR
3 LOWTHER GR
4 CHURCH CL
5 SMEATON GR
6 THE PLEASANCE
7 SPRINGWELL AV
8 WOODLAND CR
9 THE CREST
10 SPRINGWELL RD
11 SPRINGWELL AV
12 THE DRIVE
13 SCOTT CL
14 ST MARY'S AV
15 PRIMROSE HL DR
16 PRIMROSE HL GR

D1
1 TATEFIELD PL
2 HANOVER PL
3 THE INTAKE
4 APPLE TREE LA
5 APPLE TREE MS
6 CHURCHFIELD LA
7 APPLE TREE WALK

For full street detail of Garforth see
Philip's STREET ATLAS of West Yorkshire

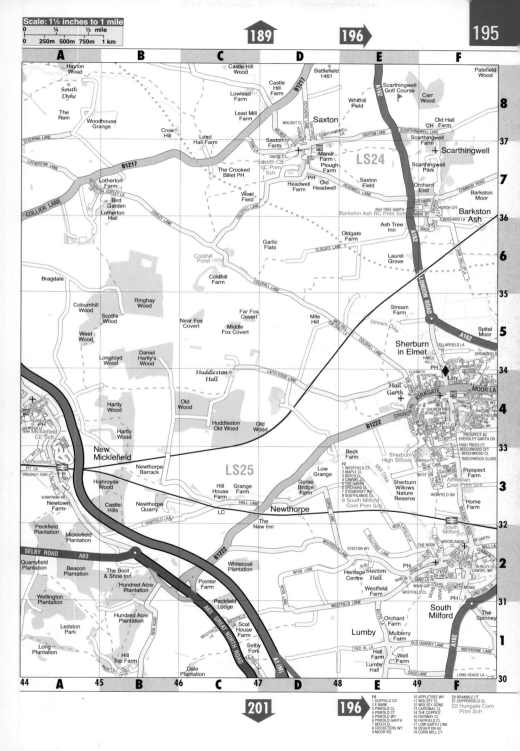

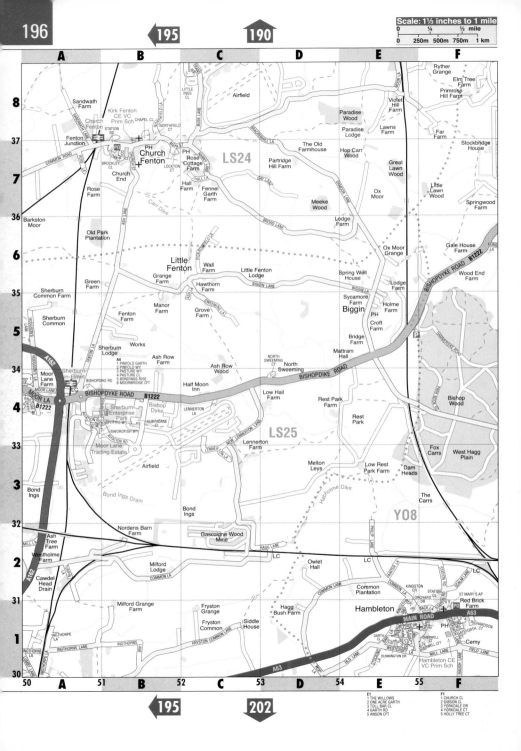

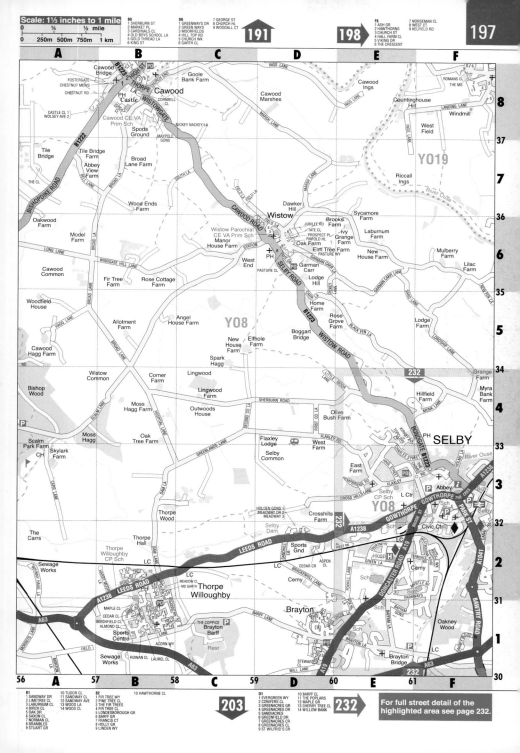

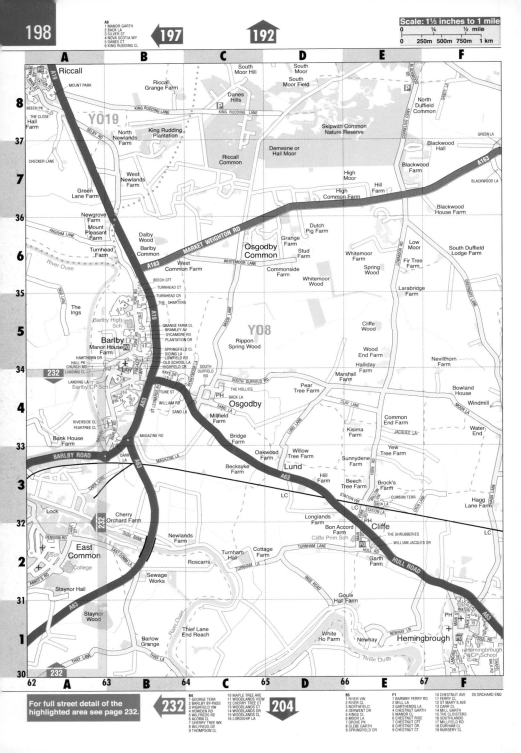

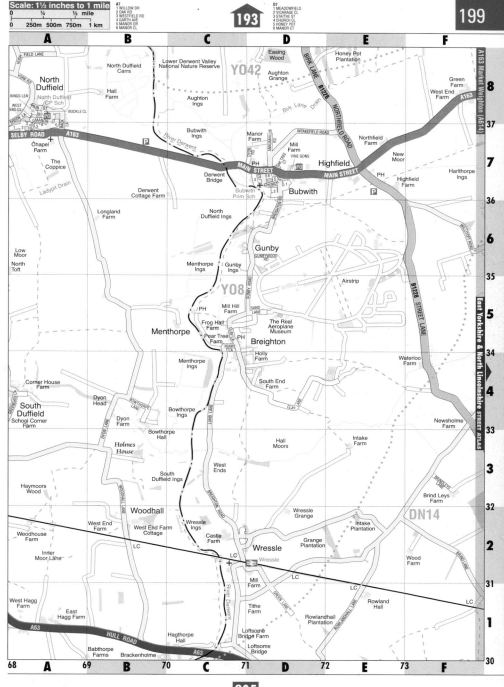

Scale: 1⅓ inches to 1 mile

0   ¼   ½   mile
0   250m   500m   750m   1 km

A7
1 WILLOW DR
2 OAK RD
3 WESTFIELD RD
4 GARTH AVE
5 MANOR DR
6 MANOR CL

D7
1 MEADOWFIELD
2 VICARAGE CL
3 STAITHE ST
4 CHURCH CL
5 HONEY POT
6 MANOR CT

Field Lane
North Duffield
York Rd
Kings Lea
West End Cl
North Duffield CP Sch
Green La
Manor
PO
Back La
Main St
Selby Road A163
Chapel Farm
The Coppice
Ladypit Drain

North Duffield Carrs
North Duffield Ings
Hall Farm
Aughton Ings
Bubwith Ings
River Derwent
Derwent Bridge
Derwent Cottage Farm

Lower Derwent Valley National Nature Reserve
YO42
Easing Wood
Aughton Grange

Honey Pot Plantation
Birk Lane
Birk Lane Drain
Northfield Road
West End Farm
Green Farm
A163

Manor Farm
Annumdale Rd
Mill Farm
Vine Gdns
Oak Tree La
PO
Intakefield Road
Highfield
Main Street
Northfield Farm
New Moor
Highfield Farm
Harlthorpe Ings
PH
A163 Market Weighton (A614)

Main Street
Church La
Bubwith Prim Sch
Bubwith
P

Longland Farm
North Duffield Ings

Low Moor
North Toft

Menthorpe Ings
Gunby Ings
Gunby
Gunbywood Rd
Gunby Road
YO8
Airstrip
Waterloo Farm
B1228 Street Lane

PH
Mill Hill Farm
Sand Lane
Frog Hall Farm
Pear Tree Farm
Menthorpe
PH
Breighton
The Real Aeroplane Museum
Ferry La
Old La
Holly Farm
South End Farm
Clay Lane

Menthorpe Ings
Newsholme Farm

Corner House Farm
Greenwell La
South Duffield
School Corner Farm
Dyon Head
Dyon Farm
Bowthorpe La
Dyon Lane
Bowthorpe Ings
Bowthorpe Hall
South Duffield Ings
West Ends
Brackley's Lane
Brind Leys Farm
Hall Moors
Intake Farm

Haymoors Wood
Holmes House
Woodhall
Wressle Ings
Castle Farm
West Ends Farm Cottage
Woodhall Lane
Brighton Road
West End Farm
Wressle Grange
Grange Plantation
Intake Plantation
DN14

Woodhouse Farm
Inner Moor Lane
LC
LC
Wressle
Wressle
LC
Grange Plantation
Wood Farm
Brind Rd

West Hagg Farm
East Hagg Farm
A63
Hull Road
Mill Farm
Tithe Farm
Green Lane
Rowlandhall Plantation
Rowland Hall
LC
Rowlandhall Lane
LC

Babthorpe Farms
Brackenholme
Hagthorpe Hall
River Derwent
Loftsome Bridge Farm
Loftsome Bridge
A63

East Yorkshire & North Lincolnshire STREET ATLAS

8 37 7 36 6 35 5 34 4 33 3 32 2 31 1 30

68 69 70 71 72 73
A   B   C   D   E   F

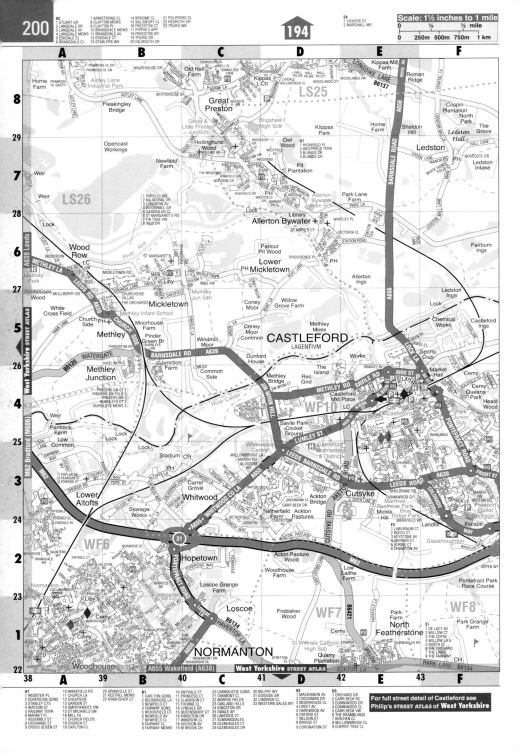

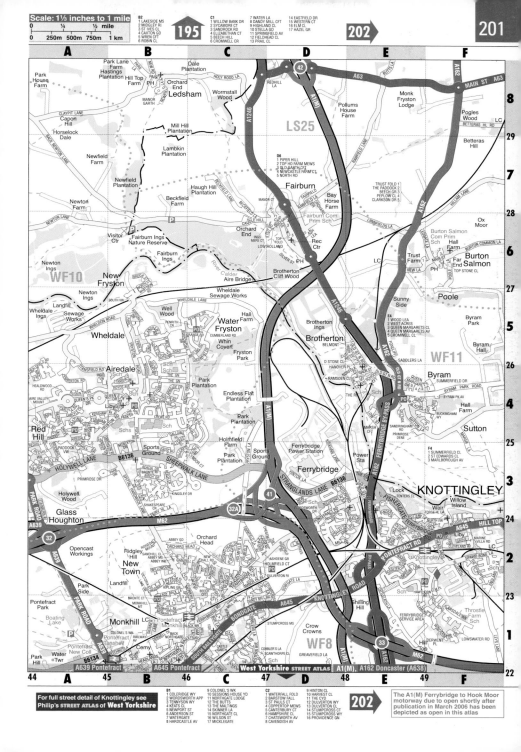

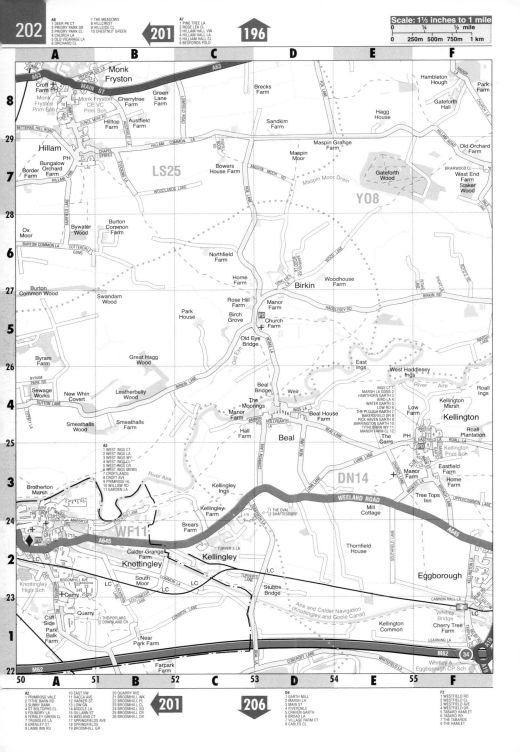

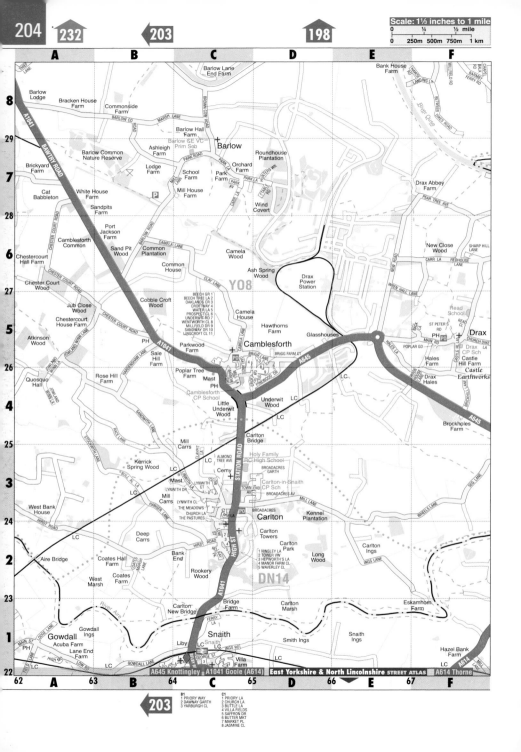

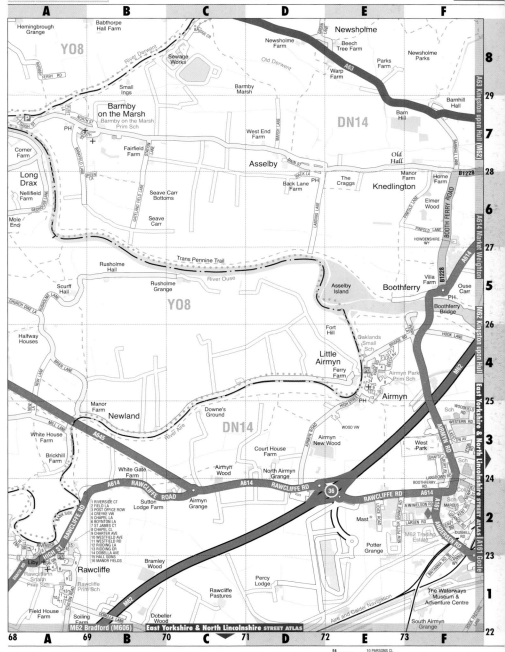

E4
1 BEECH GR
2 CHESTNUT AVE
3 BEECH AVE
4 PERCY DR
5 HALL CL
6 PARK CL
7 COURTS CL
8 WOODLAND WY
9 ST DAVID'S VW
10 PARSONS CL
11 PARSON'S WK
12 CHURCH VW
13 THE CROSSINGS
14 THE PADDOCK

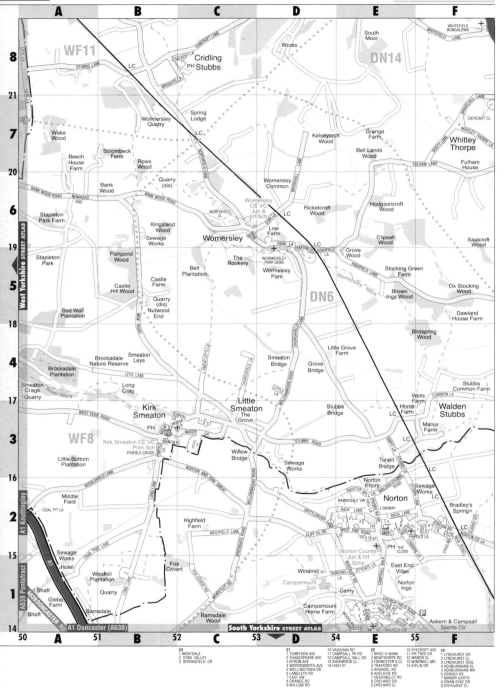

West Yorkshire STREET ATLAS

A1 Knottingley

A639 Pontefract A639 DONCASTER RD

WF11

WF8

WF8

DN14

DN6

Cridling
Stubbs
PH

Spring
Lodge

Wake
Wood

Beech
House
Farm

Scrombeck
Farm

Rows
Wood

Wormersley
Quarry

Bank
Wood

Quarry
(dis)

Kingsland
Wood

Sewage
Works

Works

South
Moor

WHITEFIELD
BUNGALOWS

WHITEFIELD
LANE

Kelseycroft
Wood

Grange
Farm

Whitley
Thorpe

Bell Lands
Wood

Fulham
House

Womersley
Common

Womersley
CE VC
Jun &
Inf Sch

Ricketcroft
Wood

Hodgsoncroft
Wood

Saulcroft
Wood

Womersley

Belt
Plantation

Low
Farm

The
Rookery

Wormesley
PARK GDNS

Wormesley
Park

Clipsall
Wood

Grove
Wood

Stocking Green
Farm

Brown
Ings Wood

Ox Stocking
Wood

Dawland
House Farm

Stapleton
Park Farm

Stapleton
Park

Fishpond
Wood

Castle
Hill Wood

Castle
Farm

Quarry
(dis)
Nutwood
End

Sod Wall
Plantation

Birdspring
Wood

Smeaton
Leys

Brockadale
Nature Reserve

Brockadale
Plantation

Long
Crag

Little Grove
Farm

Smeaton
Bridge

Grove
Bridge

Stubbs
Common Farm

Smeaton
Crags
Quarry

River Went

Kirk
Smeaton

PH

Kirk Smeaton CE VC
Prim Sch

PINFOLD CROSS

Little
Smeaton
The
Grove

Stubbs
Bridge

Wells
Farm

Home
Farm

Manor
Farm

Walden
Stubbs

Willow
Bridge

Sewage
Works

Tanpit
Bridge

Norton
Priory

Sewage
Works

Bradley's
Spring

Little Bottom
Plantation

Middle
Field

COAL PIT LA

Norton

Highfield
Farm

Sewage
Works

Hotel

Windhill
Plantation

Quarry

Glebe
Farm

Shaft

Shaft

Barnsdale

Fox
Covert

Barnsdale
Wood

Windmill

Campsmount
Sch

Cemy

Campsmount
Home Farm

Norton County
Jun & Inf
Schs

East End
Villas

Norton
Ings

Askern & Campsall
Sports Ctr

PH
THE
CLOSE

A1 Doncaster (A638)

South Yorkshire STREET ATLAS

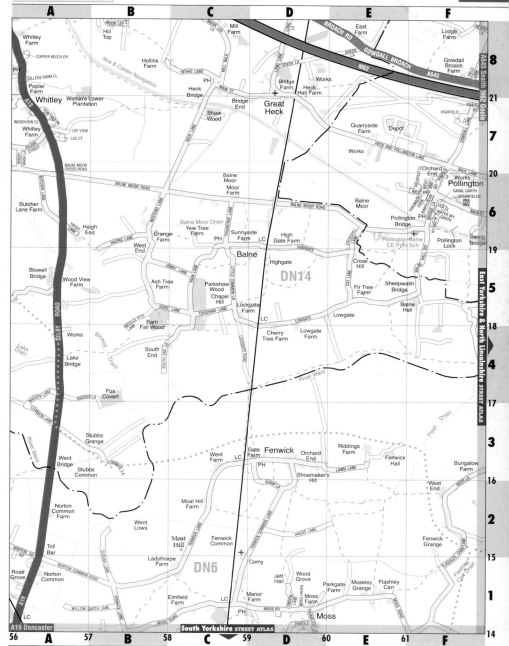

Scale: 1⅓ inches to 1 mile

0 ¼ ½ mile
0 250m 500m 750m 1 km

Row 8
Whitley Farm
Hill Top
MOOR LEE LA
Mill Farm
MOOR LEE LA
BROACH RD
East Farm
GOWDALL BROACH
Lodge Farm
COPPER BEECH DR
Hollins Farm
Aire & Calder Navigation
INTAKE LANE
GREEN LA
GREEN LA
M62
Gowdall Broach Farm
A645 Snaith
PH
COLLEGE FARM CL
Poplar Farm
Heck Bridge
MAIN ST
PH
Bridge Farm
Works
Heck Hall Farm
M62 Goole
A645
Whitley
Watkin's Lower Plantation
Bridge End
Great Heck
YEW TREE PK
21

WOODVIEW CL
Whitley Farm
LEE VIEW
LEE CT
Shaw Wood
Quarryside Farm
Depot
HIGHFIELD
A19
SHEEN LA
HAIGH LANE
SILVER STREET
BALNE MOOR CROSS ROAD
BALNE MOOR ROAD
Balne Moor Farm
Works
HECK AND POLLINGTON LAKE
Orchard End
Works
Pollington
BALK LANE
20

BUTCHER LANE
Butcher Lane Farm
BALNE MOOR ROAD
Balne Moor
Pollington
CANAL GARTH
GREENFIELDE RD
Pollington Bridge
HECK LANE
MAIN ST
WATER WY GARTH
6

Haigh End
HAZING LANE
WESTERN LANE
Grange Farm
Balne Moor Drain
Yew Tree Farm
THORNTREE LANE
Sunnyside Farm
PH
LC
High Gate Farm
HIGHGATE
Pollington-Balne CE Prim Sch
Pollington Lock
Swing Bridge
19

Blowell Bridge
Wood View Farm
West End
JENNY LANE
PARK LANE
Balne
Highgate
CASSON LANE
CAT LANE
Cross Hill
DN14
Fir Tree Farm
Sheepwash Bridge
Balne Hall
5

Ash Tree Farm
GORE LANE
NEVILLE PITS LANE
Parkshaw Wood
Chapel Hill
LITTLE COMMON LANE
TOADHAM LANE
Lockgate Farm
LC
LOWGATE
Lowgate
18

Works
Blowell Drain
Barn Fall Wood
SOUTH END LA
South End
LOCKGATE ROAD
Cherry Tree Farm
Lowgate Farm
East Yorkshire & North Lincolnshire STREET ATLAS
4

Lake Drain
Lake Bridge
River Went
Fleet Drain
17

BADGER LANE
COMMON LANE
Fox Covert
BADGER LA
Stubbs Grange
Went Farm
LC
Gate Farm
Fenwick
Orchard End
Riddings Farm
Fenwick Hall
Bungalow Farm
3

River Went
Went Bridge
COMMON LA
Stubbs Common
PH
SHAW LA
Shoemaker's Hill
LAWN LANE
West End
WEST LA
16

Norton Common Farm
Went Lows
Moat Hill Farm
FENWICK COMMON LANE
FENWICK COMMON LANE
HAGGS LANE
Fenwick Grange
2

NORTON CO RD
Toll Bar
CLOUGH LANE
NORTON COMMON ROAD
Moat Hill
Fenwick Common
Cemy
FLASHLEY CARR LANE
Flashley Carr Drain
15

Rose Grove
A19
LC
Norton Common
FENWICK LANE
WILLOW GARTH LANE
Ladythorpe Farm
DN6
Elmfield Farm
LC
Manor Farm
PH
Jett Hall
Wood Grove
LONDON LANE
Parkgate Farm
Moseley Grange
Flashley Carr
MOSS HAVEN LA
MOSS ROAD
1

MOSS ROAD
South Yorkshire STREET ATLAS
MOSS RD
PINFOLD LA
Moss
14

56 A 57 B 58 C 59 D 60 E 61 F

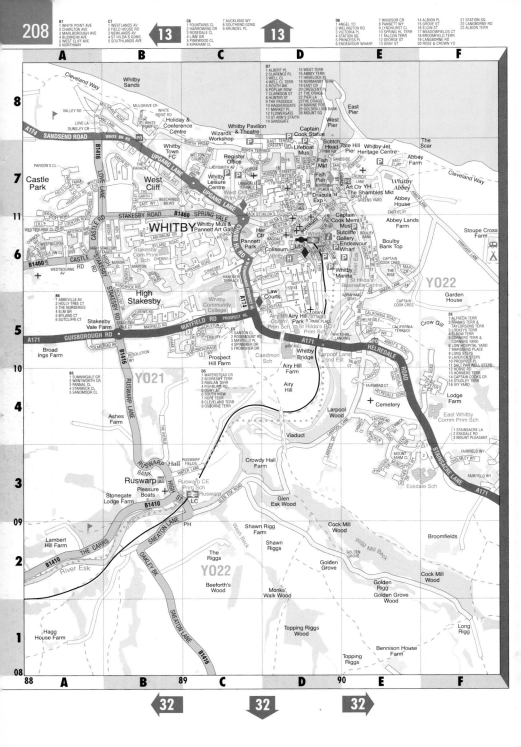

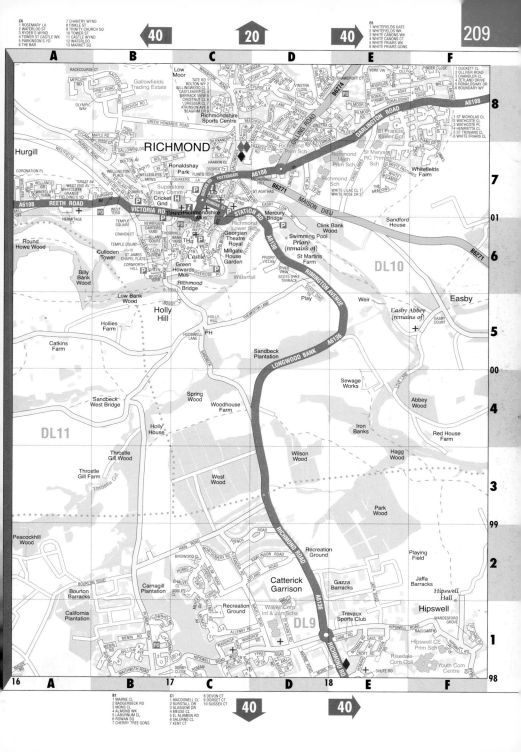

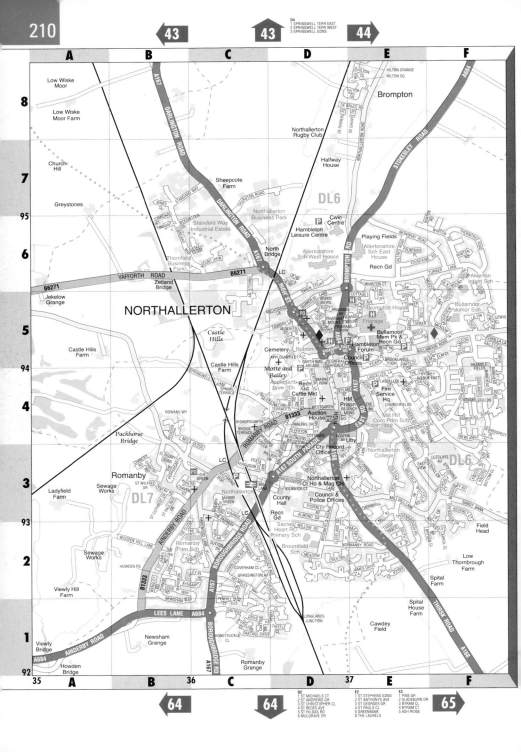

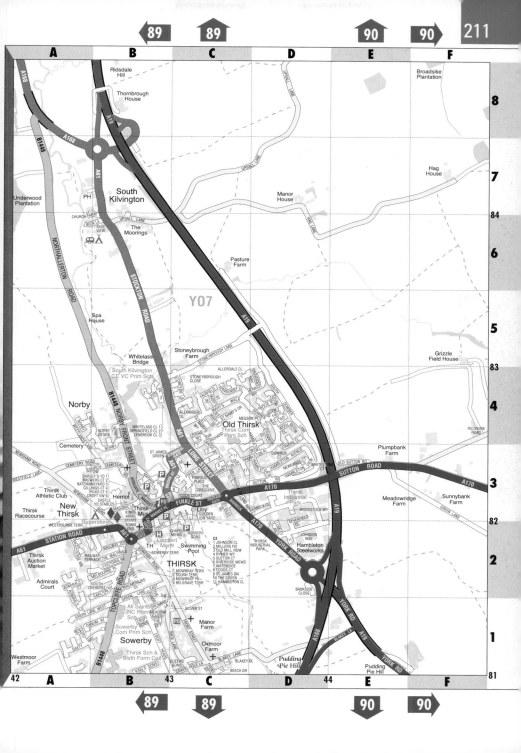

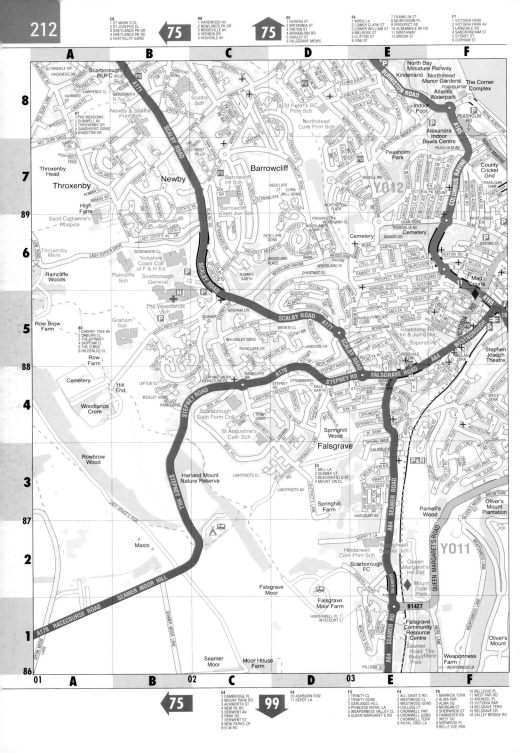

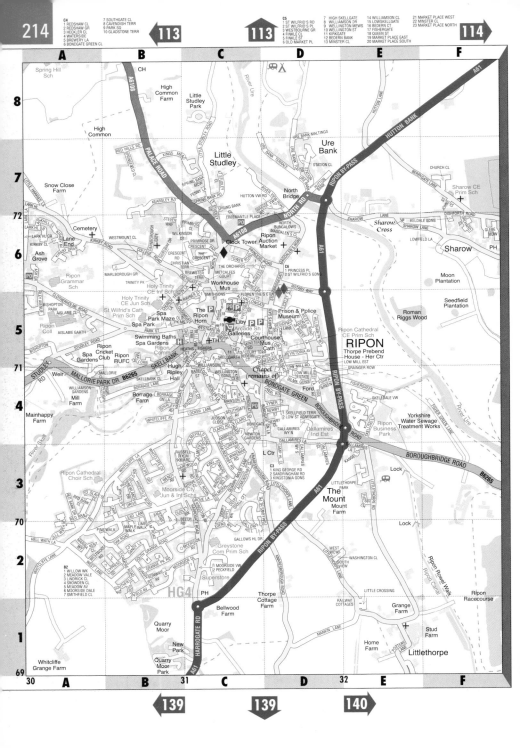

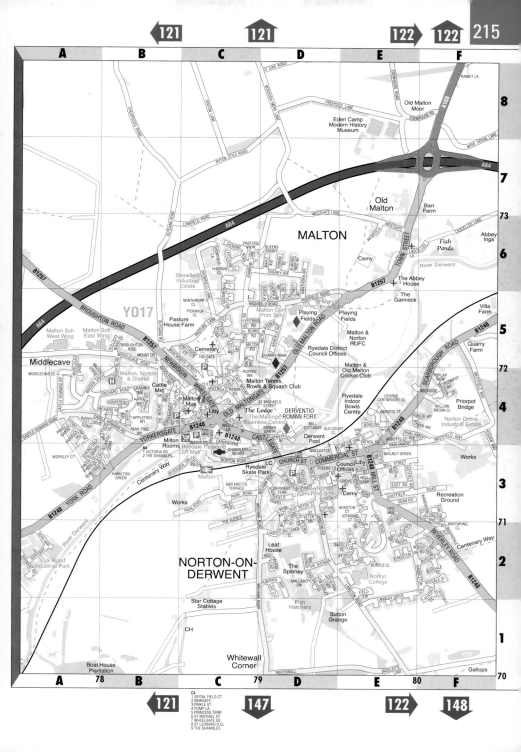

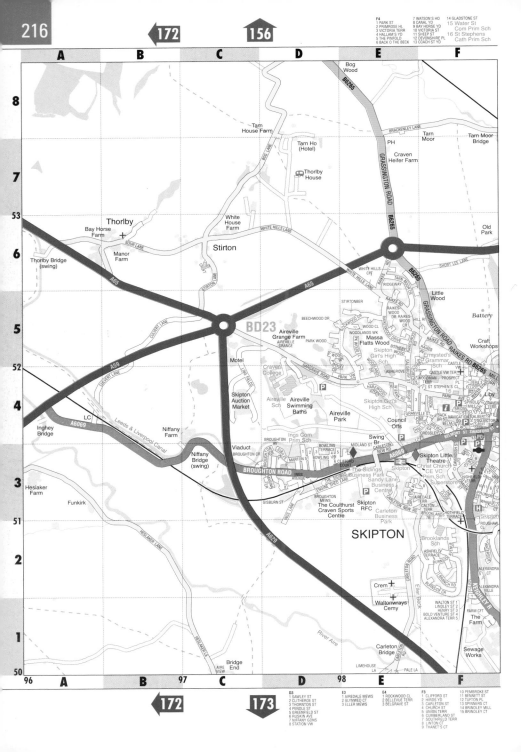

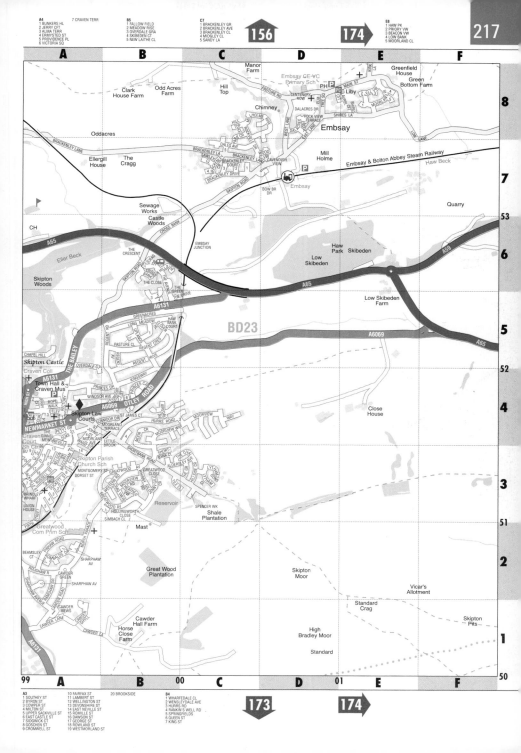

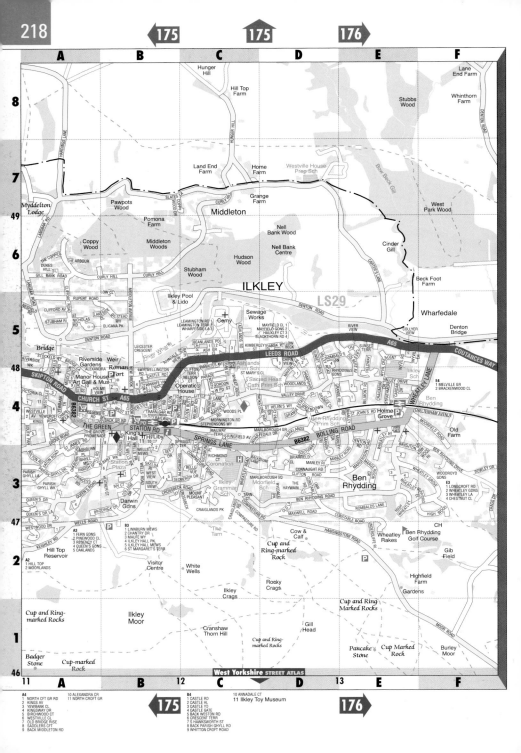

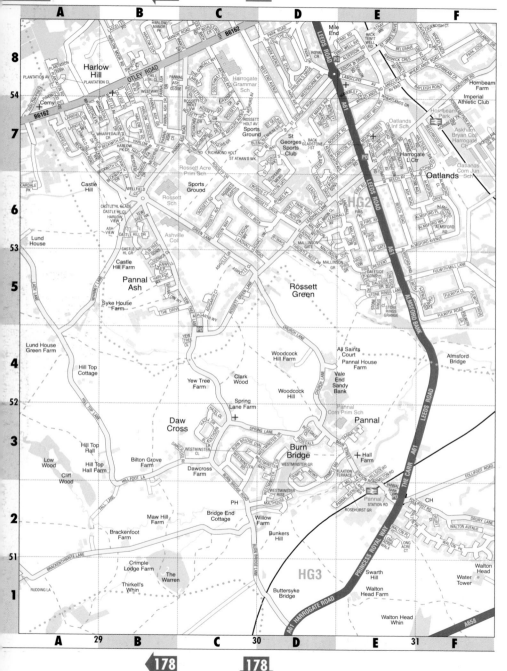

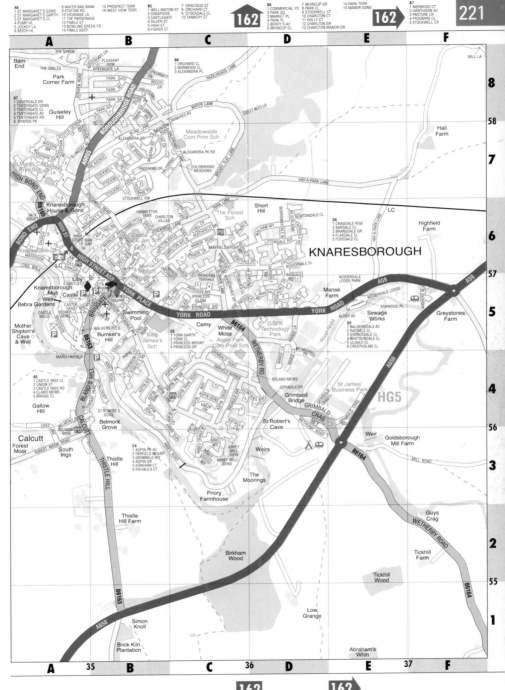

A6
1 ST MARGARET'S GDNS
2 ST MARGARET'S GARTH
3 ST MARGARET'S CL
4 PUMP HL
5 JOCKEY LA
6 BEECH HL

8 WATER BAG BANK
9 STATION RD
10 VICARAGE LA
11 THE PARSONAGE
12 FINKLE ST
13 BOWLING GREEN YD
14 FINKLE KEEP

15 PROSPECT TERR
16 WEST VIEW TERR

B5
1 WELLINGTON ST
2 CHEAPSIDE
3 CASTLEGATE
4 SILVER ST
5 HIGH ST
6 FISHER ST

7 GRACIOUS ST
8 ORCHARD CT
9 STOCKDALE CL
10 TANNERY CL

162

B6
1 COMMERCIAL YD
2 PARK SQ
3 MARKET PL
4 PARK PL
5 BERRY'S AV
6 WHINCUP GR

7 WHINCUP GR
8 PARK CL
9 STOCKWELL CT
10 CHARLTON CT
11 HOLLY CT
12 CHARLTON GR
13 CHARLTON MANOR DR

14 PARK TERR
15 MANOR GDNS

162

B7
1 NORWOOD CT
2 HAWTHORN AV
3 PASTURE CR
4 FROGMIRE CL
5 STOCKWELL CR

A7
1 COVERDALE DR
2 TENTERGATE GDNS
3 TENTERGATE CL
4 TENTERGATE AV
5 TENTERGATE RD
6 BYARDS PK

B8
1 ORCHARD CL
2 NORWOOD CL
3 ALEXANDRA PL

D6
1 CRAGDALE RISE
2 BARDALE CL
3 BRANSDALE GR
4 FLAXDALE CL
5 FOSSDALE CL

D5
1 BALDERDALE AV
2 RAYDALE CL
3 STONESDALE CL
4 WHITSUNDALE CL
5 ULDALE CL
6 CRESTHOLME CL

C5
1 YORK GARTH
2 YORK CL
3 PRINCESS MOUNT
4 PRINCESS GR

C4
1 ASPIN PK AV
2 FARFIELD MOUNT
3 GRIMBALD WY
4 ASPIN GR
5 KIRKHAM CT
6 RIEVAULX CT

A5
1 CASTLE INGS CL
2 UNION ST
3 CASTLE INGS RD
4 CLARO MEWS
5 BRIDGE CL

KNARESBOROUGH

HG5

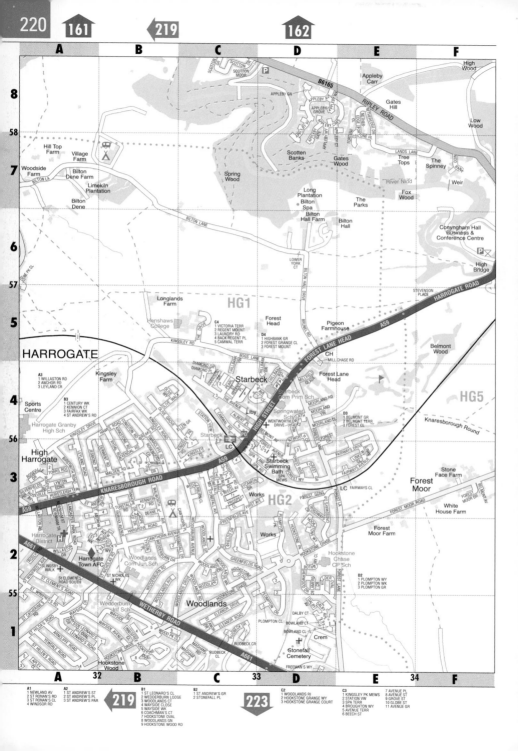

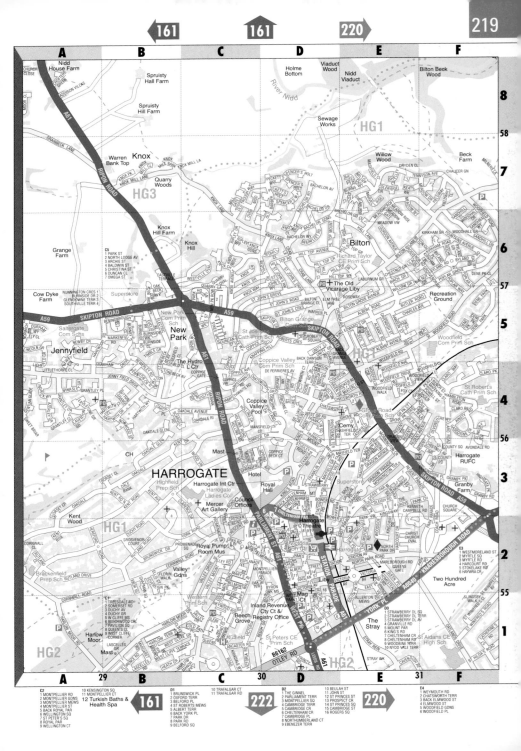

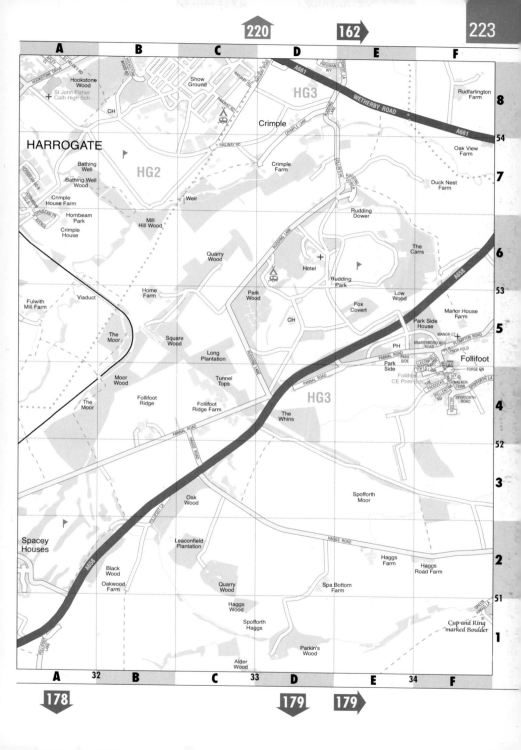

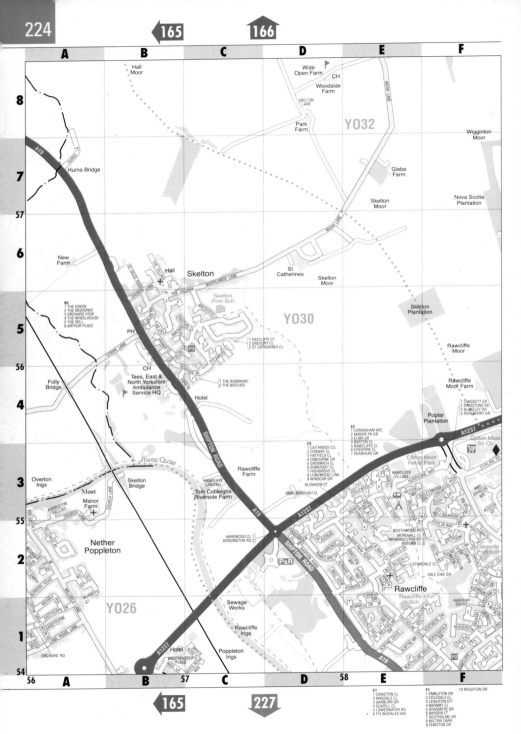

Hall Moor

Wide Open Farm
CH
Woodside Farm

SKELTON LANE

Park Farm

YO32

Wigginton Moor

MOOR LANE

Glebe Farm

Skelton Moor

Nova Scotia Plantation

New Farm

Hall

Skelton

St Catherines

Skelton Moor

Skelton Plantation

YO30

Skelton Plantation

Hurns Bridge

HURNS LANE

A19

ST GILES BOROUGH LANE
THE VILLAGE
CHURCH LANE

MOORLANDS LANE

Skelton Prim Sch

BECKFIELD LANE

Rawcliffe Moor

BS
1 THE GREEN
2 THE MEADOWS
3 ORCHARD VIEW
4 THE WHEELHOUSE
5 THE DELL
6 ARTHUR PLACE

PH

PO

1 RATCLIFFE CT
2 GREGORY CL
3 ST CATHERINES CL

Rawcliffe Moor Farm

Poplar Plantation

F1
1 CANGSETT GR
2 RINGSTONE RD
3 BLAKELEY GR
4 ROSEBERRY GR

Folly Bridge

STRIPE LANE

CH

Tees, East & North Yorkshire Ambulance Service HQ

Hotel

SYCAMORE AV

1 THE ROWMANS
2 THE BEECHES

E2
1 CONINGHAM AVE
2 MANOR PK GR
3 ELMA GR
4 BARTON CL
5 RAWCLIFFE CL
6 CHESHIRE CL
7 DEANHEAD GR

A1237

Clifton Moor Sh Ctr

STIRLING RD

E3
1 CAITHNESS CD,
2 CONWAY CL
3 HATFIELD CL
4 OSBOURNE DR
5 GRENWICH CL
6 SOMERSET CL
7 HIGHGROVE CL
8 LONGWOOD LINK
9 WINSCAR GR

BLENHEIM CT

MARLBOROUGH CL

Clifton Moor Retail Park

Rawcliffe Village

HURRICANE WAY

AMY JOHNSON WY

AVENTINE WY

River Ouse

Overton Ings

Skelton Bridge

Moat

Manor Farm

POPPLETON HALL GD

CHURCH LANE

FISH GARTH

Rawcliffe Farm

Rawcliffe LANDING

Tom Cobleighs Riverside Farm

A19

A1237

SHIPTON ROAD

HOLLYWOOD

BOOTHWOOD RD
MOREHALL CL
WHARNSCLIFFE DR
RYBURN CL

Lakeside Prim Sch

Nether Poppleton

HAREWOOD CL 1
KENSINGTON RD 2

P&R

MANOR LA
RANCLIFFE CL
ST MARK S GR

STANDALE GR

DALE DIKE GR

YO26

NURSERY ROAD

LONG RIDGE LANE

SANDSTONE

EASTHORPE DR

Sewage Works

SHIPTON ROAD

HOWARD RD

BOWNESS DR

FURNESS DR

Rawcliffe

Rawcliffe Inf Sch

Park GR

HAVERAH COURT

BEAVERDYKE

ORCHARD RD

Hotel

WESTMINSTER PLACE

A1237

Rawcliffe Ings

Poppleton Ings

A19

PO

E1
1 CONISTON CL
2 WASDALE CL
3 GARBURN GR
4 SCAFELL CL
5 LOWESWATER RD
6 FYLINGDALES AVE

F1
1 EMBLETON DR
2 COLEDALE CL
3 LEIGHTON CFT
4 BARMBY CL
5 GRASMERE GR
6 BARDEN CT
7 SOUTHOLME DR
8 MILTON CARR
9 FEWSTON DR

10 REIGHTON DR

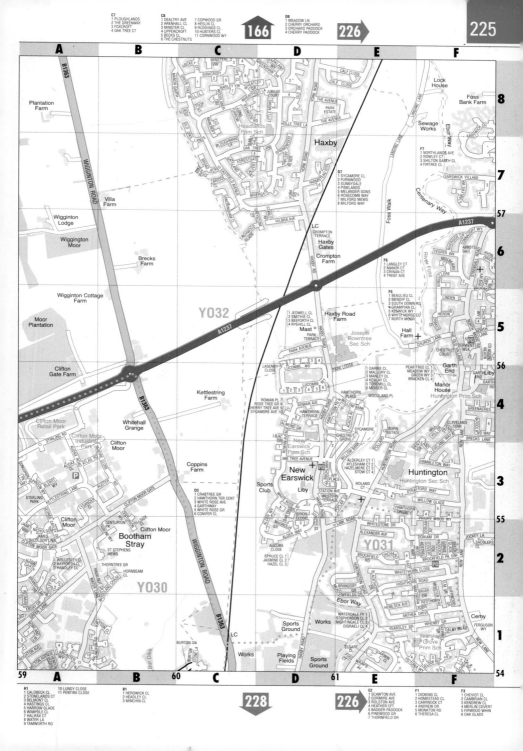

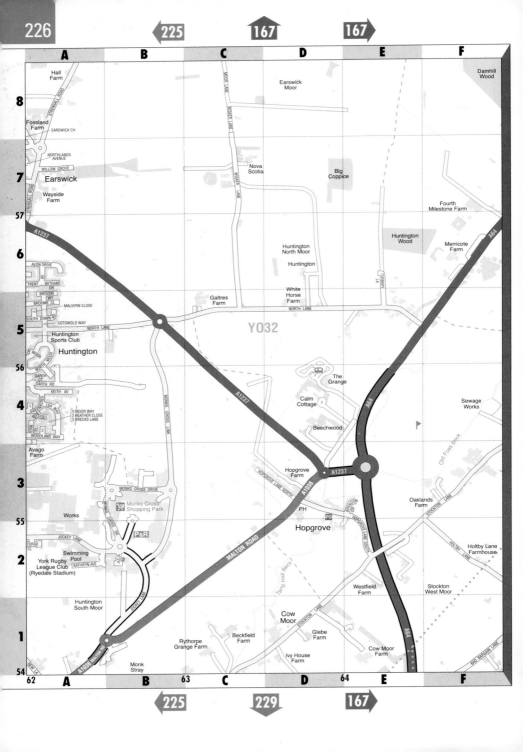

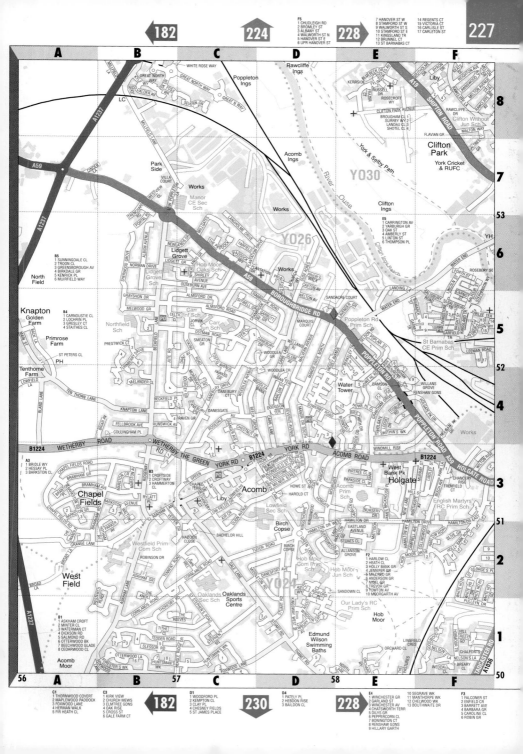

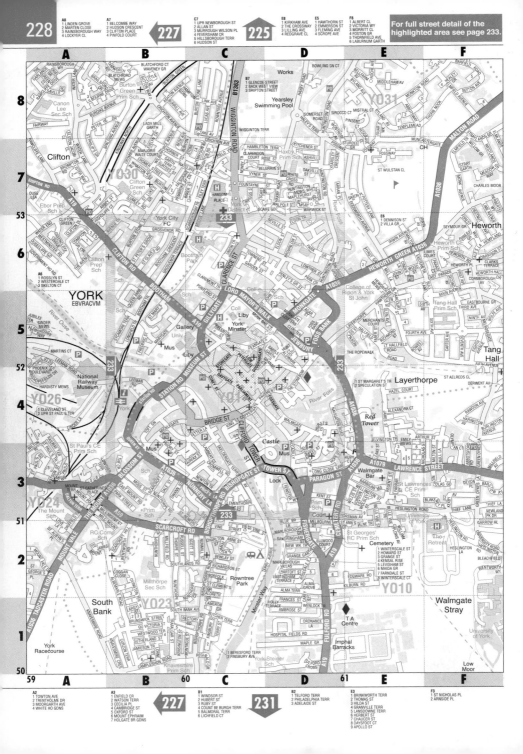

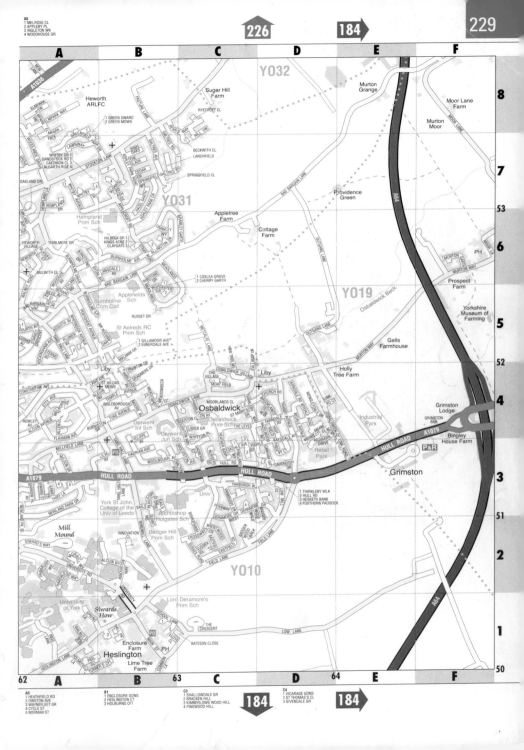

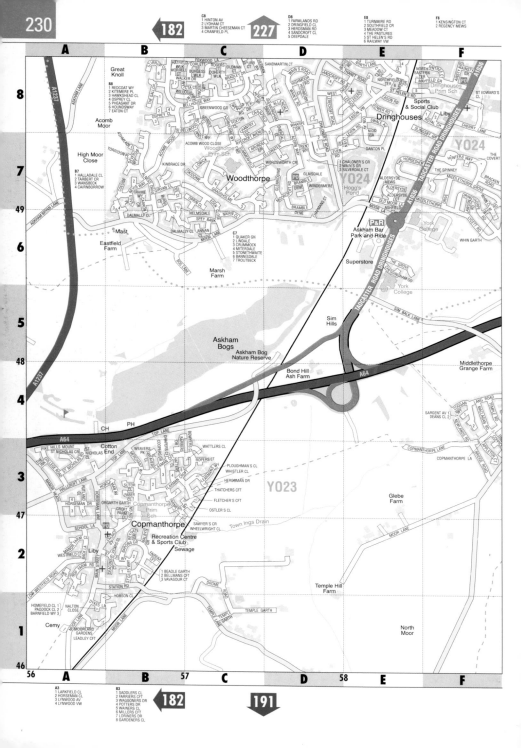

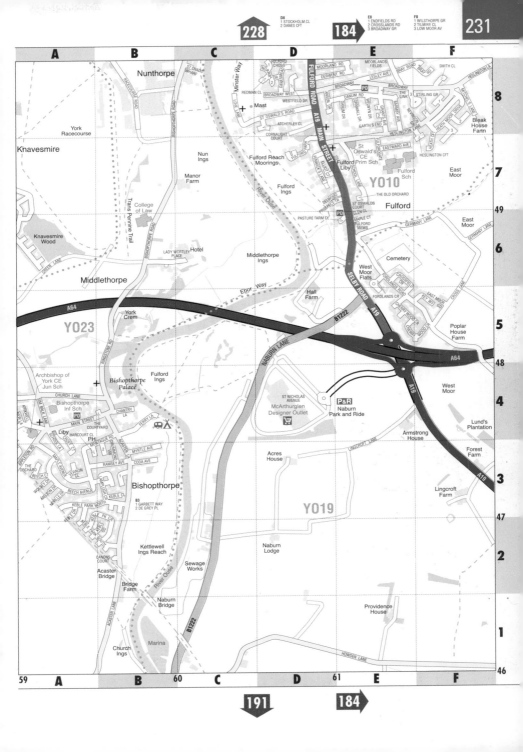

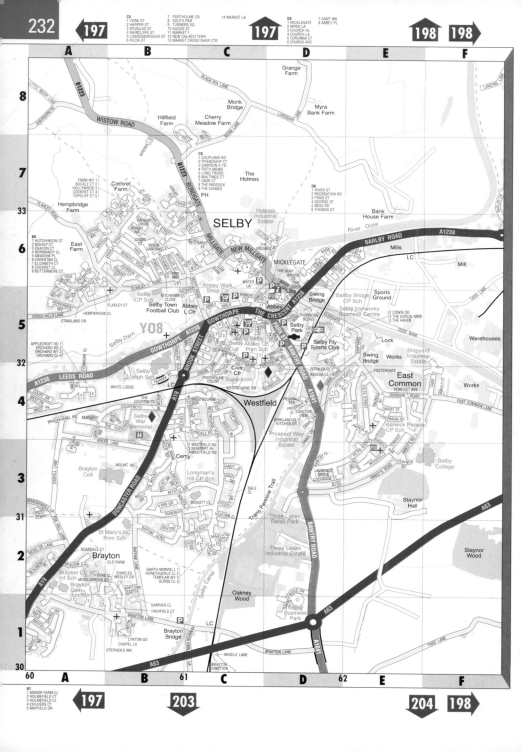

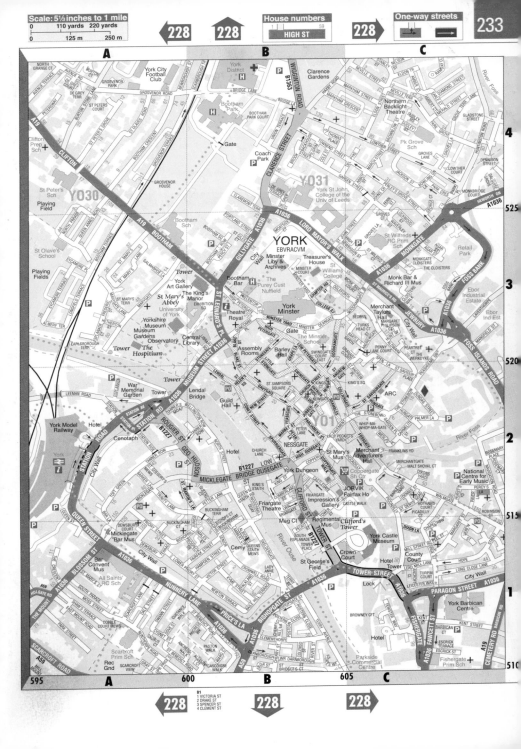

Index

Place name May be abbreviated on the map

Location number Present when a number indicates the place's position in a crowded area of mapping

Locality, town or village Shown when more than one place has the same name

Postcode district District for the indexed place

Page and grid square Page number and grid reference for the standard mapping

Church Rd **6** Beckenham BR2.........**53** C6

Public and commercial buildings are highlighted in magenta   Places of interest are highlighted in blue with a star ★

Abbreviations used in the index

Acad	Academy	Comm	Common	Gd	Ground	L	Leisure
App	Approach	Cott	Cottage	Gdn	Garden	La	Lane
Arc	Arcade	Cres	Crescent	Gn	Green	Liby	Library
Ave	Avenue	Cswy	Causeway	Gr	Grove	Mdw	Meadow
Bglw	Bungalow	Ct	Court	H	Hall	Meml	Memorial
Bldg	Building	Ctr	Centre	Ho	House	Mkt	Market
Bsns, Bus	Business	Ctry	Country	Hospl	Hospital	Mus	Museum
Bvd	Boulevard	Cty	County	HQ	Headquarters	Orch	Orchard
Cath	Cathedral	Dr	Drive	Hts	Heights	Pal	Palace
Cir	Circus	Dro	Drove	Ind	Industrial	Par	Parade
Cl	Close	Ed	Education	Inst	Institute	Pas	Passage
Cnr	Corner	Emb	Embankment	Int	International	Pk	Park
Coll	College	Est	Estate	Intc	Interchange	Pl	Place
Com	Community	Ex	Exhibition	Junc	Junction	Prec	Precinct

Prom	Prom	St	Street
Rd	Road	Sta	Station
Recn	Recreation	Terr	Terrace
Ret	Retail	TH	Town Hall
Sh	Shopping	Univ	University
Sq	Square	Wk, Wlk	Walk
		Wr	Water
		Yd	Yard

Index of localities, towns and villages

A

Aberford 194 F7
Acaster Malbis 191 D8
Acaster Selby 191 B4
Acklam
  Middlesbrough 6 E8
  Stamford Bridge ..169 E8
Acomb 227 C3
Addingham 174 F5
Agglethorpe 60 A1
Ainderby Quernhow ..88 C4
Ainderby Steeple 64 B7
Ainthorpe 29 C6
Airedale 201 B4
Aire View 173 D1
Airmyn 205 E4
Airton 155 A6
Airy Hill 208 D4
Aiskew 63 A3
Aislaby
  Egglescliffe 5 C3
  Pickering 95 D8
  Whitby 31 F7
Aldborough 141 C5
Aldbrough St John 2 A2
Aldfield 139 A8
Aldwark 142 C2
Allerston 97 C5
Allerton Bywater 200 D6
Allerton Mauleverer ..163 E4
Alne 142 F4
Alne Station 143 A5
Amotherby 121 B4
Ampleforth 92 C1
Angram
  Keld 35 E6
  York 182 C3
Appersett 56 C5
Appleton-le-Moors 70 F2
Appleton-le-Street 120 F4
Appleton Roebuck 190 F5
Appleton Wiske 24 B3
Appletreewick 157 D7
Archdeacon Newton 2 F7
Arkendale 163 B8
Arncliffe 107 D2
Arrathorne 62 A8
Asenby 115 B6
Askham Bryan 182 F3

Askham Richard 182 D3
Askrigg 57 F6
Askwith 176 D3
Asselby 205 D7
Aughton 193 C1
Austwick 130 E7
Aysgarth 58 E3
Azerley 113 A5

B

Bagby 90 C3
Bainbridge 57 D5
Baldersby 88 D1
Baldersby St James 114 E8
Balne 207 C5
Bank Newton 172 B8
Barden 61 A8
Barkston Ash 195 F7
Barlby 198 B5
Barlow 204 C7
Barmby on the Marsh ..205 B7
Barnoldswick
  Earby 171 D1
  Ingleton 103 A2
Barrowcliff 212 D7
Barton 21 D7
Barton Hill 146 D3
Barton-le-Street 120 E5
Barton-le-Willows 146 D1
Barwick in Elmet 194 B8
Battersby 27 D6
Beadlam 93 C7
Beal 202 D4
Beamsley 174 F7
Beckermonds 80 D3
Beckwithshaw 178 A7
Bedale 63 B2
Bedlam 161 A8
Bell Busk 155 A3
Bellerby 60 D7
Beningbrough 165 D4
Bent 187 D7
Bewerley 137 B3
Bickerton 181 A5
Biggin 196 E5
Bilbrough 182 D1
Bilton 219 E6
Bilton in Ainsty 181 E4

Binsoe 86 F2
Birdforth 116 E6
Birdsall 148 B4
Birkby 23 B1
Birkin 202 D6
Birstwith 160 E6
Bishop Monkton 140 A5
Bishop Thornton 138 F2
Bishopthorpe 231 B3
Bishopton 113 D2
Bishop Wilton 169 F2
Black Banks 3 D2
Blackwell 3 B4
Blades 37 B5
Blazefield 137 E4
Blubberhouses 159 D2
Boltby 66 F1
Bolton Abbey 174 E8
Bolton Bridge 174 F8
Bolton-on-Swale 41 F6
Bolton Percy 190 D4
Boosbeck 9 E8
Bootham Stray 225 F3
Boothferry 205 F5
Booze 17 F1
Bordley 133 D3
Boroughbridge 141 C5
Borrowby
  Northallerton 65 E4
  Whitby 11 D6
Bossall 168 D7
Boston Spa 188 F8
Bouthwaite 110 E2
Bracewell 171 C3
Brackenbottom 105 E3
Brafferton 116 A1
Braidley 83 B2
Bramham 188 F5
Brandsby 118 C3
Branksome 2 F6
Branton Green 142 A1
Brawby 94 F1
Brawith 26 A6
Braythorn 177 E4
Brayton 232 A2
Brearton 162 A7
Breighton 199 D5
Bridge Hewick 114 B1
Bridgehouse Gate 137 B4
Briggswath 32 B7

Briscoerigg 177 F5
Brockfield 167 E2
Brompton 43 F3
Brompton-by-Sawdon ..98 C5
Brompton-on-Swale 41 B7
Brookfield 6 E6
Brotherton 201 D5
Broughton
  Malton 121 D4
  Skipton 172 E6
Broxa 74 C6
Brunthwaite 174 D1
Bubwith 199 D7
Buckden 107 E8
Bugthorpe 169 D4
Bullamoor 44 B1
Bulmer 146 B6
Burley in Wharfedale ..176 B1
Burn 203 D7
Burn Bridge 222 D3
Burneston 87 E7
Burniston 75 C8
Burnsall 157 B8
Burnt Yates 160 F8
Burrill 62 E2
Burtersett 56 E4
Burton Fleming 126 E3
Burton in Lonsdale 102 F3
Burton Leonard 140 B2
Burton Salmon 201 F6
Burythorpe 147 F3
Buttercrambe 168 E5
Butterwick
  Brawby 120 E8
  Foxholes 125 B2
Byland Abbey 91 E1
Byram 201 F4

C

Calcutt 221 A3
Caldbergh 84 B7
Caldwell 1 B4
Calton 155 B6
Camblesforth 204 D5
Camp Hill 87 F5
Cantsfield 102 B4
Carlbury 2 B7
Carlesmoor 111 E4
Carleton in Craven 173 A4

Carlton
  Camblesforth 204 D3
  Darlington 1 F3
  Helmsley 68 E1
  West Witton 83 E7
Carlton Husthwaite 116 F7
Carlton in Cleveland ...26 A3
Carlton Miniott 89 C4
Carperby 58 E4
Carthorpe 87 E6
Castle Bolton 59 A6
Castleford 200 C4
Castleton 29 A6
Castley 178 A1
Cattal 164 A1
Catterick 41 D5
Catterick Bridge 41 D6
Catterick Garrison 209 D2
Catterton 190 B8
Catton 88 F1
Cawood 197 B8
Cawthorne 71 D4
Cawton 119 C7
Cayton 100 C6
Chantry 59 D2
Chapel Fields 227 A3
Chapel Haddlesey 203 C5
Chapel-le-Dale 104 C8
Charltons 9 C6
Chop Gate 46 F6
Church Fenton 196 B7
Church Houses 48 F4
Clapham 130 C8
Clapham Green 160 C5
Claxton 168 B7
Cleasby 2 F4
Cliffe
  Darlington 2 B6
  Selby 198 E2
Clifford 188 E7
Clifton
  Ilkley 176 F3
  York 228 A4
Clifton Park 227 F7
Clint 161 A6
Clints 39 C7
Clough 55 A7
Cloughton 54 C2
Cloughton Newlands ...54 C2
Coates 171 E4
Cobby Syke 159 F2

Cockayne...48 A5
Cockerton...3 B6
Cock Hill...165 B2
Colburn...41 A5
Cold Cotes...103 F2
Cold Kirby...91 D7
Collingham...188 A8
Colsterdale...84 E4
Colton...190 E7
Commondale...9 D1
Coneysthorpe...120 D2
Coneythorpe...163 A5
Coniston Cold...155 A1
Conistone...173 C2
Cononley...173 C3
Cononley Woodside...173 C3
Constable Burton...61 C5
Coomboots...75 B6
Copgrove...140 C2
Copmanthorpe...230 B2
Copt Hewick...114 C2
Cotterdale...55 F8
Cotton Tree...186 A2
Coulby Newham...7 A5
Coulton...119 B5
Countersett...57 C2
Coverham...60 C1
Cowan Bridge...102 D7
Cowesby...66 C4
Cowling
  Bedale...62 D2
  Glusburn...187 B6
Cowthorpe...180 E7
Coxwold...117 D8
Crackpot...37 B3
Cracoe...156 C7
Crag...187 D6
Crakehill...115 E4
Crambe...146 F3
Crambeck...146 F6
Crathorne...25 A6
Cray...81 E2
Crayke...118 A1
Cridling Stubbs...206 C8
Crimple...223 D8
Cringles...174 C3
Crockey Hill...184 A1
Croft-on-Tees...22 D8
Cropton...71 B4
Crosby Court...65 B6
Crossgates...99 E7
Cross Hills...187 E7
Cross Lanes...143 D3
Crowdon...54 A4
Cubeck...57 A6
Cundall...115 E3
Cutsyke...200 E3

D

Dacre...159 F7
Dacre Banks...159 F8
Dalby...119 B2
Dalesbridge Centre...130 E6
Dallow...111 F2
Dalton
  Newsham...19 D7
  Topcliffe...115 F7
Dalton Gates...22 D4
Dalton-on-Tees...22 E6
Danby...29 C7
Danby Wiske...43 C5
Darley...160 A6
Darlington...3 B6
Daw Cross...222 B3
Deepdale...80 F2
Deerstones...175 B8
Deighton
  Brompton...44 A8
  Escrick...192 A7
Denton...176 A3
Dishforth...115 A4
Downholme...39 D4
Draughton...174 B7
Drax...204 F5
Drebley...157 D6
Dringhouses...230 E8
Duggleby...149 B6
Dunkeswick...178 E2
Dunnington...184 F7
Dunsley...12 F2

E

Eaglescliffe...5 E5
Earby...172 B1
Earswick...226 A7
Easby
  Richmond...209 F5
  Stokesley...27 B7
Easington...11 A8
Easingwold...143 D8
East Appleton...99 B8
East Ayton...12 C3
East Barnby...3 E4
Eastburn...187 F7
Eastby...156 F1

East Common...232 E4
East Cottingwith...193 C5
East Cowton...22 F2
Easterside...7 A7
East Garforth...194 E4
East Harlsey...44 E6
East Hauxwell...61 D8
East Heslerton...124 A7
East Knapton...123 C6
East Layton...20 C8
East Lutton...150 C8
East Marton...26 F8
East Ness...93 C2
East Newton...94 B1
East Rounton...24 E2
East Row...13 A3
East Witton...61 A1
Eavestone...138 B7
Ebberston...97 E5
Eggborough...202 F2
Egglescliffe...5 E4
Egton...31 B5
Egton Bridge...31 A4
Eldroth...130 E4
Ellerbeck...44 F3
Ellerburn...96 E1
Ellerton
  Catterick...41 F4
  Wheldrake...193 C2
Ellingstring...85 D6
Ellington...5 C8
Elton...185 B2
Elvington...185 B2
Embsay...217 D8
Enterpen...25 C4
Eppleby...1 E4
Eryholme...23 A7
Escrick...192 B5
Eshton...155 D3
Everley...74 F4
Exelby...63 D1

F

Faceby...25 F2
Fadmoor...69 F4
Fairburn...201 D7
Falsgrave...212 D3
Fangdale Beck...47 A1
Farlington...144 F6
Farnham...162 D7
Farnhill...173 E1
Farnley...177 B2
Faverdale...3 A6
Fawdington...115 F3
Fearby...85 E4
Feetham...37 C5
Feizor...131 B6
Felixkirk...90 C7
Fenwick...207 D3
Ferrensby...162 F7
Ferrybridge...201 D3
Fewston...159 F1
Fewston Bents...159 F1
Filey...101 C3
Finghall...61 D4
Firby
  Bedale...63 A1
  Westow...147 A5
Firth Moor...3 F4
Fishpool...177 C2
Flasby...155 E3
Flawith...142 E4
Flaxby...163 B4
Flaxton...145 F1
Fleets...156 A7
Flixton...99 F2
Folkton...100 B2
Follifoot...223 F5
Fordon...1 D3
Forcett...126 A6
Foredale...131 C8
Forest...42 B7
Forest Moor...220 F3
Foston...146 B4
Foul Green...9 E1
Foxholes...125 D3
Foxton...44 E3
Foxup...106 C7
Fremington...38 D6
Fryton...120 A6
Fulford...231 E7
Full Sutton...169 A2
Fylingthorpe...33 B3

G

Gainford...1 D8
Galphay...112 F3
Gammersgill...83 C5
Ganthorpe...120 A1
Ganton...125 B8
Garforth...194 C4
Gargrave...155 D1
Garriston...61 B7
Gateforth...203 A7
Gate Helmsley...168 B2
Gatenby...64 D1

Gauber...78 F1
Gayle...56 D4
Gayles...19 E6
Gerrick...10 C3
Giggleswick...131 C2
Gill...187 A6
Gillamoor...70 A5
Gilling East...118 F8
Gilling West...20 E4
Girsby...23 D7
Glaisdale...30 D4
Glass Houghton...201 A3
Glasshouses...137 D4
Glusburn...187 D8
Goathland...51 E8
Goldsborough
  Knaresborough...163 A2
  Whitby...12 D5
Gollinglith Foot...85 B3
Goulton...25 E3
Gowdall...204 A1
Gowthorpe...169 C1
Grafton...141 D2
Grange...57 D5
Grassington...134 E3
Great Ayton...7 F2
Great Barugh...95 A1
Great Broughton...26 E5
Great Burdon...3 F8
Great Busby...26 C4
Great Crakehall...62 E4
Great Edstone...94 C7
Great Fencote...63 C8
Great Habton...121 C7
Great Heck...207 D7
Great Langton...42 D3
Great Ouseburn...164 B8
Great Preston...200 C8
Great Smeaton...23 C3
Great Thirkleby...90 D1
Green Close...130 A8
Green Hammerton...164 C3
Green Hill...194 F8
Greenhow...136 D3
Grewelthorpe...112 D7
Greygarth...111 F3
Greystonegill...129 C8
Grimston...229 E3
Grindale...127 D2
Grinton...38 C5
Gristhorpe...100 D3
Grosmont...31 D3
Grunsagill...153 A1
Guisborough...8 D7
Gunby...199 D6
Gunnerside...36 F4

H

Hackforth...62 E8
Hackness...74 F5
Hall Garth...184 F6
Halton East...174 C8
Halton Gill...106 E7
Halton West...154 A1
Hambleton
  Selby...196 F1
  Skipton...174 D8
Hampsthwaite...160 F5
Hanlith...155 A8
Hardgate...139 A1
Hardraw...56 C6
Harlow Hill...160 E4
Harmby...60 E4
Harome...93 C4
Harrogate...219 D1
Harrogate Hill...3 C8
Harrogate Village...3 E8
Hartforth...20 D5
Hartley...14 A7
Hartlington...157 C8
Harton...168 C8
Hartwith...160 B8
Haughton Le Skerne...3 F6
Hawes...56 D4
Hawkswick...107 F1
Hawnby...67 F4
Haxby...225 D7
Hazlewood...175 A8
Healaugh...37 F6
Healey...85 E3
Heathfield...136 F6
Heathwaite...45 E8
Hebden...135 A1
Hellifield...154 B3
Hellifield Green...154 B3
Helm...57 D6
Helmsley...92 F7
Helperby...142 A8
Helperthorpe...124 D1
Helwith Bridge...131 D8
Hemingbrough...198 F1
Hemlington...6 F4
Hensall...203 D2
Heslington...229 B1
Hessay...182 C8
Hetton...155 F5
Hew Green...160 D5
Heworth...228 F6

Heyshaw...159 D8
High Bentham...129 B8
High Birstwith...160 D5
High Bradley...173 E4
High Catton...185 D8
High Coniscliffe...2 C6
High Ellington...85 F6
High Grantley...138 D8
High Harrogate...220 A3
High Hawsker...33 B6
High Hutton...147 B7
High Kilburn...91 B2
High Leven...6 A3
High Marishes...96 B1
High Mowthorpe...149 D7
High Shaw...56 D7
High Stakesby...208 B5
High Worsall...24 A8
Hillam...202 A7
Hilton...6 C2
Hinderwell...11 F7
Hipswell...203 F3
Hirst Courtney...213 D7
Hole Bottom...135 A3
Holgate...227 E3
Hollinthorpe...194 A2
Holly Hill...209 B5
Holme...88 D5
Holme Green...190 F4
Holtby...167 F1
Hopetown...200 C2
Hopgrove...226 D2
Hopperton...163 E3
Hornby
  Bedale...62 B8
  Croft-on-Tees...23 E4
Horton...171 B5
Horton in Ribblesdale...105 C3
Houlsyke...29 F6
Hovingham...119 F6
Howe...88 E3
Howgill...157 E6
Howsham...146 F1
Hubberholme...81 C1
Huby
  Harrogate...178 B2
  Stillington...144 A4
Hudswell...40 A7
Hummersknott...3 A5
Hunmanby...126 F8
Hunsingore...180 F8
Huntington...225 E3
Hurgill...209 A7
Hurworth-on-Tees...3 E1
Hurworth Place...3 D1
Hut Green...203 A2
Hutton Bonville...43 C7
Hutton Buscel...98 E7
Hutton Conyers...114 A4
Hutton Gate...8 D6
Hutton Hang...61 D3
Hutton-le-Hole...70 C5
Hutton Mulgrave...12 D1
Hutton Rudby...25 C5
Huttons Ambo...147 B6
Hutton Sessay...116 D7
Hutton Village...8 E4
Hutton Wandesley...182 A5

I

Ickornshaw...187 A6
Ilkley...218 B4
Illon...85 E1
Ingerthorpe...139 C5
Ingleby Arncliffe...45 B8
Ingleby Barwick...6 B4
Ingleby Cross...45 A7
Ingleby Greenhow...27 C5
Ingleton...103 D3
Ingmanthorpe...180 E5
Inholmes...189 C6
Ireby...102 F6
Irton...99 D6
Ivelet...36 D5

J

Jennifield...219 A5
Junction...187 F8

K

Keasden...130 A5
Kelbrook...186 A8
Keld...35 E8
Keldholme...70 D1
Keld Houses...136 C2
Kelfield...191 D1
Kellingley...202 C2
Kellington...202 F4
Kepwick...66 C6
Kettleness...12 D6

Kettlesing...160 C3
Kettlesing Bottom...160 C3
Kettlewell...108 B3
Kexby...185 C6
Key Green...31 A3
Kilburn...91 B2
Kildale...27 E8
Kildwick...187 F8
Killerby...100 C5
Killinghall...165 C5
Kilnsey...134 B6
Kilton Thorpe...10 B8
Kiplin...42 B4
Kippax...194 E1
Kirby Grindalythe...149 E6
Kirby Hill...20 A5
Kirby Knowle...66 C2
Kirby Misperton...95 D2
Kirby Sigston...44 D1
Kirby Underdale...170 A5
Kirby Wiske...88 F8
Kirkbridge...62 F5
Kirkby...26 D5
Kirkby Fleetham...42 D1
Kirkby Hill...141 B7
Kirkby Malham...154 F8
Kirkby Malzeard...112 D5
Kirkby Mills...94 C8
Kirkbymoorside...70 B1
Kirkby Overblow...179 A4
Kirkby Wharfe...190 A3
Kirk Deighton...180 B5
Kirkham...147 A4
Kirk Hammerton...164 C2
Kirklevington...24 F8
Kirklington...88 A4
Kirk Smeaton...206 B3
Knapton...227 A5
Knaresborough...221 A6
Knavesmire...231 A7
Knayton...65 F2
Knedlington...205 E6
Knottingley...201 F3
Knox...219 B7

L

Lane End...171 C2
Lane Ends...187 C6
Laneshaw Bridge...186 C4
Langbar...175 B6
Langbaurgh...7 F2
Langcliffe...131 E3
Langthorne...62 E5
Langthorpe...141 A6
Langthwaite...17 E1
Langtoft...151 D5
Langton...147 F6
Lastingham...70 F5
Laverton...112 D4
Lawkland...130 F5
Lawkland Green...131 A4
Layerthorpe...228 E4
Leake...65 F5
Lealholm...30 B6
Lealholm Side...30 D7
Leathley...177 D2
Leavening...147 E1
Lebberston...116 C2
Leck...102 E7
Ledsham...201 B8
Ledston...200 F7
Ledston Luck...194 F1
Leeming...63 D4
Leeming Bar...63 C5
Leighton...85 C2
Leppington...169 C8
Levisham...72 D5
Leyburn...60 D5
Leysthorpe...93 B1
Lindley...177 C4
Lingdale...9 F7
Lingerfield...162 B6
Lingfield...3 F5
Linton
  Grassington...134 D1
  Wetherby...180 A1
Linton-on-Ouse...164 E7
Little Airmyn...205 E4
Little Ayton...8 B1
Little Barugh...62 D5
Little Crakehall...62 D5
Little Fencote...63 C8
Little Fenton...196 B6
Little Habton...121 A8
Little Heck...203 D1
Little Hutton...116 B7
Little Ouseburn...164 A7
Little Ribston...180 A8
Little Sessay...116 C5
Little Skipwith...192 D1
Little Smeaton
  North Cowton...23 C2
  Norton...206 C3
Little Stainforth...131 D6
Little Studley...214 C7
Littlethorpe...214 F1
Litton...107 A5

Liverton ... 10 D6
Liverton Mines ... 10 C8
Lockton ... 72 D4
Lodge Green ... 36 F5
Lofthouse ... 110 C4
Londonderry ... 63 E2
Long Drax ... 205 A6
Long Lease ... 33 A7
Long Marston ... 182 A6
Longnewton ... 5 A7
Long Preston ... 153 F5
Longscales ... 160 C4
Loscoe ... 200 C1
Lothersdale ... 187 A8
Low Bentham ... 128 F8
Low Bradley ... 173 E3
Low Catton ... 185 C8
Low Coniscliffe ... 2 F4
Low Dalby ... 72 F2
Low Dinsdale ... 4 C1
Low Ellington ... 86 A6
Lower Altofts ... 200 A3
Lower Dunsforth ... 142 A4
Lower Mickletown ... 200 D6
Lower Westhouse ... 103 B4
Low Garth ... 29 F4
Low Gate ... 138 F6
Low Gatherley ... 21 D1
Lowgill ... 128 F3
Low Grantley ... 112 E1
Low Green ... 160 A6
Low Hawsker ... 33 A6
Low Hutton ... 147 C6
Low Laithe ... 137 F2
Low Marishes ... 122 C8
Low Mill ... 48 E2
Lowna ... 70 A6
Low Row ... 37 C4
Low Snaygill ... 173 D4
Low Town ... 5 B1
Low White ... 37 D5
Low Worsall ... 24 A8
Lumb ... 187 A4
Lumby ... 195 E1
Lund ... 198 D3
Lythe ... 12 E4

M

Malham ... 133 A1
Maltby ... 6 C4
Malton ... 215 C4
Manfield ... 2 B4
Manor Park ... 176 B2
Margrove Park ... 9 D6
Markington ... 139 D3
Marrick ... 38 F5
Marsett ... 57 A1
Marske ... 39 C7
Marton
  Boroughbridge ... 141 D1
  Middlesbrough ... 7 B7
  Pickering ... 94 F6
Marton-in-the-Forest ... 144 E7
Marton-le-Moor ... 114 F1
Masham ... 86 B3
Masongill ... 103 A6
Maunby ... 64 D1
Meagill ... 159 D3
Mearbeck ... 153 D7
Melmerby
  Carlton ... 83 F8
  Ripon ... 114 C7
Melsonby ... 21 A7
Menethorpe ... 147 D6
Menthorpe ... 199 C5
Merrybent ... 2 E5
Methley ... 200 B5
Methley Junction ... 200 A4
Mewith Head ... 129 E6
Mickleby ... 12 A4
Micklefield ... 194 F4
Mickletown ... 200 B5
Mickley ... 112 F7
Middlecave ... 215 A5
Middleham ... 60 E2
Middlesmoor ... 110 B5
Middlethorpe ... 231 B6
Middleton
  Glusburn ... 187 A6
  Ilkley ... 218 C2
  Pickering ... 95 E8
Middleton One Row ... 4 D3
Middleton-on-Leven ... 25 D8
Middleton Quernhow ... 88 B1
Middleton St George ... 4 B4
Middleton Tyas ... 21 D5
Milby ... 141 B6
Mill Dam ... 129 C6
Mill Hirst ... 159 F7
Minskip ... 141 A3
Monk Fryston ... 202 B8
Monkhill ... 201 B1
Monkroyd ... 186 D4
Moor End ... 188 D8
Moor Monkton ... 165 A3
Moorsholm ... 10 B5
Morton-on-Swale ... 64 A6
Moss ... 207 D1
Moulton ... 21 D3
Mount Pleasant ... 7 B5
Mowden ... 3 A6
Moxby ... 144 D5
Muker ... 36 A5
Murton ... 184 D7
Muscoates ... 94 A3
Muston ... 100 F2

Myton-on-Swale ... 141 F5

N

Naburn ... 191 D8
Nappa ... 171 B8
Nawton ... 93 E7
Neasham ... 4 A1
Nesfield ... 175 B4
Nether Burrow ... 102 B6
Netherby ... 179 B1
Nether Poppleton ... 224 A2
Nether Silton ... 66 B7
Newall ... 176 F1
Newbiggin
  Askrigg ... 57 F6
  Filey ... 101 A5
  Thoralby ... 82 D8
Newbridge ... 96 A8
Newby
  Ingleton ... 104 A1
  Middlesbrough ... 7 A3
  Ripon ... 140 D6
  Scarborough ... 75 E5
Newby Cote ... 104 B1
Newby Wiske ... 64 E2
New Earswick ... 225 D3
New Fryston ... 201 B6
Newholm ... 13 A1
New Houses ... 105 C4
Newland ... 205 B3
New Micklefield ... 195 A3
New Park ... 219 B5
New Road Side ... 187 B5
New Row ... 8 F1
Newsham
  Barnard Castle ... 19 D8
  Thirsk ... 89 A8
Newsholme
  Asselby ... 205 E8
  Barnoldswick ... 171 A6
New Thirsk ... 211 A3
Newthorpe ... 195 D3
Newton Kyme ... 189 B7
Newton-le-Willows ... 62 B4
Newton Morrell ... 21 E8
Newton Mulgrave ... 11 E6
Newton-on-Ouse ... 165 B6
Newton-on-Rawcliffe ... 72 A5
Newton under Roseberry ... 8 B4
Newton upon Derwent ... 185 E4
New Town ... 201 B2
New York ... 137 F1
Nidd ... 161 E6
Norby ... 211 A4
Normanby ... 94 F4
Normanton ... 200 C1
Northallerton ... 210 C5
North Cowton ... 22 C3
North Deighton ... 180 B6
North Duffield ... 199 A8
North Featherstone ... 200 E1
North Grimston ... 148 E6
North Ings ... 119 D1
North Kilvington ... 89 E8
North Lees ... 113 E4
North Otterington ... 64 D4
North Rigton ... 178 B5
North Stainley ... 113 D7
Norton ... 206 E2
Norton-le-Clay ... 115 C2
Norton-on-Derwent ... 215 D3
Nosterfield ... 87 B3
Nun Appleton ... 190 F3
Nun Monkton ... 165 A4
Nunnington ... 93 E2
Nunthorpe
  Middlesbrough ... 7 D5
  York ... 231 B8
Nunwick ... 114 A5

O

Oakdale ... 161 B2
Oak Tree ... 4 E4
Oatlands ... 222 F6
Octon ... 151 F8
Old Byland ... 91 F8
Old Malton ... 215 E7
Old Micklefield ... 194 F4
Oldstead ... 91 C3
Old Thirsk ... 211 C4
Ormesby ... 7 C8
Osbaldwick ... 229 C4
Osgodby
  Seamer ... 100 B7
  Selby ... 198 C4
Osgodby Common ... 198 C6
Osmotherley ... 45 C4
Oswaldkirk ... 93 A1
Otterburn ... 154 E4
Oughtershaw ... 80 C4
Oulston ... 117 E5
Outhgill ... 34 A8
Over Burrow ... 102 B7
Over Silton ... 66 B8
Overton ... 165 F2
Overtown ... 102 C7
Oxton ... 190 A6

P

Padside ... 159 B6
Padside Green ... 159 C6
Painsthorpe ... 170 B5

Pannal ... 222 E3
Pannal Ash ... 222 B5
Park ... 186 F5
Park End ... 7 B8
Parlington ... 194 E6
Pateley Bridge ... 137 C4
Patrick Brompton ... 62 C5
Pickering ... 95 E6
Pickhill ... 88 C6
Picton ... 24 D6
Piercebridge ... 2 A6
Place Newton ... 123 C3
Pockley ... 69 B1
Pollington ... 207 F6
Poole ... 201 F5
Port Mulgrave ... 11 F8
Potterton ... 188 C1
Potto ... 25 A8
Preston-on-Tees ... 5 F7
Preston-under-Scar ... 59 E6
Primrose Valley ... 101 C1

R

Rainton ... 114 E6
Ramsgill ... 110 E1
Raskelf ... 116 E2
Rathmell ... 153 C6
Ravenscar ... 54 A8
Ravenseat ... 15 C2
Ravensworth ... 20 A7
Raw ... 33 B4
Rawcliffe
  Carlton ... 205 A1
  York ... 224 E2
Raydale ... 57 A1
Raygill ... 186 E8
Red Hill ... 201 A4
Redmire ... 59 C6
Reeth ... 38 B6
Reighton ... 127 D6
Riccall ... 198 A8
Richmond ... 209 C7
Rievaulx ... 91 F8
Rillington ... 122 F5
Ripley ... 161 C7
Ripon ... 214 E5
Risplith ... 138 E7
Robin Hood's Bay ... 33 D4
Roecliffe ... 140 F4
Romanby ... 210 B3
Rookwith ... 62 A1
Rosedale Abbey ... 49 E3
Rossett Green ... 222 D5
Roundhill Village ... 5 F5
Rowden ... 161 E6
Roxby ... 11 C7
Rudby ... 25 D5
Rufforth ... 182 C6
Runswick Bay ... 12 A7
Rushton ... 98 D6
Ruswarp ... 208 B3
Rylstone ... 156 E8
Ryther ... 190 F1
Ryton ... 121 F6

S

Sadberge ... 4 B8
St John's ... 194 F8
Salton ... 94 D3
Sandhutton ... 89 A4
Sand Hutton ... 168 B5
Sandsend ... 13 A3
Satron ... 36 D4
Sawdon ... 98 C7
Sawley ... 138 F6
Saxton ... 195 D8
Scackleton ... 119 C4
Scagglethorpe ... 122 D3
Scalby ... 75 D6
Scaling ... 11 A4
Scaling Dam ... 11 A4
Scampston ... 123 A6
Scarborough ... 213 B5
Scarthingwell ... 195 F7
Scawton ... 91 E6
Scorton ... 41 F7
Scotton
  Harrogate ... 162 A6
  Richmond ... 40 F2
Scrayingham ... 168 F7
Scriven ... 162 D5
Scruton ... 63 D7
Seamer
  Middlesbrough ... 6 F1
  Scarborough ... 99 E6
Seave Green ... 47 A7
Sedbusk ... 56 E6
Selby ... 232 C6
Selly Hill ... 32 A8
Selside ... 105 A6
Sessay ... 116 B6
Settle ... 131 E3
Settrington ... 122 D1
Sexhow ... 25 D4
Sharow ... 214 F6
Shaw Mills ... 138 F1
Sherburn ... 124 D8
Sherburn in Elmet ... 195 E5
Sheriff Hutton ... 145 C5
Shipton ... 165 F5
Sicklinghall ... 179 E3
Silpho ... 74 E7
Silsden ... 174 C2
Simonstone ... 56 D6

Sinderby ... 88 C4
Sinnington ... 95 A8
Skeeby ... 21 A1
Skelton ... 224 C6
Skelton on Ure ... 140 E7
Skerne Park ... 3 C3
Skewsby ... 119 A1
Skipton ... 216 F4
Skipton-on-Swale ... 88 E2
Skipwith ... 192 E1
Skirethorns ... 134 C2
Skirpenbeck ... 169 A4
Skyreholme ... 157 E7
Slapewath ... 9 C6
Sledmere ... 150 A4
Sleights ... 32 A6
Slingsby ... 120 C6
Small Banks ... 174 F3
Smelthouses ... 137 F3
Snainton ... 98 A5
Snaith ... 204 C1
Snape ... 87 A7
Sneaton ... 32 D6
Sneatonthorpe ... 32 F5
Sockburn ... 23 C6
Sourby ... 176 D8
South Bank ... 228 B1
South Duffield ... 199 A4
South Holme ... 120 B8
South Kilvington ... 211 B7
South Loftus ... 10 E8
South Milford ... 195 F1
South Otterington ... 64 F2
South Stainley ... 139 E2
Sowerby ... 211 B1
Spacey Houses ... 223 A2
Spaunton ... 70 E4
Speeton ... 127 F2
Spennithorne ... 60 F3
Spofforth ... 179 E5
Sproxton ... 92 F4
Stackhouse ... 131 D4
Stainburn ... 177 F3
Stainforth ... 131 E6
Stainsacre ... 32 F7
Stainton
  Marrick ... 39 C3
  Middlesbrough ... 6 D5
  York ... 167 B5
Staintondale ... 54 B5
Stalling Busk ... 81 B8
Stamford Bridge ... 168 E2
Stanwick-St-John ... 1 E2
Stape ... 71 F8
Stapleton ... 3 A2
Starbeck ... 220 C4
Starbotton ... 107 F5
Staupes ... 160 C4
Staveley ... 140 F1
Staxton ... 99 E2
Stead ... 176 A1
Stean ... 110 A4
Stearsby ... 118 F2
Stillingfleet ... 191 C3
Stillington ... 144 C6
Stirton ... 216 C6
Stock ... 171 C3
Stockton on the Forest ... 167 D4
Stokesley ... 26 D7
Stonegate ... 30 D8
Stonegrave ... 119 D8
Stone House ... 78 F8
Stranghow ... 9 F6
Street ... 29 F3
Street Houses ... 190 C8
Streetlam ... 42 F5
Strensall ... 167 A7
Strensall Camp ... 167 B6
Studfold ... 105 D1
Studley Roger ... 113 C1
Studley Royal ... 113 C1
Stutton ... 189 D4
Suffield ... 75 A5
Summerbridge ... 138 A1
Summerscales ... 158 C1
Sutton ... 201 F4
Sutton Howgrave ... 87 F1
Sutton-in-Craven ... 187 F6
Sutton-on-the-Forest ... 144 C3
Sutton-under-
  Whitestonecliffe ... 90 E5
Sutton upon Derwent ... 185 C1
Swainby ... 45 E8
Swaledale ... 37 C4
Swartha ... 174 E6
Swathgill ... 119 B4
Swetton ... 111 F4
Swillington ... 194 A1
Swillington Common ... 194 A3
Swincliffe ... 160 E4
Swinden ... 154 C1
Swinithwaite ... 59 C4
Swinton
  Malton ... 121 C4
  Masham ... 86 B2

T

Tadcaster ... 189 D6
Tame Bridge ... 26 A7
Tang ... 160 D4
Tang Hall ... 228 F5
Tanton ... 7 C1
Temple Hirst ... 204 E3
Terrington ... 119 F1
Theakston ... 87 E8
The Mount ... 214 D3
The Spa ... 213 B4

Thimbleby ... 45 A2
Thirlby ... 90 E7
Thirn ... 86 B8
Thirsk ... 211 C2
Thixendale ... 170 E7
Tholthorpe ... 142 D5
Thoralby ... 58 E1
Thorganby ... 193 B4
Thorgill ... 49 C3
Thorlby ... 216 B6
Thormanby ... 116 F5
Thornaby-on-Tees ... 6 A7
Thornborough ... 87 C2
Thorns ... 35 E2
Thornthwaite ... 159 D6
Thornton ... 6 E4
Thornton-in-Craven ... 172 A3
Thornton in Lonsdale ... 103 C4
Thornton-le-Beans ... 65 B5
Thornton-le-Clay ... 146 A4
Thornton-le-Dale ... 96 D5
Thornton-le-Moor ... 65 B3
Thornton-le-Street ... 65 D1
Thornton Rust ... 58 B4
Thornton Steward ... 61 D1
Thornton Watlass ... 86 D8
Thorp Arch ... 188 F8
Thorpe ... 156 F8
Thorpe Bassett ... 123 A4
Thorpe Underwood ... 164 C6
Thorpe Willoughby ... 197 C2
Threshfield ... 134 D2
Thrintoft ... 64 A8
Throxenby ... 212 A7
Thruscross ... 159 A5
Thwaite ... 35 F5
Thwing ... 126 B1
Timble ... 176 D7
Tockwith ... 181 D7
Tollerton ... 143 A3
Tollesby ... 7 A6
Topcliffe ... 115 B7
Tosside ... 152 F3
Toulston ... 189 B7
Town Head ... 174 C1
Towthorpe
  Sledmere ... 149 D1
  York ... 167 B5
Towton ... 189 E2
Trawden ... 186 B1
Tunstall
  Catterick ... 41 B2
  Cowan Bridge ... 102 B4

U

Uckerby ... 21 E1
Ugglebarnby ... 32 C6
Ugthorpe ... 11 F2
Ulleskelf ... 190 C2
Ulshaw ... 61 A2
Upper Dunsforth ... 142 A2
Upper Helmsley ... 168 B3
Upper Poppleton ... 165 F1
Upsall ... 66 B2
Ure Bank ... 214 D7
Urlay Nook ... 5 B5
Ura ... 47 A8

V

Vicar's Green ... 39 F7

W

Waithwith Banks ... 40 B5
Wake Hill ... 111 F1
Walden Stubbs ... 206 F3
Walkerville ... 41 A4
Walmgate Stray ... 228 F1
Walshford ... 180 D8
Walton ... 181 A2
Warlaby ... 64 D6
Warsill ... 138 C4
Warthermarske ... 86 A1
Warthill ... 167 F2
Washfold ... 18 D1
Wass ... 91 F2
Water Fryston ... 201 C5
Wath
  Hovingham ... 119 F6
  Pateley Bridge ... 137 A6
  Ripon ... 114 A7
Weaverthorpe ... 124 E1
Weeton ... 178 C1
Welburn
  Pickering ... 94 A7
  Westow ... 146 D2
Welbury ... 24 E1
Well ... 87 A4
Wennington ... 102 B1
Wensley ... 60 A4
Wensleydale ... 57 A5
Wescoe Hill ... 178 B1
West Appleton ... 41 C1
West Ayton ... 99 A7
West Barnby ... 12 C3
West Burton ... 58 F1
West Cliff ... 208 B2
Westerdale ... 28 E4
Westfield ... 232 C4
West Field ... 227 A2
West Garforth ... 194 B3
West Haddlesey ... 203 A5
West Harlsey ... 44 D5

West Heslerton 123 F7
Westhouse.............103 C4
West Knapton.........123 B6
West Layton 20 A8
West Lilling...........145 C4
West Lutton 150 B8
West Marton..........171 F5
West Ness 94 B1
Weston...............176 E2
Westow...............147 B4
West Rounton 24 D2
West Scrafton 83 F6
West Stonesdale 15 E1
West Tanfield 87 A1
West Witton 59 E3
Wetherby.............180 D4
Wharfe 131 A8

Wharram le Street 149 A4
Whashton 20 A5
Whashton Green 20 A5
Whaw 17 B3
Wheldale.............201 B5
Wheldrake............192 F8
Whenby 145 B8
Whinfield 3 F8
Whitby 208 C6
Whitewall Corner 215 C1
Whitley.............207 A7
Whitley Thorpe 206 F7
Whittington..........102 A7
Whitwell 42 B6
Whitwell-on-the-Hill ...146 E4
Whitwood 200 C3
Whixley 164 A5

Whorlton 25 E1
Wiganthorpe 119 E3
Wigginton 166 D5
Wigglesworth.........153 C4
Wighill 181 D1
Wilberfoss...........185 F6
Willerby.............99 C2
Wilsill 137 E3
Wilton...............97 A5
Winewall............186 B2
Winksley 112 F2
Winsley.............160 D8
Winterburn 155 D5
Winton 44 C3
Wintringham 123 C4
Wistow 197 D6
Wold Newton 126 A3

Wombleton 93 F7
Womersley 206 C6
Woodale.............83 A2
Woodhall
   Selby 199 B2
   Thoralby.........58 B5
Woodhouse...........200 A1
Woodlands 220 C1
Wood Row...........200 A6
Woodthorpe 230 C7
Worton 57 F5
Wray 128 A6
Wrayton.............102 B3
Wrelton 71 C1
Wressle 199 D2
Wycoller............186 C2
Wydra 160 A1

Wykeham
   Malton 122 B6
   Seamer 98 E6

Y

Yafforth 43 C1
Yarm 5 D3
Yearsley 118 C5
Yedingham 97 D2
Yockenthwaite 81 A1
York...............233 B3
Youlthorpe 169 C2
Youlton.............142 E2

A

Abber La LS24 ....182 A2
Abbeville Ave 1 YO21 ..208 B6
Abbey Cl 12 LS29 ......175 A4
Abbey Crags Way
HG5 ....221 C3
Abbey Gdns WF8 ......201 B2
Abbey Hill BD23 ......155 C5
Abbey Inf Sch DL3 .....3 B5
Abbey Jun Sch DL3 ....3 B5
Abbey La YO22 ....208 E7
Abbey Leisure Ctr
YO8 ....232 C5
Abbey Mews WF8 .....201 B2
Abbey Mill Gdns HG5 ..221 C3
Abbey Mill View HG5 ..221 C3
Abbey Pl 1 YO8 ......233 D5
Abbey Rd Darlington DL3 ..3 B5
Knaresborough HG5 ...221 B3
Sadberge DL2 ....4 C7
Abbey St YO30 ....228 A7
Abbey Terr 16 YO21 ..208 D7
Abbey Wlk
Pontefract WF8 ......201 B2
Selby YO8 ....232 C5
Abbey Wh Sch Ctr
YO8 ....232 C6
Abbey Yd YO8 ....232 C5
Abbeyfield Dr 10 TS16 ..5 D5
Abbot St YO31 ....233 C4
Abbot Rd Selby YO8 ..232 E3
Whitby YO22 ....208 E5
Abbot's Garth YO12 ...99 D6
Abbot's Rd Selby YO8 .232 E3
Abbots Gait YO32 ....225 F6
Abbots Way HG5 .....221 C3
Abbotsford Rd YO10 .228 F3
Abbotsway YO31 .....228 E8
Abbotts Cl LS25 .....194 F8
Abbotts Ct YO17 .....215 E4
Abelton Gr 33 YO32 ..166 E5
Aberbran Ct 41 TS17 ..5 F4
Aberdeen La 10 YO11 213 A6
Aberdeen Pl DL1 .....213 A6
Aberdeen Rd DL1 .....3 B8
Aberdeen St 20 YO11 213 A6
Aberdeen Terr 21 YO11 213 A6
Aberdeen Wlk 16 YO11 213 A6
Aberford CE Prim Sch
LS25 ....194 F8
Aberford Rd
Barwick in Elmet & Scholes
LS15 ....194 C8
Bramham cum Oglethorpe
LS23 ....188 E5
Garforth LS25 ....194 D4
Abrahams Quay YO22 208 E5
Abram's View YO11 ..213 B2
Acacia Ave YO32 ....225 E4
Acacia Dr WF10 .....201 B3
Academy Gdns DL2 ...1 D8
Acaster Ave YO23 ...191 A3
Acaster Dr LS25 .....194 D3
Acaster La
Acaster Malbis YO23 .231 B1
Acaster Selby YO23 ..191 A4
Accommodation Rd
YO25 ....151 D6
Acer Cl 4 BD20 .....187 F7
Acklam Grange Sch TS5 ..6 D7
Acklam Rd TS17 ......6 C8
Acklam Whin Prim Sch
TS5 ....6 D6
Ackton La WF7 ......200 D1
Ackton Pasture La
WF7 ....200 D3
Ackton Pastures Prim Sch
WF10 ....200 D3
Ackworth St 3 YO12 .212 E4
Acomb Prim Sch
YO24 ....227 A3
Acomb Rd YO24 .....227 D3
Acomb Wood Cl YO24 230 C7
Acomb Wood Dr YO24 230 B7
Acorn Cl 8 Barlby YO8 198 B4
Middleton St George DL2 ..4 D4
Acorn Way
Gateforth YO8 ....197 B1
York YO24 ....230 D7
Acre Fold 21 LS29 ...174 F4
Acre Mdw 1 BD22 ...187 B6
Acre Rd 2 BD22 .....187 B6
Acres Cl 24 YO62 ....92 F6
Acres La Brompton YO13 ..98 C4
Helmsley YO62 ....93 A6
Scrayingham YO41 ..169 B8
Acres The
Addingham LS29 .....175 A5
Glusburn BD20 ......187 E6
Stokesley TS9 ....26 C8
Acresfield 6 BB8 ....186 A3
Adam's Field La YO61 117 F4
Adcott Rd TS5 ....6 E7
Addingham Prim Sch
LS29 ....174 F5
Addingham Wharfedale Rd
LS29 ....174 E4
Addison Ave 18 WF6 .200 B1
Addison Rd TS9 ......8 A1
Addison Villas HG3 ..219 A8
Addlethorpe La LS22 179 C3

Adelaide Rd
Middlesbrough TS7 ....7 B6
6 Norton DN6 ....206 E2
Adelaide St 3 YO23 ..228 B2
Adlington Cl 8 YO32 .167 A7
Admirals Ct YO7 .....211 A2
Admirals' Ct YO7 ....211 A2
Agar St YO31 ....233 C3
Agnes Ing La LA2 ...128 A7
Agnesgate HG4 ......214 D5
Aikengill Rd LA2 ....129 A4
Ailcey Rd HG4 ......214 D5
Ainderby Rd DL7 ....210 B2
Ainderby Steeple CE Prim Sch
DL7 ....64 A7
Ainsford Way TS7 ....7 D8
Ainstable Rd TS7 ....7 D8
Ainsty Ave YO24 ....230 F8
Ainsty Dr 2 LS22 ...180 C4
Ainsty Gr YO24 .....230 F8
Ainsty Rd
Harrogate HG1 ......219 F4
Wetherby LS22 ......180 C4
Ainsty View
Acklam YO17 ....169 E8
Whixley YO26 ....164 A4
Ainsworth Way TS7 ..7 D8
Ainthorpe La YO21 ..29 C7
Aintree Ct
9 Darlington DL1 ....3 F6
York YO24 ....230 F8
Aire Cres BD20 .....187 E7
Aire Rd LS22 ....180 B4
Aire St Castleford WF10 200 E4
Glusburn BD20 ......187 F7
Knottingley WF11 ...202 A3
Aire Valley Cl BD20 .173 D3
Aire Valley Dr BD20 .173 D3
Aire Valley Mount
WF10 ....201 A4
Aire View BD23 .....216 C1
Aire View Inf Sch
BD20 ....174 C1
Airedale Ave
Gargrave BD23 ......155 D1
Skipton BD23 ....217 B4
Airedale Dr 8 WF10 .201 B5
Airedale High Sch
WF10
Airedale Inf Sch WF10 201 B4
Airedale Mews 1 BD23 216 E3
Airedale Rd
Castleford WF10 .....201 A4
Scotton DL9 ....40 D4
Airedale Terr 8 BD23 216 E3
Airedale Trading Pk
BD20 ....187 F8
Airedale View 1 BD20 187 F8
Aireside Ave BD20 ..173 D1
Aireside Terr BD20 ..173 D2
Aireville Dr BD20 ...174 C1
Aireville Grange BD23 216 D5
Aireville Sch BD23 ..216 D4
Aireville Swimming Baths
BD23 ....216 D5
Aireyholme La TS9 ...8 B2
Airmyn Pk Prim Sch
DN14 ....205 E4
Airmyn Rd DN14 ....205 D3
Airy Hill DL7 ....208 D5
Airy Hill Com Prim Sch
YO21 ....208 D5
Airy Hill La TS12 ....9 D8
Aiskew Leeming Bar CE Sch
DL7 ....63 C4
Aislabie Cl HG4 .....214 A5
Aislabie Garth HG4 .214 A5
Aislaby Carr La WF10 95 C7
Aislaby La Aislaby YO21 32 A8
Aislaby YO18 ....95 C6
Aislaby Rd TS16 .....5 D4
Aismunderby Cl HG4 214 C3
Aismunderby Rd HG4 214 C4
Aisne Rd DL9 ....209 C1
Aketon Rd WF10 ...200 D1
Alanbrooke Com Prim Sch
YO7 ....89 A1
Alanbrooke Ind Est
DL7 ....115 C8
Alandale Cres LS25 .194 B3
Alandale Rd LS25 ...194 B4
Albany Ave HG1 ....219 E5
Albany Rd
Harrogate HG1 ......219 E5
Middlesbrough TS7 ...7 B6
Albany St 3 YO26 ..227 F5
Albany Wlk LS29 ...218 A3
Albatross Way DL1 ..3 E5
Albemarle Back Rd 10
YO11 ....212 F6
Albemarle Cres 18
YO11 ....213 A6
Albemarle Rd YO23 .228 B2
Albert Dr 8 DL9 .....40 F5
Albert Cl 1 YO32 ...228 F8
Albert Hill
Harrogate HG1 ......220 C4
1 Whitby YO21 .....208 D7
Albert Pl
Eaglescliffe TS16 ....5 E5
12 Glusburn BD20 ..187 E7
Harrogate HG1 ......219 E5
1 Scarborough YO12 213 A7
Albert Simmons Way St 40
LS29 ....176 C1
Albert Sq BD23 .....216 F4
Albert St 33 Earby BB18 172 A1

Albert St continued
Glusburn BD20 ......187 F7
Harrogate HG1 ......219 D2
Normanton South WF6 200 B2
8 Scarborough YO12 213 A7
York YO10 ....233 C1
Albert Terr
5 Harrogate HG1 ...219 D1
Skipton BD23 ....216 F4
Albion Ave YO26 ....227 B6
Albion Cres 3 YO11 213 A4
Albion Pl 14 YO11 ..208 D6
Albion Rd 25 Earby BB18 172 A1
Scarborough YO11 ..213 A4
Albion St Boosbeck TS12 ..9 E7
Boston Spa LS23 ....188 E7
Castleford WF10 ....200 E4
24 Earby BB18 .....172 A1
York YO1 ....233 B1
Albion Terr
8 Boston Spa LS23 .188 E7
25 Whitby YO21 ....208 D6
Alcelina Ct YO23 ...233 B1
Alcuin Ave YO10 ...229 A4
Alcuin Way YO10 ...229 B2
Aldborough Gate 18
YO51 ....141 B4
Aldborough Way YO26 227 F5
Aldborough & Boroughbridge
Com Prim Sch YO51 141 C5
Aldenham Rd TS14 ..8 E5
Alder Ave HG5 ......221 E5
Alder Carr La YO18 .49 E2
Alder Hill St 4 BB18 172 A1
Alder Rd HG1 ....219 F5
Alder Way YO32 ....225 D2
Alderley Ct YO32 ...225 E3
Alderman Leach Prim Sch
DL3 ....3 B6
Alders Rd YO18 .....49 C4
Aldersley Ave BD23 217 B3
Alderson Cres YO12 99 E7
Alderson Rd HG2 ...222 E8
Alderson Sq HG2 ...222 E8
Aldersyde YO24 ....230 E7
Aldersyde Ct YO24 .230 E7
Aldersyde Mews YO24 230 E7
Aldreth Gr YO23 ...228 C2
Aldridge Rd 7 TS18 .5 D8
Aldwark YO1 ....233 C3
Aldwych Cl TS6 .....7 E8
Alexander Ave
8 East Ayton/West Ayton
YO13 ....99 B8
Alexander Cl YO7 ...211 C4
Alexander Rd DL9 ..209 C2
Alexandra Cres 10 LS29 218 B4
Alexandra Ct
Skipton BD23 ....216 F2
York YO10 ....228 E4
Alexandra Gr DL10 .209 C7
Alexandra Pk YO12 .212 D5
Alexandra Pl
Ilkley LS29 ....218 A4
3 Knaresborough HG5 221 B8
Alexandra Rd
Harrogate HG1 ......219 D3
Stensall YO32 ....167 A6
Alexandra Terr BD23 216 F2
Alexandra Ville BD23 216 F2
Alexandra Way DL10 209 C7
Alexandria Dr DL2 ..4 D4
Alfreda Terr 1 YO22 208 E6
Alga Terr YO11 .....213 A4
Algarth Rd YO31 ....229 B7
Algarth Rise YO31 ..229 B7
All Saint's Rd 1 YO12 212 F4
All Saints CE Jun & Inf Sch
WF7 ....200 E1
All Saints RC Sch
HG3 ....179 A4
All Saints' RC Sch
YO24 ....233 A1
Allan St Darlington DL1 ..3 D6
2 York YO30 ....228 C7
Allans Ct YO10 .....209 B6
Allanson Gr YO26 ..227 E2
Allatson Cl WF8 ....206 A3
Allen Cl YO10 ......229 A4
Allen Gr TS9 ....26 B7
Allenby Rd
20 Hemsley YO62 ...92 F6
Hipswell DL9 ....209 C1
Allendale YO24 .....230 D8
Allendale Rd TS7 ...7 D8
Allenson Gr YO31 ..225 F1
Allerby La TS14 .....5 D5
Allensway TS17 .....6 C2
Allerdale Cl YO11 ..211 C4
Allerston La YO18 ..97 C4
Allerton Balk TS15 .5 E2
Allerton Bywater Prim Sch
WF10 ....200 D7
Allerton Dr 22 YO26 165 F1
Allerton La HG5 ....163 D4
Allerton Mews HG1 219 E5
Allerton Pk House*
DL6 ....63 E8
Allerton Sch E House
DL6 ....210 E6
Allerton Wath Rd DL6 65 C4
Allertonshire W House Sch
DL6 ....210 D6
Allhallowgate HG4 .214 C5
Allington Dr YO31 ..229 B6

Allington Way
Darlington DL1 ......3 F5
Great Burdon DL1 ...4 A5
Allison Ave TS17 ....6 B4
Allison St LS14 ......8 E6
Allotments La YO61 143 F3
Alloway Gr TS8 .....6 F5
Alma Gdns HG4 ....214 D4
Alma Gr YO10 .....228 D2
Alma Par 4 YO11 ..212 F5
Alma Pl DL10 ......209 C7
Alma Rd BD8 ....186 B3
Alma Sq 3 YO11 ...212 F5
Alma Terr York YO10 228 D2
York YO10 ....228 D2
Alma Way 2 YO18 ..96 A6
Almery Terr YO30 ..233 A3
Almond Cl 7 Filey YO14 101 B4
Hambleton YO8 .....197 B1
Almond Ct 4 TS14 ..8 F6
Almond Gr 11 Filey YO14 101 B4
Northallerton DL7 ..210 D3
Scarborough YO12 ..212 D5
York YO32 ....225 D4
Almond Tree Ave
Carlton DN14 ....204 C3
Malton YO17 ....215 D6
Almscliffe Dr LS17 .178 B2
Almscliffe Garth LS17 178 B4
Almsford Ave HG2 .222 E5
Almsford Bank HG2 222 E5
Almsford Cl HG2 ...222 F6
Almsford Dr
Harrogate HG2 .....222 F6
York YO26 ....227 C5
Almsford End HG2 .222 E6
Almsford Oval HG2 222 E6
Almsford Pl HG2 ...222 E6
Almsford Rd
Harrogate HG2 .....222 F6
York YO26 ....227 C5
Almsford Wlk HG2 .222 E6
Almshouse Hill 1 LS23 188 E5
Alne CP Sch YO61 .142 F4
Alne Rd
Easingwold YO61 ..143 B8
Tollerton YO61 ....143 A3
Alne Terr YO10 ....228 E2
Alness Dr YO24 ...230 B7
Alpine Ct 5 WF10 .200 F3
Altofts La WF10 ...200 B3
Altofts Rd WF10 ..200 A4
Alum House La TS9 26 D6
Alverton Cl HG2 ...222 F7
Alverton Dr DL3 ...3 B8
Alverton Inf Sch DL6 210 F6
Alverton La DL7 ...210 D4
Alvin Wlk 6 YO41 .185 B2
Alvis Gr YO10 .....231 D8
Alwyn Rd DL3 .....3 D8
Alwyne Dr YO30 ..224 E1
Alwyne Gr YO30 ..224 E1
Amber Ct YO31 ...233 C4
Amber St YO31 ...233 C4
Amberly St 4 YO26 227 E5
Amble Cl YO62 ....70 B2
Ambler St WF10 ..200 E4
Ambler's La YO30 .165 F7
Ambleside Ave
16 Barnoldswick BB18 171 D2
York YO10 ....229 B4
Ambleside Gr TS5 .6 E8
Ambleside Wlk DL1 3 F4
Ambrey Cl 18 YO14 126 F8
Ambrose Rd HG4 ..214 C4
Ambrose St YO10 .228 D1
America La BD20 ..187 F4
Amesbury Cres TS8 6 E5
Amiens Cres 9 DL9 209 D1
Amotherby Com Prim Sch
YO17 ....121 A4
Amotherby La YO17 121 A6
Amplecarr YO61 ...117 B5
Ampleforth Coll YO62 92 C1
Ampleforth Coll Jun Sch
YO62 ....118 F7
Ampleforth St Benedicts RC
Prim Sch YO62 ....92 C1
Amy Johnson Way
YO30 ....225 A3
Anchor Rd 2 HG1 .220 A3
Anchorage Hill DL10 209 D8
Anchorage La DL7 .210 C5
Anchorage Way YO21 208 C5
Anchorite La 7 YO10 95 F7
Ancress Wlk YO23 .233 A1
Ancroft Cl YO1 ....233 C1
Anderson Gr 8 YO24 227 F2
Anderson St WF6 .200 A1
Anderton St 6 BB18 187 E8
Andrew Dr 4 YO32 225 F1
Andrew La YO10 ..71 B4
Anfield Ct 8 DL1 ..3 F6
Angel Ct YO1 .....233 B2
Angel Yd 8 YO12 .208 D6
Angelica Ct 12 HG3 161 B3
Angram Cl YO30 ..224 F1
Angram La
Barlby with Osgodby
YO19 ....198 A6
Muker DL11 ....35 E6
Tollerton YO61 ...143 B3
Angram Rd YO26 .182 A5
Angrove Ct TS9 ...7 F1
Angrove Dr TS9 ..7 F1
Annan Cl YO24 ...230 C6

Annandale Ct 10 LS29 218 B4
Annandale Gr 1 YO11 75 D5
Annas Garth DL8 ...60 F4
Anne St TS17 ......6 B4
Annie St YO8 ......232 C6
Annumhills Rd YO8 199 D7
Anserdale La YO62 70 E5
Anson Croft 5 YO8 196 E1
Anson Dr YO10 ...231 D8
Anteforth View DL10 20 E3
Anthea Dr YO31 ..225 E1
Anthony La HG4 ..114 E1
Anvil Sq 2 DL11 ..38 B6
Anvil Way DL7 ....22 C2
Anzio Rd DL9 .....209 C1
Apedale Rd
Castle Bolton with East &
West Bolton DL8 ...37 F1
Redmire DL8 ......59 C8
Apley Cl HG2 .....220 A1
Apollo St 9 YO10 .228 E3
Apple Garth
16 Easingwold YO61 117 D1
18 Poppleton YO26 165 F1
Apple Tree Gdns 2
LS29 ....175 C2
Apple Tree La 4 LS25 194 D1
Apple Tree Mews 5
LS25 ....194 D1
Apple Tree Wlk 8 LS25 194 D1
Appleby Ave HG5 .220 D8
Appleby Cres HG5 .220 D8
Appleby Ct HG5 ..220 D8
Appleby Gate HG5 220 D7
Appleby Glade YO32 225 D7
Appleby Gr HG5 ..220 D8
Appleby La
Aldbrough DL11 ..1 F1
Kirkby Malzeard HG4 112 B4
Appleby Pl 3 YO31 229 A5
Appleby Way HG5 .220 D7
Appleby Wlk HG5 .220 D7
Applecroft Rd
Selby YO8 ....232 A4
York YO31 ....229 B7
Applefields Sch YO31 229 B5
Applegarth
Barnoldswick BB18 171 E2
Coulby Newham TS8 7 A4
Applegarth Ct DL7 210 D5
Applegarth Prim Sch
DL7 ....210 D4
Applegarth St 18 BB18 172 A1
Applegarth La YO23 230 F3
Appleton La
Appleton-le-Street with
Easthorpe YO17 ...120 F4
Coneysthorpe YO60 120 E2
Appleton Rd YO23 .231 A3
Appleton Roebuck Prim Sch
1 YO23 ....190 F5
Appleton Wiske Com Prim
Sch DL6 ....24 B3
Appletree Dr YO8 .196 E1
Appletree Way
Malton YO17 ......215 B4
16 Sherburn in Elmet LS25 195 F4
Appletreewick Stone Circ*
BD23 ....135 E2
Appley Cl TS16 ...5 E7
Apron La HG3 ....140 B2
Apsley Way TS17 .5 F5
Arbour The
2 Glusburn BD20 .173 E1
Ilkley LS29 ....218 A6
Arbour Way YO17 215 E4
ARC* YO1 ....233 C2
Arc The LS29 ....218 B4
Arcade Sh Ctr* HG4 214 C5
Archbishop Holgate's Sch
YO10 ....229 B3
Archbishop of York CE Jun
Sch YO23 ....231 A4
Archer La HG3 ...140 B3
Archers Gn The DL10 41 C7
Archers Mdw HG5 221 F5
Archie St 8 HG1 .220 C5
Arden Cl DL7 ....210 D5
Arden La YO62 ..92 B8
Arden Mews DL7 210 D5
Arena View 12 DL10 41 D5
Arenhall Cl 2 YO32 225 C8
Argam Dikes* YO25 127 B2
Argam La YO25 ..127 D3
Argill 3 DL8 ......60 F5
Argyle Rd YO21 .208 C7
Argyle St YO23 ..228 B1
Arkendale La HG5 141 A2
Arkendale Rd HG5 162 F8
Arkengarthdale CE Prim Sch
DL11 ....17 D1
Arkengarthdale Rd
DL11 ....38 B7
Arkle Cres DL1 ...3 C3
Arlington Rd
Middlesbrough TS5 6 F8
York YO30 ....225 A1
Armoury Rd YO8 232 B5
Armstrong Ct 7 WF6 200 A2
Armstrong Way DL7 226 E3
Army Foundation Coll
HG2 ....161 A2
Arncliffe CE VC Prim Sch
BD23 ....107 D2
Arncliffe Dr WF11 .201 D2
Arncliffe Rd HG2 ..220 A1

Ardnale Way **8** YO14 ....101 B4
Arnold Rd DL1 ....3 E6
Arnside Cres WF10 ....201 B4
Arnside Pl **2** YO10 ....228 F3
Arran Ct DL25 ....194 C3
Arran Dr DL25 ....194 C3
Arran Pl YO31 ....228 D7
Arrows Cres **10** YO51 ..141 B5
Arrows Terr **9** YO51 ....141 B5
Art Ctr The* YO22 ....208 E7
Arthington Ave HG1 ....219 E2
Arthur Pl **6** YO30 ....224 B5
Arthur St
  8 Barnoldswick BB18 ..171 D2
  Earby BB18 ....186 A8
  Great Ayton TS9 ....8 E2
  York YO10 ....228 E4
Arthurs Ave HG2 ....222 C7
Arthurs Cl HG2 ....222 C7
Arthurs Gr HG2 ....222 C7
Arundel Ct TS17 ....5 F6
Arundel Gr YO24 ....230 C7
Arundel Pl
  12 Scarborough YO11 ..212 F5
  2 Whitby YO21 ....208 C6
Arundel Rd **4** DN6 ....206 E2
Ascot Rd DL25 ....194 C1
Ascot Way YO14 ....227 D1
Ascough Wynd DL8 ....63 D3
Ash Bank Ave HG4 ......113 D2
Ash Bank Cl **1** HG4 ..113 D2
Ash Bank Rd HG4 ....113 D2
Ash Cl **1** Ilkley LS29 ..175 C2
  Newton on Derwent
    YO41 ....185 E4
  York YO31 ....229 B7
Ash Croft **7** DL10 .....41 D5
Ash Gn TS8 ....7 A4
Ash Gr
  18 Barnoldswick BB18 ..171 D1
  Danby YO21 ....29 A6
  12 Filey YO14 ....101 B4
  Glusburn BD20 ....187 E7
  1 Ilkley LS29 ....218 C5
  1 Kirkbymoorside YO62 ..70 B1
  1 Kirklevington TS15 ....24 E8
  Northallerton DL6 ......210 F5
  1 Riccall YO19 ....197 F8
  Ripon HG4 ....214 A6
  Scarborough YO12 ......212 C7
  Whitby YO21 ....208 B6
Ash Hill TS8 ....7 B5
Ash La
  Church Fenton LS24 ....196 B6
  Garforth LS25 ....194 D4
  1 Haxby YO32 ....166 E5
  Little Fenton LS25 .....196 C5
Ash Lea Danby YO21 .....29 A6
  Fairburn WF11 ....201 D6
Ash Rd **15** Filey YO14 ..101 B4
  Guisborough TS14 ....8 F7
  Harrogate HG2 ....220 E3
Ash Ridge **3** DL6 ......210 E3
Ash St **11** Glusburn BD20 ..187 E7
  Ilkley LS29 ....218 C5
  Trawden BB8 ....186 B1
  York YO26 ....227 E4
Ash Tree Cl DL8 ....62 F2
Ash Tree Garth LS24 ....195 E7
Ash Tree Rd
  8 Bedale DL8 ....63 A2
  Knaresborough HG5 ....221 B6
Ash View HG2 ....222 B6
Ashbank La Filey YO14 ..62 F1
  Sheriff Hutton YO60 ...145 F6
Ashberry Nature Reserve*
  YO62 ....92 B7
Ashbourne Cl **12** YO51 ..141 B4
Ashbourne Rd **10** YO51 ..141 B4
Ashbourne Way YO24 ..230 C8
Ashburn Pl LS29 ....218 A3
Ashburn Rise **10** YO11 ..212 E4
Ashburn Way LS22 .....180 B4
Ashburnham **4** DN6 ..206 F2
Ashburnham Wlk **5**
  DN6 ....206 F2
Ashdale Cl DL2 ....4 E4
Ashdale La LS22 ....180 B4
Ashdale Rd
  10 Dunnington YO19 ..184 F7
  Helmsley YO62 ....92 B8
Ashdene Gr WF8 ....201 D2
Ashdown Rise YO13 .....75 C8
Ashdowne Cl DL8 ....62 E5
Ashdowne Ct DL8 ....62 E5
Ashes The DL10 ....21 C7
Ashfield
  2 Grassington BD23 ..134 E3
  Wetherby LS22 ....180 C3
Ashfield Ave YO17 .....215 D5
Ashfield Cl
  2 Constable Burton DL8 ..61 C5
  2 Pateley Bridge HG3 ..137 B4
Ashfield Ct YO24 ....230 E7
Ashfield Ct Rd **10** HG3 ..137 B4
Ashfield Rd Danby YO21 ..29 A6
  Harrogate HG1 ....219 B2
  6 Pickering YO18 ......96 A6
  3 Selby WF6 ....200 A2
Ashfield Terr
  Harrogate HG1 ....219 A4
  Skipton BD23 ....216 F2
Ashford Ave TS5 ....6 D8
Ashford Pl YO24 ....227 D2
Ashgap La WF6 ....200 A2
Ashgarth Cl HG2 ....222 C5
Ashgarth Way HG2 .....222 C5

Ashgrove BD23 ....216 E4
Ashgrove Cres LS25 ....194 D2
Ashlands Cl DL6 ....210 F4
Ashlands Dr DL6 ....210 F4
Ashlands Dr **2** DL6 ....63 C5
Ashlands Prim Sch
  LS29 ....218 C5
Ashlands Rd
  Ilkley LS29 ....218 C5
  Northallerton DL6 .....210 F4
Ashlea Cl YO8 ....232 D4
Ashlea Rd DL2 ....210 D4
Ashley Ct **2** YO14 ....101 B3
Ashley Pk Cres YO31 ..229 B6
Ashley Pk Rd YO31 ....229 B7
Ashmead **4** LS23 .....188 E7
Ashmeade Cl YO24 ....230 B8
Ashney Ave YO30 ......228 B8
Ashton Cl BD23 ....154 B3
Ashton Rd WF10 ....200 E3
Ashtree Dr YO8 ....197 D1
Ashville Ave
  Eaglescliffe TS16 ....5 E6
  Scarborough YO12 .....212 F6
Ashville Cl HG2 ....222 C5
Ashville Coll HG2 ......222 B6
Ashville Dr **9** DL2 .....22 E8
Ashville Gr HG2 ....222 C5
Ashville St YO31 ....228 D7
Ashwood Cl **5** YO62 ..92 F7
Ashwood Dr TS9 ....26 C8
Ashwood Glade YO62 ..92 F7
Ashwood Pl HG5 ....221 E5
Ashworth Rd WF8 .....201 C2
Askam Ave WF8 ....201 C2
Aske Ave DL10 ....209 E8
Aske Hall* DL10 ....20 D2
Askern & Campsall Sports Ctr
  DN6 ....206 F1
Askew Dale TS14 ....8 D6
Askew Rigg La YO18 ....71 A5
Askham Bog Nature
  Reserve** YO23 ......230 C5
Askham Bryan YO23 ...182 F2
Askham Bryan Coll Harrogate
  Ctr HG2 ....223 A7
Askham Bryan La
  YO23 ....230 A6
Askham Croft **1** YO24 ..227 B1
Askham Fields La
  YO23 ....182 F2
Askham La **2** YO24 ..227 B2
Askrigg Prim Sch DL8 ..57 E5
Askwith Com Prim Sch
  LS21 ....176 D3
Askwith La LS21 ....176 D3
Askwith Moor Rd
  LS21 ....176 D5

Aspen Cl
  3 Dunnington YO19 ..184 F7
  Pickering YO18 ....95 F7
  Selby YO8 ....197 D2
Aspen Way
  Slingsby YO62 ....120 B5
  Tadcaster LS24 ....189 D6
Aspin Ave HG5 ....221 B4
Aspin Chase HG5 ......221 B4
Aspin Dr HG5 ....221 C4
Aspin Gdns HG5 ....221 C4
Aspin Gr **4** HG5 ......221 C3
Aspin La HG5 ....221 C3
Aspin Oval HG5 ....221 B4
Aspin Pk Ave **1** HG5 ..221 C4
Aspin Pk Com Prim Sch
  HG5 ....221 B4
Aspin Pk Cres HG5 ....221 B4
Aspin Pk Dr HG5 ......221 B4
Aspin Pk La HG5 ......221 C4
Aspin Pk Rd HG5 ......221 C3
Aspin View HG5 ....221 C4
Aspin Way HG5 ....221 C4
Aspinall Rise **8** BD23 ..154 B3
Asquith Ave
  Scarborough YO12 ....212 E3
  York YO31 ....229 A5
Assembly St **7** WF6 ..200 A1
Astbury TS8 ....7 C4
Asterley Dr TS5 ....6 D8
Astley Ave LS26 ....194 A1
Astley La
  Great & Little Preston
    LS26 ....200 B8
  Swillington LS26 ......194 A1
Astley La Ind Pk LS26 ..200 B8
Astley Way LS26 ......200 A8
Atcherley Cl YO10 ....231 D8
Athelstan Com Prim Sch
  LS25 ....195 F3
Athelstan Cl LS21 .....177 A1
Athelstans Ct LS25 ....195 F4
Athol Sq YO17 ....215 C4
Atkinson Ave DL10 ....209 D8
Atkinson Ct WF6 ......200 A1
Atkinson La WF8 ......201 C1
Atlantis Wr Pk* YO12 ..212 F8
Atlas Rd YO30 ....225 A3
Atlas Wynd TS16 ....5 E3
Attermire Cave*
  BD24 ....132 A3
Atterwith La YO26 ....182 A7
Auborough St **5** YO11 ..213 A6

Auckland Ave DL3 ....3 B6
Auckland Oval DL3 ......3 B6
Auckland St TS14 ....8 F7
Audax Way **2** YO21 ..208 C6
Aucuba Cl YO17 ....225 D2
Audax Cl YO30 ....225 A3
Audax Rd YO30 ....225 A3
Audby La LS22 ....180 C4
Audus St **10** YO8 ....232 C5
Augusta Cl DL1 ....3 D5
Aumit La YO62 ....92 E1
Aunums Cl **8** YO10 ....96 D5
Auster Bank Ave LS25 ..189 F7
Auster Bank Cres
  LS24 ....189 F7
Auster Bank Rd LS24 ..189 F7
Auster Bank View
  LS24 ....189 F7
Auster Rd YO30 ....225 B3
Austfield La LS25 ......202 B8
Austin Dr DL9 ....41 A5
Austin Rd WF10 ....201 B4
Austwick CE Prim Sch
  BD24 ....130 E7
Austwick Rd DL2 ......131 C8
Autumn Ave **8** LS22 ..8 C4
Ava Rd DL9 ....40 C4
Avalon Ct TS8 ....6 E5
Avens Way TS17 ....6 A5
Avenue A LS23 ....181 A2
Avenue B LS23 ....181 A1
Avenue Bank HG4 ....86 C4
Avenue C E LS23 ......181 B1
Avenue C W LS23 .....181 A1
Avenue Cl HG2 ....220 D4
Avenue D LS23 ....181 A1
Avenue E E LS23 ......181 B1
Avenue E W LS23 .....189 A8
Avenue G LS23 ....181 B1
Avenue Gr **11** HG2 ..220 D3
Avenue House Cl HG5 ..162 F3
Avenue P **1** HG2 ....220 C3
Avenue Prim Sch The
  TS7 ....7 D6
Avenue Rd
  Harrogate HG2 ....220 C3
  Scarborough YO12 ....212 E4
  York YO30 ....233 A4
Avenue St **8** HG2 ....220 C3
Avenue Terr
  5 Harrogate HG2 ....220 C3
  York YO30 ....233 A4
Avenue The
  Campsall DN6 ....206 E1
  Collingham LS22 ......180 A1
  Dalby-cum-Skewsby
    YO60 ....119 B2
  Eaglescliffe TS16 ....5 E6
  26 Filey YO14 ....101 B3
  Gilling East YO62 .....118 E7
  Great Ribston with Walshford
    LS22 ....180 C8
  Guisborough TS14 ......8 D6
  Harrogate HG1 ....220 C4
  5 Haxby YO32 ......166 D5
  Knaresborough HG5 ..221 A7
  Masham HG4 ....86 C3
  Middlesbrough TS5 ....6 F8
  Norton YO17 ....215 C2
  Nun Monkton YO26 ..165 A4
  Nunnington YO62 .....93 E1
  6 Pateley Bridge HG3 ..137 C4
  Richmond DL10 ....209 C7
  Rufforth YO23 ....182 C6
  Skipton BD23 ....217 B6
  Skutterskelfe TS15 ....25 E6
  1 Sleights YO22 ......32 A6
  Snape with Thorp DL8 ..87 A7
  South Milford LS25 ...195 F2
  Stainton Dale YO13 ....54 A8
  Stokesley TS9 ....26 C7
  Thirkleby High & Low
    with Osgodby YO7 ..116 D8
  West Hauxwell DL8 ....61 C8
  Whitby YO21 ....208 B4
  Wighill LS24 ....181 D2
  York YO19 ....228 A6
Avenue Victoria YO11 ..213 A3
Aviation Rd LS25 .....196 A4
Aviator Ct YO30 ......224 F3
Aviemore Ct **10** DL1 ..3 F6
Aviemore Rd TS8 ....6 F5
Avocet Cres **11** YO12 ..99 F6
Avon Dr
  Barnoldswick BB18 ...171 E2
  Guisborough TS14 ......8 E6
  York YO32 ....225 F6
Avon Garth LS22 .....180 B3
Avon Rd **2** DL2 ......22 D8
Avondale Rd HG1 .....219 F4
Avro Cl TS18 ....5 F7
Awnhams La YO42 ....169 D2
Axminster Rd TS8 ......6 F5
Axton Cl TS17 ....6 A6
Aylesham Ct YO30 ....225 E3
Aylton Dr TS5 ....6 E6
Aynham Cl **2** BD23 ..3 D4
Aynholme Cl DL8 .....60 E2
Aynholme Dr **1** LS29 ..174 F4
Ayresome Way **1** TS5 ..6 E6
Aysgarth Falls* DL8 ...58 F3
Aysgarth Gr DL7 ......210 B2
Aysgarth Rd DL1 ....3 D4
Aysgarth Sch DL8 ......62 A4
Ayton Castle* YO13 ...99 A8
Ayton Rd YO12 ....99 C7
Azerley Gr HG3 ....219 A4

Azerley La HG4 ....112 F3

B

Babyhouse La BD20 ...173 A1
Bachelor Ave HG1 ....219 D7
Bachelor Dr HG1 ......219 D7
Bachelor Gdns HG1 ..219 D6
Bachelor Hill YO24 ...227 D2
Bachelor Rd HG1 .....219 D7
Bachelor Way HG1 ...219 D6
Back Ave Victoria **2**
  YO11 ....213 A3
Back Beck La LS29 ....174 F4
Back Bridge St BD23 ..216 F4
Back Cheltenham Mount
  HG1 ....219 D3
Back Colne Rd **9** BD20 ..187 E7
Back Dawson Terr
  HG1 ....219 D5
Back Dragon Par HG1 ..219 D3
Back Dragon Rd HG1 ..219 D3
Back Elmwood St **3**
  HG1 ....219 E4
Back Gate LA6 ....103 D3
Back Gladstone St
  HG1 ....222 D7
Back Gn BD23 ....153 F5
Back Gr Rd LS29 .....218 B4
Back Grange Ave HG1 ..219 D5
Back High St **3** HG3 ..137 B4
Back La
  Acaster Selby YO23 ...191 B3
  Airton BD23 ....155 A6
  Askew DL7 ....63 C5
  Aike YO61 ....142 F4
  Ampleforth YO62 ......92 C1
  Appleton Roebuck YO23 ..191 A5
  Appleton-le-Moors YO62 ..70 F2
  Asselby DN14 ....205 D6
  Bagby YO7 ....90 B3
  Barkston Ash LS24 ...195 F6
  Barlby with Osgodby
    YO8 ....198 C4
  Barton DL10 ....21 C7
  Barton-le-Street YO17 ..120 E5
  1 Bedale DL8 ....182 D1
  Birstwith HG3 ....160 D5
  Bolton-on-Swale DL10 ..41 E5
  7 Boroughbridge YO51 ..141 B5
  Borrowby YO7 ....65 E4
  Bradleys Both BD20 ..173 E4
  10 Brafferton YO61 ..115 F1
  Bramham LS23 ....188 E6
  Burley in Warfedale
    LS29 ....176 C1
  Carlton Miniott YO7 ...89 B3
  Carthorpe DL8 ....87 E7
  Cold Kirby YO7 ....91 C6
  Copmanthorpe YO23 ..230 A2
  Cost Henwick HG4 ....114 B2
  Cottingwith YO42 ....193 C5
  Crakehall DL8 ....62 E4
  Crathorne TS15 ....24 F6
  Dalton YO7 ....115 A4
  Dishforth YO7 ....115 A4
  Drax YO8 ....204 F5
  Eaglescliffe TS16 ....5 E4
  Easingwold YO61 .....117 D1
  East Tanfield DL8 ......87 D2
  Ebberston & Yedingham
    YO13 ....97 D5
  Ellerton YO42 ....193 C1
  Fewston HG3 ....159 F1
  Flaxton YO60 ....145 F1
  Giggleswick BD24 ....130 F2
  Great & Little Broughton
    TS9 ....26 E5
  Great Ouseburn YO26 ..164 A8
  Great Preston WF10 ..200 D6
  Gristthorpe YO14 ....100 E5
  Guisborough TS9 ....8 A4
  Hambleton YO8 ......196 F1
  Harome YO62 ....93 C5
  Hawsker-cum-Stainsacre
    YO22 ....32 F5
  11 Haxby YO32 ......166 D5
  Hebden BD23 ....135 A2
  Hellifield BD23 ......154 B3
  Hemingbrough YO8 ...198 F1
  Hetton BD23 ....135 F5
  Hirst Courtney YO8 ...203 F4
  Holtby YO19 ....184 E8
  Hunsingore LS22 ....180 E8
  Hutton-le-Hole YO62 ..70 C4
  Huttons Ambo YO60 ..147 B7
  Kirby Wiske YO7 ......88 E7
  Kirkby Malham BD23 ..154 F8
  Kirkby Malzeard HG4 ..112 D5
  Lockton YO18 ....72 E4
  Long Preston BD23 ...153 F5
  Longnewton TS21 ......4 F8
  Low Coniscliffe & Merrybent
    DL2 ....2 E4
  Low Worsall TS15 .....24 D7
  Luttons YO17 ....150 B8
  Malham BD23 ....132 F2
  Markington with Wallerthwaite
    HG3 ....139 C3
  Marton YO62 ....94 F5
  Marton cum Grafton
    YO51 ....141 D1
  Melmerby HG4 ....114 B7
  1 Middleham DL8 .....60 E2
  Morton-on-Swale DL7 ..64 A6
  Moulton DL10 ....21 D4

Back La continued
  Newby Wiske DL7 ......64 D3
  Newholm-cum-Dunsley
    YO21 ....13 A1
  Newton-on-Ouse YO30 ..165 B6
  North Cowton DL7 .....22 B3
  North Duffield YO8 ...199 A7
  Norton DN6 ....206 E2
  Osmotherley DL6 ......45 B4
  Raskelf YO61 ....116 F2
  Rathmell BD24 ....153 C6
  Reeth, Fremington & Healaugh
    DL11 ....38 B6
  2 Riccall YO19 ......198 A8
  Rookwith HG4 ....86 A8
  Scorton DL10 ....41 E6
  Settrington YO17 .....148 D8
  Sicklinghall LS22 ....179 E3
  Sinnington YO62 ......95 A8
  Sutton-under-Whitestonecliffe
    YO7 ....90 E5
  Thirkleby High & Low
    with Osgodby YO7 ..116 D8
  Thirsk YO7 ....211 B1
  Tholthorpe YO61 .....142 D5
  Thormanby YO61 .....116 F6
  Thornton Steward DL8 ..61 C2
  Topcliffe YO7 ....115 C7
  Trawden BB8 ....186 A1
  Tunstall DL10 ....102 A4
  Weaverthorpe YO17 ..124 E1
  Weeton LS17 ....178 C2
  Wennington LA2 ......102 C2
  West Tanfield HG4 .....87 A1
  West Witton DL8 ......59 C4
  Westerdale YO21 ......35 A5
  Whixley YO26 ....164 A3
  Whorlton DL6 ....45 D8
  Wilberfoss YO41 .....185 F5
  Wold Newton YO25 ...126 A4
  Wombleton YO62 ......93 E7
  Wray-with-Botton LA2 ..128 A6
  York YO26 ....227 A5
Back La S
  Middleton YO18 ....95 E8
  Wheldrake YO19 .....192 F7
Back Middleton Rd **1**
  LS29 ....218 A4
Back Newton La
  WF10 ....201 A7
Back Nook **1** DL8 ....58 F1
Back Northgate WF8 ..201 B1
Back O' Newton YO41 ..185 E3
Back of Parks Rd YO62 ..70 C2
Back of the Beck **5**
  BD23 ....216 F4
Back Parish Ghyll Rd **8**
  LS29 ....218 B4
Back Pk St YO8 ......232 D5
Back Rd Birstwith HG3 ..160 B5
  Thormanby YO61 .....116 F5
Back Regent Pl **4** HG1 ..220 C4
Back Royal Par **5** HG1 ..219 C2
Back Sea View YO14 ..101 C1
Back Side YO17 ....149 B5
Back St
  Boroughbridge YO51 ..141 C5
  Bramham LS23 ....188 E6
  Burton Fleming YO25 ..126 E3
  Langtoft YO25 ....151 D5
  10 Middleham DL8 ....60 E2
  Wold Newton YO25 ...126 A4
Back St Hilda's Terr
  YO21 ....208 D7
Back Sta Rd **17** BD20 ..187 E8
Back Syke DL8 ....57 D5
Back Tewit Well Rd
  HG2 ....222 E8
Back W View **2** YO30 ..228 B7
Back Weston Rd **5**
  LS29 ....218 B4
Back York Pl **1** HG1 ..219 C2
Backhouse St YO31 ...233 B4
Backside La YO8 ....93 E6
Backstone La LS29 ....218 C3
Backstone Way LS29 ..218 C4
Bacon Ave WF6 ....200 B2
Bad Bargain La YO31 ..229 A5
Baden Cl TS17 ....6 B6
Bader Prim Sch TS17 ..6 B6
Badger Butt La BD23 ..155 B5
Badger Cl BD23 ......134 D3
Badger Gate **33** LS29 ..175 C2
Badger Hill Dr **14** DL8 ..63 B3
Badger Hill Prim Sch
  YO10 ....229 B2
Badger La DN6 ....207 A3
Badger Paddock **3**
  YO31 ....225 E2
Badger Wood Glade
  YO10 ....229 D3
Badgerbeck Rd **2** DL8 ..209 B1
Badgers Gate LS29 ...175 C6
Badminton Ct **18** DL1 ..3 F6
Baek Chapel St **24** BB18 ..171 D1
Baffam Gdns YO8 ....232 B2
Baffam La YO8 ....232 B2
Bagby La YO7 ....90 B2
Bagdale YO21 ....208 C6
Bagdale Ct YO21 .....208 D6

Baghill La WF8 ....201 C1
Baildon Ave LS25 ....194 D2
Baildon Cl 3 YO26 ....227 C4
Baile Hill Terr YO1 ....233 B1
Bailey Ct DL7 ....210 C4
Bailey La BD23 ....152 E3
Bailey St BB18 ....172 E1
Bailey The BD23 ....217 A4
Bainbridge CE Prim Sch DL8 .....57 D5
Bainbridge Dr YO8 ....232 C4
Bairnswood Sch YO12 ..212 B6
Baker St
Appleton Wiske DL6 ......24 A3
York YO30 ....228 C7
Bakersfield Dr DN14 ....202 F3
Bakewell Mews 6 DL3 ..3 A7
Bala Cl 2 TS17 ....5 F4
Baldersby Garth
Baldersby YO7 ....88 D1
Rainton YO7 ....114 F6
Baldersby St James CE VC Prim Sch YO7 ....114 E7
Baldersdale Ave 1 HG5 ...221 D5
Baldoon Sands TS5 ......6 D6
Baldwin St 4 HG1 ....219 C5
Balfour St YO26 ....227 F5
Balfour Terr TS5 ....6 D8
Balfour Way YO32 ....167 A6
Baliol Croft TS21 ....5 A7
Balk La DN14 ....207 F7
Balk The
Bishop Wilton YO41 ......169 C2
Marton-le-Moor HG4 ....114 E1
Slingsby YO62 ....120 B5
Balk Top YO7 ....115 B1
Balkscyde YO62 ....120 B5
Ball Gr Dr BB8 ....186 A3
Ballhall La YO42 ....193 E6
Balmer Hill DL2 ....1 C8
Balmoral Ave TS17 ......6 C8
Balmoral Dr LS26 ....200 B6
Balmoral Rd
Barmpton DL1 ....3 E8
Lingdale TS12 ....9 F6
Middlesbrough TS5 ......7 C8
Ripon HG4 ....214 C3
Balmoral Terr 5 YO23 ..228 B1
Balne Hall Rd DN14 ....207 F5
Balne Moor Rd DN14 ..207 B6
Balshaw Rd LA2 ....129 B3
Baltimore Way DL1 ......3 D7
Bamburgh Ct TS17 ......5 F5
Banbury Rd WF8 ....201 C2
Bancroft Fold 8 BB18 ..171 D1
Bancroft Steam Mus* BB18 ....171 D1
Bands La DL8 ....56 C4
Bank Bottom LA6 ....103 C3
Bank Cl 2 YO22 ....32 A6
Bank Dike Hill HG3 ......159 A4
Bank Hall Cl LA6 ....103 D4
Bank House La LA6 ......103 B5
Bank La Egton YO21 ....30 E5
Faceby TS9 ....25 F1
Grassington BD23 ....134 E3
Great & Little Broughton TS9 ....26 F3
Silsden BD20 ....174 C4
Bank Rd Glusburn BD20 ..187 E8
Selby YO8 ....232 D6
Bank Side
2 Eastfield YO11 ....100 A7
Rawcliffe DN14 ....205 A2
Bank St
2 Eastfield YO11 ....100 A7
Castleford WF10 ....200 E4
1 Wetherby LS22 ....180 C3
Bank The DL10 ....41 D4
Bank Top LA6 ....103 D3
Bank Top La 4 TS13 ....12 A7
Bank Wood Rd WF4 ....206 A6
Bank Yd DL10 ....209 C6
Bankfield La DN14 ....205 A7
Bankfield St BB8 ....186 A2
Bankhead Cl DL6 ....210 F4
Bankhead Rd DL6 ....210 F4
Banklands Ave BD20 ....174 C1
Banklands La BD20 ......174 C1
Banks Bridge Cl BB18 ..174 F3
Banks Hill 1 BB18 ....171 D1
Banks La DL10 ....41 E2
Banks Rd Brompton DL6 ..44 A2
Darlington DL1 ....3 E6
Banksfields Ct TS6 ......7 F8
Bankside Cl
3 Poppleton YO26 ....165 F1
Thirsk YO7 ....211 D2
Bankwell Rd BD24 ......131 D2
Bannisdale 6 YO24 ......230 C7
Bannister Cl BB8 ....186 B2
Bannister Wlk BD22 ....187 A6
Banqueting House* LS21 ....176 D1
Bar Convent Mus* YO24 ....233 A1
Bar Knotts Terr YO17 ..215 C3
Bar La
Bramham cum Oglethorpe LS23 ....188 F7
Garforth LS25 ....194 D4
Hambleton YO8 ....196 E1
Knaresborough HG5 ....162 D5
Roecliffe YO51 ....141 A5

Bar La continued
York YO1 ....233 A2
Bar Pl HG1 ....219 D5
Bar St YO11 ....213 A6
Bar The 6 DL10 ....209 C6
Barbara Gr 4 YO24 ......227 F3
Barbeck YO7 ....211 C3
Barbeck Cl YO7 ....211 D3
Barberry YO7 ....7 B4
Barberry Cl Ingleby TS17 ..6 B5
20 Killinghall HG3 ....161 B3
Barbers Dr YO23 ....230 B4
Barbican Ct YO10 ....233 C1
Barbican Mews YO10 ..228 E3
Barbican Rd YO10 ......233 C1
Barbondale Gr HG5 ......221 C5
Barbondale Rd LA10 ....77 A7
Bardale Cl 2 HG5 ....221 D6
Barden Ct 6 YO30 ......224 F1
Barden Fell View 3 BD23 ....134 E2
Barden La DL8 ....40 B1
Barden Moor Rd DL1 ..3 E4
Barden Pl YO14 ....101 A3
Barden Rd BD23 ....157 A1
Barden Twr* BD23 ......157 C4
Bardney Rd YO14 ....126 F8
Bardsley Cl TS16 ....5 E7
Barefoot St HG4 ....214 C4
Barff Bank DL8 ....61 A2
Barff La YO41 ....169 D4
Barff Gr 16 YO8 ....197 D1
Barff Gr 6 YO8 ....197 B2
Barff La YO8 ....197 C1
Barff View YO8 ....203 D7
Barfield Rd YO31 ....228 F8
Bargate DL10 ....209 B6
Bark House La 1 LA2 ..131 B8
Bark La
Addingham LS29 ....175 A5
Embsay with Eastby BD23 ....157 A1
Barker Bsns Pk HG4 ....114 C6
Barker Dr YO8 ....232 B6
Barker La YO1 ....233 A2
Barker's La
Newholm-cum-Dunsley YO21 ....13 A1
Snainton YO13 ....98 A4
Barkery The 7 YO8 ......7 B3
Barkhouse Bank HG3 ..138 F4
Barkhouse Wood La WF11 ....202 D6
Barkston Ash Cath Prim Sch LS24 ....195 E7
Barkston Ave 1 YO26 ..227 B3
Barkston Cl 3 YO26 ....227 A3
Barkston Gr YO26 ....227 A3
Barkston Rd YO26 ......227 B3
Barlby Bridge CP Sch YO8 ....232 D5
Barlby By-pass 2 YO8 ..198 B4
Barlby CP Sch YO8 ....198 B4
Barlby Cres YO8 ....232 F7
Barlby High Sch YO8 ..198 B5
Barlby Rd YO8 ....232 E6
Barley Cl YO17 ....215 D3
Barley Hall* YO1 ....233 B3
Barley Horn Rd LS24 ..190 B2
Barley Rise YO32 ....167 A6
Barleycorn Yd YO1 ......233 C2
Barleyfields La LS22 ....211 C1
Barleyfields Rd 4 LS22 ..180 C3
Barleyfields Rd 4 LS22 ..180 C3
Barleyhill Rd LS25 ......194 B4
Barley's Yd YO7 ....211 B3
Barlow CE VC Prim Sch YO8 ....204 C7
Barlow Cl TS14 ....8 F6
Barlow Common Nature Reserve* YO8 ....204 B7
Barlow Comm Rd YO8 ..204 B8
Barlow Rd YO8 ....204 B6
Barlow St YO26 ....227 D4
Barmby Ave YO10 ......231 E8
Barmby Cl YO30 ....224 F1
Barmby Ferry Rd 1 YO8 ....198 F1
Barmby on the Marsh Prim Sch DN14 ....205 B7
Barmoor Cl YO13 ....75 D6
Barmoor Gn YO13 ......75 C6
Barmpton La DL1 ....3 F7
Barn Field Cl BB8 ....186 A3
Barnaby Pl TS14 ....8 E7
Barnard La YO13 ....98 C4
Barnard's Rd YO21 ......31 A4
Barnbow La LS15 ....194 A6
Barnes Rd
Castleford WF10 ....200 E3
Darlington DL3 ....3 A6
Barney La YO60 ....146 A1
Barnfield Way YO23 ....230 A2
Barnhill La DN14 ....205 F7
Barningham Rd DL11 ..18 G7
Barnoldswick CE Prim Sch BB18 ....171 E1
Barnoldswick La LA6 ..103 A2
Barns Wray 2 YO61 ....117 D1
Barnsdale Est WF10 ....200 D3
Barnsdale View
Ledston WF10 ....200 F7
Mickletown LS26 ....200 B5
Barnsdale View DN6 ..206 E2
Barnwell Cres HG2 ......222 B5
Barnwood Cres BB18 ..172 A5

Barnwood Rd BB18 ....172 A1
Barnygate La YO60 ....147 A2
Barons Cres YO23 ......230 B2
Barr La YO22 ....162 D4
Barrack View DL10 ......209 C8
Barracks Bank DL10 ....21 A2
Barret St 18 BD18 ......172 A1
Barrett Ave 3 YO24 ....227 F3
Barrett Rd DL3 ....3 A5
Barrington Garth DN14 ....202 F3
Barrowby La
Austhorpe LS15 ....194 A4
Kirkby Overblow HG3 ..179 A3
Barrowcliff Com Jun Sch YO12 ....212 C7
Barrowcliff Cty Jun Sch YO12 ....212 C7
Barrowcliff Inf Sch YO12 ....212 C7
Barrowcliff Rd YO12 ....212 D7
Barry Bank YO21 ....11 F1
Barry's La YO12 ....212 E2
Barse Beck La HG3 ....160 D5
Barstow Ave YO10 ......228 F3
Barstow Fall 2 WF11 ..201 C2
Bartindale Rd YO14 ....127 A5
Bartle Garth YO1 ....233 C3
Barton CE Prim Sch DL10 ....21 D7
Barton Cl 4 YO31 ....225 E3
Barton St DL1 ....3 E6
Bartons Garth YO8 ....232 B2
Barugh La
Barugh (Great & Little) YO17 ....95 B2
Normanby YO62 ....94 F4
Barwic Par YO8 ....232 E4
Barwick Fields TS17 ....6 A5
Barwick La Ingleby TS17 ..6 A4
Ingleby Barwick TS5 ....5 F5
Barwick Par CP Sch YO8 ....232 E4
Barwick Rd LS15 ....194 C5
Barwick St YO12 ....212 F5
Barwick Terr 1 YO12 ..212 F5
Barwick View TS17 ....6 A5
Barwick Way TS17 ......6 A5
Barwick-in-Elmet CE Sch LS15 ....194 C8
Bassett St YO30 ....232 C3
Bassleton La TS17 ......6 A5
Baston La YO61 ....143 E4
Batemans Yd YO7 ......211 B3
Bates Ave DL3 ....3 B7
Bateson Cl YO10 ....229 C1
Bath St LS29 ....218 C5
Battersby Ave YO9 ......27 C7
Battersby Sta TS9 ......27 C7
Battle of Bramham Moor (site of)* LS24 ....188 F4
Battle of Marston Moor (site of)* YO26 ....181 E7
Battle of Standard Hill (site of)* DL6 ....43 E4
Battle of Towton (site of)* LS24 ....195 D8
Battlefields Way YO11 ..168 D2
Battling Hills La YO18 ..49 B5
Bawhead Rd 28 BB18 ..172 A1
Bawtry Cl YO8 ....232 D3
Bawtry Rd YO8 ....232 D3
Baxby Manor* YO61 ..117 B6
Baxby Terr 2 DL2 ....22 D8
Baxter Cl YO61 ....143 D8
Baxtergate YO21 ....208 D6
Baxton's Sprunt 1 YO62 ..92 F7
Bay Cl YO14 ....101 B2
Bay Bolton Ave DL8 ....59 F3
Bay Horse Yd 5 BD23 ..216 F4
Baydale Rd DL3 ....3 A4
Baysdale Cl TS14 ....8 F6
Baysdale Rd TS17 ......6 B7
Bazeley's La YO17 ......215 E1
Beach Rd The YO14 ....101 B3
Beach The YO14 ....101 B3
Beacon Bank YO62 ....92 D1
Beacon Brow Rd DL3 ..75 A7
Beacon Grange Pk DL2 ..4 C7
Beacon Hill DL2 ....4 C7
Beacon Rd
Millington YO42 ....170 B1
Seamer YO12 ....99 D7
Beacon Rise 4 LS29 ....175 C2
Beacon St 5 LS29 ......175 A4
Beacon View BD23 ....217 E8
Beacon Way YO22 ......32 D6
Beacons La TS17 ....6 A4
Beaconsfield Mews YO24 ....227 C4
Beaconsfield St
Northallerton DL7 ....210 D4
3 Scarborough YO12 ..212 E3
York YO24 ....227 D3
Beadlam Ave YO7 ......7 D6
Beadle Garth YO23 ....230 B2
Beagle Croft YO41 ......168 D2
Beagle Ridge Dr YO24 ..227 C1
Beagle Spinney YO41 ..168 C1
Beal La Beal DN14 ......202 D4
Cridling Stubbs WF11 ..202 C1
Beale Cl TS17 ....6 B5
Beamsley Ct BD23 ......217 A2
Beamsley La BD23 ......174 F7
Beamsley View 18 LS29 ..175 C2
Bean Sheaf La YO17 ....96 A3
Beancroft Rd WF10 ....200 E3

Beancroft St WF10 ....200 E3
Beanland La YO32 ......167 D2
Beanlands Dr 7 BD20 ..187 E7
Beanlands Par LS29 ....218 C5
Beanlands Pl 8 BD20 ..187 E7
Bean's Way YO31 ....229 B8
Beatswell Lawn HG4 ..114 C8
Beaufighter Cl DL10 ....41 F6
Beaufort Cl YO10 ....229 B3
Beaulieu Cl 1 YO32 ....225 F5
Beaumont Hill Sch DL1 ..3 D8
Beaumont Pl YO8 ......232 A2
Beaverdyke YO30 ......224 F1
Becca La LS25 ....194 F8
Beck Cl 6 YO41 ....185 B2
Beck Closes Rd YO26 ..142 A1
Beck Hole 9 YO11 ......100 B6
Beck Isle Mus of Rural Life* YO18 ....95 F7
Beck La Cloughton YO13 ..54 C1
Collingham LS22 ....180 A1
Farndale East YO62 ....48 F2
Leavening YO17 ....147 E1
Lebberston YO11 ....100 D5
South Kilvington YO7 ..211 B6
Wheldrake YO19 ....193 A8
Beck Mdw LS15 ....194 C7
Beck Mill Cl YO17 ......215 D3
Beck Row YO41 ....169 D5
Beck Side BD23 ....173 B4
Beck Side Cl BD20 ......173 D1
Beckbridge La 2 WF6 ..200 B1
Beckbridge Way WF6 ..200 B1
Beckclose La DL8 ....87 F6
Beckdale Rd YO62 ......92 E7
Beckett Cl 8 YO62 ......93 D7
Beckfield Cl 5 BD20 ....187 E7
Beckfield La
Fairburn WF11 ....201 C7
York YO26 ....227 B5
Beckfields Ave TS17 ....6 A4
Becklands Cl YO51 ......141 A5
Becklands La YO51 ....141 A4
Becks Brow BD23 ......153 C3
Becks Cl 9 YO32 ....225 C8
Beckside Catterick DL10 ..41 E4
7 Elvington YO41 ....185 B2
Malton YO17 ....210 B4
4 Staithes TS13 ....13 K2
Wilberfoss YO41 ....185 F6
Beckside Cl
18 Addingham LS29 ....174 F4
20 Burley in Wharfedale LS29 ....176 C1
Beckwith Ave HG2 ....222 B7
Beckwith Cl
Harrogate HG2 ....222 A6
York YO30 ....229 C7
Beckwith Cres HG2 ....222 B6
Beckwith Dr HG2 ......222 B6
Beckwith Head Rd HG3 ....178 C8
Beckwith Rd HG2 ......222 A7
Beckwith Wlk HG2 ....222 A7
Beckwithshaw Com Prim Sch HG3 ....178 A8
Bedale Ave
Scarborough YO12 ......212 E8
York YO30 ....229 D4
Bedale CE Prim Sch DL8 ....63 A2
Bedale High Sch DL8 ..63 A3
Bedale La HG4 ....114 A8
Bedale Mus* DL8 ....63 A3
Bedale Rd Aiskew DL7 ..63 A2
Scotton DL9 ....40 F2
Well DL8 ....63 A3
Bedburn Dr DL3 ....2 F5
Bede Ave YO30 ....228 B2
Bedern YO1 ....233 C3
Bedern Bank 13 HG4 ..214 C5
Bedern Ct 18 HG4 ......214 C5
Bedford Rd TS7 ....7 D6
Bedford St YO23 ....233 A1
Bedfords Fold 6 LS25 ..202 A7
Bedlam Hill YO7 ....65 C4
Bedlam La
Fewston HG3 ....159 F2
Staveley HG5 ....140 E1
Beech Ave
3 Airmyn DN14 ....205 E4
Bishopthorpe YO23 ....231 A3
1 Early BB18 ....172 A1
Harrogate HG2 ....222 E6
4 Topcliffe YO7 ....89 B1
York YO24 ....227 F7
Beech Cl Baldersby YO7 ..88 D1
3 Eastfield YO11 ....100 B7
Elvington YO41 ....185 B2
Farnham HG5 ....162 D5
Great Ayton TS9 ....7 F1
Hunton DL9 ....40 E2
Scruton DL7 ....63 C7
7 Sherburn in Elmet LS25 ..195 F4
Snape with Thorp DL8 ..87 A7
3 South Milford LS25 ..195 F2
Tadcaster LS24 ....189 F6
Beech Cres
Castleford WF10 ....201 B3
Whitwell-on-the-Hill YO60 ....146 E4

Beech Croft
Barlby with Osgodby YO8 ....198 B6
Pontefract WF8 ....201 C2
Beech Ct
Bishopthorpe YO23 ....231 A3
2 Eastfield WF10 ....200 F3
Hellifield BD23 ....154 B3
Beech Dr
6 Kirkbymoorside YO62 ..70 B1
12 Scalby YO13 ....75 D5
South Milford LS25 ....195 F2
Beech End Model Village* DL8 ....60 D6
Beech Glade YO31 ....225 F2
Beech Gr
1 Airmyn DN14 ....205 E4
Burton Salmon LS25 ..201 F6
Camblesforth YO8 ......204 C5
Harrogate HG2 ....219 C1
Knaresborough HG5 ..221 B8
Maltby TS8 ....6 C4
Northallerton DL6 ......210 E5
Selby YO8 ....232 C5
Sowerby YO7 ....211 C1
Whitby YO21 ....208 B6
York YO26 ....227 C4
Beech Hill
Carleton BD23 ....173 A4
6 Knaresborough HG5 ..221 A6
6 Pontefract WF8 ....201 C1
Beech Hill Rd BD23 ....173 A4
Beech La
8 East Ayton/West Ayton YO13 ....99 A7
3 Sportforth HG3 ....179 E6
Beech Pk YO19 ....198 A8
York YO24 ....167 A6
Beech Rd
Boston Spa LS23 ....188 E8
Campsall DN6 ....206 E1
Darlington DL3 ....3 F7
Harrogate HG2 ....222 E6
Ripon HG4 ....214 B3
Beech Rise LS23 ....188 F8
Beech St
28 Barnoldswick BB18 ..171 D1
10 Glusburn BD20 ......187 E7
2 Harrogate HG2 ....220 C3
Beech Tree Ct 2 YO30 ..164 F7
Beech Tree La YO8 ....204 C5
Beech View LS25 ......194 E8
Beech Way 2E YO26 ..165 F1
Beech Wlk
5 Eastfield YO11 ....100 A7
Tadcaster LS24 ....189 D6
Beechcroft Cl 2 YO9 ..9 F6
Beeches End LS23 ......188 F8
Beeches The
Middleton St George DL2 ..4 D4
Skelton YO30 ....224 C4
3 Wetherby LS22 ....26 C7
Wetherby LS22 ....180 C4
Beechfield
Coulby Newham TS8 ..7 A5
Hawsker-cum-Stainsacre YO22 ....33 A6
Newby Wiske DL7 ......64 F2
Norton-on-Ouse YO30 ..165 B6
Beechfield Cl DL8 ......197 B1
Beechfield Rd LS25 ....209 C8
Beechings Mews YO21 ....208 B7
Beechnut La WF8 ......201 B1
Beechtree Rd LS24 ....189 D5
Beechville Ave YO12 ..212 F6
Beechwood Ave 2 TS9 ..26 C8
Beechwood Cl
14 Bedale DL8 ....63 A2
Markington with Wallerthwaite HG3 ....139 C4
Sherburn in Elmet LS25 ..195 F3
Beechwood Cres 8 HG2 ....219 C1
Beechwood Croft LS25 ....195 F3
Beechwood Dr BD23 ..216 D5
Beechwood Glade
Sherburn in Elmet LS25 ..195 F3
7 York YO24 ....227 B1
Beechwood Gr
Harrogate HG2 ....222 F7
18 Ilkley LS29 ....218 C5
Knaresborough HG5 ..221 D5
Beechwood Rise 1 LS22 ....180 C4
Beedham Cl BD23 ......225 D5
Beeston's La LS17 ......178 C4
Beggarmans Rd DL8 ..80 C8
Belbrough Cl 3 TS15 ..25 C5
Belbrough La TS15 ....25 C5
Belcombe Way 1 YO30 ..222 F4
Belford La HG4 ....112 A3
Belford Pl 3 HG1 ......219 D1
Belford Rd 4 HG1 ......219 D1
Belford Sq 9 HG1 ......219 D1
Belfry Way 3 WF6 ....200 B1
Belgrave Cres
Harrogate HG2 ....222 E8
York YO12 ....212 F5
Belgrave St
3 Skipton BD23 ....216 E4
York YO31 ....228 C7
Belgrave Terr
3 Hurworth-on-Tees DL2 ..22 D8
14 Scarborough YO11 ..212 F5
Thirsk YO7 ....211 B2

Bell Cl Haxby YO32 . . . . .225 C8
[S] Seamer YO12 . . . . .99 D6
Bell End Gn YO18 . . . . .49 D3
Bell Hall* YO19 . . . . . .191 E6
Bell La Cawood YO8 . . . . . .197 A7
Huby YO61 . . . . .144 A4
Hursthwaite YO61 . . . . .117 B5
Rawcliffe DN14 . . . . .205 A2
Ulleskelf LS24 . . . . .190 C2
Bellaby Pk [7] YO62 . . . . . .93 D7
Bellburn La DL3 . . . . .3 B7
Belle Hill BD24 . . . . .131 D3
Belle Vue LS29 . . . . .218 C3
Belle Vue Cres [33] YO14 . .101 B3
Belle Vue Par [9] YO11 . .212 F5
Belle Vue Pl [10] YO11 . . .212 F5
Belle Vue St
[34] Filey YO14 . . . . .101 B3
Scarborough YO12 . . . . . .212 F5
York YO10 . . . . .228 E3
Belle Vue Terr
Whitby YO21 . . . . .208 D7
York YO10 . . . . .228 E3
Bellerby Camp DL8 . . . . . .60 B7
Bellerby Rd DL8 . . . . .60 D6
Bellerburn Rd YO17 . . . . .95 F2
Bellevue Terr
Ripon HG4 . . . . .214 C5
[2] Skipton BD23 . . . . .216 E4
Bellfarm Ave YO31 . . . . . . .228 E8
Bellground La YO30 . . . . .165 D4
Bellhouse La HG2 . . . . .29 C7
Bellhouse Way YO24 . . . . .230 B8
Bellingham Cl YO7 . . . . . . .211 C3
Bellman Wlk HG4 . . . . .113 D2
Bellmans Croft YO23 . . . . .230 B2
Bell's Ct [3] YO62 . . . . .92 F6
Bellwood Ave
Boston Spa LS23 . . . . .188 E7
Lockwood TS12 . . . . .9 E7
Bellwood Dr YO24 . . . . . . .230 B8
Belmangate TS14 . . . . .8 F6
Belmont WF11 . . . . .201 D5
Belmont Ave
Harrogate HG2 . . . . .220 D4
[10] Otley LS21 . . . . .176 F1
Belmont Cl [3] YO30 . . . . .225 A1
Belmont Gr [1] HG2 . . . . .220 D3
Belmont Prim Sch TS14 . . .8 F6
Belmont Rd
Harrogate HG2 . . . . .219 C2
Ilkley LS29 . . . . .218 E4
Scarborough YO11 . . . . . . .213 A4
Belmont St BD23 . . . . .216 D4
Belmont Terr [2] HG2 . . . .220 D3
Belmont View HG5 . . . . . . .221 A4
Belmont Wharf BD23 . . . . .216 F4
Belthorpe La YO42 . . . . . . .169 E1
Belton Pk Dr [7] YO11 . . . . .40 E4
Belvedere Hospl YO11 . . . .213 A3
Belvedere Pl YO11 . . . . . . .213 A3
Belvedere Rd YO11 . . . . . . .213 A3
Belvoir Ave [3] YO41 . . . . .185 B2
Belvoir Dr WF11 . . . . .201 F2
Belvoir Terr [9] YO11 . . . . .213 A5
Ben La BB18 . . . . .171 E2
Ben Rhydding Dr LS29 . . .218 F3
Ben Rhydding Prim Sch
LS29 . . . . .218 E4
Ben Rhydding Rd
LS29 . . . . .218 F4
Bence The YO42 . . . . .170 C3
Benedict Ave YO8 . . . . .232 E4
Beningbrough Hall &
Gdns* YO30 . . . . .165 D4
Beningbrough Dr HG3 . . . .219 B5
Beningbrough La
YO30 . . . . .165 D5
Benjamin Thomas
Woodwork* BD24 . . . . .131 C2
Benjy La YO19 . . . . .192 E7
Benkhill Dr [10] DL8 . . . . . . .63 A2
Bennett St [11] BD23 . . . . . .216 F3
Bennions Way [5] DL10 . . . .41 E4
Bennison La YO21 . . . . .13 A1
Bennymoor La YO8 . . . . . . .198 C4
Bensham Rd DL1 . . . . .3 D8
Benson La WF6 . . . . .200 D2
Bent La Colne BB8 . . . . . . .186 A3
Sutton BD20 . . . . .187 E7
Bent Rigg La YO13 . . . . .54 B7
Bentham Moor Rd
LA6 . . . . .103 A2
Bentham Rd LA6 . . . . .103 B3
Bentham Sta LA2 . . . . .129 A7
Bentinck Ave TS5 . . . . .6 F8
Bentley Wynd TS16 . . . . . . .5 D3
Benton Cap La BD22 . . . . .187 B7
Bents La YO18 . . . . .71 A5
Beresford Cl DL10 . . . . .41 F6
Beresford Terr YO23 . . . . . .228 C1
Berghill La YO7 . . . . .66 A7
Berkeley Terr YO26 . . . . . . .227 E5
Berkley Dr TS14 . . . . .8 F5
Bernard La YO26 . . . . .164 B3
Bernica Gr TS17 . . . . .6 A4
Berry Bank DL11 . . . . .1 A6
Berry La LS26 . . . . .200 C8
Berrygate La HG4 . . . . .214 E7
Berry's Ave [5] HG5 . . . . . . .221 B6
Berwick Rd
Archdeacon Newton DL3 . . .3 A7
[18] Scotton DL9 . . . . .40 E4
Bestmire La DL6 . . . . .65 A4
Betteras Hill Rd LS25 . . . .202 A8

Betton Farm Visitor Ctr*
YO13 . . . . .99 C8
Betton Rise YO13 . . . . .99 B8
Between Dikes Rd
YO8 . . . . .204 F8
Beulah St [10] HG1 . . . . . . .219 D2
Beulah Terr YO11 . . . . .212 F5
Beverley Balk YO41 . . . . . .168 B2
Beverley Cl [12] YO11 . . . .100 B6
Beverley Gate YO12 . . . . . . .99 D1
Beverley Rd
[11] Eastfield YO11 . . . . . .100 B6
Middlesbrough TS7 . . . . .7 C6
Norton YO17 . . . . .215 E3
Beverley Rise YO11 . . . . . .212 F5
Beverley Rise LS29 . . . . . .175 C2
Beverley Sch TS4 . . . . .6 F8
Bewerley Rd [1] HG5 . . . . .219 B5
Bewley Gr YO23 . . . . .228 C2
Bewley Gr TS5 . . . . .6 F8
Bexhill Cl WF8 . . . . .201 C1
Bexley Dr TS6 . . . . .7 E8
Bickerton Way LS21 . . . . . .176 F1
Bickley Gate YO13 . . . . .73 F6
Bickley Howe YO12 . . . . . .212 B4
Bickley Rd YO12 . . . . .212 B4
Bielby Cl [3] Bedale BD8 . . . .63 B3
[33] Scalby YO12 . . . . .75 D5
Big Mdw Dr [5] LS29 . . . . .174 E4
Big Sheep & Little Cow
Farm* DL8 . . . . .63 B3
Bilsdale Cl
Northallerton DL7 . . . . . . .210 C2
York YO30 . . . . .224 E2
Bilsdale Gr HG5 . . . . .221 D6
Bilsdale Midcable Chop Gate
CE VC Prim Sch TS9 . . . .46 F6
Bilton Cl HG1 . . . . .219 E6
Bilton Dr HG1 . . . . .219 D4
Bilton Gr Ave HG1 . . . . . . .219 E5
Bilton Grange CE HG1 . . . .219 D5
Bilton Grange Com Prim Sch
HG1 . . . . .219 D5
Bilton Hall Dr HG1 . . . . . . .220 D6
Bilton La HG1 . . . . .219 E6
Binks Cl DL6 . . . . .210 B7
Binnington Carr La
YO12 . . . . .99 B1
Binnie La BD20 . . . . .187 D7
Binsley La YO61 . . . . .117 E2
Binsoe La YO61 . . . . .86 F3
Sleights YO22 . . . . .32 A6
Birch Cl [3] Filey YO14 . . . .101 B3
[8] Hunton DL9 . . . . .40 F2
[2] Kirklevington TS15 . . . . .24 E8
[4] Thorpe Willoughby YO8 .197 B1
York YO32 . . . . .225 D3
Birch Copse YO24 . . . . . . .227 D2
Birch Cres [10] YO22 . . . . . .32 A6
Birch Dr [2] Faceby TS9 . . . .25 F1
Kippax LS25 . . . . .194 C2
Birch Gr
Castleford WF10 . . . . .201 B3
Harrogate HG2 . . . . .219 E6
Kippax LS25 . . . . .194 D1
Birch Hall La BB18 . . . . . . .172 B1
Birch La [9] YO32 . . . . .166 E5
Birch Rd DL1 . . . . .3 D8
Birch View [3] YO18 . . . . . . .96 A6
Birch Way YO61 . . . . .143 D8
Birchen Cl [7] WF10 . . . . . .200 D3
Birches The TS8 . . . . .7 A5
Birchfield Dr TS16 . . . . .5 D5
Birchwood Cl [10] BD24 . . . .131 D2
Birchwood Cl [5] LS29 . . . . .218 A4
Birchwood Mews YO32 . . . .227 F7
Birchwood Rd TS7 . . . . .7 C6
Bird Gdn* LS25 . . . . .195 B7
Bird La Hensall DN14 . . . . .203 D2
Kellington DN14 . . . . .202 F4
Bird Ridding La DL8 . . . . . . .60 B1
Birdale Field La LS23 . . . . .188 E5
Birdforth Way [1] YO62 . . . .92 C1
Birds of Prey & Conservation
Area* YO7 . . . . .88 F7
Birdwood Cl DL10 . . . . . . .209 C2
Birk Brow Rd TS12 . . . . .9 D5
Birk Field Bank YO21 . . . . .28 F6
Birk Head La YO22 . . . . .70 F4
Birk La YO42 . . . . .199 D8
Birkby La DL7 . . . . .23 B1
Birkdale Ave HG5 . . . . .221 D5
Birkdale Gr [4] YO26 . . . . . .227 B5
Birker La
Newton on Derwent
YO41 . . . . .185 D4
Wilberfoss YO41 . . . . .185 F6
Birkett La CA17 . . . . .14 B7
Birkhills HG3 . . . . .140 A3
Birkin La WF11 . . . . .202 B4
Birkin Rd YO8 . . . . .203 A5
Birklands [1] YO62 . . . . .93 D7
Birkwith La LA2 . . . . .128 F7
Birmham Rocks*
HG3 . . . . .138 B4
Birstwith CE Prim Sch
HG3 . . . . .160 E6
Birstwith Dr YO26 . . . . .227 E4
Birstwith Grange HG3 . . . .160 E6
Birstwith Rd HG3 . . . . .160 A3
Birthwaite La HG3 . . . . .161 C8
Birtley Ave TS5 . . . . .6 F7
Bishop Cl [1] HG3 . . . . .160 E6
Bishop Ct [2] YO8 . . . . .232 B6
Bishop Garth [2] HG3 . . . .137 C4

Bishop Monkton CE Prim Sch
HG3 . . . . .140 A5
Bishop Monkton Rly Cutting
Nature Reserve*
HG3 . . . . .139 F5
Bishop Thornton CE VC Prim
Sch HG3 . . . . .139 F2
Bishop Thornton RC Prim
Sch YO42 . . . . .169 F2
Bishop Way [3] HG3 . . . . . .137 C4
Bishop Wilton CE VC Prim
Sch YO42 . . . . .169 F2
Bishopdale Cl HG5 . . . . . . .221 D6
Bishopdale Dr [7] LS22 . . . .180 A1
Bishopdike Rd
Cawood YO8 . . . . .197 A6
Sherburn in Elmet LS25 . . .196 A4
Bishopgate St YO23 . . . . . .233 B1
Bishophill Jun YO1 . . . . . . .233 A1
Bishophill Senior YO1 . . . .233 B1
Bishops Ct YO1 . . . . .233 B1
Bishops Way DL10 . . . . .41 D5
Bishopsfields Dr YO26 . . . .228 A5
Bishopsgarth DL7 . . . . .210 C4
Bishopsway YO10 . . . . .229 C3
Bishopthorpe Inf Sch
YO23 . . . . .231 A4
Bishopthorpe Pal*
YO23 . . . . .231 B4
Bishopthorpe Rd
YO23 . . . . .231 B5
Bishopton HG4 . . . . .214 A5
Bishopton La
Great Burdon DL1 . . . . .4 A7
Ripon HG4 . . . . .113 D2
Bishopton Pk HG4 . . . . . . .214 A5
Bisley Ct [3] DL1 . . . . .3 D7
Bismarck St YO26 . . . . .227 E5
Bitterdale La YO62 . . . . .70 A3
Black Abbey La [1] BD20 . . .187 E8
Black Bank HG4 . . . . .130 E3
Black Diamond Way [3]
TS16 . . . . .5 D5
Black Dike La YO26 . . . . . . .182 F8
Black Fen La YO8 . . . . .232 C8
Black Gill La
Airton BD23 . . . . .154 B8
Settle BD23 . . . . .132 A1
Black Hill HG2 . . . . .222 B8
Black Hill Rd HG3 . . . . .157 F8
Black Horse La TS15 . . . . . .25 C3
Black Sike La YO13 . . . . . . .98 A4
Black Wlk WF8 . . . . .201 B1
Blackbird Way [3] YO12 . . . .99 F6
Blackburn La WF11 . . . . . . .202 B2
Blacklee CA17 . . . . .14 B7
Blacksmith Bank DL8 . . . . .62 E5
Blacksmith Ct DL7 . . . . . . .22 C2
Blacksmith Hill YO22 . . . . .53 A7
Blackthorn TS8 . . . . .7 B4
Blackthorn Dr YO31 . . . . . .225 E2
Blackthorn La HG3 . . . . . . .222 C3
Blackthorn Way LS25 . . . . .218 D5
Blackwell DL3 . . . . .3 B4
Blackwell La HG3 . . . . .3 B4
Blackwood La HG3 . . . . . . .198 F7
Blackwood Rd YO8 . . . . . . .198 E8
Blair Ave YO17 . . . . .215 D2
Blair Pk HG5 . . . . .221 C5
Blake Ct YO10 . . . . .193 A8
Blake Gate HG3 . . . . .136 E1
Blake St YO1 . . . . .233 B3
Blakeley Cres [3] BB18 . . . .171 D2
Blakeney Pl YO10 . . . . .228 F3
Blakeney Rd YO62 . . . . .49 B5
Blakey Cl YO21 . . . . .211 C1
Blakey La YO7 . . . . .211 C1
Blakey Rd YO62 . . . . .70 B6
Bland La YO26 . . . . .227 A4
Bland's Cliff [27] YO11 . . . .213 A6
Bland's Hill HG5 . . . . .221 A4
Blandford Rd DL9 . . . . .40 E3
Blands Ave WF10 . . . . .200 D7
Blands Cres [3] WF10 . . . . .200 D7
Blands Gr [4] WF10 . . . . . .200 D7
Blands Terr WF10 . . . . .200 D7
Blansby La YO17 . . . . .121 C8
Blansby Pk La YO18 . . . . . . .96 A8
Blatchford YO30 . . . . .228 B8
Blatchford Mews
YO30 . . . . .228 B8
Blawath Rd YO18 . . . . .51 A2
Blayshaw La HG3 . . . . .110 B4
Blazefield Bank HG3 . . . . .137 D3
Blea Moor Rd LA6 . . . . .78 F2
Blea Pit La HG4 . . . . .140 E8
Bleaberry La YO41 . . . . . . .169 B5
Bleachfield YO10 . . . . .228 F2
Blean La DL8 . . . . .57 D3
Bleara Rd BB18 . . . . .186 B8
Blenheim Ave [4] YO21 . . . .208 B7
Blenheim Cl DL10 . . . . .41 F6
Blenheim Ct
Harrogate HG2 . . . . .222 D1
Rawcliffe YO30 . . . . .224 D3
Blenheim St [12] YO12 . . . .213 A7
Blenheim Terr YO12 . . . . . .213 A7
Blenheim Way HG2 . . . . . . .222 D1
Bleriot Way YO30 . . . . .225 A3
Blewhouse La DL8 . . . . .61 E3
Blind La Aiskew DL8 . . . . . . .63 B3
Barton DL10 . . . . .21 D7
Burton in Lonsdale LA6 . . .102 F3
Guisborough HG5 . . . . .8 C6
Hurworth DL2 . . . . .22 B7
Knaresborough HG5 . . . . . .221 B7
Scorton DL10 . . . . .42 B8

Blind La continued
Tockwith YO26 . . . . .181 B8
Blind Piece La YO7 . . . . . . .116 A6
Bloe Beck La LA2 . . . . .129 E6
Bloody Beck Hill YO13 . . . . .54 A7
Bloomp Ct [2] TS17 . . . . .5 F4
Blorenge Cl WF10 . . . . .200 D3
Blossom St YO24 . . . . .233 A1
Blossom Way WF10 . . . . . .200 D3
Blossomgate HG4 . . . . .214 B5
Blue Bank 32 A4
Blue Barn La TS15 . . . . .25 C6
Blue Bell Dr YO8 . . . . .232 B6
Blue Bridge La YO10 . . . . . .228 D2
Blue Nile Way [2] DL9 . . . . .41 A5
Blue Ridge Pk WF10 . . . . .200 E3
Blue Slates Cl YO19 . . . . . .193 A8
Bluebeck Dr YO30 . . . . . . .227 E8
Bluebell Mdw [18] HG5 . . . .161 B3
Bluebell Wlk HG4 . . . . .161 B3
Blyth Cl YO8 . . . . .232 A5
Boar La TS17 . . . . .6 B5
Boat La Barforth DL11 . . . . . .1 C7
Great Ouseburn YO26 . . . .164 C8
Kirby Hall YO26 . . . . .162 A5
Mickletown LS26 . . . . .200 C5
Boatcliffe Rd YO14 . . . . . . .127 D7
Boathouse La DL2 . . . . .2 E4
Bob La YO7 . . . . .65 E3
Bodmin Dr WF6 . . . . .200 A2
Bodner Hill YO61 . . . . .118 F1
Boeing Way TS18 . . . . .5 F7
Bog Hall YO21 . . . . .208 D5
Bog La
Askham Bryan YO24 . . . . .230 B6
Barwick in Elmet & Scholes
LS15 . . . . .194 A7
Stirton with Thorlby
BD23 . . . . .216 D7
Boggart La LS24 . . . . .190 C2
Boggy La DL10 . . . . .209 B5
Boghole Bank DL6 . . . . .45 B3
Boghouse La TS13 . . . . .10 F3
Bogs La
Bridge Hewick HG4 . . . . . .114 C1
Harrogate HG1 . . . . .220 C5
Bolckow St TS14 . . . . .8 F7
Boid Venture St BD23 . . . . .216 F2
Boldron Cl [8] TS18 . . . . . . .5 D8
Bolland St [8] BB18 . . . . . . .171 D2
Bolling Rd LS29 . . . . .218 D4
Boltby Rd YO30 . . . . .224 F2
Bolton Abbey Sta
BD23 . . . . .174 D8
Bolton Ave DL10 . . . . .209 B7
Bolton Castle* DL8 . . . . . . .59 B6
Bolton Cross DL10 . . . . .41 D5
Bolton Ct YO7 . . . . .211 B2
Bolton St [8] HG1 . . . . .219 D4
Bolton Way
[18] Leyburn DL8 . . . . .60 D5
Richmond DL10 . . . . .209 C8
Bolton-on-Swale Nature
Reserve* DL10 . . . . .41 F5
Bonby La YO8 . . . . .192 E2
Bond End HG5 . . . . .221 A6
Bond La
Appleton Roebuck YO23 . . .190 F5
Settle BD23 . . . . .131 D2
Bond St WF8 . . . . .201 C1
Bondgate Helmsley YO62 . . .92 F6
Pontefract WF8 . . . . .201 C1
Ripon HG4 . . . . .214 C5
Selby YO8 . . . . .232 B7
Bondgate Ct HG4 . . . . .214 C5
Bondgate Gn HG4 . . . . .214 C4
Bondgate Gn Cl [6] HG4 . . .214 C4
Bondgate La LS25 . . . . .194 C2
Bondings Rise [8] LS25 . . . .196 A4
Bonington Ct [7] YO26 . . . .227 E4
Bonny Dr TS8 . . . . .7 C5
Bonnygate YO61 . . . . .118 F3
Bonnygrove Way TS8 . . . . . .7 B4
Bonnywell La YO7 . . . . .114 C6
Boosbeck Rd TS12 . . . . .9 F7
Boot St [28] BB18 . . . . .172 A1
Booth Bridge La BD23 . . . .172 A3
Booth Ferry Rd DN14 . . . . .205 F6
Booth St [27] LS29 . . . . .175 A4
Bootham* YO30 . . . . .233 A3
Bootham Bar* YO31 . . . . . .233 B3
Bootham Cres YO30 . . . . . .233 A4
Bootham Pk YO31 . . . . .233 A4
Bootham Pk Ct YO31 . . . . .233 A4
Bootham Pk Hospl
YO31 . . . . .233 B4
Bootham Row YO31 . . . . . .233 B4
Bootham Sch YO30 . . . . . . .233 A4
Bootham Sq YO31 . . . . .233 B4
Bootham Terr YO30 . . . . . . .233 A4
Boothwood Rd YO30 . . . . .224 E2
Booty La DN14 . . . . .206 F7
Borage Rd [3] HG1 . . . . . . .161 B3
Bore Tree Baulk YO19 . . . .184 D6
Borogate [2] YO62 . . . . .92 F6
Borough Mere La
YO17 . . . . .215 D8

Borough Rd
Darlington DL1 . . . . .3 D5
Richmond DL10 . . . . .208 D7
Boroughbridge High Sch
YO51 . . . . .141 B5
Boroughbridge Prim Sch
YO51 . . . . .141 B5
Boroughbridge Rd
Bishop Monkton HG3 . . . .140 B5
Bridge Hewick HG4 . . . . . .114 B1
Dishforth YO7 . . . . .115 A2
Knaresborough HG5 . . . . .221 B5
Northallerton DL7 . . . . .64 E6
Ripon HG4 . . . . .214 E3
Scriven HG5 . . . . .162 E6
Westwick YO51 . . . . .140 D4
Whixley YO26 . . . . .164 B4
York YO26 . . . . .227 D5
Borrage Gn La HG4 . . . . . .214 B4
Borrage La HG4 . . . . .214 B4
Borrowby Ave DL6 . . . . . . .210 F3
Borrowby La
HG5 . . . . .221 D6
Borrowdale Dr
Castleford WF10 . . . . .201 B5
York YO30 . . . . .224 F1
Boss Moor La BD23 . . . . . .155 F8
Boston Ave DL6 . . . . .210 D4
Boston Dr TS7 . . . . .7 B5
Boston Rd Clifford LS23 . . .188 E7
Wetherby LS22 . . . . .180 C2
Boston Spa Comp Sch
LS23 . . . . .188 B8
Botheby Wood BD23 . . . . .216 E5
Botton House La YO22 . . . .33 B5
Bottoms La YO22 . . . . .33 B6
Botton Rd LA2 . . . . .128 E2
Boulby Bank YO22 . . . . . . .208 E6
Bouldershaw La DL11 . . . . .17 D1
Boulsworth Dr BB8 . . . . . . .186 B1
Boulsworth Gr [4] BB8 . . . .186 A3
Boundary Ave BD20 . . . . . .187 E7
Boundary Way DL8 . . . . . . .209 F8
Bourlon Rd DL9 . . . . .209 A2
Bourn Ave DL1 . . . . .3 E5
Bournemouth Rd TS3 . . . . . .7 D8
Bouthwaite Dr [13] YO26 . .227 E4
Bow Bridge Dr BD23 . . . . .217 D7
Bow Bridge La YO21 . . . . . .29 A7
Bow Bridge View
LS24 . . . . .189 F7
Bow St TS14 . . . . .8 F7
Bowbridge La YO7 . . . . .63 A8
Bowcarr La YO26 . . . . .163 D8
Bowcliffe Rd LS23 . . . . .188 E5
Bowe Cres [3] DL8 . . . . .63 B2
Bowen Rd HG1 . . . . .219 D3
Bower St HG1 . . . . .219 D2
Bower Wlk YO17 . . . . .215 E4
Bowes Ave YO11 . . . . .100 F5
Bowes La YO14 . . . . .100 F5
Bowes Pk HG2 . . . . .222 D6
Bowesfield Cres TS18 . . . . . .6 A8
Bowesfield Ind Est TS18 . . .6 A8
Bowesfield La TS18 . . . . .6 A7
Bowland Cl HG2 . . . . .220 D1
Bowland Cl HG2 . . . . .220 D1
Bowland La YO42 . . . . .193 E2
Bowland View LA6 . . . . . . .103 E3
Bowling Gn YO30 . . . . .225 A1
Bowling Gn Ct YO31 . . . . .228 D8
Bowling Gn La
[9] Hunmanby YO14 . . . . .126 F8
Manfield DL2 . . . . .2 B4
York YO31 . . . . .233 C4
Bowling Gn Yd DL6 [16] HG5 .221 B6
Bowling La YO11 . . . . .215 E4
Bowling Terr BD23 . . . . . . .216 D3
Bowling View BD23 . . . . . . .216 D3
Bowman St DL3 . . . . .3 D7
Bowmess Dr YO30 . . . . . . .224 D1
Bowthorpe La YO8 . . . . . . .199 B4
Bowyers Cl YO23 . . . . .230 C4
Box Hill YO12 . . . . .212 C3
Box La WF8 . . . . .201 C1
Boyle & Petyt Sch The
BD23 . . . . .174 F8
Boyle The [15] LS29 . . . . . . .194 B8
Boynton La
Barton-le-Street YO17 . . . .120 F8
Rawcliffe DN14 . . . . .205 A1
Boynton Rd DL7 . . . . .22 E2
Braburn Gdns TS6 . . . . .6 F5
Bracewell La BD23 . . . . . . .171 B4
Bracewell St [3] BB18 . . . . .171 D2
Bracken Cl
Whitby YO22 . . . . .208 E4
York YO32 . . . . .225 F4
Bracken Cres TS14 . . . . .8 D6
Bracken Field BD23 . . . . . .134 B3
Bracken Hill
Scarborough YO12 . . . . . .212 C7
[2] York YO10 . . . . .229 C3
Bracken Rd YO24 . . . . .230 F7
Brackenber Cl DL2 . . . . . . .131 C2
Brackenber La DL2 . . . . . . .131 C1
Brackenfield Prep Sch
HG1 . . . . .219 A2
Brackenhill Ave YO8 . . . . . .232 A4

Brackenhill La
Brayton YO8 ....232 A3
Church Fenton LS24 ....196 C8
Sleights YO22 ....32 A5
Brackenhills YO26 ....165 F1
Brackenley Ave 2
BD23 ....217 C7
Brackenley Cl BD23 ...217 C7
Brackenley Cres BD23 .217 C7
Brackenley Ct BD23 ...217 C7
Brackenley Dr BD23 ...217 C7
Brackenley Gn 1 BD23 .217 C7
Brackenley La BD23 ...217 A7
Brackenthwaite La
HG3 ....222 A1
Brackenwell La LS17 ..178 B4
Brackenwood Cl 2
LS29 ....218 E4
Brackit La YO61 ......91 B2
Bracknell Rd TS17 ....6 C8
Bradfords Cl 8 LS23 ..188 E6
Bradley Ave
Castleford WF10 ......200 E4
Northallerton DL6 ....210 F2
Bradley Cres YO23 ....182 D6
Bradley Dr YO24 ......230 C8
Bradley Gr BD20 ......174 B1
Bradley La YO23 ......182 C5
Bradley Rd
Pickering YO18 ....71 F4
Silsden BD20 ....174 B2
Bradley Rise BD20 ....174 B1
Bradleys Both Com Prim Sch
BD20 ....173 E3
Bradleys Terr 2 TS9 ..8 A2
Bradworth Cl 3 YO11 ..100 B7
Bradworth Dr 2 YO11 ..100 B7
Braeburn Inf Sch & Com Jun
Sch YO11 ....100 A6
Braegate La LS24 .....190 E7
Braemar Dr TS25 ......194 D4
Braeside TS15 ....24 E8
Braeside Gdns YO24 ...227 E3
Brafferton Hall Gdn 3
YO61 ....115 F1
Braham La HG5 ....159 F7
Brailsford Cres YO30 ..228 A8
Braimber La YO51 .....141 C1
Braithegayte YO19 ....192 F8
Braithwaite Hall DL8 ..84 D8
Braithwaite La
Dacre HG3 ....159 A7
East Witton Town DL8 ..84 E8
Braker La YO26 ....163 F4
Bramall La 8 DL1 .....3 F6
Bramble Cl
8 Colburn DL9 ......41 A5
1 Killinghall HG3 ....161 B3
Bramble La 20 LS25 ...195 F4
Bramble Dene YO24 ....230 D7
Bramble Wlk YO17 ....215 B4
Bramblefields DL6 ....210 F4
Brambles 8 YO8 ......197 B1
Brambles The 8 LS29 ..175 C2
Brambling Fields La
YO17 ....122 C2
Bramblings The 6
WF10 ....200 D3
Bramcote Prep Sch for Boys
YO11 ....213 A3
Brame La HG3 ....177 A8
Bramfield Way 6 TS17 .6 D6
Bramham Ave YO26 .....227 A3
Bramham Dr HG3 ....219 A4
Bramham Gr YO26 .....227 A3
Bramham La LS23 ......186 A4
Bramham Pk* LS23 ....188 C4
Bramham Pk Gdns*
LS23 ....188 C4
Bramham Prim Sch
LS23 ....188 E6
Bramham Rd
Boston Spa LS23 ......188 E7
Thorner LS14 ....188 A3
York YO26 ....227 A2
Bramley Ave YO8 ......198 B5
Bramley Garth YO31 ...229 B6
Bramley Head La HG3 ..158 E5
Bramper La DL7 ....42 E1
Branch Rd BD23 ....174 B2
Brandon Gr YO32 ......226 E3
Brandsby Bank YO61 ...118 D3
Brandsby Gr YO31 .....225 E2
Brandsby Rd YO61 .....118 A1
Brandsby St YO61 .....118 A1
Brankin Dr DL1 ....3 E4
Brankin Rd DL1 ....3 D3
Branklyn Gdns TS17 ...6 A4
Branksome Gr 1 TS18 ..5 E8
Branksome Sch DL3 ....3 A6
Bransdale TS14 ....8 D6
Bransdale Ave
Northallerton DL7 ....210 C2
1 Pontefract WF6 ....200 A2
Bransdale Cl 6 WF6 ...200 A2
Bransdale Gr 3 HG5 ...221 D6
Bransdale Mews 10
WF6 ....200 A2
Bransdale Rd YO62 ....48 B1
Bransdale Wlk WF6 ....200 A2
Bransholme Dr YO30 ...225 A2
Brant Bank La LS29 ...175 B3
Brant La LS24 ....189 D4
Branton Ct YO26 ......142 A1

Branton Ct YO26 ......142 A1
Branton La YO26 ......142 A1
Branton Pl YO26 ......227 A3
Brass Castle La TS8 ...7 C3
Brat La LS21 ....177 A7
Bravener Ct YO30 .....165 B6
Brawby La YO62 ....94 E1
Bray Gate YO42 ......169 E2
Bray Rd YO10 ....231 F8
Braygate Balk YO18 ...72 C5
Braygate La YO18 .....72 D5
Braygate St YO17 .....121 A2
Braythorne La LS21 ...177 E4
Brayton CE VC Sch
YO8 ....232 A2
Brayton Coll YO8 .....232 C1
Brayton Com Jun Sch
YO8 ....232 A2
Brayton Junc YO8 .....232 C1
Brayton La YO8 ....232 B1
Breakmoor Ave BD20 ...174 C2
Brearlands BD23 ......172 A3
Brearton La HG3 ......161 E8
Breary Cl YO24 ....227 F1
Breary Flat La HG5 ...221 C7
Brechin Dr TS17 ......6 B6
Breckenbrough La
DL10 ....41 A3
Breckenbrough Sch
YO7 ....89 A6
Breckney La YO17 .....122 D5
Breckon Hill YO62 ....49 A1
Brecks La Kippax LS25 .194 C2
Pockley YO62 ....93 B8
Strensall YO32 ....167 B7
Swillington LS26 .....194 B2
York YO32 ....225 F4
Brecksfield YO30 .....224 C5
Brecon Cres TS17 .....5 F4
Breedycroft La YO17 ..121 C4
Breighton Rd
Bubwith YO8 ....199 D6
Wressle YO8 ....199 C3
Brendon Gr TS17 ......6 A3
Brentwood DL8 ....60 D5
Brentwood Cres YO10 ..229 C2
Brewers Ct YO7 ......211 B3
Brewerton St HG5 .....221 A5
Brewery La
5 Ripon HG4 ....214 C4
Skipton BD23 ....216 F4
Brewery Rd LS29 ......218 C4
Brewery Visitor Ctr*
HG4 ....86 C4
Brewster Terr HG4 ....214 C6
Briar Ave YO26 ....227 B4
Briar Cliffe YO8 .....232 A3
Briar Dr YO23 ....225 F2
Briar Pk 5 YO62 .....93 D7
Briar Rd TS17 ....6 B7
Briar Wlk DL3 ....3 B3
Briardene Ave 2 YO12 .75 E5
Briarfield Cl LS29 ....218 D3
Briars Ct YO23 ....190 E5
Briars Dr YO23 ......190 E5
Briars The HG5 ....221 B7
Briarwood Cl YO8 .....202 F7
Brick Kiln La YO8 ....203 D6
Brick Lands La YO8 ...203 F4
Brickfield La YO51 ...141 D4
Brickhill La YO8 .....204 F4
Brickkiln La
Aldbrough DL11 ....2 A3
Forcett & Carkin DL11 .20 C8
Brickyard La YO7 .....89 C6
Brickyard Rd YO51 ....141 A4
Bridge La Ilkley LS29 .218 A5
Poppleton YO26 ....165 F8
York YO30 ....233 B4
Bridge Mews LA6 ......103 C4
Bridge Rd
Bishopthorpe YO23 ....230 B7
Boston Spa LS23 ......188 F8
Brompton-on-Swale DL10 .41 B6
Glusburn BD20 ....187 E7
Hurworth DL2 ....3 B3
Malton YO17 ....215 C5
Old Byland & Scawton
YO7 ....91 F7
1 Stokesley TS9 ......26 C7
10 Bridge St 5 Bedale DL8 .63 A3
12 Castleford WF10 ...200 F4
Egglescliffe TS16 .....5 D4
12 Helmsley YO62 .....92 F6
8 Normanton South WF6 .200 B2
18 Pickering YO18 ....95 F7
Richmond DL10 ....209 B6
Skipton BD23 ....216 F4
Tadcaster LS24 ....189 E6
Thirsk YO7 ....211 B3
Whitby YO22 ....208 C4

Bridge St continued
York YO1 ....233 B2
Bridge Terr
Northallerton DL7 ....210 C4
Richmond DL10 ....209 B6
Bridge View Rd HG4 ...214 C7
Bridges Ct YO8 ......232 D6
Bridges La YO42 .....193 E4
Bridgestones* YO18 ..73 B6
Bridle Wlk YO8 ......227 A3
Bridle Way 6 YO8 ....232 C4
Bridlington Rd
Hunmanby YO14 ....127 A7
Sledmere YO25 ....150 C4
1 Stamford Bridge YO41 .168 D2
Wold Newton YO25 ....126 A4
Bridlington St YO14 ..126 F8
Brier Hill YO21 ......29 C7
Brier La YO8 ....205 A4
Briercliffe YO12 .....212 C7
Briergate YO12 ......225 C2
Brierlands Cl LS25 ...194 D4
Brierlands La LS25 ...194 E4
Brierley Rd YO12 .....194 B1
Briery Cl YO12 ......175 C2
Brigg Farm Ct YO8 ...204 D5
Brigg La YO8 ....204 D5
Brigg Rd 5 YO14 .....101 B3
Brigg's Ave WF10 .....200 F3
Briggate HG5 ....221 B5
Briggs St YO33 ......228 C2
Bright St 10 Colne BB8 .186 A3
Darlington DL1 ....3 E1
18 Trawden BB8 ......186 A3
York YO26 ....227 F5
Bright Terr BB8 .....186 A1
Bright Wlk YO8 ......232 B6
Brighton Rd LS29 .....218 E3
Brigshaw Dr WF10 ....200 C8
Brigshaw High Sch
WF10 ....200 C8
Brigshaw La WF10 ....200 C8
Brimham Rocks*
HG3 ....138 B4
Brind La DN14 ....199 F2
Brindle Pk Dr WF10 ..201 A3
Brindley Cl 8 BD23 ..216 F3
Brindley Mill BD23 ...216 F3
Brindley Wharf BD23 ..217 A3
Brindleys La DN14 ....199 F3
Brinkburn Ave DL3 ....3 B7
Brinkburn Rd
Darlington DL3 ....3 B6
4 Darlington DL1 ....212 E5
Brinklow Way HG2 ....222 B5
Brinkworth Terr 1
YO7 ....211 C3
Briscoe Ridge La HG3 .177 F6
Briscoe Way TS8 .....6 E5
Britannia St 2 YO12 ..212 E5
Broach La Heck DN14 ..203 D1
Kellington DN14 .....202 F3
Broach Rd Heck DN14 ..207 D8
Hensall DN14 ....203 C1
Broad Acres YO32 .....225 C7
Broad Balk YO17 .....149 A5
Broad Balk La YO7 ...115 B1
Broad Carr Rd HG3 ...110 D2
Broad Cl TS8 ....6 D5
Broad Dubb Rd HG3 ...177 C8
Broad Gate
Brompton YO13 ......98 B7
Hunsingore LS22 .....180 F8
Marton cum Grafton
YO26 ....141 F1
Broad Gate Rd YO21 ..28 E4
Broad Head La BD22 ..187 E2
Broad Highway YO12 ..192 F8
Broad La
Appleton Roebuck YO23 .191 A6
6 Beal DN14 ....202 A4
Catton YO41 ....185 C7
Cawood YO8 ....197 A6
Church Fenton LS24 ..196 B6
Hurworth YO23 ....222 A2
Wistow YO8 ....197 A5
Broad Oak YO61 ......168 D6
Broad Oak La 18 YO32 .166 E5
Broadacres DN14 .....204 D3
Broadacres Ave DN14 ..204 D3
Broadacres Garth
DN14 ....204 D3
Broadfield La HG4 ....138 B8
Broadfield Way 6 LS29 .174 E4
Broadgate Rd TS5 ....6 E8
Broadlands
2 Roundhill Village TS17 .6 A5
Wheldrake YO19 ......192 F8
Broadlands Dr 5 YO13 .99 B8
Broadmanor YO8 ......141 F1
Broadmires La YO18 ..95 E6
Broadrum La YO18 ....95 E6
Broadstone Way YO30 .224 E3
Broadway
1 Darlington DL1 ....212 D7
York YO10 ....231 E8
Broadway Gr 3 YO10 ..231 E8
Broadway The DL1 ....3 E5
Broadway W YO10 .....231 D8
Brockadale Nature Reserve*
WF8 ....206 B4
Brockfield Pk Dr YO31 .225 F2
Brockfield Rd YO31 ...225 E2
Brockholme La DL6 ...65 A4

Brocklesby Rd TS14 ...8 F5
Brockley Cl LS24 .....196 B7
Broc-o-bank 1 DN6 ...206 E2
Brodrick Dr LS29 .....218 A3
Brogden La BB18 .....171 B1
Brokes La DL11 ......40 B6
Bromley La TS8 ......7 B3
Bromley St 2 YO26 ...227 F5
Brompton & Sawdon Com
Prim Sch YO13 ....98 C5
Brompton Ave 4 TS14 ..8 F7
Brompton Carr La
YO13 ....98 B4
Brompton Com Prim Sch
DL6 ....43 F3
Brompton Hall Sch
YO13 ....98 C5
Brompton House Day Hospl
DL6 ....210 E5
Brompton Ings Rd
YO13 ....98 D3
Brompton La DL6 .....43 E4
Brompton Rd
Newton-le-Willows DL8 ..62 B4
Northallerton DL6 ....210 D5
York YO30 ....228 A7
Brompton-on-Swale CE Prim
Sch DL10 ....41 B7
Bronaber Cl 1 TS17 ...5 F4
Bronte Cl
Brompton on Swale DL10 .41 C7
Scarborough YO12 ....212 D5
Bronte Ct WF8 ....201 B1
Bronte Dr DL9 ....41 A5
Bronte Rise WF10 ....201 B3
Brook House Croft
BD24 ....131 E6
Brook La Danby YO21 ..29 E6
Halton West BD23 ....153 F1
Thornton Dale YO18 ..96 D6
Weeton LS17 ....178 C2
Brook Pk YO21 ....32 A7
Brook St
Castleford WF10 .....201 B6
18 Earby BB18 ....172 A1
Hebden BD23 ....135 A2
Hellifield BD23 .....154 B3
Ilkley LS29 ....218 B4
12 Scarborough YO12 .212 F6
Selby YO8 ....232 C4
Skipton BD23 ....216 F4
York YO31 ....233 B4
Brook View BD23 .....173 B4
Brookacre 7 LA6 .....103 D3
Brooke Cl
Harrogate HG1 ....219 E7
12 Knaresborough YO62 .70 B1
Brookfield HG3 ......160 F5
Brookfield Cl HG3 ....161 A5
Brookfield Cres HG3 ..161 A5
Brookfield Garth HG3 .161 A5
Brookfield Way
7 Earby BB18 ....172 A1
Hampsthwaite HG3 ....160 F5
Brookland La LA6 ....102 F2
Brooklands
4 Filey YO14 ....101 B3
York YO10 ....229 D4
Brooklands Cl 44 YO14 .101 B3
Brooklands Cres DL6 ..63 D6
Brooklands Sch BD23 ..216 F2
Brooklands Terr BD23 .216 F3
Brooksbank Rd TS7 ...7 D7
Brookside
Collingham LS22 .....188 A8
Hovingham YO62 .....119 E6
Skelton & Brotton TS12 .9 D8
Skipton BD23 ....217 A3
Sleights YO22 ....32 B6
Brookside Cl 1 DL6 ...63 D6
Brookside Cl 2 DL8 ...63 B2
Brookwood Way TS16 ...5 E4
Broom Hill Ave 6 TS16 .6 D5
Broom Rise La
Egton YO21 ....30 F4
1 Newby YO21 ....12 B2
Broom Rd LS24 ....189 D5
Broom Wlk YO12 .....212 C7
Broome Cl
14 Pontefract WF6 ...200 A2
York YO30 ....225 F5
Broome Way YO32 .....226 A5
Broomfield HG3 ......160 E6
Broomfield Ave DL7 ...210 D2
Broomfield Com Prim Sch
DL7 ....210 D2
Broomfield Terr 18
YO21 ....208 D6
Broomhill WF10 ......201 A3
Broomhill Cl 28 WF11 ..202 A2
Broomhill Cres 2
WF11 ....202 A2
Broomhill Dr 3 WF11 ..202 A2
Broomhill Gr 19 WF11 ..202 A2
Broomhill Pl 22 WF11 ..202 A2
Broomhill Sq 11 WF11 ..202 A2
Brotes La BD23 ......169 C8
Brotes Wlk BD23 .....164 B5
Brotherton & Byram Com
Prim Sch WF11 ......201 A4
Brough Ave 5 DL6 ....43 F4
Brough La TS14 ......8 D6
Brough Hall* DL10 ....41 A4
Brough Mdws 2 DL10 ..41 D5
Brough Rd 28 DL9 ....40 E4
Brougham Cl YO30 ....227 B4

Brougham St
Darlington DL3 ....3 C7
Skipton BD23 ....217 A3
Broughton Cres BD23 ..216 C3
Broughton Gn La
YO17 ....121 C4
Broughton Gr BD23 ...216 D3
Broughton Mews
BD23 ....216 D3
Broughton Rd
11 East Ayton/West Ayton
YO13 ....99 A7
Malton YO17 ....215 A5
Skipton BD23 ....216 D3
Broughton Rise YO17 ..215 B5
Broughton Way 1
4 Harrogate HG2 .....220 C3
York YO10 ....229 B4
Brow La LA2 ....129 D6
Browcliff BD20 ......174 C2
Brown Bank La BD20 ..174 C2
Brown Bank Rd
Kirkby Malzeard HG4 ..111 F5
Norwood HG3 ....177 B8
Brown Cow Rd YO13 ...204 C8
Brown Howe Rd YO18 ..51 A1
Brown La YO13 ....141 F1
Brown Moor 22 YO41 ..168 D2
Brown Rigg Rd YO13 ..53 F5
Brown's Terr 4 TS13 ..11 F7
Browney Croft YO10 ...233 C1
Browning Cl 3 DL9 ...40 E4
Brownlow St YO1 .....233 C4
Brownmoor La
Huby YO61 ....144 A2
Sutton-on-the-Forest
YO61 ....166 B8
Brownroyd 14 BB18 ...172 B1
Browns Ct 4 BD20 ....173 E3
Brownsea Rd TS18 ....5 D5
Brownsfield Rd 2 LS29 .174 F4
Broxa Hill YO13 ......74 C6
Broxa La YO13 ....74 D5
Broxa Moor La YO13 ..74 C7
Bruce Way 5 YO10 ....95 F6
Brunel Ct 12 YO7 ....227 F5
Brunel Rd HG1 ....219 B2
Brunel Way DL1 ......3 A5
Brunsell La YO26 ....163 F7
Brunswick Cl 2 YO32 .167 B8
Brunswick Dr HG1 ....219 B2
Brunswick Pl 1 HG1 ..219 D1
Brunswick Sch Ctr
YO11 ....213 A5
Brunswick St
Whitby YO21 ....208 D6
York YO23 ....228 B1
Brunt Acres Est DL8 ..59 A5
Brunt Acres Rd DL8 ..54 D6
Brunthwaite La BD20 ..174 E1
Brunton Bank DL8 ....59 A5
Brunton La HG5 ......163 B6
Brunton Rd LA2 ......131 A6
Bry Hills YO12 ......99 D6
Bryan Cl 16 DL2 .....3 E1
Bryden Cl DL6 ....210 E5
Bryony Cl YO8 ......232 B2
Bryony Ct YO8 ......232 B2
Bryony Rd 4 HG3 ....161 B3
Bryony Way 5 HG3 ...161 B3
Bubwith Prim Sch
YO8 ....199 D7
Buck Haw Brow BD24 ..131 A4
Buck La YO61 ....147 B6
Buck Stone La BD22 ..187 C5
Buckden Cl 13 YO61 ..143 D8
Buckden Wood La
BD23 ....107 D8
Buckingham Ct YO1 ..233 A1
Buckingham Sq 8 YO62 .92 F6
Buckingham St YO1 ..233 B2
Buckingham Terr YO1 .233 B2
Buckingham Way
WF11 ....201 F4
Buckle Cl YO8 ....199 A8
Buckle Cl YO8 ....232 B7
Buckle La WF6 ......200 A1
Bucks La 1 BD24 ....131 D2
Buess La DL1 ....4 A7
Buffet Hill La LA2 ..129 C7
Bugthorpe La YO41 ..169 D5
Bugthorpe La Town E
YO41 ....169 E5
Bull Alley La DN14 ..204 B3
Bull Balk YO41 ......185 E4
Bull Hill DL8 ....61 E8
Bull Ing La BD23 ....134 D3
Bull La Huby YO61 ...166 B7
York YO61 ....228 F3
Bull Moor La YO60 ...168 A8
Bull Piece La YO17 ..122 D3
Bullamoor Cl DL6 ....210 F5
Bullamoor Jun Sch
DL6 ....210 F5
Bullamoor Rd DL6 ....210 E6
Buller St YO8 ....232 B6
Bullock Cl
Newsham YO7 ....88 F8
Newsham with Breckenbrough
YO7 ....89 A8
Bullytree La LS25 ...195 E2
Bulmer Hill YO60 ....145 B6
Bungalow Rd BD20 ...187 D7
Bunkers Hill
Aberford LS25 ....194 F7
1 Skipton BD23 ......217 A4

Burdale Cl
 ☑ Eaglescliffe TS16 . . . . .5 D5
 Norton YO17 . . . . .215 F2
Burdike Ave YO30 . . . . .228 A8
Burdock Cl ☑ HG3 . . . . .161 B3
Burdon Garth TS17 . . . . .6 D5
Burgate YO18 . . . . .95 F7
Burgess Wlk YO24 . . . . .230 C8
Burghley Dr ☑ TS17 . . . . . . .6 A5
Burgoyne Cl HG4 . . . . .113 D3
Burke Rd YO17 . . . . .215 C5
Burke St HG1 . . . . .219 E5
Burlands La YO26 . . . . .182 F7
Burley Ave HG3 . . . . .161 A2
Burley Bank Cl HG3 . . . . . . .161 A3
Burley Bank Rd HG3 . . . . . . .161 A3
Burley Cl
 South Milford LS25 . . . . .195 F2
 Thornton-le-Street YO7 . . . . . .65 B1
Burley La ☑ HG3 . . . . .161 A3
Burley Oaks Prim Sch ☑
 LS29 . . . . .176 C1
Burlington Ave YO10 . . . . . . .228 F4
Burlyn Rd ☑ YO14 . . . . .127 A8
Burma Rd DL2 . . . . .3 F7
Burn Bridge La HG3 . . . . . . .222 C2
Burn Bridge Oval HG3 . . . . . .222 C3
Burn Bridge Rd HG3 . . . . . . .222 C3
Burn Est YO32 . . . . .225 E4
Burn Hall Cl YO8 . . . . .203 D7
Burn La YO8 . . . . .203 D6
Burn Wood Ct TS21 . . . . .5 A7
Burn Rd ☑ HG1 . . . . .219 B5
Burneston CE VA Prim Sch
 DL8 . . . . .87 E8
Burneston Hargill DL8 . . . . . . .87 F8
Burnett Cl HG3 . . . . .140 A2
Burnham Rd LS25 . . . . .194 C3
Burnholme Ave YO31 . . . . . .229 B6
Burnholme Com Coll
 YO31 . . . . .229 A5
Burnholme Dr YO31 . . . . . . .229 A6
Burnholme Gr YO31 . . . . . . .229 A5
Burniston Gdns YO13 . . . . . . .75 D7
Burniston Gr YO10 . . . . .229 A4
Burniston Rd YO12 . . . . .212 E8
Burnley Rd BB8 . . . . .186 A1
Burnleys Ct LS26 . . . . .200 B4
Burnleys Dr LS26 . . . . .200 B4
Burnleys Mews LS26 . . . . . . .200 B4
Burnleys View LS26 . . . . .200 B4
Burnmoor Cres LA6 . . . . .103 D3
Burnmoor Dr TS6 . . . . .5 D5
Burnroyd Ave ☑ BD20 . . . . .187 E7
Burns Cl YO24 . . . . .230 B7
Burns Hill ☑ LS29 . . . . .174 F4
Burns Way
 Boston Spa LS23 . . . . .188 E7
Burnsall Cl ☑ YO14 . . . . . . .101 A3
Burnsall Dr YO26 . . . . .227 E4
Burnsall La BD23 . . . . .135 A1
Burnsall Mews BD20 . . . . . . .178 B2
Burnsall VA Prim Sch
 BD23 . . . . .157 B8
Burnside ☑ YO11 . . . . .100 A6
Burnside Ave BD23 . . . . .216 F2
Burnside Cl ☑ HG1 . . . . .219 B5
Burnside Cres BD23 . . . . . . .216 F2
Burnside Dr HG1 . . . . .219 B5
Burnside Rd
 Darlington DL1 . . . . .3 E4
 Harrogate HG1 . . . . .219 B5
Burnside Wlk HG1 . . . . .219 B5
Burnt La HG4 . . . . .87 A1
Burnt Yates CE Prim Sch
 HG3 . . . . .160 F8
Burnthouse Bank DL6 . . . . . . .45 B3
Burr Bank ☑ YO17 . . . . .213 B6
Burrard Ave DL10 . . . . .209 B7
Burrill Ave YO30 . . . . .228 B8
Burrill Dr ☑ YO32 . . . . .166 D5
Burrill Rd DL8 . . . . .62 F2
Burrow Rd LA6 . . . . .102 E5
Burstall Dr ☑ DL9 . . . . .209 C1
Burtersett Rd DL8 . . . . .56 D4
Burton Ave YO30 . . . . .228 B7
Burton Comm La
 LS25 . . . . .202 A6
Burton Ct YO30 . . . . .233 A4
Burton Fields Cl ☑
 YO41 . . . . .168 D2
Burton Fields Rd ☑
 YO41 . . . . .168 D2
Burton Fleming Rd
 YO25 . . . . .126 B3
Burton Gn YO30 . . . . .228 B8
Burton Gn Prim Sch
 YO30 . . . . .228 B8
Burton Hill ☑ LA6 . . . . .102 F3
Burton La YO61 . . . . .141 D8
Burton Leonard Lime
 Quarries Nature Reserve*
 HG3 . . . . .140 A1
Burton Leonard CE Prim Sch
 HG3 . . . . .140 A2
Burton Rd LA2 . . . . .128 E8
Burton Riggs Nature
 Reserve* YO11 . . . . .99 F6
Burton Salmon Com Prim
 Sch LS25 . . . . .201 F6
Burton Stone La YO30 . . . . . .233 A4
Burtondale Rd ☑ YO12 . . . . .99 F7
Burtree Ave YO30 . . . . .224 B4
Burtree Ave YO30 . . . . .224 B4
Burwains La BD23 . . . . .155 F5
Burwen Castle (Roman
 Fort)* BD23 . . . . .172 C4

Burwen Castle Rd
 BD23 . . . . .172 C4
Busby La TS9 . . . . .26 C4
Busk La LS24 . . . . .196 C8
Busky Dike La LS21 . . . . .159 E2
Butcher La Potto DL6 . . . . . . .25 C2
 Whitby DN14 . . . . .207 D6
Butcher Terr YO23 . . . . .228 C1
Butcher's La YO25 . . . . .126 E3
Butler Rd HG1 . . . . .219 E5
Butt Fields La DN14 . . . . . . .203 F1
Butt Hedge YO26 . . . . .182 A5
Butt Hill ☑ Haxby YO32 . . . . .166 D5
 Kippax LS25 . . . . .194 D1
Butt Hills* YO25 . . . . .126 A3
Butt La
 Carlton Husthwaite YO7 . . . . .116 F7
 Guisborough TS14 . . . . .9 A6
 Wold Newton YO25 . . . . .126 A3
Butter Mkt ☑ DN14 . . . . . . .204 C1
Butterbur Way ☑ HG3 . . . . .161 B3
Buttercrambe Rd
 YO41 . . . . .168 C3
Buttercup Cl ☑ HG3 . . . . . . .161 B3
Butterfield Cl HG3 . . . . .140 B5
Butterfield Dr TS16 . . . . .5 D5
Butterfly World* YO18 . . . . . .5 E6
Buttermere Ave
 Middlesbrough TS5 . . . . .6 E8
 ☑ Wetherby LS22 . . . . .180 B3
Buttermere Ct ☑ YO8 . . . . . .232 B6
Buttermere Dr YO30 . . . . . . .224 E1
Butters Cl ☑ YO32 . . . . .166 D5
Butterwick La YO17 . . . . . . .120 F8
Butterwick Rd
 Barton-le-Street YO17 . . . . . .120 E5
 Foxholes YO17 . . . . .125 B7
 Langtoft YO25 . . . . .151 C7
Butthouse Rigg DL11 . . . . . . .35 F8
Buttle La ☑ DN14 . . . . .204 C1
Butts YO8 . . . . .171 D1
Butts Cl ☑ YO41 . . . . .168 D2
Butts Hill YO14 . . . . .127 C6
Butts La Bainbridge DL8 . . . . .81 B8
 Barton-le-Willows YO60 . . . . .146 D2
 Bentham LA2 . . . . .129 A8
 Eaglescliffe TS16 . . . . .5 D4
 Monk Fryston LS25 . . . . .202 A8
 South Milford LS25 . . . . .195 E1
Butts The ☑ WF8 . . . . .201 B1
Buxton Ave TS7 . . . . .7 B5
Byards Pk ☑ HG5 . . . . .221 A7
Byefield Gr YO13 . . . . .99 B8
Byemoor Ave TS9 . . . . .8 A1
Byemoor Cl TS9 . . . . .8 A1
Byland Abbey (rems of)*
 YO61 . . . . .91 E1
Byland Ave
 Northallerton DL6 . . . . .210 E5
 Thirsk YO7 . . . . .211 C3
 York YO31 . . . . .228 E8
Byland Ct ☑ YO21 . . . . .208 B6
Byland Gr HG1 . . . . .219 A6
Byland Mews HG5 . . . . .221 D4
Byland Pl
 Harrogate HG1 . . . . .219 A6
 ☑ Northallerton DL6 . . . . . . .210 E5
Byland Rd
 Harrogate HG1 . . . . .219 A6
 Whitby YO21 . . . . .208 B6
Bylands Way DL3 . . . . .3 A6
Byng Rd DL9 . . . . .209 F1
Byram Cl ☑ DL6 . . . . .210 E3
Byram Ct ☑ DL6 . . . . .210 E3
Byram Pk Ave WF11 . . . . . . .201 F4
Byram Pk Rd WF11 . . . . .202 A4
Byron Ave ☑ DN6 . . . . .206 E1
Byron Cl DL2 . . . . .22 D7
Byron Dr YO30 . . . . .227 F8
Byron St ☑ BD23 . . . . .217 A3
Byron Wlk Mews HG2 . . . . . .219 C2
Byward Dr YO12 . . . . .99 F7
Byway The DL1 . . . . .3 E5
Byways HG2 . . . . .222 B6

C

Cabin La ☑ HG3 . . . . .137 F1
Caburn Cl ☑ YO12 . . . . .212 B8
Caedmon Ave YO21 . . . . . . .208 B8
Caedmon Cl YO31 . . . . .229 A7
Caedmon Sch YO21 . . . . . . .208 B8
Cairn View LS29 . . . . .218 D5
Cairnborrow ☑ YO24 . . . . . .230 B7
Caithness Cl ☑ YO30 . . . . . .224 E3
Calcaria Ct LS24 . . . . .189 D5
Calcaria Rd LS24 . . . . .189 E5
Calcutt HG5 . . . . .221 A4
Caldbeck Cl ☑ YO30 . . . . . . .225 A1
Calder Ave ☑ YO26 . . . . . . .227 B8
Calder Cres DN14 . . . . .207 F6
Caldey Gdns ☑ TS17 . . . . .5 F4
Caledonia St YO12 . . . . .212 E5
Caledonian Way DL1 . . . . .3 F8
Calf Cl YO32 . . . . .225 D8
Calf Fall LA6 . . . . .76 C2
Calf Hall La BB18 . . . . .171 D1
Calf Wood La BD20 . . . . .172 E1
California Ct ☑ TS9 . . . . .7 A2
California Dr WF10 . . . . .200 B3
California Gr ☑ TS9 . . . . .8 A2
California Terr YO22 . . . . .208 E5
Callum Cl DL3 . . . . .3 A7
Calton La BD23 . . . . .155 A6
Calton Terr BD23 . . . . .216 F3
Calvert Ct YO32 . . . . .225 C7

Calvert Hos DL11 . . . . .36 C4
Calverts Garth YO60 . . . . . . .145 D5
Cam Gill Rd BD23 . . . . .108 B4
Cam High Rd BD23 . . . . .79 D5
Cam La BD23 . . . . .172 A3
Camblesforth CP Sch
 YO8 . . . . .204 C4
Cambrian Cl YO32 . . . . .5 F4
Cambrian Cl ☑ YO32 . . . . . . .225 F3
Cambridge Ave TS7 . . . . .7 B5
Cambridge Cres ☑
 HG1 . . . . .219 D2
Cambridge Pl
 ☑ Harrogate HG1 . . . . .219 D2
 ☑ Scarborough YO12 . . . . . .212 E4
Cambridge Rd
 Harrogate HG1 . . . . .219 D2
 Middlesbrough TS5 . . . . .6 E8
Cambridge St
 ☑ Harrogate HG1 . . . . .219 D2
 Normanton South WF6 . . . . . .200 A1
 Scarborough YO12 . . . . .212 F6
 ☑ York YO24 . . . . .228 A3
Cambridge Terr
 ☑ Harrogate HG1 . . . . .219 D2
 ☑ Scarborough YO11 . . . . . .213 A4
Camden Rd WF10 . . . . .201 B4
Camela La YO8 . . . . .204 B6
Cameron Gr YO23 . . . . .228 C1
Camm La DN14 . . . . .204 C3
Cammock La BD24 . . . . .131 D2
Camp Hill Cl HG4 . . . . .114 C2
Camp the (Earthworks)*
 YO11 . . . . .126 C7
Campbell Ave
 Ripon HG4 . . . . .113 D3
 York YO24 . . . . .227 E2
Campbell St ☑ BD20 . . . . . . .187 E8
Campion Cl ☑ YO13 . . . . .75 D5
Campion Dr TS14 . . . . .8 D6
Campion Gr
 Coulby Newham TS7 . . . . .7 B6
 ☑ Harrogate HG3 . . . . .161 B3
Campion La TS15 . . . . .25 A6
Campion Rd DL1 . . . . .3 D7
Campleshon Rd YO23 . . . . . .228 B1
Campsall Balk YO8 . . . . .206 E1
Campsall Hall Rd ☑
 DN6 . . . . .206 E1
Campsall Pk Rd ☑ DN6 . . . . .206 E1
Campsmount Sch
 DN6 . . . . .206 D1
Camwal Rd HG1 . . . . .220 C4
Camwal Terr ☑ HG1 . . . . . . .220 C4
Cana La HG4 . . . . .114 C2
Canaan La DL8 . . . . .60 E2
Canal Garth DN14 . . . . .207 F6
Canal Rd
 Cottingwith YO42 . . . . .193 C5
 Ripon HG4 . . . . .214 D4
 Selby YO8 . . . . .232 D4
Canal St BD23 . . . . .216 F4
Canal View YO8 . . . . .232 D3
Canal Yd ☑ BD23 . . . . .216 F4
Canberra Rd TS7 . . . . .7 B6
Canby La ☑ HG3 . . . . .179 E6
Candler Ave ☑ YO13 . . . . .99 A7
Candler St YO12 . . . . .212 E5
Canham Gr YO10 . . . . .229 D3
Cannon Hall La DN14 . . . . . .202 F1
Cannon St WF10 . . . . .200 F3
Canns La LS25 . . . . .5 E2
Canon Lee Sec Sch
 YO30 . . . . .228 A8
Canons Ct YO30 . . . . .231 B2
Canons Garth La ☑ YO62 . . .192 F6
Canterbury Cl
 ☑ Haxby YO32 . . . . .166 D5
 Whitby YO21 . . . . .208 C5
Canterbury Ct ☑ WF8 . . . . . .201 C2
Canton Gdns TS5 . . . . .6 E6
Caper Hill YO21 . . . . .29 F1
Captain Cook & Staithes
 Heritage Ctr* TS13 . . . . .13 K2
Captain Cook Birthplace
 Mus* TS7 . . . . .7 B7
Captain Cook Cres
 YO22 . . . . .208 E6
Captain Cook Meml Mus*
 YO22 . . . . .208 E7
Captain Cook Prim Sch
 TS7 . . . . .7 B6
Captain Cook's Cl
 Hinderwell TS13 . . . . .11 D8
 Staithes TS13 . . . . .13 K1
Captain Cook's Cres TS7 . . . . .7 C6
Captain Cook's Mon*
 TS9 . . . . .8 D1
Captain Cook's Schoolroom
 Mus* TS9 . . . . .8 A1
Captain Cook's Way TS9 . . . . .8 A1
Captain Cooks Cres ☑
 YO22 . . . . .208 E6
Cardan Pk HG3 . . . . .222 A6
Cardan Dr LS29 . . . . .218 E4
Cardinal Cl ☑ LS25 . . . . .195 F4
Cardinal Gdns DL3 . . . . .3 B5
Cardinals Cl ☑ YO8 . . . . .197 B8
Careless House La
 HG3 . . . . .138 E4
Carentan Cl ☑ YO8 . . . . .232 B6
Carey St YO10 . . . . .228 D1
Cargate Hill ☑ YO14 . . . . . . .101 B3
Cargo Fleet La ☑ TS3 . . . . . . .7 C8
Carl St YO23 . . . . .228 B2
Carla Beck La BD23 . . . . .173 B4
Carlbury Ave TS5 . . . . .6 D6
Carlbury Cres DL3 . . . . .3 A5

Bur - Cas 243

Carr La continued
 Roecliffe YO51 . . . . .140 E3
 Sheriff Hutton YO60 . . . . .145 E6
 Stillington YO61 . . . . .144 C6
 Sutton-on-the-Forest
 YO61 . . . . .144 D2
 Thirlby YO7 . . . . .90 F1
 Thormanby YO61 . . . . .116 E4
 Wetherby LS22 . . . . .180 D4
 Wistow YO8 . . . . .197 A3
 York YO26 . . . . .227 D5
Carr Leys La YO7 . . . . .66 A5
Carr Mill Mews BD22 . . . . . . .187 B5
Carr Rd ☑ BB18 . . . . .171 D2
Carr Side Rd YO26 . . . . .163 F8
Carr The HG3 . . . . .222 E2
Carr Wood Rd WF10 . . . . . . .200 F3
Carrbank La YO23 . . . . .167 E3
Carrfield YO24 . . . . .230 C8
Carrfield Dr LS15 . . . . .194 B8
Carrfield Rd LS15 . . . . .194 B8
Carriage Wlk ☑ TS16 . . . . . . .5 D5
Carrick Gdns YO23 . . . . .227 E3
Carrier's Row BB8 . . . . .186 B2
Carrington Ave ☑ YO26 . . . . .227 E5
Carrnock Ct ☑ YO32 . . . . . . .225 F1
Carrol Cl DL6 . . . . .210 F3
Carrol Pl ☑ DL2 . . . . .22 C8
Carron Cres YO24 . . . . .230 B7
Carrs Mdw YO19 . . . . .192 B5
Carrs The YO21 . . . . .208 A2
Carrside ☑ YO11 . . . . .99 F6
Carseylands Hill BD23 . . . . . .155 A4
Carts Riggin YO7 . . . . .66 A8
Carter Ave YO31 . . . . .228 F5
Carter La ☑ YO62 . . . . .70 B1
Carter's La Ilkley LS29 . . . . . .218 E6
 Longnewton TS16 . . . . .5 A4
Carters Yd DL10 . . . . .209 B6
Cartmell Dr St George DL2 . . . . .4 C3
Cass House Rd TS8 . . . . .6 E4
Cass La
 Knaresborough HG5 . . . . .221 A4
 South Milford LS25 . . . . .195 E1
Castelo Gr ☑ YO18 . . . . .96 A6
Castle Bank DL6 . . . . .25 E1
Castle CE Jun Sch
 HG5 . . . . .221 B6
Castle Cl Cawood YO8 . . . . . .197 A8
 ☑ Haxby HG3 . . . . .166 D5
 Killinghall HG3 . . . . .161 C5
 Middleton St George DL2 . . . . .4 C3
Castle Dr ☑
 Northallerton DL7 . . . . .210 D5
 ☑ Spofforth HG3 . . . . .179 E6
 ☑ Thornton Dale YO18 . . . . . .96 D5
Castle Cres ☑ YO13 . . . . .213 B7
Castle Ct TS15 . . . . .25 A5
Castle Dyke Wynd TS16 . . . . . .5 E3
Castle Earthworks*
 DL8 . . . . .204 F4
Castle End DL8 . . . . .59 B6
Castle Garth
 Pontefract WF8 . . . . .201 C1
 ☑ Thornton Dale YO18 . . . . . .96 D5
Castle Gate ☑ LS29 . . . . .218 B4
Castle Gdns YO11 . . . . .213 B6
Castle Hill
 ☑ Humanby YO14 . . . . .126 F8
 ☑ Ilkley LS29 . . . . .218 B4
 Richmond DL10 . . . . .209 C6
 ☑ Settle BD24 . . . . .131 E2
Castle Hill Cl HG2 . . . . .222 B6
Castle Hill Dr HG2 . . . . .222 B6
Castle Hill Glade HG2 . . . . . .222 B6
Castle Hill Gr HG2 . . . . .222 B6
Castle Hill La ☑ YO8 . . . . . . .204 F5
Castle Howard*
 YO60 . . . . .120 D1
Castle Howard Dr
 YO17 . . . . .215 A4
Castle Howard Rd
 YO17 . . . . .215 A4
Castle Ings ☑ HG3 . . . . .179 E5
Castle Ings Cl ☑ HG5 . . . . . .221 A5
Castle Ings Rd ☑ HG5 . . . . . .221 A5
Castle La Danby YO21 . . . . . . .29 D6
 ☑ East Ayton/West Ayton
 YO13 . . . . .99 B8
Castle Mdws DL8 . . . . .87 A7
Castle Mills HG5 . . . . .221 A5
 ☑ Ilkley LS29 . . . . .218 B4
 Killinghall HG3 . . . . .161 C5
 ☑ Pickering YO18 . . . . .95 F7
 Scarborough YO11 . . . . .213 A6
 Thornton Dale YO18 . . . . .96 D5
 Whitby YO21 . . . . .208 A6
Castle Rise ☑ YO13 . . . . .99 A7
Castle Side YO60 . . . . .145 C5
Castle St Skipton BD23 . . . . . .217 A3
 ☑ Spofforth HG3 . . . . .179 E6
Castle Steads (Fort)*
 DL8 . . . . .84 C8
Castle Steads* DL11 . . .19 D6
Castle Terr
 ☑ Richmond DL10 . . . . .209 C6
 ☑ Scarborough YO11 . . . . . .213 B6
Castle View
 ☑ Newby & Scalby YO13 . . . . .75 D5
 Richmond DL10 . . . . .209 B6
 Sheriff Hutton YO60 . . . . .145 C5
Castle View Terr BD23 . . . . . .216 F4
Castle Wlk YO11 . . . . .233 C2
Castle Wynd ☑ DL10 . . . . . . .209 C6

244 Cas - Chu

Castle Yd **3** Ilkley LS29 ..218 B4
Knaresborough HG5 .....221 A5
Castle Yd Stables
Coll YO7 ..211 B3
Castlebergh Hospl
BD24 ..131 C2
Castlebergh La **6** BD24 ..131 E2
Castleford High Sch Tech
Coll WF10 ..200 F4
Castleford La
Featherstone WF7 ..200 D2
Knottingley WF11 ..201 B2
Castleford Mkt Pl*
WF10 ..200 D4
Castleford Mus Rm*
WF10 ..200 E4
Castleford Normanton &
District Hospl WF10 ..200 D3
Castleford Rd WF6 ..200 B2
Castleford Redhill Jun Sch
WF10 ..201 B4
Castleford Sta WF10 ..200 E4
Castleford Three La Ends
Prim Sch WF10 ..200 D4
Castlegate
East Ayton/West Ayton
YO13 ..99 A7
Castlekeep Cl YO30 ..209 C8
Castlemount Ave YO13 ..75 C6
Castlereagh Cl TS21 ..5 A7
Castleton Ave
Middlesbrough TS5 ..6 D8
Northallerton DL7 ..210 C1
Castleton Com Prim Sch
YO21 ..29 A7
Castleton Moor Sta
YO21 ..29 A7
Castleton Rd DL9 ..40 F4
Castley La LS21 ..178 A1
Cat Bank DL11 ..39 C6
Cat La Balne DN14 ..207 E5
Bilbrough YO23 ..182 D1
Cat Pottery* DL8 ..58 F1
Cathcart Cl DN14 ..206 F7
Cathedral Cl HG4 ..214 D5
Catherine Love Dr **18**
YO61 ..143 C8
Catherine St **2** TS12 ..9 F7
Cattal Moor La YO26 ..181 B8
Cattal St YO26 ..164 A2
Cattal St YO26 ..164 A2
Cavalry Ct **9** YO12 ..75 F5
Cavendish Ave
Harrogate HG2 ..219 E1
Pontefract WF8 ..201 C2
Cavendish Ct HG2 ..222 F8
Cavendish Gr YO10 ..229 D3
Cavendish Rd TS4 ..7 A8
Cavendish St
Barnoldswick BB18 ..171 D1
Harrogate HG1 ..219 E5
Skipton BD23 ..216 F3
Cavendish Terr **8** HG4 ..214 C4
Cavendish View BD23 ..217 D7
Caversham Rd TS4 ..7 A8
Cawcliff La YO18 ..97 A5
Cawdel Cl LS25 ..195 F2
Cawdel Way LS25 ..195 F2
Cawder Ghyll BD23 ..217 A1
Cawder La BD23 ..217 A2
Cawder Mews BD23 ..217 A1
Cawder Rd BD23 ..217 A2
Cawood CE VA Prim Sch
YO8 ..197 B8
Cawood Cres LS24 ..190 C1
Cawood Dr TS5 ..6 F7
Cawood Rd
Stillingfleet YO19 ..191 D3
Wistow YO8 ..197 C2
Cawthorn Ave HG2 ..220 B2
Cawthorn Pl HG2 ..220 B3
Cawthorne Cres YO14 ..101 A3
Cawthorne La YO18 ..71 D3
Cawton Rd YO62 ..118 F8
Caxton Ave YO26 ..227 D6
Caxton Cl **11** DL10 ..41 C7
Caxton Gdns **4** WF8 ..201 B2
Caxton Way YO11 ..99 F6
Cayley Cl YO30 ..224 F1

Cayley La YO13 ..98 C5
Caymer Rd YO11 ..100 A7
Cayton Com Prim Sch
YO11 ..100 B6
Cayton Low Rd YO11 ..99 F6
Cayton Low Rd Ind Est
YO11 ..100 A6
Cecil Rd **7** YO14 ..127 A8
Cecil St
Barnoldswick BB18 ..171 D2
Harrogate HG1 ..219 E5
Cecilia Pl **3** YO24 ..228 A3
Cedar Cl
Hambleton YO8 ..197 B1
Ripon HG4 ..214 B3
Cedar Cres YO8 ..197 D2
Cedar Dr
Coulby Newham TS8 ..6 D4
Tadcaster LS24 ..189 D6
Cedar Glade YO19 ..184 E7
Cedar Gr Barton DL10 ..21 C7
3 Filey YO14 ..101 B4
Middleton One Row DL2 ..4 D3
Sutton BD20 ..187 E7
York YO31 ..229 B7
Cedar Mews **4** BD22 ..22 D8
Cedar Rd DL3 ..3 B6
Cedar Ridge LS25 ..194 E5
Cedar Vale **6** BD22 ..70 B1
Cedarhurst Dr TS12 ..9 F7
Cedarwood **3** DL2 ..4 C4
Cedarwood Ave **1** TS9 ..26 C8
Cedarwood Cl **3** YO24 ..227 B1
Cedarwood Glade TS8 ..6 E4
Celtic Cl YO30 ..227 B5
Cemetery La DL3 ..3 A5
Cemetery Rd
10 Earby BB18 ..172 A1
Normanton South WF6 ..200 B1
Thirsk YO7 ..211 A3
York YO10 ..233 C1
Cennon St **3** TS17 ..5 F4
Centenary Row BD23 ..217 D8
Central Arc DL61 ..210 D5
Central Av **6** YO11 ..143 D8
Central Dr
Castleford WF10 ..200 C4
Northallerton DL61 ..210 E4
Central St TS16 ..5 E3
Central Way **1** TS9 ..8 A2
Centre La LS24 ..189 E6
Centre Rd BD20 ..186 D7
Centurian Cl **7** DL10 ..41 E4
Centurion Pk YO30 ..225 B2
Centurion Way
Clifton YO30 ..225 B3
Crossgates YO12 ..99 E6
Century Wlk **1** HG2 ..220 B3
Ceres Rd LS22 ..180 C3
Chacksfield Rd **6** DL10 ..41 E4
Chadderton Cl TS13 ..9 E8
Chadderton Dr TS17 ..6 C7
Chafer Wood Nature
Reserve* YO13 ..97 D6
Chain Bar La HG3 ..161 A4
Chain La HG5 ..221 C6
Chair Wlk HG4 ..139 B8
Chaldon Cl **4** YO30 ..167 A6
Chaldron Way TS16 ..5 D6
Chalfield Cl TS17 ..6 B4
Chalfonts YO24 ..227 F1
Chalford Oaks TS5 ..6 D8
Challacombe Cres TS17 ..6 A3
Challoner Rd TS15 ..5 D2
Chaloner St TS14 ..8 F6
Chaloner's Cres YO24 ..230 C7
Chaloner's Rd YO24 ..230 D8
Chamber End Fold **5**
BD23 ..134 E3
Champion Ave **8** WF10 ..200 F3
Chancel Way YO21 ..208 A6
Chancery Ct YO24 ..227 C3
Chancery Rise
Stockton-on-Tees TS18 ..6 A6
York YO24 ..227 F3
Chandler Cl DL10 ..209 F8
Chandlers Ct YO11 ..213 B2
Chandlers Ridge Prim Sch
TS7 ..7 D5
Chandlers Wharf
YO7 ..215 C3
Chantilly Ave DL1 ..3 F7
Chantry Ave **1** YO60 ..146 E6
Chantry Ave **14** YO26 ..165 F1
Chantry Bank DL8 ..59 D3
Chantry Cl YO24 ..230 C8
Chantry Ct HG3 ..161 C7
Chantry Dr
East Ayton/West Ayton
YO13 ..99 B8
2 Ilkley LS29 ..218 B3
Chantry Gap **11** YO26 ..165 F1
Chantry Garth DL8 ..59 D3
Chantry Gr **13** YO26 ..165 F1
Chantry La
Bishopthorpe YO23 ..231 B4
Stutton with Hazlewood
LS24 ..189 B3
Chantry Rd
5 East Ayton/West Ayton
YO13 ..99 B8
Northallerton DL7 ..210 B3
Chantry Wynd **7** YO26 ..165 F1
Chapel Balk Rd YO8 ..198 F1
Chapel Bridge* DL11 ..1 C7

Chapel Cl
Bilton-in-Ainsty with Bickerton
LS22 ..181 B5
Church Fenton LS24 ..196 B8
21 Helmsley YO62 ..92 F6
Rawcliffe DN14 ..205 A1
Chapel Cres DL7 ..63 C8
Chapel Croft **8** BD23 ..134 E3
Chapel Ct
Gargrave BD23 ..155 D1
Huby YO61 ..144 A4
Chapel Fields Rd
YO26 ..227 A3
Chapel Fold **6** BD20 ..134 E3
Chapel Garth
Dalton YO7 ..115 E7
Markington with Wallerthwaite
HG3 ..139 C3
Thorntoft DL7 ..63 F7
Chapel Gate
Kirkby Malham BD23 ..154 F8
Malham BD23 ..132 F1
Sherburn YO17 ..124 D6
Chapel Haddlesey CE VC
Prim Sch YO8 ..203 B5
Chapel Hill
Boroughbridge YO51 ..141 C5
Kearby with Netherby
LS22 ..179 B1
Skipton BD23 ..217 A5
Chapel Hill La LS21 ..178 A1
Chapel House Mews **9**
BD23 ..173 B4
Chapel La
Askham Bryan YO23 ..182 F3
Barwick in Elmet LS15 ..194 C8
Boston Spa LS23 ..188 E7
Brayton YO8 ..232 B1
Brompton YO13 ..98 B7
5 Burton in Lonsdale LA6 ..102 F3
10 Easingwold YO61 ..143 C8
18 Eastfield YO11 ..100 B6
Fingall DL8 ..61 E4
Halton East BD23 ..174 C8
Harome YO62 ..93 C4
Hebden BD23 ..135 A2
Horton in Ribblesdale
BD24 ..105 C3
Ilkley LS29 ..218 A4
Langtoft YO25 ..151 D5
Little Smeaton WF8 ..206 B3
Marton-le-Moor HG4 ..114 F1
Rawcliffe DN14 ..205 A2
Reighton YO14 ..127 E5
3 Riccall YO19 ..192 A1
2 Spofforth HG3 ..179 E5
3 Thornton Dale YO18 ..96 D5
Tollerton YO61 ..143 A3
Westow YO60 ..147 B4
Chapel Mews YO7 ..211 C2
Chapel of Our Lady*
YO11 ..213 C7
Chapel Rd
22 Scarborough YO11 ..213 A6
Settrington YO17 ..122 D1
Chapel Riggs **8** DL10 ..41 E4
Chapel Row YO10 ..233 C1
Chapel Sq **2** BD23 ..131 E2
Chapel St
3 Addingham LS29 ..174 F4
6 Beadlam YO62 ..93 D7
Carleton BD23 ..173 B4
Cattal YO26 ..164 A1
12 Earby BB18 ..172 A1
27 Filey YO14 ..101 B3
Grassington BD23 ..134 E3
Hambleton YO8 ..196 F1
Hillam LS25 ..202 B2
Kirk Hammerton YO26 ..164 C2
Knaresborough HG5 ..221 B5
Middleton St George DL2 ..4 C4
Nunnington YO62 ..93 E2
12 Settle BD24 ..131 D2
Tadcaster LS24 ..189 E6
Thirsk YO7 ..211 B2
Chapel Terr YO24 ..227 C3
Chapel Wlk
Long Preston BD23 ..153 F5
3 Riccall YO19 ..192 A1
Chapman Cl **1** YO22 ..167 C8
Chapman Ct BB18 ..171 D2
Chapman La **8** HG4 ..86 C3
Chapman Sq HG1 ..219 B2
Chapman's La YO30 ..165 E7
Chapman's Ct YO24 ..230 D6
Chapter House St YO1 ..233 B3
Charles Ave HG1 ..219 E5
Charles Ct DL10 ..209 F7
Charles Moor YO31 ..228 F7
Charles St YO8 ..232 B6
Charles Wesley Dr
YO8 ..232 B2
Charlock TS8 ..7 B4
Charlton Ave
Knaresborough HG5 ..221 B6
2 Whitby YO21 ..208 B7
Charlton Ct **10** HG5 ..221 B6
Charlton Dr HG5 ..221 B6
Charlton Gr **2** HG5 ..221 B6
Charlton Manor Dr **8**
HG5 ..221 B6
Charlton St YO23 ..228 C2
Charlton Villas HG5 ..221 B6
Charnwood Dr TS7 ..7 D6
Charrington Ave TS17 ..6 A6
Charter Ave DN14 ..205 A1
Charters The YO8 ..198 B5
Chartwell Cl TS17 ..6 B4

Chase Garth Rd **18**
YO61 ..143 C8
Chase Side Ct YO24 ..230 E8
Chase The
9 Boroughbridge YO51 ..141 B4
Garforth LS25 ..194 D4
Hurworth-on-Tees DL2 ..3 E1
Knaresborough HG5 ..221 D5
Norton YO17 ..215 E2
17 Wetherby LS22 ..180 C3
Chastworth Ct HG1 ..219 D4
Chatham Rd HG4 ..113 D2
Chatsworth Ave **7** WF8 ..201 C2
Chatsworth Dr
16 Haxby YO32 ..166 F5
2 Wetherby LS22 ..180 B3
Chatsworth Gdns
YO12 ..212 E7
Chatsworth Gr
4 Boroughbridge YO51 ..141 B5
Harrogate HG1 ..219 C4
Chatsworth Pl **1** HG1 ..219 D4
Chatsworth Rd HG1 ..219 D4
Chatsworth Terr
2 Harrogate HG1 ..219 E4
4 York YO26 ..227 E4
Chaucer Gn HG1 ..219 F7
Chaucer La HG1 ..69 F5
Chaucer St **7** YO10 ..228 E3
Chaumont Way **1** YO32 ..167 D2
Chauvent Cl YO7 ..209 C2
Cheapside
2 Knaresborough HG5 ..221 B5
11 Normanton South WF6 ..200 A1
11 Settle BD24 ..131 D2
Cheapsides Rd YO17 ..215 B8
Checker La YO19 ..198 A7
Checkstone Ave
WF10 ..200 D2
Chelkar Way YO30 ..224 F1
Chelmsford Rd HG1 ..219 E2
Cheltenham Ave
Ilkley LS29 ..218 E4
Middlesbrough TS7 ..7 B5
Cheltenham Cres **6**
HG1 ..219 D2
Cheltenham Mount
HG1 ..219 D3
Cheltenham Par HG1 ..219 D3
Cheltenham Rd **8** HG1 ..219 D3
Chelwood Wlk **2** YO26 ..227 E4
Chepstow Ct **14** DL1 ..3 F6
Cherry Ave
Malton YO17 ..215 D6
Swinton YO17 ..121 B4
Cherry Cl YO21 ..208 B6
Cherry Garth HG1 ..219 E4
Cherry Garth Rd DL7 ..210 C3
Cherry Gr **7** Bedale DL8 ..63 B3
2 Ilkley LS29 ..175 C2
10 Poppleton YO26 ..165 F1
Cherry Hill La YO23 ..233 B1
Cherry La YO24 ..230 F8
Cherry Orch **2** YO22 ..225 D8
Cherry Paddock
4 Haxby YO32 ..225 D8
Kexby YO41 ..168 C2
Cherry Rd **1** YO14 ..127 A8
Cherry St YO23 ..233 B1
Cherry Tree Ave
Newton-on-Ouse YO30 ..165 B6
1 Scarborough YO12 ..212 B5
York YO32 ..225 D3
Cherry Tree Cl
13 Brayton YO8 ..197 D1
5 Castleford WF10 ..200 F3
Cherry Tree Cr **12** YO8 ..198 B5
Cherry Tree Dr YO14 ..101 A4
Cherry Tree Gdns **7**
DL9 ..209 B1
Cherry Tree Way **14** DL9 ..41 A5
Cherry Tree Wlk
Amotherby YO17 ..121 A4
2 Barlby YO8 ..198 B4
Cherry Wood Cres
YO19 ..231 E5
Cherrytree Cl **9** HG4 ..140 E7
Cherrywood Ave **4** TS9 ..26 C8
Chervil Ct TS8 ..7 B4
Cherwell Croft YO8 ..196 F1
Cherwell Ct YO8 ..196 F1
Cheshire Ave YO32 ..167 A6
Cheshire Cl **6** YO32 ..226 E4
Cheshire Sq YO7 ..89 B1
Chesler-pit La YO61 ..117 F2
Chesney Fields **4** YO24 ..227 F3
Chessingham Gdns
YO24 ..230 E6
Chessingham Pk YO19 ..184 F6
Chester Ct Rd YO8 ..204 A6
Chester La DL6 ..65 D8
Chester Rd TS17 ..6 A6
Chestnut Ave
2 Airmyn DN14 ..205 E4
Harrogate HG1 ..219 F3
Malton YO17 ..215 D6
Thornton Dale YO18 ..96 D6
2 Topcliffe YO7 ..89 A1
Welburn YO60 ..146 E6
York YO31 ..228 F8

Chestnut Cres
6 Catterick Garrison DL9 ..40 F5
1 Catton YO7 ..89 A1
Chestnut Croft **7** YO8 ..198 F1
Chestnut Ct
8 Hemingbrough YO8 ..198 F1
York YO32 ..225 F5
Chestnut Dr
17 Barnoldswick BB18 ..171 D1
8 Hemingbrough YO8 ..198 F1
Middlesbrough TS7 ..7 C6
Chestnut Garth **4** YO8 ..198 F1
Chestnut Gn **10** LS25 ..202 A8
Chestnut Gr
Acomb YO23 ..227 C4
Harrogate HG1 ..219 E6
Huntington YO32 ..225 E4
Norton YO17 ..215 F2
Chestnut Mews **5** YO7 ..197 A8
Chestnut Rd
Cawood YO8 ..197 A8
Eaglescliffe TS16 ..5 E6
Chestnut Rise **6** YO8 ..198 F1
Chestnuts The
8 Haxby YO32 ..225 C8
Hensall DN14 ..203 D2
Pontefract WF8 ..201 C2
Scarborough YO12 ..212 B7
Chevin Dr YO14 ..101 A3
Cheviot Cl **1** YO32 ..225 F3
Chew La
Gargrave BD23 ..155 D1
Seamer YO12 ..99 D6
Chichester Cl **18** YO13 ..75 D5
Chieftain Rd DL9 ..40 C4
Chiltern Ave WF10 ..200 C3
Chiltern Way YO32 ..225 F5
Chilvers Ct **9** YO22 ..232 A1
Chimes Rd YO8 ..232 C6
Chimes The **9** YO8 ..232 C6
China St DL3 ..3 D7
Chippendale Rise **8**
LS21 ..177 A1
Chippenham Rd TS4 ..7 A7
Cholmley Way YO22 ..208 F3
Christ Church CE Prim Sch
BB8 ..186 A3
Christ Church CE VC Prim
Sch BD23 ..216 F3
Christ Church Oval
HG1 ..219 E2
Christina St **3** HG1 ..219 C5
Christ's Hospl DL8 ..63 A1
Christy Gate Rd YO21 ..28 E4
Chubb Hill Rd YO21 ..208 C6
Chudleigh Rd
Harrogate HG1 ..219 F4
3 York YO26 ..227 F5
Church Ave
Clapham LA2 ..130 C8
4 Dacre HG3 ..137 F1
Harrogate HG1 ..219 D5
York YO31 ..232 C6
Church Balk YO19 ..184 E7
Church Bank
Aysgarth DL8 ..58 F3
Hunton DL8 ..61 F7
Kirkby Malzeard HG4 ..112 D5
Church Cl
Askham Bryan YO23 ..182 F3
Bagby YO7 ..90 C3
4 Bubwith YO8 ..199 D7
Carleton BD23 ..173 B4
18 Filey YO14 ..101 B4
1 Hambleton YO8 ..196 F1
Killinghall HG3 ..219 A8
Kirby Hill YO51 ..141 B7
Middleton St George DL2 ..4 C3
Newby & Scalby YO13 ..75 C5
Redmire DL8 ..59 C5
Sawley HG4 ..138 E6
Sharow HG4 ..214 F7
4 Swillington LS26 ..194 A1
5 Tollerton YO61 ..143 B3
Wheldrake YO19 ..193 A7
Church Cliff Dr **9** YO14 ..101 B4
Church Cres
Stutton with Hazlewood
LS24 ..189 D4
Swillington LS26 ..194 A1
Church Croft
Barkston Ash LS24 ..195 F7
Gargrave BD23 ..172 C8
Church Cswy LS23 ..188 F8
Church Dike La **3** WF6 ..200 A1
Church Dike La YO8 ..204 F5
Church Dr
Great Ayton TS9 ..7 F1
Lockwood TS12 ..9 E7
Church End
Cawood YO8 ..197 B8
Sheriff Hutton YO60 ..145 D5
Church Farm Cl YO7 ..211 A6
Church Farm Ct LS23 ..182 C6
Church Farm View
LS15 ..194 C8
Church Fenton La
LS24 ..196 A8
Church Fenton Sta
LS24 ..196 A8
Church Field La **2**
YO26 ..164 A8
Church Field Rd DN6 ..206 E1
Church Garth DL6 ..25 D2
Church Gdns LS25 ..194 C3
Church Gn **3** YO41 ..185 C2

Church Hill
4 Bramham LS23 ....188 E5
Crayke YO61 ....118 A1
Easingwold YO61 ....117 C1
10 Hunmanby YO14 ....126 F8
Hunsingore LS22 ....180 E8
Malton YO17 ......215 C4
Newby & Scalby YO13 ...75 C5
North Rigton LS17 ...178 B3
Reighton YO14 ......127 C6
3 Selby YO8 ......232 D5
Sherburn in Elmet LS25 .195 E4
4 Spofforth HG3 ....179 E6
Stillingfleet YO19 ....191 D3
Thorner LS14 ......188 A3
Thornton Dale YO18 ....96 D6
8 Wistow YO8 .....197 D6

Church La
Allerston YO18 ....97 B5
Appleton Roebuck YO23 .190 F4
Aysgarth DL8 ....58 F3
Bagby YO7 ....90 C3
Barton DL10 ......21 C8
Bishopthorpe YO23 ...231 A4
Bolton Percy YO23 ...190 D4
Boroughbridge YO51 ..141 B5
Brompton YO13 ......98 C5
Burnsall BD23 .....157 A8
Carlton DN14 ......204 C3
Catton YO41 ......185 D8
Cayton YO11 ......100 B6
Collingham LS22 ....180 A1
Cropton YO18 ......71 B4
Cundall with Leckby
YO61 ....115 E3
Dunnington YO19 ....184 E7
Eislack BD23 ......172 D4
4 Elvington YO41 ...185 C2
Faceby TS9 ....25 F1
Fylingdales YO22 ....33 C4
Garforth LS25 ......194 C4
Gargrave BD23 .....172 D8
Gateforth YO8 ......202 F6
Gilling East YO62 ...118 F7
Guisborough TS7 .....7 E5
Hampsthwaite HG3 ...161 A6
17 Haxby YO32 .....166 E5
Hebden BD23 ......135 A1
Hensall DN14 ......203 C1
Hutton Buscel YO13 ....98 F7
Ingleby Greenhow TS9 ..27 B5
Kelbrook & Sough BB18 .186 A8
Kellington DN14 ....202 E3
Kirby Hill YO26 .....164 B7
Kirby Hill YO51 ....141 B7
Knaresborough HG5 ..221 A6
Langtoft YO25 ......151 C1
Low Worsall TS15 .....24 A8
Marton cum Grafton
YO51 ....141 D1
Martons Both BD23 ...172 A5
Mickletield LS25 ....194 F4
Mickletown LS26 ....200 B5
Middlesbrough TS5 .....6 E7
Middleton YO18 ......95 E8
Middleton St George DL2 ..4 C3
Milby YO51 ......141 B7
4 Monk Fryston LS25 ..202 A8
Moor Monkton YO26 ..224 B3
Nether Poppleton YO26 .224 B3
New Earswick YO32 ...165 E5
2 Normanton South WF6 .200 A1
North Featherstone
WF7 ....200 E1
Pannal HG3 ......222 D4
Poppleton YO26 ....224 A3
Rainton YO7 ......114 E6
Redmire DL8 ....59 C5
Ripon HG4 ......214 B5
Sadberge DL2 ....4 C7
Scarborough YO11 ...213 B7
4 Selby YO8 ......232 D5
Sessay YO7 ......116 C6
Settrington YO17 ...122 D1
Sinnington YO62 .....71 A1
Skelton YO30 ......224 B5
Slingsby YO62 .....120 B6
2 Snaith DN14 .....204 C1
South Stainley with Cayton
HG3 ....139 E2
5 Spofforth HG3 ....179 E6
Stainburn LS21 .....177 E3
Stainforth BD24 ....131 E6
10 Stamford Bridge YO41 .168 D2
Stensall YO32 .....167 A7
Stutton with Hazlewood
LS24 ....189 E4
Swillington LS26 ....194 A1
Terrington YO60 ....119 F1
Thormanby YO61 ...116 F5
Thornton Dale YO18 ...96 D6
Thwing YO25 ......126 A1
Tunstall LA6 ......102 B4
Walton YO60 ......146 E6
Weston LS21 ......176 D1
Westow YO60 ......147 B4
Wheldrake YO19 ....193 A4
Whitby YO22 ......208 E7
Whorlton DL6 ......25 D1
Wigginton YO32 ....183 D1
Wighill LS24 ......181 D1
Wintringham YO17 ...123 C4
York YO1 ....233 B2
Church Mdw DL10 ....21 D8
Church Mdw 9 LS23 ..188 E6

Church Mews
Barlby YO8 ......198 A5
13 Boroughbridge YO51 .141 B5

Church Mews continued
Sherburn in Elmet LS25 .195 F4
2 York YO26 ......227 C3

Church Rd
5 Glusburn BD20 ....187 E7
Great Preston LS26 ...200 C8
Linton BD23 ......134 E2
Pontefract WF6 ....200 A3
Scotton DL9 ....40 E4
Stainton Dale YO13 ....54 A7
Stamford Bridge YO41 ..168 D2
Thornton in Craven
BD23 ....171 F3
York YO10 ......229 D4
Church Rise YO19 ...167 F1

Church Row
Hurworth-on-Tees DL2 ...3 E1
Melsonby DL10 ......20 F7
Church Side LS26 ...200 B5

Church Sq
Harrogate HG1 ......219 F3
Whitby YO21 ......208 C7

Church St
Addingham LS29 ....175 A4
Amotherby YO17 ....121 B4
Asenby YO7 ......115 B7
Barkston Ash LS24 ...195 F7
Bellerby DL8 ....60 D7
Bilton-in-Ainsty with Bickerton
YO26 ....181 D5
Boston Spa LS23 ...188 E8
Broughton BD23 ....172 D7
Bubwith YO8 ......199 D7
Carleton BD23 .....173 B4
Church Fenton LS24 ..196 B7
Copmanthorpe YO23 ..230 B2
Danby YO21 ....29 B7
Dunnington YO19 ....184 E7
5 Easingwold YO61 ..143 C8
5 Filey YO14 ......101 B3
Gargrave BD23 .....155 D1
16 Glusburn BD20 ....187 E8
Goldsborough HG5 ...163 A3
Guisborough TS14 .....8 F7
8 Helmsley YO62 ....92 F6
Heslerton YO17 ....123 F7
Hovingham YO62 ...119 E6
Ilkley LS29 ......218 A4
Ingleton LA6 ......103 D4
Kirk Hammerton YO26 .164 C2
Kirkby Malzeard HG4 ..112 D5
24 Kirkbymoorside YO62 ..70 B1
Knottingley WF11 ...201 E4
Long Preston BD23 ...153 F4
6 Masham HG4 .....86 C3
6 Middleham DL8 .....60 E2
Norton YO17 ......215 D3
Nunnington YO62 ....93 E2
2 Scarborough YO11 ..213 B6
Settle BD24 ......131 D3
5 Skipton BD23 .....216 F3
5 Staithes TS13 ......13 K2
Trawden BB8 ......186 B1
Ulleskelf LS24 .....190 C3
Well DL8 ....87 A4
West Tanfield HG4 ....87 A1
14 Wetherby LS22 ....180 C3
Whitby YO22 ......208 E6
Whixley YO26 .....164 A5
York YO1 ....233 A2
Church St St 3 YO11 .213 B6

Church View
12 Airmyn DN14 ....205 E4
5 Brompton DL6 .....43 F3
16 Hurworth DL2 ......3 E1
Kirby Hill YO51 ....141 B7
Ledston LS25 ......194 E1
Norton DN6 ......206 E1
Sherburn YO17 ....124 D8
Sherburn in Elmet LS25 .195 F4
South Milford LS25 ...195 F2
Thirsk YO7 ......211 C1
Church View Mews 7
LS23 ....188 E7

Church Wind
Aine YO61 ......142 F4
.Burneston DL8 ......87 E7

Church Wlk
Lindrick with Studley
Royal & Fountains HG4 .139 B7
1 Willerby YO12 ......99 D2
8 Wistow YO8 .....197 D6
Church Wynd DL10 ..209 C7
Churchfield Dr 28 YO32 .166 E5

Churchfield La
Castleford WF10 ....200 F3
8 Kippax LS25 .....194 D1
Little Smeaton DN6 ..206 C4
Churchfields DL6 ...210 E4
Churchill Cl 3 TS9 ....8 A2
Churchill Way 4 BD20 .187 E8
Churchside Villas
LS26 ....200 B5
Churchville LS25 ...194 F4
Churchville Ave LS25 .194 F4
Churchville Dr LS25 ..194 F4
Churchville Terr LS25 .195 A4
Churwell Cl WF10 ...200 E2

Cinder La
Castleford WF10 ....200 E4
Clifford LS23 ......188 F7
Lindley LS21 ......177 C3
Upper Poppleton YO26 .227 A4
York YO1 ....228 A4
Cinder Mews YO26 ..228 A5
Citadilla Cl 5 DL10 ...41 C7
Clack La DL8 ......45 A4
Clapdale Dr LA2 ....130 C8

Clapdale Way 2 LA2 ..130 C8
Clapgate Bank DL11 ...39 D8
Clapham CE VC Prim Sch
LA2 ....130 C7
Clapham Sta LA2 ...130 D6
Clare Ave DL3 ....3 A5
Claremont 28 YO14 ..101 B3
Claremont Dr TS7 .....7 C5
Claremont La HG3 ...140 B5
Claremont La BB18 ..186 A3
Claremont Terr YO11 .233 B4
Claremont Ave 49 YO14 .101 B3
Clarence Dr Filey YO14 .101 B3
Harrogate HG1 .....219 B3

Clarence Pl
7 Scarborough YO11 ..213 A6
2 Whitby YO21 .....208 D7

Clarence Rd
Middlesbrough TS7 ....7 D5
2 Scarborough YO12 ..213 A7
Scorton DL10 ....41 F7

Clarence St
2 Barnoldswick BB18 ..171 E1
8 Colne BB8 ......186 A3
9 Trawden Forest BB8 .186 B1
York YO31 ......233 B4
Clarendon Ct YO31 ..228 C7

Clarendon Rd
Boston Spa LS23 ...188 E8
Great Burdon DL1 .....3 F3
Clarendon St 10 BB8 .186 A3
Clareton La HG5 ....163 B6
Clark Ct WF7 ......200 E1
Clark St 7 YO12 ....213 A7
Clarke's Croft YO7 ..115 A4
Clarks Terr YO21 ...228 F6
Clarkson Ct 12 WF6 ..200 B1
Clarkson Dr LS25 ...201 F6
Clarkson St 7 YO21 ..208 D7
Claro Ave HG1 .....219 F4
Claro Mews 4 HG5 ..221 A5
Claro Pk HG1 .....219 F4

Claro Rd
Harrogate HG1 ......219 F3
Ripon HG4 ......214 C4
Claro Way HG1 ....219 F4
Claude Ave TS5 ......6 E8
Claudius Dr YO12 ...99 E6
Claver Cl DL6 .....45 D8
Clavery Ley La YO62 ..67 E1
Claxton Ave DL3 .....3 A6
Clay Bank TS9 .....27 A3
Clay Hill YO41 .....169 C3
Clay La Bubwith YO8 .199 C5
Camblesforth YO8 ...204 C6
Cliffe YO8 ......198 D4
Clay Pit La YO51 ...144 A4
Clay Pl 3 YO24 ....227 D1
Claygate YO31 .....229 B6

Claypit La
Carlton DN14 ......204 C8
Ledston WF10 .....201 A8
Clayton Fold 5 BD20 .187 F7
Clayton Hall Rd BD20 .187 F7
Clayton Mews 8 WF6 .200 A2
Clayton Pl 9 WF6 ...200 A2
Clayton St 7 BB18 ..171 E1
Cleasby La DL2 .....2 F1
Cleasby Way TS16 ....5 D6
Clement St 4 YO23 ..233 B1
Clementhorpe YO23 ..233 B1
Clevedon House Sch
LS29 ....176 A1
Clevegate TS7 ......7 C5
Cleveland 1 TS16 ....5 D4

Cleveland Ave
Darlington DL3 ......3 C5
Knottingley WF11 ...201 F2
Scalby YO12 ......212 D8
Stokesley TS9 .....26 C8
Cleveland Coll of Art &
Design TS5 ....6 E8

Cleveland Dr
Middlesbrough TS7 ....7 B6
Northallerton DL7 ...210 D2
Cleveland Inf Est DL1 ...3 D6
Cleveland Rd Boltby YO7 .91 B8
Catterick Garrison DL9 .40 F4
Scarborough YO12 ...212 E6
Scorton DL10 ....41 F7
Cleveland Rein YO7 ..66 A3

Cleveland St
Darlington DL1 ......3 D6
Great Ayton TS9 .....8 A2
Guisborough TS14 .....8 E6
York YO24 ......228 A4

Cleveland Terr
Darlington DL3 ......3 D5
8 Whitby YO21 ....208 D5
York YO24 ......227 F4
Cleveland Trad Est DL1 ...3 D6
Cleveland View 1 TS9 .25 F1

Cleveland Way
1 Carlton Miniott YO7 ..89 C4
Helmsley YO62 .....92 E6
York YO22 ......225 F3
Cliff Bridge Pl 6 YO11 .213 A5
Cliff Bridge Terr 7
YO11 ....213 A5
Cliff Brow YO13 .....11 C7
Cliff Cres LS25 ....194 E1
Cliff Dr 24 DL8 .....60 D5
Cliff Gate Rd DL11 ...35 E4
Cliff Hill Rd DN6 ...206 D2

Cliff La
Newholm-cum-Dunsley
YO21 ....13 B2

Cliff La continued
Snainton YO13 ......97 F5
Whitwell-on-the-Hill
YO60 ....146 A4
Wilton YO18 ......97 A5
Wilton YO18 ......95 B8

Cliff Rd
Stainton Dale YO13 ....54 A8
Staithes TS13 ......13 K2
Cliff St YO21 .....208 D7
Cliff The YO22 .....32 J6
Cliffe Mews YO60 ..119 E1
Cliffe Rd HG2 .....219 C1
Cliffe VC Prim Sch
YO8 ....198 E2
Clifford Ave LS29 ...218 A5
Clifford Ct BD23 ....216 D3
Clifford Moor Rd
LS23 ....188 D8

Clifford Rd
Boston Spa LS23 ...188 F8
Ilkley LS29 ......218 A6

Clifford St
8 Barnoldswick BB18 ..171 E1
2 Skipton BD23 .....216 F3
York YO1 ....233 B2
Clifford's Terr 28 YO14 .101 B3
Clifford's Twr* YO1 .233 B1
Clifton YO30 ......233 A4
Clifton Dale YO30 ...228 A7
Clifton Gn YO30 ...228 A6
Clifton Gn Jun Sch
YO30 ....228 B7
Clifton La YO21 ...176 F3
Clifton Moor Gate
YO30 ....225 A2
Clifton Moor Ind Pk*
YO30 ....225 A4
Clifton Moor Ret Pk
YO30 ....224 E3
Clifton Moor Sh Ctr
YO30 ....224 F3
Clifton Moorgate
YO30 ....225 B3
Clifton Pk Ave YO30 .227 E8
Clifton Pl 3 YO30 ...228 A7
Clifton Prep Sch
YO30 ....233 A4
Clifton Rd Darlington DL1 ..3 D4
Ilkley LS29 ......218 D3
Clifton St Earby BB18 .186 A8
5 Scarborough YO12 ..212 F6
Trawden Forest BB8 ..186 A1
Clifton Terr LS29 ...218 C4
Clifton Without Jun Sch
YO30 ....227 F8
Clint Bank HG3 ....160 E6
Clint Bank La HG3 ..160 F6
Clint Garth HG3 ....160 E6
Clipt La YO7 ......65 D2
Clitheroe St 2 BD23 ..216 D3
Clive Gr YO24 .....227 F2
Clive Rd 1 YO24 ...179 E6
Clock Twr* HG4 ...214 C6
Clockhill Field La
YO26 ....163 F3
Clockwood Gdns TS16 ..5 E3
Clogger La BD23 ...172 D3
Cloggerby Rigg DL11 ..35 E5

Cloisters The
18 Hemingbrough YO8 .198 F1
Wilberfoss YO41 ....185 E6
York YO31 ......233 C3
Cloisters Wlk YO31 ..233 C3
Close La BD22 ....187 B5
Close Rd WF10 ....200 F4

Close The
Barwick in Elmet LS15 .194 B7
Boroughbridge YO51 ..141 A3
Boston Spa LS23 ...188 E8
Cawood YO8 .....197 A7
8 Collingham LS22 ...188 A8
11 East Ayton/West Ayton
YO13 ....99 B8
4 Fylingdales YO22 ...33 D1
Hunmanby Sands YO14 .101 C1
Kirkby Fleetham DL7 ..42 C1
Longnewton TS21 ....4 F7
Neasham DL2 ......4 A1
Northallerton DL7 ...210 D2
Norton DN6 ......206 E2
Riccall YO19 ......198 A8
Scalby YO12 ......212 B8
Studley Roger HG4 ..113 F1
Thirsk YO7 ......211 C1
Thornes LS14 .....188 A3
Thornton Dale YO18 ...96 D5
Towton LS24 ......189 D3
Wilton YO18 ......96 A7
Cliothermole Rd HG4 .214 A5
Clough La DN6 ....207 B2
Clover Hill BD23 ...217 B5
Clover Way 3 HG3 ..161 B3
Cloverley Cl YO41 ..168 C2
Clowbeck Ct DL3 .....3 B8
Clydach Gr 22 TS17 ...5 F8
Clyde Gr TS18 .....5 F8

Coach La
18 Hurworth-on-Tees DL2 ..3 E1
Lindley LS21 ......177 D3

Coach Rd
Harrogate HG1 ......219 F2
Sheriff Hutton YO60 ..145 D4
Sleights YO22 .....32 A6
Coach St BD23 ....216 F4

Coach St Yd 16 BD23 .216 F4
Coachman's Ct 6 HG2 .220 B1

Coal Pit La
Kirk Smeaton WF8 ...206 A2
Rimington BB7 ....171 A1
Coalmire La DL6 ....45 D7
Coalpits La 10 DL3 ...3 A7
Coarse La HG3 .....159 A4
Coastal Rd YO13 ...75 D7
Coastguard Hill YO14 .127 E5
Coate Cl TS8 ......6 E5
Coate's La BD20 ...173 F2
Coates Ave BB18 ...171 E2
Coates Fields BB18 .171 E2

Coates La
Barnoldswick BB18 ..171 E2
Kettlewell with Starbotton
BD23 ....107 F5
Coates La Prim Sch
BB18 ....171 E2
Coates Marsh La
DN14 ....204 B2
Coatham Ave DL2 ....4 D3
Coatham La TS21 ....5 B7
Cob Castle* DL8 ....63 B1
Cob La BB18 .....186 A6
Cobble Carr TS14 ....8 E6
Cobble Ct Mews YO24 .233 A1
Cobbler's La WF8 ...201 C1
Cobblers La WF8 ...201 C1
Cobblers La Inf Sch
WF8 ....201 D1
Cobby Syke Rd HG3 .159 F1
Cobcroft La WF11 ...206 B8

Cobden St
Barnoldswick BB18 ..171 D1
Darlington DL1 ......3 E5
Thornaby TS17 .....6 B8
Cobham Way YO32 ..226 D3
Cobham Way HG3 ..145 D5
Cobshaw La DL8 ...62 F6
Cochrane St YO8 ...232 D3
Cock Garth YO17 ..122 D1
Cock La Gainford DL2 ..1 E8
Piercebridge DL2 ....2 A7
Cock Lodge (site of)*
YO7 ....115 C6
Cock Lodge (site of)*
Cockburn St 8 TS12 ..9 F7
Cocked Hat HG4 ...139 C8
Cockerhill La YO62 ..93 E7
Cockerton CE Prim Sch
DL3 ....3 A6
Cockerton Gn DL3 ...3 B6
Cockhill La BB8 ...186 A4
Cocking La LS29 ...174 E3
Cockpit Cl HG4 ....113 C7
Cockrah Rd YO13 ...74 A1
Cockret Cl 2 YO8 ..232 B6
Cockret Ct YO8 ...232 B6
Cockret Rd YO8 ...232 B7
Cockshaw Bank La
HG4 ....113 B4
Cockshott Pl 5 LS29 .174 F4
Coda Ave YO23 ...231 B3
Codlin Rd 4 TS15 ...25 C5
Coeside YO24 .....230 B7
Coggan Cl YO23 ...228 B2
Coggan Way YO23 .230 F4
Colber La HG3 ....138 F2
Colbert Ave LS29 ...218 E5
Colburn Com Prim Sch
DL9 ....41 A5
Colburn Dr DL9 ....40 F5
Colburn La DL9 ....40 F6
Colburn Sidings DL9 .40 F4
Cold Bath Pl HG2 ..219 C1
Cold Bath Rd HG2 .219 C1
Cold Cotes Rd HG3 .160 B4
Cold Kirby Rd YO7 ..91 C8
Coldhill La LS25 ...195 C6
Coldie Hill 11 TS15 ..25 C5
Coldstone La YO7 ...88 B2
Coldyhill La YO12 ..212 B8
Colaton St DL1 ....233 B4
Colebrooke Mdws
HG5 ....221 C7
Coledale Cl 2 YO30 .224 F1
Colenso St YO23 ..233 B1
Coleridge Dr HG1 ..219 C7
Coleridge Gdns DL1 ..3 D3
Coleridge Way 1 WF8 .201 B1
Colescliffe Cres YO12 .212 C8
Colescliffe Rd YO12 .212 C8
Colin St 3 BB18 ...171 D2
Coliseum* YO21 ..208 D6
Coll of Ripon & York St John
YO31 ....228 E6

College Ct
1 Low Bradley BD20 ..173 E4
4 Scarborough YO11 .213 A2
College Dr LS29 ...218 B3
College Farm Cl DL10 .209 C8
College Farm La LS22 .180 A2
College La YO62 ....92 F6

College La
Bradleys Both BD20 ..173 E3
5 Masham HG4 ....86 C3
Scarborough YO11 ...213 A1
College of Law YO23 .231 B7
College of Ripon & York St
John HG4 ......214 B6

College Rd
Bradleys Both BD20 173 E3
Copmanthorpe YO23 230 A3
Harrogate HG2 222 B8
Ripon HG4 214 B6
College St
Harrogate HG2 222 B8
York YO1 233 B3
Colley Broach Rd
YO61 117 F7
Collier Hag La YO23 182 B3
Collier La
Lotherton cum Aberford
LS25 195 A6
West Layton DL11 20 A8
Colliergate YO1 233 B2
Collin Ave TS4 6 F8
Collin Bank HG3 160 E6
Collinge Rd 9 BD22 187 B6
Collingham Way 12
YO14 101 A3
Collingsway 4 DL3 3 A7
Collingwood Ave
YO24 227 F2
Collingwood Gdns
YO17 215 A3
Collingwood Rd WF6 200 A2
Collin's Hill HG3 223 D7
Collinsons La YO17 122 F5
Colliwath La DL8 60 F4
Collyer View LS29 218 E5
Colne & Broughton Rd
BD23 172 C4
Colne Rd
Barnoldswick BB18 171 D1
Cowling BD22 187 A5
Earby BB18 172 A1
Kelbrook & Sough BB18 186 A8
Sutton BD20 187 C7
Trawden Forest BB8 186 A1
Colonel's Wlk 9 WF8 201 B1
Colorado Way WF10 200 F2
Colstan Rd DL6 210 E3
Colton La YO23 190 E6
Coltsgate Hill HG4 214 B6
Columbine Gr 33 HG3 161 B3
Columbus Ravine
YO12 212 F7
Columbus Way DL10 41 C7
Colville Cres 8 DL9 41 A5
Colville Rd 12 DL9 41 A5
Comercial St
9 Barnoldswick BB18 171 D1
Harrogate HG1 219 D3
Norton YO17 215 D3
Scarborough YO12 212 E5
Tadcaster LS24 189 E6
Comercial Yd 1 HG5 221 B6
Comets Garth 11 DL3 3 A7
Comfort La DL10 20 C5
Comfrey Cl 32 HG3 161 B3
Comfrey Manor TS8 7 B4
Commercial St 9 BD24 131 E2
Common Croft La
YO26 165 E1
Common La Beal DN14 202 D3
Burn YO8 203 E7
Catton YO41 185 E8
Dunnington YO19 184 F5
Fangfoss YO41 169 B1
Knottingley WF11 202 B1
Norton DN6 206 E2
Sutton upon Derwent
YO41 193 C8
Temple Hirst YO8 203 F4
Thorganby YO19 192 F5
Walden Stubbs DN6 206 F4
Warthill YO19 167 F2
York YO10 229 B1
Common Rd
Dunnington YO19 184 F7
Skipwith YO8 192 E1
Comon Balk La HG3 140 A3
Comon Holme La
LS29 175 C3
Comon La
Carlton Husthwaite YO7 116 F8
Coverham with Agglethorpe
DL8 60 A2
Glaisdale YO21 29 F1
Hambleton YO8 196 D2
Harome YO62 93 E5
Hartley CA17 14 A8
Scruton DL7 63 E7
South Milford LS25 195 F2
Ulleskelf LS24 190 C2
West Witton DL8 59 F2
Comon Rd
Barkston Ash LS24 195 F7
Church Fenton LS24 196 A7
Strensall YO60 145 D1
Comondale Sta YO21 9 E1
Compton La LS23 188 A7
Compton St YO30 228 A6
Conan Dr DL10 209 D8
Conan Gdns DL10 209 D8
Concorde Pk YO30 225 A3
Concorde Way TS18 5 F7
Coney Moor Gr LS26 200 C6
Coney St YO1 233 B2
Coneycroft 10 YO19 184 F7
Coneygarth La
Dunnington YO19 184 E5
Tunstall LA6 102 A4
Conference Cl YO17 215 B4
Conifer Cl 6 YO32 225 D3
Conifers Cl 2 YO8 197 D1
Coningham Ave 1
YO30 224 E2
Coniscliffe Mews DL3 3 A4
Coniscliffe Rd DL3 3 A4
Coniston Ave BB18 171 D2
Coniston Cl 1 YO30 224 E1
Coniston Dr
Castleford WF10 201 C4
York YO10 229 B4
Coniston Gdns 6 YO12 99 F7
Coniston Gr TS5 6 E7
Coniston Rd HG1 220 B4
Coniston Way
3 Eastfield YO12 99 F7
Thirsk YO7 89 C4
Conistone La BD23 108 B3
Connaught Rd
Ilkley LS29 218 D3
Middlesbrough TS7 7 D6
Connaught Way YO32 225 F6
Cononley Com Prim Sch
BD20 173 D2
Cononley La BD20 173 D1
Cononley Rd BD20 187 D8
Cononley Sta BD20 173 D1
Conowl Cl 23 YO62 92 F6
Conroy Cl 11 YO61 143 D8
Consort St BD23 217 B4
Constable Burton Hall*
DL8 61 C6
Constable Rd
Hunmanby YO14 127 A8
Ilkley LS29 218 D3
Constable Ridge Rd
HG3 160 B2
Constantine Ave
10 Colburn DL9 41 A5
York YO10 229 A4
Constantine Gr 11 DL9 41 A5
Constitution Hill 3
BD24 131 E2
Conway Cl 2 YO30 224 E3
Conway Cres BB18 171 E1
Conway Gr 8 TS17 5 F4
Conyers Ave DL3 3 A6
Conyers Cl DL10 209 D8
Conyers Ings YO13 99 A7
Conyers La DL8 61 D6
Conyers Rd DL7 22 E2
Conyers Sch TS15 5 E2
Conyngham Hall HG5 220 F6
Cook Cl DL10 41 C7
Cook's Row 5 YO11 213 B6
Cookgate TS7 7 C5
Cooks Cl 2 DL6 45 A7
Cooks Gdns 3 YO13 75 D5
Cookson Way DL9 41 A5
Coolham La BB18 186 B8
Coombe Dr DL1 3 F6
Coombes Cl YO61 144 C3
Coomboots Brow YO13 75 A6
Cooper Cl DL6 25 D2
Cooper La
Blubberhouses LS21 159 C1
Potto DL6 25 D2
Cooper La Shepherd
LS21 159 C2
Cooper Rd 49 Filey YO14 101 B3
18 Wetherby LS22 180 C3
Coopers Dr YO23 230 B3
Copgrove La HG5 162 D8
Copgrove Rd HG3 140 A2
Cophill La YO7 66 A4
Copley La LS25 195 B7
Copmanroyd LS21 177 A2
Copmanthorpe La
YO23 230 E3
Copmanthorpe Prim Sch
YO23 230 B3
Copmanthorpe Sports Club
YO23 230 B2
Copper beech Cl
YO26 182 F8
Copper Beech Dr
DN14 207 A8
Copper Beeches The 2
YO19 184 E7
Copperclay Wlk YO61 117 D1
Copperfield Cl
Malton YO17 215 C5
21 Sherburn in Elmet LS25 195 F4
Coppergate
1 Riccall YO19 191 F1
York YO1 233 B2
Coppergate Sh Ctr
YO1 233 B2
Coppergate Wlk YO1 233 B2
Coppertop Mews 4
WF8 201 C2
Coppice Ave HG1 219 C4
Coppice Beck Ct HG1 219 D3
Coppice Cl
Harrogate HG1 219 C4
10 Haxby YO32 166 E5
Coppice Dr HG1 219 C3
Coppice Gate HG1 219 C4
Coppice La
14 Hellifield BD23 154 B3
Wrelton YO18 71 B1
Coppice Rise HG1 219 C5
Coppice The
Barwick in Elmet LS15 194 B7
Bishopthorpe YO23 230 F4
Brayton YO8 197 C1
Ilkley LS29 218 A6
Leeming DL7 63 F3
Coppice The *continued*
14 Sherburn in Elmet LS25 195 F4
19 Sutton BD20 187 E7
Coppice Valley Com Prim
Sch HG1 219 C5
Coppice Valley Pool
HG1 219 D4
Coppice View HG1 219 C4
Coppice Way HG1 219 C5
Coppy La
Cononley BD20 173 C2
Sutton BD22 187 E4
Coppy Rd LS29 174 F4
Coppy Wood Dr LS29 218 B7
Copse Hill 1 YO14 101 A4
Copse The
3 North Featherstone
WF7 200 E1
5 Scarborough YO12 212 B5
Copsewood Wlk 5 TS9 26 C8
Copwood Gr 7 YO32 225 C8
Corban La YO32 166 B6
Corban Way 21 YO32 166 D5
Corber Hill 7 DL6 43 F3
Corbie Way YO18 96 A7
Corby Ave TS5 6 D8
Cordike La
Birdsall YO17 148 D6
Langton YO17 147 F6
Cordilleras La DL11 39 C8
Corlett Ct YO24 230 C8
Corn Mill Ct 19 LS25 195 F4
Corn Mill Gdns YO12 212 D7
Corn Mill La 39 LS29 176 D1
Cornaught Ct YO10 231 D8
Cornbell Gate 4 HG4 113 D2
Cornborough Av YO31 228 F6
Cornborough Rd
YO60 145 C5
Cornel Rise 26 HG3 161 B3
Cornelian Ave YO11 100 B8
Cornelian Cl YO11 213 C1
Cornelian Dr YO11 213 C1
Cornelius Cswy YO8 198 E8
Corner Cl 17 YO32 166 D5
Corner Complex The*
YO12 212 F8
Corners Terr 5 YO22 208 E6
Corners Yd 5 YO22 208 E6
Cornerstones Cl LS29 175 A4
Cornfield Rd TS17 6 A8
Cornflower Way 1 HG3 161 B3
Cornforth Hill DL10 209 B6
Cornlands YO17 215 D2
Cornlands Rd YO24 227 B1
Cornmill Cl YO8 197 B8
Cornmill Sh Ctr DL1 3 C5
Cornwall Ave
Darlington DL1 3 E6
Silsden BD20 174 B1
Cornwall Cl HG1 219 A2
Cornwall Dr YO10 231 E8
Cornwall Rd HG1 219 B2
Cornwood Way 11 YO32 225 C8
Coronation Ave
6 Colburn DL9 41 A5
Harrogate HG2 222 E7
1 Hinderwell TS13 11 F7
Coronation Gr HG2 222 E7
Coronation Hospl
LS29 218 C3
Coronation Pl DL10 209 A7
Coronation Rd
Crakehall DL8 62 E5
Harrogate HG2 222 E7
Coronation St
8 Barnoldswick BB18 171 E1
Castleford WF6 200 B2
Corporation Rd DL3 3 C6
Corporation Rd Jun & Inf Sch
DL3 3 C6
Corporation Rd Prim Sch
DL3 3 C6
Corpse Rd
North Otterington DL7 64 E5
Thornton-le-Moor DL6 65 A4
Corunna Ct 5 YO8 232 D5
Cosmo Ave YO31 229 A5
Costa La YO18 95 D6
Costa Way YO18 95 E7
Cotchers La LS24 195 D8
Cotcliffe Ave DL6 210 F3
Cotcliffe Bank DL6 65 E5
Cote Hill Rd HG3 160 B4
Cote La Healey HG4 85 D5
Sproxton YO62 92 C4
Cotescue Bank DL8 60 C1
Cotherstone Cl TS16 5 C5
Cotswold Dr LS25 194 C3
Cotswold Way YO32 226 A5
Cottage Cl DL6 210 E5
Cottage La YO60 145 C4
Cottagers La DL2 2 C3
Cottam La YO25 151 C5
Cottee Way 16 DL9 41 A5
Cotterdale Cl HG5 221 C6
Cotterdale Gdns LS25 202 A6
Cotterdale Holt 9 LS22 180 A1
Cottom La YO42 193 C2
Cotton Tree La BB8 186 A3
Coulby Farm Way TS8 7 A5
Coulby La YO18 97 A6
Coulby Manor Way TS8 6 F6
Coulby Newham Sch
TS8 7 A5
Coulson Cl 5 YO32 167 C8
Coulter Beck La LA6 102 D7
Coulthurst Craven Sports Ctr
The BD23 216 F3
Coulton La YO62 119 A6
Count De Burgh Terr 4
YO23 228 B1
County Par HG1 219 F3
County Sq HG1 219 F3
Coupland Rd
Garforth LS25 194 C4
1 Selby YO8 232 C6
Courby Hill HG4 86 F2
Courcey Gr YO26 227 C4
Court Dr YO8 232 A4
Court Gn Cl YO13 54 D1
Court La BD23 217 A4
Court Moor La YO62 70 A4
Court Terr HG4 214 C5
Court The 6 DL8 63 A2
Courthouse Mus*
HG4 214 C5
Courtneys Selby YO8 232 B4
Wheldrake YO19 193 A8
Courtneys The YO8 232 B4
Courts Cl 7 DN14 205 E4
Courtyard The
Bishopthorpe YO23 231 B4
11 Pontefract WF8 201 C2
Coutances Way LS29 218 F5
Cove Rd BD23 132 F2
Cover La
Carlton Town DL8 83 E7
Marton-le-Moor HG4 114 E1
Coverdale Dr
1 Knaresborough HG5 221 A7
Scarborough YO12 212 B4
Coverdale Garth 2
LS22 188 A8
Coverdale La TS13 12 A4
Coverham Abbey (rems of)*
DL8 60 C1
Coverham Cl DL7 210 C2
Coverham La DL8 60 C1
Covert The
9 Topcliffe YO7 89 B1
York YO24 230 F7
Cow & Calf Rocks*
LS29 218 D2
Cow Cl La
Kirkby Malham BD23 154 E8
Lockwood TS12 10 B4
Cow Gate La BD23 171 B7
Cow La Cowling BD22 187 B6
Knottingley WF11 202 A2
Lothersdale BD20 172 F1
Middleton Tyas DL10 21 E5
Womersley DN6 206 C6
Cow Pasture La YO42 193 C3
Cow Wath Bank YO22 51 E8
Cow Wath Cl 30 YO12 75 D5
Cowbar Bank 1 TS13 13 K2
Cowbar La TS13 13 J2
Cowcliff Hill YO17 148 F6
Cowgarth La 15 BB18 172 B1
Cowgill St 17 BB18 172 A1
Cowhouse Bank YO62 68 F3
Cowie Dr YO8 232 D5
Cowland La YO7 88 D3
Cowley Cl TS16 5 E7
Cowley Rd TS5 6 E7
Cowling Com Prim Sch
BD22 187 A6
Cowling Hill La BD22 186 F7
Cowling La DL8 62 D3
Cowling Rd DL8 62 D2
Cowlings Cl 16 YO14 127 A8
Cowpasture Rd LS29 218 C3
Cowper La YO23 191 C8
Cowper St 3 BD23 217 A3
Cowton Castle* DL7 22 D1
Cowton La YO14 127 C6
Cowton Way TS16 5 D6
Coxlea Gr YO31 229 B6
Coxwain Cl YO14 101 B2
Coxwold Dr DL1 3 D4
Coxwold Hill 5 LS22 180 C4
Coxwold Pottery*
YO61 117 D7
Coxwold View 1 LS22 180 C3
Crab La Harrogate HG1 219 D6
Seamer YO12 99 E6
Crab Tree La WF8 206 A1
Crabmill La YO61 143 D8
Crabtree Gn LS22 188 A8
Crabtree Gr 1 YO32 225 D3
Crabtree Hill LS22 188 A8
Cracoe & Rylstone VC CE
Prim Sch BD23 156 B6
Cradley Dr TS5 6 E6
Cradoc Gr 14 TS17 5 F4
Craft Ctr* DL11 38 B6
Crag Bank YO21 28 B8
Crag Cl 33 BD20 187 E7
Crag Gdns LS23 188 E5
Crag Hill La HG3 161 B6
Crag Hill Rd YO13 53 F8
Crag La
Bradleys Both BD20 173 E2
Felliscliffe HG3 160 D4
Huby LS17 178 B2
Killinghall HG3 161 B1
Knaresborough HG5 221 B5
North Rigton LS17 178 B3
Pannal HG3 178 C8
Sutton BD20 187 D6
Crag Side Rd DL8 57 B2
Crag The 3 LS23 188 E5
Crag View
Cononley BD20 173 D1
Crag View *continued*
Skipton BD23 217 B6
Threshfield BD23 134 B3
Weeton LS17 178 B2
Crag View Rd BD23 217 B3
Cragdale 18 BD24 131 D2
Cragdale Rise 1 HG5 221 D6
Cragg Bottom Rd
BD22 187 C1
Cragg Dr LS29 218 F3
Cragg Hill Rd BD24 105 C3
Cragg La LA2 130 C4
Cragg The 21 YO21 208 D7
Craggs La
Arrathorne DL10 41 A1
Tatham LA2 129 A3
Craig St DL3 3 C6
Craiglands Pk LS29 218 C3
Craiglands Rd LS29 218 C3
Craigmore Dr LS29 218 E4
Craigs Way YO7 211 C4
Crake La HG3 159 F6
Crakehall CE Prim Sch
DL8 62 E4
Cranberry TS8 7 B5
Cranbrook Ave YO26 227 C5
Cranbrook Rd YO26 227 C5
Cranbrooks The YO19 192 F8
Cranesbill Cl HG3 161 B3
Cranfield Pl 4 YO24 230 C8
Cranford Gdns TS5 6 D8
Crank La DL7 63 B7
Crankley La YO61 143 B7
Cranwell Gr TS17 6 B6
Craven Bank La BD24 131 B3
Craven Coll
Settle BD24 131 D2
Skipton BD23 217 A4
Craven Cres 3 LS29 174 F4
Craven Ct
Cowling BD22 187 C6
Northallerton DL7 210 B3
Richmond DL10 209 B6
Silsden BD20 174 C1
Skipton BD23 217 A4
Craven Ct Sh Ctr
BD23 217 A4
Craven Dr BD20 174 C1
Craven Garth 5 DN14 202 D4
Craven Mus* BD23 217 A4
Craven Ridge La BD24 131 A2
Craven Ridge La Ends
BD24 131 B3
Craven St 3 Colne BB8 186 A3
Harrogate HG1 219 D4
Scarborough YO11 213 A4
Skipton BD23 216 F3
Craven Terr BD23 216 F4
Craven Way
5 Boroughbridge YO51 141 B4
Dent LA10 78 B8
Cravendale Rd 4 DL9 40 F5
Cravengate DL10 209 B6
Craven's Hill YO13 54 C3
Crawford Cl YO26 181 C7
Crawley Way YO31 229 B6
Cray Thorns Cres YO7 115 A4
Crayke Castle* YO61 117 F1
Crayke CE VC Prim Sch
YO61 117 F1
Crayke La YO61 117 F2
Crayke Manor* YO61 118 A2
Crescent Arts* YO11 213 A5
Crescent Ave YO21 208 C7
Crescent Back Rd 8
YO11 213 A5
Crescent Ct LS29 218 B4
Crescent Gdns HG1 219 C2
Crescent Hill 53 YO14 101 B3
Crescent Par HG4 214 C6
Crescent Pl 20 YO21 208 D7
Crescent Rd
Harrogate HG1 219 C2
Ripon HG4 214 B6
Crescent Terr 6 LS29 218 B4
Crescent The
13 Bedale DL8 63 B3
Burton Fleming YO25 126 E3
Carlton TS9 26 A2
Eaglescliffe TS16 5 D4
Filey YO14 101 B3
Garforth LS25 194 D4
17 Helmsley YO62 92 F6
Ilkley LS29 218 E5
Kelfield YO19 191 D1
Kexby YO41 185 C5
Kippax LS25 194 D1
Micklefield LS25 195 A3
Middlesbrough TS7 7 D6
Middleton St George DL2 4 E4
North Rigton LS17 178 B3
Northallerton DL6 210 E4
Otley LS21 177 A1
6 Riccall YO19 197 F8
Richmond DL10 209 D7
Ripon HG4 214 B6
Scalby YO12 212 B7
Scarborough YO11 213 A5
Sicklinghall LS22 179 E3
Skipton BD23 217 B6
Stainton Dale YO13 54 A8
Stamford Bridge YO41 168 D2
2 Summerbridge HG3 138 A1
Thirsk YO7 211 C3
Thornaby TS17 6 B8
Thornton Dale YO18 96 D5
York YO24 233 A1
Crest The LS26 194 A1

Crestbrooke DL7 ....210 D2
Crestholme CI ⬛ HG5 ...221 D5
Crewe Rd WF10 ....201 B4
Creyke View DN14 .....205 A1
Cribyn Ct ⬛ TS17 ....7 E8
Crichton Ave YO30 ....228 B8
Cricket La TS6 ....7 E8
Cricketers CI LS25 ....194 D3
Cricketers Way ⬛ 195 F4
Cridling Gdns DN6 ....220 D7
Crimple Ave LS22 .....180 A8
Crimple La HG3 ....223 D7
Crimple Mdws HG3 ....222 D3
Crinan Ct
  Pontefract WF6 ......200 A2
  ⬛ York YO32 ....225 F6
Crindle Carr La DL7 ...65 B3
Cringle Moor Chase
  TS9 ....26 F4
Cringles La BD20 .....174 C4
Cringley La DL8 ....57 E5
Crocus Ct ⬛ DL9 .....41 A5
Croft Ave
  ⬛ Knottingley WF11 ..202 A3
  Middlesbrough TS5 .....6 D8
  ⬛ Normanton South WF6 .200 B2
  Otley LS21 ....176 F1
Croft CE Prim Sch ⬛ DL2 ..22 C8
Croft CI
  Carlton Husthwaite YO7 ..116 F7
  ⬛ Kexwold YO61 .....143 C8
  Ingleton LA6 ....103 D3
Croft Ct YO23 ....231 A4
Croft Dr LS23 ....188 E6
Croft Farm Ct YO23 ...230 B3
Croft Gdns YO7 ......211 B1
Croft Head Terr ⬛
  BD20 ....187 E7
Croft Heads YO7 .....211 B1
Croft House La Carthorpe DL8 ..87 E6
  ⬛ Glusburn BD20 ....187 E7
Croft Hills TS9 ....26 A7
Croft House St ⬛ LS21 .176 F1
Croft House Fold ⬛
  LS29 ....175 A4
Croft House La BD23 ..135 A1
Croft La
  Carlton Husthwaite YO7 ..116 F8
  Newton Kyme cum Toulston
  LS24 ....189 B7
  Snainton YO13 ....97 F5
  Walton LS23 ....181 A2
Croft Motor Racing Circut*
  DL2 ....22 C5
Croft Rd
  Bramham cum Oglethorpe
  LS23 ....188 C6
  Camblesforth YO8 ....204 D4
  Catterick Garrison DL9 ..209 E1
  Eaglescliffe TS16 .....5 D4
  Hurworth DL2 ....3 B2
  Ingleton LA6 ....103 D3
Croft St ⬛ Earby BB18 ..172 B1
  ⬛ Glusburn BD20 ....187 E6
Croft The Beadlam YO62 ..93 D7
  Burton in Lonsdale LA6 ..102 F3
  Castleford WF10 .....200 F3
  ⬛ Collingham LS22 ...188 A8
  Draughton BD23 .....174 B7
  ⬛ Filey YO14 ....101 B3
  Knottingley WF11 ....202 A3
  Langthorpe YO51 .....141 A7
  Scalby YO12 ....212 B7
  Sheriff Hutton YO60 ..145 D5
  Stirton with Thorlby
  BD23 ....216 C6
  Thirsk YO7 ....211 B1
  West Tanfield DL8 ....87 B3
Croft View YO7 ......211 B3
Crofters Gn HG3 .....219 A8
Crofters Mill BD20 ...187 F6
Croftlands ⬛ WF11 ...202 A3
Crofts Ave
  ⬛ Pickering YO18 ....96 A6
  Richmond DL10 ......209 B7
Crofts The
  ⬛ Glusburn BD20 ....173 F1
  ⬛ Sutton BD20 ......187 E6
Croftside ⬛ YO26 ....227 B3
Croftway
  Barwick in Elmet LS15 ..194 C8
  Camblesforth YO8 ....204 C5
  Selby YO8 ....232 C4
  Sherburn in Elmet LS25 ..199 F4
  ⬛ York YO26 ....227 B3
Crombie Ave YO30 ...228 B7
Cromer St YO30 .....228 B7
Crompton Terr YO32 ..225 D6
Cromwell Ave ⬛ YO14 .101 B3
Cromwell CI ⬛ WF11 ..200 E4
Cromwell Cres ⬛ WF8 .201 C1
Cromwell Dr YO7 .....64 A6
Cromwell Gdns ⬛ YO11 .212 F4
Cromwell Par ⬛ YO11 .212 F4
Cromwell Rd
  Harrogate HG2 ....222 E7
  Scarborough YO11 ....212 F4
  York YO1 ....233 B1
Cromwell Rise LS25 ..194 C1
Cromwell St ⬛ BD23 ..217 A3
Cromwell Terr ⬛ YO11 .212 F4
Crook La HG4 ....85 E5
Crooked La YO26 ....164 C2
Crookland La YO32 ...166 F5
Croom Medieval Village*
  YO25 ....150 B4
Croome Dale La YO17 ..150 C6

Croome Rd YO25 .....150 B4
Cropstones LS23 .....188 F5
Cropton Brewery & Visitor
  Ctr* YO18 ....71 B3
Cropton La YO18 .....71 B2
Cropton Rise YO12 ...212 B4
Cropton Way TS8 ......7 B5
Crosby Rd DL6 ......210 C4
Crosby St DL3 ....3 C7
Crosland CI ⬛ YO62 ..92 F6
Cross Bank BD23 ....217 B6
Cross End Fold ⬛ LS29 .175 A4
Cross Gate YO13 ....97 D5
Cross Haw La ⬛ LA2 ..86 A4
Cross Head Bank DL8 ..60 D7
Cross Hill
  Fairburn WF11 ....201 D6
  Sutton-under-Whitestonecliffe
  YO7 ....90 D5
Cross Hills La YO8 ...232 A5
Cross La Bentham LA2 ..128 E8
  Brompton YO13 ......98 C5
  Burneston DL8 ....87 A5
  Burniston YO13 ......75 D7
  Farndale East YO62 ...48 E4
  Flaxton YO60 ....167 E8
  Fulford YO19 ....231 F5
  Giggleswick BD24 ....130 F2
  Great Ouseburn YO26 ..116 B8
  Little Ayton TS9 ......27 A8
  Pickhill with Roxby YO7 ..88 C6
  Scalby YO12 ....212 C8
  Sinnington YO62 .....95 A8
  Snainton YO13 ....97 F3
  Stonebeck Up HG3 ...110 B5
Cross La Hospl YO12 ..212 B8
Cross Lanes DL10 ...209 E7
Cross Queen St ⬛ WF6 .200 A1
Cross Rd LA2 ....128 E7
Cross Rein Bank DL7 ..23 A1
Cross Row Boosbeck TS12 ..9 D7
  Swillington LS15 .....194 A3
Cross St ⬛ Cowling BD22 .187 B6
  ⬛ Earby BB18 ....172 A1
  Scarborough YO11 ....213 A6
  Skipton BD23 ....216 F3
  ⬛ York YO24 ....227 C3
Cross The LS15 ......194 B8
Cross Top DL8 ....57 E7
Crossbeck CI BD23 ...218 B3
Crossbeck Rd
  Ilkley LS29 ....218 B3
  Northallerton DL6 ....210 F5
Crossbeck Way TS7 ...7 D8
Crosscliff TS8 ....6 F5
Crossdale Rd YO18 ..72 E3
Crossfield CI ⬛ DL2 ..3 E1
Crossfield Cres YO19 .231 E6
Crossfields TS8 ......7 F4
Crossgate La ⬛ YO18 ..95 F6
Crossgates HG3 .....138 B5
Crosshill La DN14 ...207 E6
Crosshills BD20 .....173 D1
Crossings The ⬛ DN14 .205 F4
Crosslands Rd ⬛ YO11 .231 E8
Crossley PI BD23 ....216 F4
Crossley St ⬛ LS22 ..180 C3
Crossley St Prim Sch
  LS22 ....180 C3
Crossman Dr ⬛ WF6 ..200 A2
Crossmoor La YO32 ..166 E6
Crossway The
  Darlington DL1 ....3 E5
  ⬛ York YO31 ....228 E8
Crossways YO10 .....229 C2
Crossways Cres HG2 ..220 D3
Crossways Dr HG2 ...220 D3
Crossways The LS21 ..177 A1
Crosswell Pk ⬛ TS17 ..5 F4
Crow Hill La HG3 ....160 C4
Crow Nest Rd LA2 ...130 F6
Crowberry Dr HG3 ...161 B3
Crowdy CI YO7 ......208 C4
Crowfoot La DL6 .....43 D5
Crowgarth HG4 .....140 D7
Crown Cres YO11 ....213 A4
Crown Gr YO8 ......197 B8
Crown Sq ⬛ YO7 ....200 B1
Crown St
  ⬛ Burley in Warfedale
  ....176 C1
  Darlington DL1 ....3 C5
Crown Terr YO11 ....213 A4
Crowood Ave TS9 ....26 C8
Crowtrees LA2 ......130 E8
Crummack La LA2 ...130 E8
Crummock ⬛ YO24 ..230 C7
Cswy The YO21 ......12 E3
Cuddy Brown CI ⬛ YO18 ..96 A6
Cuddy La DL6 ....45 B4
Culloden Twr (Heritage)*
  DL10 ....209 B6
Culvert La BD23 ....216 A4
Cumberland CI ⬛ YO32 .167 B6
Cumberland Gdns
  DL10 ....209 C7
Cumberland St
  ⬛ Skipton BD23 ....216 F3
  York YO1 ....233 B2
Cumbernauld Rd TS17 ..6 C7
Cumbrian Ave ⬛ YO32 .167 B6
Cundall CI ⬛ HG4 ...214 D4
Cundall CI ⬛ YO7 ...115 B6
Cundall CI ⬛ DL9 ...167 C8
Cundall Manor Sch
  YO61 ....115 E3
Cundall Way HG2 ....222 D8
Cunliffe Rd LS29 ....218 B4

Cunningham Ave TS17 ..6 B6
Cunningham Rd DL9 ..40 F4
Cupid's Alley YO17 ...149 B6
Curfew Rd HG4 ......214 C3
Curlew CI ⬛ HG3 ....211 D8
Curlew CI ⬛ Ilkley LS29 .175 C2
  Leyburn DL8 ....60 E4
Curlew Cres ⬛ DL9 ..40 F2
Curlew Dr
  Crossgates YO12 .....99 E6
  ⬛ Filey YO14 ....101 A3
Curlew Glebe ⬛ YO19 .184 E7
Curly Hill LS29 ......218 C7
Currer La LS29 ......175 B6
Currie CI YO8 ....209 C2
Curson Terr YO8 ....198 E3
Curtain CI DL11 ......1 D5
Curtain The DL11 ....1 D4
Curteis Dr DL1 ......41 B6
Curzon Terr YO23 ...228 B1
Custance Wlk YO23 ..233 A1
Cut Rd WF11 ....201 D6
Cut Throat La HG3 ...138 F1
Cutler La LS26 ......200 C8
Cutpurse La DL10 ...209 C8
Cutsyke Ave WF10 ...200 D3
Cutsyke Crest WF10 ..200 D3
Cutsyke Rd WF10 ....200 D2
Cycle St ⬛ YO10 ....229 C3
Cygnet CI ⬛ YO14 ..101 A4
Cygnet St YO23 .....233 A1
Cyndor Ct YO11 ....201 C3
Cypress CI DL3 ......3 B4
Cypress Gdns HG4 ..214 B2
Cypress Rd TS7 ......7 C6

D

Dacre Braithwaite CE Prim
  Sch HG3 ....159 B7
Dacre Ct LS24 ......195 D7
Dacre Hall Pk HG3 ...159 D7
Dacre La HG3 ....159 D7
Dacre Pasture La
  HG3 ....159 D6
Daffy La YO61 ......117 E1
Dacre CI YO8 ....197 D6
Daisy CI DL9 ....41 A5
Daisy Hill BD20 ....174 C1
Dakyn CI DL7 ......222 D2
Dalacres Cres BD23 ..217 D4
Dalacres Dr BD23 ...217 D4
Dalby Ave HG2 .....220 D1
Dalby Bank YO60 ...119 C2
Dalby CI YO12 ......212 B5
Dalby Ct HG2 ......220 D1
Dalby Forest Dr YO18 ..96 E8
Dalby Mead YO32 ...225 F1
Dalby Way TS8 ......7 A5
Dale Bank HG1 .....219 C5
Dale CI Burniston YO13 ..75 C8
  Hampsthwaite HG3 ...161 A5
  ⬛ Hurworth-on-Tees DL2 ..3 E1
  Selby YO8 ....232 C3
  Thornton Watlass HG4 ..86 D8
Dale Dike Dr YO30 ..224 F2
Dale Edge ⬛ YO11 ..99 F7
Dale End Danby YO21 ..29 C7
  Kirkbymoorside YO62 ..70 B1
Dale End Rd YO62 ...70 A7
Dale Garth YO12 ...212 A7
Dale Gr YO8 ....60 D6
Dale Rd Carleton BD23 ..173 A4
  Darlington DL3 ....3 B5
  Sadberge DL2 ....3 D7
Dale Rise YO13 .....75 C8
Dale St ⬛ Earby BB18 .172 A1
  York YO23 ....233 A1
Dale Stone CI WF11 ..201 D5
Dale The LS25 ......194 B8
Dale View ⬛ Earby BB18 .172 A1
  Ilkley LS29 ....218 B4
Dale Way ⬛ DL8 ....60 D5
Dalefield Ave WF11 ..201 A4
Dalefield Rd WF6 ...200 A1
Dalehouse Bank TS13 ..13 J1
Dales Ave BD23 ....217 C2
Dales Countryside Mus*
  DL8 ....56 D5
Dales Pk Rd TS8 .....6 F5
Dales Sch DL7 ......64 A7
Dalesbridge Outdoor Ctr*
  LA2 ....130 E6
Daleside Ave HG2 ...222 E5
Daleside Dr HG2 ....222 E5
Daleside Gdns HG2 ..222 E5
Daleside Pk HG3 ....160 A6
Daleside Rd
  Farndale East YO62 ...48 C3
  Farndale West YO62 ..48 B6
  Harrogate HG2 ......222 E5
  Rosedale East Side YO18 ..49 C5
  Rosedale West Side YO18 ..49 C3
Dalesview Ct YO8 ...232 B6
Dalguise Av YO31 ...233 C4
Dallamires CI ⬛ HG4 .214 D3
Dallamires Ind Est
  HG4 ....214 D4
Dallamires La HG4 ..214 D4
Dallamires Way N
  HG4 ....214 D4
Dallamires Way S
  HG4 ....214 D3
Dalmally CI YO24 ...230 B6

Dalton Hill YO19 ....193 A8
Dalton La Dalton YO7 ..115 D7
  Wothersome LS23 ...188 C5
Dalton Terr YO24 ...228 A3
Dam Bank YO8 .....232 C6
Dam Head Rd ⬛ BB18 .171 D1
Dam Hill YO23 .....182 B4
Dam La
  Appleton Roebuck YO23 ..190 F4
  Markington with Wallerthwaite
  HG3 ....139 C3
  Saxton with Scarthingwell
  LS24 ....195 C7
  Selby YO8 ....197 B3
Dame La DL8 ....58 F1
Damson CI YO26 ...227 F4
Danby Castle* YO21 ..29 D6
Danby CE VC Prim Sch
  YO21 ....29 B6
Danby La DL7 ......43 C5
Danby St YO7 ......40 F4
Dandy Mill Ave WF8 ..201 C1
Dandy Mill Croft ⬛
  WF8 ....201 C1
Dandy Mill View WF8 .201 C1
Dane Ave
  Thorpe Willoughby YO8 ..197 B1
  York YO26 ....227 C3
Dane's Graves (Tumuli)*
  YO25 ....151 C2
Danebury Cres YO26 .227 C4
Danebury Dr YO26 ..227 C4
Danebury Dr YO26 ..227 C4
Danelaw Gdns ⬛ DL6 .43 F3
Danelaw Rd ⬛ DL6 ..43 F3
Danes Croft ⬛ YO10 .231 D8
Danes Ct ⬛ YO19 ..198 A8
Danes Dyke ⬛ YO12 .75 D5
Danes Hills (Tumuli)*
  YO19 ....192 C2
Danescroft YO8 ....232 C2
Danesfort Rd YO24 ..227 D1
Danesgate YO24 ...227 D1
Danesmead YO10 ..231 D8
Danesmoor Cres DL3 ..3 B5
Danethorpe YO41 ...166 D2
Dangerous Cnr HG1 ..160 A2
Dansk Way LS29 ...218 C5
Danum Dr YO10 ....211 A1
Danum Rd YO10 ...231 E8
Danum Sch YO10 ...231 E8
D'arcy Ct YO9 ......40 F4
D'arcy Rd YO8 .....232 C4
Dark La
  Barwick in Elmet & Scholes
  LS15 ....194 B8
  Brompton YO13 ....98 C5
  Newsham DL11 .....18 C8
  Sinnington YO62 ....71 A1
  Spofforth with Stockeld
  HG5 ....179 E6
  Stainburn LS21 ....177 E2
  Spofforth HG3 .....160 A2
Darfield La WF8 ...201 C2
Darley Carr HG3 ...159 F6
Darley CI ⬛ YO41 ..168 D2
Darley Com Prim Sch
  HG3 ....160 A6
Darley Mill Ctr* HG3 .159 F6
Darley Rd HG3 ....160 A6
Darling La YO23 ...182 A3
Darlington (Bank Top) Sta
  DL1 ....3 D4
Darlington Arts Ctr* ⬛ 2
  DL3 ....3 D5
Darlington Back La DL2 ..4 E8
Darlington Coll of Tech
  DL3 ....3 B5
Darlington Meml Hospl
  DL3 ....3 C6
Darlington Rd
  Easby DL10 ....20 F1
  Longnewton TS21 ...4 F5
  Northallerton DL6 ...210 C6
  Richmond DL10 ....209 E8
  Stockton-on-Tees TS18 ..5 C8
Darlington Rly Ctr & Mus
  DL3 ....3 C6
Darnborough Gate
  HG4 ....214 B6
Darnborough St YO23 .233 B1
Darnbrook Rd ⬛ BB18 .171 D1
Darnbrook Wlk YO22 ..51 D8
Darnton Dr TS4 ......7 A7
Darrowby CI YO7 ...211 C4
Darrowby Dr DL3 ...3 A6
Darwin CI YO23 ...225 E1
Daskett Hill YO60 ..145 B7
Dauby La YO41 ....185 A3
Davenport Rd TS15 ..25 D2
David La YO18 ......72 F5
Davison Rd DL3 .....3 C7
Davison St DL1 .....3 D4
Davison St TS12 ....9 F7
Davygate YO1 .....233 B2
Daw La YO23 ......191 A5
Dawcross Rise HG3 ..222 B3
Dawes Ave WF10 ...201 A4
Dawnay La YO61 ...165 E5
Dawnay Garth
  Shipton YO30 ......165 E5
  ⬛ Snaith DN14 .....204 B1

Dawney La YO61 ...143 B6
Dawson St ⬛ BD23 ..217 A3
Dawson Terr HG1 ...219 D4
Dawson's La HG4 ...85 F4
Dawtrie St WF10 ...201 B4
Day La HG3 ....159 E4
Daysfoot Ct ⬛ YO10 .228 E3
De Bruce Rd DL6 ...210 D8
De Brus Pk TS8 .....7 C4
De Brus Way TS14 ..8 F7
De Burgh Ct DL9 ...41 A5
De Ferrers Rd DL6 ..210 D8
De Ferrieres Ave HG1 .219 D4
De Gaunte Rd DL6 ..210 D8
De Grey Ct YO30 ...233 A4
De Grey PI ⬛ YO21 .231 B3
De Grey St YO31 ...233 B4
De Grey Ter YO30 ..233 A4
De Lacy Ave ⬛ WF7 .200 E1
De Lisle Cres DL9 ..209 C2
De Mowbray Ct YO23 .182 B6
Deacon CI ⬛ YO8 ..232 B6
Deacons Ct YO23 ..230 B2
Dealtry Ave ⬛ YO32 .225 C8
Dean Edge Rd BD22 .187 C1
Dean Hall Brow YO7 ..32 C5
Dean La BD22 .....187 F7
Dean Rd Norton YO17 .215 E3
  Scarborough YO12 ..212 E6
Dean St Ilkley LS29 ..218 C5
  Trawden Forest BB8 ..186 A1
Deane PI HG2 ......220 B3
Deangate YO1 .....233 B3
Deanhead Gr ⬛ YO30 .224 E2
Deans CI YO23 ....230 F4
Deans Sq YO7 .....115 C7
Debruse Ave TS15 ..5 D2
Dee CI YO24 ....230 B7
Deep Dale LS23 ...180 E1
Deep Ghyll Fold HG4 .214 C3
Deep Ghyll Wlk HG4 .214 C3
Deepdale
  Guisborough TS14 ...8 D6
  ⬛ Hutton Rudby TS15 .25 C5
  Scarborough YO11 ..230 D8
Deepdale Ave
  Eastfield YO11 .....100 A8
  Middlesbrough TS4 ...7 A8
  Scarborough YO11 ..213 A1
Deepdale La
  Boston Spa LS23 ...180 E1
  Ingleton LA6 ....77 F8
Deepdale Way ⬛ DL1 .3 F6
Deepfurrows La YO41 .185 D3
Deeping Way TS8 ...6 E5
Deer Hill Gr YO30 ..224 F3
Deer Pk Ct ⬛ LS25 .195 F4
Deerstone Way ⬛ YO19 .184 F7
Deighton Ave ⬛ LS25 .195 F4
Deighton La
  Brompton DL6 ......43 E5
  Little Smeaton DL6 ..23 E1
Deighton Rd
  Coulby Newham TS4 ..7 A7
  Spofforth with Stockeld
  HG3 ....179 F6
  Wetherby LS22 ....180 C4
Deighton Gates Prim Sch
  LS22 ....180 C4
Del Pyke YO31 ....233 C4
Delamere CI ⬛ YO32 .166 D5
Delamere Cres HG2 ..220 B4
Delamere Rd TS3 ...7 B8
Delaney CI ⬛ DL2 ..131 D2
Delf La YO7 ....66 A4
Dell The ⬛ YO30 ..224 B5
Delves La YO22 ....30 F3
Delwood YO10 ....231 D7
Dene CI DL3 ....3 C4
Dene Gr DL3 ....3 A6
Dene Mdw ⬛ YO13 .99 B8
Dene Pk HG1 ......219 F5
Dene Rd DL6 ......210 E5
Dene Pk CI HG1 ...219 F5
Dene The YO12 ...212 E7
Denesway YO25 ...194 D3
Denevale TS15 .....5 E3
Denison Ave ⬛ YO12 .99 D6
Denison Rd YO8 ...232 E4
Dennis La BD20 ...173 C2
Dennis St YO1 .....233 C2
Dentdale Dr HG5 ..221 C6
Denton Rd LS29 ...218 A5
Denton Terr WF10 ..200 F4
Denver Dr ⬛ DL2 ..4 D4
Denver Rd BD20 ...206 F2
Denwell Terr WF8 ..201 B1
Deramore Dr YO10 ..229 C3
Deramore Dr W YO10 .229 C3
Derby CI YO9 ......209 C1
Derby Rd TS14 .....8 F6
Derby The YO11 ...213 A1
Dere St Roman Rd*
  DL10 ....2 B2
Derrings La YO41 ..142 D6
Derventio Roman Fort*
  YO17 ....215 D4
Derwent Ave
  Garforth LS25 .....194 C3
  ⬛ Scarborough YO12 .212 C4
  York YO31 ....228 F4

Derwent Cl
Elvington YO41 ....185 B3
2 Stamford Bridge YO41 .168 D2
Derwent Ct YO41 ....185 C2
Derwent Dr
4 Barlby YO8 ....198 B5
Castleford WF10 ....201 C5
Wheldrake YO19 ....192 F7
Derwent Est YO19 ....184 E7
Derwent Inf Sch YO10 .229 B4
Derwent Jun Sch
YO10 ....229 B4
Derwent Pk YO19 ....193 A8
Derwent Pl WF11 ....201 F1
Derwent Pool YO17 .215 D4
Derwent Rd
Harrogate HG1 ....220 B3
Huttons Ambo YO17 ....215 A2
Whitby YO21 ....208 A7
York YO10 ....231 D8
Derwent St 7 YO42 ....212 E4
Derwent Swimming Pool &
Fitness Ctr YO17 ....215 D4
Derwent Terr YO17 ....215 D3
Derwent Wlk YO32 ....225 F5
Desmond Dr DL2 ....4 C3
Deveron Way YO24 ....230 B8
Devil's Arrows Standing
Stones* YO51 ....141 B5
Devon Cl 8 DL9 ....209 C1
Devon Pl YO10 ....228 F3
Devonshire Dr YO12 ....212 E7
Devonshire Gn HG4 ....114 F1
Devonshire Pl
Harrogate HG1 ....219 E3
13 Skipton BD23 ....216 F4
Devonshire Rd DL1 ....3 E6
Devonshire St 13 BD23 .217 A3
Devonshire Way HG1 ....219 F4
Dew La TS7 ....7 D7
Dewberry TS8 ....7 B4
Dewsbury Ct YO1 ....233 A1
Dewsbury Terr YO1 ....233 A1
Dexta Way DL7 ....210 C3
Diamond Ct TS18 ....5 F7
Diamond Dr HG1 ....220 C4
Diamond Mews HG2 ....219 C1
Diamond Pl HG1 ....220 C4
Diamond Rd TS17 ....6 B8
Diamond St YO31 ....233 C4
Dibble Bridge Bank
YO21 ....28 F6
Dibdale Rd DL2 ....4 A1
Dick La BD22 ....187 B6
Dick Scot La DL11 ....19 D7
Dickens Cl 1 YO32 ....225 F1
Dickens Dr WF8 ....201 B2
Dickens Rd YO17 ....215 C6
Dickey La YO8 ....197 D5
Dickson Rd 8 YO24 ....227 E7
Dicky Grounds La
YO17 ....121 D8
Dijon Ave YO24 ....227 C2
Dike La HG3 ....159 C8
Dike Ray Cl YO32 ....225 C7
Dikelholln La DL8 ....85 E6
Dikelands Cl 8 YO26 .165 F1
Dikelands La YO26 ....165 F1
Dikes La TS9 ....8 C2
Diligence Way 2 TS16 ....5 D5
Dilys Gr 5 YO26 ....227 E4
Dimmingdale Rd TS12 ....10 A3
Dinas Ct 8 TS17 ....5 F4
Dinsdale Ave TS5 ....6 E7
Dinsdale Ct 7 DL2 ....4 C4
Dinsdale Cres DL1 ....3 D5
Dinsdale Cres DL1 ....3 D5
Dinsdale Dr TS16 ....5 E5
Dinsdale Sta DL2 ....4 C4
Diomed Ct TS7 ....7 B7
Dishforth Airfield
YO7 ....115 A2
Dishforth Airfield Com Prim
Sch YO7 ....115 B2
Dishforth CE VC Prim Sch
YO7 ....114 F4
Dishforth Rd
Copt Hewick HG4 ....114 B2
Sharow HG4 ....214 F6
Disraeli Cl YO32 ....225 E1
Dixon Cl YO8 ....232 B6
Dixon Gdns YO8 ....232 B6
Dixon La YO1 ....233 A1
Dixon Rd HG1 ....219 D4
Dixon St BD20 ....187 F7
Dixon Terr HG1 ....219 D4
Dixons Bank TS8 ....7 C5
Dixons Yd YO1 ....233 C2
Dob Pk Rd LS21 ....176 F4
Dock Hill YO8 ....232 C4
Doctor Laithe 8 BD23 .134 D2
Doctor's Hill LA2 ....128 E8
Doctor's La TS15 ....25 C5
Doctors La WF10 ....200 D7
Dodder Carr Rd TS13 ....10 F3
Dodford Rd TS8 ....6 F5
Dodgson La
Lothersdale BD20 ....186 D8
Thornton in Craven
BB18 ....172 C1
Dodgson Terr YO26 .227 D4
Dodmire Jun & Inf Sch
DL1 ....3 E4
Dodsworth Ave YO31 .228 E7
Doe Pk YO30 ....224 F2

Doe Pk La YO41 ....169 B4
Dog Hill DL8 ....60 E3
Dog Hill Brow BD24 .131 D6
Dog Kennel La YO16 ....96 E5
Doherty Wlk YO24 ....230 C8
Dolphin Ctr The DL1 ....3 C5
Dolegate YO41 ....168 F4
Dolly La DL7 ....64 C8
Dollyth Howe* YO17 .149 F6
Dolphin Ctr The DL3 ....3 C5
Dolphin Way YO14 ....100 F5
Don Ave YO24 ....230 E8
Don Pedro Ave WF6 ....200 B1
Don Pedro Cl WF6 ....200 B1
Donald Smith Ct DL8 ....61 C5
Doncaster Rd
Brayton YO8 ....232 B3
Knottingley WF11 ....201 E2
North Elmsall WF8 ....206 A1
Doran Cl 13 YO14 ....101 B3
Dorchester Rd LS24 .189 D5
Doriam Ave YO31 ....225 F2
Doriam Dr YO31 ....225 F2
Dorkings The TS9 ....26 E5
Dorset Cl HG1 ....219 A3
Dorset Cres HG1 ....219 A3
Dorset Ct 5 DL9 ....209 C1
Dorset St TS14 ....8 E5
Dorset St BD23 ....217 A3
Dorts Cres LS24 ....190 C1
Dotcliffe Rd BB18 ....186 A7
Doublegates Ave 6
HG4 ....113 D2
Doublegates Cl 8 HG4 .113 D2
Doublegates Ct 10 HG4 .113 D2
Doublegates Gn 9 HG4 .113 D2
Doublegates Wlk 7
HG4 ....113 D2
Doubting Castle*
YO21 ....10 D1
Douglas Cl TS18 ....5 F7
Douglas St 8 YO8 ....232 C5
Douky Bottom Cave*
BD23 ....133 F7
Dove Cl LS22 ....180 B4
Dove Cote Gdns DN14 .203 D2
Dove St YO23 ....233 A1
Dove Way YO62 ....94 C8
Dovecot Cl YO14 ....100 E4
Dovecote Dr WF10 ....200 F7
Dovecote Garth 5
YO41 ....185 B2
Dovecote Mews YO7 .115 C7
Dovedale Ave YO12 .212 D8
Dovelands 14 BD20 .187 E6
Dovey Cl 7 TS17 ....5 F4
Dowber Cl YO7 ....211 D3
Dowber Way YO7 ....211 D4
Dower Chase YO19 .192 A6
Dower Pk YO19 ....192 B6
Dowkell La LS23 ....188 F1
Downdale Rd YO13 ....54 B4
Downdinner Hill YO21 .208 C6
Downholme Rd DL9 .209 B1
Downland Cres WF11 .202 A1
Downside Rd TS5 ....6 D8
Dracula Experience*
YO21 ....208 D7
Dragon Ave HG1 ....219 E3
Dragon Par HG1 ....219 E3
Dragon Rd HG1 ....219 E3
Dragon Terr HG1 ....219 E3
Dragon View HG1 ....219 E4
Drake Cl YO21 ....208 B5
Drake St 8 YO23 ....233 B1
Drakes Cl YO22 ....225 F5
Drapers Croft YO23 ....230 B4
Drax CP Sch YO8 ....204 F5
Dreaken Fold 4 YO13 ....99 A7
Drebley La BD23 ....157 D6
Dresser Cl DL10 ....209 C8
Driffield Rd YO25 ....126 A4
Driffield Terr YO24 ....228 A2
Drift La HG4 ....138 B8
Dringfield Cl 2 YO24 ....230 D8
Dringhouses Prim Sch
YO24 ....230 F8
Dringhouses Sports Club
YO24 ....230 F8
Dringthorpe Rd YO24 .230 F7
Drive The
Harrogate HG1 ....220 C5
7 High & Low Bishopside
HG3 ....137 C4
Kippax LS25 ....194 D1
Middlesbrough TS17 ....6 A6
Skipton BD23 ....217 B5
12 Swillington LS26 .194 A1
Threshfield BD23 ....134 B3
Drome Rd YO23 ....230 C2
Drovers Ct 8 YO61 .143 C8
Drovers Way YO21 ....208 B3
Drovers Wlk BD23 .154 B3
Druggist La 8 LS29 .174 F4
Druggon Rd DL9 ....40 E3
Druids Mdw 8 YO51 .141 B5
Drummond View
YO23 ....231 B4
Drury Cl HG3 ....222 F2
Drury La HG3 ....222 F2
Drury St DL3 ....3 C6
Dryden Cl HG1 ....219 E2
Dryhurst Cl 7 DN6 .206 F2
Dubbing Garth La DL11 .37 B4
Dubb's La DL1 ....81 C1
Duchess of Kents Military
Hospl DL9 ....40 F4

Duchy Ave
3 Harrogate HG2 ....219 C1
7 Scalby YO13 ....75 C5
Duchy Gr 8 HG2 ....219 C1
Duchy Rd HG1 ....219 B2
Duck Hill HG4 ....214 C5
Duck La YO12 ....125 A8
Duck St LA2 ....128 A6
Duck St La HG3 ....136 D2
Duckett Cl DL10 ....209 F8
Duckett St BD23 ....217 A3
Duckhill La YO7 ....115 A4
Dudley Mews YO31 .233 C4
Dudley Rd DL1 ....4 A5
Dudley St YO31 ....233 C4
Dudley Wlk HG4 ....214 B3
Duffield Cres 1 LS25 .195 F4
Dugdale La BB7 ....152 C1
Duggleby Howe*
YO17 ....149 C5
Duke St
6 Burton in Lonsdale LA6 .102 F3
13 High Bentham LA2 .129 A8
Settle BD23 ....131 D2
Skipton BD23 ....217 A4
14 Trawden Forest BB8 .186 A3
Duke's La YO25 ....126 A1
Dukes Hall LS29 ....218 A6
Dukes Wharf YO23 .233 B1
Dukesway TS17 ....6 B5
Dulverton Cl
2 High Leven TS17 ....6 A3
13 Pontefract WF8 ....201 C2
Dulverton Rise WF8 .201 C2
Dulverton Way WF8 .201 C2
Dumb Tom's La LA6 .103 B1
Dumfries Sq 8 DL9 ....40 E4
Duna Way 8 YO62 ....70 C1
Duncan Cl 6 HG1 ....219 C5
Duncan St HG1 ....219 C5
Dunce Mire Rd LS25 .202 A8
Duncombe Cl
2 Eastfield YO12 ....99 F7
Malton YO17 ....215 A3
Duncombe Dr
24 Pickering YO18 ....95 F7
Stensall YO32 .167 B8
Duncombe Pk* YO62 .92 E6
Duncombe Pl YO1 .233 B3
Dundas Gdns YO21 .208 B6
Dundas St
Richmond DL10 ....209 C7
York YO1 ....233 C2
Dunderdale Cres
WF10 ....201 B5
Dunelm Wlk DL1 ....3 E7
Dunkeswick La LS17 .178 D4
Dunn Gr 8 YO11 ....100 A7
Dunnington CE Prim Sch
YO19 ....184 E7
Dunnington Dr DL2 .196 E1
Dunniwood Cl 4 WF10 .200 D3
Dunniwood Dr 8 WF10 .200 D3
Dunroyal YO61 ....141 F8
Dunroyal Cl YO61 ....141 F8
Dunsley Cres YO21 .208 A8
Dunslow Cl LS25 ....194 F4
Dunslow La YO11 ....99 F6
Dunslow Rd YO11 ....99 F6
Dunsmore Cl TS8 ....6 C4
Dunwell Ave 2 YO12 .212 B7
Durham Cl 18 YO8 .198 F1
Durham La TS16 ....5 D5
Durham La Ind Pk TS16 .5 D6
Durham La Prim Sch
TS16 ....5 D5
Durham Pl 5 YO12 .213 A7
Durham St
Castleford WF10 ....200 F3
6 Scarborough YO12 .212 F7
Durham Tees Valley Airport
DL2 ....1 C7
Durham Way HG3 ....219 A5
Durlston Dr YO30 .167 A7
Duxbury St 11 BB18 .172 B1
Dyke Hall La LA10 ....78 A8
Dykelands Cl YO19 .192 F7
Dykes La YO23 ....230 A1
Dyon La YO8 ....199 B3
Dyon Rd YO8 ....199 D7
Dyson la DL11 ....18 G7

E

Eagle Pk TS8 ....7 C5
Eaglescliffe Sta TS16 ....5 E6
Early Springfield Prim Sch
BB18 ....172 B1
Earlit La YO23 ....191 A8
Earl Crag View BD22 .187 C6
Earl Edwin Dr DL10 .209 D8
Earle St YO31 ....233 C4
Earlham St 10 BB18 .172 B1
Earls Ct Rd TS8 ....6 F5
Earls View 3 BD20 .187 E6
Earlsborough Terr
YO30 ....233 A4
Earlsdon Ave TS5 ....6 D7
Earlsway TS17 ....6 A5
Earswick Chase YO32 .225 F7
Earswick Village YO32 .225 F7
Easby Abbey (rems of)*
DL10 ....209 E5
Easby Ave TS5 ....6 F8
Easby Cl 4 Bedale DL8 ....63 B2
7 Ilkley LS29 ....175 C2

Easby Ct DL10 ....209 F5
Easby Dr LS29 ....175 C2
Easby La Easby TS9 ....27 A8
Great Ayton TS9 ....27 A8
Easby Low Rd DL10 .209 D7
Easingwold Com Prim Sch
YO61 ....117 C1
Easingwold Sch YO61 .143 C8
Eason Rd YO24 ....230 E8
Eason View YO24 ....230 E8
Easson Rd DL3 ....3 C5
East Acres WF11 ....201 F4
East Ave
8 Easingwold YO61 ....143 D8
18 Glusburn BD20 ....187 E7
21 Scalby YO13 ....75 C5
East Ayton Com Prim Sch
YO13 ....99 A8
East Barnby 2 LS25 .195 F4
East Beck Ct LS21 .176 C3
East Brow Rd YO18 ....72 D4
East Carr 8 WF10 ....200 D6
East Castle St 8 BD23 .217 A3
East Cl DL2 ....4 C7
East Cliff YO22 ....208 E7
East Comm La YO8 .232 F4
East Cowton CE Prim Sch
DL7 ....22 E1
East Cres 12 YO21 ....208 D7
East Down WF10 ....201 A4
East End YO60 ....145 D5
East Garforth Prim Sch
LS25 ....194 D4
East Garforth Sta
LS25 ....194 D3
East Gate YO13 ....98 D6
East Heslerton La
YO17 ....124 A8
East Ings La YO18 ....95 F4
East La Ampleforth YO62 .92 D1
Castle Bolton with East &
West Bolton DL8 ....59 B6
Embsay BD23 ....217 D7
Yafforth DL7 ....43 C1
East Lea YO7 ....115 C7
East Lea View 21 YO11 .100 B6
East Moor Gdns YO19 .231 F5
East Mount YO17 ....215 C4
East Mount Rd
Darlington DL1 ....3 D6
York YO24 ....233 A1
East Neville St 14 BD23 .217 A3
East Parade
Harrogate HG1 ....219 E2
Ilkley LS29 ....218 C4
York YO31 ....228 F6
East Pk Rd
Harrogate HG1 ....219 E2
15 Scalby YO13 ....75 D5
5 Spofforth HG3 ....179 E5
East Rd Melsonby DL10 ....20 F7
Northallerton DL6 ....210 E4
Norton YO17 ....215 E3
East Sandgate 14 YO11 .213 B6
East Side 5 TS15 ....25 D5
East St Gargrave BD23 .155 D1
Gayles DL11 ....19 E6
Swinton YO17 ....121 B4
East Terr YO21 ....208 D7
East Terr Crescent
YO21 ....208 D7
East View Barton DL10 ....21 D8
7 Campsall DN6 .206 E1
8 Knottingley WF11 .202 A2
Langthorpe YO51 .141 A6
Middleton St George DL2 ....4 D3
Northallerton DL6 ....210 E3
Sherburn in Elmet LS25 .211 B6
South Kilvington YO7 .211 B8
18 Trawden BB8 ....186 B1
East View Ct HG5 ....162 F3
East Way Whitby YO21 .208 B7
York YO31 ....225 E2
East Whitby Com Prim Sch
YO22 ....208 F4
East Witton Rd DL8 ....60 E2
Eastbeck Cl YO17 ....124 E8
Eastborough YO11 .213 B6
Eastbourne Comp Sch
DL1 ....3 E6
Eastbourne Gdns TS3 ....7 C8
Eastbourne Gr YO31 .228 F5
Eastbourne Rd DL1 ....3 D5
Eastburn Jun & Inf Sch
BD20 ....187 F7
Eastbury Cl TS17 ....6 B4
Eastby Rd HG1 ....219 F6
Eastern Terr YO31 .228 E6
Eastfield 8 YO60 ....145 D5
Eastfield Ave
Haxby YO32 ....225 C7
Norton YO17 ....215 E3
Richmond DL10 ....209 D8
Eastfield Cl LS24 ....189 F7
Eastfield Cres YO10 .229 C2
Eastfield Ct 2 YO32 .225 C7
Eastfield Dr 14 WF11 .201 C1

Eastfield La
Dunnington YO19 ....184 F8
Kellington DN14 ....202 F4
Spennithorne DL8 ....61 A3
Thoralby DL8 ....58 E2
Eastfield Rd
Norton YO17 ....215 E3
Pickering YO18 ....96 A6
Eastfields TS3 ....7 B8
Eastgate 16 Helmsley YO62 .92 F3
Pickering YO18 ....96 A6
3 Seamer YO12 ....99 D6
Eastholme Dr YO30 .224 E1
Easthorpe Dr YO24 .224 A1
Eastland Ave YO24 .227 E2
Eastlands LS25 ....194 C3
Easton Way DL4 ....41 D5
Eastville Terr HG1 ....219 B6
Eastward Ave YO10 .231 E7
Eastway YO11 ....100 A7
Eastway Cl 2 YO62 ....70 C1
Eaton Ct LS29 ....230 B8
Eaton Rd LS29 ....218 A3
Eavestone Gr HG3 ....222 C3
Ebberston Hall* YO13 .97 D6
Ebenezer Terr 9 HG1 ....219 D2
Ebor Cl DL10 ....21 A1
Ebor Ct
Northallerton DL7 ....210 D3
7 Selby YO8 ....232 C6
Ebor Ind Est YO31 ....233 C3
Ebor Mount LS25 ....194 D1
Ebor Prep Sch YO30 .228 A7
Ebor Rise HG1 ....219 B2
Ebor St Selby YO8 .232 C5
York YO23 ....233 B1
Ebor Way YO24 ....224 A2
Ebsay Dr YO30 ....225 A1
Eccles Cl YO30 ....224 D2
Eden Ave YO30 ....232 D3
Eden Camp Modern History
Mus* YO17 ....215 E8
Eden Cl
2 Hurworth-on-Tees DL2 ....3 D1
1 Hutton Rudby TS15 ....25 C4
York YO24 ....230 C7
Eden Cres DL1 ....3 C4
Eden Crest DL2 ....1 D7
Eden La DL2 ....1 D7
Eden Pk DL2 ....4 C4
Eden Pk Rd 2 TS15 ....25 C4
Eden Rd DL7 ....210 B2
Edendale WF10 ....200 F6
Edengarth 8 YO17 ....215 E8
Edens Way HG4 ....214 C2
Edge Dell YO12 ....99 E8
Edge La
Grassington BD23 ....134 F3
Long Preston BD23 ....153 E6
Edgehill Rd YO12 .212 E2
Edgemoor Rd DL1 ....3 E4
Edgerton Cl LS24 ....189 D6
Edgerton Ct 11 LS24 .189 D6
Edgerton Dr LS24 ....189 D6
Edgerton Garth LS24 .189 D6
Edgware Rd YO10 .228 E2
Edinburgh Dr DL3 ....3 A7
Edmondson St 8 BB18 .171 D2
Edmondson's La BD23 .172 C5
Edmund Wilson Swimming
Baths YO24 ....227 D1
Edston Dr 5 TS14 ....8 F7
Edward Pease Way DL3 ....3 A7
Edward St
27 Earlby BB18 ....172 A1
Pontefract WF6 ....200 A3
Egglescliffe CE VC Sch
TS16 ....5 E4
Eggleston CE Sch
YO12 ....212 C8
Eggleston Hill YO12 ....3 A6
Eggshall La LA2 ....130 C8
Eglington Ave TS14 ....8 F6
Egremont Cl 11 YO41 .168 D2
Egton Ave TS7 ....7 C5
Egton CE VA Prim Sch
YO21 ....31 B5
Egton Cliff YO21 ....31 A4
Egton La YO21 ....31 A4
Egton Sta YO21 ....31 A4
Eight Acre La HG4 ....113 A5
Eighth Ave YO31 ....228 F5
El Alamein Rd 8 DL9 .209 C1
Elbolton Cave* BD23 .156 E8
Elbow Terr 8 YO22 .208 E6
Elder Rd DL6 ....210 D4
Elder's St 8 YO11 .213 A6
Eldmire La YO7 ....115 D6
Eldon St YO31 ....233 C4
Eldon Terr YO31 ....233 C4
Eldroth Rd LA2 ....130 C5
Eldwick Cl YO30 .224 F2
Eleanor Dr HG2 ....220 C1
Eleanor Gr HG2 ....220 C1
Electric Ave HG1 ....219 B5
Elgar Cl YO31 ....227 C2
Elgin Rd 8 YO32 ....167 B6
Elgin St 8 YO12 .212 F6
Elizabeth Ct
7 Selby YO8 ....232 B6
Sherburn in Elmet LS25 .195 E4
Elizabeth Dr WF10 .201 B4
Elizabethan Ct 8 WF8 .201 C1
Elland Ct 8 DL1 ....3 F8
Ellarfield La LS25 ....195 F5
Ellen Cl HG2 ....220 C4
Ellenthorpe La YO51 .141 D6
Eller Gates YO21 ....30 C6

Eller Gill La BD23 ....172 D4
Eller Mews **3** BD23 .....216 E3
Ellerbeck Ct TS9 ....26 D6
Ellerbeck Way
Great & Little Broughton
TS9 ....26 D6
Middlesbrough TS7 ....7 D8
Whitby YO22 ....208 E4
Ellerburn Rd YO18 ....96 F7
Ellerby Bank TS13 ....11 F4
Ellerby La YO13 ....11 F5
Ellerclose Rd **25** DL8 .....60 D5
Ellerholme La DL11 ....38 F5
Ellerington Cl **5** LA6 ...103 D3
Ellerker La LS14 ....188 A3
Ellerker Rd LS14 ....188 A3
Ellers La 59 A2
Ellers Rd BD20 ....187 E6
Ellerton Bank Nature
Reserve* YO18 ....72 F1
Ellerton Priory (rems of)*
DL11 ....39 A4
Ellerton Rd TS18 ....5 D8
Elliot St BD23 ....231 D7
Elliot St BD23 ....216 F4
Elliott St BD20 ....174 B1
Ellis Ct HG1 ....219 B2
Ellis Gdns **6** YO13 .....75 D5
Ellis La LS25 ....194 C5
Ellison Ave **52** YO12 ....75 D5
Ellwood Cotts BD24 .....131 D4
Ellwood Ct YO10 ....228 D2
Elm Ave Kippax LS25 ....194 C2
Northallerton DL6 ....210 F5
Elm Cl
Barnoldswick BB18 ......171 D1
10 Filey YO14 ....101 B4
Hipswell DL9 ....209 F1
Northallerton DL7 ....210 F5
Elm Ct DL6 ....210 E5
Elm Dr TS7 ....7 B6
Elm End **8** YO22 ....166 E5
Elm Gn **7** YO62 ....92 F7
Elm Gr Sherburn YO17 ...124 D8
Thornaby TS17 ....6 B8
4 Whitby YO21 ....208 B6
York YO31 ....225 F2
Elm Pl WF11 ....201 F2
Elm Rd **32** Glusburn BD20 ..187 F8
Guisborough TS14 ....8 F7
Harrogate HG1 ....219 E5
Ripon HG4 ....214 B2
9 Scarborough YO12 ...212 E4
3 Topcliffe YO7 ....89 B1
Elm St YO8 ....232 D6
Elm Tree Ave
Harrogate HG1 ....219 D5
9 Poppleton YO26 .....165 F1
Elm Tree Rise HG3 ......140 B5
Elm Tree Sq BD23 ....217 D8
Elm View YO18 ....96 A6
Elm Wlk **8** DL10 ....41 D5
Elma Gr **8** YO30 ....224 E2
Elmet Dr LS15 ....194 C8
Elmet Rd LS15 ....194 C7
Elmete Ave LS25 ....195 F4
Elmete Rd WF10 ....201 B5
Elmfield Ave YO31 ......228 F8
Elmfield Rd
8 Glusburn BD20 .....187 F8
Hurworth DL2 ....3 D1
Hurworth-on-Tees DL2 ...22 D8
Elmfield Terr YO31 .....228 F7
Elmlands Gr YO31 ....228 F8
Elmpark Vale YO31 ......229 A8
Elmpark View YO31 .....229 A8
Elmpark Way YO31 ......229 A8
Elms Cl **8** YO12 ....191 F1
Elms The YO32 ....167 D2
Elmslac Cl **3** YO62 .....92 F6
Elmslac Rd **3** YO62 .....92 F7
Elmtree Gdns **8** YO12 ...92 F6
Elmville Ave YO12 ......212 E6
Elmwood Ave LS15 ......194 B8
Elmwood Chase LS15 ....194 B8
Elmwood Cl **6** TS9 .....26 C8
Elmwood La LS15 ....194 B8
Elmwood Rd TS16 ....5 E6
Elmwood St **4** HG1 ....219 E4
Elphin Bridge La
YO61 ....117 B6
Elslack La BD23 ....172 C4
Elston Cl YO30 ....228 A8
Elston Pl YO8 ....232 C6
Eltham Cres TS17 ....6 C6
Elton La HG3 ....160 E6
Elton Par DL3 ....3 B5
Elton Rd DL3 ....3 B5
Elvington CE Prim Sch
YO41 ....185 B3
Elvington Ind Est
YO41 ....185 A3
Elvington La YO19 ......184 E5
Elvington Pk YO41 ......185 A3
Elvington Terr YO10 ....228 E4
Elwick Ave TS5 ....6 F7
Elwick Gr YO10 ....229 C4
Elwick La YO26 ....164 B7
Ely Cl HG3 ....160 E5
Embleton Dr **1** YO30 ...224 F1
Embleton Rd LS26 ......200 B4
Embsay CE VC Prim Sch
BD23 ....217 D8
Embsay Sta BD23 ....217 D7
Embsay Steam Rly*
.......................217 E7
Emerald St YO31 ....233 C4
Emerson Ave TS5 ....6 F8

Emerson Cl **2** DL6 .....25 D1
Emerson Rd DL2 ....3 E1
Emery Cl DL2 ....3 E1
Emgate **8** BD23 ....63 A3
Emily Mews YO10 ....228 E4
Emley Moor Rd DL1 ....3 E4
Emley View LS25 ....194 C2
Emmerson St **2** YO31 .228 E5
Emmet La HG3 ....160 C5
Emmott Ct BB8 ....186 C3
Emmott La BB8 ....186 B4
Emsworth Dr TS16 ....5 D5
Enclosure Gdns **1**
YO10 ....229 B1
Endcliff Cres YO12 .....212 D8
Endeavour Wharf **8**
YO21 ....208 D6
Endfields Rd **1** YO10 ..231 E8
Endican La DL7 ....65 D3
Endsleigh Dr TS5 ....9 D8
Enfield Chase TS14 ......8 F5
Enfield Cres **4** DL9 ....40 E4
Enfield Cres **5** YO24 ..227 F2
Engine Shed La BD23 ...216 D3
England La WF11 ....201 F2
English Martyrs' RC Prim Sch
YO24 ....227 F3
Ennerdale Ave YO31 ....229 B5
Enter La LA6 ....103 D3
Enterpen TS15 ....25 C4
Enterprise Way
Bradleys Both BD20 .....173 D4
Sherburn in Elmet LS25 ..196 B4
Whitby YO22 ....32 F8
Eppleby Forcett CE Prim Sch
DL11 ....22 F7
Epsom Ct **11** DL1 ......3 F6
Eridge Rd DL1 ....8 F6
Ermysted St **4** BD23 ..217 A4
Ermysted's Gram Sch
BD23 ....216 F4
Eryholme La DL2 ....22 F7
Escrick CE VC Prim Sch
YO19 ....192 A5
Escrick Ct YO19 ....192 B5
Escrick Pk Gdns YO19 ..192 B5
Escrick St YO10 ....233 C1
Escrick Terr YO10 ....233 C1
Esher Ave TS6 ....7 E8
Eshington La DL8 ....58 F2
Eshton Rd BD23 ....155 D2
Esk Dr YO26 ....227 B8
Esk Rd DL1 ....3 D3
Eskdale Sch YO22 ......208 E3
Eskdale Ave
Normanton WF6 ....200 A2
York YO10 ....229 C3
Eskdale Cl
5 Pontefract WF6 .....200 A2
Sleights YO22 ....32 A5
Eskdale Croft WF6 .....200 A2
Eskdale Ct **12** WF6 .....200 A2
Eskdale Rd YO22 ....208 F3
Eskdaleside YO22 ....31 F5
Eskew La LA2 ....128 E2
Eskitt Hill YO12 ....212 D4
Esp La BB18 ....171 C1
Esplanade
Harrogate HG2 ....219 C2
Whitby YO21 ....213 A4
York YO26 ....233 A2
Esplanade Cres YO30 ...213 B2
Esplanade Gdns YO11 ..213 A4
Esplanade Rd YO11 .....213 A3
Estell La YO13 ....74 C5
Estill Ct **2** YO11 .....100 B6
Estoril Rd S DL1 ....3 F4
Ethel Cres HG5 ....221 C6
Ethel St **12** BB18 .....171 E1
Etive Pl YO24 ....230 B7
Eton Dr **7** YO32 ......166 D5
Eton Rd TS5 ....6 E8
Ettersgill Cl TS16 ....5 D5
Ettersgill Dr DL3 ....3 A5
Ettington Ave TS3 ....7 B8
Etty Ave YO10 ....229 C4
Etty Cl **24** YO41 ......168 D2
Euclid Ave HG1 ....219 B5
Eva Ave YO30 ....224 D2
Evelyn Cres YO30 ......228 B7
Evelyn Ct **5** HG3 .....161 B2
Evelyn Dr YO12 ....212 D4
Evergreen Way **1** 197 D1
Evergreen Wlk **2** TS4 ...6 F8
Everingham Rd TS15 .....5 D2
Eversley Ave LS25 ......195 F3
Eversley Ct LS25 ....195 F4
Eversley Garth Cres
LS25 ....195 F4
Eversley Mount LS25 ...195 F3
Evesham Rd TS3 ....7 B8
Evron Cir YO14 ....101 B3
Ewart St YO12 ....212 E3
Ewden Cl **16** YO14 ....101 A3
Ewe Leys La YO17 ....66 A5
Ewelands Hill YO7 ......94 D7
Exchange St **4** WF6 ...200 A1
Exelby Cl DL6 ....63 D1
Exelby La DL7 ....63 D5
Exeter Cres **10** HG3 ...161 B3
Exeter Dr DL1 ....3 F7
Exford Cl **8** TS17 ......6 A3
Exhibition Sq YO1 ......233 B3
Express Way WF6 ......200 A3
Eyre Cl YO8 ....232 A2

F

Faber Cl YO23 ....230 B3
Faber St YO31 ....228 E5
Faceby Rd TS9 ....26 A2
Fadmoor Bank YO62 ......69 E6
Fadmoor La YO62 ....69 F4
Fair Head La YO22 ....31 D4
Fairburn Dr LS25 ....194 D3
Fairburn Prim Sch
WF11 ....201 D6
Fairburn Sports & Recn Ctr
WF11 ....201 D6
Fairfax **15** YO41 ......168 D2
Fairfax Ave
Harrogate HG2 ....220 B2
North Featherstone
WF7 ....200 E1
Selby YO8 ....232 B4
Fairfax Cl
2 Ampleforth YO62 .....92 C1
Bolton Percy YO23 ......169 D4
Fairfax Cres YO26 .....181 C7
Fairfax Croft YO23 .....230 B2
Fairfax House* YO1 ....233 C2
Fairfax Rd 4 D4
Fairfax St
1 Scarborough YO12 ..212 E5
10 Skipton BD23 ......217 A3
York YO1 ....233 B1
Fairfax Wlk **3** HG2 ...220 B3
Fairfield
Fairburn WF11 ....201 D7
Thirsk YO7 ....211 C4
Fairfield Ave TS7 ....7 D7
Fairfield Cl **16** LS25 ..195 F4
Fairfield Cres YO12 ....212 E8
Fairfield La LS25 ....202 A6
Fairfield Link LS25 .....195 F4
Fairfield Rd
Stainless TS13 ....13 K2
Stokesley TS9 ....26 B7
Tadcaster LS24 ....189 E6
Fairfield St DL3 ....3 A5
Fairfield Way
3 Tadcaster LS24 ......189 E6
Whitby YO22 ....208 F3
Fairfields Dr YO30 .....224 B5
Fairheath Rd LA2 ......128 E5
Fairholme La DL7 ....64 A4
Fairmead Ct YO22 .....208 E4
Fairmead Way YO22 ...208 E4
Fairview TS21 ....5 A7
Fairview Gdns DL10 ....209 C8
Fairway
Normanton South WF6 ..200 B1
4 Scalby YO13 ....75 C5
Selby YO8 ....232 A4
York YO30 ....228 A8
Fairway App WF6 ......200 B1
Fairway Ave WF6 ......200 B1
Fairway Cl
8 Normanton South WF6 .200 B1
15 Sherburn in Elmet LS25 .195 F4
Fairway Dr
Normanton South WF6 ..200 B1
Poppleton YO26 ....165 F1
Fairway Gdns **4** WF6 ...200 B1
Fairway Mdws **9** WF6 ..200 B1
Fairway The
Darlington DL1 ....3 E5
Middlesbrough TS8 ....7 C5
8 North Featherstone
WF7 ....200 E1
Northallerton DL7 ......210 C3
Sherburn in Elmet LS25 ..195 F4
Fairways Ave HG2 ......220 E3
Fairways Dr HG2 ....220 E3
Fairways Dr HG2 ....220 D3
Fairwood Pk TS8 ....7 C5
Fairy Hill La WF8 ......201 B3
Fairy La YO18 ....71 C3
Falcon Ave **12** YO12 ...99 E6
Falcon Cl **10** Haxby YO32 .166 F5
1 Scotton DL9 ....40 F2
17 Settle BD24 ....131 D2
Falcon Dr WF10 ....200 E3
Falcon Gdns **30** YO24 .204 D1
Falcon Terr **11** YO21 ..208 D6
Falcon Way TS14 ....8 D6
Falcon Wlk TS15 ....6 C2
Falconberg Way TS15 ....5 D2
Falconer St **1** YO24 ..227 E2
Falconers Rd YO11 .....213 A5
Falconers Sq **10** YO11 .213 A5
Falkland Rd **2** DL9 ....40 F5
Falkland St YO1 ....233 B1
Fall La Pannal HG3 .....222 B2
Thornthwaite with Padside
HG3 ....159 A6
Fallow Field **1** BD23 ..217 B5
Falmer Rd DL1 ....3 D4
Falmouth Ave WF6 .....200 A2
Falmouth Cres **9** WF6 ..200 A2
Falmouth Dr DL3 ....3 C8
Falmouth Rd WF6 ......200 A2
Falsgrave Com Resource
Ctr* YO12 ....212 E1
Falsgrave Cres YO30 ...228 B7
Falsgrave Mews **6**
YO12 ....212 E5
Falsgrave Rd YO12 .....212 E5
Fanacurt Rd TS14 ....8 D5
Fancy Bank TS14 ....9 B6

Fanny La Knayton YO7 ...65 F2
Stutton with Hazlewood
LS24 ....189 D4
Far La
Hutton Buscel YO13 .....98 F8
Kettlewell with Starbotton
BD23 ....108 D5
Far Mead Croft **3** LS29 .176 C1
Farfield YO26 ....227 C6
Farfield Ave HG5 ....221 C4
Farfield La YO19 ....184 E8
Farfield lane YO19 .....167 E1
Farfield Mount **2** HG5 .221 C4
Farfields Cl TS21 ....4 F6
Farm Cl YO21 ....208 A7
Farm Croft BD23 ....216 F1
Farm Garth TS9 ....8 A2
Farm La TS17 ....6 A5
Farm Way YO8 ....232 B7
Farmanby Cl **12** YO18 ...96 D5
Farmanby Rd **1** YO24 .230 D8
Farmstead Rise YO32 ..225 D7
Farnborough Ct **10** DL2 ..4 C4
Farndale Ave
Northallerton DL7 ......210 C2
York YO10 ....229 D4
Farndale Cl **1** YO32 ..166 F5
Farndale Cres DL3 ......3 B6
Farndale Dr TS14 ....8 D6
Farndale Rd HG5 ......221 D6
Farndale St YO10 ......228 D2
Farnham La HG5 ....162 D7
Farnley CE VA Prim Sch
LS21 ....177 B3
Farnley Hall* LS21 ....177 B2
Farnley La LS21 ....177 B2
Farnley Pk LS21 ....177 C2
Farrar St YO10 ....228 E3
Farriers Croft **2** YO23 .230 B2
Farriers Ct **12** LS22 ..180 C3
Farside Garth YO13 .....75 D6
Farside Rd YO13 ....99 A7
Farthinggale Way TS8 ...6 E4
Favell Ave WF6 ....200 A1
Faven Field Rd YO7 ....211 D4
Faverdale DL3 ....3 B7
Faverdale N DL3 ....3 B7
Faverdale Rd DL3 ....3 B7
Faverdale W DL3 ....3 B7
Faversham Cl TS8 ....6 F4
Favordale Rd BB8 ......186 A3
Fawcett Ave TS8 ....6 F4
Fawcett St YO10 ....233 C1
Fawdington Rd YO61 ...115 F2
Fawkes Dr YO26 ....227 C4
Fearby Rd Fearby HG4 ...85 F4
Masham HG4 ....86 A4
7 Stockton-on-Tees TS18 ..5 D8
Fearnhead TS8 ....7 C5
Feasegate YO1 ....233 B2
Featherbeck Cl **8** LA6 .103 D3
Featherbed La
Bilton-in-Ainsty with Bickerton
LS24 ....181 C3
Ellerbeck DL6 ....44 E4
Federation St **12** BB18 .171 D1
Feeding Pasture La
YO60 ....147 B2
Feetham Ave DL1 ....3 F7
Feethams Sports Gd
DL1 ....3 C5
Felbrigg La TS17 ....6 A4
Feldom La DL11 ....19 E1
Felixkirk Rd YO7 ......211 F4
Felixstowe Dr **10** DL9 ...40 E4
Fell La Cracoe BD23 ....156 B7
Winton CA17 ....14 C8
Fell Rd LA6 ....104 A7
Fell View BD23 ....217 E8
Fell View St **4** BD23 ..134 E2
Fellbrook Ave YO26 ....227 B4
Fenby Ave DL1 ....3 E4
Fenby Gdns YO12 ......212 C4
Fence Dike La DL7 ......63 C7
Fenton Ave BB18 ......171 E2
Fenton Cl **10** YO11 ...100 B7
Fenton La Malton YO17 .215 C8
Sherburn in Elmet LS25 ..195 E2
Fenton St Boosbeck TS12 ..9 D7
38 Burley in Wharfedale
LS29 ....176 C1
Fenwick Cl **11** YO11 ..100 B6
Fenwick Comm La
DN6 ....207 D2
Fenwick La DN6 ....207 B1
Fenwick St YO23 ......228 C2
Fenwick's La YO10 .....231 D7
Ferguson Cl DL7 ....210 C3
Fergusson Rd YO30 ....225 F1
Fern Bank Ave BB18 ...171 D2
Fern Cl YO32 ....226 A4
Fern Gdns **1** LS29 ...218 A3
Fern St YO31 ....233 C4
Ferndale Rd YO8 ......232 C4
Fernie Rd TS14 ....8 D6
Fernlea Cl YO8 ....232 D6
Fernley Gn Cl **8** WF11 .202 A2
Fernway YO10 ....229 C3
Fernwood TS8 ....6 E4
Fernwood Cl **2** DL6 ...43 F3
Ferry Cl **19** YO8 ......198 F1
Ferry Farm Cl **2** YO19 .191 D8
Ferry La
Bishopthorpe YO23 .....231 B4
Bubwith YO8 ....199 C5
Snaith & Cowick DN14 ..204 C1

Ferry La continued
Thorganby YO19 ....193 B5
Ferrybridge By-pass
WF11 ....201 E3
Ferrybridge Inf Sch
WF11 ....201 E3
Ferrybridge Rd
Castleford WF10 ....200 F4
Pontefract WF8 ....201 C1
Fetter La YO1 ....233 B2
Feversham Cres **8**
YO31 ....228 C7
Feversham Dr **18** YO62 .70 B1
Feversham Rd YO62 .....92 F7
Fewster Way YO10 .....233 C1
Fewston Cl **11** YO41 ..101 A3
Fewston Cres HG1 .....219 B4
Fewston Dr **9** YO30 ..224 F1
Field Ave YO8 ....197 B1
Field Cl YO21 ....208 A7
Field Head YO41 ......185 C6
Field House Rd **2** YO62 .70 C2
Field La Aberford LS25 ..194 F8
Burniston YO13 ....75 D8
Gowdall DN14 ....207 F8
Hambleton YO8 ....196 F1
Hensall DN14 ....203 D2
Heslington YO10 ......229 C2
Newby & Scalby YO13 ...75 E5
Rawcliffe DN14 ....205 A1
Wistow YO8 ....197 C7
Field La Sports Ctr
YO8 ....197 B1
Field Rd YO8 ....203 A5
Field View
Norton YO17 ....215 E2
York YO31 ....228 C7
Fieldhead Cl **12** WF8 ..201 C1
Fieldhead Dr
Barwick in Elmet LS15 ..194 C8
16 Glusburn BD20 .....187 E7
Fieldhead Paddock
LS23 ....188 E8
Fielding's Yd DL10 ....209 A7
Fieldside YO12 ....212 D7
Fieldstead Cres YO12 ..212 D8
Fieldway
Harrogate HG1 ....219 F7
Ilkley LS29 ....218 E4
Fieldway Cl HG1 ....219 F7
Fifth Ave **24** Colburn DL9 .41 A5
York YO31 ....228 F4
Filey Ave HG4 ....214 A6
Filey Brigg Nature Reserve*
YO14 ....101 C2
Filey CE VC Inf Sch
YO14 ....101 B3
Filey Cl **12** DL9 ....40 E4
Filey Dams Nature Reserve*
YO14 ....101 B3
Filey Mus* YO14 ......101 B3
Filey Jun Sch YO14 ....101 B3
Filey Rd Folkton YO11 ..100 A2
Hunmanby YO14 ....127 A8
Scarborough YO11 .....213 A2
Filey Sch YO14 ....101 B3
Filey Terr YO30 ....228 C7
Finchley Ct TS5 ....6 E6
Finden Gdns HG3 ......160 F5
Fine Garth Cl LS23 ....188 E6
Finghall Sta DL8 ....61 E5
Finkills Way DL7 ......210 C6
Finkle Cl **14** HG5 .....214 C5
Finkle Hill LS25 ....195 F5
Finkle Keep **14** HG5 ..221 A6
Finkle St Hensall DN14 .203 D2
12 Knaresborough HG5 .221 A6
Malham BD23 ....133 A1
3 Malton YO17 ....215 C4
8 Richmond DL10 .....209 C6
9 Ripon HG4 ....214 C5
Selby YO8 ....232 C5
Sheriff Hutton YO60 ...145 C5
Thirsk YO7 ....211 C3
Finsbury Ave YO23 ....228 C1
Finsbury St YO23 .....228 C1
Fir Gr **11** YO24 ....227 C1
Fir Heath Cl **5** YO24 ..227 C1
Fir Tree Cl Hilton TS15 ...6 C2
Thorpe Willoughby YO8 .197 B2
Fir Tree Dr Filey YO14 ..101 B4
11 Norton DN6 ....206 E2
Fir Tree La YO8 ....197 B2
Fir Tree View YO8 .....197 B2
Fir Trees The YO8 .....197 B2
Firbank Cl **9** YO32 ...167 A2
Firbeck Rd LS23 ....188 E6
Firbeck Wlk TS17 ....6 C8
Firby La HG4 ....214 B5
Firby Rd Bedale DL8 ....63 A2
Richmond DL10 ....209 B8
Firs Ave Harrogate HG2 .222 E6
Ripon HG4 ....214 D4
Firs Cl HG2 ....222 E6
Firs Cres HG2 ....222 E5
Firs Dr HG2 ....222 E6
Firs Gate HG2 ....222 E6
Firs Gr HG2 ....222 E5
Firs Pk HG2 ....222 E6

Firs Rd HG2 ....222 E6
Firs View HG2 ....222 E5
First Ave 26 Colburn DL9 ...41 A5
Harrogate HG2 ....220 C3
Menwith with Darley
HG3 ....160 A4
10 Pickering YO18 ....95 F7
Sherburn in Elmet LS25 ..196 A4
5 Wetherby LS22 ....180 C3
York YO31 ....228 F6
First Comm La YO8 ....197 D4
Firth St BD23 ....217 A2
Firthfields LS25 ....194 D4
Firthland Rd YO18 ....95 F7
Firthmoor Cres DL1 ....3 E4
Firthmoor Prim Sch DL1 ...3 F4
Firtree Ave TS6 ....7 E8
Firtree Cl
4 Earswick YO32 ....225 F7
York YO24 ....227 E3
Firtree Cres LS24 ....189 D5
Firville Ave WF6 ....200 A1
Firwood Whin 5 YO32 ....225 F3
Fishbeck La BD20 ....174 D2
Fishburn Rd 4 YO21 ....208 D5
Fisher Gdns HG5 ....221 A5
Fisher Gn La HG4 ....214 F4
Fisher Row 14 HG4 ....86 C3
Fisher St 5 HG4 ....221 A5
Fishergate
3 Boroughbridge YO51 ..141 B5
Knottingley WF11 ....201 E3
17 Ripon HG4 ....214 C5
York YO10 ....233 C1
Fishergate Prim Sch
YO10 ....233 C1
Fishergreen HG4 ....214 D4
Fishers Ct HG4 ....214 C5
Fishers Garth 10 YO18 ...95 F6
Fitzalan Rd 18 DL8 ......63 A2
Fitzjohn Cl YO17 ....215 C6
Fitzwilliam Dr
Darlington DL1 ....3 D7
Malton YO17 ....215 A4
Five Hills La DL10 ....21 D5
Five La Ends HG4 ....86 D5
Flake La TS13 ....12 A3
Flamingo Land Theme Pk &
Zoo* YO17 ....95 D2
Flashley Carr La DN6 ....207 F1
Flask La DL8 ....87 C3
Flass La WF10 ....200 E3
Flat Cliffs YO14 ....101 C1
Flat La
Bolton-on-Swale DL10 ....41 E6
Hellifield BD23 ....153 F3
Flats Bank DL11 ....19 F6
Flats La
Barwick in Elmet LS15 ...194 B7
Thirkleby High & Low
with Osgodby YO7 ....90 D1
West Witton DL8 ....59 D4
Flatts La
Eston & South Bank TS6 ...7 F7
Welburn YO62 ....94 A7
Wombleton YO62 ....93 F6
Flavian Gr YO10 ....229 B4
Flaxdale Cl 4 HG5 ......221 D6
Flaxley Ct YO9 ....232 B5
Flaxley Rd YO8 ....232 A7
Flaxman Ave YO10 ......229 A4
Flaxman Croft YO23 .....230 B3
Flaxmill Cl DL11 ....18 G7
Flaxton Rd YO32 ....167 B7
Flaxton Terr HG2 ....222 E3
Fleck Way TS17 ....6 B5
Fleet Bank La YO61 .....143 C1
Fleet La
Barmby on the Marsh
DN14 ....205 A2
Mickletown LS26 ....200 A6
Tockwith YO26 ....181 C7
Fleetham La
Cundall with Leckby YO7 ...115 C4
Kirkby Fleetham with Fencote
DL7 ....63 C8
Fleets La BD23 ....156 A6
Fleming Ave 5 YO31 .....228 E5
Fletcher Ct 14 YO12 ....222 E4
Fletcher's Croft YO23 ...230 C3
Flintmill La LS23 ....180 E2
Flints Terr DL10 ....209 C2
Flixton Carr La YO11 .....99 F4
Flock Leys 2 YO13 ......75 D5
Flora Ave DL3 ....3 B5
Florence Ct 12 YO51 ....141 B5
Florence Gr YO30 ....224 D2
Florence Rd HG2 ....219 B1
Florentine's Ct HG4 ....214 C5
Florin Wlk HG1 ....219 B2
Flotmanby La YO14 .....100 D2
Flow Edge DL8 ....57 F7
Flower Ct 10 YO11 ......100 B6
Flower Garth
40 Filey YO14 ....101 B3
Scarborough YO12 ......212 C6
Flowergate 8 YO21 .....208 D7
Flywheel St DL10 ....41 F7
Fog La YO42 ....193 E4
Fold The DL8 ....187 B6
Fold The Filey YO14 ....101 B1
Thornton in Craven
BD23 ....172 A3
Foldshaw La HG3 ....159 C8
Folks Cl 18 YO32 ....166 F5

Follifoot CE Prim Sch
HG3 ....223 F4
Follifoot La HG3 ....223 B2
Follifoot Rd HG3 ....222 F3
Folliott Ward Cl YO17 ...215 B5
Folly La LS23 ....188 E5
Folly View 8 LS23 ......231 B5
Fontenay Rd DL10 ......209 D8
Fonteyn Ct TS8 ....6 F5
Forbidden Cnr The*
DL8 ....60 B1
Forcett Cl
East Layton DL11 ....20 C8
Middlesbrough TS5 ....6 E7
Forcett Gdns DL11 ....1 D3
Forcett La DL10 ....20 D5
Forden Chalk Bank Nature
Reserve* YO25 ....126 C4
Fordlands YO8 ....197 B2
Fordlands Cres YO19 ...231 E5
Fordlands Rd YO19 .....231 E6
Fordon La
Willerby YO12 ....125 E7
Wold Newton YO25 .....126 A6
Fordon Pl TS4 ....7 A8
Fordyce Rd TS8 ....6 E4
Fore La Cowesby YO7 ....66 B4
West Tanfield DL8 ....87 D3
Whorlton DL6 ....25 F1
Foreshore Rd YO11 .....213 A5
Forest Ave HG2 ....220 D3
Forest Cl
3 Harrogate HG2 ....220 D3
27 Haxby YO32 ....166 E5
Forest Cres HG2 ....220 D3
Forest Dr Colburn DL9 ...41 A5
Dishforth YO7 ....115 A4
Middlesbrough TS7 ....7 D7
Forest Gdns HG2 ....220 D3
Forest Gr
Harrogate HG2 ....220 D3
York YO31 ....228 F8
Forest Grange Cl 2
HG2 ....220 D4
Forest La Alne YO61 ....143 B5
Fulford YO19 ....184 A2
Harrogate HG2 ....220 D3
Kirklevington TS15 ......24 D8
Strensall YO32 ....167 A8
Forest La Head HG2 ....220 D3
Forest Moor Dr HG5 ....221 A3
Forest Moor Rd HG5 ....220 F3
Forest Mount 3 HG2 ....220 D4
Forest of Galtres Prim Sch
YO30 ....165 F5
Forest Rd
Appletreewick HG3 .....157 F8
Northallerton DL6 ......210 E5
Pickering YO18 ....96 A6
Forest Rise HG2 ....220 D3
Forest Sch The HG5 ....221 C6
Forest Way
Harrogate HG2 ....220 D3
York YO31 ....228 B1
Forester's Wlk YO24 ...227 B1
Foresters Ct 5 YO12 ....75 F5
Foresters Wlk YO14 ....168 C1
Forestgate YO32 ....225 C7
Forge Cl
Huntington YO32 ....226 A2
Wheldrake YO19 ....193 A7
Forge Gn HG2 ....223 F4
Forge Hill La WF11 .....201 F3
Forge La
Deighton YO19 ....192 A7
Kirkby Fleetham with Fencote
DL7 ....42 C1
Tollerton YO61 ....143 A3
Forge Valley Wood National
Nature Reserve*
YO12 ....75 A1
Forge Way DL1 ....3 D6
Forkers La YO17 ....122 D2
Forrester's Ct 3 DN6 ...206 E2
Forth St YO26 ....227 F6
Fortune Cl HG5 ....220 E7
Fortune Hill HG5 ......220 E8
Foss Ave LS22 ....180 B4
Foss Bank YO31 ....233 C3
Foss Ct YO31 ....225 E1
Foss Field La YO19 ....191 B8
Foss Garth YO41 ......185 F5
Foss Islands Rd YO31 ..233 C3
Foss La YO22 ....32 C2
Foss Wlk YO26 ....227 B5
Fossdale Cl 5 HG5 .....221 D6
Fosse Way LS25 ....194 D3
Fossgate YO1 ....233 C2
Fossland View 4 YO32 ..167 A7
Fossway
Stamford Bridge YO41 ...168 D1
York YO31 ....228 D7
Foster Ave
Normanton South WF6 ...200 A1
Silsden BD20 ....174 B1
Foster Cl 11 LS29 ......176 C1
Foster Gate YO8 ....232 D4
Foster Rd 4 BB18 ......171 D2
Foster Wlk LS25 ....195 F4
Fosterton CE VC Prim Sch
YO60 ....146 A3
Foston Gr 4 YO31 .....225 E1
Foston La YO60 ....146 B2
Fother Ingay Dr DL1 .....3 F8
Fothergill Way 3 YO51 ..141 B4
Fothill La YO13 ....98 E6
Foulbridge La YO13 .....97 F3

Foulds Rd BB8 ....186 A1
Foulgate Nook La
HG4 ....112 B6
Foundry La 5 WF11 ....202 A2
Fountain St TS14 ....8 F6
Fountains Abbey & Studley
Royal W Gdn* HG4 ....139 B7
Fountains Ave
Boston Spa LS23 ....188 E8
Harrogate HG1 ....219 F6
Ingleby LS17 ....6 B5
Fountains CE Prim Sch
HG3 ....110 B4
Fountains Gate HG4 ...112 F1
Fountains La HG4 ......139 B7
Fountains Mill* HG4 ...139 B7
Fountains Pl DL6 ....210 E6
Fountains Rd DL6 .....210 E6
Fountains View DL3 .....3 A6
Fountains Way
Knaresborough HG5 ....221 C4
Morton-on-Swale DL7 ...64 A7
Fountayne Rd 18 YO14 ..126 F8
Fountayne St YO31 ....228 C7
Four La Ends
Burythorpe YO17 ......147 D4
Lawkland BD24 ....130 F3
Four Lanes Ends BB7 ..152 C1
Four Riggs DL3 ....3 C5
Fouracre Dr 11 YO22 ...32 A6
Fourth Ave
20 Colburn DL9 ....41 A5
York YO31 ....228 E5
Fox Cl 8 DL2 ....22 D8
Fox Covert YO31 ......225 F2
Fox Covert Cl 15 DL8 ...63 B3
Fox Covert Rd WF8 ....206 C1
Fox Ct HG1 ....219 E4
Fox Garth
5 Brafferton YO61 .....115 F1
Poppleton YO26 ....224 A3
Fox Glade YO41 ....168 C2
Fox Heads La LS22 ....179 D4
Fox Hill La YO8 ....232 A3
Fox La
Chapel Haddlesey YO8 ..203 C5
Hambleton LS25 ....196 B1
Thornton-le-Dale YO18 ...96 C3
Thorpe Willoughby YO8 ..197 B1
Fox Oak Furniture Craft Ctr*
YO7 ....116 F7
Fox Terr WF8 ....201 C1
Foxberry Ave TS5 ....6 D6
Foxbridge Way WF6 ...200 C2
Foxcliff WF11 ....201 E5
Foxcroft 3 YO32 ....225 C7
Foxdale Ave YO8 ......197 B1
Foxglove Cl
2 Killinghall HG3 ......161 B3
Northallerton DL7 .....210 C1
Foxglove Ct 10 DL9 ....41 A5
Foxhill La YO8 ....232 A3
Foxholme La HG4 ....86 B3
Foxthorn Paddock
YO10 ....229 D3
Foxton Cl YO30 ....224 C8
Foxton La DL6 ....44 E2
Foxwood La 8 YO24 ...227 B1
Foxwood Sch BD24 ....105 C4
Frances Dr YO8 ....232 A6
Frances St YO10 ......228 D1
Francis Cl 7 WF8 ......201 B2
Francis Dr 27 DL9 ......41 A5
Frank La YO26 ....164 F4
Frank St 8 BB18 ......171 E1
Frank's La YO26 ......164 A5
Franklin Mews YO8 ....232 B3
Franklin Mount HG1 ...219 D4
Franklin Rd HG1 ......219 D3
Franklin Sq HG1 ......219 D3
Franklin St 7 YO12 ....212 F6
Franks Terr 2 YO22 ...208 E6
Fraser Rd 8 TS18 ....5 E8
Frazer Ct YO30 ....227 E8
Frederic St YO30 ......233 A3
Freebrough Rd TS12 ...10 A4
Freehold La YO7 ....115 A4
Freely Fields 7 LS23 ...188 E5
Freely La LS23 ....188 F5
Freeman's Way HG3 ...223 D8
Freemans Way
Leeming DL7 ....63 C4
Wetherby LS22 ....180 D3
Fremantle Pl HG4 .....214 C5
Freeport Outlet Village*
WF10 ....200 F3
Freers Yd YO17 ....215 D3
Freeston Ct 16 WF6 ...200 A2
Freeston Dr WF6 ......200 A2
Freeway Dr WF10 .....200 B3
French Rd DL9 ....41 A5
French St HG1 ....219 F4
Frenchgate DL10 ......209 C2
Friarage Ave DL6 .....210 D5
Friarage Com Prim Sch
YO11 ....213 B6
Friarage Gdns DL6 ....210 D5
Friarage Hospl DL6 ....210 D5
Friarage Mount DL6 ...210 D5
Friarage St DL6 ....210 D5
Friarage Terr DL6 .....210 D5

Friar's Gdns 10 YO11 ..213 A6
Friar's Way 11 YO11 ...213 A6
Friar's Wlk YO31 ......228 E8
Friargate
Scarborough YO11 .....213 A6
York YO1 ....233 B2
Friargate Theatre
YO1 ....233 B2
Friars Cl YO19 ....184 D7
Friars Hill YO62 ....95 A8
Friars Mdw YO10 .....231 D7
Friars Pardon DL2 ......3 E1
Friary Com Hospl
DL6 ....210 D5
Friendship Ct 2 YO8 ..232 C6
Frith Mews 4 YO8 .....232 C6
Frobisher Dr 5 YO21 ..208 C5
Frogmire Cl 4 HG5 ....221 B7
Frogmire Dr HG5 .....221 B7
Frogmire Rd HG5 .....221 B7
Front Nook 2 DL8 ......58 F1
Front St
Appleton Wiske DL6 ....24 B3
6 Bramham LS23 ......188 E5
Burton Fleming YO25 ..126 E3
Burton Leonard HG3 ...140 A2
Castleford WF10 ......200 F3
Grosmont YO22 ....31 C4
Langtoft YO25 ....151 C5
Lastingham YO62 ......70 E5
Naburn YO19 ....191 D8
Thirsk YO7 ....211 C1
Topcliffe YO7 ....115 C7
Wold Newton YO25 ....126 A4
York YO24 ....227 D4
Front The DL2 ....4 D3
Fryer Cres DL1 ....3 F7
Fryston Comm La
LS25 ....202 A8
Fryston Rd WF11 ......201 C3
Fryston Rd WF10 ......201 B5
Fryton La YO62 ....120 A7
Fryup Cres TS14 ....8 E5
Fulbeck Rd TS3 ....7 D8
Fulford Cross YO10 ....228 D1
Fulford Mews YO10 ...231 D7
Fulford Pk YO10 ......231 D7
Fulford Rd
Scarborough YO11 .....212 F3
York YO10 ....231 D8
Fulford Sch YO10 .....231 E7
Fulfordgate YO10 .....231 E7
Fulham La DN14 ......206 E7
Fuller-Good Rd 17 DL10 ...41 E4
Fullicar La DL6 ....43 F3
Fulmar Head TS14 ......8 D6
Fulthorpe Ave DL3 .....3 A5
Fulthorpe Rd DL3 ......3 A5
Fulwith Ave HG2 ......222 F5
Fulwith Cl HG2 ....222 F5
Fulwith Gate HG2 ....222 F5
Fulwith Gr HG2 ....222 F5
Fulwith Mill La HG2 ..222 F5
Fulwith Rd HG2 ......222 F5
Fummerber La LS24 ...130 C5
Furlong Rd 23 YO41 ..168 D2
Furlongs Ave YO17 ...215 F3
Furnace La HG4 ....87 A1
Furness Dr
Bentham LA2 ....129 A8
Darlington DL3 ....224 E1
Furnessford Rd LA2 ...128 D6
Furnwood 2 YO32 ....225 D7
Furrows The 16 YO11 ..100 B7
Fushetts La LA2 ......129 A8
Futurist Theatre*
YO11 ....213 A6
Fyling Rd YO12 ....208 A6
Fylingdales Ave 6
YO30 ....224 E1
Fylingdales CE VC Prim Sch
YO22 ....33 C4

G

Gable Ct YO7 ....115 A4
Gable Pk YO23 ....182 C6
Gables Cl 8 DN14 ....202 D4
Gables The
18 Hurworth-on-Tees DL2 ...3 E1
Knaresborough HG5 ...221 A8
Middlesbrough TS7 .....7 B6
Scriven HG5 ....162 C5
Gainford CE Prim Sch
DL2 ....1 C7
Gainford Wath Rd
YO13 ....53 F5
Gainsborough Cl
YO32 ....167 B8
Gainsborough Ct
BD23 ....217 B4
Gaits DL8 ....56 C4
Gale Bank DL8 ....60 B3
Gale Farm Ct 3 YO24 ..227 E3
Gale Garth YO61 .....142 F4
Gale Gate YO25 ......142 A1
Gale La Beadlam YO62 ...93 D6
Stainburn LS21 ....177 E3
Thorganby YO19 ......192 F4
York YO24 ....227 C2
Gale Rd YO61 ....142 F4
Gale The YO19 ....191 D4
Gallabar La YO11 .....141 E1
Galley Hill Prim Sch
TS14 ....8 D6
Galligap La YO10 .....229 C4

Gallogate La LS17 ....178 C1
Gallops The
Norton YO17 ....215 E2
York YO26 ....227 B5
Gallowfields Rd DL10 ..209 B7
Gallowfields Trad Est
DL10 ....209 B8
Gallowgate DL10 .....209 C7
Gallowheads La YO62 ..95 A6
Gallows Hill
Castleford WF10 ......201 B4
Ripon HG4 ....214 C2
Gallows Hill Dr HG4 ..214 C2
Gallows Hill La YO13 ..98 D5
Gallows Hill Pk HG4 ..214 D2
Galmanhoe La YO30 ...233 A3
Galphay La HG4 ......113 A3
Galtres Ave YO31 .....229 B7
Galtres Dr 7 YO61 ....143 D8
Galtres Gr YO30 ......227 F7
Galtres Rd
Northallerton DL6 ....210 E6
York YO31 ....229 B7
Gant Wlk 7 YO8 ......232 D5
Ganton Cl 1 YO21 ....208 C5
Ganton Hill YO12 .....125 B7
Ganton Pl YO24 ....230 C8
Ganton Rd YO25 .....125 C4
Gaol The YO61 ....144 E7
Gap Cres YO14 ....127 D7
Gap Rd YO14 ....127 D8
Garbett Way 1 YO23 ..231 B3
Garburn Gr YO30 ....224 E1
Garbutt Gr YO26 .....227 D5
Garbutt La 1 DL6 .....25 D1
Garbutt Wood Nature
Reserve* YO7 ....91 A6
Garbutts La TS15 .....25 B5
Garden Cl
3 Glusburn BD20 .....187 D7
Sherburn in Elmet LS25 ...195 E4
Garden Flats La YO19 ..184 B7
Garden House Cl LS26 ..200 B6
Garden La
11 Knottingley WF11 ..202 A3
Sherburn in Elmet LS25 ...195 F4
Garden Pl YO1 ....233 C2
Garden St
Castleford WF10 ......200 E3
12 Normanton South WF6 ..200 A1
York YO31 ....233 B4
Garden Village LS25 ...195 F6
Garden Way 8 YO31 ..233 B4
Gardeners Cl 3 YO23 ..230 B3
Gardeners Row YO25 ..150 B3
Gardens Rd BD23 .....155 D1
Gardens The 18 YO14 ..101 B4
Garfield Rd YO12 .....212 E6
Garfield Terr YO26 ...227 F5
Garforth Barkyhill Infants
Sch LS25 ....194 C3
Garforth Com Coll
LS25 ....194 C3
Garforth Gn La Prim Sch
LS25 ....194 D3
Garforth Leisure Ctr
LS25 ....194 C3
Garforth Sta LS25 ....194 C4
Gargrave CE VC Prim Sch
BD23 ....155 C1
Gargrave House Gdn
BD23 ....172 D6
Gargrave Rd
Broughton BD23 ......172 D6
Skipton BD23 ....216 D4
Gargrave Sta BD23 ...172 C8
Garibaldi St 1 YO11 ..213 B6
Garland St 7 YO26 ...227 E4
Garlands Hill 8 YO11 ..212 F3
Garlands The
Scarborough YO11 ....212 F3
York YO30 ....227 F8
Garman Carr La YO8 ..197 D6
Garnet Brow La LA2 ..130 D2
Garnet La 8 LS24 .....189 E6
Garnet Rd TS17 ....6 B8
Garnet Terr YO26 ....227 E5
Garrick Cl YO8 ....232 B1
Garrow Hill YO10 .....229 A3
Garrow Hill Ave YO10 ..229 A3
Garroway Way YO10 ..184 A4
Garrowby Hill YO41 ...169 F3
Garrowby Rd YO42 ...169 F2
Garrowby St YO41 ....169 E3
Garrowby View 5 YO41 ..168 D2
Garrs End La BD23 ....134 E3
Garrs La 10 BD23 .....134 E3
Gars The LS24 ....128 A6
Garsbeck Way TS7 .....7 D8
Garsdale Fold 8 LS22 ..180 A1
Garsdale Rd HG5 .....221 D6
Garsdale Sta LA10 ....55 A6
Garth Ave
Collingham LS22 .....188 A3
4 North Duffield YO8 ..199 A7
Garth Cl 1 Catterick DL10 ..41 D5
6 Wistow YO8 ....197 D6
Garth Ct YO32 ....225 C8
Garth Dr YO8 ....196 E1
Garth End
Collingham LS22 .....188 A3
Kirk Deighton LS22 ...180 B5
York YO32 ....225 F4
Garth End Rd YO13 ....99 A7

Garth Fold BD20 ....173 C1
Garth Glebe **8** Y08 ....198 B5
Garth Grange **3** Y030 ..164 F7
Garth La
  Hambleton Y08 ....196 E1
  Snainton YO13 ....98 A5
Garth Mdws **15** DL10 ....41 D5
Garth Mill DN14 ....202 D4
Garth Morrell Y08 ......232 C2
Garth Rd
  4 Hambleton Y08 ......196 E1
  York Y031 ....225 F4
Garth Terr Y030 ....228 B7
Garth The
  8 Collingham LS22 ..188 A8
  Sinnington Y062 ....95 A8
  4 Stokesley TS9 ......26 C7
  Tunstall DL10 ....41 B2
  Whitby Y021 ....208 B7
Garth View Y08 ....196 E1
Garth Way Arc DL7 ....210 D5
Garth's End Y010 ....231 E8
Garthends La **8** Y08 ...198 F1
Garthorne Ave DL3 ....3 A5
Garths End **20** Y032 ...166 F5
Garths La DL8 ....58 E3
Garthway **4** Y023 .....225 D3
Gas House La LA2 ....129 A8
Gas St BD23 ....213 F3
Gas Works La LS23 ......188 F8
Gascoigne Ave LS15 .....194 B7
Gascoigne Cres HG1 .....219 F4
Gascoigne Ct LS15 ......194 B7
Gascoigne Cres LS15 ....194 B7
Gascoigne View LS15 ....194 B7
Gascoigne Wlk Y023 ......233 B1
Gascoigne Wood Mine
  LS25 ....196 C2
Gaskell Cl DL7 ....210 C6
Gate Bridge Rd HG4 .....112 D2
Gate La Borrowby Y07 .....65 E4
  Low Coniscliffe & Merrybent
  DL2 ....2 E4
Gate Way Y021 ....29 B4
Gatecliff Brow BD23 ....155 F4
Gateforth Ct Y08 ....196 F1
Gateforth La Y08 ....196 F1
Gateforth New Rd
  Y08 ....203 A8
Gatehead La Y042 ....193 D7
Gatehowe Rd Y017 ....170 A7
Gatela Rd Y013 ....53 D2
Gateland Cl Y032 ....225 C7
Gateland Field La
  DN14 ....205 B6
Gatenby Garth Y061 .....143 B8
Gatesgarth Cl Y012 .....212 B8
Gatherley Rd DL10 ....41 C7
Gauber Rd LA6 ....78 F1
Gaudy La DL8 ....56 C3
Gauk St WF11 ....201 D6
Gaul Rd DL9 ....209 E1
Gaw La BD23 ....174 C8
Gawterske La Y062 ....94 B8
Gay La LS24 ....196 C7
Gay Mdws Y032 ....167 D2
Gaylands La BB18 ....172 B1
Gayle La DL8 ....56 C4
Gayton Sands TS5 ....6 D6
Gazelle Way Y07 ....115 B1
Geecroft La LS22 ....179 D3
Geldof Rd Y032 ....225 F1
Gemini Studios Art Gall *
  BD23 ....134 E3
General La Y042 ....193 E6
Geneva Cres DL1 ....3 D4
Geneva La DL1 ....3 D4
Geneva Rd DL1 ....3 E5
Gennell La Y060 ....145 E1
Gentian Glade HG3 ......219 A4
George Cartwright Cl
  Y017 ....215 E4
George Cayley Dr
  Y030 ....225 A3
George Ct Y031 ....233 C3
George Hudson St
  Y01 ....233 B2
George St
  15 Addingham LS29 ...174 F4
  Carleton BD23 ....173 B4
  19 Earby BB18 ....172 A1
  3 Scarborough Y012 ..213 A6
  4 Selby Y08 ....232 D6
  17 Skipton BD23 .....216 F4
  Snaith DN14 ....204 C1
  18 Whitby Y021 ......208 D6
  7 Wistow Y08 ....197 D6
  York Y01 ....233 C1
George Terr **1** Y08 ...198 B4
Georgian Theatre Royal &
  Mus * DL10 ....209 C6
Gerard Ave Y012 ....229 A5
Germain Rd Y08 ....232 E4
Germany La Y019 ....231 E6
Gerrick La TS12 ....10 C3
Gerrie St DL12 ....9 D7
Ghyll Brow Y021 ....30 D4
Ghyll Cl DL10 ....209 D8
Ghyll Way BD23 ....175 C2
Ghyll Wood BD23 ....175 C2
Ghyll Mdws BB18 ....171 E2
Ghyll Mews Y021 ....218 A3
Ghyll Royd Prep Sch
  LS29 ....176 B2
Ghyll The DL10 ....209 D8
Ghyll Way BD23 ....175 C2
Ghyll Wood BD23 ....175 C2
Gibb St BD22 ....187 B6
Gibbet Hill Y061 ....117 C5
Gibside La BD20 ....173 C1

Gibson Cl **2** Y08 .....196 F1
Gibson La LS25 ....194 D1
Giggleswick Prim Sch
  BD24 ....131 D3
Giggleswick Sch
  BD24 ....131 C2
Giggleswick Sta BD24 ..131 C1
Gilcar St WF6 ....200 B2
Gilcar Way WF6 ....200 B2
Gildercliffe Y012 ......212 C7
Giles Ave Y031 ....229 A5
Gill Bank Rd LS29 ......218 A6
Gill Cl **6** LS29 ......174 E4
Gill Croft Y061 ....117 C1
Gill La Cowling BD22 ...187 A6
  Kearby with Netherby
  LS22 ....179 C1
  Nesfield with Langbar
  LS29 ....175 B4
  Rosedale West Side YO18 .49 E2
Gillamoor Ave Y031 .....229 B5
Gillamoor Bank Y062 ....70 A5
Gillamoor CE VC Prim Sch
  Y062 ....70 A4
Gillamoor Rd Y062 ......70 A2
Gillann St WF11 ....202 A2
Gillgate Rd HG4 ....112 B4
Gilling Castle * Y062 .118 E7
Gilling Cres DL1 ....3 D4
Gilling Rd Aske DL10 ...20 E1
  Richmond DL10 ....209 D7
Gilling Way Y017 ....215 C5
Gillings Ct Y017 ....211 B3
Gillingwood Cl DL10 ....209 C8
Gillingwood Rd Y030 ....224 F1
Gills Fold BD23 ....134 E2
Gills The LS21 ....177 A1
Gillylees Y012 ....212 C5
Gilmonby Rd TS3 ....7 B8
Gilsforth Hill Y026 ....164 A3
Gilsforth La Y026 ......164 A3
Gilstead Way LS29 ......218 B5
Gisthwaite La Y062 .....164 A3
Gilwern Ct **28** TS17 ....5 F4
Gindhill La LS21 ....178 A4
Ginnel Mews The
  BD23 ....217 A4
Ginnel The **1** HG1 ...219 D2
Gipsey Cnr Y019 ....184 E3
Girls High Sch BD23 ...216 E4
Girton Wlk DL1 ....3 D7
Girvan Cl Y024 ....230 B7
Gisburn Rd
  Barnoldswick BB18 .....171 D2
  Hellifield BD23 ....155 A1
Gisburn Rd Com Prim Sch
  BB18 ....171 D1
Gisburn St
  Barnoldswick BB18 .....171 D2
  Skipton BD23 ....216 D3
Givendale Ct **3** Y010 .229 C4
Givendale Rd Y012 .....212 D8
Glade Rd Y019 ....192 B2
Glade The
  Escrick Y019 ....192 A6
  Scarborough Y012 .....212 C5
  York Y031 ....229 B7
Gladstone La Y012 .....212 E5
Gladstone Rd Y012 .....212 E5
Gladstone Rd Inf Sch
  Y012 ....212 E5
Gladstone Rd Jun Sch
  Y012 ....212 E5
Gladstone St
  Darlington DL3 ....3 C5
  Harrogate HG2 ....222 E7
  Normanton South WF6 ..200 B2
  Scarborough Y012 .....212 E6
  14 Skipton BD23 .....216 F4
  York Y031 ....228 E6
Gladstone Terr **16** HG4 .214 C4
Glaisby Ct Y031 ....229 A6
Glaisdale Y024 ....230 D7
Glaisdale Ave TS5 ....6 F8
Glaisdale Hall La Y021 .30 C4
Glaisdale Prim Sch
  Y021 ....30 D4
Glaisdale Rd TS15 ....5 F3
Glaisdale Sta Y021 .....30 E4
Glasgow Dr **3** DL9 ...209 C1
Glasshouses Com Prim Sch
  HG3 ....137 D3
Glaves Cl Y013 ....99 B7
Glebe Ave
  Full Sutton Y041 .....169 A2
  Harrogate HG2 ....219 C2
  York Y026 ....227 D5
Glebe Cl **18** Barton DL10 .21 C7
  18 Bedale DL8 ....63 A2
  Bolton Percy Y023 ....190 D4
  Kirby Hill Y051 ......141 B7
  Manfield DL2 ....1 D3
  3 Strensall Y032 ....167 B7
Glebe Ct DL10 ....21 A7
Glebe Field Dr **8** LS22 .180 B3
Glebe Gdns **3** DL8 ....11 A8
Glebe La DL2 ....2 C4
Glebe Mdw HG4 ....214 F6
Glebe Rd Campsall DN6 .206 E1
  Darlington DL3 ....3 D8
  Harrogate HG2 ....219 C2
  Scruton DL7 ....26 C7
Glebe Sq DL2 ....63 C5
Glebe St WF10 ....200 E4
Glebe Way **28** Y032 ...166 E5
Gledstone Rd BD23 .....171 E5

Gledstone View **8**
  BB18 ....171 D2
Glen Ave Y031 ....228 E5
Glen Ct
  Newby & Scalby Y013 ...75 C5
  York Y010 ....231 E6
Glen Esk Rd Y022 ......208 C3
Glen Rd Y021 ....228 E5
Glencoe Ct LS25 ....200 C8
Glencoe Croft LS25 ....200 C8
Glencoe Gdns LS25 .....200 C8
Glencoe St **1** Y030 ...228 B7
Glencoe Terr LS25 .....200 C8
Glendale
  Guisborough TS14 ....8 D5
  1 Hutton Rudby TS15 ..25 C5
Glendale Rd TS5 ....6 F8
Glendowne Terr HG1 ....219 B5
Gleneagles Ct
  28 Castleford WF6 ...200 B1
  Spofforth HG3 ....179 E5
Gleneagles Dr **22** WF6 .200 B1
Gleneagles Rd
  Darlington DL1 ....3 F8
  Middlesbrough TS4 ......7 A8
  North Featherstone
  WF7 ....200 E1
Glenfield Ave Y032 ....180 C2
Glenmore Dr Y017 ......215 E2
Glenn Cres TS7 ....7 B5
Glenridding Y024 ......230 D7
Glenside Y012 ....212 E7
Globe St
  16 Harrogate HG2 ....220 C3
  Scarborough Y011 .....213 B6
Gloucester Ave Y031 ...229 B5
Glusburn Com Prim Sch **67**
  BD20 ....187 E7
Glyder Ct **6** LS17 .....5 F4
Glynndale Dr Y012 .....212 A8
Glynved Ct **2** BD23 ...216 E3
Goat La BD24 ....131 F7
Goathland Com Prim Sch
  Y022 ....51 C8
Goathland Gr TS14 ......8 E5
Goathland Sta Y022 ....51 D8
Goats Rd DL11 ....20 B7
Godfrey Rd **8** DL10 ...41 E4
Godley Cl DL9 ....209 C2
Godwinsway **18** Y041 .168 D2
Goker La Y051 ....141 E1
Gold Thread La **3** Y011 159 A2
Golden Acres DL7 ....22 E2
Golden Butts Rd LS29 ..218 C4
Golden Gr Y022 ....208 E2
Golden Lion Bank **25**
  Y021 ....208 D7
Golden Lion Yd **7** Y07 .211 C3
Goldhill La Y07 ....90 D6
Goldsborough CE Prim Sch
  HG5 ....162 F3
Goldsborough Ct HG5 ..163 A3
Goldsborough La Y021 ..12 C4
Golf Links Ave LS25 ...189 D5
Golf Links Cres **4** LS25 189 D5
Golf Links Ct LS25 ....189 E5
Good Hope Cl WF6 ......200 B2
Goodall Cl **31** BB18 ..172 A1
Goodenber Rd LA2 ......129 A8
Goodramgate Y01 ....233 B2
Goodrick Cl Y022 ......222 B5
Goods Yd The Y08 ......232 D5
Goodwood Ave LS25 ....194 C1
Goodwood Cl
  Sadberge DL2 ....4 B8
  Scalby Y012 ....212 B6
Goodwood Gr Y024 ......227 F1
Goodwood Rd **3** DL9 ...40 E3
Goody Cross LS25 ......194 B1
Goody Cross La LS25 ...194 A1
Goose Gn Cl **2** TS16 ....5 D8
Goose Gn La BB3 ....186 A1
Goose La Y061 ....144 C1
Goose Mire La Y012 .....99 C6
Goose Tk La Y060 ......145 C3
Goosecroft Gdns DL6 ..210 D5
Goosecroft La
  East Harlsey DL6 ......44 D6
  Northallerton DL6 ....210 D5
Gooselands BD24 ....153 C6
Gooselands Hill BD23 .107 D2
Goosepastures TS16 .....5 E3
Gordale Cl **3**
  Barnoldswick BB18 .....171 D1
  Skirethorns BD23 .....134 B3
Gordale La BD23 ....133 A2
Gordale Mount HG5 .....221 C6
Gordon Ave Y031 ....219 E6
Gordon Cres DL10 ......209 D8
Gordon St
  3 Glusburn BD20 .....187 E7
  Ilkley LS29 ....218 C4
  Scarborough Y012 .....212 E5
  York Y031 ....228 D7
Gordon Terr Y021 ......173 C1
Gore La DN14 ....207 B5
Gore Sands TS5 ....6 F5
German Cl **3** TS17 .....5 F4
Gormire Ave **2** Y07 ...225 E2
Gormire Ct Y07 ....211 D3
Gorse Cl Y08 ....232 C2
Gorse Hill **1** Y019 ...195 D3
Gorse La TS14 ....8 D5
Gorse Paddock Y032 ....225 F2
Goschen St **8** BD23 ...217 A3
Gosling Gate Rd DL10 ...40 F2
Gosside Gr **31** WF6 ...200 B1
Gough Rd DL9 ....40 D4

Gouldings Cl Y011 .....100 A7
Goulton La TS9 ....25 E3
Gouthwaith Cl Y030 ....224 F7
Government House Rd
  Y030 ....228 A6
Gowans The Y061 ....144 C3
Gowdall Broach DN14 ..207 E8
Gowdall La
  Pollington DN14 ....207 F7
  Snaith & Cowick DN14 .204 B1
Gowdall Rd DN14 ....203 E2
Gower Rd Aske DL10 .....20 D1
  Richmond DL10 ....209 C8
  York Y024 ....230 E8
Gowthorpe Y08 ....232 C5
Gr Prom The LS29 ......218 A4
Gracious St Huby Y061 .144 A4
  7 Knaresborough HG5 .221 B5
Grafton Cl TS14 ....8 F6
Grafton La Y051 ....141 C4
Grafton St WF10 ....200 F3
Graham Cl Y011 ....213 B7
Graham Cres Y012 .....212 C5
Graham Dr WF10 ....201 A4
Graham Rd HG4 ....113 D3
Graham Sch Y012 ....212 B5
Grainary Wildlife Farm The *
  Y013 ....53 E3
Grainbeck La HG3 ......219 A4
Grainger Cl **8** TS16 ....5 D5
Grainger Row HG4 ......214 D5
Grainger St DL1 ....3 D4
Grains La BD23 ....154 E8
Grammar Sch La DL6 ...210 D3
Grampian Cl **4** Y032 .225 F5
Granary Ct Y01 ....233 B3
Granby Pk HG1 ....219 F3
Granby Rd HG1 ....219 F3
Grange Ave Askew DL7 ..63 C4
  Filey Y014 ....101 B3
  Garforth LS25 ....194 C3
  Harrogate HG1 ....219 D5
  3 Hurworth-on-Tees DL2 ..3 E1
  Ilkley LS29 ....218 D4
  Scarborough Y012 .....212 E4
  Spofforth HG3 ....179 E6
  Tadcaster LS24 ....189 F6
  3 Willerby Y012 .....99 D2
Grange CI **18** Bedale DL8 .63 A2
  Bishop Thornton HG3 ..138 F1
  Dishforth Y07 ....114 F4
  Full Sutton Y041 .....169 A2
  Ilkley LS29 ....218 D4
  Lebberston Y011 ......100 D5
  Northallerton DL7 ....210 C3
  Skelton Y030 ....224 B5
Grange Cl E DL7 ....63 E7
Grange Cres
  Middlesbrough TS7 .....7 B5
  10 Tadcaster LS24 ...189 E6
Grange Ct Y012 ....99 D2
Grange Dr TS9 ....26 C7
Grange Farm Cl Y08 ...198 B5
Grange Garth Y010 .....228 D2
Grange La **1** Dacre HG3 137 F1
  Rufforth Y023 ....227 A2
  Scackleton Y062 ....119 C3
  Stonebeck Down HG3 ...187 F2
Grange Pk Cl WF10 ....200 D7
Grange Pk Rd HG4 .....214 B2
Grange Rd **19** Bedale DL8 .63 A2
  Brompton-on-Swale DL10 .41 B6
  Burley in Warfedale
  LS29 ....176 C1
  8 Campsall DN6 .....206 E1
  Castleford WF10 ......201 B5
  Colburn DL9 ....40 F5
  3 Dacre HG3 ....137 F1
  Darlington DL1 ....3 C4
  Farnhill BD20 ....187 A1
  Tadcaster LS24 ....189 E6
  Thornaby TS17 ....6 B8
Grange St Y010 ....228 D2
Grange Terr HG4 ....114 B8
Grange The
  Kirby Hill Y051 ......141 A7
  York Y031 ....211 B2
Grange View
  Castleford WF6 ....176 F1
  Towton LS24 ....189 E2
Grangefield Ave **32**
  LS29 ....176 C1
Granger Ave Y026 .....227 C3
Grant Cl Dl6 ....45 B4
Grantham Dr Y026 .....227 E4
Grantley Cl HG3 ....219 A4
Grantley Dr HG3 ......219 A4
Grantley Hall Coll
  HG4 ....138 E8
Grantley Pl HG3 ......219 A4
Grants Ave Y010 ......231 E8
Granville Rd
  21 Filey Y014 .....101 B3
  4 Harrogate HG1 ....219 D3
  Scarborough Y011 .....213 A3
  4 Stokesley TS9 ....26 C7
Granville Sq **3** Y011 .213 A3
Granville St
  20 Normanton South WF6 .200 A1
  Skipton BD23 ....216 E4
Granville Terr **4** Y021 .208 E2
Grape La Whitby Y022 ..208 E7
  York Y01 ....233 B3

Grasmere Ave LS22 .....180 A3
Grasmere Cres HG2 .....222 C7
Grasmere Dr Y010 .....229 B4
Grasmere Gr **5** Y030 .224 F1
Grass Croft TS21 ....5 A7
Grass Wood La BD23 ...134 C4
Grass Wood Nature
  Reserve * BD23 ....134 C4
Grassfield Cl **8** HG3 .137 B4
Grassgill La BD23 ......59 E3
Grassholme Y024 ......230 C7
Grassholme Way TS16 ....5 D6
Grassington Ave DL7 ..210 C2
Grassington CE Prim Sch
  BD23 ....134 C4
Grassington Rd
  Middlesbrough TS4 .....7 A8
  Skipton BD23 ....216 F5
Gravel Hole La
  Sowerby Y07 ....89 E3
  Thirsk Y07 ....211 C1
Gravelhill La DN14 ....206 F7
Gravelly Hill La LS17 .178 A2
Gray St Ripon HG4 ....214 C5
Gray St **18** Whitby Y021 .208 D6
  York Y030 ....233 A1
Grays Rd Y062 ....69 F6
Grayshon Dr Y026 .....227 B5
Grayston Plain La
  HG3 ....160 F4
Graystonber La LA2 ....130 E7
Great & Little Preston Jun
  Sch LS26 ....200 C8
Great Auk TS14 ....8 D6
Great Ave DL10 ....209 A7
Great Ayton Sta TS9 ....8 B1
Great Cl Y08 ....197 B8
Great Cl Bank DL8 .....153 A6
Great Croft Cl **8** BB18 171 D2
Great Moor Rd Y013 ....74 D2
Great N Rd
  Ledsham LS25 ....195 C1
  Micklefield LS25 .....194 F5
Great W Way Y026 ......227 B8
Great Ouseburn Com Prim
  Sch 164 B8
Great Pasture LS29 ....176 C1
Great Sike Rd Y017 ...215 D6
Great Smeaton Com Prim
  Sch DL6 ....23 C3
Greatwood Ave BD23 ...217 A3
Greatwood Cl BD23 ....217 B3
Greatwood Com Prim Sch
  BD23 ....217 A2
Greavefield La WF8 ....201 C1
Greaves Smithy LS29 ..175 B4
Grebe Ave DL9 ....40 E2
Grebe Way DL9 ....95 F7
Green Ave LS25 ....194 C2
Green Balk
  Great & Little Broughton
  TS9 ....26 F5
  Millington Y042 ......170 D1
Green Bank BB18 ......171 E2
Green Bank La HG4 ....139 A6
Green Cl
  Bradleys Both BD20 ...173 D3
  2 Linton-on-Ouse Y030 .164 F8
  Middlesbrough TS7 .....7 D5
  Steeton with Eastburn
  BD20 ....187 F7
  York Y030 ....228 A8
Green Cres The Y062 ...120 B5
Green Croft Gdns **24**
  Y011 ....100 B6
Green Dike Y030 ......225 C8
Green Dikes La Y025 ..151 F1
Green Dyke La Y062 ...120 C5
Green Dykes Y017 .....215 A3
Green Dykes La Y010 ..228 F3
Green End Ave **35** BB18 172 A1
Green End Rd **34** BB18 .172 A1
Green Gate
  Exelby, Leeming & Newton
  DL8 ....63 D2
  Hawsker-cum-Stainsacre
  Y022 ....33 A6
  Kirkby Malham BD23 ..154 F8
  West Witton DL8 ......59 C3
Green Gate La
  Crakehall DL8 ....62 E5
  Kildale Y021 ....27 F8
  Long Preston BD23 ....153 F5
Green Haggs La HG3 ...160 D8
Green Hammerton CE Prim
  Sch Y026 ....164 B3
Green Head La BD22 ...161 E2
Green Hill Y062 ......118 E6
Green Hill La BD22 ...187 A5
Green Hills Y032 .....168 B7
Green Hills La DL7 ....64 B6
Green Howard's Dr **8**
  Y012 ....75 F5
Green Howards Mus *
  DL10 ....209 C6
Green Howards Rd
  Pickering Y018 ....96 A6
  Richmond DL10 ....209 B8
Green Island Y021 .....99 D7
Green La Acomb Y024 ..227 C2
  Addingham LS29 ....174 F4
  Appleton Roebuck Y023 .191 B6
  Barmby on the Marsh
  DN14 ....205 A6
  Barton-le-Street Y017 .120 E8

Green La continued
Bedale DL8 ...... 62 F3
Bishopthorpe YO24 ...... 231 A6
Boston Spa LS23 ...... 188 F7
Bradleys Both BD20 ...... 174 A3
Burton Leonard HG3 ...... 140 B2
Burton-on-Yore HG4 ...... 86 D6
Castleford WF10 ...... 200 E3
Cawton YO62 ...... 119 B6
Collingham LS22 ...... 188 A8
Coneythorpe & Clareton HG5 ...... 163 B5
Constable Burton DL8 ...... 61 A6
Cottingwith YO42 ...... 193 C5
Cundall with Leckby YO61 ...... 115 D4
Darlington DL1 ...... 3 D8
Dishforth YO7 ...... 115 A2
East Rounton TS15 ...... 24 F4
Fadmoor YO62 ...... 69 E3
Farndale West YO62 ...... 48 E1
Folkton YO11 ...... 99 F1
Garforth LS25 ...... 194 D4
Glusburn BD20 ...... 187 D7
Great Ouseburn YO26 ...... 142 A1
Halton East BD23 ...... 157 C1
Harome YO62 ...... 93 C5
Harrogate HG2 ...... 222 C6
Heck DN14 ...... 207 D8
Horton BD23 ...... 171 B5
Hudswell DL11 ...... 39 F5
Hutton Rudby TS15 ...... 25 B4
Ilkley LS29 ...... 176 C2
Ingleton LA6 ...... 103 E2
Kippax LS25 ...... 194 C2
Kirby Wiske YO7 ...... 88 F7
Kirkby Overblow LS17 ...... 178 D2
Kirklevington TS15 ...... 5 E2
Langtoft YO25 ...... 151 D5
Lebberston YO11 ...... 100 D5
Ledston WF10 ...... 200 E7
Little Ayton TS9 ...... 27 A8
Littlethorpe HG4 ...... 140 A7
Marrick DL11 ...... 38 E7
Maunby YO7 ...... 64 D1
Menwith with Darley HG3 ...... 160 A6
Mickletown LS26 ...... 200 C5
Middlesbrough TS5 ...... 6 E8
Moor Monkton YO26 ...... 164 F1
Newby TS7 ...... 7 C3
North Cowton DL7 ...... 22 B2
North Duffield YO8 ...... 198 F8
Otley LS21 ...... 176 F1
Rawcliffe YO30 ...... 225 A1
Ripon HG4 ...... 113 C3
Sawley HG4 ...... 138 E7
Scalby YO12 ...... 212 C8
Selby YO8 ...... 232 A3
South Stainley with Cayton HG3 ...... 161 E8
Shutton with Hazlewood LS24 ...... 189 D4
Sutton BD23 ...... 187 F2
Sutton-on-the-Forest YO61 ...... 144 E4
Thirsk YO7 ...... 211 F3
Weaverthorpe YO17 ...... 124 F1
Welbury DL6 ...... 44 C8
Wensley DL8 ...... 60 A4
Whitby YO22 ...... 208 E5
Whorlton DL6 ...... 45 F7
Wigginton YO32 ...... 166 D5
Winksley HG4 ...... 112 F2
Wressle DN14 ...... 205 D8
Green La E YO7 ...... 211 B1
Green La Prim Sch TS5 ...... 6 E8
Green La Villas LS25 ...... 194 D4
Green La W YO7 ...... 211 A1
Green Mdws BB8 ...... 186 A1
Green Pastures DL8 ...... 62 C5
Green Pk Ave 5 YO11 ...... 100 B6
Green Pk Rd 14 YO11 ...... 100 B6
Green Row LS26 ...... 200 B5
Green St
Castleford WF10 ...... 200 E5
7 Cowling BD22 ...... 187 B6
Darlington DL1 ...... 3 D5
Green Sward YO31 ...... 229 A7
Green Sykes Rd BD20 ...... 187 F4
Green The Brompton DL6 ...... 43 F3
Castleford WF10 ...... 201 B4
1 Clapham LA2 ...... 130 C8
Cleasby DL2 ...... 2 F4
Conistone with Kilnsey BD23 ...... 134 B6
20 Dunnington YO19 ...... 184 F7
Garforth LS25 ...... 194 D3
Hellifield BD23 ...... 154 B3
High Coniscliffe DL2 ...... 2 C6
Kettlewell with Starbotton BD23 ...... 108 B3
Kirkby Malzeard HG4 ...... 112 D5
5 Kirklevington TS15 ...... 24 E8
Knaresborough HG5 ...... 221 A8
Linton-on-Ouse YO30 ...... 164 F8
Longnewton TS21 ...... 5 A7
Middlesbrough TS17 ...... 6 D7
Northallerton DL7 ...... 210 C3
8 Otley LS21 ...... 176 F1
Rawcliffe DN14 ...... 205 A1
Richmond DL10 ...... 209 B6
Scalby YO12 ...... 212 B7
Seamer TS9 ...... 6 F1

Green The continued
6 Seamer YO12 ...... 99 D6
9 Skelton YO30 ...... 224 B5
Skipton BD23 ...... 217 B6
10 Thirsk YO7 ...... 211 C3
Tockwith YO26 ...... 181 C7
2 Tollerton YO61 ...... 143 B3
7 Topcliffe YO7 ...... 89 B1
Wistow YO8 ...... 197 D6
York YO26 ...... 227 C3
Green Village YO7 ...... 88 C5
Green Way
Glusburn BD20 ...... 187 E8
Harrogate HG2 ...... 222 C6
Middlesbrough TS7 ...... 7 D5
York YO32 ...... 225 F4
Green Ways 2 YO8 ...... 197 D6
Green Wlk 5 BB18 ...... 172 A1
Greenacre CI TS9 ...... 7 F1
Greenacres Hunton DL8 ...... 61 E7
Morton-on-Swale DL7 ...... 64 A6
Skipton BD23 ...... 217 B5
Stainton & Thornton TS8 ...... 6 D5
York YO32 ...... 225 F4
Greenacres CI 8 YO3 ...... 197 D1
Greenacres Cres 7
YO8 ...... 197 D1
Greenacres Dr 4 YO8 ...... 197 D1
Greenacres Gr 3 YO8 ...... 197 D1
Greenbank 5 DL6 ...... 210 E2
Greenbank CI WF10 ...... 200 D3
Greenbank Rd DL3 ...... 3 C6
Greenberfield La BB18 ...... 171 E2
Greencliffe Dr YO30 ...... 228 A6
Greencroft La 14 YO19 ...... 184 F7
Greencroft La 17 YO19 ...... 184 F7
Greendown CI LS29 ...... 218 D4
Greenfield Ave LS25 ...... 194 D1
Greenfield CI DL2 ...... 3 E1
Greenfield Dr
6 Brayton YO8 ...... 197 D1
Eaglescliffe TS16 ...... 5 D5
Greenfield Gdns BD20 ...... 187 F7
Greenfield Pk Dr
YO31 ...... 229 A7
Greenfield Rd 5 YO11 ...... 213 A4
Greenfield St 5 BD23 ...... 216 D3
Greenfields DN14 ...... 207 F6
Greenfields Ave HG2 ...... 220 C2
Greenfields Dr HG2 ...... 220 C2
Greenfields Rd HG2 ...... 220 C2
Greenfinch CI YO12 ...... 99 E6
Greenfoot La LA2 ...... 128 E8
Greengales Ct YO19 ...... 193 A8
Greengales La YO19 ...... 193 A8
Greengate
Malton YO17 ...... 215 C4
Scarborough YO12 ...... 212 D4
Greengate Dr HG5 ...... 221 B8
Greengate La
Cliffe YO8 ...... 198 F6
Kirkby Fleetham with Fencote DL7 ...... 42 B1
Knaresborough HG5 ...... 221 B8
Thornton-le-Dale YO18 ...... 96 C6
Greengate Rd WF8 ...... 206 C1
Greengate View HG5 ...... 221 B8
Greengates La YO61 ...... 142 E3
Greenhill Cres DL6 ...... 210 E3
Greenholme CI
1 Boroughbridge YO51 ...... 141 B6
7 Burley in Warfedale LS29 ...... 176 C1
Greenhow Hill HG3 ...... 136 C2
Greenhow Hill Rd
HG3 ...... 159 B6
Greenhow Pk LS29 ...... 176 B1
Greenhowsyke La DL6 ...... 210 E4
Greenland La YO17 ...... 95 B3
Greenlands TS15 ...... 25 C6
Greenlands La YO8 ...... 197 C3
Greenlands Rd YO18 ...... 95 F6
Greenless La DL11 ...... 1 A2
Greenmires La LS21 ...... 177 E4
Greenroyd Gr 13 BD20 ...... 187 E6
Greens Yd YO22 ...... 208 E7
Greensborough Ave 3 YO26 ...... 227 B5
Greenshaw Dr YO32 ...... 225 C8
Greenside 18 YO19 ...... 184 F7
Greenside CI 24 YO19 ...... 184 F7
Greenside Ct 9 DL2 ...... 4 C4
Greenside Wlk 23 YO19 ...... 184 F7
Greenstead Rd YO12 ...... 212 B8
Greenway The
2 Haxby YO32 ...... 225 C7
21 Middleton St George DL2 ...... 4 C4
Greenways Dr 1 YO8 ...... 197 D6
Greenways The DL7 ...... 63 D8
Greenwood Ave 7 HG3 ...... 137 B4
Greenwood Gr YO24 ...... 230 C8
Greenwood Rd 6 HG3 ...... 137 B4
Greet's Hill YO17 ...... 169 E7
Gregory CI YO23 ...... 224 C5
Grenadier Dr DL6 ...... 210 F3
Grendon Gdns 1 DL2 ...... 4 C4
Grenley St 3 WF11 ...... 202 A2
Grenville Rd TS17 ...... 6 B6
Greenwich CI 8 YO30 ...... 224 E3
Gresham CI DL1 ...... 3 D7
Gresley St 3 BD23 ...... 216 F4
Greta Ave DL10 ...... 209 D7
Greta Heath 2 LA6 ...... 102 A7
Grewelthorpe CE Prim Sch HG4 ...... 112 C7

Grey CI YO61 ...... 144 C3
Grey St HG2 ...... 222 E7
Grey Thorn La HG5 ...... 163 D3
Grey Twrs Dr TS7 ...... 7 D5
Greyfriars CI DL3 ...... 2 F5
Greylands Pk Ave
YO12 ...... 212 C8
Greylands Pk Dr YO12 ...... 212 C8
Greylands Pk Gr 3
YO12 ...... 212 C8
Greylands Pk Rd
YO12 ...... 212 C8
Greystoke Rd YO30 ...... 224 E1
Greystone Ct 2 LS29 ...... 176 C1
Greystone Com Prim Sch
HG4 ...... 214 C2
Greystone Ct YO32 ...... 225 C7
Greystone Head HG4 ...... 112 A4
Greystone La
Aldbrough DL2 ...... 2 A4
Stanwick St John DL11 ...... 1 E4
Greystonegill La LA2 ...... 129 C7
Greystones Ave HG3 ...... 161 B4
Greystones CI LS25 ...... 188 F1
Greystones La BD22 ...... 187 A6
Grimbald Crag CI
HG5 ...... 221 D4
Grimbald Crag Rd
HG5 ...... 221 D4
Grimbald Crag Way
HG5 ...... 221 D4
Grimbald Way 3 HG5 ...... 221 C4
Grimston Bar YO19 ...... 229 F4
Grimston La YO17 ...... 148 D7
Grimston Rd 12 YO11 ...... 127 A8
Grimwith Garth YO30 ...... 224 F2
Grimwith Rd BD23 ...... 135 E2
Grindale Rd YO16 ...... 127 F2
Grinkle La TS13 ...... 10 F5
Grinton Rd TS18 ...... 5 D8
Grisedale Cres TS16 ...... 5 E4
Gristhwaite La YO7 ...... 89 D1
Grosmont Gall* YO22 ...... 31 C4
Grosmont Sta YO22 ...... 31 C4
Grosvenor Cres 2
YO11 ...... 213 A4
Grosvenor Ct HG1 ...... 219 B2
Grosvenor Gdns LS17 ...... 178 B2
Grosvenor Gr HG1 ...... 219 F6
Grosvenor House
YO30 ...... 233 A4
Grosvenor House Sch
HG3 ...... 160 D6
Grosvenor Pk YO30 ...... 233 A4
Grosvenor Pl TS14 ...... 8 E6
Grosvenor Rd
Harrogate HG1 ...... 219 E6
Scarborough YO11 ...... 212 F4
Wistow YO30 ...... 233 A4
Grosvenor Sq 3 YO30 ...... 164 F8
Grosvenor Terr YO30 ...... 233 A4
Grove Ave LS29 ...... 175 C2
Grove Bank 4 TS15 ...... 24 E8
Grove Cl YO14 ...... 214 C3
Grove Cres
Boston Spa LS23 ...... 188 F8
South Milford LS25 ...... 195 F2
Grove Gdns 12 YO26 ...... 165 F1
Grove Hill Rd 4 YO14 ...... 101 B4
Grove La
Knottingley WF11 ...... 201 F2
Ripon HG4 ...... 214 C3
Grove Pk 7 YO8 ...... 198 B5
Grove Pk Ave HG1 ...... 219 E4
Grove Pk Ct HG1 ...... 219 E4
Grove Pk La HG1 ...... 219 E4
Grove Pk Terr HG1 ...... 219 E4
Grove Pk View HG1 ...... 219 E4
Grove Pk Wlk HG1 ...... 219 E4
Grove Rd
Boston Spa LS23 ...... 188 F8
14 Filey YO14 ...... 101 B4
Harrogate HG1 ...... 219 E5
Ilkley LS29 ...... 218 A3
Grove Rd Com Prim Sch
YO14 ...... 101 B4
Grove St 38 Earby BB18 ...... 172 A1
9 Harrogate HG2 ...... 220 C3
Norton YO17 ...... 215 E3
18 Whitby YO21 ...... 208 D6
Grove Terr DL8 ...... 60 E2
Grove Terr La YO31 ...... 233 C4
Grove The
Eaglescliffe TS15 ...... 5 E2
Guisborough TS14 ...... 8 D5
Harrogate HG1 ...... 219 E3
Hutton Rudby TS15 ...... 25 D5
Ilkley LS29 ...... 218 A4
Kellington DN14 ...... 203 A3
Kippax LS25 ...... 194 D1
Middlesbrough TS5 ...... 6 E6
Normanton South WF6 ...... 200 A1
Norton YO17 ...... 215 E2
1 Seamer YO12 ...... 99 D6
Skipton BD23 ...... 217 C3
Swillington LS26 ...... 194 A1
York YO24 ...... 230 E6
Grove View YO30 ...... 228 A6
Groves Ct YO31 ...... 233 C4
Groves La YO31 ...... 233 C3
Grove Way DL10 ...... 41 E4
Grunton La DL2 ...... 2 C4
Grysedale La BD23 ...... 134 B2
GSPK Tech Pk HG5 ...... 221 C6
Guadaloupe Rd DL9 ...... 40 C4
Guards Ct 10 YO12 ...... 75 F5

Guildford Rd TS6 ...... 7 E8
Guisborough Mus*
TS14 ...... 8 F7
Guisborough Priory*
TS14 ...... 8 F7
Guisborough Rd
Aislaby YO21 ...... 31 F8
Great Ayton TS9 ...... 7 F1
Lockwood TS12 ...... 10 A5
Middlesbrough TS7 ...... 7 D5
Thornaby TS17 ...... 6 B8
Whitby YO21 ...... 208 A5
Guisborough Swimming Pool
TS14 ...... 8 E7
Gunby Rd YO8 ...... 199 D5
Gunbywood Rd YO8 ...... 199 D6
Guncroft La YO62 ...... 69 D1
Guning La DL11 ...... 36 B4
Gunnergate La TS8 ...... 7 B5
Gunnerside Methodist Prim Sch DL11 ...... 36 E5
Gurney Pease Prim Sch
DL1 ...... 3 D6
Gurney St DL1 ...... 3 D6
Guy La YO7 ...... 114 F2
Gyll Hall La DL11 ...... 21 E1
Gypsy La
Castleford WF10 ...... 201 B3
Middlesbrough TS7 ...... 7 C6
Gypsy La Sta TS7 ...... 7 D6

H

Haakon CI DL10 ...... 209 C7
Habton La YO17 ...... 121 B7
Habton Rd YO17 ...... 95 D1
Hackforth & Hornby CE Prim Sch DL8 ...... 62 E8
Hackforth Rd 2 TS18 ...... 5 D8
Hackness CE VC Prim Sch
YO13 ...... 74 E5
Hackness Dr YO12 ...... 212 A8
Hackness Rd YO12 ...... 212 A8
Haddlesey Rd WF11 ...... 202 D5
Haddocks La YO61 ...... 142 B4
Haddon CI YO24 ...... 227 C2
Hadrian Ave YO10 ...... 229 B3
Hadrians Wlk YO10 ...... 99 E6
Hag La
Cottingwith YO42 ...... 193 C4
Raskelf YO61 ...... 142 E8
South Kilvington YO7 ...... 211 D6
Sproxton YO62 ...... 92 D4
Youlton YO61 ...... 142 F2
Hague Ave 3 YO12 ...... 75 D5
Hagworm Hall* YO12 ...... 75 C2
Haig Rd DL9 ...... 209 C2
Haig St YO8 ...... 232 B6
Haigh La DN14 ...... 207 A6
Hailsham Ave TS17 ...... 6 B5
Hailstone Dr DL6 ...... 210 F5
Hales La YO8 ...... 204 E5
Haley's Terr YO31 ...... 228 E7
Half Moon St 1 YO30 ...... 164 F7
Halfpenny CI HG5 ...... 221 C7
Halfpenny La HG5 ...... 221 B7
Halifax CI YO41 ...... 169 A2
Halifax Ct 1 YO30 ...... 225 A1
Halifax Way YO41 ...... 185 A3
Hall Arm La YO51 ...... 141 D5
Hall Ave 10 BD20 ...... 187 E6
Hall Brow BD23 ...... 155 A1
Hall CI 5 Airmyn DN14 ...... 205 E4
Austwick LA2 ...... 130 C7
Burley in Warfedale LS29 ...... 176 B1
Cawood YO8 ...... 191 D1
11 Glusburn BD20 ...... 187 E6
Hall Croft BD23 ...... 216 E4
Hall Ct WF11 ...... 201 E4
Hall Dr
Burley in Warfedale LS29 ...... 176 B1
Glusburn BD20 ...... 187 E6
Middlesbrough TS5 ...... 6 F7
Hall Farm CI 4 YO19 ...... 197 F8
Hall Farm Ct YO61 ...... 125 E3
Hall Farm Pk LS25 ...... 194 F4
Hall Garth 28 YO18 ...... 95 F7
Hall Garth CI LS24 ...... 190 C3
Hall Garth La TS5 ...... 16 B7
Hall Garths* LS25 ...... 195 E4
Hall Gdns Ellerburn YO18 ...... 96 E7
Barnhill BD20 ...... 173 F1
Rawcliffe DN14 ...... 205 B2
Hall Gn La LS17 ...... 178 C4
Hall Ings La YO62 ...... 70 E4
Hall La Askwith LS21 ...... 176 E5
Blubberhouses LS21 ...... 159 C2
4 Brafferton YO61 ...... 115 F1
Church Fenton LS24 ...... 196 B8
Harome HG62 ...... 93 C4
Harrogate HG1 ...... 219 E6
Hawnby DL6 ...... 46 B1

Hall La continued
Huddleston with Newthorpe LS25 ...... 195 C3
Leathley LS21 ...... 177 D1
Ledston WF10 ...... 200 F7
Myton-on-Swale YO61 ...... 142 A6
Hall Mdws BB8 ...... 186 A2
Hall Moor CI 7 TS15 ...... 24 E8
Hall Orchards Ave
LS22 ...... 180 D3
Hall Pasture 9 YO22 ...... 32 A6
Hall Pk Wistow YO8 ...... 198 A5
York YO10 ...... 229 B1
Hall Pk CI 7 YO23 ...... 75 D5
Hall Pk Croft LS25 ...... 200 D5
Hall Pk Gr 28 YO13 ...... 75 D5
Hall Pk Mdws LS25 ...... 200 D8
Hall Pk Orch LS25 ...... 200 D8
Hall Pk Rd
Hunmanby YO14 ...... 126 F8
Walton LS23 ...... 181 A2
Hall Rise
Burley in Warfedale LS29 ...... 176 B1
12 Haxby YO32 ...... 166 F5
Hall Sq 6 YO51 ...... 141 B5
Hall Twr Hill* LS15 ...... 194 B8
Hall View Gr DL3 ...... 3 A6
Hall Way 8 BD20 ...... 187 E6
Halladale CI 1 YO24 ...... 230 B7
Hallam CI YO14 ...... 101 B3
Hallam La LS21 ...... 176 D3
Hallam's Yd 6 BD23 ...... 216 F4
Hallard Way 6 YO32 ...... 167 B7
Hallcroft Dr 12 LS29 ...... 175 A4
Hallcroft La YO23 ...... 230 A3
Hallfield Ave LS25 ...... 194 F4
Hallfield La
Nawton YO62 ...... 69 C3
Wetherby LS22 ...... 180 C3
Hallfield Rd YO31 ...... 228 E5
Hallfield Terr LS25 ...... 194 F4
Hallgarth Alne YO61 ...... 142 F4
Great & Little Broughton TS9 ...... 26 E5
Hipswell DL9 ...... 209 F1
Hallwith Rd DL8 ...... 61 A3
Halnaby Ave DL3 ...... 2 F5
Halstead Rd HG2 ...... 222 E7
Hambleton Ave
Northallerton DL7 ...... 210 C2
Thirsk YO7 ...... 211 D3
York YO10 ...... 229 C4
Hambleton CE VC Prim Sch
YO8 ...... 196 F1
Hambleton CI
12 Easingwold YO61 ...... 143 D8
11 Thirsk YO7 ...... 211 C3
Hambleton Ct
Great Smeaton DL6 ...... 23 C3
Knaresborough HG5 ...... 221 C6
Hambleton Dr YO7 ...... 211 D3
Hambleton Forum* 210 E5
Hambleton Garth 3
YO61 ...... 143 C8
Hambleton Gate TS9 ...... 26 C7
Hambleton Gr HG5 ...... 221 B6
Hambleton La YO61 ...... 91 F2
Hambleton Leisure Ctr
DL6 ...... 210 D6
Hambleton Pl YO7 ...... 211 C3
Hambleton Rd
8 Catterick Garrison DL9 ...... 40 E3
Harrogate HG1 ...... 219 F4
Norton YO17 ...... 215 E2
Hambleton Terr
Knaresborough HG5 ...... 221 B6
York YO31 ...... 228 C7
Hambleton View
2 Haxby YO32 ...... 166 D5
Thirsk YO7 ...... 211 D3
4 Tollerton YO61 ...... 143 B3
Hambleton Way
Easingwold YO61 ...... 143 D8
York YO32 ...... 225 F3
Hamer Bank YO18 ...... 49 F4
Hamerton CI 11 YO14 ...... 127 A8
Hamerton Rd 10 YO14 ...... 127 A8
Hamhall La DL7 ...... 63 D6
Hamilton Ave HG2 ...... 222 E8
Hamilton CI YO13 ...... 75 C5
Hamilton Ct WF6 ...... 200 A2
Hamilton Dr
Darlington DL1 ...... 3 D8
York YO24 ...... 227 E2
Hamilton Dr E YO24 ...... 227 E2
Hamilton Dr W YO24 ...... 227 D2
Hamilton Gn YO17 ...... 215 E3
Hamilton Way YO24 ...... 227 E2
Hamlet The 8 DN14 ...... 202 F2
Hamley La YO62 ...... 70 F3
Hammer Rd HG4 ...... 85 B7
Hammersike Rd
Cawood YO8 ...... 196 F5
Wistow YO8 ...... 197 A4
Hammerton CI
Green Hammerton YO26 ...... 164 C3
3 York YO26 ...... 227 B3
Hammerton Dr
Garforth LS25 ...... 194 D3
Hellifield BD23 ...... 154 B3
Hammerton Sta YO26 ...... 164 D2
Hammond Dr DL1 ...... 3 C4
Hammond Rd YO13 ...... 54 A8

Hampden St YO1 ....233 B1
Hampden Way TS17 ....6 B6
Hampshire Cl
 Ilkley LS29 ....218 D4
 [6] Pontefract WF8 ....201 C2
Hampson Gdns YO30 ....228 B8
Hampsthwaite CE Prim Sch
 HG3 ....161 A5
Hampsthwaite Rd
 HG1 ....161 B3
Hampton Gdns YO30 ....228 C8
Hampton Rd YO12 ....212 C3
Hanbury Gdns LS25 ......194 C4
Hancow Rd
 Hartoft YO18 ....50 A1
 Rosedale East Side YO18 ...49 F3
Handale Cl TS14 ....9 A6
Handley Cl
 Stockton-on-Tees TS18 ....5 F7
 York YO30 ....225 A2
Hang Bank DL10 ....21 B8
Hanger La DN14 ....204 B3
Hanghow La DL8 ....84 C8
Hanging Stone La YO18 ...49 E4
Hangingstone Rd
 LS29 ....218 D2
Hankins La YO42 ....193 D1
Hanover Pl
 [2] Kippax LS25 ....194 D1
 Knottingley WF11 ....201 D4
Hanover Rd [6] YO11 ....212 F5
Hanover St [9] YO10 ....173 E1
Hanover St E [7] YO10 ...227 F5
Hanover St W [7] YO26 ...227 F5
Hanover Terr YO21 ....208 C6
Hansom Pl YO31 ....228 C7
Hanson Ave WF6 ....200 A1
Harborough Ct [20] YO14 ...126 F8
Harbour Rise [5] DL8 ....63 A2
Harbour View [7] DL8 ...63 A3
Harcourt Ave YO12 ......212 E3
Harcourt Cl
 Bishopthorpe YO23 ......231 A4
 Wheldrake YO19 ....192 F7
Harcourt Dr
 Addingham LS29 ....174 F5
 Harrogate HG1 ....219 E2
Harcourt Pl [4] YO11 ....213 A5
Harcourt Rd [4] YO11 ....219 E2
Harcourt St YO31 ....228 E5
Hard Gate BD23 ....134 A3
Hard Stiles DL1 ....39 B7
Hardcastle Ave [8] WF8 ..201 B1
Harden Cl YO30 ....224 F2
Harden Rd BB18 ....186 A7
Hardenshaw La YO8 .....204 B4
Hardigate Rd YO18 ....72 B7
Hardings La
 Glusburn BD20 ....187 F8
 Middleton LS29 ....218 A8
Hardisty Hill HG3 ....159 C3
Hardisty Mews YO26 .....228 A4
Hardrada Way [8] YO41 ...168 D1
Hardy Mdws [11] BD23 ....134 E4
Hardy St YO8 ....232 E4
Harebell Cl
 [17] Harrogate HG3 ....161 B3
 Northallerton DL7 ....210 C1
Harecroft Rd [6] LS21 ...177 A1
Haregill Bank HG4 ....85 E6
Harehills La BD22 ....187 E1
Haresfield Way TS17 .....6 A5
Harewell Cl HG3 ....137 D3
Harewell La [13] HG3 .....137 F1
Harewood Ave
 [5] Normanton South WF6 ..200 B2
 [6] Scalby YO12 ....212 D8
Harewood Chase DL7 ...210 B2
Harewood Cl
 Morton-on-Swale DL7 ....64 A6
 Rawcliffe YO30 ....224 D2
Harewood Dr YO32 ....166 D5
Harewood Dr [4] YO14 ...101 A3
Harewood La DL7 ....210 C3
Harewood Rd
 Collingham LS22 ....188 A8
 Harrogate HG3 ....219 A5
 Ripon HG4 ....9 D2
 Skipton BD23 ....216 E4
Harewood Way YO10 ....229 A2
Harford Rd YO11 ....100 B6
Hargill
 Gilling with Hartforth & Sedbury
 DL10 ....20 E4
 Harmby DL8 ....60 E4
 West Witton DL8 ....59 C3
Hargill Cl DL8 ....60 E4
Hargill La Finghall DL8 ...61 E4
 [6] Leeming DL7 ....63 D4
 Redmire DL8 ....59 C7
Hargill Rd DL8 ....61 A3
Hargrove Rd HG2 ....228 B2
Harington Ave YO10 .....228 F4
Harker Hill DL8 ....56 C4
Harker St [12] WF11 ....202 A2
Harkness Cl DL7 ....63 C4
Harkness Dr DL7 ....63 C4
Harland Cl YO61 ....144 C3
Harland Mount Nature
 Reserve* YO12 ....212 B3
Harlech Cl [11] TS17 ......5 F4
Harlech Way HG2 ....222 B5
Harley Cl YO12 ....40 F4
Harley Cres DL9 ....40 F4
Harley La DL9 ....40 F4
Harley St [5] DL9 ....212 E5
Harlow Ave YO12 ....222 B7

Harlow Carr RHS Gdn*
 HG3 ....161 B1
Harlow Cl [11] YO24 ......227 F2
Harlow Cres HG2 ....222 B7
Harlow Grange Pk
 HG3 ....178 C8
Harlow Manor Pk
 HG2 ....222 B8
Harlow Moor Dr HG2 ....219 B1
Harlow Moor Rd HG2 ....219 A1
Harlow Moor Rd HG2 ....222 A8
Harlow Pines HG2 ....222 A7
Harlow Pk Cres HG2 .....222 A7
Harlow Pk Dr HG2 ....222 A7
Harlow Pk Rd HG2 ....222 B7
Harlow Rd YO24 ....227 F2
Harlow Terr HG2 ....219 B1
Harlow View HG2 ....222 B6
Harlsey Castle* DL6 .....44 D5
Harlsey Cres TS18 ....5 E8
Harlsey Rd TS18 ....5 E8
Harmby Rd [12] DL8 ......60 D5
Harness La [13] YO51 .....141 B4
Harold Ct YO24 ....227 D3
Harold St YO8 ....232 F4
Harolds Way [11] YO41 ...168 D1
Harome Heads La YO62 ..93 B6
Harome Heads Rd
 YO62 ....93 C6
Harper La BD20 ....187 E6
Harper La HG3 ....159 C6
Harper St
 Barnoldswick BB18 ....171 C1
 [5] Selby YO8 ....232 C5
Harper Terr TS18 ....5 E8
Harpers Sq [12] BD20 ....187 E6
Harpers Terr DL2 ....4 B5
Harr Gill DL8 ....58 A6
Harringay Cres [20] DL1 ...3 F6
Harris Dr [5] DL10 ....41 E4
Harris St DL1 ....3 E4
Harrison Gr HG1 ....220 C4
Harrison St
 Barnoldswick BB18 ....171 E1
 York YO31 ....228 F6
Harrogate Coll [15] HG1 ..219 D2
Harrogate Ctr The* 219 D3
Harrogate District Hospl
 HG2 ....220 A2
Harrogate Gram Sch
 HG2 ....220 A4
Harrogate Granby High Sch
 HG1 ....220 A4
Harrogate Hill Inf & Jun Sch
 DL3 ....3 D7
Harrogate Ladies Coll
 HG1 ....219 C3
Harrogate Leisure Ctr
 HG2 ....222 E7
Harrogate Rd
 Bishop Monkton HG3 .....139 E5
 Boroughbridge HG5 ......141 A4
 Ferrensby HG5 ....162 E7
 Green Hammerton YO26 ..164 B3
 Kirkby Overblow HG3 ....222 D1
 Knaresborough HG5 ......220 F5
 Littlethorpe HG4 ....214 C1
 Spofforth with Stockeld
 LS22 ....180 A4
 Weeton LS17 ....178 B2
Harrogate Sta HG1 ......219 D2
Harrogate Theatre*
 HG1 ....219 D2
Harrow Cliff La YO18 ....96 E4
Harrow Glade [5] YO30 ...225 A1
Harrow Rd TS5 ....6 E8
Harrowing Dr [2] YO21 ...208 C6
Harry Moor La YO8 ....197 B2
Harryfield La YO61 ....144 C7
Hart Hill Cres YO41 .....169 A2
Hart Rhydding La
 LS29 ....174 F4
Hartburn Village TS18 ...5 E8
Hartforth La DL10 ....20 E4
Hartington St [18] BB8 ...186 A3
Hartington Way DL3 .....3 C7
Hartley La CA17 ....14 A7
Hartley Pl BD22 ....187 B6
Hartley Rd HG2 ....222 B7
Hartley St [12] BB18 ......172 A1
Hartlington Raikes
 BD23 ....157 B8
Hartoft St YO10 ....228 D2
Hartwith Ave [8] HG3 ...138 A1
Hartwith Bank HG3 ......138 A1
Hartwith Cl HG3 ....138 A1
Hartwith Dr HG3 ....219 A4
Hartwith Gn [6] HG3 ....138 A1
Hartwith Way HG1 ....219 B4
Harvard Ct YO10 ....212 A8
Harvest Croft [11] WF8 ...201 C2
Harvest Croft LS23 ......176 B1
Harvest Way YO11 ....100 B7
Harwood Dale Rd YO13 ...54 A1
Hasguard Way [12] TS17 ...5 F4
Hassacarr La YO19 ......184 F6
Hastings Cl [4] YO30 ....225 A1
Hastings Cres WF10 .....201 A4
Hatcase La [20] YO61 .....95 F7
Hatfield Ave TS5 ....6 E8
Hatfield Cl [9] YO30 .....224 E3
Hatfield Rd DL7 ....210 D3
Hatfield Wlk YO24 ....230 B8
Hathaway La [11] YO41 ...169 B1
Hatterboard Dr YO12 ....208 D7
Hatters Ct [9] YO23 ......230 B3
Haugh La YO8 ....202 F8

Haughton Com Sch DL1 ...3 E7
Haughton Rd
 Darlington DL1 ....3 D6
 YO30 ....228 C7
Haughton Rd YO30 ......225 C7
Hauling La YO23 ....191 C8
Hauxley Ct LS29 ....218 D5
Havelock Pl [17] YO21 ....208 D7
Havelock St 6 B8
Haven The Selby YO8 ....232 D5
 [6] South Milford LS25 ...195 F2
Haverah Ct YO30 ....224 F1
Havercroft Rd YO14 .....127 A8
Havernook La HG4 ....86 A3
Havers Hill YO11 ....100 A6
Haverthwaites Dr
 LS25 ....188 F1
Haverton La WF6 ....200 C1
Havikil La HG5 ....162 A5
Havikil Pk HG5 ....162 A6
Havilland Rd TS17 ....6 B6
Havre Pk [11] BB18 ....171 E1
Haw Bank Ct BD23 ......157 A8
Haw Gr BD23 ....154 B3
Haw Hill View WF6 ....200 A2
Haw La BD23 ....154 B3
Haw Pk [18] BD23 ....217 E8
Hawber Cote Dr BD20 ...174 C1
Hawber La BD20 ....174 C1
Hawdon Ave YO8 ....232 D5
Hawes Com Prim Sch
 DL8 ....56 D4
Hawes Rd HG1 ....220 B4
Hawes Visitor Ctr*
 DL8 ....56 D4
Hawke Garth [8] YO14 ...62 A3
Hawkridge Cl TS17 .....6 B8
Hawkshead Cl [5] YO24 ..230 B8
Hawkstone TS8 ....7 C4
Hawkstone Cl TS14 .....8 E6
Hawkswell La HG4 ....40 E1
Hawkswood [11] DL2 .....3 D1
Hawley St BB8 ....186 B3
Hawse Rd YO8 ....204 B7
Hawshaw Rd BD22 ......186 E7
Hawsker Cum Stainsacre CE
 VC Prim Sch YO22 ......33 A7
Hawsker Intake Rd
 YO22 ....32 F5
Hawsker La
 Hawsker-cum-Stainsacre
 YO22 ....13 F1
 Whitby YO22 ....208 F6
Hawson Cl [9] YO11 .....100 B7
Hawthorn Ave
 [6] Knaresborough HG5 ..221 B7
 Knottingley WF11 ....201 E2
 Malton YO17 ....215 D5
 Tadcaster LS24 ....189 D5
Hawthorn Cl
 [11] Addingham LS29 .....174 E4
 Hellifield BD23 ....154 B3
 [12] Leyburn DL8 ....60 D5
 [8] Pickering YO18 ....96 A6
 Stutton with Hazlewood
 LS24 ....189 E5
Hawthorn Cres TS7 .....7 C6
Hawthorn Croft [6] LS24 ..189 D5
Hawthorn Dr
 [17] Topcliffe YO7 ....89 B1
 Wilberfoss YO41 ....195 B1
 Wistow YO8 ....198 A5
Hawthorn Garth DN14 ...202 F4
Hawthorn Gr YO31 ......228 E5
Hawthorn La YO21 ......96 A6
Hawthorn Pl YO32 ....225 C4
Hawthorn Spinney
 YO32 ....225 E3
Hawthorn St [11] YO31 ...228 E5
Hawthorn Terr YO32 .....225 D4
Hawthorn Terr Cent [2]
 YO32 ....225 D3
Hawthorn Terr N
 YO32 ....225 D4
Hawthorn Terr S
 YO32 ....225 D3
Hawthorn Way YO14 ....101 C1
Hawthorn Wlk [11] YO11 ..100 A7
Hawthorne Ave
 [18] Haxby YO32 ....166 C5
 [10] Scotton DL9 ....40 F2
Hawthorne Cl
 Burniston YO13 ....75 F7
 [6] Thorpe Willoughby
 YO8 ....197 B2
Hawthorne Dr
 Barnoldswick BB18 ....171 E1
 Guisborough TS14 ....8 E6
Hawthorne Gr YO31 .....228 E5
Hawthorne Mews
 YO32 ....167 A8
Hawthorns La [11] YO8 ...197 F8
Hawthorns Cl [11] BD23 ...133 B2
Hawthorns The
 [20] Barnoldswick BB18 ...187 E7
 [11] Great Ayton TS9 ....8 A2
Haxby Moor Rd
 Haxby YO32 ....166 F7
 Towthorpe YO32 ....167 A7
Haxby Rd Clifton YO31 ...225 D1
 Middleton St George DL2 ...4 C5
 New Earswick YO32 .....225 D7
 York YO31 ....233 B4
Haxby Rd Prim Sch
 YO31 ....228 D7
Hay Brow Cl YO13 ....75 C5
Hay Brow Cres YO13 ....75 C5
Hay La YO13 ....75 C5
Hay-a-park La HG5 ....221 D7

Hayfield Ave LS23 ....188 E8
Hayforth Cl YO30 ....225 A2
Haygate La YO18 ....95 F5
Haygill Nook BD23 ....174 B5
Hayhills La BD20 ....174 B2
Hayton Wood View
 LS25 ....194 F8
Haywain The LS29 ....218 D3
Hayward Cres [6] HG1 ...219 E4
Haywra St HG1 ....219 D3
Hazel Bank HG5 ....162 D6
Hazel Brow Farm*
 DL11 ....37 C4
Hazel Cl Pannal HG3 ....222 C3
 York YO32 ....225 D8
Hazel Ct [11] Bedale DL8 ..63 B3
 York YO31 ....228 E4
Hazel Dr HG3 ....222 C3
Hazel Garth YO31 ....229 B7
Hazel Gr
 Middlesbrough TS7 ......7 C6
 Pontefract WF8 ....201 C1
 Sutton BD20 ....187 E7
Hazel Gr Rd BD20 ....187 E7
Hazel Hill YO12 ....75 A2
Hazel Old La DN14 ......33 D4
Hazel Rd
 [2] Boroughbridge YO51 ..141 B4
 [2] Filey YO14 ....101 A4
 Knottingley WF11 ....201 F1
Hazel Rise LS26 ....200 B5
Hazelheads La HG5 ......221 C8
Hazelmere Ct YO32 .....225 E3
Hazelnut Gr YO30 ....225 B2
Hazelwood Ave
 Garforth LS25 ....194 D3
 York YO10 ....229 D4
Hazing La DN14 ....207 B6
Hazler La BD23 ....157 D7
Headingley Cres [5] DL1 ...3 F6
Headingley Rd [7] DN6 ..206 E2
Headland Cl [20] YO32 ....166 E5
Headland La YO18 ....72 B4
Headlam La
 Howgrave BD8 ....87 F2
 Knottingley WF11 ....201 F2
 Pontefract WF8 ....201 B1
Headlands Prim Sch
 YO32 ....225 D8
Headlands Rd YO62 .....70 C2
Headley Cl [2] YO30 ......225 B1
Headley La LS23 ....188 F5
Heads Bank DL8 ....58 F3
Heads La BB18 ....186 A7
Heads Rd Newton YO18 ...51 B1
 Pickering YO18 ....71 F8
Headwell La LS24 ....195 E7
Healaugh La YO26 ....181 A1
Healaugh Priory*
 LS24 ....181 E1
Heald Brow BB18 ....171 D2
Heald St WF10 ....200 F4
Healdfield Rd WF10 .....201 A4
Healdwood Rd WF10 ....200 F4
Healey Gr YO31 ....228 F8
Healthfield Prim Sch
 DL3 ....3 E5
Heath Cl BD23 ....227 F2
Heath Cres BD20 ....173 E3
Heath Croft YO10 ....231 D8
Heath Dr
 Boston Spa LS23 ....188 D8
 [11] Low Bradley BD20 ...173 E3
Heath Gr HG2 ....219 B1
Heath Moor Dr YO10 ...231 E8
Heath Pk [20] LS29 ....175 C2
Heath Ride YO32 ....167 B8
Heathcliff Gdns [6]
 YO10 ....212 C8
Heather Bank
 [18] Stamford Bridge YO41 ..168 D2
 York YO10 ....229 C4
Heather Brow [16] BB18 ...172 B1
Heather Cl Selby YO8 ...232 C3
 [6] Whorlton DL6 ....45 F2
Heather Croft [4] YO31 ...225 E2
Heather Ct LS29 ....218 B3
Heather Dr YO22 ....208 E3
Heather View YO22 ......217 B3
Heather Way [11] HG3 ....161 B3
Heatherdene LS24 ....189 E6
Heatherdene Rd [6] DL8 ...60 E4
Heathfield Dr HG5 ....221 C6
Heathfield Pk DL2 ....4 C5
Heathfield Rd [11] YO10 ...229 A3
Heathness Rd LS29 ......174 E5
Heathrow TS17 ....6 C7
Heathrow La YO14 ....214 C5
Heaths Cl HG4 ....214 C4
Hedben Bank HG3 ....138 F4
Hebden Rd BD23 ....134 E2
Hebdon Rise [2] YO26 ...227 B4
Heber Dr BD23 ....172 A5
Heber's Ghyll Dr [20]
 LS29 ....175 C2
Heber's Gr [21] LS29 .....175 C2
Hebron Rd YO21 ....26 D2
Heck & Pollington Lake
 DN14 ....207 C2
Heck Gill La HG3 ....160 A5
Heckler La HG4 ....207 C7
Heckler La HG4 ....214 C4
Heddon St TS17 ....6 A3
Hedley St TS14 ....8 F7
Height La BD23 ....174 C6

Height Lands La YO23 ...182 D6
Heights La BD20 ....174 A2
Helena St LS25 ....200 C8
Helks Brow LA2 ....128 E2
Hell Wath Gr HG4 ....214 A2
Hell Wath La HG4 ....214 A2
Hellifield
 Littlethorpe HG4 ....214 A2
 Markingfield Hall HG4 ...139 E6
Hellifield Com Prim Sch
 BD23 ....154 B3
Hellifield Rd BD23 ....155 A6
Hellifield Sta BD23 ......154 B4
Helmsdale YO24 ....230 C6
Helmsley Castle*
 YO62 ....92 E6
Helmsley Com Prim Sch
 YO62 ....92 F7
Helmsley Dr TS14 ....8 E7
Helmsley Gr [16] YO32 ...166 D5
Helmsley Rd TS9 ....26 C7
Helmsley Walled Gdn*
 YO62 ....92 E6
Helmsley Way DL7 ......210 C2
Helperby & Myton La
 YO61 ....142 A7
Helperby La YO51 ....141 C7
Helredale Gdns YO22 ...208 E4
Helredale Rd YO22 ......208 E4
Helston Rd WF6 ....200 A2
Helwath Rd YO13 ....53 D5
Helwith Rd DL11 ....38 E7
Hemingbrough CP Sch
 YO8 ....198 F1
Hemingford Gdns TS15 ...5 E2
Hemishor Dr LS26 ......200 C8
Hemlington Hall Prim Sch
 TS8 ....6 E5
Hemlington Lake & Recn Ctr
 TS8 ....6 E5
Hemlock Ave YO31 ......229 B7
Hempbridge Cl YO8 ....232 A5
Hempbridge Rd YO8 ....232 A5
Hempland Ave YO31 ....228 F6
Hempland Dr YO31 ......229 A7
Hempland Jun Sch
 YO31 ....229 B6
Hempland La YO31 ......229 A6
Hempland Prim Sch
 YO31 ....229 A6
Hemsby Rd WF10 ....200 E3
Henbusk La LA2 ....130 A8
Hendon Garth YO30 ....225 A1
Henlow La YO60 ....147 B4
Henrhyd Ct [28] TS17 .....5 F4
Henrietta St YO22 ....209 F8
Henrietta St YO22 ....208 E7
Henry St BD21 ....216 F1
Hensall CP Sch DN14 ...203 C1
Hensall Sta DN14 ....203 C1
Henshaws Coll HG1 .....220 B5
Henside La BD24 ....132 A5
Henside Rd BD24 ....132 B6
Henson Gr WF10 ....201 A4
Henwick Hall La YO8 ...232 C1
Hepton Hill YO17 ....120 F2
Hepworth's La DN14 ....204 C2
Herberton Rd [11] YO31 ...228 E3
Herberts Way YO31 .....228 F7
Hercules St DL1 ....3 E7
Herdborough Rd
 YO11 ....100 A7
Herdsman Dr YO23 .....230 C3
Hereman Rd [18] YO24 ...230 B8
Herdwick Cl [2] YO30 ....225 B1
Hereford Rd HG1 ....219 A2
Hergill La Baldersby HG4 ...88 C1
 Kirby Hill DL11 ....19 F5
Heritage Ctr The* TS12 ..9 D6
Herman Wlk YO24 ......230 C8
Hermitage Cl DL10 ......209 A7
Hermitage The* HG4 ...86 C8
Hermitage Way YO22 ...32 A5
Heron Ave YO24 ....230 C8
Heron Cl [11] Bedale DL8 ...63 A3
 [6] Thornton Dale YO18 ...96 D5
Heron Ct [6] Filey YO14 ...101 A4
 [6] Hunton DL9 ....40 F2
Heron Dr DL1 ....3 E5
Heron Gate TS14 ....8 D6
Heron La YO12 ....212 F5
Heron Rise YO32 ....225 F5
Heron Tree Cl DL8 ....60 D7
Heron Way YO17 ....215 D2
Herongate YO11 ....95 F6
Herriot* YO7 ....211 B3
Herriot Dr DL9 ....41 A5
Herriot Way [11] YO7 .....211 C2
Hertford Cl [6] YO11 ....100 A7
Hertford Vale CE VC Prim
 Sch YO12 ....99 D2
Hesketh Ave TS4 ....7 A7
Hesketh Bank YO10 .....229 C4
Heslaker La BD23 ....216 C1
Hesleden Ave TS5 ....6 D6
Hesley La BD24 ....153 A6
Heslin Cl [6] YO32 ....225 C8
Heslington Croft YO10 ...231 F7
Heslington Ct [6] YO10 ...229 B1
Heslington Gdns [2] TS14 ..8 F7

Heslington La
Heslington YO10 ....229 A1
York YO10 ....228 F3
Heslington Rd YO10 ....228 E3
Hessay Pl 2 YO26 .....227 A3
Hetherton St YO30 ....233 A3
Hetton Garth 18 DL8 ....60 D5
Hewitson Rd DL1 ....3 E5
Hewitts La BD20 ......172 F2
Hewley Ave YO10 ......229 A4
Hewley Dr 9 YO13 ......99 A7
Heworth YO31 ....229 A6
Heworth CE Prim Sch
YO31 ....228 F6
Heworth Dr YO21 ......208 B6
Heworth Gn YO31 ......233 C4
Heworth Hall Dr YO31 ..228 F6
Heworth Mews YO31 ...228 E6
Heworth Pl YO31 ......228 F6
Heworth Rd YO31 ......228 F6
Heworth Village YO31 ..229 A6
Heyford Rd YO7 ....115 B1
Heygate Bank YO18 ....49 F3
Heygate La LS23 ....188 F6
Heyshaw Rd HG3 ......159 C8
Heythrop Dr
Guisborough TS14 ....8 F6
Middlesbrough TS5 ....6 D7
Heywood Rd HG2 ......219 C1
Hibernia St YO12 ......212 E5
Hicks La LS26 ....200 B6
Hickstead Ct 16 DL10 ...3 F6
Hidcote Gdns YO17 .....6 A4
High Back Side YO18 ...95 E8
High Bank
Ampleforth YO62 ....92 B2
Bradleys Both BD20 .....173 E3
5 Threshfield BD23 ....134 D2
High Bank Cl 7 LS29 ..174 F4
High Barmer YO13 .....75 B7
High Bentham Com Prim Sch
LA2 ....129 B8
High Bond End HG5 ....221 A7
High Bradley La BD20 ..173 E4
High Catton Rd YO41 ..185 D8
High Church Wynd TS16 .5 D3
High Cleugh HG4 ......214 A4
High Coniscliffe CE Sch
DL2 ....2 C6
High Cragwell YO21 ...31 F7
High Crest 6 HG3 .....137 C4
High Croft 7 YO14 ....126 F8
High Croft Way 5 BD20 .173 E1
High Ct HG5 ....221 A6
High Eggborough La
DN14 ....203 A1
High Fell Cl BD24 .....131 D1
High Field YO10 ....229 D4
High Fold BB18 ....186 A7
High Garth
Eastfield YO11 ....100 A7
Richmond DL10 ....209 B8
High Gill Rd TS7 ....7 D6
High Gn Catterick DL10 ..41 D4
Hebden BD23 ....135 A2
High Gn Dr BD20 ......174 B1
High Hill Gr St 14 BD24 .131 D2
High Hill La BD24 .....131 D2
High La Beadlam YO62 ...93 C8
Birstwith HG3 ....160 C5
Cowling BD22 ....187 A4
Cropton YO18 ....71 C4
Dalby-cum-Skewsby
YO60 ....119 A2
Dalton DL11 ....19 D7
Fylingdales YO22 ....33 C5
Gillamoor YO62 ....70 A6
Grassington BD23 ......134 E3
Grinton DL11 ....37 D4
Hawes DL8 ....56 F4
Howsham YO60 ....147 B1
Kirby Sigston DL6 ....44 E1
Leake DL6 ....65 E6
Maltby TS15 ....6 C4
Muston YO14 ....100 F1
Myton-on-Swale YO61 ..142 B6
Newsham DL11 ....18 G7
Reeth, Fremington & Healaugh
DL11 ....37 F5
Spofforth with Stockeld
HG3 ....179 C4
Sutton upon Derwent
YO41 ....185 D3
Thirlby YO7 ....90 D6
Thornton Watlass DL8 ...62 C2
West Scrafton DL8 ......83 F6
West Witton DL8 ....59 D2
High Leir La YO7 ....67 D1
High Mdw
Gowdall DN14 ....204 A1
Selby YO8 ....232 B6
High Mill Dr 1 YO12 ....75 F5
High Mill La YO12 .....175 A5
High Mkt Pl YO7 ....70 B1
High Moor Edge YO12 ..212 A7
High Moor La
Boroughbridge HG5 .....141 A2
Branton HG3 ....161 F8
Newton-on-Ouse YO30 ..165 C8
Scotton HG5 ....162 A5
High Moor Rd
North Rigton HG3 ....178 A5
Skelton HG5 ....140 F7
High Moor Way 1
YO11 ....100 A6

High Newbiggin St
YO31 ....233 B3
High Oaks YO31 ....229 B7
High Ousegate YO1 ....233 B2
High Peak TS14 ....8 F5
High Peter La HG3 .....140 A3
High Petergate YO1 ...233 B3
High Rd LA2 ....128 F5
High Riding Aske DL10 ..20 D1
Richmond DL10 ....209 C8
High Rifts TS8 ....6 E5
High Riggs La YO18 ....96 C3
High Row
Bugthorpe YO41 ....169 D4
Caldwell DL11 ....1 C4
Darlington DL1 ....3 C5
Melsonby DL10 ....20 F7
High Skellgate 7 HG4 ..214 C5
High St Airmyn DN14 ..205 E3
Ampleforth YO62 ....92 C3
Aske DL10 ....20 E2
Austwick LA2 ....130 E7
Barmby on the Marsh
DN14 ....205 A4
Barnby YO21 ....12 C4
Barton-le-Street YO17 ..120 E5
Beadlam YO62 ....93 D7
Boosbeck TS12 ....9 D8
6 Boroughbridge YO51 ..141 B5
Boston Spa LS23 ....188 E8
Bramham LS23 ....188 F6
Buckton/Bempton YO13 ..97 D6
Burniston YO13 ....75 C8
Burton in Lonsdale LA6 ..102 F3
Carlton DN14 ....204 C2
Castleford WF10 ....200 E4
Catterick DL10 ....41 D5
Cawood YO8 ....197 B8
Cottam YO25 ....150 E5
Cropton YO18 ....71 B4
Danby YO21 ....29 A6
Eaglescliffe TS15 ....5 D4
16 Eastfield YO11 ....100 A6
Gargrave BD23 ....155 D1
Glaisdale YO21 ....30 D4
Gristhorpe BD20 ....187 E6
Great Ayton TS9 ....7 F1
Great Broughton TS9 ...26 E4
Hampsthwaite HG3 .....160 F5
Harrogate HG2 ....220 C4
4 Helmsley YO62 ....92 F6
Heslerton YO17 ....123 F6
Hinderwell TS13 ....11 F7
Hovingham YO62 ......119 E6
Husthwaite YO61 ......117 B6
Ingleton LA6 ....103 D4
Kippax LS25 ....194 C2
Kirby Grindalythe YO17 ..149 D8
5 Knaresborough HG5 ...221 B5
Knottingley WF11 ......201 E5
Langtoft YO25 ....151 C8
Lastingham YO62 ....70 D5
9 Leyburn DL8 ....60 D5
Lingdale TS12 ....9 F7
Lockwood TS12 ....10 A5
Markington with Wallerthwaite
HG3 ....139 C4
Mickleby TS13 ....12 A4
Middlesbrough TS7 ......7 C8
Newton Mulgrave TS13 ..11 E4
Normanton South WF6 ..200 A1
Northallerton DL7 ......210 D6
2 Norton DN6 ....206 E1
Old Byland & Scawton
YO62 ....92 A4
Oldstead YO7 ....91 E5
Pateley Bridge HG3 ....137 B4
Rawcliffe DN14 ....205 A1
Rillington YO17 ....122 F5
Scalby YO13 ....75 D5
6 Settle BD24 ....131 E2
Settrington YO17 ....122 F1
Sherburn YO17 ....124 D7
Skipton BD23 ....217 A4
Slingsby YO62 ....120 B5
Snainton YO13 ....98 A5
Snaith DN14 ....204 B1
South Milford LS25 .....195 E2
Spofforth HG3 ....179 E5
3 Staithes TS13 ....13 K2
Stillington YO61 ....144 B6
Stokesley TS9 ....26 C7
Swinton YO17 ....121 B4
Tadcaster LS24 ....189 E6
Thornton Dale YO18 ...96 D5
Thornton-le-Clay YO60 ..146 A4
Wharram YO17 ....149 A6
Whitby YO21 ....208 B3
Whixley YO26 ....164 A4
Wilberfoss YO41 ....132 D5
Wistow YO8 ....197 D6
Wrelton DL10 ....45 D8
Wombleton YO62 ....93 E7
Wrelton YO18 ....71 C1
High St Agnesgate
HG4 ....214 C5
High Stakesby Rd
YO21 ....208 A6
High Stell DL3 ....4 C4
High Town Bank Rd
YO7 ....91 C5
High Trace DL6 ....210 E2
High View HG3 ....159 F8
High View HG3 ....160 F8
High Wheatley LS29 ...218 D3
High Wlk YO12 ....212 E7
High Wood LS29 ....218 F3
Highbank Gr 1 HG2 ...220 D4
Highbury Ave TS5 ......6 F8
Highcliff Rd TS14 ....8 C4

Highcliffe Ct YO30 .....228 A6
Highcroft
Collingham LS22 ....188 A8
9 Grassington BD23 ....134 E3
Highdale Ave 6 YO12 ..212 D8
Highdale Rd YO12 ......212 E7
Higher Hartley St 2
BD20 ....187 D7
Higher Lodge St 1
BD20 ....187 D7
Higher Rd BD23 ....152 F4
Higherlands Cl BD23 ..155 D1
Highfield
Pollington DN14 ....207 F7
Scarborough YO12 ......212 E4
Highfield Ave WF8 .....201 D2
Highfield Cl YO25 ......126 A4
Highfield Cres YO8 ....198 B5
Highfield Ct YO8 ....232 B1
Highfield Dr
Allerton Bywater WF10 ..200 C7
Castleford LS25 ....194 C3
Highfield Gn
Allerton Bywater WF10 ..200 C7
Sherburn in Elmet LS25 ..195 F3
Highfield Gr WF10 .....200 C7
Highfield La
Barwick in Elmet & Scholes
LS15 ....194 B7
Fangfoss YO41 ....169 B1
Gillamoor YO62 ....69 F5
Huddleston with Newthorpe
LS25 ....195 B2
Nawton YO62 ....69 C2
Scagglethorpe YO17 ....122 B2
Womersley DN6 ....206 D5
Highfield Pl 1 WF10 ...200 D7
Highfield Prep Sch
HG1 ....219 B3
Highfield Rd
Aberford LS25 ....194 F8
2 Earby BB18 ....172 A1
Malton YO17 ....215 C5
Ripon HG4 ....214 B3
Whitby YO21 ....208 A7
Highfield Terr BD23 ...216 F3
Highfield View 8 YO8 ..198 B4
Highfield Villas LS25 ...195 F3
Highfields La YO7 ......115 A1
Highgate Balne DN14 ..207 D8
Glusburn BD20 ....187 D8
Highgate Pk HG1 ......219 F3
Highgrove Cl YO30 ....224 E3
Highland Cl 12 WF8 ...201 C1
Highlands Ave 5 YO32 .167 B7
Highlands Cl YO14 .....101 B1
Highmoor Cl YO24 ....230 D8
Highmoor Rd
Darlington DL1 ....3 F4
York YO24 ....230 D8
Highthorn Rd YO31 ....225 E2
Highthorne La YO61 ...117 B5
Highway BD24 ....131 E3
Hilbeck Gr YO31 ......229 B6
Hilbra Ave YO32 ......225 D6
Hilda St 6 Selby YO8 ..232 C5
3 York YO10 ....228 E3
Hildenley Cl 6 YO12 ..212 B5
Hilderthorpe TS7 ....7 C6
Hildewell 3 TS13 ......11 F7
Hildyard Cl TS9 ....26 C8
Hill Bank HG5 ....163 B7
Hill Cl DL1 ....38 B6
Hill Crest YO19 ....167 F1
Hill Crest Gdns YO24 ..227 F1
Hill End La BD22 ......186 F5
Hill Field YO8 ....232 B8
Hill Foot La HG3 ......222 B2
Hill House La DL2 ....4 C8
Hill La BB8 ....186 B4
Hill Rd WF10 ....200 F3
Hill Rise
Middleton St George DL2 ..4 D3
Skipton BD23 ....216 E5
Hill Rise Ave HG2 .....222 B8
Hill Rise Cl HG2 ......222 B8
Hill Side DL2 ....3 A3
Hill St
6 Barnoldswick BB18 ...171 E1
York YO24 ....227 E5
Hill The DL8 ....56 D4
Hill Top
2 Burley in Wharfedale
LS29 ....176 C1
Castleford WF10 ....200 C4
Ilkley LS29 ....218 A2
Knottingley WF11 ......201 F2
Hill Top Ave HG1 .....219 D6
Hill Top Cl
Embsay BD23 ....217 C8
Harrogate HG1 ....219 D6
Stutton with Hazlewood
LS24 ....189 D4
Hill Top Cres HG1 .....219 D6
Hill Top Ct DL7 ....22 C3
Hill Top Gr HG1 ....219 D6
Hill Top Gr HG1 ....219 D6
Hill Top La Earby BB18 ..172 A1
Pannal HG3 ....222 E2
Hill Top Mount HG1 ...219 D6
Hill Top Rd
Harrogate HG1 ....219 D6
Whitby YO18 ....197 D6
Hill Top View HG1 .....159 F8
Hill Top Wlk HG1 .....219 D6
Hill View
Langthorpe YO51 ......141 A6

Hill View continued
Stillington YO61 ....144 C6
Hill View YO11 ....229 C7
Hillam Comm La LS25 ..202 B7
Hillam H Cl 5 LS25 ....202 A7
Hillam Hall La 4 LS25 ..202 A7
Hillam Hall View 3
LS25 ....202 A7
Hillam La
Burton Salmon LS25 ...201 F7
Hillam LS25 ....202 B7
Hillam Rd YO8 ....204 C6
Hillary Garth 9 YO26 ..227 E4
Hillbank Gr HG1 ......220 D4
Hillbank Rd HG1 ......220 D4
Hillbrook Dr 2 HG3 ....59 E3
Hillcrest
8 Monk Fryston LS25 ...202 A8
Tadcaster LS24 ....189 D5
Hillcrest Ave
Newby & Scalby YO12 ..75 E5
Poppleton YO26 ....224 A2
Silsden BD20 ....174 C1
Hillcrest Cl WF10 .....201 B3
Hillcrest Ct 2 LS24 ...189 D5
Hillcrest Dr
Castleford WF10 ....201 B3
Loftus TS13 ....10 D8
Hillcrest Gdns YO51 ..141 A7
Hillcrest Gr 2 YO12 ...75 E5
Hillcrest Mount WF10 .201 B3
Hillgarth WF11 ....201 F2
Hillgarth Ct 4 YO41 ..185 B2
Hillhouse La DL2 ....4 C7
Hillington Rd TS4 ......7 B8
Hillocks La TS12 ....10 A5
Hills La BD22 ....187 A5
Hillsborough Terr 5
YO30 ....228 C7
Hillshaw Parkway
HG4 ....214 D5
Hillside Byram WF11 ..201 E4
Follifoot HG3 ....223 F4
3 Ingleby Arncliffe DL6 ...45 A7
Skipton BD23 ....217 B6
Hillside Cl
18 Addingham LS29 ....174 F4
Bootham Stray YO30 ...225 B2
Monk Fryston LS25 .....202 A8
Threshfield BD23 ......134 B3
Hillside Cres BD23 ....217 C3
Hillside Dr BD23 ......134 B3
Hillside Gdns
Harrogate HG3 ....151 D5
Scarborough YO12 .....212 C1
Hillside Rd HG3 ....222 F3
Hillside Way YO17 ....150 B8
Hilltop Cres DL9 ....40 E4
Hilton Cl DL6 ....210 E8
Hilton Cl DL6 ....210 E8
Hilton Grange DL8 ....210 E8
Hilton La 7 HG5 ......221 A6
Hilton Rd TS9 ....6 F1
Hilton Sq DL6 ....210 E8
Hincks Hall La HG3 ...139 C3
Hinderwell Com Prim Sch
YO12 ....212 D2
Hinderwell La
Hinderwell TS13 ....11 E8
Staithes TS13 ....13 K1
Hinderwell Pl YO12 ...212 D2
Hinderwell Rd YO12 ..212 E1
Hindle Dr 10 YO14 ...101 B3
Hinsley La DN14 ......204 C2
Hinton Ave 8 YO24 ...230 C8
Hinton Cl 9 WF8 .....201 C1
Hinton La WF11 ......201 D3
Hipswell CE Prim Sch
DL9 ....209 F1
Hipswell Rd DL9 ......209 E1
Hipswell Rd W DL9 ...209 C1
Hird Ave 22 BD24 ....131 D2
Hird Rd TS15 ....5 D2
Hirds Yd 3 BD23 .....216 F3
Hirst Courtney & Temple
Hirst CP Sch YO8 ......203 E3
Hirst Rd TS9 ....160 E5
Hirst Rd YO8 ....204 A3
Hirst St WF10 ....200 C8
Hirstead Gdns YO12 ..212 B5
Hirstead Rd YO12 .....212 B8
Hob Cote La BD22 ....187 F1
Hob Moor Com Prim Sch
YO24 ....227 D2
Hob Moor Dr YO24 ...227 E2
Hob Moor Jun Sch
YO24 ....227 C2
Hob Moor Oaks Sch
YO24 ....227 C6
Hobart Rd WF10 ......201 B5
Hobb Nook La LS21 ...176 D4
Hobbs Cl YO7 ....209 C2
Hobgate YO24 ....230 D7
Hobmoor Terr YO24 ...227 E2
Hobson Cl YO23 ......230 B1
Hockney La YO8 ......200 C8
Hodge La WF8 ....206 B8
Hodgson Fold YO23 ..174 E5
Hodgson Hill YO13 ....54 B4
Hodgson La YO26 ....182 F8
Hodgson's La LS25 ...196 A5
Hogg La YO17 ....148 E6
Holbeck Ave
Middlesbrough TS5 .....6 E6
Scarborough YO12 .....213 B2
Holbeck Cl YO11 .....213 B1
Holbeck Hill YO11 .....213 B1
Holbeck Rd YO11 .....213 A2

Holbecks La YO51 ....141 F3
Holburns Croft 3 YO10 .229 B1
Holden Gdns YO8 .....197 D2
Holderness Dr 2 DL3 ...3 A7
Hole House La BB7 ...152 B2
Hole La BD20 ....174 A2
Holes La WF11 ....201 E2
Holgate DL6 ....45 E8
Holgate Bank HG5 ....161 A8
Holgate Bridge Gdn 7
YO24 ....228 A3
Holgate Ct YO17 .....215 C5
Holgate Lodge Dr
YO26 ....227 E4
Holgate Rd YO24 .....233 A1
Holl Gate DL8 ....59 E3
Hollicarrs Cl YO19 ....192 A2
Hollies The YO8 ......198 C4
Hollin Gate LS21 ......176 E1
Hollin Hall Dr LS29 ...175 C2
Hollin La LA2 ....129 F6
Hollin Top La YO21 ...29 C7
Hollies The LS26 ......200 A6
Hollington St 8 BB8 ..186 A3
Hollingwood Gate 51
LS29 ....175 C2
Hollingwood Rise 32
LS29 ....175 C2
Hollingworth Cl BD23 .217 B3
Hollinhurst Brow LA2 ..128 F2
Hollins DL8 ....60 B3
Hollins Beck Cl LS25 ..200 D8
Hollins Cl HG3 ....161 A5
Hollins Cres HG1 .....219 C4
Hollins Gr WF10 ......200 C7
Hollins Hall HG3 ......161 A4
Hollins La Firby DL8 ...63 B1
Hampsthwaite HG3 .....160 F5
Melmerby HG4 ....114 B8
Middleton Quernhow HG4 .88 C1
Rosedale East Side YO18 ..49 D4
Hollins Mews HG1 ....219 C4
Hollins Rd
10 Barnoldswick BB18 ...171 D1
Harrogate HG1 ....219 C4
Hollis Cres YO32 ......167 B6
Hollow Gill Brow
BD24 ....153 C5
Hollow Moor La DL8 ...62 E7
Hollow Bank Gr 3 YO24 .227 F2
Holly Bank Rd YO24 ..227 F2
Holly Cl
Acaster Malbis YO23 ...191 C8
Full Sutton YO41 ......169 A2
Thirsk YO7 ....211 B2
Wrelton YO18 ....71 C1
Holly Ct 11 HG5 ......221 B6
Holly Garth Cl TS9 .....7 F1
Holly Gr Selby YO8 ....232 B3
8 Thorpe Willoughby YO8 ..197 B2
Holly Hill DL10 ....209 C5
Holly Pk LS17 ....178 B3
Holly Rd 10 Bedale DL8 ..63 B3
Boston Spa LS23 ......188 D8
Holly Terr YO10 ......228 D1
Holly Tree Croft 2
YO19 ....184 F7
Holly Tree Ct
5 Hambleton YO8 ......196 F1
2 Whitby YO21 ....208 B6
Holly Tree Garth YO32 .167 E3
Holly Tree La
Dunnington YO19 ......184 F7
Haxby YO32 ....225 D8
Holly Wlk YO12 ......212 D7
Hollybush Ave TS17 ...6 B5
Hollybush Gn LS22 ...188 B8
Hollygarth La DN14 ..202 D4
Hollyhurst Ave 1 TS4 ...6 F8
Hollyhurst Rd DL3 .....3 B6
Hollyrood Rd WF10 ...224 E3
Hollywalk Ave TS6 ....7 E8
Hollywood YO8 ....232 B7
Holm Hill YO13 ......115 C2
Holme La LA2 ....130 C6
Ellerton & Aughton HG3 ..219 C4
Halton East BD23 .....174 B8
Newbiggin DL8 ....58 E1
Rudby TS9 ....25 E7
Holme St 3 BB8 ......186 A3
Holme The 1 YO9 .....26 E4
Holme Ave YO14 .....218 A4
Holmebeck La HG4 ....88 B1
Holmefield Cl 3 YO8 ..232 A1
Holmefield Cres YO4 ..214 C3
Holmefield La YO10 ..229 A1
Holmefield Rd
Glusburn BD20 ....232 A1
Ripon HG4 ....214 C3
Holmefields Rd TS6 ....7 F8
Holmes Cres YO60 ...146 E6
Holmes Dr YO19 .....192 A1
Holmes House YO8 ...199 B1
Holme Ind Est YO8 ...232 D6
Holmes The YO8 .....232 C6

Holmfield HG4 ....112 D7
Holmfield Cl WF8 ......201 C2
Holmfield Dr WF8 ......201 D2
Holmfield La WF8 ......201 C2
Holmstead Ave YO21 ..208 A5
Holmtree La HG4 ....113 B8
Holmwood Ave TS5 ......6 F8
Holnicote Cl **3** TS17 ....6 A3
Holray Pk DN14 ....204 C2
Holroyd Ave YO31 ......229 A5
Holtby Gr YO12 ....212 D5
Holtby La Holtby YO19 ..167 D1
Stockton-on-the-Forest
YO32 ....226 F2
Holy Family RC High Sch
DN14 ....204 C3
Holy Family RC Prim Sch
DL3 ....3 B6
Holy Rood La LS25 ....201 C8
Holy Trinity CE Inf Sch
HG4 ....214 B6
Holy Trinity CE Prim Sch
HG4 ....214 B5
Holyrood Ave DL3 ....3 A5
Holyrood Cl TS17 ......6 B8
Holystone Dr TS17 ......6 A4
Holywell Gn TS16 ......5 E5
Holywell Halt Sta
BD23 ....174 A8
Holywell La
Castleford WF10 ......201 A3
North Cowton DL7 ......22 C2
Home Farm Cl LA2 ....128 A6
Home Office Emergency
Planning Coll YO61 ..143 D6
Homefield Cl YO23 ....230 A2
Homestead Cl
Eggborough DN14 ....203 A2
2 York YO32 ....225 F1
Homestead Garth **1** TS17 ..6 D6
Homestead Rd HG1 ....219 E2
Honey Pot **8** YO8 ....199 D7
Honey Pot Rd **2** DL10 ..41 C6
Honeypot La DL3 ....3 C7
Honeysuckle Cl
Romanby DL7 ....210 C1
Selby YO8 ....232 C2
Honister Gr LS15 ....5 F4
Honolulu Ct **15** TS17 ....5 F4
Hood La YO13 ....54 D2
Hoodstorth La HG3 ....158 F6
Hookstone Ave HG2 ....222 E7
Hookstone Chase
HG2 ....220 D2
Hookstone Chase Com Prim
Sch HG2 ....220 D2
Hookstone Cl HG2 ....220 D2
Hookstone Dr HG2 ....223 A8
Hookstone Garth HG3 ..159 E5
Hookstone Grange Ct **3**
HG2 ....220 C2
Hookstone Grange Way **2**
HG2 ....220 C2
Hookstone Oval **7** HG2 ..220 B1
Hookstone Pk HG2 ....220 C2
Hookstone Rd HG2 ....222 E7
Hookstone Way HG2 ....220 D2
Hookstone Wood Rd **9**
HG2 ....220 B1
Hope St **10** Filey YO14 ..101 B3
Knaresborough HG5 ....221 B5
Scarborough YO12 ....213 A6
York YO10 ....233 C1
Hope Terr **7** YO21 ....208 D5
Hopetown La DL3 ......3 A6
Hopgrove La N YO32 ..226 C3
Hopgrove La S YO32 ..226 E3
Hopper Hill Rd YO11 ....99 F6
Hopper La LS21 ....159 C2
Hopperton St TS5 ......163 E4
Hopps's Rd **8** BD20 ..187 E8
Horcum Ct BD20 ......174 B3
Hornbeam Cl YO30 ....225 B2
Hornbeam Cres HG2 ....222 F8
Hornbeam Pk
Harrogate HG2 ....222 F7
Knaresborough HG2 ....223 A6
Hornbeam Pk Ave
HG2 ....222 F7
Hornbeam Pk Rd HG2 ..222 F7
Hornbeam Pk Sta
HG2 ....222 F7
Hornbeam Sq N HG2 ..223 A7
Hornbeam Sq S HG2 ..223 A7
Hornbeam Sq W HG2 ..223 A7
Hornblower Cl **5** HG4 ..113 D2
Hornby Castle* DL8 ....62 C8
Hornby Cl **1** DL2 ......3 E1
Hornby Rd
Appleton Wiske DL6 ....24 A3
Roeburndale LA2 ......128 A6
Wray-with-Botton LA2 ..128 A6
Horndale Rd **8** YO14 ..101 B4
Horne Rd DL3 ....40 F4
Horner Ave YO61 ......144 A5
Horner Cl YO61 ......144 A5
Horner St YO30 ......228 B7
Horners Terr **15** YO22 ..208 E6
Hornsea Rd TS8 ....6 E5
Hornsey Garth **22** YO32 ..166 E5
Horse Bell Gate LA6 ..103 D4
Horse Course La YO17 ..122 E1
Horse Mill La HG4 ....139 D5
Horse Rd **12** YO22 ....208 E6
Horsefair YO61 ......141 B5
Horseman Ave YO23 ..230 A3
Horseman Cl **2** YO23 ..230 A3
Horseman Dr YO23 ..230 A3

Horseman La YO23 ....230 A3
Horsemarket Rd YO17 ..215 B4
Horsemill Sq HG5 ....221 B5
Horseshoe Cave*
BD24 ....132 A3
Horseshoe Cl DL9 ......40 F4
Horseshoe The YO24 ..230 E7
Horseway Ave YO18 ....49 D4
Horsfield Way YO19 ..184 F7
Horsman Ave YO10 ..233 C1
Horton-in-Ribblesdale CE VC
Prim Sch BD24 ......105 D3
Horton-in-Ribbleside Sta
BD24 ....105 C3
Hospital Fields Rd
YO10 ....228 D1
Hospital La YO8 ......197 B4
Hospital Rd YO17 ....215 B4
Hospitium The* YO1 ..233 A3
Hostess La YO18 ....72 E4
Hotham Ave YO26 ....227 B2
Hothams Ct YO1 ......233 C2
Hothfield Jun Sch
YO10 ....174 C1
Hothfield Terr BD23 ..216 F3
Houghton Ave WF11 ..201 E4
Houghton Banks **3** TS17 ..6 D6
Houndgate DL1 ....3 C5
Houndsway **6** YO24 ..230 B8
House of Correction Mus*
HG4 ....214 D5
Hovingham CE VC Prim Sch
YO62 ....119 E6
Hovingham Dr
6 Guisborough TS14 ....8 F7
Scarborough YO12 ....212 B4
Hovingham Hall*
YO62 ....119 E6
How Hill Rd HG4 ......139 B6
How Stean Gorge*
HG3 ....110 B4
Howard Cl DL10 ....41 F7
Howard Dr YO30 ......224 E2
Howard Link YO30 ....224 D2
Howard Rd
Catterick Garrison DL9 ..209 E1
Towthorpe YO32 ......167 B6
Howard St
8 Scarborough YO12 ..213 A7
York YO10 ....228 D2
Howden Dike TS15 ......5 E2
Howden La YO19 ......231 E1
Howden Rd
4 Barlby YO8 ....198 B4
Romanby DL7 ....210 B2
Silsden BD20 ....174 C1
Howdenshire Way
DN14 ....205 F6
Howdlands La HG4 ....140 E7
Howe Ave DL10 ....41 E3
Howe Bank YO21 ......29 B7
Howe End YO62 ....70 B1
Howe Field Rd YO26 ..142 A2
Howe Hill Bank TS8 ....7 B2
Howe Hill Cl YO26 ....227 E4
Howe Hill La DL10 ....41 C6
Howe Hill Rd YO26 ....227 E4
Howe La YO41 ....170 A5
Howe Rd Malton YO17 ..122 A6
Norton YO17 ....215 E3
Howe St YO24 ....227 D3
Howes Rd **8** YO14 ..127 A8
Howgate DL8 ....57 F6
Howgill La
Barden BD23 ....157 E6
Rimington BB7 ......171 A1
Howhill Quarry Rd
HG3 ....178 B7
Howhill Rd HG3 ......178 B8
Howker La YO61 ......116 F2
Howl Gate YO41 ......185 E8
Howlbeck Rd YO11 ......8 E7
Howldale La
Appleton-le-Moors YO62 ..70 F4
3 Beadlam YO62 ......93 D7
Howlgate La YO21 ......13 A1
Howsham Gates*
YO60 ....146 F2
Howson La BD24 ......131 A4
Hoxton Rd YO12 ....212 F6
Hoylake Rd TS4 ....6 F8
Hoylake Way YO16 ......5 E4
Hubback Sq **5** DL3 ....3 A1
Hubert St **2** YO23 ..228 B1
Huby CE VC Prim Sch
YO61 ....144 A4
Huby St
3 Guisborough TS14 ....8 F7
York YO10 ....228 E3
Huby Rd YO61 ....144 B3
Hudgin La Lockton YO18 ..72 E4
Wykeham YO13 ....98 D4
Hudson Cl
Malton YO17 ....215 C6
Stamford Bridge YO41 ..168 D2
2 Tadcaster LS24 ....189 E6
15 Whitby LS22 ......180 C3
Hudson Cres **2** YO24 ..227 B1
Hudson St
Whitby YO21 ....208 D7
6 York YO30 ......228 D7
Hudson View **1** LS24 ..189 E6
Hudswell La DL10 ....209 C5
Hugden Cl YO18 ......96 A6
Hugden Way YO18 ....215 F4

Huggate Dikes* YO42 170 F2
Huggate Hill YO17 ..170 E7
Hugh Field La YO8 ..199 A8
Hugh Field N La YO8 ..193 A1
Hugh St WF10 ......200 E4
Hull Rd Cliffe YO8 ..198 E2
Hemingbrough YO8 ..199 B1
Osbaldwick YO10 ....229 D3
York YO10 ....229 B3
Humber Dr **5** YO32 ..167 B6
Humber Rd TS17 ....6 B7
Hummersknott Sch &
Language Coll DL3 ....3 A4
Humphrey Balk La
YO7 ....114 D8
Humphrey Hill DL8 ....58 D1
Hundale Rd **8** TS15 ....25 C5
Hunday Field Rd YO51 ..141 E2
Hundens Day Hospl DL1 ..3 E5
Hundens La DL1 ....3 D6
Hungate
Bishop Monkton HG3 ..140 A5
Brompton YO13 ....98 C5
Pickering YO18 ....95 F6
York YO1 ....233 C2
Hungate Cl LS24 ......195 D8
Hungate Com Prim Sch
YO25 ....195 F4
Hungate La YO11 ....126 F8
Hungate La YO14 ....126 F8
Hungate Rd LS25 ....195 F4
Hunger Hill YO1 ....218 C7
Hungerhill La YO62 ....93 F6
Hunmanby Rd
Burton Fleming YO25 ..126 E3
Reighton YO14 ......127 C6
Hunmanby St YO14 ..100 F2
Hunmanby Sta YO14 ..127 A7
Hunmanby Rd YO14 ..233 C3
Hunt House Rd YO22 ..51 B6
Hunt St WF10 ......200 D4
Hunter St **8** YO21 ..208 D7
Hunters Cl
Dunnington YO19 ....184 E7
3 Easingwold YO61 ..143 C8
13 Haxby YO32 ......225 D8
4 Hurworth-on-Tees DL2 ..3 D1
Osgodby YO11 ....100 B7
Hunters Croft BD23 ..156 F1
Hunters Gate DL2 ......4 C3
Hunters Ride DL6 ......24 B3
Hunters Row **6** YO51 ..141 B4
Hunters Way
Norton YO17 ....215 D2
Selby YO8 ....232 B4
York YO24 ....230 F7
Hunters Wlk
Barlow YO8 ....204 D7
Kirk Deighton LS22 ..180 C4
Hunters Wood Way **21**
YO19 ....184 F7
Huntington Mews
YO31 ....228 D7
Huntington Prim Sch
YO32 ....225 F4
Huntington Rd **1** YO31 ..233 C4
Huntington Sec Sch
YO32 ....225 E3
Huntington Sports Club
YO32 ....226 A5
Hunton & Arrathorne Com
Prim Sch DL8 ....61 F7
Hunton Rd DL8 ....40 E1
Huntriss Row YO11 ..213 A6
Huntsman's Wlk YO24 ..227 B1
Huntsmans La YO41 ..168 C2
Hurdle Cl YO17 ......215 D2
Hurgill Rd DL10 ......209 A7
Hurn Rd YO61 ....144 A4
Hurns La YO30 ......224 A7
Hurrell La YO18 ....96 E5
Hurricane Cl LS25 ....196 A4
Hurricane Way YO30 ..224 E3
Hurst Hill BD23 ......217 B4
Hurst Hill HG3 ......159 F7
Hurst's YO1 ....233 C2
Hurstleigh Terr HG1 ..220 A3
Hurworth Comp Sch
DL2 ....22 D8
Hurworth House Sch
DL2 ....22 D8
Hurworth Prim Sch DL2 ..3 E1
Hurworth Rd
Hurworth DL2 ....3 F1
Hurworth-on-Tees DL2 ..22 D8
Neasham DL2 ....4 A1
Hussars Ct **6** YO12 ....75 F5
Husthwaite CE VC Sch
YO61 ....117 B5
Husthwaite Rd
Coxwold YO61 ......117 D7
Easingwold YO61 ....117 B2
Hutchinson Dr DL6 ..210 E3
Hutchinson St **1** YO23 ..232 B6
Hutton Ave DL1 ......3 C4
Hutton Bank
3 Hutton Rudby TS15 ..25 D5
Ripon HG4 ....214 A3
Hutton Cl YO26 ......224 A2
Hutton Cross Rd YO13 ..98 B6
Hutton Gate YO13 ..222 D6
Hutton La
Guisborough TS14 ......8 A5
Hutton Conyers HG4 ..114 A4
Sharow HG4 ....214 D8

Hutton Rae La YO7 ....116 D7
Hutton Rudby Prim Sch
TS15 ....25 C5
Hutton Sq YO26 ......182 A5
Hutton View Rd HG4 ..214 C7
Hutton Village Rd TS14 ..8 D5
Hutton's Mon* DL11 ..39 C6
Hutts La HG4 ....112 C7
Hyde Pk Rd
Harrogate HG1 ......219 E3
Knaresborough HG5 ..221 B8
Hydro Cl LS29 ......218 F3
Hydro Leisure Ctr The
HG2 ....219 C5
Hyrst Gr **28** YO31 ....228 E6

I

Ian St TS17 ....6 B8
I'anson Cl DL8 ......60 D6
I'anson Rd DL10 ......60 D6
Ibbetson Cl **16** HG4 ....86 C3
Iburndale La YO22 ....32 A6
Iddison Dr DL8 ......63 A2
Ikin Way YO32 ......225 F6
Ilkley Gr TS14 ....8 E5
Ilkley Gram Sch LS29 ..218 C3
Ilkley Hall Mews **5**
LS29 ....218 B3
Ilkley Hall Pk **4** LS29 ..218 B3
Ilkley Pool & Lido
LS29 ....218 B5
Ilkley Rd
Addingham LS29 ......175 A4
Ilkley LS29 ....176 C1
Ilkley Sch LS29 ......218 E5
Ilkley Sta LS29 ......218 B4
Ilkley Swimming Baths
LS29 ....218 C5
Ilkley Toy Mus* ∞ 219 B4
Ilton Bank LA6 ....85 E1
Ilton Garth YO30 ....225 A2
Imperial Ave TS17 ......6 B8
In Moor La HG3 ......109 F6
Ing Dene Ave **16** BB8 ..186 A3
Ing Dene Cl BD23 ..155 E3
Ingdale Howl YO62 ..92 C7
Ingdale La YO7 ....66 C3
Ingfield La BD24 ....131 D2
Ingham Cl YO22 ......32 A6
Ingleborough Ave
YO30 ....229 B4
Ingleborough Cave*
LA2 ....104 D2
Ingleborough Dr **4**
BB18 ....171 D1
Ingleborough National
Nature Reserve*
LA6 ....104 D8
Ingleborough Pk Cl **3**
LA6 ....103 D3
Ingleborough Pk Dr **2**
LA6 ....103 D3
Inglebrook Sch WF8 ..201 B1
Ingleby Arncliffe CE VA Prim
Sch DL6 ....45 A8
Ingleby Ave TS9 ......27 B6
Ingleby Dr LS24 ......189 E6
Ingleby Greenhow CE VC
Prim Sch TS9 ......27 C5
Ingleby Manor* TS9 ..27 C4
Ingleby Mill Prim Sch
TS17 ....6 A4
Ingleby Rd
Great & Little Broughton
TS9 ....27 A5
Great Broughton TS9 ..26 E5
Ingleby Way TS17 ......6 B5
Ingleton Dr DL7 ......210 D3
Ingleton Inst Est LA6 ..103 D3
Ingleton Mid Sch LA6 ..103 D3
Ingleton Prim Sch
LA6 ....103 D3
Ingleton Wlk **3** YO31 ..229 A5
Ingman Lodge Rd BD24 ..78 F1
Ingramgate YO17 ....211 C3
Ingrish La YO23 ......182 C1
Ings Active YO8 ......216 D3
Ings Cl **6** Pickering YO18 ..95 F6
5 Willerby YO12 ......99 D2
Ings Com Prim Sch
YO8 ....216 D3
Ings Dr
Low Bradley BD20 ....173 E3
Mickletown LS26 ......200 A5
Ings Field Rd YO26 ..142 A3
Ings La
Ainderby Quernhow YO7 ..88 D4
Beal DN14 ....202 D4
Bishop Monkton HG3 ..140 B5
Bishop Wilton YO42 ..169 D2
Bradleys Both BD20 ..173 E2
Brompton YO13 ....98 B4
Carlton DN14 ....204 E2
Cawood YO8 ....197 D8
Cononley BD20 ......173 D2
Cottingwith YO42 ....193 C5
Crakehall DL8 ....62 F5
Ebberston & Yedingham
YO13 ....97 C4
Great Preston WF10 ..200 E6
Harome YO62 ....93 D4
Hensall DN14 ....203 D1
Husthwaite YO61 ....117 A6
Hutton Buscel YO13 ..99 A3

Ings La *continued*
Kellington DN14 ......202 F4
21 Kirkbymoorside YO62 ..70 B1
Kirkbymoorside YO62 ..94 B7
Lastingham YO62 ......70 F5
Lillings Ambo YO60 ..145 C2
Nether Poppleton YO26 ..224 B1
Pickering YO18 ....95 E4
Riccall YO19 ....197 E8
Roundhill Village TS15 ..5 D2
Skipton BD23 ....216 D2
Snape with Thorp DL8 ..87 B7
Stillington YO61 ......144 A6
Thorganby YO19 ......193 B5
Thorp Arch LS23 ....189 A8
Tollerton YO61 ......143 B2
Welburn YO62 ....94 A5
Wheldrake YO19 ....193 B7
Wighill LS24 ....189 D8
Wilstow YO8 ....99 D2
Wistow YO8 ....198 A6
York YO10 ....229 A1
Ings Mere Ct WF11 ..201 C6
Ings Rd Cliffe YO8 ....198 D2
Dunsforths YO26 ......142 A3
Snaith DN14 ....204 C1
Thorganby YO19 ....193 B4
Ullesket LS24 ......190 C3
West Ayton YO13 ......99 B6
Wilberfoss YO41 ....185 E6
Ings Terr YO22 ......31 C4
Ings View **3** Bedale DL8 ..63 B3
Castleford WF10 ....201 A4
Mickletown LS26 ....200 C6
York YO30 ....224 D2
Ingsgarth 95 F6
Ingthorne La LS25 ..195 F1
Ingthorpe La LS25 ..195 F1
Ingthorpe La
Martons Both BD23 ..171 E7
Monk Fryston LS25 ..196 A1
Inhams La YO22 ......141 F2
Inholmes La
Tadcaster LS24 ......189 D6
Walton LS23 ....181 B2
Inman Gr HG5 ....221 B8
Inman Terr YO26 ....227 D4
Inman Wlk HG5 ......221 B8
Innisfree Cl HG2 ....220 B1
Innovation Cl YO10 ..229 B2
Innovation Way YO10 ..229 B2
Institute St **4** BD20 ..187 E7
Intake Ave YO30 ......228 C8
Intake La
Acaster Malbis YO23 ..191 C7
Beal WF11 ....202 D5
Carlton Miniott YO7 ..209 C2
Dunnington YO19 ....184 F7
Grassington BD23 ....134 E3
Habton DN14 ....121 E7
Heck DN14 ....207 C8
Tollerton YO61 ......143 B4
West Haddlesey YO8 ..202 F6
Intake The
3 Kippax LS25 ......194 D1
Osgodby YO11 ....100 B7
Intakefield Rd YO8 ..199 D7
Invicta Ct YO24 ......230 B8
Ireby Rd LA6 ....102 F3
Ireton St **2** YO31 ..228 C7
Iron Row LS29 ......176 C1
Irton Moor La YO12 ..212 A1
Irvine Way YO24 ....230 B7
Irwin Ave YO31 ......228 E6
Isabella Rd LS25 ....194 D5
Island Heritage* HG4 ..214 B8
Islebeck La YO7 ......115 F8
Iver Cl YO26 ....227 C5
Ivy Bank Ct **4** LS25 ....75 D5
Ivy Cl Follifoot HG3 ..223 F4
Marton YO19 ....141 D1
Ivy Cotts DL7 ....210 D4
Ivy Cres DL8 ....62 B4
Ivy Ct LS29 ....218 B3
Ivy House Cl **1** YO11 ..100 B6
Ivy House Gdns BD23 ..155 D1
Ivy La LS23 ....188 E8
Ivy Pl YO32 ....225 D3
Ivy Yd **18** YO22 ......208 E6

J

Jack Field La BD20 ..187 D6
Jack Hill La LS21 ....176 F6
Jack Hole YO61 ......142 F4
Jack La Crayke YO61 ..118 A1
Stillington YO61 ......144 C7
Wigglesworth BD23 ..153 C4
Jackson Cl YO11 ....100 B6
Jackson Dr TS9 ......26 C8
Jackson La YO41 ....185 E4
Jackson St
24 Glusburn BD20 ..187 E7
York YO31 ....233 C4
Jackson's La
Bradleys Both BD20 ..173 F3
Eastfield YO11 ......100 A8
Scarborough YO11 ..100 A8
Jacobs Cl YO8 ......199 D7
Jacobi Cl YO13 ......228 A7
Jacques Gr BD20 ....174 C1
Jacques' La YO8 ....198 E4
Jaffa Rd DL9 ....209 E2
Jagger La DL10 ....20 E6

Jagoe Rd **6** BB18 ....172 A1
James Backhouse Pl
YO24 ....227 E3
James Cl LS25 ....194 D4
James Ct DL10 ....209 F7
James La DL10 ....41 A2
James Nicholson Way
YO30 ....225 A2
James Nicolson Link
YO30 ....225 A2
James Pl **2** YO12 .....213 A6
James St
Castleford WF10 ....200 E5
20 Earby BB18 ....172 A1
18 Glusburn BD20 ....187 E8
Harrogate HG1 ....219 D2
Scarborough YO12 ......213 A6
Selby YO8 ....232 C5
York YO10 ....228 E4
Jameson Cres YO12 .212 D5
Jamesville Way YO7 .115 B6
Jamieson Terr YO23 .228 B1
Janesway LS25 ....194 C1
Janet's Foss* BD23 .133 B2
Jasmine Cl
16 Snaith DN14 ....204 C1
York YO32 ....225 D2
Jasper La HG3 ....179 A3
Jay Ave TS17 ....6 B4
Jaywick Cl YO32 ....167 B8
Jedburgh Dr DL3 ....2 F7
Jedwell Cl YO32 ....225 D5
Jerry Carr Bank YO62 .92 B1
Jerry Croft **2** BD23 ...217 A4
Jerry La BD20 ....174 F1
Jersey Ct YO12 ....99 C7
Jervaulx Abbey* HG4 .85 D8
Jervaulx Dr HG5 ....221 D4
Jervaulx Rd DL7 ....64 A6
Jervis Ct YO41 ....185 C1
Jervis Rd YO24 ....230 E8
Jesmond Ct YO17 ....215 E3
Jesmond Gr **5** TS18 .....5 E8
Jesmond Rd
Darlington DL1 ....3 F7
Harrogate HG1 ....220 A3
Jew Leys La YO23 .....190 F3
Jewbury YO31 ....233 C3
Jewitt La LS22 ....188 B8
Jin Whin Ct WF10 .....200 D4
Jin-Whin Hill WF10 ...200 C4
Jobbing Cross YO61 ..116 C3
Jockey La
Huntington YO32 ....225 F2
5 Knaresborough HG5 ..221 A6
Joffre Ave WF10 ....200 F3
John Breckon Rd YO21 .28 A5
John Dixon La DL1 ....3 D5
John of Gaunt's Castle*
HG3 ....160 B1
John Smiths Brewery*
LS24 ....189 E6
John St Darlington DL1 ..3 D6
11 Earby BB18 ....172 A1
33 Filey YO14 ....101 B3
Great Ayton TS9 ....8 A2
11 Harrogate HG1 ....219 D2
Selby YO8 ....232 D6
Whitby YO21 ....208 D7
York YO31 ....228 E6
Johnson Cl
Brompton on Swale DL10 ..41 C7
1 Thirsk YO7 ....211 C3
Johnson St YO8 ....232 B6
Johnson Way YO7 .....211 D2
Joilby La Cleasby DL10 ....2 E1
Croft-on-Tees DL2 ....22 B8
Newton Morrell DL10 ...21 F8
Jonah's La HG3 ....160 B1
Jonathan Garth **17** LS29 .174 F4
Jorvik* YO1 ....233 C2
Jorvik Cl YO26 ....227 C5
Joseph Rowntree Sec Sch
YO32 ....225 E5
Jowett's La BD20 ......174 B4
Jowland Winn La YO8 .204 A4
Jubbergate YO1 ....233 B2
Jubilee Bank TS7 ....7 C8
Jubilee Cave* BD24 ..131 F4
Jubilee Ct BD23 ....216 D3
Jubilee Croft BD23 ....153 F5
Jubilee Ct
Richmond DL10 ....209 E8
6 Tollerton YO61 ....143 B3
Wigginton YO32 ....225 D8
Jubilee Rd
Norton YO17 ....215 E3
Wistow YO8 ....197 D6
Jubilee Terr YO26 .....227 F5
Judson Cl HG4 ....214 C4
Julia Ave YO32 ....226 B2
Junction Farm Prim Sch
TS16 ....5 D5
Juniper Cl YO32 ....225 D3
Juniper Gr TS21 ....5 C8
Juniper Way **28** HG3 ...161 B3
Jura Dr DL1 ....3 E8

Jute Rd YO26 ....227 B5
Jutland Rd DL9 ....209 C2

K

Kader Ave TS5 ....6 D7
Kader Prim Sch TS5 .....6 E7
Kail La BD23 ....156 F8
Kangel Cl HG4 ....214 E3
Kaneon Ave **3** YO12 ...99 E6
Kathryn Ave YO32 .....226 A2
Kay House La TS15 .....24 D5
Kaye Dr YO8 ....198 B4
Kays Bank YO61 ....117 C5
Kearby Cliff LS22 ......179 B1
Kearsley Cl TS16 ....5 E7
Kearsley Rd HG4 ......214 B7
Kearton DL11 ....37 D6
Keasden Rd LA2 ....130 A3
Keats Cl
4 Pontefract WF8 .....201 B1
York YO30 ....227 F8
Keats Wlk HG1 ....219 E2
Keble Cl YO23 ....231 B3
Keble Dr YO23 ....231 A2
Keble Garth LS25 .....194 E1
Keble Gdns YO23 .....231 B2
Keble Pk Cres YO23 ..231 A2
Keble Pk N YO23 ......231 A3
Keble Pk S YO23 ....231 A2
Keeper's Cl YO61 .....118 A1
Keeper's Hill YO25 ...150 A1
Keepers Gate **18** YO18 .95 F6
Keepers Way **11** YO19 .184 F7
Keighley Rd
Bradleys Both BD20 ...173 D3
1 Colne BB8 ....186 A3
Cowling BD22 ....187 B6
Glusburn BD20 ....187 F7
Ilkley LS29 ....218 A2
Laneshaw Bridge BB8 .186 D3
Skipton BD23 ....216 F2
Trawden Forest BB8 ...186 B3
Keilder Rise TS8 ....6 F5
Keith Ave YO32 ....226 A4
Kelber La TS4 ....6 F8
Kelbrook Prim Sch
BB18 ....186 A7
Kelbrook Rd BB18 .....171 D1
Kelcbar Cl LS24 ....189 D6
Kelcbar Hill LS24 ......189 D6
Kelcbar Way LS24 ....189 D6
Kelcow Caves* BD24 .131 D3
Keld Cl Melmerby HG4 .114 B6
Pickering YO18 ....95 E7
Scalby YO12 ....212 B8
Keld Head Orch **1** YO62 .70 B1
Keld Head Rd YO62 ....70 A1
Keld La
Hutton-le-Hole YO62 ...70 C5
Newton YO18 ....70 A5
Thorpe Bassett YO17 .123 A3
Keld Runnels Rd YO13 .75 A4
Keldale **4** YO32 ......166 F5
Keldale Gdns HG4 .....214 F6
Keldgate Rd YO18 ......72 A3
Keldhead YO18 ....95 E8
Keldheads La DL8 ......59 F5
Kelfield Rd **8** YO19 ..197 F8
Kell Bank HG4 ....214 A8
Kell Bank CE Prim Sch
HG4 ....85 E3
Kell Beck **1** YO21 ....176 F1
Kell Syke La BD23 ....155 A6
Kellington La DN14 ...202 F2
Kellington Prim Sch
DN14 ....202 F3
Kelvin Terr DL7 ....210 D4
Kemmel Cl DL9 ....40 E2
Kempton Cl **2** YO24 .227 D1
Kempton Ct **13** DL1 .....3 F6
Kendal Cl
8 Dunnington YO19 ..184 F7
Hellifield BD23 ....154 B3
Kendal Dr WF10 ....201 B4
Kendal Gate YO26 ....180 D7
Kendal La YO26 ....181 D7
Kendal Rd
Harrogate HG1 ....220 B3
Long Preston BD23 .....154 A3
Kendalmans **4** BD24 .131 D2
Kendrew St **3** DL3 ....3 C6
1 York YO32 ....167 B7
Kenilworth Ave HG2 .220 D7
Kenilworth Dr **3** BB18 .172 A1
Kenlay Cl YO32 ....225 D4
Kennedy Dr **32** YO32 .166 E5
Kennels La LS14 ....188 A4
Kennet La LS25 ....194 D3
Kenneth Campbell Rd
HG1 ....219 E2
Kennion Ct **2** HG2 ..220 B3
Kennion Rd HG2 ....220 B3
Kenrick Pl **5** YO26 ..227 B5
Kensal Rise YO10 .....228 D2
Kensington
Eston & South Bank TS6 ..7 E8
Thorner LS14 ....188 A3
Kensington Ct **1** YO24 .230 F8
Kensington Gdns DL1 ..3 E5
Kensington Sq **16** HG2 .220 C3
Kensington St YO23 .228 B1
Kent Ave HG1 ....219 B3
Kent Cl HG4 ....214 A6
Kent Ct **7** DL9 ....209 C1
Kent Dr HG1 ....219 B3

Kent Rd Guisborough TS14 ..8 E5
Harrogate HG1 ....219 B3
Selby YO8 ....232 A6
Kent Rd N HG1 ....219 B3
Kent Rise HG1 ....219 A2
Kent St YO10 ....233 C1
Kentmere Dr YO30 ....224 F1
Kenton Cl **4** TS18 ......5 E8
Kerride YO30 ....227 E8
Kershaw Ave WF10 ...201 A4
Kerver La YO19 ....184 F7
Kesteven Rd TS4 ....7 A7
Kestrel Dr **7** DL9 ......40 F2
Kestrel Mews **21** WF6 .200 A1
Kestrel View **7** YO12 ..99 E6
Kestrel Wood Way
YO31 ....225 F2
Keswick Dr WF10 .....200 C5
Keswick Gr
Darlington DL1 ....3 D4
Middlesbrough TS5 ....6 D7
Keswick Way **5** YO32 .225 F5
Kettle End DL10 ....21 C7
Kettle Spring La HG3 .139 B1
Kettlesbeck Brow LA2 .130 C5
Kettlesing Felliscliffe Com
Prim Sch HG3 ....160 C4
Kettlestring La YO30 .225 A5
Kettlewell La DL8 ......57 A5
Kettlewell Prim Sch
BD23 ....108 A3
Kew at Castle Howard*
YO60 ....146 C8
Kex Gill Rd HG3 ....158 F2
Kexby Ave YO10 ......228 F3
Kexby Bridge* YO41 .185 C6
Kexby Stray YO41 ....185 B5
Key La YO61 ....118 A1
Key Way YO19 ....231 F5
Keys Beck Rd YO18 ...71 F8
Keystone Ave **3** WF10 .200 F3
Khyber Pass YO11 ....213 A6
Kiddal La LS15 ....188 C2
Kidstones Bank DL8 ...81 E3
Kielder Dr DL3 ....3 E7
Kielder Oval HG2 .....220 D2
Kilburn Rd YO10 ......228 D2
Kildale Sta YO21 ....27 E8
Kildare Garth **3** YO62 ..70 C1
Kildwick CE VC Prim Sch
BD20 ....187 F8
Kilgram La HG4 ....85 E8
Kilham Rd YO25 ....151 D5
Killerby Dr **8** DL10 ...41 E4
Killerby La YO11 ....100 C5
Killin Rd DL1 ....3 E7
Killinghall CE Prim Sch
HG3 ....161 C5
Kilmarnock Rd DL1 .....3 E8
Kiln Hill La
Lawkland LA2 ....131 A6
Silsden BD20 ....174 A1
Kiln La LA2 ....128 A6
Kilners Croft **11** LS29 .174 F4
Kilnsey Fold BD20 .....174 A1
Kilnsey Pk* BD23 .....134 B6
Kilnwick Ct DL7 ....210 D3
Kilton La TS12 ....9 F7
Kilton Thorpe La TS13 ..10 B8
Kimberley St LS29 ....218 C5
Kimberlows Wood Hill **3**
YO10 ....229 C3
Kinbrace Dr YO24 .....230 B7
Kinderland* YO12 ....213 E8
King Edward Ave
WF10 ....200 C7
King Edward St
27 Glusburn BD20 ....187 E7
Normanton South WF6 .200 A1
King Edward's Dr
HG1 ....219 D5
King George Rd **1** HG4 .214 C3
King Hill YO14 ....101 A4
King James Rd HG5 ..221 B5
King James's Sch
HG5 ....221 B5
King Rudding Cl **6**
YO19 ....198 A8
King Rudding La YO19 .198 B8
King St
Castleford WF10 ....200 F3
6 Cawood YO8 ....197 B8
Muston YO14 ....101 B2
Normanton South WF6 .200 A1
Pateley Bridge HG3 ...137 B4
Richmond DL10 ....209 C6
Ripon HG4 ....214 C4
Scarborough YO11 .....213 A6
York YO1 ....233 B2
King's Cl **8** DL10 ......41 D5
King's Gate LA2 ....130 D3
King's Gdns YO7 ....211 B1
King's Manor Sch TS5 ..6 E7
King's Rd **6** HG1 .....219 D3
King's Sq YO1 ....233 C2
King's St BD23 ....217 B4
King's Staith YO1 .....233 B2
Kingfisher Cl **7** YO12 ..99 F6
Kingfisher Ct
22 Pontefract WF10 ...200 A1
3 Scotton DL9 ....40 F2
Kingfisher Dr
3 Bedale DL8 ....63 B3
Bishopthorpe YO13 ......63 D6
10 Pickering YO18 ....95 F6
Whitby YO22 ....208 E3

Kingfisher Reach
17 Boroughbridge YO51 .141 B5
8 Collingham LS22 ....180 A1
Kings Acre YO31 ....229 B6
Kings Arms Ct YO7 ...211 B3
Kings Ave **2** LS29 ....218 A4
Kings Cl **5** Barlby YO8 .198 B5
Kings Hall* LS29 ....218 B4
Kings Keld Bank DL8 ..86 F8
Kings La YO13 ....97 D5
Kings Lea YO8 ....199 A8
Kings Mdws YO7 ....89 E3
Kings Mead HG4 ....214 B7
Kings Moor Rd YO32 .167 D2
Kings Rd Ilkley LS29 .218 A4
Knaresborough HG5 ..221 C6
Kingsclere YO32 ....225 F6
Kingsland Terr **11** YO26 .227 F5
Kingsley Ave WF11 ..201 D3
Kingsley Cl HG1 ....220 C3
Kingsley Dr
Castleford WF10 ....201 B3
Harrogate HG1 ....220 C3
2 Middleham DL8 ....60 E2
Kingsley Pk Mews **1**
HG1 ....220 C3
Kingsley Pk Rd HG1 .220 C3
Kingsley Rd
Harrogate HG1 ....220 B5
Trawden Forest B88 ...186 B3
Kingsthorpe YO24 .....227 D2
Kingston Ave YO24 ...214 C3
Kingston Cres YO30 .196 E2
Kingston Dr
24 Castleford WF6 .....200 B1
Hambleton YO8 ....196 E1
18 Normanton WF6 .....200 B1
Norton YO17 ....215 E2
Kingston Garth **2** YO22 ..33 C3
Kingston Gr **5** YO12 .212 B7
Kingstonia Gdns **3**
HG4 ....214 C5
Kingsway
Garforth LS25 ....194 B3
Harrogate HG1 ....219 E3
Pontefract WF8 ....201 B2
Scalby YO12 ....212 C8
8 Stamford Bridge YO41 .168 D2
Weeton LS17 ....178 B2
Kingsway Dr
Harrogate HG1 ....219 E2
4 Ilkley LS29 ....218 A4
Kingsway Garth LS25 .194 B3
Kingsway N YO30 ....227 D8
Kingsway W YO24 ....227 D1
Kingswood Gr YO24 .227 D2
Kinloss Cl TS17 ....6 C7
Kinsey Cave* BD24 ..131 C4
Kintyre Dr **1** YO7 ......6 B6
Kiplin Dr **14** DN6 .....206 E2
Kiplin Hall* DL10 ....42 B4
Kippax Ash Tree Prim Sch
LS25 ....194 D1
Kippax Greenfield Prim Sch
LS25 ....194 D1
Kippax Leisure Ctr
LS25 ....200 D8
Kippax N Jun & Inf Sch
LS25 ....194 D1
Kir Cres YO24 ....227 C2
Kirby Hill CE Prim Sch
YO51 ....141 B7
Kirby La
Ebberston & Yedingham
YO17 ....97 E1
Sledmere YO25 ....150 A4
Kirby Misperton La
YO17 ....121 C7
Kirby Misperton Rd
YO17 ....95 F2
Kirk Balk YO17 ....169 E8
Kirk Balk La YO60 ....168 B7
Kirk Bank
Conistone with Kilnsey
BD23 ....133 D3
Kirkby Malzeard HG4 .112 A5
Kirk Fenton Parochial CE VC
Prim Sch LS24 ....196 B8
Kirk Gate
Brompton YO13 ....98 C7
Silpho YO13 ....74 E6
Kirk Hammerton CE Prim Sch
YO26 ....164 C2
Kirk Hammerton La
YO26 ....164 C3
Kirk Hills LS14 ....188 A3
Kirk Ings La YO7 ....66 B7
Kirk La
Embsay with Eastby
BD23 ....217 E8
Tockwith YO26 ....181 C7
Kirk Rd Eaglescliffe TS15 ..5 F2
Northallerton DL7 .....210 B3
Kirk Smeaton CE VC Prim
Sch **49** LS25 ....206 B3
Kirk Syke La BD23 ...155 A6
Kirk View **1** YO26 ...227 C3
Kirkby & Great Broughton CE
VA Prim Sch TS9 ....26 B5
Kirkby Ave Ripon HG4 .214 A6
Selby YO8 ....232 B7
Kirkby Cl HG4 ....214 A6
Kirkby Dr HG4 ....214 A6

Kirkby Fleetham CE Prim Sch
DL7 ....42 C1
Kirkby in Malhamdale United
VA Prim Sch BD23 ....154 F8
Kirkby La
Gillamoor YO62 ....70 A3
Kearby with Netherby
HG3 ....179 B2
Kirkby TS9 ....26 D6
Kirkby Fleetham with Fencote
DL7 ....42 C2
Sicklinghall LS29 ....179 D3
Kirkby Malzeard CE Prim Sch
HG4 ....112 D5
Kirkby Overblow CE Prim Sch
HG3 ....179 A4
Kirkby Rd
North Stainley with Sleningford
HG4 ....113 C4
Ripon HG4 ....214 A6
Selby YO8 ....232 B7
Kirkbymoorside Com Prim
Sch YO62 ....70 A1
Kirkcaldy Fold WF6 ..200 B1
Kirkcroft YO32 ....225 C8
Kirkdale La YO62 ....93 F8
Kirkdale Rd YO10 .....229 D4
Kirkdale Way HG2 ....219 C1
Kirkfield Ave LS14 ...188 A3
Kirkfield Cres LS14 ..188 A3
Kirkfield La LS14 .....188 A3
Kirkfield Rd DL3 ....3 D8
Kirkgate
Knaresborough HG5 ..221 A6
7 Middleham DL8 ....60 E2
Ripon HG4 ....214 C5
Settle BD24 ....131 D2
Sherburn in Elmet LS25 .195 E4
Silsden BD20 ....174 C1
Thirsk YO7 ....211 B3
Kirkgate La YO62 ....70 F4
Kirkham Augustinian Priory
(rems of)* YO60 ......146 F4
Kirkham Ave **1** YO31 .228 E8
Kirkham Bridge*
YO60 ....146 F4
Kirkham Cl **6** YO21 ..208 C6
Kirkham Cl LS25 ......221 C4
Kirkham Gr HG1 ......219 F6
Kirkham Pl HG1 ....219 F6
Kirkham Rd
Harrogate HG1 ....219 F6
Middlesbrough TS7 ....7 D6
Whitby YO21 ....208 C6
Kirkham View YO60 .147 B4
Kirkland Cl YO10 ......228 E8
Kirklands **1** WF11 ..201 D3
Kirklands YO32 ....167 B6
Kirklands La **1** YO32 .169 C2
Kirklevington Prim Sch
TS15 ....24 E8
Kirkstall Dr BB18 .....171 E2
Kirkstone Dr YO31 ...229 A6
Kirkstone Rd HG1 ....220 B4
Kirkwell YO23 ....231 A4
Kit La BD20 ....174 B8
Kitchen Dr YO8 ....232 D4
Kitchener Cl YO8 .....232 D4
Kitchener Rd
Ripon HG4 ....113 D3
Scotton DL9 ....40 E4
Kitchener St Selby YO8 .232 B6
York YO31 ....228 D7
Kitemere Pl **2** YO24 .230 B8
Kitter La YO21 ....31 C8
Kitty Garth YO19 .....193 A7
Kitty Hill (Tumulus)*
YO41 ....169 C3
Knapping Hill HG1 ...219 C5
Knapton Cl **11** YO32 .167 B6
Knapton La YO26 .....227 B4
Knapton Wold Rd
YO17 ....122 A3
Knaresborough Ave TS7 ..7 B5
Knaresborough Castle*
HG5 ....221 A5
Knaresborough House &
Gdns* HG5 ....221 A5
Knaresborough Mus*
HG5 ....221 A5
Knaresborough Rd
Bishop Monkton HG3 ..140 B4
Follifoot HG3 ....223 F5
Harrogate HG2 ....219 F2
Little Ribston LS22 .....180 A8
Ripon HG4 ....214 C6
Knaresborough Sta
HG5 ....221 A6
Knaresborough Swimming
Pool HG5 ....221 B5
Knavesmire Cl YO10 ..93 C5
Knavesmire Cres
YO23 ....228 B1
Knavesmire Prim Sch
YO23 ....228 B1
Knavesmire Rd **1** YO23 .228 A1
Knayton CE VC Prim Sch
YO7 ....65 E3
Kneeton La DL10 ....21 C5
Knightsway LS25 .....194 B3
Knipe Point Dr **8** YO11 .100 B8
Knoll The
3 Bramham LS23 .....188 E6
York YO24 ....227 B2
Knolls Cl **11** YO11 ....100 B7
Knolls La YO62 ....67 F5
Knot La BB7 ....171 A5

Knott La
  Easingwold YO61 ....143 C8
  Steeton with Eastburn
  BD20 ....187 F7
Knott Rd YO18 ....49 D5
Knottingley England La Jun &
  Inf Sch WF11 ....201 A2
Knottingley High Sch
  WF11 ....201 A2
Knottingley Rd WF8 ....201 D1
Knottingley Sta WF11 ...201 F2
Knotto Bottom Cl DL6 ...210 F3
Knotto Bottom Way
  DL6 ....210 F3
Knotts La BD23 ....152 E1
Knowle La
  Ilton-cum-Pott HG4 .....85 D1
  Kirby Knowle YO7 ....66 C2
Knowles Cl **5** TS15 .....24 E8
Knox Ave HG1 ....219 C5
Knox Chase HG1 ....219 C6
Knox Cl HG1 ....219 C6
Knox Dr HG1 ....219 C6
Knox Gdns HG1 ....219 C6
Knox Gr HG1 ....219 C6
Knox La Harrogate HG1 .219 D6
  Scarborough YO11 ......213 B1
Knox Mill Bank HG3 .....219 B7
Knox Mill Cl HG3 ....219 B7
Knox Mill La HG3 ....219 B7
Knox Pk HG3 ....219 B7
Knox Rd HG1 ....219 C6
Knox Rise HG1 ....219 C6
Knox Way HG1 ....219 C5
Kyle Cl **3** YO61 ....143 B3
Kyle Way YO61 ....227 B8
Kyme Castle* LS24 .....189 C7
Kyme St YO1 ....233 B1

L

La Bassee Rd DL9 ......209 D1
Laburnum Ave
  Fylingdales YO22 ....33 C4
  Thornaby TS17 ....6 B7
Laburnum Cl
  5 Catterick Garrison DL9 .209 B1
  Rufforth YO23 ....182 C6
  3 Snaith DN14 ....204 C1
  3 Thorpe Willoughby YO8 .197 B1
Laburnum Ct **1** WF10 ..200 F7
Laburnum Dr HG2 ....140 A5
Laburnum Garth **6**
  YO31 ....228 F8
Laburnum Gr
  Harrogate HG1 ....219 E6
  Richmond DL10 ....209 D8
  Stillingfleet YO19 ......191 D4
  Whitby YO21 ....208 B6
Laburnum Rd TS7 ....7 D8
Lacey Ave YO12 ....209 D7
Lachman Rd BB8 ....186 A2
Lack La YO62 ....93 C2
Lackon Bank HG3 ....160 D6
Lacy Gr LS22 ....180 C2
Ladgate La TS5 ....6 F6
Lady Anne Ct YO1 ......233 B1
Lady Balk La WF8 ......201 B1
Lady Edith's Ave YO12 .212 B6
Lady Edith's Cres
  YO12 ....212 B6
Lady Edith's Dr YO12 ...212 A6
Lady Edith's Pk YO12 ...212 B7
Lady Elizabeth Hastings CE
  Prim Sch LS23 ....180 F1
Lady Elizabeth Hastings CE
  Sch LS22 ....180 A1
Lady Grace's Ride
  YO12 ....212 A3
Lady Hamilton Gdns
  YO24 ....227 E2
Lady Hartley Ct BB8 ...186 B3
Lady Hullocks Ct **12** TS9 .26 C7
Lady La HG3 ....222 A5
Lady Lumley's Sch
  YO18 ....95 F7
Lady Mill Garth YO30 ..228 B8
Lady Peckitts Yd YO1 ..233 B2
Lady Rd YO30 ....228 B8
Lady Wortley Pl YO23 ..231 B6
Ladycarr La YO61 ......143 E8
Ladysmith Ave YO21 ...208 C7
Ladysmith Mews **13**
  YO32 ....167 A7
Ladysmith Rd DL9 ......40 C4
Ladywell La YO51 ......141 C5
Ladywell Rd YO51 .....141 B5
Lairs Cres YO13 ....98 A5
Lairs La YO13 ....98 A5
Lairum Rise LS23 ......188 E7
Laith Staid La LS25 ....195 D4
Laithbutts La LA2 ......130 B8
Lake View HG4 ....201 B2
Lakeber Ave LA2 ......129 A8
Lakeber Dr LA2 ....129 A8
Lakeside
  Acaster Malbis YO23 ...191 C7
  Darlington DL1 ....3 C4
  Hunmanby Sands YO14 .101 B1
Lakeside Cl LS29 ......218 A5
Lakeside Ct **20** WF6 ..200 B1
Lakeside Mdws **1** WF8 .201 B2
Laking La YO25 ....126 A3

Lamb Inn Rd **9** WF11 ..202 A2
Lamb La TS17 ....6 A4
Lamb's La TS9 ....27 B4
Lambert Ct YO1 ....233 B1
Lambert Meml Hospl
  YO7 ....211 B2
Lambert St
  11 Skipton BD23 ....217 A3
  2 Trawden BB8 ....186 B1
Lambeth St **8** BB8 ....186 A3
Lambourne Dr TS7 ....7 C6
Lambs La **13** YO10 ....55 F7
Lamel St YO10 ....229 A3
Lamplugh Cres YO23 ...223 B1
Lanacar La DL8 ....56 A4
Lancar Cl **18** YO32 ...166 D5
Lancaster Cl **9** YO13 ...75 D5
Lancaster Pk Rd HG2 ..220 A3
Lancaster Rd
  Harrogate HG2 ....219 C1
  North Cowton DL7 ......22 C2
Lancaster St **6** YO11 ..213 A6
Lancaster Way
  Middlesbrough TS17 ......6 B6
  17 Scalby YO13 ....75 D5
  York YO30 ....225 A1
Lancers Ct **4** YO12 ...75 F5
Landalewood Rd YO30 ..224 F2
Landau Ct YO30 ....227 F8
Landing La
  Asselby DN14 ....205 D6
  Barlby with Osgodby
  YO8 ....232 F8
  Haxby YO32 ....225 B4
  Hemingbrough YO8 .....204 F8
  Riccall YO19 ....197 F8
Landing Rd YO8 ....232 F5
Landings The **21** YO32 .166 F5
Lands La HG5 ....220 E7
Lane Ends La BD22 ....187 B7
Lane Foot Rd HG3 ......159 E8
Lane House La BB8 .....186 B1
Lane House Rd BD22 ...187 A6
Lane The
  Gate Helmsley YO41 ...168 B2
  Mickleby TS13 ....12 A4
Lanehead La DL11 ......18 H8
Lanehouse Rd TS17 ......6 B8
Laneshaw Bridge Prim Sch
  BB8 ....186 B3
Lang Ave YO10 ....229 A4
Lang Gate YO13 ....74 E4
Lang Kirk Cl **2** BD20 ..173 F1
Lang Rd
  Bishopthorpe YO23 ....230 F4
  York YO32 ....225 F6
Langbar Rd LS29 ......218 A6
Langbaurgh Cl TS9 ......8 A2
Langbaurgh Rd TS15 ...25 C4
Langber End La LA6 ...103 D1
Langber La BD23 ....154 A6
Langborne Rd **10** YO21 .208 D6
Langborne Rd YO21 ....208 D6
Langburn's Bank YO21 ..29 A7
Langcliffe Ave HG2 ....220 B3
Langcliffe Ave E HG2 ..222 B8
Langcliffe Com Prim Sch
  BD24 ....131 E4
Langcliffe Garth BD23 ..131 D3
Langcliffe Rd BD24 ....131 D3
Langdale **4** YO24 ......230 C7
Langdale Ave
  3 Pontefract WF6 .....200 A2
  York YO31 ....229 B6
Langdale Dr **2** WF6 ...200 A2
Langdale Gr YO8 ......232 B3
Langdale Mews **4** WF6 .200 A2
Langdale Rd **3** YO12 ..212 F7
Langdale Terr YO21 ....208 C7
Langdon Way TS16 ......5 D5
Langfield La HG3 ......160 B5
Langford Cl **21** LS29 ..176 C1
Langford Ct **17** LS29 ..176 C1
Langford La LS29 ......176 C1
Langford Mews **19** LS29 176 C1
Langford Rd LS29 ......176 C1
Langford Ride **30** LS29 176 C1
Langholm Cres DL3 ......3 C5
Langholme Dr YO26 ...227 C6
Langholme Dr **2** DL11 ..38 B6
Langley Ave YO12 .....212 A8
Langley Ct **1** YO12 ...225 F6
Langley Dr **6** YO12 ...215 E1
Langnaby Rd DN6 ......205 F6
Langrickgate La YO42 ..193 C5
Langsett Ave **7** YO14 ..101 A3
Langsett Gr YO30 .....224 F1
Langstrothdale Rd
  BD24 ....105 D7
Langthwaite La DL8 ....59 C3
Langton Prim Sch
  YO25 ....151 C1
Langton Crossroads
  YO17 ....148 B6
Langton Ct **1** YO32 ...167 A6
Langton La YO17 ......148 C8
Langton Prim Sch
  YO17 ....147 F5
Langton Rd
  Norton YO17 ....215 E2
Langwith Ave LS22 ....188 A8
Langwith Stray YO10 ..184 C7
Lansdown Way **7** YO32 166 F5
Lansdowne Cl YO17 ...215 E4

Lansdowne Terr **5**
  YO10 ....228 E3
Lanshaw Bank BD23 ...175 A7
Lanshaw Croft YO30 ..224 F1
Lansbury Dr TS13 ......10 D8
Larch Gr **8** Filey YO14 .101 B4
  Pannal HG3 ....222 E2
Larch Rd **6** YO7 ......89 A1
Larch Rise **4** YO61 ...117 D1
Larchfield YO31 ....229 C7
Larchfield Com TS8 .....6 F4
Larchfield Sports Ctr
  DL3 ....3 C5
Larchfield St DL3 ....3 C5
Lark Hill HG4 ....214 A7
Lark Hill Cres **15** HG4 .113 D2
Lark Hill Dr HG4 ......214 A6
Lark La HG4 ....214 A6
Larkfield Cl
  1 Copmanthorpe YO23 .230 A3
  Harrogate HG2 ....222 A7
Larkfield Dr HG2 ......222 A7
Larkfield Rd
  Harrogate HG2 ....222 A7
  Selby YO8 ....232 A4
Larkfield Way HG2 ....222 A7
Larkhill YO14 ....214 A6
Larkspur Gr **14** HG4 ...161 B3
Larkspur Rd TS7 ....7 A6
Larpool Cres YO22 ....208 C2
Larpool Dr YO22 ......208 D3
Larpool La YO22 ......208 D4
Larpool La Ind Est
  YO22 ....208 D5
Larun Beat The TS15 ....5 E2
Lascelles Ct DL6 ......210 E4
Lascelles Gr HG2 .....222 B7
Lascelles La
  Malton YO17 ....215 E6
  Northallerton DL6 .....210 E4
Lascelles Rd HG2 .....222 B8
Lascelles La
  YO10 ....228 D2
Latimer La TS14 ....8 E6
Latimer Rd DL1 ....3 E7
Lauderdale Dr TS14 .....8 F6
Laughton Ave YO12 ...212 C5
Laundry La LA6 ....103 D3
Laundry Rd
  4 Filey YO14 ....101 B3
  3 Harrogate HG1 .....220 C4
Lauradale La BD23 ....134 D1
Laurel Ave TS4 ....7 A4
Laurel Cl Burniston YO13 .75 D8
  Gateforth YO8 ....197 B1
Laurel Garth Cl YO32 ..217 D8
Laurels The **6** DL6 ...210 E2
Laurence Gr YO8 ......232 D3
Laurence Jackson Sch
  TS14 ....8 F7
Lavender Ct **21** YO14 ..41 A5
Lavender Gr YO31 .....228 E8
Laveracks Ind Est
  YO41 ....185 B3
Laverick Terr **9** YO14 ..208 E6
Laverton Gdns HG3 ...219 A4
Law La HG3 ....138 F1
Lawn Ave YO30 ....176 C1
Lawn La DN6 ....207 E3
Lawn Rd **35** LS29 ....176 C1
Lawnfield Dr HG3 .....140 B5
Lawnfield Rd HG3 .....140 B5
Lawns The HG2 ....222 C8
Lawnswood Dr YO30 ..227 F8
Lawnway YO31 ....229 A7
Lawrence Cl YO12 ....212 A8
Lawrence Cres DL10 ..209 D8
Lawrence St YO10 ....228 E4
Lawrence St YO10 ....212 A8
Lawsings Brow LA2 ...130 B5
Lawson Ave **1** YO51 ..141 B4
Lawson Rd YO24 ......230 F7
Lawsons Cl YO14 .....126 F7
Laycock Fields **11** BD22 .187 B6
Layerthorpe YO31 .....233 C3
Layfield Prim Sch TS15 ..5 D2
Lazenby Dr **10** LS22 ..180 B3
Lazenby Moor La HG5 ..141 A4
Le Cateau Com Prim Sch
  DL9 ....40 F4
Le Cateau Rd **10** DL9 ..40 E4
Lea Croft LS23 ....188 E7
Lea La YO8 ....204 F5
Lea Way YO32 ....225 E3
Lead La Brompton DL6 ..43 F3
  Nether Silton YO7 .....66 B7
  Ripon HG4 ....214 B3
  Westerdale YO21 ......28 E4
Lead Mill La YO1 ......233 C1
Leadhall Ave HG2 .....222 A6
Leadhall Cres HG2 ....222 B6
Leadhall Dr HG2 ......222 A6
Leadhall Gdns HG2 ...222 A6
Leadhall Gr HG2 ......222 A6
Leadhall La HG2 ......222 A6
Leadhall Rd HG2 .....222 A6
Leadhall View HG2 ....222 A6
Leadhall Way HG2 ....222 A6
Leading Post St **8**
  YO11 ....213 B6
Leadley Croft YO23 ...230 A1
Leafield Rd DL1 ....3 D4
Leahope Ct TS17 ....6 C8
Leahurst Cl YO17 .....215 E4

Leake Cl YO7 ....65 F6
Leake St
  Castleford WF10 ....200 F4
  York YO10 ....228 E3
Lealholm Cres TS3 ......7 C8
Lealholm La YO21 ......30 B5
Lealholm Prim Sch
  YO21 ....30 C6
Lealholm Sta YO21 .....30 C6
Leamington Rd LS29 ...218 C5
Leamington Terr LS29 ..218 C5
Learmans Way YO23 ..230 B1
Learning La DN14 .....202 F1
Leas Head Rd YO22 ....32 B2
Leas La YO18 ....99 F5
Leas The
  1 Brafferton YO61 ....115 F1
  Darlington DL1 ....3 D8
  8 Eastfield YO11 .....99 F7
Lease Rigg La YO22 ....31 A3
Leases La DL10 ....41 E2
Leases Rd DL7 ....63 C5
Leasmires Ave **10** YO61 .143 D8
Leat Cl YO17 ....215 D2
Leather Bank LS22 ....176 C1
Leathley La LS21 ......177 D1
Leavening Com Prim Sch
  YO17 ....147 E2
Leazon Hill **8** TS17 .....6 D6
Leazon Hill **8** TS17 .....6 D6 (see below)
Lebberston CE Prim Sch
  LA6 ....102 E7
Leconfield Garth HG3 ..223 F5
Ledbury Way TS14 .....8 E6
Ledsway **1** BD23 .....134 E3
Ledgate La LS25 ......201 E6
Ledston Ave LS25 .....194 D3
Ledston Hall* WF10 ...200 F8
Ledston Mill La WF10 ..200 F8
Lee Ct DL6 ....207 A7
Lee View DN14 ....207 A7
Lee Way WF10 ....200 F3
Leech La DL10 ....41 E4
Leeds Barnsdale Rd
  WF10 ....200 D3
Leeds La LS26 ....194 A3
Leeds Rd
  Allerton Bywater WF10 .200 D7
  Barwick in Elmet & Scholes
  LS15 ....194 A7
  Castleford WF10 ....200 C4
  Collingham LS22 ......188 A8
  Great Preston WF10 ...200 C7
  Harrogate HG2 ....219 D1
  Ilkley LS29 ....218 D5
  Kippax LS25 ....194 C2
  Micklefield LS25 ......200 A6
  Pannal HG3 ....222 F3
  Selby YO8 ....232 A4
  Tadcaster LS24 ....189 D5
Leeman Rd YO26 ......233 A2
Leeming & Londonderry Com
  Prim Sch DL7 ....63 D4
Leeming Bar Ind Est
  DL7 ....63 C5
Leeming Bar Sta DL7 ...63 C5
Leeming La
  Brough with St Giles
  DL10 ....41 D5
  Burneston DL8 ....87 F8
  4 Burton in Lonsdale LA6 .102 F3
  Kirklington-cum-Upsland
  YO7 ....88 A4
  Langthorpe YO51 .....141 B6
  Melmerby HG4 ....63 C4
  Theakston DL7 ....63 E1
  Thornthwaite with Padside
  HG3 ....159 D5
Leeming RAF Com Prim Sch
  DL7 ....63 F3
Lees La DL7 ....210 B1
Leeside YO24 ....230 E8
Legion St LS25 ....195 F2
Legram La YO26 ......163 D8
Legram Rd YO26 ......163 D8
Leicester Cres LS29 ...218 B5
Leicester Way
  Aislaby TS16 ....5 D4
  York YO1 ....233 C1
Leighton Cl YO30 ......99 E6
Leighton Croft **3** YO30 .224 F1
Leighton Rd **8** TS18 ....5 D8
Leisure Pk YO32 ......226 A2
Leith Rd DL3 ....3 A5
Lelaburn Bar Sta DL7 ...63 C5
Lendal YO1 ....233 B2
Lendales La YO18 ......95 E3
Lennerton La LS25 ....196 C3
Lennox Ave DL10 .....209 D7
Lennox Pl HG4 ....214 B7
Lennox Pl **14** YO24 ...227 A2
Leonard St **18** BB18 ..171 D1
Leppington Dr YO12 ..212 C4
Leppington La YO17 ..147 D1
Lercroft Rd YO24 .....230 B8
Lesley Ave YO10 .....231 E8
L'Espec St DL6 ....210 E5
Leven Bank Rd TS15 ...5 D4
Leven Cl TS16 ....5 D4
Leven La TS15 ....25 C5
Leven Rd Eaglescliffe TS15 .5 E3
  Stokesley TS9 ....26 C7
  York YO24 ....230 D7
Leven Wynd **8** TS9 ...26 C7
Levendale Prim Sch
  TS15 ....5 F3

Levens Cl HG3 ....161 A3
Levenside Great Ayton TS9 .7 F1
  4 Hutton Rudby TS15 ...25 D5
  Stokesley TS9 ....26 C7
Levick Cres HG3 ....6 D8
Levisham St YO10 ....228 D2
Levisham Sta YO18 ....72 B5
Lewis Cl
  1 Croft-on-Tees DL2 ...22 C8
  Northallerton DL6 ....210 F5
Lewis Rd DL6 ....210 F5
Lexden Ave TS5 ....6 D8
Leyburn Com Prim Sch
  DL8 ....60 D5
Leyburn La **5** TS18 ....5 D8
Leyburn Old Globe Nature
  Reserve* DL8 ....60 B4
Leyburn Pl **8** YO14 ...101 A3
Leyburn Rd Askrigg DL8 .57 F6
  Darlington DL1 ....3 D7
  Masham HG4 ....86 B4
  Middleham DL8 ....60 E3
  Scotton DL9 ....40 C4
Leyburn Sta DL8 ....60 D5
Leyes The YO10 ......229 C4
Leyfield Cl **13** YO32 ..167 A7
Leyland Cl BB8 ....186 A2
Leyland Cres **3** HG1 ..220 A3
Leyland Rd
  Harrogate HG1 ....220 A3
  York YO31 ....229 A5
Leys La
  Boston Spa LS23 .....188 D8
  Darrington WF11 .....206 A8
  Glusburn BD20 ....187 B8
  Knottingley WF11 ....201 F1
  Little Smeaton WF8 ..206 A7
Leys Rd WF11 ....206 A7
Leyshorpe La YO62 ....93 B2
Liardet Rd **18** DL10 ...41 E4
Libanus St **16** TS17 ....5 F4
Library Sq YO1 ....233 B3
Lichfield Ct **3** YO23 ..228 B1
Lichfield Gr HG3 ......219 A4
Lickley St HG4 ....214 B6
Lidget Croft BD20 ....173 E3
Lidget La HG5 ....163 B5
Lidget Rd BD20 ....173 E3
Lidgett Gr YO26 ......227 B6
Lidgett Gr Sch YO26 ..227 B6
Lidgett La LS25 ......194 C3
Lidice Rd DN14 ......205 E2
Lidsty Hill YO62 ....70 C5
Lifeboat Mus* YO21 ..208 D7
Light Bank La BD20 ...174 C2
Light La DL8 ....59 E5
Lightfoot Ave YO12 ...212 D3
Lightfoots Cl YO12 ...212 D3
Lightfoots La YO12 ...212 D3
Lightfoots Rd YO12 ...212 D3
Lightmire La YO26 ....142 A1
Lightwater Valley Miniature
  Rly* HG4 ....113 C6
Lightwater Valley Theme
  Pk* HG4 ....113 C6
Lilac Ave
  Appleton Roebuck YO23 .190 F5
  Thornaby TS17 ....6 B7
  York YO31 ....229 B3
Lilac Cl **7** LS29 ......175 A4
Lilac Gr Harrogate HG1 .219 E6
  New Earswick YO32 ...225 D4
Lilac Rd TS7 ....7 D7
Lilac Wlk YO12 ....212 D7
Lilbourne Dr YO30 ....228 A8
Lile Cl DL10 ....209 C7
Lilla Cl YO21 ....208 A6
Lilla Gr **8** YO31 .....228 E8
Lilling La YO60 ....145 E3
Lilly Gate La HG3 .....162 A8
Limber Hill YO21 ......30 E4
Lime Ave YO31 ....229 A3
Lime Chase **18** YO62 ...70 B1
Lime Cl **16** LS29 ....174 E4
Lime Gr Harrogate HG1 .219 F3
  4 Whitby YO21 ......208 C6
Lime Kiln La LS22 ....180 B5
Lime La DL8 ....87 F2
Lime Rd Eaglescliffe TS16 ..5 E6
  Guisborough TS14 ......8 E7
  Sinnington YO62 ....94 D8
Lime St HG1 ....219 F3
Lime Tree Ave
  Boston Spa LS23 .....188 E8
  1 Easingwold YO61 ...117 D1
  Malton YO17 ....215 D6
  York YO32 ....225 D3
Lime Tree Gr **1** YO8 ..197 B1
Lime Tree Mews **18**
  YO19 ....184 F7
Lime Wlk HG4 ....214 B2
Limebar Bank Rd
  YO51 ....141 D1
Limebar La YO51 .....141 C2
Limegarth **10** YO26 ..165 F1
Limehouse La BD23 ...116 C1
Limekiln Bank HG4 ....113 C1
Limekiln La HG5 ......150 B3
Limekiln La
  Burton Leonard HG3 ..140 A1
  East Layton DL11 ......1 F2
  3 Eastfield YO11 .....100 B6
  Halton West BD23 ....154 A1

Limekiln La *continued*
North Stainley with Sleningford HG4 113 C5
Snape with Thorp HG4 86 D5
Limekiln Rd YO7 65 F5
Limes Ct YO31 228 F6
Limes The
Burniston YO13 75 C8
Helmsley YO62 92 F6
Stockton-on-the-Forest YO32 167 D2
Limestone Gr YO13 75 C8
Limestone La YO13 75 A5
Limestone Rd YO13 75 B7
Limestone Way YO13 75 C8
Limetree Cl 2 YO8 197 B1
Lime-tree Cres LS25 194 E1
Limetrees WF8 201 D2
Limpsey Gate La YO18 72 D6
Limpton Gate TS15 5 E2
Linacre Way DL1 3 D7
Lincoln Gr HG3 219 A5
Lincoln Rd 30 BB18 172 A1
Lincoln St YO26 227 F5
Lindale 2 YO24 230 C7
Linden Ave Darlington DL3 3 B5
Great Ayton TS9 7 F1
Linden Cl Great Ayton TS9 7 F2
4 Hutton Rudby TS15 25 C4
Sleights YO21 32 B7
York YO32 225 F5
Linden Cres
Great Ayton TS9 7 F1
5 Hutton Rudby TS15 25 C4
Middlesbrough TS7 7 B6
Linden Dr Hurworth DL2 3 D1
1 Hurworth-on-Tees DL2 22 D8
Linden Gdns DL10 209 D7
Linden Gr Great Ayton TS9 7 F1
Thornaby TS17 6 B8
1 York YO30 228 A8
Linden Rd 9 Earby BB18 172 A1
Great Ayton TS9 7 F1
Northallerton DL6 210 E4
Scalby YO12 212 A8
Linden Way
9 Thorpe Willoughby YO8 197 B2
Wetherby LS22 180 B4
Lindhead Sch YO13 75 C8
Lindhead Rd YO13 75 B8
Lindisfarne Rd TS3 7 C8
Lindley Rd YO30 224 F1
Lindley St Skipton BD23 216 F2
York YO24 227 F3
Lindley Wood Gr YO30 224 E3
Lindon Rd DL10 20 F1
Lindrick Cl
32 Castleford WF6 200 B1
3 Ripon HG4 214 B2
Lindrick Way HG3 219 A4
Lindsay Rd LS25 194 C3
Lindsey Ave YO26 227 D4
Linen Way 10 DL6 43 F3
Ling Croft LS23 188 D8
Ling Fields BD23 216 C4
Ling Gill National Nature Reserve* BD23 79 C1
Ling Hill YO12 212 B7
Ling La YO41 185 F6
Ling Trod YO17 123 D4
Lingcrag Gdns BD22 187 B6
Lingcroft Cl YO8 204 D4
Lingcroft La
Naburn YO19 231 E3
Tockwith LS22 181 A6
Lingdale Prim Sch TS12 9 F7
Lingdale Rd
Lockwood TS12 9 E7
Thornaby TS17 6 C7
Lingfield Ash TS8 7 A5
Lingfield Cl DL1 3 F5
Lingfield Cres YO24 227 F1
Lingfield Prim Sch TS7 7 B5
Lingfield Rd TS15 5 F3
Lingfield Way DL1 4 A5
Lingham La YO7 115 A3
Linghaw La LA2 129 C7
Lingholm Cres 9 YO11 99 F7
Lingholm La YO11 100 D4
Lingmoor La YO62 70 E3
Lingrow Cl 3 TS13 12 A7
Link Ave YO30 228 C8
Link Rd YO31 225 E2
Link Rd Ct YO19 229 D4
Link The
Copmanthorpe YO23 230 A3
Middlesbrough TS3 7 C8
Northallerton DL7 210 B2
Selby YO8 232 A4
York YO10 231 E8
Link Wlk 5 YO11 100 A6
Linkfoot La YO62 93 A6
Links Cl HG2 220 E3
Links Dr LA2 129 A8
Links Prim Sch The TS16 5 E5
Links The
7 North Featherstone WF7 200 E1
Tadcaster LS24 189 E5
Links Way HG2 220 E3
Linkway DN6 206 E2
Linnburn Mews 1 LS29 218 B3
Linnet Way YO24 230 C8
Linton Ave 9 LS22 180 B3
Linton Cl
Cloughton YO13 54 D1
10 Filey YO14 101 B3
Linton Com LS22 179 F1
Linton Ct 8 BD23 216 F3
Linton Falls 1 BD23 134 E2
Linton La LS22 180 B2
Linton Mdw 5 YO30 164 F7
Linton Mdws 7 LS22 180 B3
Linton on Ouse Prim Sch YO30 165 A7
Linton Pl 4 YO30 164 F7
Linton Rd
Collingham LS22 180 A1
Poppleton YO26 224 A1
Wetherby LS22 180 B3
Linton Rise 17 DL9 40 E4
Linton St 5 YO26 227 E5
Linton Woods YO30 165 A7
Linton Woods La YO30 165 A8
Linwith La DN14 204 C3
Linwood Ave TS9 26 C8
Lippersley La BD20 174 D3
Lisheen Ave WF10 200 F4
Lismore Pl YO12 212 E1
Lismore Rd YO12 212 E1
Lister Hill 5 BD20 187 E6
Lister St LS29 218 A4
Lister Way YO30 228 A7
Lisvane Ave YO12 212 D4
Litley Bank YO7 66 B5
Little Ave YO30 228 B8
Little Ayton La
Great Ayton TS9 8 A1
27 Roundhill Village TS17 5 F4
Little Beck Bank YO22 32 C4
Little Beck La YO22 32 B3
Little Beck Wood Nature Reserve* YO22 32 B3
Little Brook BD23 217 B4
Little Catterton La LS24 190 A7
Little Church La LS26 200 B5
Little Comm La DN14 207 C5
Little Croft HG3 139 C4
Little Crossing HG4 214 E2
Little Field La YO18 72 C5
Little Garth YO26 224 A2
Little Hallfield Rd YO31 228 E5
Little Harries La HG4 214 A7
Little Heck Comm La DN14 203 D1
Little Hutton La DL11 1 A4
Little Ings Cl LS24 196 C8
Little Ings La YO51 141 C5
Little King St 5 HG3 137 B4
Little La Brompton DL6 44 A3
12 Easingwold YO61 143 C8
Ellerton YO42 193 C1
11 Haxby YO32 166 E5
Ilkley LS29 218 C4
Little Smeaton DN6 206 D4
North Stainley with Sleningford HG4 113 C4
Little Mdws YO32 225 D8
Little Moor Cl YO13 54 C1
Little Moor La YO8 232 A8
Little Pasture 3 TS17 6 D5
Little Stonegate YO1 233 B3
Little Studley Cl HG4 214 C7
Little Studley Pk HG4 214 C8
Little Studley Rd HG4 214 C7
Little Westfield YO25 151 C3
Little Wood St YO17 215 E3
Littlebeck Dr DL1 3 E7
Littleboy Dr TS17 6 C8
Littledale YO18 95 F7
Littlefield Cl 5 YO26 165 F1
Littleside DL8 83 E7
Littlethorpe Cl
Harrogate HG3 219 A4
7 Strensall YO32 167 B8
Littlethorpe La HG4 214 D2
Littlethorpe Pk HG4 214 E3
Littlethorpe Potteries* HG4 140 A7
Littlethorpe Rd HG4 214 E3
Littondale Ave HG5 221 D6
Liverton La TS13 10 D6
Liverton Mill Bank TS12 10 B6
Liverton Rd TS13 10 D7
Livingstone Rd YO12 212 E6
Livingstone St YO26 227 F5
Lloyd Cl YO10 229 B1
Lob La YO41 168 D2
Lochrin Pl 2 YO26 227 B4
Lock Cl DN14 207 F6
Lock La
Castleford WF10 200 E5
Normanton WF6 200 A3
Lock La Sports Ctr WF10 200 F5
Lock Wlk DL10 41 E4
Locker La HG4 214 C4
Lockey Croft YO32 225 C8
Lockeys Terr 3 YO22 208 E6
Lockfield Dr BB18 171 E2
Lockgate Rd DN14 207 C4
Lockheed Cl TS18 5 F7
Lockton Cres TS17 6 A6
Lockton Ct LS24 196 B7
Lockton La YO18 72 E4
Lockton Rd YO21 208 A6
Lockwood Chase YO13 54 D1
Lockwood Prim Sch TS12 9 D7
Lockwood St YO31 233 C3
Lockyer Cl 4 YO30 228 A8
Locomotion Ct 5 TS16 5 D5
Loders Gn 5 YO11 99 F6
Lodge Cl 7 YO11 100 B6
Lodge Gdns
Gristlthorp YO14 100 E4
5 Snaith DN14 204 C1
Lodge La 5 Brompton DL6 43 F3
Danby YO21 29 D7
Gowdall DN14 203 F1
Newby with Mulwith HG4 140 E6
Wennington LA2 102 B1
Lodge Rd
Hutton-le-Hole YO62 70 C5
Lythe YO21 12 E3
Settle BD24 153 E8
Lodore Gr TS5 6 D7
Lofthouse La YO41 185 D7
Loftus Cl YO12 212 B4
Lombards Wynd DL10 209 C7
Londesborough Gr 5 YO8 197 B2
Londesborough Pk 10 YO12 99 D6
Londesborough Rd YO12 212 E4
Londesborough St 5 YO8 232 C5
London La DN6 207 D1
Long Acre Ct HG3 222 E2
Long Acre Wlk HG3 222 E2
Long Ashes Leisure Ctr BD23 134 B3
Long Band DL8 58 A8
Long Bank DL11 19 C6
Long Bank La BD23 153 E1
Long Barrow*
Thixendale YO17 170 A7
Willerby YO12 125 E7
Long Cl La YO10 233 C1
Long Crag View 1 HG3 161 B2
Long Cswy
Arkengarthdale DL11 16 C6
Halton East BD23 174 B8
Thirkleby High & Low with Osgodby YO7 90 D1
Long Cswy Rd
Danby YO21 29 E3
Hutton Buscel YO13 99 A4
Long Furrow YO32 225 C8
Long Gate BD22 187 D4
Long Gn 7 BB18 172 B1
Long Heads La LS25 195 F1
Long Hill End BD22 187 B5
Long Ing La BB18 171 E1
Long La
Barwick in Elmet LS15 194 C7
Borrowby YO7 65 E5
Brompton DL6 44 A6
Catton YO41 185 D6
Cawood YO8 197 A6
Cowling BD22 187 B7
East Ayton YO13 99 B7
Ellerton YO42 193 F1
Farndale East YO62 48 F4
Felliscliffe HG3 160 E3
Gayles DL11 19 E6
Heck DN14 207 D8
Heslington YO10 184 C3
Kirk Smeaton WF8 206 B1
Laneshaw Bridge BB8 186 B4
Lockwood TS12 10 B5
Normanby YO62 95 A4
Picton TS15 24 E6
Seamer YO12 99 E6
Slingsby YO62 120 D6
Tatham LA2 128 E7
Well DL8 87 C4
Long Level LA6 102 C8
Long Mann Hills Rd YO8 232 B4
Long Marston CE VC Prim Sch YO26 182 A6
Long Mdw 7 Colne BB8 186 A3
Skipton BD23 217 B5
Long Mdw Gate LS25 194 C2
Long Mdws
Garforth LS25 194 C3
6 Ilkley LS29 176 C1
Rillington YO17 122 F5
Long Newton La TS21 5 A6
Long Preston Endowed VA Prim Sch BD23 153 F5
Long Preston Sta BD23 153 F4
Long Rampart YO42 193 D3
Long Riddings LS29 174 F5
Long Ridge Dr YO26 224 A1
Long Ridge La YO26 224 A1
Long Royd Rd BB18 172 A1
Long St Asenby YO7 115 B6
Easingwold YO61 143 C8
Thirsk YO7 211 C3
Topcliffe YO7 115 C6
Long Stoop Standing Stone* HG3 160 A2
Long Stps 8 YO22 208 E6
Long Swales La HG4 112 D5
Long Trods 5 YO8 232 C6
Long Wlk
Knaresborough HG5 221 A6
Scarborough YO12 212 D7
Longacre WF10 200 E3
Longbank Rd TS7 7 D7
Longber La LA6 102 D4
Longbow Ave LS26 200 B6
Longcroft 2 YO32 166 E5
Longcroft Rd 1 LS29 218 E3
Longdale Ave 18 BD24 131 D2
Longdike La
Kippax LS25 200 E8
Thornton Steward HG4 61 E1
Longfield Comp Sch DL3 3 C8
Longfield Ct 21 BB18 171 D1
Longfield Rd DL3 3 C7
Longfield Terr YO30 233 A3
Longland La YO26 164 A3
Longlands Field Rd YO26 163 D8
Longlands La
Boroughbridge YO51 141 A3
Danby YO21 29 B6
Hetton BD23 155 F5
Sicklinghall LS22 179 E3
Thornton-le-Dale YO18 96 E5
Longlands Rd YO17 123 B3
Longmans Hill CP Sch YO8 232 C3
Longtons La BD23 152 F4
Longwestgate YO11 213 B6
Longwood Bank DL10 209 D5
Longwood Link 8 YO30 224 E3
Longwood Rd YO30 224 F3
Lonsdale Mdws LS23 188 E8
Lonsdale Pl 12 YO13 99 B8
Lonsdale Rd YO11 213 A3
Loos Rd DL9 40 F3
Loraine Cres DL1 3 C4
Lord Ave TS17 6 B5
Lord Deramore's Prim Sch YO10 229 C1
Lord Mayor's Wlk YO31 233 B3
Lord's Cl 23 BD24 131 D2
Lord's Cl Rd LA2 129 B3
Lord's La DL8 63 C2
Lords La
Ainderby Mires with Holtby DL8 41 F1
Hackforth DL8 62 E8
Upper Poppleton YO26 165 E2
Lords Moor La YO32 167 C7
Lordship La
16 Barlby YO8 198 A4
Wistow YO8 232 D8
Loriners Dr 7 YO23 230 B3
Loring Rd YO13 54 A7
Lorne St YO23 228 B1
Lorraine Ave 3 YO41 185 B2
Loscoe Cl WF6 200 C2
Loshpot La LS22 180 C5
Lothersdale Com Prim Sch BD20 186 F8
Lothersdale Rd BD20 187 B8
Lotherton La LS25 195 A7
Lotherton Way LS25 194 C4
Louisa St DL1 3 D5
Lousy Hill La YO22 32 C3
Louvain St 5 BB18 171 D2
Love La Brawby YO17 94 F1
Castleford WF10 200 E3
Easby DL10 209 E4
8 Leyburn DL8 60 D5
Nunthorpe YO10 231 C8
Whitby YO21 208 A7
York YO24 228 A2
Lovers' La DL7 64 F2
Low Bank
4 Embsay BD23 217 E8
Over Silton DL6 66 A8
Low Beck LS29 218 D5
Low Bentham Com Prim Sch LA2 128 F8
Low Bentham Rd LA2 128 F8
Low Catton Rd YO41 185 C8
Low Cl LS29 218 A5
Low Comm LS26 200 C4
Low Croft 6 YO32 167 A7
Low Demesne LA6 103 D3
Low Demesne Cl 4 LA6 103 D3
Low Farm LS26 200 C8
Low Farm Cl
Bolton Percy YO23 190 D4
Thornton TS8 6 D4
Low Field La
Cold Kirby YO7 91 D7
Goldsborough HG5 163 A1
Marton cum Grafton YO51 141 E2
Staveley HG5 140 E1
Low Fields Dr YO24 227 C3
Low Fold BB18 186 A7
Low Garth YO22 32 A6
Low Garth Link 17 LS25 195 F4
Low Garth Rd LS25 195 F4
Low Gate DL8 57 F5
Low Gate La HG4 138 F7
Low Gn Catterick DL10 41 D4
Copmanthorpe YO23 230 B2
13 Knottingley WF11 202 A2
Menwith with Darley HG3 160 A6
Low Holland WF11 201 C6
Low Hospl Yd 6 YO22 208 E6
Low House La
Carlton Miniott YO7 89 C2
Dishforth YO7 115 B2
Low Hutton Pk YO60 147 C6
Low La Askrigg DL8 58 B4
Low La *continued*
Carperby-cum-Thoresby DL8 58 F4
Cononley BD20 173 C2
Cowling BD22 187 A8
Cropton YO18 71 B4
Dalby-cum-Skewsby YO60 119 B2
Dalton DL11 19 D7
Embsay with Eastby BD23 217 E8
Grassington BD23 134 E3
Grinton DL11 37 E5
Heslington YO10 229 D1
Howsham YO60 147 A1
Hutton-Sessay YO7 116 B7
Leck LA6 102 D7
Leyburn DL8 60 C4
Lythe YO21 12 D3
Maltby TS17 6 B3
Menwith with Darley HG3 159 F6
Mickleby TS13 12 A3
Middlesbrough TS5 6 E6
Muker DL11 36 C4
Newsham DL11 18 H7
Reeth, Fremington & Healaugh DL11 37 F5
Silsden BD20 174 B3
Spofforth with Stockeld HG3 179 C4
Stainburn LS21 177 F3
Sutton-under-Whitestonecliffe YO7 90 E6
Swinton YO17 121 C4
Thirkleby High & Low with Osgodby YO7 90 C1
West Rounton DL6 24 D3
Westow YO60 147 C4
Wigglesworth BD23 153 D3
Low Mdw YO8 232 C6
Low Mill* DL8 57 D5
Low Mill Cl YO10 229 D3
Low Mill Est HG4 214 E5
Low Mill La LS29 175 A4
Low Mill Rd HG4 214 D4
Low Moor Ave 3 YO10 231 F8
Low Moor La
Askham Richard YO23 182 D3
Brearton HG5 162 B7
East Harlsey DL6 44 C7
Fearby HG4 85 F3
Hessay YO26 182 C8
Rillington YO17 122 E6
Low Moor Rd YO18 71 F5
Low Moor S La YO17 122 D6
Low Moorgate YO17 122 F5
Low Ousegate YO1 233 B2
Low Peter La HG3 140 A3
Low Petergate YO1 233 B3
Low Pk Rd LS29 176 A3
Low Poppleton La YO26 227 B7
Low Rd Gainford DL2 1 C7
Gowdall DN14 204 A1
Irton YO12 75 B3
Kellington DN14 202 F4
Kirby Grindalythe YO17 149 F7
Newby & Scalby YO12 212 A6
Thirkleby High & Low with Osgodby YO7 116 E8
Low Skellgate HG4 214 C5
Low Sleights Rd LA6 104 B7
Low St Aiskew DL7 63 C6
Austwick LA2 130 E7
Burton in Lonsdale LA6 102 F3
Carlton DN14 204 C2
Husthwaite YO61 117 B6
Kirkby Fleetham with Fencote DL10 41 F2
Knottingley WF11 201 E4
Lastingham YO62 70 E5
Nunnington YO62 93 E2
Oswaldkirk YO62 92 F3
Ripon HG4 214 D5
22 Scalby YO13 75 D5
Sherburn in Elmet LS25 195 F4
Thornton-le-Clay YO60 146 A4
Low St Agnesgate HG4 214 D4
Low Stanghow Rd TS12 9 F6
Low Thorpe DL8 85 D8
Low Town Bank Rd YO61 91 B4
Low Tun Way YO62 69 A2
Low Wath Rd HG3 137 B4
Low Way 5 LS23 188 E5
Low Well Pk YO19 192 F7
Low Westfield Rd YO23 230 A1
Low Wood La
Glaisdale YO21 30 C6
Leyburn DL8 60 C4
Low Wood Rise LS29 218 F3
Lowcroft
9 Collingham LS22 188 A8
High Bentham LA2 129 B8
Lowcross Ave TS14 8 E5
Lowcross Dr TS9 26 E5
Lowdale Ave YO12 212 E8
Lowdale Ct 4 YO22 32 A6
Lower Clark St
2 Scarborough YO12 212 F6
13 Scarborough YO12 213 A7
Lower Constable Rd LS29 218 D3
Lower Croft St 39 BB18 172 A1

Lower Darnborough St YO23 ...233 B1
Lower Derwent Valley Nat Nature Reserve* YO42 ...199 C8
Lower Flat Cliffs YO14 ...101 C1
Lower Friargate YO1 ...233 B2
Lower Greenfoot **15** BD24 ...131 D2
Lower Mickletown LS26 ...200 C6
Lower Oxford St WF10 ...200 E4
Lower Pk Marina* BB18 ...171 E1
Lower Priory St WO1 ...233 A1
Lower Sta Rd **8** WF6 ...200 A1
Lower Union St BD23 ...216 F3
Lower Wellington Rd LS29 ...218 B4
Lower William St **8** YO12 ...212 F6
Lower York Ct HG1 ...220 D6
Loweswater Rd **5** YO30 ...224 E1
Lowfield **3** Eastfield YO11 ...100 A6
Hawes DL8 ...56 C4
Lowfield Dr YO32 ...166 E5
Lowfield La
Beamsley BD23 ...174 F7
Kirkby Fleetham with Fencote DL7 ...42 D2
Langthorpe YO51 ...141 A6
Rufforth YO26 ...227 A4
Scrayingham YO41 ...169 A7
Sharow HG4 ...214 F6
Snape with Thorp DL8 ...87 A7
Lowfield Rd
Barlby with Osgodby YO8 ...198 B5
Hillam LS25 ...202 C8
Malton WO17 ...215 C6
Lowfield Sec Sch YO24 ...227 D3
Lowfields Ave
Ingleby Barwick TS17 ...6 A5
Roundhill Village TS17 ...6 D5
Lowfields La YO7 ...88 C6
Lowgate DN14 ...207 D5
Lowgill La LA2 ...128 F4
Lowick LA2 ...230 C7
Lowkber La LA6 ...103 E2
Lowlands Dr DL7 ...63 C5
Lowmoor Rd YO8 ...198 E6
Lown Hill YO24 ...227 C2
Lowna Rd YO62 ...70 B5
Lownorth Rd BD23 ...53 C2
Lowskellgate **16** HG4 ...214 C5
Lowswater Rd YO21 ...201 F1
Lowther Cres **8** LS26 ...194 A1
Lowther Ct YO31 ...233 C4
Lowther Dr
Garforth LS25 ...194 C3
Selby YO8 ...232 E3
2 Swillington LS26 ...194 A1
Lowther St YO31 ...233 C4
Lowther Terr YO24 ...228 A3
Loxley Cl YO30 ...224 F2
Loyne Pk LA6 ...102 A7
Lucas Gr YO30 ...228 C8
Lucas Gr S YO26 ...181 C7
Lucas Gr S YO26 ...181 C7
Lucas Rd YO26 ...181 C7
Luccombe Cl **17** TS17 ...6 A3
Lucerne Dr TS14 ...8 E6
Lucia La TS14 ...8 E6
Lucky La YO7 ...89 E8
Lucombe Way YO32 ...225 D4
Luddith Rd YO17 ...148 D5
Ludlow Ave LS25 ...194 D4
Ludsgate TS17 ...6 C7
Lumb Gill La LS29 ...175 A3
Lumb La BD22 ...187 A5
Lumb Mill Way BD23 ...157 F2
Lumby Hill LS25 ...202 A8
Lumby La
Monk Fryston LS25 ...202 A8
South Milford LS25 ...196 A1
Lumley Cl YO7 ...211 D2
Lumley La Azerley HG4 ...112 D2
Kirkby Fleetham with Fencote DL7 ...42 B1
Lumley Rd YO30 ...228 B7
Lumley St WF10 ...200 D3
Lunar Pk YO1 ...213 C6
Luncarr La HG4 ...114 B2
Lund Cl YO32 ...225 C8
Lund Head La HG3 ...179 B2
Lund La Bubwith YO8 ...199 C4
Cliffe YO8 ...198 D4
Hampsthwaite HG3 ...161 A5
Lund Rd YO62 ...70 B7
Lund Sand La
Easingwold YO61 ...143 A8
Raskelf YO61 ...117 A1
Lund Side La LS25 ...195 F2
Lund's Twr* BD20 ...187 D5
Lundgreen La YO61 ...144 A3
Lundy Cl **10** YO30 ...225 A1
Lunebeck Wlk TS17 ...6 C6
Lunedale Ave
Knaresborough HG5 ...221 C5
Middlesbrough TS5 ...6 E8
Lunedale Rd DL3 ...3 A6
Lunn La DN14 ...202 D3
Lunnfields La WF11 ...201 E6

Lupton Bank HG3 ...137 D3
Lupton Cl HG3 ...137 D3
Lutton La YO17 ...123 F4
Luttons CP Sch YO17 ...150 B8
Lutyens The **22** LS29 ...175 C2
Lycett Rd YO24 ...230 F6
Lych Gate **14** DL2 ...3 E1
Lydford Rd **18** DL10 ...41 C4
Lydham Ct **2** YO24 ...230 C8
Lyell St YO12 ...212 F6
Lynbrook Cl YO7 ...211 B4
Lyndale LS25 ...200 D8
Lyndale Ave YO10 ...229 C3
Lyndale Gr **14** WF6 ...200 B1
Lynden Way YO24 ...227 D3
Lyndhurst Cl
2 Norton DN6 ...206 F2
8 Whitby YO21 ...208 D6
Lyndhurst Dr **8** DN6 ...206 F2
Lyndhurst Rise **8** DN6 ...206 F2
Lyndon Ave
Bramham LS23 ...188 E6
Garforth LS25 ...194 C4
Lyndon Cl **8** LS23 ...188 E6
Lyndon Cres **4** LS23 ...188 E6
Lyndon Rd LS23 ...188 E6
Lyndon Sq **2** LS23 ...188 E6
Lyndon Way LS23 ...188 E6
Lynndale Ave **6** BD20 ...187 F8
Lynton Ave LS23 ...188 E8
Lynton Cl YO8 ...232 B1
Lynton Gdns
Brayton YO8 ...232 B1
Darlington DL1 ...3 E5
Harrogate HG1 ...220 A3
Lynton Way HG3 ...160 A6
Lynwith Cl DN14 ...204 C3
Lynwith Ct DN14 ...204 C3
Lynwith Dr DN14 ...204 C3
Lynwood Ave **8** YO23 ...230 A3
Lynwood Cl YO23 ...230 A3
Lynwood View **4** YO23 ...230 A3
Lynx La YO7 ...115 B1
Lyon Rd BD20 ...187 F7
Lyonette Rd DL1 ...3 E7
Lys Cres DL9 ...209 D1
Lys Cres DL9 ...209 C8
Lytham Cl BD23 ...217 C3
Lytham Gdns BD23 ...217 C3
Lytham Rd DL1 ...3 D8
Lythe Bank Lythe YO21 ...12 F4
Sutton with Howgrave DL8 ...87 F2
Lythe CE VC Prim Sch YO21 ...12 F5
Lythe Fell Rd LA2 ...129 B2
Lythe La LA2 ...129 A2

M

MacArthurs Cl YO7 ...211 B2
MacDonell Cl **1** DL9 ...209 C1
MacKeridge La YO62 ...48 F4
Mackie Dr TS14 ...8 F7
MacKinnon Ave **1** WF6 ...200 B2
MacLagan Rd YO2 ...230 D2
Mafeking St HG1 ...219 F4
Magazine La YO8 ...198 B3
Magazine Rd YO8 ...198 B4
Magdalen's Cl HG4 ...214 D6
Magdalen's Rd HG4 ...214 D6
Magister Rd TS17 ...6 B7
Magnia Gr YO32 ...225 D2
Magpie Garth YO12 ...99 E6
Maida Gr YO10 ...228 D2
Maiden Bower (Motte & Bailey)* YO7 ...115 D5
Maiden Castle* DL11 ...38 A5
Maiden Greve YO17 ...215 A4
Maidensgrave Henge* YO25 ...126 F1
Maidstone Dr TS7 ...7 C6
Main Ave YO8 ...232 E5
Main Rd Drax YO8 ...204 F5
Gainford DL2 ...1 D7
Hambleton YO8 ...196 E1
Hellifield BD23 ...154 B3
Stainforth BD24 ...131 E6
Steeton with Eastburn BD20 ...187 F7
Weaverthorpe YO17 ...124 E1
Main St Aberford LS25 ...194 F8
Addingham LS29 ...174 F4
Allerston YO18 ...97 B5
Alne YO61 ...142 F4
Amotherby YO17 ...121 A4
Appleton Roebuck YO23 ...190 F5
Askham Bryan YO23 ...182 F3
Askrigg DL8 ...57 E6
Bagby YO7 ...90 C3
Balne DN14 ...205 D7
Austwick LA2 ...130 E7
Aysgarth DL8 ...58 E3
Barkston Ash LS24 ...195 E7
Barwick in Elmet LS15 ...194 B8
8 Beal DN14 ...202 D4
Bentham LA2 ...128 E8
Bishop Monkton HG3 ...140 B5
Bishopthorpe YO23 ...231 A4
Bolton Percy YO23 ...190 E5
Brafferton YO61 ...116 E7
Bubwith YO8 ...199 C7
Bugthorpe YO41 ...169 D4

Main St continued
Burley in Warfedale LS29 ...176 C1
Burton Salmon LS25 ...201 F6
Church Fenton LS24 ...196 B7
Cliffe YO8 ...198 E2
Cononley BD20 ...173 D1
Copmanthorpe YO23 ...230 A2
Cottingwith YO42 ...193 C5
Darley HG3 ...160 A6
Deighton YO19 ...192 A7
Earby BB18 ...186 A7
East Acton/West Ayton YO13 ...99 A7
Eastfield YO11 ...100 B6
Ebberston & Yedingham YO13 ...97 D5
Elldraton YO42 ...193 C1
Elvington YO41 ...185 C2
Embsay BD23 ...217 E8
Escrick YO19 ...192 B5
Farnhill BD20 ...173 E1
Folkton YO11 ...100 A2
Follifoot HG3 ...223 F5
Foston YO60 ...146 A6
Garforth LS25 ...125 A8
Garforth LS25 ...194 C3
Gillamoor YO62 ...70 A4
Gilling East YO62 ...118 F7
Glusburn BD20 ...187 E7
Gowdall DN14 ...204 A1
8 Grassington BD23 ...134 E3
Great Ouseburn YO26 ...164 B8
Great Preston WF10 ...200 D6
Gristithorp YO14 ...100 E4
Harome YO62 ...93 C5
Healaugh LS24 ...181 F2
Heck DN14 ...207 C8
Helperby YO61 ...142 A8
Hemingbrough YO8 ...198 F1
Hensall DN14 ...203 D2
Heslington YO10 ...229 B1
Hessay YO26 ...182 B8
High Bentham LA2 ...128 A8
Hovingham YO62 ...119 E6
Huby YO61 ...144 A4
Ingleton LA6 ...103 D3
Irton YO12 ...99 C6
Kelfield YO19 ...191 D1
Kellington DN14 ...202 F3
Kirk Deighton LS22 ...180 B5
Kirk Smeaton WF8 ...206 B3
Kirkby Malham BD23 ...154 F8
Kirkby Malzeard HG4 ...112 C5
Knapton YO26 ...227 A5
Langcliffe BD24 ...131 E4
Ledston WF10 ...200 F7
Linton LS22 ...180 A1
Little Ouseburn YO26 ...164 A7
Long Preston BD23 ...153 F5
Low Bradley BD20 ...173 E3
Menwith with Darley HG3 ...160 A4
Mickletown LS26 ...200 B6
Middleton YO18 ...95 E8
Monk Fryston LS25 ...201 F8
1 Naburn YO19 ...191 D8
Newton Kyme cum Toulston LS24 ...189 C7
North Duffield YO8 ...199 A8
Nunthorpe YO18 ...231 D8
Pannal HG3 ...222 D3
Pollington DN14 ...207 F6
Poppleton YO26 ...165 F1
Rathmell BD24 ...153 C6
Reighton YO14 ...127 E5
Riccall YO19 ...198 A8
Ryther cum Ossendyke LS24 ...190 E2
Saxton with Scarthingwell LS24 ...195 D7
Scholes LS15 ...194 D7
Scotton HG5 ...162 A6
Seamer YO12 ...99 D6
Sheriff Hutton YO60 ...145 D5
Shipton YO30 ...165 F5
Sicklinghall LS22 ...179 D3
Sinnington YO62 ...95 A8
Stainforth BD24 ...131 E6
Stamford Bridge YO41 ...168 D2
Staveley HG5 ...140 E1
Stillington YO61 ...144 C6
Threshfield BD23 ...134 C2
Thwing YO25 ...126 B1
Tollerton YO61 ...143 A3
Ulleskelf LS24 ...190 C3
Walton LS23 ...181 A2
Wath HG4 ...114 A8
Weeton LS17 ...178 C1
West Tanfield HG4 ...87 A1
Westow YO60 ...147 B4
Wheldrake YO19 ...192 F7
Whittington LA6 ...102 A7
Wilberfoss YO41 ...185 E5
Wombleton YO62 ...93 E6
Womersley DN6 ...206 C6
Wray-with-Botton LA2 ...128 A6
Mains La YO60 ...146 D5
Mains The BD24 ...131 D3
Mainsfield Cl **8** BD24 ...131 D3
Mainsfield Rise **2** BD24 ...131 D3
Maison Dieu DL10 ...209 D7
Major St DL3 ...3 C6
Malbys Gr YO23 ...230 B3
Malbys Gr YO23 ...230 A3
Malden Rd HG1 ...220 B3
Malham Gr YO31 ...229 B5

Malham Moor La BD23 ...133 F4
Malham Rakes BD23 ...133 A2
Malham Tarn* BD24 ...132 F6
Malham Tarn Field Ctr* BD24 ...132 F6
Malham Tarn National Nature Reserve* BD24 ...132 E5
Malham Visitor Ctr* BD23 ...133 A1
Malim Rd DL1 ...221 C2
Mallard Cl **8** Filey YO14 ...101 A4
12 Pickering YO18 ...95 F7
Mallard Rd **4** DL9 ...40 F2
Mallard View YO17 ...215 D2
Mallard Way
4 Eastfield YO12 ...99 F6
11 Haxby YO32 ...166 E5
Mallard Wlk **14** YO51 ...141 B5
Mallinson Cl HG2 ...222 D6
Mallinson Cres HG2 ...222 E6
Mallinson Gate HG2 ...222 E6
Mallinson Oval HG2 ...222 D6
Mallinson Way HG2 ...222 D6
Mallison Hill Dr **8** YO61 ...117 D1
Mallorie Cl HG4 ...214 A5
Mallorie Ct HG4 ...214 B5
Mallorie Pk Dr HG4 ...214 A4
Mallory Cl YO12 ...212 B8
Mallory Ct **17** DL1 ...3 F6
Mallowdale TS7 ...7 C5
Malltraeth Sands TS17 ...6 D6
Malpas Dr DL7 ...210 D4
Malpas Rd
Brompton YO13 ...98 C4
Northallerton DL7 ...210 D3
Malsis Prep Sch BD20 ...187 C7
Malt Dubs Cl LA6 ...103 D3
Malt Kiln La YO23 ...190 F5
Malt Kiln Terr LS24 ...189 D4
Malt Shoval Ct YO11 ...233 C2
Maltby Rd TS8 ...6 F4
Malthouse La HG3 ...222 D2
Maltings Bsns Ctr The LS25 ...215 C3
Maltings Ct **8** Alne YO61 ...143 A5
8 Selby YO8 ...232 C6
Maltings The
8 Brafferton YO61 ...115 F1
18 Pontefract WF8 ...201 B1
Thirsk YO7 ...211 B2
Maltkiln La
Castleford WF10 ...200 F4
Killinghall HG3 ...161 C6
Maltings The LA6 ...102 A7
Malton & Norton Hospl YO17 ...215 B4
Malton Ave **8** YO31 ...228 E6
Malton Com Hospl YO17 ...215 A5
Malton Com Prim Sch YO17 ...215 D5
Malton Gate YO18 ...96 D5
Malton La
Allerston YO18 ...97 B4
Flaxton YO60 ...146 A1
Kirby Grindalythe YO17 ...150 A8
Malton Mus* YO17 ...215 C4
Malton Rd
Hunmanby YO14 ...126 F8
Huntington YO32 ...226 A1
Leavening YO17 ...147 E2
Pickering YO18 ...95 F6
Rillington YO17 ...122 F4
Scampston YO17 ...123 B7
Slingsby YO62 ...120 B5
Swinton YO17 ...121 C4
York YO31 ...228 F7
Malton Sch YO17 ...215 A5
Malton Sta YO17 ...215 C3
Malton Way YO30 ...227 F8
Malvern Ave YO26 ...227 D5
Malvern Cl
Huntington YO32 ...226 A5
8 Hurworth-on-Tees DL2 ...3 E1
Stokesley TS9 ...26 C7
Malvern Cres
Darlington DL3 ...3 C5
Scarborough YO12 ...212 D5
Malvern Rd
Middlesbrough TS5 ...6 E6
Stokesley TS9 ...26 C7
Malvern Way WF11 ...201 F2
Manchester Rd BB18 ...171 D1
Mancroft YO32 ...225 C8
Mandale Mill Prim Sch TS17 ...6 B8
Mandale Rd TS5 ...6 D8
Manfield CE Prim Sch DL2 ...1 D5
Mangrill La LS14 ...188 C3
Manham Hill YO11 ...99 F7
Mankin La HG4 ...214 D1
Manley Cl YO32 ...225 D4
Manley Gr LS29 ...218 E4
Manley Gr LS29 ...218 E4
Manley Rise LS29 ...218 D3
Manor Ave YO12 ...212 D6
Manor Beeches The **8** YO19 ...184 E7

Manor CE Sec Sch YO26 ...227 C7
Manor Chase YO26 ...181 F6
Manor Cl
Burton in Lonsdale LA6 ...102 F3
8 Hemingbrough YO8 ...198 F1
Ingleton LA6 ...103 D3
15 Kirkbymoorside YO62 ...70 B1
Low Worsall TS15 ...24 B8
6 North Duffield YO8 ...199 A7
12 Norton DN6 ...206 E2
8 Stokesley TS9 ...26 C7
Topcliffe YO7 ...115 C6
Upper Poppleton YO26 ...182 F8
Wath HG4 ...114 A8
Whitby YO21 ...208 B6
Manor Cres HG5 ...221 C6
Manor Croft YO42 ...169 F1
Manor Ct
6 Bubwith YO8 ...199 D7
Fairburn WF11 ...201 D7
Follifoot HG3 ...223 F5
Kirkby Malzeard HG4 ...112 D5
Knaresborough HG5 ...221 B5
2 York YO32 ...225 F6
Manor Dr
2 Brafferton YO61 ...115 F1
Camblesforth YO8 ...204 C4
4 Dunnington YO19 ...184 E7
Harrogate HG2 ...222 C8
Hilton TS15 ...6 C2
Kirby Hill YO51 ...141 A7
Knaresborough HG5 ...221 C6
8 North Duffield YO8 ...199 A7
North Featherstone WF7 ...200 E1
Pickering YO18 ...95 E7
Stokesley TS9 ...162 A6
Manor Dr N YO26 ...227 C8
Manor Dr S YO26 ...227 C8
Manor Farm Cl
1 Brayton YO8 ...232 A1
Carlton DN14 ...204 C2
Copmanthorpe YO23 ...230 A2
Manor Farm Ct YO8 ...203 A4
Manor Farm Way TS8 ...6 F5
Manor Fields DN14 ...205 B2
Manor Fold YO8 ...223 F5
Manor Garth
Haxby YO32 ...225 B8
6 Kellington DL9 ...202 F3
12 Kirklevington TS15 ...24 E8
Ledsham LS25 ...201 B8
7 Norton DN6 ...206 F2
1 Riccall YO19 ...198 A8
7 Southmith HG4 ...112 E6
Manor Garth Rd LS25 ...194 E1
Manor Gdns
6 Hummanby YO14 ...127 A8
Killinghall HG3 ...161 C5
Knaresbymoorside YO62 ...70 B1
15 Knaresborough HG5 ...221 B6
Scarborough YO12 ...212 E6
Thornton LS14 ...188 A3
Manor Gn
Northallerton DL7 ...210 C3
Patrick Brompton DL8 ...62 C5
Great Broughton TS9 ...26 E5
Manor Heath YO23 ...230 A3
Manor House Art Gall & Mus* LS29 ...218 B4
Manor Inf Sch HG5 ...221 C6
Manor La
Healaugh LS24 ...181 E1
Rawcliffe YO30 ...224 D2
Manor Orchards HG5 ...221 B6
Manor Pk
Arkendale HG5 ...163 A7
Cowling BD22 ...187 B6
Ledston WF10 ...200 F7
Swinton YO17 ...121 C1
Manor Pk Ave
North Featherstone WF7 ...200 D7
Pontefract WF8 ...201 C2
Manor Pk Cl YO30 ...224 E2
Manor Pk Gr **2** YO30 ...224 E2
Manor Pk Rd YO30 ...224 E2
Manor Pl Beal DN14 ...202 C4
Darlington DL3 ...3 C4
Fylingdales YO22 ...33 C4
Harrogate HG2 ...222 B8
Hurworth-on-Tees DL2 ...3 D1
Killinghall HG3 ...161 C5
Knaresborough YO12 ...212 E5
Manor House Mus* LS29 ...189 D4
Manor Rise LS29 ...218 D4
Manor Vale **25** YO62 ...70 B1
Manor View
Castleford WF10 ...200 D7
Oswaldkirk YO62 ...93 A1
Rillington YO17 ...122 F5
Manor View Rd YO11 ...100 C5
Manor Way
Glusburn BD20 ...187 E6
York YO30 ...224 E2
Manor Wood TS8 ...6 F6
Manorcroft WF6 ...200 A1
Manorfields **11** DL2 ...3 E1
Manse Cres **23** LS29 ...176 C1

Manse La HG5 ....221 D4
Manse Rd LS29 ....176 C1
Manse Way BD20 ....187 E7
Mansfield Ave TS17 ......6 B8
Mansfield Ct HG1 ....219 C4
Mansfield Rd LS29 ......176 B1
Mansfield St YO31 ......233 C3
Manston La TS14 DL2 ....4 C4
Manston La LS15 ....194 A5
Manton Ave TS5 ....6 D8
Maple Ave
Bishopthorpe YO23 ....231 A3
Malton YO17 ....215 D6
5 Colburn DL9 ....40 F5
Hambleton YO8 ....197 B1
8 South Milford LS25 ...195 F2
Maple Croft YO61 ......144 A5
Maple Ct
Wheldrake YO19 ....192 D8
York YO10 ....231 E6
Maple Dr YO12 ....212 D7
Maple Garth HG4 ......114 B7
Maple Gr **12** Brayton YO8 197 D1
7 Linton-on-Ouse YO30 ..164 F7
York YO10 ....228 D1
Maple La YO61 ....144 A5
Maple Rd DL10 ....209 A8
Maple Tree Ave **10** YO8 .198 B4
Maple Wlk HG4 ....214 B2
Maplehurst Ave YO8 ...228 D7
Maplewood Paddock **2**
YO24 ....227 C1
Mar Head Balk HG5 ....163 A7
Marage Rd YO7 ....211 B3
Marazion Dr YO13 ....3 C8
Marbeck La HG5 ......140 F2
March Ave HG5 ....221 A4
March St
Normanton South WF6 ..200 A1
York YO31 ....233 C4
Marchby La YO7 ....90 C7
Marderby La YO7 ....90 C7
Maresfield Rd DL9 .....40 E3
Margaret Philipson Ct
YO31 ....233 C3
Margaret Rd HG2 ......219 B1
Margaret St YO10 .....233 C1
Margerison Cres LS29 ..218 E3
Margerison Rd LS29 ...218 E3
Maria St **13** LS29 ......176 C1
Marias Ct **9** YO11 ....213 A6
Marigold Cl YO8 ......232 C2
Marina Ave **8** DN14 ...204 B1
Marina Cres BD23 .....216 D3
Marina Rd DL3 ....3 D8
Marina Way HG4 ......214 A2
Marine Dr YO11 ....213 C7
Marine Espl YO13 ......54 A8
Marine Par **24** YO21 ..208 D7
Marine Villa Rd WF11 ..201 F2
Mariner's Terr **18** YO14 .101 B3
Marion Ave TS16 ....5 D4
Marishes La
Allerston YO17 ....97 A2
Thornton-le-Dale YO17 ..96 E1
Marishes Low Rd
YO17 ....122 B8
Marjorie Waite Ct
YO30 ....228 B7
Mark House La BD23 ...155 C1
Mark La
Fylingdales YO22 ....33 C3
Kirk Deighton LS22 ...180 B5
Markenfield Hall*
HG4 ....139 D6
Markenfield Rd HG3 ...219 B5
Market Cross Sh Ctr **15**
YO8 ....232 C5
Market Flat La HG5 ...162 C6
Market Hall YO11 .....213 B6
Market La **14** YO8 ....232 C5
Market Pl Askrigg DL8 ..57 E5
4 Bedale DL8 ....63 A3
2 Cawood YO8 ....197 B8
12 Easingwold YO61 ...143 C8
Hawes DL8 ....56 C4
10 Helmsley YO62 ......92 F6
25 Kirkbymoorside YO62 .70 B1
5 Knaresborough HG5 ..221 B6
Malton YO17 ....215 C4
5 Masham HG4 ....56 C2
8 Middleham DL8 ......60 E2
6 Normanton South WF6 ..200 A1
Pickering YO18 ....95 F7
Richmond DL10 ....209 C6
11 Selby YO8 ....232 C5
10 Settle BD24 ....131 D2
8 South DN14 ....204 C1
Thirsk YO7 ....211 B3
12 Wetherby LS22 .....180 C3
11 Whitby YO22 ....208 D7
Market Pl E **14** HG4 ..214 C5
Market Pl N **23** HG4 ..214 C5
Market Pl S **20** HG4 ..214 C5
Market Pl W **27** HG4 ..214 C5
Market Row DL7 ......210 D4
Market Sq DL10 ......209 C6
Market St Malton YO17 .215 C4
Normanton South WF6 ..200 A1
York YO1 ....233 B2
Market Way **2** YO11 ..213 A6
Market Weighton Rd
YO8 ....198 B6

Markham Cres YO31 ....233 B4
Markham St YO31 .....233 B4
Markington CE Prim Sch
HG3 ....139 C3
Marl Hill La BD20 .....186 D8
Marlborough Ave
3 Byram WF11 ....201 F4
Tadcaster LS24 ....189 D5
1 Whitby YO21 ....208 B7
Marlborough Cl YO30 ..224 D3
Marlborough Dr
Darlington DL1 ....3 C4
Tadcaster LS24 ....189 D5
Marlborough Gr
Ilkley LS29 ....218 D3
Ripon HG4 ....214 B6
York YO10 ....228 D2
Marlborough Rd HG1 ..219 E2
Marlborough Sq LS29 ..218 C3
Marlborough St **11**
YO12 ....213 A7
Marlborough Villas
YO10 ....228 D2
Marmion Dr **2** YO32 ..167 D2
Marmion Ct HG4 ....87 A1
Marmion Twr* HG4 ....87 A1
Marne Cl **1** DL9 .....209 B1
Marne Rd DL9 ....209 D1
Marquis Ct YO26 .....227 D5
Marr The YO14 ....100 F5
Marrick Priory (rems of)*
DL11 ....38 C4
Marrick Rd TS18 ....5 D8
Marridales DL8 ....56 D4
Marriforth La HG4 .....61 F2
Marrtree Bsns Pk
WF10 ....200 E3
Mars La TS13 ....11 A4
Marsdens Pl **7** YO22 ..208 E6
Marsett La DL8 ....57 B2
Marsh Croft WF11 ....201 E4
Marsh End WF11 ......202 A3
Marsh La Asselby DN14 .205 D7
Barlow YO8 ....204 B8
2 Beal DN14 ....202 D4
Bolton Percy YO23 ....190 D3
Byram cum Sutton WF11 .201 F4
Cawood YO8 ....197 D8
Ingleby Greenhow TS9 ..27 B5
Knottingley WF11 .....202 A2
West Haddlesey YO8 ...202 F5
Marsh La Gdns DN14 ..202 F4
Marsh Rd WF10 ....200 D3
Marshall Dr YO18 ......96 A7
Marshall Mews **2**
WF10 ....200 E4
Marshfield Rd **7** BD24 .131 D2
Marston Ave YO26 ....227 B3
Marston Bsns Pk
YO26 ....181 B7
Marston Cres YO26 ....227 B3
Marston La
Long Marston YO26 ...182 A8
Moor Monkton YO26 ..165 A1
Marston Moor Rd DL1 ..3 F4
Marston Rd YO26 .....181 D7
Marston Way **3** LS22 .180 B3
Marston Cl **2** YO30 ..228 A8
Martin Cheeseman Ct **3**
YO24 ....230 C8
Martindale Rd DL1 .....3 D7
Martinet Cl TS17 ......6 A7
Martinet Rd TS17 ......6 A7
Martinhoe Cl **4** TS17 ..6 A3
Martins Ct YO26 ......228 A5
Marton Abbey (Priory)*
YO61 ....144 C3
Marton Ave TS4 ....7 B8
Marton Ct YO10 ......208 B6
Marton cum Grafton CE VA
Prim Sch YO51 ......141 D1
Marton La
Arkendale HG5 ....163 B8
Wrelton YO18 ....95 C7
Marton Manor Prim Sch
TS7 ....7 B6
Marton Moor Rd TS7 ...7 D5
Marton Rd
Coulby Newham TS4 ....7 A7
Gargrave BD23 ....172 C8
Marton YO62 ....94 F6
Sinnington YO62 ....95 A7
Marton St BD23 ......216 D3
Marton Sta TS7 ....7 C7
Marvelstone Way TS4 ...7 A8
Marvell Rise HG1 .....219 E7
Marwood CE VA Sch TS9 .7 F1
Marwood Dr TS9 ....7 F1
Mary La YO16 ....141 F3
Mary St **3** BD20 .....173 F1
Marygate Barton DL10 .21 D7
York YO30 ....233 A3
Marygate La YO30 ....233 A3
Marykirk Rd YO7 ....6 B6
Masefield Cl HG1 .....219 E7
Masham Bank HG4 .....85 D8
Masham CE VA Prim Sch
HG4 ....86 C3
Masham Cl HG2 ......220 C1
Masham La HG4 ....87 A4
Masham Rd Firby DL8 ..62 F1
Harrogate HG2 ....220 C1
Snape with Thorp DL8 ..86 E8
Mask La YO61 ....185 D4
Masongill Fell La LA6 ..103 A6
Masonic La YO7 ......211 B3
Maspin Moor Rd LS25 .202 C7

Massa Flatts Wood
BD23 ....216 E5
Massey St YO8 ....232 C5
Master Rd TS17 ....6 B7
Master's Gate YO18 ...49 D4
Mastil Cl DL8 ....62 D5
Mastil La DL8 ....62 D5
Mastiles La BD23 .....134 A6
Matfen Ave YO7 ....7 D6
Matthew La
Bradleys Both BD20 ...173 E3
Green Hammerton YO26 .164 C4
Mattison Way YO24 ...227 E2
Maud La LS21 ....177 A6
Maude Rd DL9 ....209 A1
Maudon Ave YO18 .....96 A6
Maudon Gr YO17 .....214 B6
Maufe Way **1** LS29 ..218 B3
Maunby La YO7 ....64 D1
Mawson Gr DL6 ....65 B5
Mawson La HG4 ......214 C4
Maxim Cl **5** DL9 .....40 E4
Maxwell Rd LS29 .....218 D3
May Beck Farm Trail
YO22 ....32 D1
Mayfair Ave TS6 ....7 E8
Mayfair Rd DL1 ....3 D8
Mayfield DL7 ....64 F2
Mayfield Ave
Ilkley LS29 ....218 D4
7 Scalby YO12 ....75 E5
Mayfield Cl
3 Glusburn BD20 ....187 E7
Ilkley LS29 ....218 D4
Mayfield Cres TS16 .....5 D5
Mayfield Dr
Brayton YO8 ....232 A1
4 Seamer YO12 ....99 D6
Mayfield Gdns LS29 ..218 D5
Mayfield Gr
Harrogate HG1 ....219 D3
Knaresborough HG5 ...221 C6
York YO24 ....230 E8
Mayfield Pl
Harrogate HG1 ....219 D3
3 Whitby YO21 ....208 C5
Mayfield Rd
Brayton YO8 ....232 A1
Ilkley LS29 ....218 C4
Middlesbrough TS7 ......7 D6
Whitby YO21 ....208 B5
Mayfield Terr HG1 ....219 D3
Maypole Gdns YO8 ...197 B8
Maypole Gr **3** YO19 .191 D8
Maypole Mews LS15 ..194 B8
Maythorn Rd YO31 ...225 E2
Maythorpe YO23 .....182 C6
Mayville Ave YO12 ....212 E6
Mcan Cl YO10 ....228 E3
McArthur Designer Outlet
YO19 ....231 D4
McBean Stps* YO11 ..213 A5
McDonald Rd HG4 ....113 D3
McMullen Rd DL1 ......3 E6
Mead Cres TS17 ....6 C8
Meadlands YO31 .....229 B6
Meadow Ave **5** HG4 ..214 B2
Meadow Brook Chase **10**
WF6 ....200 B1
Meadow Cl
Cononley BD20 ....173 D2
7 Eastfield YO11 .....100 A6
Hampsthwaite HG3 ....160 F5
Northallerton DL7 ....210 D2
Thorpe Willoughby YO8 .197 C2
Meadow Croft
Brayton YO8 ....232 A2
Cononley BD20 ....173 C2
Meadow Ct
Rillington YO17 ......122 F5
Scruton DL7 ....63 E7
9 Willerby YO12 ....99 E8
9 York YO24 ....230 E8
Meadow Dale Ct TS12 ...9 F7
Meadow Dr
7 East Ayton/West Ayton
YO13 ....99 B8
Harrogate HG1 ....219 E7
Scruton DL7 ....63 E7
Thorpe Willoughby YO8 .197 B2
Meadow Garth
2 Tadcaster LS24 .....189 F6
Thirsk YO7 ....211 B1
Thorpe Willoughby YO8 .197 C2
Meadow Gate HG1 ....219 E6
Meadow Gr **2** DL8 ....63 A2
Meadow La
Cononley BD20 ....173 C2
2 Darley HG3 ....160 A6
8 Eastfield YO11 .....100 A6
1 Haxby YO32 ....166 E5
Northallerton DL6 ....210 E6
Snape DL8 ....87 A7
Meadow La **24** BD20 ..187 E7
Meadow Pl **5** YO8 ...232 B6
Meadow Rd
Garforth LS25 ....194 D4
Knaresborough HG5 ...221 B7
2 Pickering YO18 ......95 F7
Meadow Rise
Harrogate HG1 ....219 E2
2 Skipton BD23 ....217 B5
Meadow Springs Way **3**
YO61 ....143 D8
Meadow Vale
Green Hammerton YO26 .164 C3
2 Ripon HG4 ....214 B2

Meadow View
Barwick in Elmet & Scholes
LS15 ....194 B8
Harrogate HG1 ....219 E6
Sherburn in Elmet LS25 .195 F4
Meadow Way
Barnoldswick BB18 ....171 E2
Harrogate HG1 ....219 E7
Heworth YO31 ....228 F7
Huntington YO32 .....225 F4
York YO31 ....228 F7
Meadowbank Rd TS7 ...7 D7
Meadowbeck Cl YO10 ..228 E2
Meadowcroft
Draughton BD23 ......174 B7
Harrogate HG1 ....219 E6
Meadowcroft Dr HG3 ..140 A5
Meadowfield
Amotherby YO17 .....121 A4
8 Bedale DL8 ....63 B3
1 Bulwith YO8 ....199 D7
Lythe YO21 ....13 A3
8 Stokesley TS9 ....26 C8
Meadowfield Dr TS16 ...5 D5
Meadowfield Rd
6 Colburn DL9 ....41 A5
Darlington DL3 ....3 A7
Meadowfields HG2 ...208 C6
Meadowfields Cl **9**
YO21 ....208 C6
Meadowfields Ct **17**
YO21 ....208 D6
Meadowfields Dr
YO31 ....225 D2
Meadowings The TS15 ...5 D2
Meadowlands Cl **2** TS13 .11 A8
Meadows The
Carlton DN14 ....204 C3
Castleford LS25 ......200 C7
Coulby Newham TS8 ....7 B5
Hambleton YO8 ......196 F1
8 Middleton St George DL2 .4 C4
7 Monk Fryston LS25 ..202 A8
Riccall YO19 ....197 F8
Richmond DL10 ......209 E7
Scalby YO12 ....212 B7
2 Skelton YO30 ......224 B5
South Milford LS25 ...195 F2
Meadowside Com Prim Sch
HG5 ....221 C7
Meads La **3** YO11 .....99 F6
Meads The **3** YO11 ...99 F6
Meadway YO11 ....197 D2
Meadway Dr YO8 .....197 D2
Meagill La LS21 ......159 E4
Meagill Rise LS21 ....176 E1
Meam Cl YO10 ....229 D4
Meanee Rd **11** DL9 ...40 F2
Medbourne Gdns TS5 ...6 E7
Megson Pl YO7 ......211 C4
Melander Cl YO10 ....229 D4
Melander Gdns **3** YO32 .225 D7
Melbourne Dr YO7 ....90 E5
Melbourne Rd YO7 ...211 B2
Melbourne St YO10 ..228 D2
Melcombe Ave **11** YO32 .167 A7
Meldyke La TS8 ....6 D5
Melling St Wilfred CE Prim
Sch LA6 ....102 A2
Melltown's Gn YO7 ....88 C6
Melmerby Gn La HG4 .114 C6
Melmerby Gn Rd HG4 .114 B6
Melmerby Ind Est
HG4 ....114 B6
Melrose Cl **1** YO31 ..229 A5
Melrose Cres
Bishop Monkton HG3 .140 A5
Guisborough TS14 ......9 A6
Melrose Dr **16** LS29 ..176 C1
Melrose Rd HG4 .....140 A5
Melrose St **4** YO12 ..212 E6
Melrosegate YO10 ....228 F5
Melsonby Methodist Prim
Sch DL10 ....20 F7
Melton Ave YO30 ....227 F8
Melton Dr
Bishopthorpe YO23 ...231 A3
York YO30 ....227 F8
Melville Sr **1** LS29 ..218 E4
Melville Terr **22** YO14 .101 B3
Melwood Gr YO26 ....227 B5
Memorial Dr TS7 ......7 B6
Mendip Cl **2** YO32 ..225 F5
Menethorpe La YO17 .147 D7
Menin Rd DL9 ....209 B1
Menwith Hill Rd HG3 .159 D4
Mercer Art Gall*
HG2 ....219 C3
Mercer Dr DL9 ....209 C1
Merchant Adventurers Hall*
YO1 ....233 C2
Merchant Way YO11 ..230 B3
Merchant's Row **10**
YO11 ....213 B6
Merchantgate YO1 ....233 C2
Merchants Ct YO31 ...228 E5
Mere La YO11 ....214 F1
Mere Gdns YO11 ......99 F8
Merefield Way WF10 ..200 E4
Merewood Rd WF10 ..200 E4
Merioneth St TS17 .....6 A5
Merlin Covert **4** YO31 .225 F3
Merlin Rd **3** HG3 ....159 D4
Merrimoon Ave **2** TS17 ..6 D6
Merry Dale YO11 .....100 A7
Merrybank La LS17 ...178 A3

Merrybent Dr DL2 ......2 F5
Merryfield HG2 ....222 B7
Mesnes La DL8 ....59 D3
Messines Rd DL9 .....40 E3
Metcalfe La YO19 ....229 C5
Metcalfes Ct HG4 ....214 C6
Metes La YO12 ....99 E5
Methley Inf Sch LS26 .200 B5
Methley Jun Sch LS26 .200 B6
Methley La LS26 .....200 A6
Methley Pk Hospl
LS26 ....200 A6
Methley Rd WF10 ....200 D4
Methodist Prim Sch
DL11 ....36 E5
Meuse Cl **4** DL9 ....209 C1
Mewburn Rd DL3 ......3 C8
Mewith La LA2 ....129 B6
Mews Tw WF6 ....200 A2
Meynell Rd DL3 ....3 C7
Meyrick Ave LS22 ....180 C4
Michael Mount Rd
YO11 ....213 C1
Michael Syddall CE Aided
Prim Sch DL10 ....41 E5
Mickleberry La HG4 ...86 A3
Mickleby Dr YO21 ....208 B6
Mickleby La TS13 ......11 F4
Mickledale La YO26 ..163 D8
Micklefield CE Sch
LS25 ....195 A4
Micklefield Sta LS25 .195 A3
Micklegate
17 Pontefract WF8 ...201 B1
1 Selby YO8 ....232 D5
York YO1 ....233 A2
Micklegate Bar Mus*
YO24 ....233 A1
Micklethwaite View
LS22 ....180 C2
Mickletown Rd LS26 ..200 B6
Micklewaite Gr LS22 .180 C2
Middle Bank Rd TS7 ...7 D7
Middle Banks **2** YO32 .166 E5
Middle Head Rd YO18 ..71 E8
Middle La Brayton YO8 .232 C1
Brompton YO13 ....98 C7
Collingham LS22 .....180 B1
Hutton Buscel YO13 ...74 E1
Kettlewell with Starbotton
BD23 ....108 A3
14 Knottingley WF11 ..202 A2
Snainton YO13 ....97 F4
Middle Moor La DL11 ..39 F5
Middle Oxford St
WF10 ....200 E4
Middle Rd YO11 ....6 A5
Swinton YO17 ....121 B4
Wilberfoss YO41 .....185 F5
Middle Wlk YO12 .....212 E7
Middlebrook Gdns
YO8 ....232 A2
Middlecave Dr YO17 ..215 A4
Middlecave Cl YO17 ..215 A4
Middlecave Rd YO17 ..215 A4
Middlecroft Dr YO32 ..167 A7
Middlecroft Gr **2** YO32 .167 B7
Middlefield Cl
10 Osgodby YO11 ....100 B7
Weaverthorpe YO17 ..124 E1
Middlefield La
Kirk Smeaton WF8 ...206 A2
Melmerby DL8 ....84 A8
Middleham Ave YO11 .228 E8
Middleham Castle*
DL8 ....60 E2
Middleham CE Aided Prim
Sch DL8 ....60 E2
Middleham La DL8 .....60 E2
Middlesbrough Rd TS7 ..7 E6
Middlethorpe Dr
YO24 ....230 E7
Middlethorpe Gr YO24 .230 F7
Middleton Ave
Ilkley LS29 ....218 A4
Thornaby TS17 ....6 B6
Middleton Carr La
YO18 ....95 D7
Middleton Cl
Egglescliffe TS16 ......5 C5
Settrington YO17 ....122 D1
Middleton La
Middleton YO18 ....95 E8
Middleton St George DL2 .4 C3
Middleton Rd
Hutton Rudby TS15 ....25 D6
Ilkley LS29 ....218 A4
Pickering YO18 ....95 E7
Sadberge DL2 ....4 C7
York YO24 ....230 F7
Middleton St George Prim
Sch DL2 ....4 C4
Middleton Tyas CE Prim Sch
DL10 ....21 B4
Middleton Tyas La
DL10 ....21 B4
Middlewood Cl
3 Fylingdales YO22 ...33 C3
Rufforth YO23 ....182 C6
Middlewood Cres **5**
YO22 ....33 C3
Middlewood Garth **4**
YO22 ....33 C3
Middycar Bank HG4 ..138 F6
Midge Hall Cl **18** LS29 .176 C1

Midgeley Gate HG5 . . . . .162 F2
Midgeley La HG5 . . . . . .163 A3
Midgley Cl
4 Embsay BD23 . . . . .217 C7
7 Stamford Bridge YO41 .168 D2
Midgley Rd LS29 . . . . . . .176 C1
Midgley Rise **3** WF4 . . .201 B2
Midhope Way **19** YO14 . .101 A3
Midland St BD23 . . . . . . .216 E3
Midway Ave YO26 . . . . . .224 A1
Mightens' Bank DL8 . . . .60 D4
Milbank Rd DL8 . . . . .3 B5
Milburn La YO7 . . . . .89 D3
Mildred Gr **5** YO24 . . . .227 F2
Mildred Sylvester Way
WF6 . . . . .200 B1
Mile Hill Coldhill La
LS25 . . . . .195 E5
Mile Planting DL10 . . . .209 F8
Milestone Ave YO23 . . .182 C6
Milford Mews **17** YO32 .225 D7
Milford Rd LS25 . . . . . . .195 F3
Milford Way **8** YO32 . .225 D7
Milking Hill YO61 . . . . . .118 B4
Mill Balk DN14 . . . . .207 C8
Mill Bank
Bishop Thornton HG3 . . . .138 F1
Fylingdales YO22 . . . . .33 D2
Lindrick with Studley
Royal & Fountains HG4 . .113 A3
Norton YO17 . . . . .215 E3
Mill Bank Rd YO18 . . . . .72 D5
Mill Bridge BD23 . . . . . .216 F4
Mill Brow LA2 . . . . .128 E2
Mill Brow Rd BB18 . . . .172 B1
Mill Chase Rd HG2 . . . .220 D5
Mill Cl
Monk Fryston LS25 . . . . . .202 A8
Ravensworth DL11 . . . . . . .19 F6
Settle BD24 . . . . .131 D2
6 Spofforth HG3 . . . . . .179 E6
Mill Cotts YO17 . . . . . . .215 D4
Mill Croft
Cowling BD22 . . . . .187 B6
Richmond DL10 . . . . .209 A7
Mill Dam LS23 . . . . .188 F7
Mill Dam La WF8 . . . . . .201 C1
Mill Dike La YO7 . . . . . .116 F8
Mill Field La YO61 . . . . . .90 B1
Mill Field Rd YO8 . . . . . .203 B5
Mill Flats La DL8 . . . . . . .60 F3
Mill Garth **14** YO8 . . .198 F1
Mill Gate
Gilling with Hartforth & Sedbury
DL10 . . . . .20 E3
Harrogate HG1 . . . . .219 C7
Knayton with Brawith YO7 . .65 E2
Mill Gn Way The YO22 . . .51 D8
Mill Hill Escrick YO19 . . .192 B5
10 Normanton South WF6 .200 A1
Mill Hill Cl DL6 . . . . .43 F3
Mill Hill Com Prim Sch
DL6 . . . . .210 C4
Mill Hill Cres DL6 . . . . .210 C3
Mill Hill Dr YO32 . . . . . .225 F4
Mill Hill La
Giggleswick BD24 . . . . . .131 C3
Northallerton DL6 . . . . . .210 E3
Mill Hills La DL11 . . . . . .38 E4
Mill House YO7 . . . . .65 D1
Mill La
Acaster Malbis YO23 . . . .191 C8
Ampleforth YO62 . . . . . .118 C8
Askham Richard YO23 . . .182 D2
Askrigg DL8 . . . . .57 E6
Aysgarth DL8 . . . . .58 E3
Barlow YO8 . . . . .204 B7
Bellerby DL8 . . . . .60 E8
Bentham LA2 . . . . .128 F7
3 Beverley HG4 . . . . . .137 B4
Boroughbridge YO51 . . . .141 B5
Brayton YO8 . . . . .203 C8
Buckton/Bempton YO13 . . .97 D5
Burniston YO13 . . . . .75 C8
Burton Leonard HG3 . . . .140 B2
Carlton DN14 . . . . .204 D3
Castleford WF10 . . . . . . .200 E5
Cayton YO11 . . . . .100 C6
Constable Burton DL8 . . . .61 C5
Darlington DL1 . . . . .3 F6
Earby BB18 . . . . .172 B1
Easingwold YO61 . . . . . .117 D1
3 East Ayton/West Ayton
YO13 . . . . .99 A7
Eskdaleside cum Ugglebarnby
YO22 . . . . .32 B6
Exelby, Leeming & Newton
DL7 . . . . .63 D3
Faceby TS9 . . . . .25 F2
Farndale East YO62 . . . . .48 E4
Gargrave BD23 . . . . .155 D1
Great Ouseburn YO26 . . .164 C8
Hambleton YO8 . . . . .196 F1
Haxby YO32 . . . . .166 D5
Hebden BD23 . . . . .135 A1
2 Hemingbrough YO8 . . .198 F1
Hessay YO23 . . . . .182 B7
High Coniscliffe DL2 . . . . . .2 C6
Kearby with Netherby
LS22 . . . . .179 C2
Kirk Hammerton YO26 . . .164 C2
Knaresborough HG5 . . . .221 F8
Langtoft YO25 . . . . .151 C7
Leyburn DL8 . . . . .60 E4
6 Long Preston cum YO30 .164 F7
Long Preston BD23 . . . . .153 F4
Longnewton DL2 . . . . .4 F1
Low Bradley BD20 . . . . .173 E3

Mill La continued
Mickletown LS26 . . . . . . .200 B6
Middleton St George DL2 . . .4 D5
Muston YO14 . . . . .101 A2
Nether Silton YO7 . . . . . .66 B6
Newland YO8 . . . . .205 A3
Northallerton DL7 . . . . . .210 C3
Pannal HG3 . . . . .222 E2
Pickering YO18 . . . . .95 F6
Pontefract WF8 . . . . . . .201 C2
Rawcliffe DN14 . . . . .204 F1
Redmire DL8 . . . . .59 C5
1 Riccall YO19 . . . . . . .192 A1
Ryther cum Ossendyke
LS24 . . . . .190 E1
1 Scarborough YO12 . . .212 E3
Scruton DL7 . . . . .63 E5
Sherburn in Elmet LS25 . .195 F2
Skipton BD23 . . . . .216 F3
Sledmere YO25 . . . . .149 F3
Snape with Thorp DL8 . . . .87 B7
South Milford LS25 . . . . .195 F2
Spofforth with Stockeld
HG3 . . . . .179 E6
Stillington YO61 . . . . . . .144 C6
Stutton with Hazlewood
LS24 . . . . .189 E4
Swinden BD23 . . . . .154 B1
Thirkleby High & Low
with Osgodby YO7 . . . . . .90 C2
Thormanby YO61 . . . . . .116 E5
Threlnoft DL7 . . . . .63 F8
Whitwood WF10 . . . . . . .200 B2
Wilberfoss YO41 . . . . . . .185 E6
York YO31 . . . . .228 E6
York YO10 . . . . .142 F2
Mill La Ave YO60 . . . . . .145 C5
Mill Mount YO24 . . . . . .228 A3
Mill Mount Ct YO24 . . . .228 A3
Mill Race The **4** DL2 . .22 B8
Mill Rd
Burton Fleming YO25 . . . .126 D4
Gillamoor YO62 . . . . .70 A5
Goldsborough HG5 . . . . .221 F3
Mill Riggs TS9 . . . . .26 D7
Mill Rise DL6 . . . . .210 E2
Mill Row BD20 . . . . .187 F7
Mill St
8 Barnoldswick BB18 . . .171 D1
Glusburn BD20 . . . . .187 F7
Guisborough TS14 . . . . . . .8 F6
Harome YO62 . . . . .93 C4
Malton YO17 . . . . .215 E3
Scarborough YO12 . . . . .212 F5
York YO1 . . . . .233 C2
Mill View
8 Burley in Warfedale
LS29 . . . . .176 C1
Knottingley WF11 . . . . . .201 D2
Mill Wynd TS16 . . . . .5 E3
Millbank Ct YO7 . . . . . . .89 D4
Millbeck Gn LS22 . . . . . .188 A8
Millenium Rd BD20 . . . . .173 D4
Millers Cl YO17 . . . . . . .215 D2
Millers Croft **6** YO23 . .230 B3
Millers La TS12 . . . . .9 F6
Millers Rd **2** YO7 . . . .211 C3
Millfield YO51 . . . . .141 D2
Millfield Ave
Northallerton DL6 . . . . . .210 C3
York YO10 . . . . .228 F3
Millfield Cl
Eaglescliffe TS16 . . . . .5 D4
1 Leeming DL7 . . . . . . .63 D4
Pickering YO18 . . . . .95 F6
Wilberfoss YO41 . . . . . . .185 E5
Millfield Cres DL6 . . . . . .210 E3
Millfield Ct YO19 . . . . . .192 F7
Millfield Dr YO8 . . . . . . .204 D4
Millfield Gdns YO26 . . . .224 A2
Millfield Glade HG2 . . . .220 D4
Millfield La
Easingwold YO61 . . . . . . .117 C1
Nether Poppleton YO26 . .227 B8
Poppleton YO26 . . . . . . .224 A2
York YO10 . . . . .229 A3
Millfield Rd
17 Hemingbrough YO8 . .198 F1
Hemingbrough YO8 . . . . .204 F8
Thirsk YO7 . . . . .211 B3
Millfield Rise YO61 . . . . .117 C1
Millfield St **4** HG3 . . . .137 B4
Millfields BD20 . . . . . . .187 E8
Millgarth Ct **17** LS22 . .188 A8
Millgarth **18** Masham HG4 .86 C3
Richmond DL10 . . . . .209 C6
Selby YO8 . . . . .232 C6
Thirsk YO7 . . . . .211 B3
Millgate House Gdn*
DL10 . . . . .209 C2
Millgates YO26 . . . . . . .227 C6
Millholme Rise BD23 . . . .217 C8
Millings La YO51 . . . . . .141 B7
Millrace Cl YO17 . . . . . .215 D2
Millside YO17 . . . . .215 D2
Millthorpe Sec Sch
YO23 . . . . .228 B2
Millway YO10 . . . . .92 C1
Milner La LS24 . . . . .195 D8
Milner Rd DL1 . . . . .3 D4
Milner St YO24 . . . . .227 D3
Milners La HG1 . . . . .219 C2
Milnthorpe Cl **6** LS23 . .188 E6
Milnthorpe Garth **7**
LS23 . . . . .188 E6
Milnthorpe Gdns **5**
LS23 . . . . .188 E6

Milnthorpe La LS23 . . . .188 E6
Milnthorpe Way LS23 . . .188 D5
Milson Gr YO10 . . . . . . .229 A3
Milton Ave
Malton YO17 . . . . .215 D5
Scarborough YO12 . . . . .212 E3
Milton Carr **8** YO30 . . .224 F1
Milton Cl HG1 . . . . .219 E7
Milton Gr **11** BB18 . . . .171 D2
Milton Rd Malton YO17 . .215 C5
Milton Rd HG1 . . . . .222 E3
Milton Rms* YO17 . . . . .215 B4
Milton St Darlington DL1 . . .3 E5
4 Skipton BD23 . . . . . .217 A3
York YO10 . . . . .228 F3
Minchin Cl **3** YO30 . . .225 C8
Mine Mus* BD23 . . . . . .172 A2
Minors Cres DL3 . . . . .3 A7
Minskip Rd HG5 . . . . . . .140 F2
Minster Ave YO7 . . . . . .225 F2
Minster Cl
3 Haxby YO32 . . . . . . .225 C8
26 Ripon HG4 . . . . . . .214 C5
Minster Ct YO31 . . . . . .233 B3
Minster Rd HG4 . . . . . . .214 C5
Minster Sch The YO1 . . .233 B3
Minster View YO32 . . . .225 C8
Minster Wlk **12** DL2 . . . .4 D3
Minster Yd YO1 . . . . . . .233 B3
Minsterley Dr TS5 . . . . . . .6 D7
Minter Cl **2** YO24 . . . .227 B1
Mire Bank La DL8 . . . . . .56 F4
Mire Cl La BD22 . . . . . . .187 A8
Mire Ridge BB8 . . . . . . .186 A2
Mire Syke La HG5 . . . . .162 A5
Mires La Carthorpe DL8 . . .87 D6
Ulleskelf LS24 . . . . .190 B1
Mirkhill Rd YO8 . . . . . . .232 B6
Miry La LS15 . . . . .188 C1
Missies La HG4 . . . . .112 C3
Mistral Ct YO31 . . . . . . .228 E8
Mitchell Ave TS17 . . . . . . .6 B7
Mitchell La Alne YO61 . . .142 F4
Catton YO41 . . . . .185 D8
Settle BD24 . . . . .131 E1
Mitchell Way YO30 . . . . .224 E2
Mitchel's La YO10 . . . . . .231 F8
Miterdale **8** YO24 . . . .230 C7
Mitford Cl **8** YO14 . . . .126 F8
Mitford Rd **2** YO14 . . .126 F8
Mitford St **20** YO14 . . .101 B3
Mitton La BD20 . . . . . . .172 D1
Moat Field YO10 . . . . . .229 C4
Moat Way YO8 . . . . .197 D1
Moatside Ct YO31 . . . . .233 B3
Mock Beggar Hall*
BD23 . . . . .157 D7
Moins Ct YO10 . . . . .229 D4
Moiser Cl YO32 . . . . . . .225 D4
Mole End **10** YO18 . . . . .95 F6
Monarch Way YO26 . . . .227 D6
Monash Ave DL9 . . . . . .209 C1
Monckton Dr WF10 . . . .201 B3
Monk Ave YO31 . . . . . . .228 F7
Monk Bar & Richard III Mus*
YO31 . . . . .233 C3
Monk Fryston CE VC Prim
Sch LS25 . . . . .202 A8
Monk Fryston Prim Sch
LS25 . . . . .202 A8
Monk Gdns La YO62 . . . .93 A7
Monk Gn YO61 . . . . .142 F4
Monk Ing Rd HG3 . . . . . .159 E8
Monk La YO8 . . . . .232 C7
Monk Pk Farm* YO7 . . . .90 D4
Monk's Rd BD23 . . . . . .107 D2
Monkbridge Ct YO31 . . .233 C4
Monket House Bank
YO62 . . . . .48 C4
Monkgate Cloisters
YO31 . . . . .233 C3
Monkhill Ave WF8 . . . . .201 B1
Monkhill Dr WF8 . . . . . .201 B1
Monkhill La WF8 . . . . . .201 B1
Monkhill Mount WF8 . . .201 B1
Monkholme La BD23 . . . .134 C2
Monkroyd Ave BB18 . . . .171 D1
Monks Cross Dr YO32 . . .226 A3
Monks Cross Link
YO32 . . . . .226 B4
Monks Cross Sh Pk
YO32 . . . . .226 B4
Monkswell Pk HG5 . . . . .221 D5
Monkton Rd **3** YO31 . .225 F1
Monkton Rise **7** TS14 . . .8 F7
Monmouth Dr TS16 . . . . . .5 E3
Monmouth St **5** BB8 . .186 A3
Mons Cl **3** DL9 . . . . . .209 B1
Mons Rd DL9 . . . . .40 F4
Montage Studio Gall*
YO21 . . . . .29 A7
Montague Cres LS25 . . . .194 D4
Montague Rd YO23 . . . .231 A3
Montague St YO23 . . . . .228 C1
Montague Wlk **6** YO26 .165 F1
Montagu's Harrier TS14 . .8 D6
Montgomery Rd DL9 . . . .209 C2
Montgomery St BD23 . . .217 A3
Montpellier Cl **11** HG2 .219 C2
Montpellier Gdns **2**
HG1 . . . . .219 C2
Montpellier Hill HG2 . . . .219 C2
Montpellier Mews **3**
HG1 . . . . .219 C2
Montpellier Par HG1 . . . .219 C2

Montpellier Rd **1** HG1 . .219 C2
Montpellier Sq **3** HG1 . .219 C2
Montpellier St **4** HG1 . .219 C2
Montrose Ave YO31 . . . .228 E8
Moody Sty La **8** BD23 . .134 E3
Mook St YO60 . . . . .169 B8
Moons Acre LA2 . . . . . . .129 A8
Moor Ave **1** LS23 . . . .188 E7
Moor Carr La YO8 . . . . . .198 B5
10 Kirklevington TS15 . . .24 E8
Moor Cl Killinghall HG3 . .219 A8
Lockwood TS12 . . . . .10 A5
Wistow YO8 . . . . .192 F8
Moor Cres BD23 . . . . . . .217 B4
Moor Croft **8** BD23 . . . .134 E3
Moor End La
Crakehall DL8 . . . . .62 C3
Sowerby YO7 . . . . .90 A2
Moor End Rd YO13 . . . . . .53 F2
Moor Gn TS7 . . . . .7 D5
Moor Gr YO24 . . . . .230 E8
Moor Hill YO17 . . . . . . .147 E7
Moor House La YO61 . . . .116 B1
Moor La
Addingham LS29 . . . . . . .174 D5
Aislaby YO21 . . . . .31 F7
Aldfield HG4 . . . . .138 F8
Arkendale HG5 . . . . .162 F7
Arrathorne DL10 . . . . .41 A2
Askwith LS21 . . . . .176 D4
Bagby YO7 . . . . .90 C4
6 Barlby YO8 . . . . .198 B5
Bilbrough LS24 . . . . .182 B1
Bilton-in-Ainsty with Bickerton
YO26 . . . . .181 D5
Bishopthorpe YO23 . . . . .230 E2
Borrowby TS13 . . . . .11 C6
Brawby YO17 . . . . .94 F2
Brompton YO13 . . . . .74 B1
Broughton YO17 . . . . . . .121 C4
Burton Leonard HG3 . . . .140 B4
Carthorpe DL8 . . . . .87 D4
Catterton LS24 . . . . .190 A8
Cleasby DL2 . . . . .2 F2
Cliffe YO8 . . . . .198 F4
Cloughton YO13 . . . . .54 C1
Collingham LS23 . . . . . . .188 C8
Coneythorpe & Clareton
HG5 . . . . .163 B6
Copmanthorpe YO23 . . . .230 A1
Crayke YO61 . . . . .118 A6
Crosby DL6 . . . . .65 C5
Dalton DL11 . . . . .19 C6
Dalton YO7 . . . . .115 A8
Danby YO21 . . . . .29 C8
Dishforth YO7 . . . . .114 F3
Earswick YO32 . . . . .226 C8
East Ayton/West Ayton
YO13 . . . . .99 B8
East Layton DL11 . . . . . . .20 B8
Eastfield YO11 . . . . .100 A6
Eslack BD23 . . . . .172 D3
Embsay with Eastby
BD23 . . . . .156 F1
Full Sutton YO41 . . . . . . .168 F1
Grassington BD23 . . . . . .134 E3
Great Ouseburn YO26 . . .163 D7
Great Ribston with Walshford
YO26 . . . . .180 E8
Halton East BD23 . . . . . .157 B1
Haxby YO32 . . . . .166 D7
Hunton DL8 . . . . .61 E8
Hutton-le-Hole YO62 . . . .70 C5
Kearby with Netherby
HG3 . . . . .179 B2
Kelfield YO19 . . . . .191 E2
Kirby Hill HG4 . . . . .140 F8
Long Preston BD23 . . . . .153 F5
Milby YO51 . . . . .141 F7
Murton YO19 . . . . .229 F8
Myton-on-Swale YO61 . . .142 B5
Naburn YO19 . . . . .191 D8
Nether Silton DL6 . . . . . . .66 C8
Newsham DL11 . . . . .19 A7
Newsham with Breckenbrough
YO7 . . . . .65 A1
Newton-on-Ouse YO30 . .165 C7
Rufforth YO23 . . . . .182 E6
Ryther cum Ossendyke
LS24 . . . . .196 A6
Scalby YO12 . . . . .212 A8
Settrington YO17 . . . . . .122 C1
Sherburn in Elmet LS25 . .195 F4
Skelton YO30 . . . . .224 D6
Snape with Thorp DL8 . . . .86 E6
Steeton with Eastburn
BD20 . . . . .187 F7
Stillington YO61 . . . . . . .143 F6
Strensall YO32 . . . . .167 B7
Stutton with Hazlewood
LS24 . . . . .189 D4
Thirkleby High & Low with
Osgodby YO7 . . . . .90 C1
Thirsk YO7 . . . . .89 D5
Thornaby YO61 . . . . .116 E5
Thornton Steward HG4 . . .84 F2
Thornton-le-Clay YO60 . .145 F2
Thornton-le-Moor DL6 . . .65 F1
Threshfield BD23 . . . . . .134 B2
Welburn YO62 . . . . .94 A5
West Tanfield HG4 . . . . . .87 B2
Weston LS21 . . . . .176 E2
Wilstrop YO26 . . . . .181 B8
Yafforth DL7 . . . . .43 B2
York YO24 . . . . .230 C6
Moor La Trad Est
LS25 . . . . .196 A3

Mid - Mor **261**

Moor Lee La
Eggborough DN14 . . . . . .207 B8
Heck DN14 . . . . .203 B1
Moor Pk TS7 . . . . .7 D5
Moor Pk Ave LS29 . . . . .174 F4
Moor Pk Cl
2 Addingham LS29 . . . .174 F4
Pannal HG3 . . . . .178 A8
Moor Pk Cres **3** LS29 . .174 F4
Moor Pk Dr LS29 . . . . . .174 E4
Moor Pk Gr **2** LS29 . . .174 F4
Moor Pk Way **1** LS29 . .174 F4
Moor Rd Askrigg DL8 . . . .57 E6
Bishop Monkton HG3 . . . .139 F5
Filey YO14 . . . . .101 B1
Hunmanby YO14 . . . . . . .127 B7
Ilkley LS29 . . . . .218 F1
Knayton with Brawith YO7 . .65 F3
Leyburn DL8 . . . . .60 C5
Marton cum Grafton
YO51 . . . . .141 C2
Melsonby DL10 . . . . .20 F6
Muston YO14 . . . . .101 A2
9 Sherburn in Elmet LS25 .195 F4
Stamford Bridge YO41 . . .168 D2
Wykeham YO13 . . . . .74 B4
Moor Side LS23 . . . . . . .188 E8
Moor View **8** TS13 . . . .11 F7
Moor Way YO22 . . . . . . .226 A4
Moorber La BD23 . . . . . .171 F8
Moorberries TS15 . . . . . . .6 C2
Moorbridge Croft **6**
LS25 . . . . .196 A4
Moorcock La HG3 . . . . . .159 F5
Moorcroft Rd YO24 . . . .230 D7
Moore Ave YO10 . . . . . .229 B4
Moorfield Dr YO41 . . . . .185 E6
Moorfield Rd LS29 . . . . .218 F4
Moorfield Sch LS29 . . . .218 C3
Moorfield Way YO41 . . . .185 E6
Moorfields
Raskelf YO61 . . . . .116 F2
3 Wistow YO8 . . . . . . .197 D6
Moorfields La YO62 . . . . .93 E5
Moorfoot La BD20 . . . . .173 D2
Moorgarth Ave **6** YO24 .227 D3
Moorgate YO24 . . . . . . .227 D3
Moorgate Dr LS25 . . . . .194 D1
Moorgate Rd LS25 . . . . .194 D2
Moorhill La YO17 . . . . . .147 E6
Moorhouse Cl **3** WF6 . .200 B2
Moorhouse La YO7 . . . . . .89 E8
Moorland Ave
6 Earby BB18 . . . . . . .172 B1
Skipton BD23 . . . . .217 A4
Moorland Cl
5 Embsay BD23 . . . . . .217 E8
Harrogate HG2 . . . . .220 D4
Moorland Garth **2**
YO32 . . . . .167 A7
Moorland Gdns YO23 . . .230 A1
Moorland Rd
Harrogate HG2 . . . . .220 D4
Scarborough YO12 . . . . .212 F7
York YO10 . . . . .231 D8
Moorland Terr BD23 . . . .217 B4
Moorland View HG2 . . . .220 D4
Moorlands Ilkley LS29 . . .218 A2
Skelton YO32 . . . . .166 B5
Moorlands Cl YO10 . . . . .229 C4
Moorlands Fields
YO10 . . . . .231 E8
Moorlands La
Skelton YO30 . . . . .224 C6
1 Tollerton YO61 . . . . .143 B3
Moorlands Nature Reserve*
YO32 . . . . .166 B5
Moorlands Pk YO21 . . . . .29 A6
Moors Ctr The*
Danby YO21 . . . . .29 D7
Ilkley LS29 . . . . .218 A4
Moorsholm La TS13 . . . . .10 C6
Moorside
Melling-with-Wrayton
LA6 . . . . .102 A2
Scalby YO12 . . . . .212 A8
Moorside Ave HG4 . . . . .214 B2
Moorside Cl LA6 . . . . . . .102 A2
Moorside Cty Jun & Inf Schs
HG4 . . . . .214 B2
Moorside Dale **6** HG4 . .214 B2
Moorside La
Addingham LS25 . . . . . . .175 A2
Askwith LS21 . . . . .176 C4
Moorside Rd DL10 . . . . .209 E8
Moorside View HG4 . . . .214 C2
Moorview Rd
Northallerton DL6 . . . . . .210 F5
Skipton BD23 . . . . .217 B3
Moorview Way BD23 . . . .217 B4
Morcar Rd YO41 . . . . . . .168 D1
Morehall Cl YO30 . . . . . .224 F2
Morgan Dr TS14 . . . . .8 E6
Morgan St **4** YO12 . . . .212 F5
Morlais Ct **8** TS17 . . . . .5 F4
Morlais Dr **10** TS17 . . . .99 A7
Morley Gate DL11 . . . . . .37 E5
Mornington Cres HG1 . . .219 E4
Mornington Dr LS29 . . . .218 C4
Mornington Terr HG1 . . .219 E3
Morpeth Ave
Coulby Newham TS4 . . . . .7 A7
Darlington DL1 . . . . .3 E7
Morpeth Gate DL8 . . . . . .58 F1
Morrell Ct YO24 . . . . . . .230 B8

Morrell Way YO10 ....229 A2
Morrets La YO8 ....197 A1
Morris Fields 22 WF6 ....200 B1
Morrison Rd TS14 ....8 F7
Morritt Cl 8 YO31 ....228 F8
Morton Carr La TS7 ....7 E6
Morton La YO8 ....203 A8
Morton Rd DL1 ....4 A5
Mosber La BD23 ....172 C8
Moss Arc HG4 ....214 C5
Moss End La BD22 ....186 F5
Moss Gn La
  Brayton YO8 ....232 A4
  Hirst Courtney YO8 ....203 F3
Moss Haven DN6 ....207 D1
Moss Hill La YO26 ....164 D5
Moss Rd DN6 ....207 B1
Moss Side BD18 ....171 E1
Moss St YO24 ....233 A1
Moss Way TS18 ....5 F7
Mossburn Dr YO62 ....119 E6
Mossdale Gr TS14 ....8 D6
Mossra La HG4 ....85 F4
Mosswood Cres TS5 ....6 D7
Mosswood La YO61 ....118 A1
Mossy La DL8 ....56 C4
Mother Shipton's Cave &
  Well* HG5 ....221 A5
Moule Rise LS25 ....194 E5
Moulton Hall* DL10 ....21 D2
Moulton La DL7 ....22 C3
Mounstrall La HG2 ....43 C1
Mount Ave YO8 ....232 B3
Mount Bank DL6 ....45 A5
Mount Cres YO17 ....215 B5
Mount Dr DL8 ....60 D5
Mount Ephraim 6
  YO24 ....228 A3
Mount Farm Cl YO22 ....208 E3
Mount Gdns YO22 ....222 E7
Mount Gr YO8 ....232 B3
Mount Grace Priory*
  DL6 ....45 B5
Mount Leven Rd TS15 ....5 F7
Mount Par
  5 Harrogate HG1 ....219 D3
  York YO24 ....228 A3
Mount Pk YO19 ....198 A8
Mount Pk Ave YO12 ....212 E6
Mount Pk Rd 2 YO12* 212 E4
Mount Pleasant
  20 Addingham LS29 ....174 F4
  High Bentham LA2 ....129 A8
  Ilkley LS29 ....218 C3
  Kippax LS25 ....200 D8
  Newby & Scalby YO13 ....75 C5
  Whitby YO22 ....208 F3
Mount Pleasant Cl 9 DL2 ....4 C4
Mount Pleasant E 2
  YO22 ....33 D4
Mount Pleasant Grange
  TS18 ....6 A8
Mount Pleasant N 1
  YO22 ....33 D4
Mount Pleasant Prim Sch
  DL3 ....3 A7
Mount Pleasant S 3
  YO22 ....33 A7
Mount Rd Malton YO17 ....215 B4
  Northallerton DL6 ....210 F6
  Mount Sch The YO24 ....228 A3
  Mount Side Pk YO11 ....212 D8
Mount Sq 24 YO12 ....208 C7
Mount St HG2 ....222 E7
Mount Terr YO24 ....228 A3
Mount The
  Barwick in Elmet & Scholes
    LS15 ....194 B7
  Castleford WF10 ....201 B4
  Malton YO17 ....215 B4
  Middlesbrough TS6 ....7 E8
  Selby YO8 ....232 B3
  8 Thornton Dale YO18 ......96 D5
  York YO24 ....228 A3
Mount Vale YO24 ....228 A2
Mount Vale Dr YO24 ....228 A2
Mount View
  Muston YO14 ....101 A2
  Northallerton DL7 ....210 C6
Mount View Ave YO12 ....212 E3
Mount View Cl 4 YO12 ....212 E3
Mount View Rd 3 YO11 ......100 B6
Mountside YO11 ....212 F3
Mouseman Visitor Ctr*
  YO61 ....91 B2
  Mowbray Castle (site of)*
  HG4 ....112 D5
Mowbray Cres
  17 Bedale DL8 ....63 A2
  Hovingham YO62 ....119 E6
  Kirkby Malzeard HG4 ....112 D5
Mowbray Dr
  4 Hurworth-on-Tees DL2 ....3 E1
  York YO26 ....227 C4
Mowbray Pl 7 YO7 ....211 B2
Mowbray Rd
  5 Catterick DL10 ....41 D5
  Northallerton DL6 ....210 E6
  Thirsk YO7 ....63 A2
Mowbray Sq HG1 ....219 D3
Mowbray Terr
  Thirsk YO7 ....211 B2
  West Tanfield HG4 ....87 A2
Mowden Inf Sch DL3 ....3 A6
Mowthorp Rd YO12 ....75 A3

Mowthorpe La YO60 ....145 F8
Mowthorpe Medieval
  Village* YO17 ....149 C6
Moxby La YO61 ....144 D5
Moxby Priory* YO61 ....144 D5
Muddy La LS22 ....180 A1
Muff La TS8 ....7 A3
Muirfield TS7 ....7 D5
Muirfield Ave WF7 ....200 E1
Muirfield Rd TS16 ....5 E5
Muirfield Way 6 YO26 ....227 B5
Mulberry Ct YO32 ....225 F6
Mulberry Dr 7 YO32 ....166 E5
Mulberry Garth LS23 ....188 F8
Mulgrave Castle*
  YO21 ....12 E2
Mulgrave Cres YO21 ....208 B8
Mulgrave Dr 6 DL7 ....210 D2
Mulgrave Pl YO11 ....213 B7
Mulgrave Rd YO21 ....208 A8
Mulgrave View YO22 ....32 F7
Mulberry Gdns LS26 ....200 A5
Mulwith Cl YO31 ....229 A6
Mulwith La HG4 ....140 E6
Muncaster Way YO22 ....208 E3
Muncastergate YO31 ....228 E7
Murchison Pl 8 YO12 ....212 F6
Murchison St YO12 ....212 E6
Murray St 3 Filey YO14 .....101 B3
  Scarborough YO12 ....212 F5
  York YO24 ....227 F3
Murray Wlk DL3 ....3 A5
Murrayfield Way 5 DL1 ....3 F6
Murrough Wilson Pl 3
  YO31 ....228 C7
Murton Bank YO62 ....67 E3
Murton Garth YO19 ....229 F6
Murton La YO19 ....184 D7
Murton Way YO19 ....229 E5
Mus of Victorian Whitby*
  YO22 ....208 D7
Muscoates La YO62 ....93 F3
Museum of Craven Life*
  BD24 ....131 E2
Museum St YO1 ....233 B2
Musham Bank Rd YO11 ....99 F7
Music in Miniature Ex*
  YO22 ....33 D3
Musterfield La HG4 ....113 B7
Muston Rd Filey YO14 ....101 A3
  Hunmanby YO14 ....126 F8
Mutton Scalp Rd TS12 ....9 F7
My Love La HG3 ....159 C5
Myer's Gn La HG3 ....161 B5
Myers La DL7 ....64 A8
Myra Bank La YO61 ....117 F3
Myron Rd TS17 ....5 F5
Myrtle Ave
  Bishopthorpe YO23 ....231 B3
  Selby YO8 ....232 B3
Myrtle Gdns DL1 ....3 D8
Myrtle Rd
  Eaglescliffe TS16 ....5 E6
  3 Harrogate HG2 ....219 E3
Myrtle Sq 2 HG1 ....219 E3
Myson Ave WF8 ....201 C2
Myton La YO61 ....142 C5
Myton Rd TS17 ....6 A4

N

Nab View BD20 ....174 C2
Nabs View YO12 ....212 A7
Naburn CE Prim Sch
  YO19 ....191 D8
Naburn La
  Deighton YO19 ....192 A7
  Fulford YO19 ....231 D4
Naburn Pk Mews
  YO9 ....191 E8
Nairn Cl YO24 ....230 C6
Nairnhead Cl TS8 ....6 E5
Nalton Cl YO23 ....230 A1
Nalton St YO8 ....232 C5
Nanny Goat La
  Barwick in Elmet & Scholes
    LS25 ....194 B4
  Hunton DL8 ....61 F8
Nanny La LS24 ....196 C7
Nansen St YO12 ....212 E6
Nap Cote La HG4 ....112 E4
Napier Cres YO12 ....99 D7
Napier Rd HG4 ....113 D3
Nares St YO12 ....212 E6
Narrow La YO42 ....193 D7
Narrowfield 8 YO22 ....32 A6
Nat La LS17 ....178 A3
National Ctr for Early
  Music* YO1 ....233 C2
National Railway Mus*
  YO26 ....228 A4
Nattrass Wlk 7 DL8 ....63 B2
Navigation Rd YO1 ....233 C2
Navigation Sq BD23 ....216 F4
Navigator Ct TS18 ....6 D8
Nawton Com Prim Sch
  YO62 ....93 D7
Nawton Rd YO62 ....93 E7
Neasham Ct TS9 ....26 C8
Neasham Hill DL2 ....4 B1
Neasham Rd
  Darlington DL1 ....3 D4
  Low Dinsdale DL2 ....4 B3
Neile Cl YO7 ....210 B4
Nell Bank Ctr* LS29 ....218 D6
Nelson Dr YO24 ....218 C4
Nelson Rd YO29 ....218 B4

Nelson St
  7 Normanton South WF6 ....200 B2
  Scarborough YO12 ....212 F6
  Skipton BD23 ....217 A3
  York YO31 ....233 C4
Nelson's La YO24 ....227 F1
Nesfield Cl
  17 Eastfield YO11 ....100 B6
  Harrogate HG1 ....219 B5
Nesfield Rd LS29 ....218 A5
Nesfield View 12 LS29 ......175 C2
Ness La
  Pickhill with Roxby YO7 .....88 B6
  Tockwith YO26 ....181 C8
Ness Rd 5 YO8 ....232 D6
Nessgate YO1 ....233 B2
Nesfield Cl WF8 ....201 B2
Nestfield Ind Est DL1 ....3 D6
Nether Way 20 YO26 ....165 F1
Netherby Cl 5 YO22 ....32 A6
Netherby La
  Huttons Ambo YO60 ....147 B6
  Sinnington YO62 ....71 A1
Netherdale Ct LS22 ....180 D4
Netheredge Dr HG5 ....220 E8
Netheredge Dr HG5 ....220 E8
Netherfield Cl WF10 ....200 C3
Nethergill La BD23 ....173 B1
Netherside Hall Sch
  BD23 ....134 C4
Netherwindings 18
  YO32 ....166 F5
Netherwoods 8 YO22 ....167 B8
Netherside Cl 1 TS13 ....12 A7
Nettledale La YO13 ....97 F6
Nevern Cres TS17 ....5 F4
Neville Cl DL2 ....1 D8
Neville Cres BD23 ....155 D1
Neville Dr YO23 ....231 A3
Neville Gr LS26 ....194 A1
Neville Pits La DN14 ....207 B4
Neville Rd Darlington DL3 ....3 B5
  Gargrave BD23 ....155 D1
Neville Row DL8 ....87 D7
Neville St
  Normanton South WF6 .....200 A1
  Skipton BD23 ....217 A4
  York YO31 ....233 C4
Neville Terr YO31 ....233 C4
Neville Wlk DL10 ....41 D5
Nevinson Gr YO10 ....231 E8
Nevis Way YO24 ....230 B7
Nevison Ave WF8 ....201 C2
New Brook St LS29 ....218 B5
New Church Terr 12
  YO8 ....232 C5
New Cl La LA2 ....130 C7
New Dales La BD20 ....173 D4
New Earswick Prim Sch
  YO32 ....225 D4
New Earswick Sports Club
  YO32 ....225 D4
New Fen La YO8 ....197 F6
New Forge Ct 15 YO32 .....166 F5
New Hall Rd WF8 ....201 C2
New House Farm Malham
  National Nature Reserve*
  BD23 ....133 D3
New House La BD23 ....153 F5
New Ings La YO18 ....96 E4
New Inn La
  Carthorpe DL8 ....87 F6
  10 Easingwold YO61 ......143 C8
New La Aislaby YO18 ....95 D8
  Beal DN14 ....202 D3
  Bishopthorpe YO23 ....231 B4
  Burton Salmon WF11 ....201 E6
  Hawes DL8 ....56 E4
  Holgate YO24 ....227 E3
  Huntington YO32 ....225 F1
  Kildwick BD20 ....173 F1
  Lillings Ambo YO60 ....145 C8
  Little Ouseburn YO26 ......164 A8
  Long Marston YO23 ....182 B3
  Neasham DL2 ....4 A1
  Newland YO8 ....205 A3
  Ravensworth DL11 ....20 A7
  Selby YO8 ....232 C5
  Sherburn in Elmet LS25 ....195 F3
  Sheriff Hutton YO60 ....145 D5
  Stainburn LS21 ....177 E4
  West Tanfield DL8 ....167 B8
  New Lennerton La
    LS25 ....196 C3
New Mill La LS25 ....188 F7
New Millgate YO8 ....232 C6
New Parks Cres 8
  YO12 ....212 E4
New Pk Com Prim Sch
  HG1 ....219 C5
New Pk Rd 4 YO12 ....212 E4
New Pk Row YO1 ....219 C5
New Potter Grange Rd
  DN14 ....205 E2
New Quay Rd YO1 ....208 D6
New Queen St 10 YO12 ......213 A7
New Rd Allerston YO13 ......73 D6
  Allerton Mauleverer
    with Hopperton HG5 ......163 E4
  Appleton Roebuck YO23 ....190 E5
  Appletreewick BD23 ....157 E8
  Beningbrough YO30 ....165 C6
  Birstwith HG3 ....160 D6
  Bramham LS23 ....188 E6
  Earby BB18 ....172 A1

New Rd continued
  Fylingdales YO22 ....33 D4
  Glaisdale YO21 ....29 F3
  Guisborough TS14 ....8 F6
  Heck DN14 ....203 D1
  Hessay YO26 ....182 C8
  Hunmanby YO14 ....126 F7
  Kirby Grindalythe YO17 ....149 B6
  Kirby Hill YO26 ....164 B8
  Kirkbymoorside YO62 ....70 B1
  Knottingley WF11 ....201 D3
  Ledsham LS25 ....201 B8
  Lillings Ambo YO60 ....145 D3
  Long Drax YO8 ....204 E6
  Newsham DL11 ....18 J8
  North Stainley with Sleningford
    HG4 ....112 B8
  Norton DN6 ....206 F2
  Raskelf YO61 ....116 E3
  Reighton YO14 ....127 E5
  Richmond DL10 ....209 C6
  Rosedale East Side YO18 ....49 F3
  Scotton HG5 ....162 A5
  24 Skelton YO30 ....131 D2
  Settrington YO17 ....122 D1
  Spaunton YO62 ....70 E5
  Stapleton YO8 ....206 B5
  Terrington YO60 ....119 E2
  Thornton in Lonsdale
    LA6 ....103 B4
  Ulleskelf LS24 ....190 B3
  Westerdale YO21 ....28 F6
  Wheldrake YO19 ....192 C7
  Whixley YO26 ....164 A4
New Row
  10 Boroughbridge YO51 ....141 B5
  Eppleby DL11 ....1 D4
  Trawden Forest BB8 ....186 B2
New St Carleton BD23 ......173 B4
  Kippax LS25 ....194 D1
  Langcliffe BD24 ....131 E4
  Tadcaster LS24 ....189 E6
  York YO1 ....233 B2
New Sturton La LS25 ....194 D4
New Way YO31 ....29 C4
New Wlk Terr YO10 ....228 D2
Newall Carr Rd LS21 ....176 F3
Newall Hall Pk 10 LS21 .....176 F3
Newbiggin
  Malton YO17 ....215 B5
  Richmond DL10 ....209 B6
Newbiggin Cl TS16 ....5 C5
Newbiggin La YO62 ....94 A8
Newborough St YO30 ....233 A4
Newbridge La BD23 ....174 B8
Newburgh Priory*
  YO61 ....117 E7
Newbury Ave YO24 ....227 D1
Newby & Scalby Prim Sch
  YO12 ....212 B8
Newby Cl HG4 ....214 B4
Newby Cres HG3 ....219 A4
Newby Farm Cl YO12 ....75 D5
Newby Farm Cres 30
  YO12 ....75 D5
Newby Farm Rd YO12 ....75 D5
Newby Hall & Gdns*
  HG4 ....140 C2
Newby La DN14 ....207 F8
Newby Pk* HG4 ....140 D6
Newby Terr YO31 ....228 C7
Newby & Scalby Prim Sch
  YO12 ....212 B8
Newcastle Farm Ct 4
  WF11 ....201 D6
Newchase Ct YO11 ....99 F6
Newcroft YO8 ....232 B4
Newdale 3 YO12 ....166 F5
Newfield Ave 6 WF6 ....200 B1
Newfield Cl 7 WF6 ....200 B1
Newfield Cres
  Middlesbrough TS1 ....6 D7
  Normanton South WF6 ......200 B1
Newfield La LS25 ....201 B8
Newgate 2 Malton YO17 ....215 C4
  York YO1 ....233 B2
Newgate Bank YO62 ....68 A4
Newgate Ct 36 TS17 ....6 B7
Newgate Ct YO1 ....233 B2
Newham Bridge Prim Sch
  TS5 ....6 E8
Newham Way TS8 ....7 B5
Newhay La YO8 ....198 E1
Newhold YO25 ....194 D4
Newington Rd TS4 ....7 A8
Newkin DL8 ....57 D5
Newlaithes Cres WF6 ....200 B1
Newland Ave 11 HG2 ....220 A1
Newland Pk Cl YO10 ....229 A3
Newland Pk Dr YO10 ....228 F3
Newlands DL6 ....210 F4
Newlands Ave
  Scarborough YO12 ....212 E8
  8 Whitby YO21 ....208 C7
Newlands Cl YO7 ....211 D3
Newlands Dr
  2 Glusburn BD20 ....187 F8
  Ripon HG4 ....214 B3
  Wistow YO8 ....197 B6
Newlands La
  Burniston YO13 ....54 D1
  Upper Poppleton YO26 ......182 E8
  Wintringham YO17 ....123 F3

Newlands Pk Ave
  YO12 ....212 D8
Newlands Pk Cres
  YO12 ....212 D8
Newlands Pk Dr YO12 ......212 D8
Newlands Pk Gr 2
  YO12 ....212 D8
Newlands Pk Rd YO12 ......212 D8
Newlands Rd
  Bishopthorpe YO23 ....230 F4
  Darlington DL3 ....3 B6
  Newlands Sch TS4 ....6 F7
Newlyn Dr DL3 ....3 C8
Newmarket St BD23 ....217 A4
Newnham St HG2 ....220 A3
Newnham Terr HG2 ....220 A3
Newport Ave YO8 ....232 B4
Newport St 5 WF8 ....201 B1
Newroad End WF8 ....206 A6
Newsam Rd TS16 ....5 D5
Newsham Hill DL11 ....18 J8
Newsham La
  Barugh (Great & Little)
    YO17 ....95 A1
  Habton YO17 ....121 A8
Newsham Rd YO7 ....211 A3
Newsham Way DL7 ....210 B1
Newstead La HG4 ....85 C7
Newsteads 2 DL6 ....63 B3
Newthorpe Rd 2 DN6 ....206 E2
Newton Cres 4 DL7 ....63 D4
Newton Dr YO7 ....6 B6
Newton Gdns HG4 ....214 C4
Newton House Ct
  YO12 ....144 B3
Newton La
  Archdeacon Newton DL2 .....2 F8
  Ledsham WF10 ....201 A6
  Newton Mulgrave TS13 .....11 F6
Newton Pk YO30 ....165 B7
Newton Rd
  Great Ayton TS9 ....8 A2
  Tollerton YO61 ....143 B3
Newton St YO21 ....208 D6
Newton Terr YO1 ....233 B1
Newton Way 15 BD23 ......154 B3
Newtondale Forest Dr
  YO18 ....72 B6
Newtondale Halt Sta
  YO18 ....51 D1
Nicholas Gdns YO10 ....228 E3
Nicholas St YO10 ....228 F3
Nicholls Way LS27 ....160 A6
Nicholson Ave HG4 ....113 D3
Nickey Nackey La YO8 ......197 B8
Nicklaus Dr TS16 ....5 E5
Nickstream La DL3 ....3 A7
Nidd Bank HG5 ....220 F7
Nidd Cl YO26 ....227 B8
Nidd Dr WF10 ....200 D8
Nidd Gr YO24 ....230 E8
Nidd La Birstwith HG3 ....160 E7
  Ripley HG3 ....161 D7
Nidd Orch 4 HG3 ....160 A6
Nidd Rise HG3 ....160 A6
Nidd Viaduct* HG3 ....219 E8
Nidd Wlk 1 HG3 ....137 B4
Nidderdale Dr 6 HG5 ......220 D5
Nidderdale High Sch & Com
  Coll HG3 ....137 B4
Nidderdale Lodge
  HG4 ....214 E5
Nidderdale Lodge Pk
  HG5 ....221 C5
Nidderdale Mus*
  HG3 ....137 B5
Nidderdale Recn Ctr
  HG3 ....137 A5
Nidside HG3 ....160 A6
Nidfany Gdns 7 BD23 ......216 D3
Nigel Gr 7 YO24 ....227 F2
Nightingale Cl YO32 ....225 E1
Nightingale Dr HG2 ....220 B3
Nightingale La 9 YO12 ......99 F6
Nile Rd LS29 ....218 B4
Ninelands La LS25 ....194 D3
Ninelands Prim Sch
  LS25 ....194 D3
Ninelands Spur LS25 ....194 C3
Ninevah La WF10 ....200 C2
Ninth Ave YO31 ....228 F5
Niso Terr YO11 ....213 A6
Noel's Ct DL10 ....41 E4
Nolton Ct 32 TS17 ....5 F4
Nook The Selby YO8 ....232 D6
  South Milford LS25 ....195 F2
Nookfield Cl YO23 ....230 C3
Nooking The YO61 ....117 B6
Nora Ave HG5 ....221 C6
Norby YO7 ....211 B3
Norby Est YO7 ....211 B4
Norby Front St YO7 ....211 B4
Norfolk Cl WF11 ....201 E4
Norfolk Cres TS3 ....7 C8
Norfolk Gdns YO26 ....181 C7
Norfolk Rd HG2 ....222 D7
Norfolk St YO23 ....228 C2
Norman Cl
  22 Pickering YO18 ....95 F7
  3 Thorpe Willoughby YO8 ..197 B1
Norman Ct YO11 ....101 B3
Norman Dr YO26 ....227 B6
Norman Rd Aske DL10 ....20 D1
  Catterick Garrison DL9 .....209 E1
  Richmond DL10 ....209 C8
Norman Sq DL10 ....209 D8

Norman St 5 YO10 229 A3
Normanby Prim Sch TS6 7 F8
Normanby Rd
Middlesbrough TS7 7 D8
Northallerton DL7 210 D2
Normanby Terr 18 YO21 208 D7
Normandy Cl 4 YO8 232 B6
Normanton Com Sch WF6 200 B2
Normanton Freeston High Sch WF6 200 A1
Normanton Ind Est WF6 200 B1
Normanton Public Baths WF6 200 A1
Normanton Sta WF6 200 A2
Normanton Town Mid Sch WF6 200 A1
Norseman Cl 7 YO19 197 F8
Norseway 2 YO41 168 D1
North & S Cowton Com Prim Sch DL7 22 C3
North App LS24 189 A2
North Ave
Castleford WF10 200 C4
12 Glusburn BD20 187 E6
North Back La
Stillington YO61 144 C6
Terrington YO60 119 E1
North Baileygate WF8 201 B1
North Bay Rly* YO12 212 E8
North Bglws HG4 214 D6
North Burton La YO14 127 B4
North Cl 5 WF7 200 E1
North Cliff Ave YO12 75 F5
North Cliff Ctry Pk* YO14 101 C4
North Cotes Rd
Hunmanby YO25 126 C5
Wold Newton YO25 125 E5
North Cres LS25 195 F5
North Croft Gr Rd 1 LS29 218 A4
North Dr Kippax LS25 194 D2
Sherburn in Elmet LS25 195 F5
North Duffield CP Sch YO8 199 A8
North Eastern Terr YO24 230 E8
North End Bedale DL8 63 A3
2 Hutton Rudby TS15 25 C5
Osmotherley DL6 45 B4
North Field Ave YO23 190 F5
North Field Cl YO23 190 F5
North Field La
Askham Bryan YO23 182 F3
Upper Poppleton YO26 182 F7
North Field Way YO23 190 F5
North Garth La YO60 145 D5
North Gr 2 LS22 180 C3
North Gr Ave 6 LS22 180 C4
North Grange Ct YO30 233 A4
North Hill Rd YO7 115 B2
North La
Dringhouses YO24 230 E8
Eastfield YO11 100 B6
Gainford DL2 1 D8
Great Timble LS21 176 E8
Huntington YO32 225 F5
Hutton Hang DL8 61 C4
Wheldrake YO19 192 F7
North Leas Ave YO12 212 D8
North Lodge Ave 2 HG1 219 C5
North Marine Rd YO12 212 F7
North Moor 7 YO32 225 F5
North Moor Gdns YO32 225 F5
North Moor La YO61 118 C5
North Moor Rd
Easingwold YO61 117 B2
York YO32 225 F5
North Parade
10 Burley in Wharfedale LS29 176 C1
Ilkley LS29 218 C4
Skipton BD23 217 A2
York YO30 233 A3
North Pk Dr HG1 219 E2
North Pk Rd HG1 219 E2
North Prom YO21 208 C7
North Rd Darlington DL1 3 D7
5 Fairburn WF11 201 D6
Glusburn BD20 187 E7
Grosmont YO22 31 C4
Hackforth DL8 62 E8
3 Middleham DL8 60 E2
Norton YO17 215 E3
Ripon HG4 214 D6
Stokesley TS9 26 C7
Whitby YO21 208 D6
North Rd Prim Sch DL1 3 D7
North Rd Sta DL1 3 D6
North Riding Rise DL7 65 B3
North Rigton CE Prim Sch LS17 178 C4
North Side TS15 25 C5
North St
Addingham LS29 175 A4
Barmby on the Marsh DN14 205 A7
Barnoldswick BB18 171 D1
Castleford WF10 201 B6
Folkton YO11 100 A2
Gargrave BD23 155 D1
31 Glusburn BD20 187 E7
Newby & Scalby YO13 75 C6
North St *continued*
Ripon HG4 214 C6
Scarborough YO11 213 A6
Silsden BD20 174 C1
Wetherby LS22 180 C3
York YO1 233 B2
North St La 22 YO11 213 A6
North Stainley CE Prim Sch HG4 113 C8
North Sweeming Ct LS25 196 D5
North Terr Gainford DL2 1 D7
4 Scarborough YO11 213 A6
Whitby YO21 208 C7
North View
Knottingley WF11 201 F2
Little Ribston LS22 180 A8
North Yorkshire Moors Rly* YO18 95 F7
Northallerton Bsns Pk DL6 210 C7
Northallerton Coll DL6 210 E4
Northallerton Rd
Brompton DL6 210 E7
Dalton-on-Tees DL2 22 E6
Leeming DL7 63 C4
Thirsk YO7 211 A6
Thornaby TS17 6 B7
Northallerton Rigg DL6 43 D4
Northallerton Sta DL7 210 C3
Northcarrs La YO61 144 A4
Northcliffe Gr 3 TS15 25 C5
Northcote Ave YO24 227 E3
Northcote Fold 3 LS22 180 A1
Northcroft 5 YO32 166 F5
Northcroft Gr 11 LS29 218 A4
Northern Backlight Theatre YO31 233 C4
Northfield 3 YO8 198 B5
Northfield Cl
Stokesley TS9 26 C7
Womersley DN6 206 C6
Northfield Ct LS24 196 B8
Northfield Dr
Pontefract WF8 201 C1
Stokesley TS9 26 C8
Northfield La
Church Fenton LS24 196 B8
Pockley YO62 69 B2
3 Riccall YO19 191 F1
South Milford LS25 195 E2
Womersley DN6 206 C7
Northfield Mews 15 LS22 180 C2
Northfield Pl LS22 180 C3
Northfield Rd YO8 199 E8
Northfield Sch YO26 227 B5
Northfield Terr YO24 230 E8
Northfield Way YO13 75 D6
Northfields
4 Hutton Rudby TS15 25 C5
5 Strensall YO32 167 B8
Northfields Ave 4 BD24 131 D3
Northfields Cres 5 BD24 131 D3
Northfields La YO61 142 C6
Northgate Darlington DL1 3 D5
Guisborough TS14 8 F7
Hunmanby YO14 126 F8
Muston YO14 100 F1
Pontefract WF8 201 B1
Northgate Cl 15 WF8 201 B1
Northgate Jun Sch TS14 8 F7
Northgate La
1 Linton LS22 180 A1
Warthill YO41 168 A3
Northgate Lodge 11 WF8 201 B1
Northgate Rise 2 LS22 180 A1
Northlands Ave 1 YO32 225 F7
Northleach Dr TS8 6 F5
Northminster Bsns Pk YO26 182 F7
Northolme Dr YO30 224 E1
Northstead Com Prim Sch YO12 212 D8
Northstead Flats YO12 212 D7
Northstead Manor Dr YO12 212 E7
Northumberland Ct 8 HG1 219 D2
Northumberland Rd TS17 6 B8
Northway Pickering YO18 95 E7
11 Scarborough YO12 212 F6
6 Whitby YO21 208 B7
Northwell Gate LS21 176 F1
Northwold Rd YO11 100 A7
Norton & Kirk Smeat WF8 206 C3
Norton Back La DL2 4 D8
Norton Cl HG4 114 A8
Norton Coll YO17 215 E2
Norton Com Prim Sch YO17 215 E3
Norton Comm La DN6 206 F2
Norton Comm Rd DN6 207 A1
Norton Conyers* HG4 113 F7
Norton Cres DL2 4 C8
Norton Cty Jun & Inf Schs DN6 206 E2
Norton Gr Ind Est YO17 215 F4
Norton Mill La DN6 206 E2
Norton Priory DN6 206 E2
Norton Rd
Norton YO17 215 C3
Sadberge DL2 4 C7
Norton Twr* BD23 156 B4
Norway Dr YO10 231 D8
Norwich Cl YO13 75 D6
Norwich Dr HG3 219 A5
Norwood Ave LS29 176 C1
Norwood Bottom Rd LS21 177 A5
Norwood Cl
36 Burley in Warfedale LS29 176 C1
2 Knaresborough HG5 221 B8
Norwood Ct 1 HG5 221 B7
Norwood Gr HG3 219 B4
Norwood La
Glusburn BD20 187 B8
Pannal HG3 177 E7
Norwood Pl 8 YO12 212 F5
Norwood St
Normanton WF6 200 B2
Scarborough YO12 212 F5
Nossill La DL8 59 C3
Nosterfield Nature Reserve* HG4 87 B2
Nosterfield Rd HG4 87 B2
Notagreen Rd DL11 39 F6
Nought Bank Rd HG3 137 B3
Nought Moor Rd HG3 137 B2
Nova Scotia Way 4 YO19 198 A8
Nuffield Hospl HG2 219 C1
Nun Monkton Foundation Prim Sch YO26 165 A5
Nun's Cl DL10 209 B7
Nuneaton Dr TS8 6 E5
Nunmill St YO23 228 C2
Nunnery La
Darlington DL3 3 A5
York YO23 233 B1
Nunnington Cl TS17 6 B5
Nunnington Cres HG3 219 A5
Nunnington Hall* YO62 93 F2
Nunnington Studios* YO62 93 E2
Nuns Gn La YO21 29 E3
Nunthorpe Ave YO23 228 B2
Nunthorpe Cres YO23 228 B1
Nunthorpe Gdns TS7 7 D5
Nunthorpe Gr YO23 228 B2
Nunthorpe Prim Sch TS7 7 E6
Nunthorpe Rd YO23 233 A1
Nunthorpe Sta TS7 7 E6
Nurseries The
3 Easingwold YO61 143 C8
East Ayton YO13 99 C8
10 Leyburn DL8 60 D5
3 Whitby YO21 208 B6
Nursery Cl 19 YO8 198 F1
Nursery Ct YO26 224 A2
Nursery Dr YO24 227 E3
Nursery Gdns
Thirsk YO7 211 C3
York YO10 229 C3
Nursery La 4 LS29 175 A4
Nursery Rd YO26 224 A2
Nursery Way 8 LS23 188 E7
Nutgill La Bentham LA2 129 D8
Ingleton LA2 103 D1
Nutwith La HG4 112 B8
Nydd Vale Rd HG1 219 D3
Nydd Vale Terr 10 HG1 219 D3

O

Oak Ave
Appleton Roebuck YO23 190 E3
Garforth LS25 194 C4
Killinghall HG3 161 B2
Oak Beck Rd HG1 219 B5
Oak Beck Way HG1 219 B6
Oak Busk La YO60 145 F1
Oak Cl Filey YO14 101 B4
9 Kirkbymoorside YO62 70 B1
Oak Cres LS25 194 C4
Oak Dr Garforth LS25 194 C4
5 Thorpe Willoughby YO8 197 B1
3 Topcliffe YO7 89 A1
Oak Field YO8 232 A1
Oak Field Ave YO22 51 D8
Oak Glade 6 YO31 225 F3
Oak Gr DL6 210 E6
Oak Hill TS8 7 B5
Oak La HG3 159 F8
Oak Rd Egglescliffe TS16 5 E6
Garforth LS25 194 C4
Guisborough TS14 8 F7
2 North Duffield YO8 199 A7
Ripon HG4 214 B2
Scarborough YO12 212 D4
Tockwith LS22 180 E7
Whitby YO21 208 B6
Oak Ridge 6 LS22 180 B3
Oak Rise 4 YO26 227 C3
Oak St 3 YO26 227 E5
Oak Terr HG2 219 C2
Oak Tree Cl
2 Bedale DL8 63 A2
Strensall YO32 167 B7
Tees-side Airport DL2 4 E4
Oak Tree Ct
Bubwith YO8 199 D7
Oak Tree Ct *continued*
4 Wigginton YO32 225 D7
Oak Tree Dr DL8 62 F2
Oak Tree Gr YO32 225 D3
Oak Tree La YO32 225 C7
Oak Tree Rd 7 DL8 63 A2
Oak Tree Way 10 YO32 167 B7
Oak Wood Rd LS22 180 B4
Oakbank HG1 219 C4
Oakburn Rd LS29 218 A3
Oakbusks La YO61 142 F4
Oakdale HG1 219 A3
Oakdale Ave HG1 219 B4
Oakdale Glen HG1 219 B3
Oakdale Manor HG1 161 B2
Oakdale Pl HG1 219 B4
Oakdale Rd YO30 224 F2
Oakdale Rise HG1 219 C4
Oakenshaw Dr TS5 6 E7
Oaker Bank HG3 161 B2
Oakfields DL10 21 D4
Oakhill Cres 3 YO32 167 A6
Oakland Ave YO31 229 A7
Oakland Dr YO31 229 A7
Oakland Hills 23 WF6 200 B1
Oaklands
Camblesforth YO8 204 C5
9 Great Ayton TS9 8 A2
5 Ilkley LS29 218 A3
5 Pickering YO18 96 A6
6 Strensall YO32 167 B7
Oaklands Cres YO8 204 C5
Oaklands Rd TS6 7 F8
Oaklands Sec Sch YO24 227 C2
Oaklands Small Sch DN14 205 E4
Oaklands Sports Ctr YO24 227 C2
Oaklands The DL2 4 D3
Oaklands Way YO61 143 D8
Oakley Bank YO22 208 B2
Oakley Cl TS14 8 F5
Oakley Rd TS12 9 E7
Oakmont Cl 21 WF6 200 B1
Oakney Wood Dr YO8 232 D1
Oakridge Com Prim Sch TS13 11 F7
Oakridge View 3 HG3 161 B3
Oaks La LS23 188 E8
Oaks The
Coulby Newham TS8 6 E5
Dalton YO7 115 F7
7 Masham HG4 86 C3
Oak Tree DL2 4 E4
Oaksfield LS26 200 B5
Oaktree Ave DL9 40 E2
Oaktree Bank YO7 65 F3
Oaktree Dr DL7 210 C1
Oaktree Gr 5 TS18 5 D8
Oaktree Hill DL6 43 D6
Oaktree Junc DL2 4 D4
Oakville Ave YO12 212 E6
Oakville St YO31 228 D7
Oakwood Cl LS24 196 B7
Oakwood Pk DN14 207 F6
Oatlands Com Jun Sch HG2 222 F7
Oatlands Dr
Harrogate HG2 222 F8
11 Otley LS21 177 A1
Oatlands Gr 3 TS13 11 A8
Oatlands Inf Sch HG2 222 E7
Occaney La HG3 162 D8
Occupation La LS24 188 E2
Occupation Rd TS6 7 F8
Ocean Rd YO21 208 C7
Ocean Terr YO14 100 F6
Ochrepit Hill YO42 170 A2
Oddie's La LA6 103 D5
Offerton Dr TS8 6 F5
Ogleforth YO31 233 B3
Okehampton Dr TS7 7 B6
Olav Rd DL10 209 C7
Old Barber HG1 219 D6
Old Boys Sch La 4 YO8 197 B8
Old Brewery Gdns 5 LS24 189 F6
Old Bridge Rise 7 LS29 218 A4
Old Chapel Cl 7 HG3 161 B2
Old Church Gn YO26 164 C2
Old Church La 9 HG3 137 C4
Old Church Sch DL8 60 E2
Old Coach Rd HG3 137 F2
Old Coppice 14 YO32 166 F5
Old Courthouse Mus* HG5 221 A5
Old Cricket Field La YO7 116 B6
Old Ct Cl YO17 215 D4
Old Dike Lands YO32 225 C8
Old Farm Cl 5 YO18 95 F7
Old Farm Way YO8 232 B2
Old Farmyard The* HG3 161 C7
Old Favourites Wlk 8 DL3 3 A7
Old Garth Croft 3 WF11 201 D6
Old Gayle La DL8 56 D4
Old Great N Rd WF11 201 E4
Old Hall Cl BD20 187 D7
Old Hall Croft BD23 155 D1
Old Hall La
Gilling with Hartforth & Sedbury DL10 20 D3
Kexby YO41 185 C5
Old Hall Rd BD20 187 D7
Old Hall Way BD20 187 D7
Old Hospl Compound 25 DL9 40 E3
Old House Gdns YO8 203 A5
Old La Addingham LS29 175 B3
Broughton BD23 172 D5
Cowling BD22 187 B5
Earby BB18 172 A2
Hambleton YO8 196 E1
Hirst Courtney YO8 203 F3
Horton in Ribblesdale BD24 105 A7
Ilkley LS29 218 D3
Kelbrook & Sough BB18 186 A6
Long Marston YO26 182 A6
Old La Ct LS24 190 E7
Old London Rd LS24 189 D3
Old Malton Rd
Malton YO17 215 D5
7 Willerby YO12 99 D2
Old Maltongate YO17 215 C4
Old Mill Cl 8 LS29 176 C1
Old Mill La LS23 188 F7
Old Mill Row 3 YO7 211 C3
Old Mill View YO60 145 C5
Old Mill Wynd TS9 8 A1
Old Mkt Pl 6 HG4 214 C5
Old Moor La YO24 230 E7
Old Moor Rd LA2 128 B8
Old Oliver La BD24 152 F6
Old Orchard YO32 225 D8
Old Orchard The
1 Easingwold YO61 143 C8
Fulford YO10 231 E7
Shipton YO30 165 F5
Old Pk La YO21 31 D6
Old Pk Mews HG4 214 B5
Old Quarry La LS25 195 E1
Old Raike BD23 152 F4
Old Rd
Appleton Roebuck YO23 190 E5
Clapham LA2 130 C8
Garsdale LA10 55 A6
Ingleton LA6 103 E3
Kirkby Overblow LS17 178 E1
Kirkbymoorside YO62 70 B1
Thornton in Craven BD23 172 A3
Old Sawmill The BD24 153 B7
Old Sch Cl DL8 59 D3
Old Sch La YO8 198 B5
Old St The LS24 190 C8
Old Sta Rd 4 YO62 92 C1
Old Sta Way 20 LS29 174 F4
Old Sta Yd* YO62 92 F6
Old Stone Trough La BB18 186 A6
Old Stubble The 6 TS13 13 K2
Old Sutton Rd YO7 211 E3
Old Trough Way HG1 219 C6
Old Vicarage La 5 LS25 202 A8
Old Village The YO32 225 F5
Old Wife's Way YO18 73 A8
Olde Mkt The TS16 5 D3
Oldfield Cl LS25 195 A4
Oldfield La
Collingham LS22 180 C1
Spaunton YO62 70 E4
Sutton BD22 187 F1
Oldgate La LS25 195 D6
Oldham Cl TS12 9 E8
Oldham St TS12 9 D7
Oldman Ct YO24 230 C8
Oldstead Rd YO61 91 B3
Olicana Pk LS29 218 B5
Olive Gr HG1 220 B4
Olive Way HG1 220 B4
Olive Wlk HG1 220 B4
Oliver La YO17 121 C8
Oliver St 4 YO11 213 A4
Oliver's Cl 18 YO14 126 F8
Oliver's Mount Rd YO11 212 F2
Olliver La DL10 20 F1
Olliver Rd DL10 209 E8
Olympia Cres YO8 232 E6
Olympian Ct YO10 228 F4
Olympic Way DL10 209 B8
Omega St 7 HG1 219 C5
Onams La YO62 69 F4
One Acre Garth 2 YO8 196 E1
Onhams La YO60 146 E4
Opera House Casino* YO11 213 B6
Oran La DL10 41 E4
Orcaber La LA2 130 E6
Orchard Cl
Appleton Roebuck YO23 190 F5
Barkston Ash LS24 195 E7
Dalton-on-Tees DL2 22 D7
1 Great Ayton TS9 8 A2
6 Hartwith cum Winsley HG3 137 F1
1 Knaresborough HG5 221 B8
6 Monk Fryston LS25 202 A8
9 Norton DN6 206 E2
Selby YO8 232 A4
Sharow HG4 214 F6
6 South Milford LS25 195 F2
Wilberfoss YO41 185 E6
York YO24 227 E1
Orchard Cotts 4 YO19 184 F7
Orchard Ct
Bramham cum Oglethorpe LS23 188 F5

Orchard Ct continued
8 Knaresborough HG5 .....221 B5
Orchard Dr
Fairburn WF11 ....201 D7
Hambleton YO8 ....196 F2
Linton LS22 ....180 A2
Orchard End 20 YO8 ....198 F1
Orchard Gdns YO23 .....230 B2
Orchard Gdns YO31 .....225 E2
Orchard Gr
4 Brompton DL6 ....43 F3
1 Castleford WF10 ......200 D3
Orchard Head Cres
WF8 ....201 C2
Orchard Head Dr WF8 ..201 C2
Orchard Head Jun & Inf Sch
WF8 ....201 C2
Orchard Head La WF8 ..201 B2
Orchard La
8 Addingham LS29 ......175 A4
Barkston Ash LS24 .....195 F6
Hebden BD23 ....135 A2
Ripley HG3 ....161 C7
Thirsk YO7 ....211 B1
Orchard Paddock 3
YO32 ....225 D8
Orchard Rd
Malton YO17 ....215 B4
Selby YO8 ....232 A4
3 Sleights YO22 ....32 A6
Upper Poppleton YO26 ..224 A1
Orchard The
5 Ampleforth YO62 ......92 C1
Bishopthorpe YO23 .....231 A3
Burniston YO13 ....75 D8
Heslington YO10 ....229 A1
6 North Featherstone
WF7 ....200 E1
5 Roundhill Village TS17 ..6 D5
Sadberge DL2 ....4 C7
Scalby YO12 ....212 C7
Snainton YO13 ....98 A4
Thirsk YO7 ....211 C4
Tholthorpe YO61 ....142 D5
Orchard View
Markington with Wallerthwaite
HG3 ....139 E3
5 Skelton YO30 ....224 B5
Orchard Way
Hensall DN14 ....203 C2
Middlesbrough TS7 ......7 D8
Selby YO8 ....232 A4
1 Strensall YO32 ....167 B7
Thorpe Willoughby YO8 .197 B2
York YO24 ....227 E1
Orchards The
2 Beadlam YO62 ....93 D7
6 Brafferton YO61 ......115 F1
Leavening YO17 ....147 E1
Mickletown LS26 ....200 B5
Ripon HG4 ....214 C6
Weston WY60 ....147 B4
Orchid Cl 17 DL9 ....41 A5
Orchid Way 8 HG3 ......161 B3
Ordmerstones La YO10 ..96 C4
Ordnance La YO10 ......228 D1
Oriel Bank YO11 ....212 F3
Oriel Cl YO11 ....212 F3
Oriel Cres YO11 ....212 F3
Oriel Gr YO30 ....228 A8
Ormesby Bank TS7 ......7 D7
Ormesby Cres DL7 .....210 D2
Ormesby Prim Sch TS7 ..7 C8
Orms Gill Gn La BD23 ..154 D6
Orpington Rd TS3 ....7 C8
Orrin Cl YO24 ....230 C7
Osbaldwick La YO10 ....229 B4
Osbaldwick Link Rd
YO19 ....229 D4
Osbaldwick Prim Sch
YO10 ....229 C4
Osbaldwick Village
YO10 ....229 C4
Osborne Cl HG1 ....219 D4
Osborne Gdns HG1 .....219 D4
Osborne Pk YO12 ......212 D5
Osborne Rd HG1 ....219 D4
Osborne Terr 9 YO21 ..208 D5
Osborne Wlk HG1 ......219 D4
Osbourne Dr 4 YO30 ...224 E3
Osgodby 5 YO11 ....100 B8
Osgodby Cres YO11 ....100 B7
Osgodby Gr 11 YO11 ...100 B8
Osgodby Hall Rd YO11 .100 B7
Osgodby Hill YO11 ....100 B8
Osgodby La 12 YO11 ...100 B8
Osgodby Way 11 YO11 ..100 B8
Osgoodby Bank YO7 ....90 F3
Osmington Gdns 10
YO32 ....167 A7
Osmotherley Prim Sch
DL6 ....45 B4
Osprey Cl
4 Collingham LS22 .....180 A1
Guisborough TS14 ......8 D6
5 Scotton DL9 ....40 F2
4 York YO24 ....230 B8
Osprey Garth 4 YO12 ..99 E6
Ostler's Cl YO23 ......230 C3
Ostman Rd YO26 ....227 C5
Oswaldene DL6 ....45 B4
Oswaldkirk Bank YO3 ..93 A1
Oswestry Gn TS4 ....7 A7
Oswin Gr DL10 ....20 E4

Oswy Cotts YO21 ......208 D5
Oswy St 5 YO21 ....208 D5
Otley Rd
Harrogate HG2 ....222 B8
Killinghall HG3 ....161 B4
Pannal HG3 ....178 A7
Skipton BD23 ....217 B4
Stainburn HG3 ....177 F6
Otley St BD23 ....217 A4
Otter Dr 15 YO18 ......95 F6
Otter Way TS17 ....6 A5
Otterbeck Way 18 DL8 .63 B3
Otterwood Bank 6
YO24 ....227 B1
Otterwood La YO24 ....227 B1
Otterwood Paddock
YO41 ....168 C2
Oucher La HG3 ....140 B2
Oughtershaw Rd BD23 .80 B6
Ouiston Rd YO61 ......117 D1
Our Ladys RC Prim Sch
YO24 ....227 E1
Ouse Acres YO26 ......227 D6
Ouse Bank YO8 ....232 E5
Ouseburn Ave YO26 ....227 C6
Ouseburn Ave YO30 ....228 A6
Ousecliffe Gdns YO30 .228 A6
Ousegate YO8 ....232 D5
Ouston Cl LS24 ....189 A4
Ouston La LS24 ....189 F6
Out Gang La BD23 .....107 F1
Outgaits Cl 4 YO14 ..126 F8
Outgaits La
Hunmanby YO14 ....127 A8
Muston YO14 ....100 F1
Outgang La
Osbaldwick YO19 ......229 D6
2 Pickering YO18 ....95 F6
Thornton-le-Dale YO18 .96 E6
Outgang Rd
Malton YO17 ....215 B5
Pickering YO18 ....96 A6
Scampston YO17 ....122 F7
Outgang The YO17 .....122 F4
Outgate Cnr DL6 ......23 F4
Outwood La LS24 ......190 C2
Oval The
Harrogate HG2 ....222 D8
Hurworth DL2 ....3 F1
Kellingley DN14 ....202 C3
Middlesbrough TS5 ....6 E6
Otley YO21 ....176 F1
3 Scarborough YO11 ...100 B8
Skipton BD23 ....217 B3
Over Nidd HG1 ....219 C6
Overburn Rd 8 BD20 ..187 E8
Overdale YO11 ....100 A7
Overdale Cl YO24 .....230 D8
Overdale Com Prim Sch 7
YO11 ....100 A7
Overdale Ct BD23 .....217 A5
Overdale Grange 3
BD23 ....217 B5
Overdale Rd TS3 ....7 C8
Overgreen Cl YO13 ....75 D4
Overgreen La YO13 ....75 C4
Overgreen View YO13 .75 D4
Overscar La YO18 .....72 E3
Overton Rd YO30 .....165 F3
Overton Terr YO11 ....213 B6
Ovington La DL11 .....1 A6
Ovington Terr YO23 ...228 B2
Owler Pk Rd LS29 .....175 C3
Owlwood Cl 7 YO19 ...184 E7
Owlwood La 8 YO19 ...184 E7
Owmen Field La YO62 .93 C5
Owston Ave 2 YO10 ...229 A3
Owston Rd 8 YO14 ....126 F8
Ox Calder Cl 16 YO19 .184 F7
Ox Carr La YO32 ......167 B6
Ox Cl YO41 ....168 D2
Ox Cl La
Eldmire with Crakehill
YO7 ....115 E5
Myton-on-Swale YO61 .141 F5
North Deighton LS22 ..180 B7
Whixley YO26 ....163 F5
Ox Moor La
Cattal YO26 ....164 A1
Hunsingore LS22 ......180 E8
Oxcliff YO12 ....212 C8
Oxclose La YO61 ......144 B4
Hutton-le-Hole YO62 ..70 C4
Oxcroft 28 YO62 ......70 B1
Oxen La YO8 ....198 E3
Oxenby Pl 12 YO61 ...117 D1
Oxford Dr LS21 ....194 D1
Oxford Pl HG1 ....219 D2
Oxford St
Harrogate HG1 ....219 D2
6 Normanton South WF6 .200 B2
Scarborough YO12 .....212 F6
Skelton & Brotton TS12 .9 D7
5 York YO24 ....228 A3
Oxford Terr 2 HG1 ....219 D1
Oxmoor La LS24 ....196 D7
Oxpasture Cl YO12 ....212 C4
Oxton Dr LS24 ....189 F6
Oxton La LS24 ....189 F6
Oyster Pk Jun Sch
WF10 ....201 B4

P

Packhorse Bridge*
Dacre HG3 ....159 D6
Romanby DL7 ....210 B4

Pad Cote La BD22 .....187 A5
Padbury Ave 50 YO14 .101 B3
Padbury Cl 46 YO14 ..101 B3
Paddock Cl
Askham Richard YO23 ..182 D3
Knaresborough YO23 ..230 A2
Norton YO17 ....215 E3
2 Pickering YO18 ......95 F6
Paddock Farm Wr Gdns*
DL2 ....22 D4
Paddock Hill YO17 ....215 A4
Paddock House La
LS22 ....179 E1
Paddock Rise 13 YO61 .117 D1
Paddock The
14 Airmyn DN14 ....205 E4
Appleton Wiske DL6 ...24 B3
Burton Salmon LS25 ..201 F6
Catterick DL10 ....41 D4
Knaresborough HG5 ...221 C5
Melmerby HG4 ....114 B7
Middleton St George DL2 ..4 C3
Newby Wiske DL7 .....64 C4
Normanton South WF6 .200 A1
6 Selby YO8 ....232 C6
Stokesley TS9 ....26 C8
9 Whitby YO21 ....208 D7
Wilberfoss YO41 ......185 E5
York YO26 ....227 C6
Paddock View WF10 ...201 A3
Paddock Way YO26 ....227 C6
Paddocks The HG3 ....223 F4
Page La YO62 ....93 E6
Pagnell Ave YO8 .....232 E4
Painsthorpe La YO41 .170 B5
Painter La YO8 ....196 F2
Palace Rd HG4 ....214 B7
Pale La Carleton BD23 .216 E1
Gateforth YO8 ....202 F7
Paley Gn La BD24 ....131 B2
Pallet Hill 10 DL10 ...41 D5
Pallister Ave YO31 ...232 F8
Palm Gdns DL2 ....4 C3
Palmer La YO8 ....232 A3
Palmes Cl YO19 ......191 E8
Palms Ct DL2 ....4 A5
Panman La YO19 .....184 F8
Pannal Ash Cl HG2 ...222 C8
Pannal Ash Cres HG2 .222 B7
Pannal Ash Dr HG2 ..222 B7
Pannal Ash Rd HG2 ..222 B7
Pannal Ave HG3 ......222 E2
Pannal Bank HG3 ....222 E2
Pannal Cl 3 YO21 ...208 B5
Pannal Com Prim Sch
HG3 ....222 E3
Pannal Gn HG3 ......222 E2
Pannal Rd HG3 ....223 B4
Pannal Sta HG3 ......222 E2
Pannett Art Gall*
YO11 ....208 C6
Pannierman La TS9 ...7 D1
Panorama Cl 10 HG3 .137 C4
Panorama Dr LS29 ...175 C1
Panorama Wlk HG3 ...137 C4
Pant La LS24 ....130 E7
Parade Ct YO31 ......228 F6
Parade The
Harrogate HG1 ....219 E2
Whitby YO21 ....208 B7
Paradise YO11 ....213 B7
Paradise Cotts YO17 .170 F8
Paradise Field Est 2
YO61 ....143 D8
Paradise La Dalton YO7 .115 F8
Stutton with Hazlewood
LS24 ....189 A3
Paradise Rd YO7 .....67 A2
Paragon St YO10 .....233 C1
Parcevall Hall Gdns*
BD23 ....157 E8
Parish Ghyll Dr LS29 .218 A3
Parish Ghyll La LS29 .218 A3
Parish Ghyll Rd LS29 .218 A3
Parish Ghyll Wlk LS29 .218 A3
Parison Ct WF10 .....200 F3
Park Ave Barlow YO8 .204 F4
Castleford WF10 .....200 F4
Glusburn BD20 ....187 E7
Great Preston WF10 ..200 E6
Harrogate HG2 ....219 C1
Hellifield BD23 ......154 B3
Kippax LS25 ....194 E1
Knaresborough HG5 ..221 D5
New Earswick YO32 ..225 D5
Normanton South WF6 .200 A1
Scarborough YO12 ...212 D4
Sherburn in Elmet LS25 .195 E4
Skipton BD23 ....216 F4
Swillington LS26 ....194 A1
Thornaby TS17 ....6 B8
Park Ave S HG2 ......222 D8
Park Bank 1 YO61 ....29 E7
Park Chase
Harrogate HG1 ....219 E3
Hornby DL8 ....62 C8
Park Cl 6 Airmyn DN14 .143 D8
1 Easingwold YO61 ...143 C8
3 Kippax LS25 ....194 E1
Skelton YO30 ....224 B4
Park Cres
6 Addingham LS29 ....175 A4
Castleford WF10 .....201 B4
Darlington DL1 ....3 D7
Embsay BD23 ....217 C7
Hellifield BD23 ......154 B3

Park Cres continued
York YO31 ....233 C4
Park Crest HG5 ....221 B6
Park Dale WF10 ......200 D3
Park Dr Campsall DN6 .206 E1
Glusburn BD20 ....187 E7
Harrogate HG2 ....222 D8
Knaresborough HG5 ..221 B6
18 Masham HG4 ....86 C3
Park Edge HG2 ......222 F8
Park End Prim Sch TS3 .7 C8
Park Est YO32 ....225 D8
Park Gate
Knaresborough HG5 ..221 B6
Strensall YO32 ......167 B8
Park Gr
Knaresborough HG5 ..221 C5
Norton YO17 ....215 C3
Selby YO8 ....232 B3
Swillington LS26 ....200 A8
York YO31 ....233 C4
Park Gr Sch YO31 ...233 C4
Park Head La HG3 ...171 E1
Park House Gn
Harrogate HG1 ....219 C5
7 Spofforth HG3 .....179 E5
Park House La LA2 ..125 D5
Park Jun Sch WF10 ..200 F4
Park La Balne DN14 ..207 C5
Barlow YO8 ....204 C7
Bishop Wilton YO42 ..169 F1
Borrowby YO7 ....65 E4
Buckden BD23 ....81 E2
Burn YO8 ....203 D7
Carleton BD23 ......173 A3
Cowling BD22 ....186 F5
Darlington DL1 ......3 D4
53 Easington TS13 ...11 A8
Glusburn BD20 ......187 E7
Great Preston WF10 .200 E7
Guisborough TS14 ...8 E6
Kippax LS25 ....194 D1
Kirkbymoorside YO62 .70 B1
Knaresborough HG5 ..221 C6
Ledsham LS25 ....201 B8
Luttons YO17 ....150 C8
Micklewton LS26 ....200 A5
5 Middleham DL8 ....60 E2
North Featherstone WF7 ..200 F1
North Stainley with Sleningford
HG3 ....113 E5
Spofforth with Stockeld
HG3 ....179 D5
Tatham LA2 ....128 B8
West Tanfield HG4 ...185 E5
Wilberfoss YO41 ....185 E5
Womersley DN6 .....206 D6
York YO24 ....227 F3
Park Lea Cl YO42 ....169 F1
Park La Coll YO42 ...180 C3
Park La Trl St14 ....8 F7
Park Lands 4 HG5 ...179 E5
Park Lodge YO32 ....225 D4
Park Mount HG5 .....179 E5
Park Nook Rd YO8 ...196 F4
Park Par
Harrogate HG1 ....219 F2
Knaresborough HG5 ..221 B6
Park Pl Darlington DL2 .3 D5
Hellifield BD23 ......154 B3
4 Knaresborough HG5 .221 B6
York YO31 ....233 C4
Park Rd Airmyn DN14 .205 E4
Asenby YO7 ....115 B6
Barlow YO8 ....204 F4
Castleford WF10 ....201 A3
Cowling BD22 ......186 B6
Glusburn BD20 .....187 E8
8 Harrogate HG2 ....222 D8
Norton-on-Derwent
YO17 ....215 C3
6 Scarborough YO12 .212 E4
Spofforth HG3 ......179 E5
Park Row
Knaresborough HG5 ..221 B5
Selby YO8 ....232 D5
Park Side Earby BB18 .186 A8
Follifoot HG3 ....223 E5
Park Sq
2 Knaresborough HG5 .221 B6
1 Ripon HG4 ....214 C4
Park St 18 Glusburn BD20 .187 E8
1 Knaresborough HG5 .219 C5
11 Masham HG4 ....86 C3
Pickering YO18 ....95 F7
Ripon HG4 ....214 B5
Scarborough YO12 ...212 D4
Selby YO8 ....232 D5
1 Skipton BD23 ......216 F4
York YO24 ....233 A1
Park Terr
14 Knaresborough HG5 .221 B6
Whitby YO21 ....208 D6
York YO32 ....225 D7
Park The TS17 ....75 D5
Park View
Castleford WF10 ....201 B3
Glaisdale YO21 .....30 D4
Harrogate HG1 ......219 E2
2 Leyburn DL8 ....60 D5
Middleton Tyas DL10 .21 C4
Skipton BD23 ....216 D4
Swillington LS26 ...194 A1
York YO24 ....233 A1
Park View Dr BD23 ..134 B3

Park Way
Kirk Hammerton YO26 .164 C2
Knaresborough HG5 ..221 B6
Park Wood BD23 ......216 D5
Park Wood Cl BD23 ..216 E5
Park Wood Cres BD23 .216 D5
Park Wood Way BD23 .216 D5
Park Wynd DL10 .....209 C6
Parker Ave YO26 .....227 B2
Parker Dr 21 DL8 ....63 A2
Parker La YO26 ......164 C3
Parker St
Barnoldswick BB18 ..171 C2
15 Barnoldswick BD20 .187 E8
Parkers Mount 20 YO62 .70 B1
Parkfield YO61 ....144 C6
Parkfield Ave TS5 ....6 E8
Parkfield Cl YO12 ....212 D4
Parkfield Gdns YO12 .212 D4
Parkfield La WF7 ....200 E1
Parkgate DL1 ....3 D5
Parkgate La DL10 ....41 B7
Parkin Ave YO8 .....232 C3
Parkinson App LS25 ..194 C4
Parkinson's La LS21 .159 E2
Parkinson's Yd 5 DL10 .209 C6
Parkland Dr
Darlington DL3 ....3 A6
Tadcaster LS24 ......189 A6
Parkland Way YO32 ..225 D8
Parklands
Castleford WF10 ....200 F4
Ilkley LS29 ....218 D4
Parklands The
1 Ingleby Arncliffe DL6 ..45 A7
Scruton DL7 ....63 D7
Parkshill Ct DL10 ...20 F7
Parkside DL1 ....3 C4
Parkside Cl YO24 ....227 E3
Parkside Commercial Ctr
YO23 ....233 C1
Parkstone Pl TS16 ...5 E4
Parkway The YO12 ...212 B7
Parkways YO8 ....232 B3
Parkwood Dr 8 TS18 .5 E8
Parliament Ave YO7 .215 E4
Parliament St
Harrogate HG1 ......219 C3
Norton YO17 ....215 E3
York YO1 ....233 B2
Parliament Terr 2 HG1 .219 D2
Parlington Ct LS15 ..194 C8
Parlington La LS25 ..194 E7
Parlington La LS25 ..194 E7
Parlington Mdw LS15 .194 C8
Parlington Villas LS25 .194 E8
Parracombe Cl 8 TS17 ..6 A3
Parrock St 7 BB18 ...171 D1
Parsley Mews LS26 ..200 B6
Parson Back La DL6 ..25 B2
Parsonage Rd LS26 ..200 C6
Parsonage The 11 HG5 .221 B6
Parson's Cl YO21 ....208 A7
Parson's La
1 Addingham LS29 ...174 E4
Hutton Rudby DL6 ...25 A2
Parson's Wlk 11 DN14 .205 E4
Parsons Cl 10 DN14 ..205 E4
Parsons Cl La BD20 ..131 A2
Parsons La YO10 ....165 E1
Pasley Rd HG4 ....113 D3
Paston Wlk YO30 ....233 B1
Pasture Ave LS25 ....196 A4
Pasture Cl
Barnoldswick BB18 ..171 E2
4 Sherburn in Elmet
LS25 ....196 A4
Skelton YO30 ....224 B5
Skipton BD23 ....217 B5
2 Strensall YO32 ....167 B6
Wistow YO8 ....197 D6
Pasture Cres
Filey YO14 ....101 A4
3 Knaresborough HG5 .221 B6
Pasture Ct LS25 .....195 F4
Pasture Dr Bedale DL8 .63 A2
Castleford WF10 ....200 D3
Pasture Farm Cl YO10 .231 D6
Pasture Field La YO22 .32 C5
Pasture Fold 4 LS29 .176 C1
Pasture Hill YO18 ...169 E8
Pasture La
Ellerton YO42 ....193 C1
Helperby YO61 ......142 B8
Heworth YO31 ......229 B8
Hovingham YO62 ....119 E6
Kirkby with Netherby
LS22 ....179 C1
Malton YO17 ....215 C5
Marton-le-Moor HG4 .140 D8
2 Seamer YO12 .....99 D6
Pasture Rd
Embsay with Eastby
BD23 ....217 C8
Lockton YO18 ....73 A5
Pasture The TS17 ....7 C6
Pasture View
Malton YO17 ....215 C6
Sherburn in Elmet LS25 .195 F4
Pasture Way
Castleford WF10 ....200 D3
Sherburn in Elmet LS25 .195 F4
Wistow YO8 ....197 D6
Pastures The
Catton DN14 ....204 C3
Coulby Newham TS8 ..7 B5
18 Eastfield YO11 ...100 B6
Sherburn YO17 ......124 D7

Pastures The *continued*
4 York YO24 . . . . .230 E8
Pateley Moor Cres DL2 . . . .3 E3
Pately PI 1 York YO26 . . . . .227 D4
Paterson Cres DL6 . . . . . .210 E4
Patience La HG4 . . . . .114 D3
Patrick Pool YO1 . . . . .233 B2
Patterdale Dr YO30 . . . . . .224 E1
Patterham La DL8 . . . . . . .59 D4
Pavement YO1 . . . . .233 B2
Paver La YO1 . . . . .233 C2
Pavilion Sq
7 Harrogate HG2 . . . . . . .219 C1
11 Scarborough YO11 . . . . .213 A5
Pavilion Terr 12 YO11 . . . .213 A5
Peacock's CI DL7 . . . . .63 E7
Peacocks CI TS9 . . . . .26 C8
Peak Alum Works* YO13 . . . . .53 F8
Peak Scar Rd YO62 . . . . . . .67 C3
Pear Tree Acre LS23 . . . . .180 F1
Pear Tree Ave
Long Drax YO8 . . . . .204 F7
8 Poppleton YO26 . . . . . .165 F1
Pear Tree CI
Skeeby DL10 . . . . .20 F1
York YO32 . . . . .225 F4
Pear Tree Gdns LS15 . . . . .194 D7
Pear Tree Wlk YO17 . . . . .215 B4
Pearl Rd TS17 . . . . .6 B8
Pearl St HG1 . . . . .220 C4
Pearson Garth YO13 . . . . . .99 A7
Pearson St WF6 . . . . .200 A3
Peart La BD23 . . . . .154 C8
Pease Ct YO1 . . . . .233 C3
Pease Ct
1 Eaglescliffe TS16 . . . . . . .5 D5
Guisborough TS14 . . . . . . .8 D5
4 Lingdale TS12 . . . . .9 F7
8 Lingdale TS12 . . . . .9 F7
Peasey Hills Rd YO17 . . . .215 C5
Peasholm Ave YO12 . . . . .212 F7
Peasholm Cres YO12 . . . . .212 F7
Peasholm Ct YO12 . . . . . . .212 F7
Peasholm Gap YO12 . . . . .212 F8
Peasholm Gdns YO12 . . . . .212 F7
Peasholm Rd YO12 . . . . . .212 F8
Peasholme Bridge YO12 . . . . .212 E7
Peasholme Gn YO1 . . . . . .233 C2
Peasland La YO7 . . . . .66 B5
Peaslands La YO18 . . . . . . .96 D5
Peat La HG3 . . . . .137 B3
Peatmoor La DL8 . . . . .58 E5
Peckett's Holt HG1 . . . . . .219 D7
Peckett's Way HG1 . . . . . .219 D7
Peckfield HG4 . . . . .214 C2
Peckfield CI HG3 . . . . .160 F5
Peckitt St YO1 . . . . .233 B1
Peel CI YO10 . . . . .229 C4
Peel Gn BD23 . . . . .154 B2
Peel PI 1 LS29 . . . . .176 C1
Peel St Thornaby TS17 . . . . .6 B8
York YO1 . . . . .233 C1
Peel Terr YO12 . . . . .213 A7
Pelham La YO17 . . . . .170 F4
Pegman CI TS14 . . . . .8 F7
Peirse CI DL8 . . . . .63 A2
Pelham PI 15 YO32 . . . . . .167 A7
Pellentine Rd HG3 . . . . . .223 F4
Pemberton Cres TS4 . . . . . .7 A8
Pemberton Rd WF10 . . . . .201 A4
Pembroke St
18 Skipton BD23 . . . . .216 F3
York YO30 . . . . .228 B2
Pembury Mews DL10 . . . . .41 B6
Penberry Gdns 33 TS17 . . .5 E6
Penders La TS15 . . . . .5 E1
Penderyn Cres TS17 . . . . . .5 F4
Pendle St 8 BD23 . . . . . . .216 D3
Pendleton Rd DL1 . . . . .3 D7
Pendragon Castle* CA17 . . . . .14 A1
Penfold 8 BD23 . . . . .154 B3
Penhill Ct DL7 . . . . .210 C1
Penhowe La YO17 . . . . . . .147 D4
Penistone Rd TS3 . . . . .7 C8
Penley's Gr St YO31 . . . . .233 C4
Penn La DL8 . . . . .56 D4
Penn Rd DL10 . . . . .209 B7
Pennine Way BD20 . . . . . .172 E2
Pennine Ct YO32 . . . . .225 F4
Pennine View
Burneston DL8 . . . . .87 E8
Northallerton DL7 . . . . . . .210 B2
Pennine Way
11 Barnoldswick BB18 . . . . .171 D1
Ingleby TS17 . . . . .6 A4
Penniston La YO13 . . . . . . .97 C4
Penny Gn BD24 . . . . .131 D1
Penny La
1 Easingwold YO61 . . . . . .117 D1
Ripon HG4 . . . . .214 C4
Penny La CI YO1 . . . . .233 C3
Penny Pot Gdns 4 HG3 . . .161 B2
Penny Pot La HG3 . . . . . . .160 D2
Penny Pot La or Rough Rd HG3 . . . . .161 A2
Penny Royal CI 7 HG3 . . . .161 B3
Pennycarr La YO61 . . . . . .143 D7
Pennyman Prim Sch TS3 . . . . .7 C8
Pennypot La TS18 . . . . .5 E7
Penrigg Gr 18 HG3 . . . . . . .161 B3
Penrith Cres WF10 . . . . . .201 B5
Penrith Rd TS3 . . . . .7 B8

Pentire CI 11 YO30 . . . . . .225 A1
Pentland Dr YO30 . . . . . . .225 E3
Penton Rd 20 YO11 . . . . . .100 B6
Penyghent Ave YO31 . . . . .229 A5
Pen-y-ghent Way 6 BB18 . . . . .171 D1
Penyghent Way TS17 . . . . . .6 A3
Peplow Ct LS25 . . . . .201 F6
Peppercorn CI 6 YO26 . . . .227 E4
Peppergarth The DL7 . . . . .210 B3
Peppermint Dr 22 DL9 . . . .41 A5
Peppermint Way YO8 . . . .232 A5
Per Ardua Way 6 DL10 . . . .41 E4
Percy Cross Rigg YO21 . . . . .9 A1
Percy Ct HG5 . . . . .162 A6
Percy Rd Darlington DL3 . . . .3 C7
14 Hunmanby YO14 . . . . . .127 A8
Percy St YO31 . . . . .233 B3
Percy's La YO1 . . . . .233 C2
Perie Ave HG4 . . . . .113 D3
Perry Ave TS17 . . . . .6 B5
Peter Hill Dr YO30 . . . . . . .228 A8
Peter La
Burton Leonard HG3 . . . . . .140 A2
York YO1 . . . . .233 B2
Petercroft La 5 YO19 . . . .184 F7
Petercroft La YO19 . . . . . .184 F7
Peterhouse Cl DL1 . . . . .3 D7
Petersbottom La LA2 . . . . .129 B4
Petersway YO30 . . . . .233 A4
Petre Ave YO8 . . . . .232 E3
Petty Whin CI 28 HG3 . . . .161 B3
Petyt Gr BD23 . . . . .217 A4
Pew Tree Ct YO1 . . . . .185 E6
Pheasant Dr 5 YO24 . . . . .230 B8
Philadelphia Terr 2 DL1 . . . . .228 B2
Philip La YO8 . . . . .196 E2
Philip St 27 BB18 . . . . . . .171 D1
Philippa's Dr YO12 . . . . . .222 D8
Philpin La LA6 . . . . .104 C8
Phlashetts La DL8 . . . . . . .87 A4
Phoenix Bvd YO26 . . . . . . .228 A4
Phoenix PI TS8 . . . . .6 F6
Piave Rd DL9 . . . . .40 D4
Picadilly Ct YO1 . . . . .233 C2
Piccadilly YO1 . . . . .233 C2
Pick Haven Garth DN14 . . . . .202 F3
Pickard La BB18 . . . . .171 E2
Pickard La BD20 . . . . .174 C1
Pickering Castle* YO18 . . . . .95 F7
Pickering Com Inf Sch YO18 . . . . .96 A7
Pickering Com Jun Sch 28 YO18 . . . . .95 F7
Pickering Rd
East Ayton/West Ayton YO13 . . . . .99 A7
Thornaby TS17 . . . . .6 B8
Thornton-le-Dale YO18 . . . . .96 C6
Pickeringmoor La YO7 . . . . .64 C2
Pickhill CE Prim Sch YO7 . . . . .88 C6
Picking Croft La HG3 . . . . .161 B5
Picknowfield La LS25 . . . . .196 C6
Picks Ct YO7 . . . . .211 B3
Pickwick Ct YO17 . . . . . . .215 C5
Piece Croft 2 BD23 . . . . . .134 D2
Piece Fields 4 BD23 . . . . . .134 D2
Pier La 22 YO21 . . . . .208 D7
Pierall Terr HG2 . . . . .220 B1
Piercy End YO62 . . . . .70 B1
Pierremont Rd DL3 . . . . .3 B6
Piggy La DL2 . . . . .1 C7
Pighill Nook Rd LS25 . . . . .202 C7
Pike Hills Mount YO23 . . . . .230 A3
Pike La BD24 . . . . .131 E4
Pike Rd 8 YO18 . . . . .95 F6
Pikepurse La DL10 . . . . . . .209 D8
Pilgrim St YO31 . . . . .233 B4
Pill White La LS21 . . . . . . .177 C3
Pilmoor CI DL10 . . . . .209 E8
Pilmoor Dr DL10 . . . . .209 E8
Pinar Leisure Ctr YO11 . . . . .100 A6
Pindar Rd YO11 . . . . .100 A6
Pindar Sch YO11 . . . . .100 A6
Pindars Way YO8 . . . . .198 B4
Pinder CI DL10 . . . . .209 F8
Pinders Cres WF11 . . . . . .201 E3
Pinders Gn LS26 . . . . .200 B5
Pinders Gn LS26 . . . . .200 B5
Pinders Gn Dr LS26 . . . . . .200 B5
Pinders Gn Fold LS26 . . . .200 B5
Pine CI
Castleford WF10 . . . . .200 F3
Skipton BD23 . . . . .216 E4
Pine Croft 1 HG3 . . . . .112 F2
Pine Gr 1 DL6 . . . . .210 E3
Pine Hill TS8 . . . . .7 B5
Pine Rd Guisborough TS14 . . .8 E7
Middlesbrough TS7 . . . . .7 B6
Pine Tree Ave YO17 . . . . . .215 E5
Pine Tree Ave YO17 . . . . . .215 E5
Pine Tree CI YO7 . . . . .197 B2
Pine Tree La 1 LS25 . . . . .202 A7
Pine Wlk YO12 . . . . .214 D2
Pinelands 4 YO32 . . . . . . .225 D7
Pinelands Way YO10 . . . . .229 C3
Pines Gdns 2 LS29 . . . . . .175 C2
Pines The LS17 . . . . .178 B2
Pinetree Gr DL2 . . . . .4 C4
Pinewood Ave YO14 . . . . . .101 B4

Pinewood CI
5 Easington TS13 . . . . .11 A8
2 Ilkley LS29 . . . . .218 A3
5 Whitby YO21 . . . . .208 C6
Pinewood Dr
Cambelsforth YO8 . . . . . . .204 D4
Scarborough YO12 . . . . . . .212 D5
Pinewood Gate HG2 . . . . . .222 A7
Pinewood Gr
3 York YO31 . . . . .225 E2
Pinewood Hill 4 YO10 . . . .229 C3
Pinewood Rd TS7 . . . . .7 C6
Pinewood Wlk 8 TS9 . . . . .26 C8
Pinfold Ave LS25 . . . . .195 F4
Pinfold CI
Bilton-in-Ainsty with Bickerton LS22 . . . . .181 B5
3 Riccall YO19 . . . . .192 A1
4 Sherburn in Elmet LS25 . .195 F4
Pinfold Ct
Kirkby Malzeard HG4 . . . . . .112 D5
4 Sherburn in Elmet LS25 . .195 F4
Pinfold Garth
Malton YO17 . . . . .215 A4
6 Sherburn in Elmet LS25 . .195 F4
Pinfold Gn HG5 . . . . .140 E1
Pinfold Hill YO8 . . . . .197 D6
Pinfold La
Asselby DN14 . . . . .205 F6
Kirk Smeaton WF8 . . . . . . .206 B3
Mickletown LS26 . . . . .200 C5
Moss DN6 . . . . .207 D1
Norton DN6 . . . . .206 E2
Pollington DN14 . . . . .207 F6
Pinfold PI YO7 . . . . .211 C3
Pinfold Rise LS25 . . . . . . .194 F8
Pinfold The 8 BD23 . . . . . .216 F4
Pinfold View DN14 . . . . . .207 F6
Pinfold Way 8 LS25 . . . . . .195 F4
Pinhaw Rd BD23 . . . . .217 A2
Pinnacle View BD22 . . . . .187 A5
Pinsent Ct YO31 . . . . .228 E8
Pioneer Way WF10 . . . . . .200 C2
Piper Hill 1 WF11 . . . . . . .201 D6
Piper La Cowling BD22 . . . .187 B5
Thirsk YO7 . . . . .211 C3
Piper Rd DL6 . . . . .45 F6
Pipers Acre 4 YO18 . . . . . .95 F7
Pipers La YO23 . . . . .141 F1
Pippin Rd YO17 . . . . .215 B4
Pippin's App 17 WF6 . . . . .200 A2
Pit Ings La YO7 . . . . .115 F6
Pit La Laxton Luck LS25 . . . .194 F4
Micklefield LS25 . . . . .195 A4
Mickletown LS26 . . . . .200 D5
Pitman Rd YO17 . . . . .215 C5
Place Hill DL11 . . . . .38 B6
Plane Tree Way YO14 . . . .101 A4
Planetree La
Kirkby Fleetham with Fencote DL7 . . . . .42 A1
Thornville YO26 . . . . .164 A1
Plantation Ave HG3 . . . . . .222 A8
Plantation Cl YO12 . . . . . .222 A8
Plantation Dr
Barlby with Osgodby YO8 . . . . .198 B5
York YO26 . . . . .227 C6
Plantation Gr YO26 . . . . . .227 C6
Plantation Rd HG2 . . . . . .222 A8
Plantation Terr HG2 . . . . .222 A8
Plantation The BD23 . . . . .152 E3
Plantation Way YO32 . . . . .166 C5
Player Ct TS16 . . . . .5 D5
Pleasance The 6 LS26 . . . .194 A1
Pleasant Row HG5 . . . . . . .221 C6
Pleasant View 5 BB18 . . . .172 B1
Plews Way DL7 . . . . .63 C5
Plompton CI HG2 . . . . .220 D2
Plompton Dr HG2 . . . . . . .220 D2
Plompton Gr 3 HG2 . . . . . .220 D2
Plompton Rd HG3 . . . . . . .223 F5
Plompton Way HG2 . . . . . .220 D2
Plompton Wlk 2 HG2 . . . . .220 D2
Plough Garth The
DN14 . . . . .202 F3
Ploughlands 1 YO32 . . . . .225 C7
Ploughman's CI YO23 . . . .230 C2
Ploughmans Ct 14 YO11 . .100 B7
Ploughmans' La YO30 . . . .225 C7
Plover Gdns 4 YO12 . . . . . .99 F6
Plum St YO17 . . . . .215 D3
Plumer Ave YO31 . . . . . . .229 A5
Plumer Rd DL9 . . . . .209 B1
Plumpton La HG4 . . . . . . .139 D8
Plumpton Pk HG2 . . . . . . .220 D3
Plumpton Rocks* HG5 . . . . .179 D8
Pluntrain Dale La YO18 . . . .96 B7
Pocklington La YO42 . . . . .169 F2
Pockthorpe La YO25 . . . . .151 F2
Pocock PI DL10 . . . . .41 E4
Polam Hall Sch DL1 . . . . . .3 C4
Polam La DL1 . . . . .3 C4
Polam Rd DL1 . . . . .3 C4
Pole Rd BD22 . . . . .186 F1
Pollard CI YO32 . . . . .225 E3
Pollard Gdns YO12 . . . . . .212 C4
Pollington Balne CE Prim Sch DN14 . . . . .207 F6
Polperro CI 2 WF6 . . . . . .200 A2
Pond Farm CI TS13 . . . . . . .11 F7
Pond Field CI DL3 . . . . .3 A4
Pond St 3 YO8 . . . . .232 D6

Pond View DL6 . . . . .65 F7
Pondfields Dr LS25 . . . . . .194 D1
Pontefract Castle*
WF8 . . . . .201 C1
Pontefract Monkhill Sta
WF8 . . . . .201 B1
Pontefract Mus*
WF8 . . . . .201 B1
Pontefract New Coll
WF8 . . . . .201 A1
Pontefract Pk Racecourse*
WF8 . . . . .200 F2
Pontefract Rd
Castleford WF10 . . . . .200 F4
Knottingley WF11 . . . . . . .201 D2
Normanton South WF6 . . . .200 B2
Pool Ct 20 YO18 . . . . .95 F6
Pool Rd YO26 . . . . .164 E4
Poole La LS25 . . . . .201 F6
Pope St WF6 . . . . .200 B3
Poplar Ave
Castleford WF10 . . . . .201 B4
6 Hutton Rudby TS15 . . . . .25 D5
4 Kirkbymoorside YO62 . . . .70 B1
8 Wetherby LS22 . . . . . . .180 C4
Poplar Cres
Harrogate HG2 . . . . .219 F6
Northallerton DL7 . . . . . . .210 C2
Poplar Dr WF6 . . . . .200 A3
Poplar Gdns YO8 . . . . .204 F5
Poplar Gn HG5 . . . . .162 A6
Poplar Gr
Harrogate HG2 . . . . .219 F6
York YO32 . . . . .225 E3
Poplar PI TS14 . . . . .8 E7
Poplar Row 6 YO21 . . . . . .208 D7
Poplar St YO26 . . . . .227 E5
Poplar View YO17 . . . . . . .215 B4
Poplar Way HG2 . . . . .219 F6
Poplars La YO17 . . . . .123 A7
Poplars The
11 Brayton YO8 . . . . .197 D1
2 Glusburn BD20 . . . . . . .187 E6
1 Whitby YO21 . . . . .202 A1
Poppleton Hall Gdn
YO26 . . . . .224 A3
Poppleton Rd YO26 . . . . . .227 E5
Poppleton Rd Prim Sch
YO26 . . . . .227 E5
Poppleton Sta YO26 . . . . .182 F8
Poppy CI YO8 . . . . .232 C1
Poppy Ct DL9 . . . . .41 A5
Porch Farm CI YO62 . . . . .120 B5
Porch The DL10 . . . . .21 D7
Pornic Ave YO13 . . . . .75 D5
Portal La YO17 . . . . .99 D7
Portal Rd YO26 . . . . .227 B6
Portholme Cres 7 YO8 . . . .232 C5
Portholme Ct YO8 . . . . . . .232 C4
Portholme Dr YO8 . . . . . . .232 C5
Portholme Rd YO8 . . . . . . .232 C5
Portisham PI 12 YO32 . . . .167 A7
Portland Cres HG1 . . . . . . .219 D4
Portland St YO31 . . . . .233 B4
Portland Way DL7 . . . . . . .210 C3
Portman Rise TS14 . . . . .8 E5
Post Office Row DN14 . . . .205 A1
Postern CI YO23 . . . . .233 B1
Postern La YO42 . . . . .193 D6
Pot Bank HG3 . . . . .178 A8
Potlands DL7 . . . . .63 C4
Pott Bank HG4 . . . . .85 A1
Pott Moor High Rd
HG4 . . . . .110 F8
Potter Cl YO13 . . . . .99 B8
Potter Hill 11 YO18 . . . . . .95 F7
Potter La DL7 . . . . .64 A5
Potter's Side La YO21 . . . . .9 D1
Pottergate
Gilling East YO62 . . . . .118 F7
14 Helmsley YO62 . . . . . . .92 F6
Richmond DL10 . . . . .209 C7
Potters Dr 4 YO23 . . . . . . .230 B3
Potterton CI LS15 . . . . . . .194 C8
Potterton La
Barwick in Elmet LS15 . . . .194 C8
Barwick in Elmet & Scholes LS15 . . . . .188 C1
Pottery La
Bishop Monkton HG4 . . . . .140 A6
Knottingley WF11 . . . . . . .201 E3
Littlethorpe HG4 . . . . .214 E1
York YO31 . . . . .228 E7
Pottery St WF10 . . . . .200 D4
Potticar Bank YO62 . . . . . .119 D4
Pounteys CI 4 DL2 . . . . .4 C4
Powell St
Harrogate HG1 . . . . .219 F4
Selby YO8 . . . . .232 B6
Prail CI 13 WF8 . . . . .201 C1
Precentor's Ct YO31 . . . . .233 B3
Preen Dr TS5 . . . . .6 F6
Premier Rd TS7 . . . . .7 D7
Premiere Pk 30 LS29 . . . . .175 C2
Preseli Gr 20 YO32 . . . . . .225 F1
Preston Field Cross Rd
YO13 . . . . .74 E1
Preston La
Great Preston WF10 . . . . . .200 D7
Preston-on-Tees TS18 . . . . . .5 E7
Preston View LS26 . . . . . . .194 A1
Preston Way TS9 . . . . .26 C8
Prestwick Ct
15 Middleton St George DL2 . .4 C4
Rufforth YO23 . . . . .227 B5
Pretoria St WF10 . . . . . . .200 F4

Price's La YO23 . . . . .233 B1
Priest Bank Rd 4 BD20 . . .173 F1
Priest CI YO14 . . . . .126 F8
Priest Gill Bank DL11 . . . . .19 F5
Priest La
Dunnington YO19 . . . . . . .184 F5
Ripon HG4 . . . . .214 D4
Priestcarr La YO26 . . . . . .163 D8
Primrose Ave
Hunmanby Sands YO14 . . . .101 B1
Swillington LS26 . . . . .194 A1
Primrose CI
Guisborough TS14 . . . . .8 E6
18 Killinghall HG3 . . . . . . .161 B3
Ripon HG4 . . . . .214 B6
Primrose Ct 18 DL9 . . . . . .41 A5
Primrose Dr
Castleford WF10 . . . . .201 D3
Filey YO14 . . . . .101 B1
Ripon HG4 . . . . .214 C6
Primrose Gr YO8 . . . . .232 A6
Primrose Gr
3 Knottingley WF11 . . . . . .202 A3
2 Skipton BD23 . . . . .216 F4
Primrose Hill CI LS26 . . . . .194 A1
Primrose Hill Dr
Great & Little Preston LS26 . . . . .200 A8
2 Swillington LS26 . . . . . .194 A1
Primrose Hill Garth
LS26 . . . . .200 A8
Primrose Hill Gdns
LS26 . . . . .200 A8
Primrose Hill Gn LS26 . . . .194 A1
Primrose Hill Gr 13 LS26 . . . . .194 A1
Primrose La
Great & Little Preston LS26 . . . . .188 E8
Primrose La Prim Sch 5 LS23 . . . . .188 E8
Primrose Vale 1 WF11 . . . .202 A2
Primrose Valley Rd
YO14 . . . . .101 B1
Prince Henry Rd LS21 . . . .177 A1
Prince Henrys Gram Sch
LS21 . . . . .177 A1
Prince of Wales Terr
YO11 . . . . .213 A4
Prince Rupert Dr
YO26 . . . . .181 C7
Prince St WF10 . . . . .200 C8
Princes Cres BD23 . . . . . . .217 A4
Princes Sq TS17 . . . . .6 C8
Princes Villa Rd HG1 . . . . .219 E2
Princess Ave LS25 . . . . . . .221 C5
Princess CI
Knaresborough HG5 . . . . . .221 C5
Ripon HG4 . . . . .214 C6
Princess Ct 11 WF6 . . . . . .200 A2
Princess Dr
Knaresborough HG5 . . . . . .221 C5
West Haddlesey YO8 . . . . .203 A5
York YO26 . . . . .227 D6
Princess Gr 4 HG5 . . . . . . .221 C5
Princess La 12 YO11 . . . . .213 B6
Princess Mead HG5 . . . . . .163 A3
Princess Mount 3 HG5 . . . .221 C5
Princess PI
1 Ripon HG4 . . . . .214 C6
5 Whitby YO21 . . . . .208 D6
Princess Rd
Darlington DL3 . . . . .3 D8
Ilkley LS29 . . . . .218 A3
Malton YO17 . . . . .215 C4
Ripon HG4 . . . . .214 C6
Strensall YO32 . . . . .167 B7
Princess Royal La 4
YO11 . . . . .213 A4
Princess Royal Pk 1
YO11 . . . . .213 A3
Princess Royal Rd
HG4 . . . . .214 C3
Princess Royal Terr
HG3 . . . . .213 A3
Princess Royal Way
HG3 . . . . .222 E1
Princess Sq 11 YO11 . . . . .213 B6
Princess St
Castleford WF10 . . . . .200 F5
Normanton South WF6 . . . .200 A1
Scarborough YO11 . . . . . . .213 B6
Princess Terr
Knaresborough HG5 . . . . . .221 C6
Scarborough YO11 . . . . . . .213 B6
Prior Ave DL10 . . . . .209 D7
Prior Pursglove Coll
TS14 . . . . .8 E5
Prior Wath Rd YO13 . . . . . .54 A5
Prior's La BD23 . . . . .174 C8
Prior's Wlk YO26 . . . . .227 D6
Priorpot Way YO17 . . . . . .215 F4
Priorwood Gdns TS17 . . . . . .6 A4
Priory CI
Guisborough TS14 . . . . .8 F7
Northallerton DL6 . . . . . . .210 E5
Wilberfoss YO41 . . . . .185 F6
Priory Dr YO21 . . . . .208 A6
Priory La DL10 . . . . .204 C1
Priory Pk 6 LS29 . . . . .175 C2
Priory Pk CI 13 LS25 . . . . .202 A8
Priory Pk Gr 14 LS25 . . . . .202 A8
Priory PI YO11 . . . . .100 B7
Priory Rd or Hall La
DN6 . . . . .206 E2

Priory St YO1 ....233 A1
Priory View 2 BD23 ...217 E8
Priory Villas DL10 ......209 D6
Priory Way
Barnoldswick BB18 ....171 D1
Ingleby Arncliffe DL6 ...45 A7
Snaith DN14 ....204 B1
Priory Wood Way
YO31 ....225 F2
Prison & Pol Mus*
HG4 ....214 D5
Prissick Sports Ctr TS4 ..7 B8
Pritchett Rd TS3 ....7 C8
Promenade La HG1 ......219 C3
Promenade Sq HG1 .....219 C2
Prospect Ave
Normanton South WF6 ...200 A2
Sherburn in Elmet LS25 ..195 F4
Prospect Bank
Bramham cum Oglethorpe
LS23 ....188 F6
Scarborough YO12 ....212 D6
Prospect Cl
Camblesforth YO8 ....204 D5
Harrogate HG2 ....220 C3
Pollington DN14 ....207 F6
Prospect Cres
Harrogate HG1 ....219 D2
Scarborough YO12 ....212 D6
Prospect Ct 3 LS24 ....189 E6
Prospect Dr LS24 ....189 E6
Prospect Field 5 YO22 ...33 D4
Prospect Hill YO21 .....208 C5
Prospect Mount Rd
YO12 ....212 C6
Prospect Pk YO12 ....212 D6
Prospect Pl
Harrogate HG1 ....219 D2
Northallerton DL6 ....210 F4
Scarborough YO11 ....213 A6
Skipton BD23 ....216 F4
Thornton-le-Dale YO18 ...96 D6
Whitby YO22 ....208 E6
Wistow YO8 ....197 D6
Prospect Rd
Harrogate HG2 ....220 C3
Scarborough YO12 ......212 F6
Prospect St 14 BD20 ....187 E7
Prospect Terr
Fulford YO10 ....231 D6
Knaresborough HG5 .....221 A6
Lindgale TS12 ....9 F7
Micklefield LS25 ....195 A3
York YO1 ....233 B1
Prospect View DL6 .....210 E4
Prospect Way
Leeming DL7 ....63 D4
Selby YO8 ....232 D4
Prospect Way Ind Est
YO8 ....232 D4
Providence Gn 18 WF8 ..201 C2
Providence Pl
Filey YO14 ....101 B3
Mickletown LS26 ....200 D6
Scarborough YO11 ......213 A6
Skipton BD23 ....217 A4
Providence Terr HG1 ...219 D4
Pry Hills La
Hartoft YO18 ....71 A8
Rosedale East Side YO18 ..49 F2
Pudding Hill Rd DL11 ....1 B6
Pudding La YO13 ....159 A1
Pudding Pie Hill*
YO7 ....211 D1
Pudsley Wlk DL1 ....3 D4
Pulleyn Cl 8 YO22 .....167 C8
Pulleyn Dr YO24 ....227 F1
Pump Hill 4 HG5 ....221 A6
Pump La
Kirklevington TS15 ....24 E8
Malton YO17 ....215 C4
Purey Cust Nuffield Hospl
The YO31 ....233 B3
Pye Busk Cl LA2 ....129 B8
Pye La HG3 ....160 F8

Q

Quad Squad The*
YO13 ....97 C6
Quaker Cl
Reeth, Fremington &
Healaugh DL11 ....38 B6
Scarborough YO12 ......212 C5
Quaker Gn 1 YO24 ......230 C7
Quaker La DL6 ....210 D5
Quaker's La DL6 ....44 D7
Quakers La DL10 ....209 B7
Quant Mews YO10 ......229 B3
Quarry Ave 20 WF11 ...202 A2
Quarry Banks YO7 .....116 E7
Quarry Dr TS8 ....6 E5
Quarry Gate YO13 ......74 C1
Quarry Hill YO17 ....120 F4
Quarry Hill La LS22 ....180 B3
Quarry La
Harrogate HG1 ....219 C6
Osmotherley DL6 ....45 C5
Pateley Bridge HG3 .....137 C4
Quarry Moor La HG4 ...214 C3
Quarry Mount YO12 ....212 E3
Quarry Oval HG1 ....219 C6

Quarry Rd
Eaglescliffe TS18 ....5 F7
Norton DN6 ....206 F2
Richmond DL10 ....209 B7
Ripon HG4 ....214 B2
Quay St YO11 ....213 A6
Quay The YO8 ....232 D6
Queen Annes Ct 3 DL8 ..63 A2
Queen Annes Dr 4 DL8 ..63 A2
Queen Annes Rd
YO30 ....233 A3
Queen Dike* YO17 .....170 B8
Queen Elizabeth Dr 10
YO13 ....75 D5
Queen Elizabeth Way
TS18 ....6 D6
Queen Elizabeth's Sixth Form
Coll 11 HG1 ....219 D4
Queen Ethelburga's Coll
YO26 ....164 C6
Queen Ethelburga's Dr 8
HG3 ....161 B2
Queen Ethelburga's Par 8
HG3 ....161 B2
Queen Margaret's Dr
WF11 ....201 E4
Queen Margaret's Ind Est
YO11 ....212 E2
Queen Margaret's Rd 6
YO11 ....212 F3
Queen Margaret's Sch
YO19 ....192 A5
Queen Margarets Ave 4
YO11 ....201 E4
Queen Margarets Cl 3
WF11 ....201 E4
Queen Marys Sch YO7 ..115 A7
Queen St
Cowling BD22 ....187 B6
Great Preston LS26 .....200 C7
Normanton South WF6 ..200 A1
Ripon HG4 ....214 C5
Scarborough YO11 ......213 A6
Skelton & Brotton TS12 ...9 D7
York YO24 ....233 A2
Queen Victoria St
YO23 ....228 B1
Queen's Cl 8 HG2 ......219 C1
Queen's Crt YO1 ....233 B2
Queen's Dr LS29 ....218 A3
Queen's Dr La LS29 ....218 A3
Queen's Gdns
Ilkley LS29 ....218 A3
Tadcaster LS24 ....189 E6
Queen's Par YO12 ......213 A7
Queen's Pk Dr WF10 ..201 A4
Queen's Rd
Harrogate HG2 ....219 C1
Ilkley LS29 ....218 A3
Queen's St 6 BD23 ....217 B4
Queen's Staith Rd
YO1 ....233 B2
Queen's Terr
Ilkley LS29 ....101 B3
Scarborough YO12 .....213 A7
Queens Ave DL9 ....40 E3
Queens Ct
Malton YO17 ....215 D6
Richmond DL10 ....209 C7
Queens Dr
Stokesley TS9 ....26 C8
Whitby YO22 ....208 E3
Queens Garth BD23 ....172 A3
Queens Gate HG1 ......219 E2
Queens Gdns YO7 .....211 C1
Queens Rd
Knaresborough HG5 ....221 C6
Richmond DL10 ....209 C7
Queens Staith Mews
YO1 ....233 B1
Queensbury Ct 15 WF6 ..200 B1
Queensway WF10 ......201 C2
Queensway YO7 ....211 C1
Quentin Rd DL9 ....40 E4
Quernmore Dr BB18 ...186 A7

R

Rabbit La YO17 ....215 F8
Raby La DL7 ....22 E3
Raby Pk LS22 ....180 B3
Raby Terr DL3 ....3 C5
Racca Ave 11 WF11 ....202 A2
Racca Gn WF11 ....202 A2
Race La Carlton YO8 ...204 B4
Sessay YO61 ....116 C4
Racecourse Ct DL10 ...209 A8
Racecourse La DL7 ....210 D3
Racecourse Mews
YO7 ....211 A2
Racecourse Rd
East Ayton/West Ayton
YO13 ....99 B8
Irton YO12 ....212 A1
Richmond DL10 ....209 B8
York YO23 ....231 B8
Rachel La DL11 ....20 B5
Rag Robin Turn YO7 ....66 D6
Raghill La YO61 ....142 A2
Ragian Terr 3 YO11 ...208 D5
Raikes Ave BD23 ....216 F5
Raikes La BD23 ....156 A6
Raikes' La YO22 ....32 E3
Raikes Rd BD23 ....216 F5
Raikes The HG3 ....137 E3

Raikeswood Cres
BD23 ....216 E5
Raikeswood Dr BD23 ..216 E5
Raikeswood Rd BD23 ..216 E5
Railer Bank HG4 ....112 E6
Railway Ave WF8 ......201 B1
Railway Cotts HG4 ....214 D1
Railway Rd
Follifoot HG3 ....223 C7
Ilkley LS29 ....218 B4
Railway St 16 Leyburn DL8 ..60 D5
Norton YO17 ....215 C3
Slingsby YO62 ....120 B5
Railway Terr
Hurworth-on-Tees DL2 ...22 D8
Ilkley LS29 ....218 C4
Normanton South WF6 ..200 A1
Thirsk YO7 ....211 B2
York YO24 ....228 A4
Railway View
Darlington DL1 ....3 D4
Northallerton DL7 ......210 D3
York YO24 ....230 E8
Raincliffe Ave
24 Filey YO14 ....101 B3
Raincliffe Cres YO12 ..212 C5
Raincliffe Cres YO12 ..212 C4
Raincliffe Gr YO12 ....212 C4
Raincliffe St 4 YO8 ...232 C5
Raindale Rd YO18 ......71 F6
Raines Dr 5 BD20 .....173 E3
Raines La BD23 ....134 D3
Raines Lea BD23 ......134 D3
Raines Mdws 6 BD23 ..134 D2
Raines Rd BD24 ....131 C1
Rainford Cl 7 YO12 ....99 D6
Rainhall Cres BB18 ....171 E1
Rainhall Rd BB18 .....171 D1
Rainham Cl TS17 ....6 B4
Rainsborough Way 3
YO30 ....228 A8
Rainsburgh La YO25 ..126 A3
Raisdale Rd YO18 ......26 C1
Rake La YO21 ....30 D6
Rake The LA6 ....103 D4
Rakehill Rd LS15 ......194 B8
Raker Cl YO19 ....192 F7
Rakes BD23 ....134 C1
Rakes La BD23 ....171 B5
Raleigh St YO12 ....6 A1
Ralph Butterfield Prim Sch
YO32 ....166 F5
Ralph Garth YO26 .....181 D7
Rampart The YO23 ....190 D4
Ramsay Cl YO11 ....233 C4
Ramsden St YO11 .....201 D4
Ramsden St LS25 .....200 C8
Ramsey Ave YO23 .....231 B3
Ramsey Cl YO12 ......212 E6
Ramsey St YO12 ......212 E6
Ramshaw Dr BD23 ....217 A4
Ramshill Rd YO11 .....213 A4
Randal La HG3 ....160 D4
Range Rd DL8 ....40 A2
Rankin's Well Rd 4
BD23 ....217 B4
Rantreefold Rd LA2 ...128 F4
Rape Cl La YO62 ......118 E4
Rape La YO62 ....93 B7
Raper La YO61 ....117 B3
Raper View LS25 ......194 F8
Rarber Top La LA6 ....103 D2
Rarey Dr YO17 ....124 E1
Raskelf Rd
Brafferton YO61 ....115 F1
Easingwold YO61 ......117 B1
Ratcliffe Cl YO30 .....224 C5
Ratcliffe St YO30 .....228 B7
Rathmall La YO26 .....164 C2
Rattan Row YO25 .....151 C6
Ratten Row Hunton DL8 ..61 E7
Seamer YO12 ....99 C5
Raven Cl 10 YO12 ......99 F6
Raven Gr YO26 ....227 C4
Raven Hall Rd YO13 ....53 F7
Ravens Cl Brow LA2 ...102 C1
Ravenscroft Way
BB18 ....171 E2
Ravensdale Rd BD23 ...3 B4
Ravensthorpe Prep Sch
DL11 ....20 A6
Ravensworth Castle*
DL11 ....20 A6
Ravensworth CE Prim Sch
DL11 ....20 A6
Ravine Hill 17 YO14 ..101 B4
Ravine Rd YO14 ......101 B4
Ravine Top 7 YO14 ...101 B3
Raw Bank DL11 ....37 E8
Raw Gap HG5 ....221 A6
Raw La Fylingdales YO22 ..33 A4
Kirkby Wharfe with
North Milford LS24 .....190 A3
Towton LS24 ....189 F3
Raw Pasture Bank
YO22 ....33 B5
Raw Pasture La YO22 ..33 C1
Rawcliff Rd YO18 ......72 A5
Rawcliffe Ave YO30 ...227 F8
Rawcliffe Cl 5 YO30 ..224 E2
Rawcliffe Croft YO30 ..227 E8
Rawcliffe Dr YO30 ....227 F8
Rawcliffe in Snaith Prim Sch
DN14 ....205 A1

Rawcliffe Inf Sch
YO30 ....224 E1
Rawcliffe La YO30 .....224 F1
Rawcliffe Landing
YO30 ....224 C3
Rawcliffe Rd DN14 ....205 A2
Rawcliffe Village
YO30 ....224 E2
Rawcliffe Way YO30 ..224 E2
Rawdon Ave YO10 ....228 F4
Rawfield La WF11 .....201 D7
Rawlinson Rd DL9 ....209 D2
Rawson St HG1 ....219 E5
Ray Bridge La BD23 ...155 D1
Ray La HG4 ....114 B1
Raydale Cl 2 HG5 ....221 D5
Raygill La BD23 ....186 E8
Rayleigh Rd HG2 .....222 E8
Raylton Ave TS7 ....7 B5
Rayner St HG4 ....214 C5
Read Cl YO8 ....204 F5
Read Sch YO8 ....204 F5
Real Aeroplane Mus The*
YO8 ....199 D5
Reamsbottom Gr YO23 ..228 C1
Reasty Hill YO13 ....53 E1
Reasty Rd YO13 ....53 D2
Recreation Rd
17 Pickering YO18 ......95 F6
2 Selby YO8 ....232 D6
Rectory Cl
Bolton Percy YO23 ....190 D4
Heslerton YO17 ....123 F6
Rectory Gdns YO23 ...228 B1
Rectory La
Guisborough TS14 ......8 E6
Hurworth-on-Tees DL2 ..22 C8
Longnewton TS21 ......5 A7
Nunnington YO62 ......93 E2
Skipton BD23 ....217 A4
Thornton-le-Dale YO18 ..96 E5
Red Bank Dr HG4 .....214 A3
Red Bank La HG4 .....214 A3
Red Bank Rd HG4 ....214 A3
Red Barnes Way DL3 ...3 E6
Red Brae Bank HG3 ..137 A3
Red Brow YO13 ....74 C5
Red Gate DL8 ....57 C6
Red Hall La TS15 ....6 A1
Red Hall Prim Sch DL1 ..3 F8
Red Hill La LS25 ......195 E1
Red Hills La HG3 .....140 B3
Red Hills Rd HG4 ....214 B7
Red La
Green Hammerton YO26 ..164 C3
4 Masham HG4 ....86 C3
Red Lion St BB18 .....172 B1
Red Rose Cl DL3 ....3 A7
Red Scar Dr YO12 ....212 A7
Red Scar La
Newby & Scalby YO12 ...75 C4
Scarborough YO12 .....212 A8
Red Twr* YO1 ....228 E4
Red Way Brompton DL6 ..43 F4
Danby YO21 ....29 E6
Farndale East YO62 .....48 E4
Nether Silton DL6 ......45 D1
Redbarn Dr YO10 .....229 D4
Redcap La YO42 ......193 C5
Redcar Rd
Guisborough TS14 ......8 F7
Thornaby TS17 ....6 B7
Redcliff Cl 17 YO11 ...100 B7
Redcliffe Ct YO12 ....212 D7
Redcliffe Gdns YO12 ..212 C6
Redcliffe La YO11 ....100 D6
Redcliffe Rd YO12 ....212 D6
Redcoat Way 1 YO24 ..230 B8
Redeness St YO31 ....228 E5
Redfearn Mews HG2 ..222 D6
Redgrave Cl 4 YO31 ..228 E8
Redhill Ave WF10 .....201 D6
Redhill Cl WF10 ......201 D6
Redhill Dr WF10 ......201 A3
Redhill Field La YO23 ..182 D1
Redhill Inf Sch WF10 ..201 B4
Redhill La LS25 ....201 A4
Redhill Rd
Castleford WF10 ......201 A4
Harrogate HG1 ....219 C6
Redhouse La WF10 ...204 F6
Redlish Rd HG3 ......136 E1
Redman Cl YO10 .....231 C8
Redmayne Sq YO32 ..167 B8
Redmire Sta DL8 ......59 C6
Redmires Cl YO30 ...225 A2
Redruth Dr 22 WF6 ..200 A2
Redshaw Cl 1 YO12 ..212 A8
Redshaw Gr 2 HG4 ..214 C4
Redthorn Dr YO31 ....225 F1
Redwood Dr 8 YO32 ..166 E5
Reebys La LA6 ....103 A2
Reedsham La BD23 ...186 F5
Reeth Com Prim Sch
DL11 ....38 B6
Reeth Rd
Middlesbrough TS5 ......6 E8
Richmond DL10 ....209 B6
Reeval Cl 16 BB18 ....172 B1
Reeves The YO24 ....227 C1
Regency Ave TS6 ....7 E8
Regency Ct
3 Ilkley LS29 ....218 A4
Northallerton DL6 .....210 F3
Regency Mews
Northallerton DL6 .....210 D4

Regency Mews continued
2 Helmsley YO62 .....230 F8
Regency Pk TS17 ....6 B4
Regent Ave
Harrogate HG1 ....219 E3
Skipton BD23 ....217 B5
Regent Cres BD23 ....217 B5
Regent Dr HG1 ....219 E4
Regent Mount 2 HG1 ..220 C4
Regent Par HG1 ......219 E3
Regent Pl HG1 ....220 C4
Regent Rd Ilkley LS29 ..218 A4
Skipton BD23 ....217 B5
Regent St
Castleford WF10 ......200 E4
Harrogate HG1 ....219 F3
Normanton WF6 ......200 B2
1 Scarborough YO11 ..213 A6
York YO10 ....228 E3
Regent Terr HG1 .....219 E3
Regents Ct 14 YO26 ..227 F5
Regimental Mus*
YO1 ....233 B1
Reginald Gr YO23 ....228 C1
Reginald Terr YO8 ....232 D4
Reid St Prim Sch DL3 ...3 C7
Reid Terr DL3 ....8 F6
Reighton Ave YO30 ...227 F8
Reighton Dr 10 YO30 ..224 F1
Rein Ct LS25 ....194 F8
Reins HG5 ....163 A7
Reivaulx Dr TS5 ....6 F8
Renfield Gr WF6 .....200 B2
Renshaw Gdns 8 YO26 ..227 E4
Renton Cl HG3 ....140 B5
Reservoir La 4 HG4 ....86 C3
Residence La HG4 ...214 D5
Resolution Way YO21 ..208 B5
Retreat Hospl The
YO10 ....228 F4
Reygate Gr YO23 ....230 B2
Reynard Crag La HG3 ..160 C6
Reynolds St 18 YO14 ..101 B3
Rhobell View 3 TS17 ...5 F4
Rhode's Hill La LS23 ..188 F6
Rhodes La LS23 ....188 D7
Rhodes St WF10 .....200 D4
Rhyddings Gdns YO10 ..218 D4
Ribambow La YO17 ....3 C6
Ribble Dr DL1 ....3 C3
Ribblehead Sta LA6 ....78 E1
Ribblehead Viaduct*
LA6 ....78 D2
Ribston Rd
Little Ribston LS22 ....180 A7
Spofforth with Stockeld
HG3 ....179 F6
Ribstone Gr YO31 ....229 B6
Riccal Dr
22 Helmsley YO62 ......92 F6
Huttons Ambo YO17 ..121 C1
Riccal Moor La YO62 ..93 E4
Riccall CP Sch YO19 ..191 F1
Riccall La YO19 ....191 D1
Rice Gate YO13 ....74 D8
Rice La Aldwark YO61 ..142 C2
Flaxton YO60 ....145 F2
Richard Gossop Ct 11
LS29 ....176 C1
Richard St YO8 ......232 B5
Richard Taylor CE Prim Sch
HG1 ....219 E6
Richard Thorntons CE VA
Prim Sch LA6 ....102 A3
Richardson Cl YO8 ...196 F1
Richardson Rd TS17 ....6 A7
Richardson St YO23 ..228 C2
Richmond Ave
Harrogate HG2 ....222 C7
Knottingley WF11 ....201 D3
Richmond Castle*
DL10 ....209 C6
Richmond CE Prim Sch
DL10 ....209 D7
Richmond Cl HG2 ....222 C7
Richmond Cl LS29 ...218 D3
Richmond Garth HG4 ..112 C5
Richmond Holt HG2 ..222 C7
Richmond Lower Sch
DL10 ....209 C6
Richmond Methodist Prim
Sch DL10 ....209 C7
Richmond Rd
22 Barnoldswick BB18 ..171 D2
Barton DL10 ....21 A8
Brompton-on-Swale DL10 ..41 A6
Croft-on-Tees DL2 ......21 F6
Harrogate HG2 ....222 C7
Hipswell DL9 ....209 D1
Richmond Catterick Garrison
DL9 ....60 D5
Richmond Rise DL10 ..210 C3
Richmond Sch DL10 ..209 D7
Richmond St YO31 ...228 E7
Richmond Swimming Pool
DL10 ....209 D6
Richmondfield Ave
LS15 ....194 C7
Richmondfield Cl
LS15 ....194 C7
Richmondfield Cres
LS15 ....194 C7
Richmondfield Cross
LS15 ....194 C7
Richmondfield Dr
LS15 ....194 B7

Richmondfield Garth
LS15 ....194 C8
Richmondfield Gr
LS15 ....194 C7
Richmondfield La
LS15 ....194 C7
Richmondfield Mount
LS15 ....194 C7
Richmondfield Way
LS15 ....194 C8
Richmondshire Mus*
DL10 ....209 C7
Richmondshire Sports Ctr
DL10 ....209 C8
Ridding Cres DN14 ...205 A1
Ridding Gate 5 LS21 ...176 F1
Ridding La DN14 ....205 A1
Riddings Rd LS29 .....218 B3
Riders La YO60 ....146 F2
Ridge Gn YO13 ....75 D5
Ridge La Roxby TS13 ....11 A6
Silsden BD20 ....174 B4
Sleights YO21 ....32 B7
Staithes TS13 ....13 H1
Ridge Rd LS25 ....200 E8
Ridge The
Coulby Newham TS8 .....7 A4
Linton LS22 ....188 B2
Ridgedale Mount WF8 ..201 B2
Ridgeway
Coulby Newham TS8 .....7 D5
Darlington DL3 ....3 C8
10 Eastfield YO11 ....99 F7
Skipton BD23 ....216 E6
York YO26 ....227 B3
Ridgeway The WF11 ...201 F2
Riding Cl 4 BB18 ....171 E1
Ridings The
7 Boroughbridge YO51 ..141 B4
Norton YO17 ....215 D2
Ridley Ave TS5 ....6 E8
Ridleys Fold 1 LS29 ..174 F4
Ridsdale St DL1 ....3 D5
Rievaulx Abbey* YO62 ..92 B8
Rievaulx Ave HG5 ....221 C4
Rievaulx Bank YO62 ..92 B8
Rievaulx Cl HG5 ......221 C4
Rievaulx Ct 6 HG5 ...221 C4
Rievaulx Dr DL7 ....64 A6
Rievaulx Rd YO21 ....208 C6
Rievaulx Terr* YO62 ..92 B7
Rievaulx Way TS14 .....8 F6
Riffa La LS21 ....177 E2
Rigg Bank HG4 ....85 E3
Rigg The TS15 ....5 E2
Rigg View YO22 ....32 F7
Riggs Rd YO17 ....121 F5
Riggs Spring 8 HG3 ..137 F1
Rigton Hill LS17 ......178 B4
Riley St 41 BB18 .....172 A1
Rillington Com Prim Sch
YO17 ....122 F5
Rimington Ave DL10 ..209 D6
Rimington Way YO11 ..100 B7
Ringing Keld Hill YO13 ..54 A3
Rings The TS17 ....5 F5
Ringstone Rd
Bishopthorpe YO23 .....231 B5
York YO30 ....224 F3
Ringstones La LA2 ....129 A4
Ringway LS25 ....194 B3
Ringway Gr 1 DL2 .....4 C4
Ringwood Rd YO9 .....40 F3
Riparian Way BD20 ...187 F8
Ripley Bank HG3 .....137 C4
Ripley Castle* HG3 ..161 C7
Ripley Cl
11 Kirkbymoorside YO62 ..70 B1
Normanton South WF6 ..200 B8
Ripley Dr
Harrogate HG1 ....219 C6
Normanton South WF6 ..200 B2
Ripley Gr 3 YO32 ....166 E5
Ripley Rd
Knaresborough HG5 ....220 E8
Nidd HG3 ....161 E6
Scotton HG5 ....162 A5
Ripley Way HG1 ....219 C6
Ripley's Rd YO13 .....54 B1
Ripon & District Hospl
HG4 ....214 B5
Ripon Bsns Pk HG4 ...214 E4
Ripon By-pass HG4 ...214 C2
Ripon Cath HG4 ....214 C2
Ripon Cath CE Prim Sch
HG4 ....214 D5
Ripon Cath Choir Sch
HG4 ....214 A3
Ripon Coll HG4 ....214 A5
Ripon Courthouse*
HG4 ....214 C5
Ripon Gr DL11 ....3 D4
Ripon Gram Sch HG4 ..214 A4
Ripon Greystone Com Prim
Sch HG4 ....214 C2
Ripon Horn The*
HG4 ....214 C5
Ripon Leisure Ctr
HG4 ....214 D3
Ripon Loop Nature Reserve*
HG4 ....113 F4
Ripon Racecourse*
HG4 ....214 F2
Ripon Rd
Harrogate HG3 ....219 A7
Middlesbrough TS7 ......7 E6

Ripon Rd continued
Ripley HG3 ....161 D8
South Stainley with Cayton
HG3 ....139 E2
Ripon Swimming Baths
HG4 ....214 B5
Ripon Way
Carlton Miniott YO7 .....89 C4
Harrogate HG1 ....219 C5
Rise Carr Prim Sch DL3 ..3 C7
Rise The
Huttons Ambo YO60 ....147 C6
Knottingley WF11 ......201 E4
Leavening YO17 ....147 E1
Thornton Dale YO18 .....96 D5
Whitby YO22 ....208 E6
Riseber DL8 ....60 C5
Risedale Com Coll
DL9 ....209 F1
Risedale Rd DL9 .....209 B1
Risewood YO41 ......168 B2
Rishworth Gr YO30 ...224 F2
Rivadale View LS29 ..218 B5
Rivelin Way
10 Filey YO14 ....101 A3
York YO30 ....224 F2
Rivendell BD23 ....134 B3
River Cl 2 YO8 ....198 B5
River La
Brompton-on-Swale DL10 ..41 B6
Kilburn High & Low YO61 ..91 B2
West Haddlesey YO8 ....203 A5
River Pl BD23 ....155 D1
River Rd HG4 ....91 C2
River St 1 Selby YO8 ..232 D6
Trawden BB8 ....186 B2
York YO23 ....233 B1
River View
1 Barlby YO8 ....198 B5
Boston Spa LS23 ....188 F8
Ilkley LS29 ....218 E5
Thornton DL10 ....209 D6
River View Rd HG4 ...214 C7
Riverdale 4 DN14 ....202 D4
Riverdale Gdns LS29 ..188 F8
Rivergarth DL1 ....3 F7
Riverside
17 Haxby YO32 ....166 F5
5 Settle BD24 ....131 D2
Riversdene TS9 ....26 B7
Riverside Clapham LA2 ..130 C8
Gargrave BD23 ......155 D1
Rawcliffe DN14 ......205 A2
28 Scalby YO12 ....75 D5
Riverside Ave LS25 ...177 A1
Riverside Cl
1 Elvington YO41 .....185 C2
Ilkley LS29 ....177 A1
West Haddlesey YO8 ...203 A5
Riverside Com Prim Sch
LS24 ....189 E6
Riverside Cres
5 Otley LS21 ....177 A1
York YO32 ....225 F6
Riverside Ct DN14 ....205 A2
Riverside Dr 3 LS21 ..177 A1
Riverside Gdns
2 Boroughbridge YO51 ..141 B6
2 Elvington YO41 .....185 C2
2 Poppleton YO26 .....165 F1
Riverside Mews 6 YO7 ..211 C3
Riverside Pk 4 LS21 ..177 A1
Riverside Rd DL10 ....209 C6
Riverside View YO17 ..215 B3
Riverside Way DL1 ......3 E7
Riverside Wlk
Airton BD23 ....155 A6
Ilkley LS29 ....218 A5
9 Poppleton YO26 ....165 F1
5 Strensall YO32 ....167 A7
Riverslea TS9 ....26 B7
Riversvale Dr 21 YO26 ..165 F1
Riversway BD23 ......155 C1
Riverview Ind Est DL1 ..3 D6
Roach Grange Ave
LS25 ....194 D2
Roall La DN14 ....202 F4
Robert St
Harrogate HG1 ....219 D1
Selby YO8 ....232 C5
Robert Wilkinson Prim Sch
YO32 ....167 A7
Roberts Cres HG1 ....219 D5
Roberts Sq HG1 ......219 D5
Robertson Rd
Colburn DL9 ....40 F4
Ripon HG4 ....113 D3
Robin Cl 6 WF8 ....201 B2
Robin Gr 6 YO24 .....227 F3
Robin Hood Cl YO21 ...29 A6
Robin Hood Rd YO13 ...53 F8
Robin Hood's Bay Mus*
Robin Hood's Bay Rd
YO22 ....33 A3
Robin La Bentham LA2 ..103 A1
High Bentham LA2 .....129 A8
Huby YO61 ....144 A4
Robinson Ct YO1 .....233 C2
Robinson Dr
Harrogate HG1 ....222 B6
Ripon HG4 ....227 B2
Robinson St 16 DL10 ...41 E4
Robinson Wlk WF10 ..200 D6
Robson Ave TS17 ......6 B5
Roche Ave
Harrogate HG1 ....219 F6
York YO31 ....228 E8

Rock Hill WF10 ....201 A3
Rock Terr WF10 ......201 A3
Rock View Terr BD23 ..217 D8
Rockingham Ave
YO31 ....229 A5
Rockingham Cl YO17 ..215 A3
Rockingham Ct LS24 ..189 E7
Rockingham Dr YO12 ..212 B7
Rockland Gdns YO12 ..212 D5
Rockley Grange Gdn
LS25 ....194 B3
Rocks La YO13 ....75 D7
Rocks La Cl YO13 ......75 D7
Rockville Dr BD23 ....217 C8
Rockwell Ave DL1 ......3 E7
Rockwood Cl 1 BD23 ..216 E4
Rockwood Dr BD23 ...216 E5
Rodney Terr 15 HG4 ....86 C3
Roe La LS25 ....202 C7
Roebuck La LS21 .....176 F2
Roecliffe CE Prim Sch
YO51 ....140 F4
Roecliffe La YO51 ....141 B5
Roedean Dr TS16 ......5 E4
Roger La TS8 ....6 C4
Rogers Ct YO24 ......230 C8
Rogers Sq 14 HG1 ....219 D2
Roker Cl DL1 ....3 F6
Roker Rd HG4 ....219 E4
Roland Ct YO32 ......225 E3
Rolston Ave 3 YO11 ..225 E2
Roman Ave 4 17 YO41 ..168 D2
Roman Ave S 5 YO41 ..168 D1
Roman Camps* YO30 ..225 B2
Roman Cl
Newby & Scalby YO12 ..212 A7
4 Tadcaster LS24 ....189 E6
Roman Cres DL9 .....209 C1
Roman Garth YO17 ...215 D4
Roman Rd TS5 ....6 E8
Roman Signal Sta*
YO21 ....12 D6
Roman Town Mus*
YO51 ....141 C5
Roman Way YO12 ....212 A7
Romanby Prim Sch
DL7 ....210 B2
Romanby Rd DL7 .....210 C3
Romany View YO19 ...197 F8
Romany Rd 11 TS9 .....8 A2
Rombald's View LS29 ..218 D5
Rombalds Dr BD23 ...217 A2
Rombalds Grove LS29 ..218 E3
Rombalds View LS21 ..176 F1
Romille St 15 BD23 ...217 A3
Ronaldshay Cl DL10 ..209 E8
Ronaldshay Dr DL10 ..209 E8
Ronway Ave HG4 .....214 B2
Rook St
28 Barnoldswick BB18 ..171 D1
Lothersdale BD20 ......186 F8
Rookery Rd BB18 .....171 E1
Rookwood Ave LS25 ..200 C8
Rookwood Rd TS7 ......7 D6
Roomer La HG4 ....86 B1
Rope Wlk BD23 ....217 A4
Roper Ct DL10 ......209 C7
Ropers Ct YO23 .....230 C3
Ropery La YO17 ......124 E1
Ropery The
15 Pickering YO18 .....95 F7
Whitby YO22 ....208 E6
Ropery Wlk YO17 ....215 C4
Ropewalk The YO31 ..228 E5
Ropner Gdns DL2 ......4 C3
Rosamund Ave 21 YO18 ..95 F7
Rose & Crown Yd 20
YO21 ....208 D6
Rose Ave
Sherburn in Elmet LS25 ..195 F3
Whitby YO21 ....208 B7
Rose Cres
Richmond DL10 ....209 B7
Sherburn in Elmet LS25 ..195 F3
Rose Ct LS25 ....194 D4
Rose Hill Dr 18 TS9 ....26 C7
Rose Hill Way TS9 ....26 C7
Rose La LS29 ....196 A7
Rose Lea Cl 2 LS25 ..202 A7
Rose St YO31 ....228 C7
Rose Tree Gr YO32 ...225 D4
Rose Wood Prim Sch
TS8 ....7 A4
Roseberry Ave
Great Ayton TS9 ....8 A2
Stokesley TS9 ....26 D8
Roseberry Cres 6 TS9 ...8 A2
Roseberry Dr 8 TS9 .....8 A2
Roseberry Gn HG4 ...113 C7
Roseberry Gr YO30 ...227 F8
Roseberry La
Guisborough TS9 ....8 B3
Newton under Roseberry TS9 ..8 A2
Roseberry Mount TS14 ..8 E6
Roseberry Rd TS9 ......8 A2
Roseberry Topping*
TS9 ....8 C3
Rosebery Ave YO12 ..212 E3
Rosebery St YO30 ....227 F6
Rosecomb Way 6
YO32 ....225 D7
Rosecroft Ave TS13 ...10 D5
Rosecroft Sch TS13 ...10 D8

Rosecroft Way YO30 ..227 E8
Rosedale HG3 ....222 D3
Rosedale Abbey Com Prim
Sch YO18 ....49 E2
Rosedale Ave YO26 ..227 C4
Rosedale Chy Bank
YO18 ....49 E1
Rosedale Cl
Pannal HG3 ....222 D3
3 Whitby YO21 ....208 C6
Rosedale Cres
Darlington DL3 ....3 A6
Guisborough TS14 ....8 D6
Rosedale La
Hinderwell TS13 ....11 F8
Staithes TS13 ....13 L1
Rosedale St YO10 ...228 D2
Rosehill TS9 ....8 A1
Rosehill Sq 11 HG5 ...221 B5
Rosehurst Gr HG3 ....222 E2
Roseland Dr TS7 ......7 C7
Rosemary Ct
20 Easingwold YO61 ...143 C8
6 Tadcaster LS24 ....189 E6
York YO1 ....233 C2
Rosemary La 1 DL10 ..209 C6
Rosemary Pl YO1 ....233 C2
Rosemary Row 5 LS24 ..189 E6
Rosemoor Cl
Coulby Newham TS8 .....7 B5
19 Hunmanby YO14 ...126 F8
Rosemount Dr WF6 ...200 C1
Rosemount Rd 2 YO21 ..208 C5
Rosendale Ave YO17 ..203 C7
Rosevale Terr YO12 ..212 E5
Roseville Ave
Harrogate HG1 ....220 A3
Scarborough YO12 .....212 E6
Roseville Dr HG1 .....220 A3
Roseville Rd HG1 ....220 A3
Roseway HG1 ....219 E5
Rosewood Cres HG1 ..220 A3
Roseworth TS9 ....26 E5
Rosley St HG3 ....186 B3
Roslyn Rd HG2 ....220 A2
Rossett Acre Prim Sch
HG2 ....222 C7
Rossett Beck HG2 ....222 C6
Rossett Cres HG2 ....222 C6
Rossett Dr HG2 ......222 C6
Rossett Garth HG2 ...222 C6
Rossett Gdns HG2 ...222 C6
Rossett Gn La HG2 ...222 C6
Rossett Holt Ave HG2 ..222 C7
Rossett Holt Cl HG2 ..222 C7
Rossett Holt Dr HG2 ..222 C7
Rossett Holt Gr HG2 ..222 C7
Rossett Holt View
HG2 ....222 C7
Rossett Pk Rd HG2 ...222 D6
Rossett Sch HG2 .....222 C5
Rossett Way HG2 ....222 C7
Rossiter Dr WF11 ....201 E2
Rosslyn Ct HG2 ....5 F8
Rosslyn St 1 YO30 ...228 A6
Rossway DL2 ....3 F8
Rostle Top Rd 10 BB18 ..172 A1
Rotary Way HG4 .....214 D6
Roth Hill La YO19 ....192 E3
Rothbury Cl HG2 .....220 D2
Rothbury St YO12 ...212 E5
Rothesay Gr TS7 ......7 D6
Rotunda Mus* YO11 ..213 A5
Rough Rd HG3 ....161 A2
Roughaw Cl BD23 ...216 F2
Roughaw Rd BD23 ..217 A2
Roughley Bank DL7 ...63 C5
Round Hill Link YO30 ..227 F8
Roundell Rd BB18 ...171 E2
Roundhill Ave TS17 ...5 F4
Roundhill Cl 5 BD23 ..23 E1
Roundhill Jun Sch
WF11 ....201 D3
Routh Wlk 5 YO21 ...208 D7
Rowan Ave
3 Filey YO14 ....101 A4
Malton YO17 ....215 D6
York YO32 ....225 D4
Rowan Cl
Gateforth YO8 ....197 B1
Scarborough YO12 .....212 C6
Rowan Ct
8 Catterick DL10 .....41 D5
Leyburn DL8 ....60 D5
Rowan Dr HG3 ....222 D3
Rowan Fields YO22 ...99 E2
Rowan Garth 22 BD20 ..187 E7
Rowan La
16 Hellifield BD23 ....154 B3
Skirethorns BD23 ......134 B3
Rowan Lea HG2 ......222 B7
Rowan Rd YO7 ....115 F7
Rowans Way DL7 ....210 B4
Rowden La HG3 ......160 F5
Rowedale Cl 13 YO14 ..126 F8
Rowen Ave 6 YO61 ..117 D1
Rowland Keld TS14 ....8 E5
Rowland St 18 BD23 ..217 A3
Rowlandhall La DN14 ..199 E1
Rowley Ct 2 LS29 ....218 F3
Rowley Dr LS29 .....218 F3
Rowmans The YO30 ..224 C4
Rowntree Ave YO30 ..228 A8

Roxburghe Dale WF7 ..200 C1
Roxby Ave TS14 ....8 E5
Roxby Gdns
4 Eastfield YO12 .....99 F7
18 Thornton Dale YO18 ..96 D5
Roxby La Roxby TS13 ...11 C7
Staithes TS13 ....13 J1
Roxby Rd YO18 ....96 D5
Roxby Terr 6 YO18 ....96 D5
Royal Albert Dr YO12 ..212 F8
Royal Ave YO11 .....212 F4
Royal Chase YO24 ...230 F8
Royal Cres
Harrogate HG2 ....222 D8
12 Scarborough YO11 ..213 A4
Whitby YO21 ....208 C2
Royal Cres La 8 LS21 ..212 F4
Royal Gr LS21 ....5 D5
Royal Hall* HG1 .....219 D3
Royal Par 8 HG1 .....219 C2
Royal Pump House Mus*
HG2 ....219 C2
Royd Cl 18 BD20 ....187 E7
Royd St YO13 ....5 D2
Royd's Rd YO8 ....202 F6
Royds Ave WF10 .....201 B4
Ruby St 3 YO23 .....228 B1
Rudbeck Cl HG2 .....220 C1
Rudbeck Cres HG2 ..220 C1
Rudbeck Dr HG2 .....220 C1
Rudby Bank TS15 .....25 D5
Rudby Lea TS15 ......25 D6
Rudcarr La YO19 ....167 E1
Rudda Rd YO13 ......53 F8
Rudding Dower HG3 ..223 E7
Rudding La
Follifoot HG3 ....223 C5
North Rigton HG3 .....222 A1
Ruddings YO19 ......193 A8
Ruddings Cl 9 BD23 ..225 C8
Ruddings La
Cowesby YO7 ....66 C4
Crakehall DL8 ....62 D4
Ellerton YO42 ....193 E2
Ruddings Rd YO18 ....72 B3
Ruddings The YO8 ...232 B4
Rudgate
Bilton-in-Ainsty with Bickerton
YO26 ....181 B6
Newton Kyme cum Toulston
LS24 ....189 B6
Walton LS23 ....181 B1
Rudgate Gr YO26 ....164 A4
Rudgate Pk LS23 ....181 A2
Rudstone Gr LS25 ...195 F4
Ruebury La DL6 ....45 B4
Rues La LS21 ....176 C8
Ruff La YO61 ....142 B5
Ruffa La YO18 ....96 A6
Ruffhams Cl YO19 ...192 F8
Ruffin La YO17 ......147 D5
Rufford Cl TS14 ....3 E5
Rufforth Prim Sch
YO23 ....182 C6
Rumford Way DL10 ...60 D6
Rumple Croft 4 LS21 ..176 F1
Runnymede TS7 ......7 D5
Runs Bank DL8 ....60 D8
Runswick Ave
Middlesbrough TS5 .....6 E6
Whitby YO21 ....208 A6
York YO26 ....227 B4
Runswick La TS13 ....11 F7
Rupert Rd LS29 ......218 A5
Rushmere TS8 ....7 B5
Rusholme La YO8 ....205 A5
Rushton Ave 8 BB18 ..172 A1
Rushwood Cl YO32 ...166 F5
Ruskin Ave
Middlesbrough TS5 .....6 D7
9 Skipton BD23 .....216 D3
Ruskin Cl DL2 ....22 D7
Russell St
Harrogate HG2 ....222 E7
Skipton BD23 ....217 A3
York YO23 ....228 B2
Russell Terr HG2 ......63 D2
Russet Dr YO31 .....229 B5
Russet Gr YO12 .....212 C8
Russett Rd YO17 ....215 B4
Ruston La YO13 ....98 D7
Ruswarp CE VC Prim Sch
YO21 ....208 B3
Ruswarp Fields YO22 ..208 B4
Ruswarp La YO21 ....208 B4
Ruswarp Pleasure Boats*
YO21 ....208 B3
Rutland Cl
Copmanthorpe YO23 ...230 A3
Harrogate HG1 ....219 A2
Rutland Dr HG1 ......219 A2
Rutland Pl 4 YO62 ....92 F7
Rutland Rd HG1 .....219 B2
Rutland St 4 YO62 ....92 F7
Rutland Terr YO12 ...213 A7
Rutmoor Rd YO18 ....71 E8
Rutson Hospl DL7 ....210 D5
Ryburn Cl YO30 .....224 F2
Rycroft Rd 3 YO12 ....75 E5

268 Ryd - St W

Rydal Ave
Middlesbrough TS5 ....6 E8
York YO31 ....229 A6
Rydal Cl 2 YO7 ....89 C4
Rydal Cres 1 YO12 ....99 F7
Rydal Rd Darlington DL1 ....3 E4
Harrogate HG1 ....220 B3
Rydale Pal Sh Mall*
YO17 ....215 C3
Ryder Cres 3 YO62 ....70 B1
Ryder Sq YO17 ....215 C4
Ryder's Wynd 3 DL10 ....209 C6
Rye Cl Haxby YO32 ....225 C8
Huttons Ambo YO17 ....121 C1
Rye Hill Way TS8 ....7 B4
Rycroft 7 YO32 ....167 A6
Ryecroft Ave
10 Norton DN6 ....206 E2
York YO24 ....230 C7
Ryecroft Cl YO31 ....229 C8
Ryecroft Gdns DN14 ....203 A2
Ryecroft Rd
Glusburn BD20 ....187 D8
Norton DN6 ....206 E1
Ryecroft Way 2 BD20 ....187 E8
Ryedale Cl
Helmsley YO62 ....92 F7
Norton YO17 ....215 F1
Pontefract WF6 ....200 A3
Ulleskelf LS24 ....190 B2
Ryedale Folk Mus*
 ....70 C5
Ryedale Leisure Ctr
YO18 ....95 F7
Ryedale Pk LS29 ....218 D3
Ryedale Pl WF6 ....200 A3
Ryedale Sch YO62 ....93 D7
Ryedale State Pk
YO17 ....215 C3
Ryedale Swimming Pool
YO62 ....93 D4
Ryedale View 2 YO62 ....70 B1
Ryedale Way YO8 ....232 C3
Ryefield Cl 3 YO12 ....99 F7
Ryefield Rd 1 YO11 ....100 A6
Ryegate 3 YO62 ....92 F6
Ryehill Cl YO32 ....225 D5
Ryeland St 5 BD20 ....187 E8
Ryelands Pk 1 TS13 ....11 A8
Ryemoor Rd YO32 ....225 C8
Rylatt Pl YO26 ....227 B3
Rylstone Dr 1 BB18 ....171 D1
Rymer Way 4 YO7 ....211 C3
Ryndle Cres YO12 ....212 E8
Ryndle Wlk YO12 ....212 E8
Ryndleside YO12 ....212 E7
Ryngwoode Dr YO17 ....215 C6
Ryton Old La YO17 ....121 F5
Ryton Old Rd YO17 ....122 A5
Ryton Stile Rd YO17 ....215 C7

S

Sackville Rd BD20 ....174 C1
Sackville St
20 Barnoldswick BB18 ....171 D1
Skipton BD23 ....217 A3
Sacred Heart Prim Sch
LS29 ....218 D4
Sacred Heart RC Prim Sch
DL7 ....210 D2
Sadberge CE Sch DL2 ....4 C8
Sadberge Rd YO10 ....229 C3
Sadberge Rd DL2 ....4 C5
Saddle Cl YO17 ....215 D2
Saddlers Cl
1 Copmanthorpe YO23 ....230 B3
Huntington YO32 ....225 F2
Saddlers Croft 8 LS29 ....218 A4
Saddlers La WF11 ....201 E5
Saddlers Way YO26 ....182 A6
Sadler Dr TS7 ....7 D6
Sadler Forster Way TS17 ....6 B5
Sadlers Ct YO61 ....143 A5
Saffron Dr 8 DN14 ....204 C1
Saffron Mdw 19 HG3 ....161 B3
Sails Dr YO10 ....229 B3
St Aelreds RC Prim Sch
YO31 ....229 B5
St Agathas Cl DL10 ....209 C7
St Aidan's Rd 3 DL10 ....209 D1
St Aidans CE High Sch
HG2 ....219 F1
St Aidans Rd DL10 ....209 C8
St Alkelda's Rd 1 DL8 ....60 E2
St Andrew Pl YO1 ....233 C2
St Andrew's Ave HG2 ....220 A3
St Andrew's Cres HG2 ....220 A3
St Andrew's Gr 1 HG2 ....220 B2
St Andrew's Par 3 HG2 ....220 B2
St Andrew's Pl 2 HG2 ....220 A2
St Andrew's Rd
Castleford WF10 ....201 B5
4 Harrogate HG2 ....220 B3
St Andrew's St 1 HG2 ....220 A2
St Andrew's Wlk HG2 ....220 A2
St Andrewgate YO1 ....233 B2
St Andrews Dr WF7 ....200 E1
St Andrews Gate 4 HG2 ....112 D5
St Andrews Gr 2 DL7 ....210 D2
St Andrews Mdws
HG4 ....112 D5
St Andrews Rd YO21 ....208 B5

St Ann Ct YO10 ....228 E2
St Ann's Ct YO10 ....228 D2
St Ann's Staith 15 YO21 ....208 D7
St Anne's Cres 3 DL10 ....41 E4
St Annes Gdns DL2 ....4 C3
St Anthonys Ave 2 DL7 ....210 E2
St Athan's Wlk HG2 ....222 C7
St Aubyn's Pl YO24 ....228 A2
St Augustine's Cath Sch
YO12 ....212 C4
2 Darlington DL1 ....3 C5
St Barnabas' CE Prim Sch
YO26 ....227 F5
St Barnabas St 18 YO26 ....227 F5
St Bedes Ave 4 DL7 ....210 D2
St Bedes RC Prim Sch
DL1 ....3 D8
St Benedict Rd YO23 ....233 A1
St Benedicts Cath Prim Sch
LS25 ....194 C4
St Benedicts RC Prim Sch
YO62 ....92 C1
St Bernadette's RC Prim Sch
TS7 ....7 D6
St Boltophs Cl 4 WF11 ....202 A2
St Brides Cl 30 TS17 ....5 F4
St Bridget's Ct YO23 ....233 B1
St Catherine's Rd HG2 ....219 F1
St Catherines YO30 ....224 D6
St Catherines Cl YO30 ....224 C5
St Catherines Pl YO24 ....228 A3
St Chads Wharf YO23 ....231 C8
St Christopher Cl 3
DL7 ....210 D2
St Christophers Dr 27
LS29 ....174 F4
St Clare's RC Prim Sch
TS5 ....6 D6
St Clares Abbey DL3 ....3 B5
St Clement's Gr YO23 ....228 C2
St Clement's Rd HG2 ....220 A2
St Clements Rd S
HG2 ....220 A2
St Cuthbert Dr DL7 ....210 B3
St Cuthbert's Ave 4 DL9 ....41 A5
St Cuthbert's Gn DL10 ....21 D8
St Cuthberts CE Sch
HG3 ....137 B4
St Cuthberts Wlk DL10 ....10 D8
St David's RC Tech Coll
TS5 ....6 E7
St David's View 34 TS17 ....5 F4
St Davids Rd DL1 ....3 F8
St Davids Rd 1 DL10 ....176 F1
St Denys' Rd YO1 ....233 C2
St Edmund's Cl 1 DL10 ....230 F8
St Edmunds Cl 11 DL10 ....41 C6
St Edward's Cl YO24 ....230 F8
St Edward's Com Prim Sch 1
LS23 ....188 E8
St Edwards Cl 2 WF11 ....201 F4
St Edwin's Cl DL2 ....2 C6
St Francis Xavier Sch
DL10 ....209 E8
St Gabriels RC Sch TS7 ....7 D8
St George's Ave HG2 ....222 D7
St George's Gate DL2 ....4 B5
St George's Pl YO24 ....227 F2
St Georges Gate YO10 ....228 D2
St George's Rd HG2 ....222 D7
St George's Wlk HG2 ....222 D7
St Georges Gr 3 DL2 ....210 E2
St Georges Terr TS13 ....10 D8
St Giles' Cl 1 DL9 ....41 A5
St Giles Cl YO7 ....211 C3
St Giles Rd YO30 ....224 B5
St Giles Way YO23 ....230 A2
St Gregory's Cl DL8 ....62 E4
St Gregory's Mews
YO1 ....233 A2
St Hedda's RC Prim Sch
YO21 ....31 A4
St Helena 11 YO51 ....141 B5
St Helen's Dr LS25 ....194 F4
St Helen's La
Borrowby YO7 ....65 E4
Reighton YO14 ....127 C6
St Helen's Rd
Harrogate HG2 ....223 A8
5 York YO24 ....230 E8
St Helen's Rise YO19 ....193 A7
St Helens Sq
23 Barnoldswick YO11 ....213 A6
York YO1 ....233 B2
St Helen's Way LS29 ....218 D4
St Helens Cl DL7 ....64 A7
St Helens Rd DL7 ....64 A7
St Helens Wlk TS13 ....10 D8
St Hilary Cl DL10 ....209 B7
St Hilda's Bsns Ctr
YO22 ....208 E6
St Hilda's Cres YO17 ....124 E8
St Hilda's Gdns 4 YO21 ....208 C7
St Hilda's RC Prim Sch
YO21 ....208 D5
St Hilda's Rd HG2 ....219 F1
St Hilda's St YO17 ....124 D7
St Hilda's Terr YO21 ....208 D6
St Hilda's Wlk YO21 ....208 C7
St Hildas Ampleforth CE VC
Sch YO62 ....92 C1
St Hildas Mews YO10 ....229 B4

St Hildas Rd 5 DL7 ....210 D2
St Ians Croft 22 LS29 ....174 F4
St Ives Cl 3 WF8 ....201 B2
St Ives Cres WF10 ....201 B3
St James' Bsns Pk
 ....221 E4
St James CE Prim Sch
LS22 ....180 C3
St James Chapel Flats
DL10 ....209 B6
St James Cl
Melsonby DL10 ....20 F7
York YO30 ....224 E3
St James Ct
Rawcliffe DN14 ....205 A1
Skipton BD23 ....217 B4
St James Dr 7 DL7 ....210 D2
St James Gn 9 YO7 ....211 C3
St James Mdw 18 YO51 ....141 B5
St James Mount YO24 ....228 A2
St James Pl 5 YO24 ....227 D1
St James' St LS29 ....218 A3
St James Rd
Northallerton DL7 ....210 B2
Scarborough YO12 ....212 E4
St James Terr YO8 ....232 C5
St James's St 7 LS22 ....180 C3
St John Fisher Cath High Sch
HG2 ....223 A8
St John Mews YO8 ....232 B7
St John of God Hospl
DL10 ....41 F7
St John St
Harrogate HG1 ....219 D2
York YO31 ....233 B3
St John the Baptist RC Jun & Inf
Prim Sch WF6 ....200 B1
St John's Ave
42 Filey YO14 ....101 B3
Milby YO51 ....141 B7
Scarborough YO12 ....212 E5
St John's Cl
Aberford LS25 ....188 F1
Bishop Monkton HG3 ....140 B5
St John's Cres
Bishop Monkton HG3 ....140 A5
Harrogate HG1 ....219 D5
3 Leeming DL7 ....63 D4
York YO31 ....233 C4
St John's Dr
Harrogate HG1 ....219 D6
North Rigton LS17 ....178 B4
St John's Garth 3 LS25 ....194 F8
St John's Gr HG1 ....219 C5
St John's Rd
Bishop Monkton HG3 ....140 A5
Clifford LS23 ....188 E7
Harrogate HG1 ....219 D5
Ilkley LS29 ....218 E4
2 Leeming DL7 ....63 D4
Scarborough YO12 ....212 E5
Scotton HG5 ....162 A6
5 Stamford Bridge YO41 ....168 D2
St John's View LS23 ....188 E8
St John's Way
Bishop Monkton HG3 ....140 A5
Harrogate HG1 ....219 D6
St John's Wlk
Bishop Monkton HG3 ....140 A5
Milby YO51 ....141 B7
St Johns Ave 25 YO12 ....174 F4
St Johns Cath Sch for the
Deaf 7 LS23 ....188 E8
St Johns CE Prim Sch
DL1 ....3 E4
St Johns Cl
Northallerton DL6 ....210 E2
Sharow HG4 ....214 F7
St Johns Ct
Skipton BD23 ....217 A4
Ulleskelf LS24 ....190 C3
St Johns Pk DL11 ....2 A1
St Johns Rd DL10 ....209 F1
St Joseph's Cl 8 YO12 ....212 C8
St Joseph's Ct LS25 ....194 C3
St Joseph's St LS24 ....189 E6
St Josephs Cath Prim Sch
Harrogate HG1 ....219 C5
5 Tadcaster LS24 ....189 E6
Wetherby LS22 ....180 C3
St Josephs RC Prim Sch
Castleford WF10 ....200 F4
Loftus TS13 ....10 D8
12 Pickering YO18 ....95 F7
St Josephs RC Sch
BB18 ....171 D2
St Lawrences CE Prim Sch
YO10 ....228 E3
St Leonard's Cl
1 Harrogate HG2 ....220 B1
3 Malton YO17 ....215 C4
St Leonard's Cres
YO12 ....212 D8
St Leonard's Oval
HG2 ....220 A1
St Leonard's Pl YO30 ....233 B3
St Leonard's Rd HG2 ....220 A1
St Leonards Ave YO8 ....198 B4
St Leonards 30 LS29 ....174 F4
St Leonards Rd TS14 ....8 E6
St Luke's Cl
6 Boston Spa LS23 ....188 E7
Harrogate HG1 ....219 D4
St Luke's Cres YO12 ....212 C6
St Luke's Gr YO30 ....228 A5
St Luke's Mount YO11 ....214 D4

St Lukes Cl DL7 ....22 C2
St Lukes Hospl TS4 ....7 A8
St Margaret's Ave
LS26 ....200 B5
St Margaret's Cl 3 HG5 ....221 A6
St Margaret's Garth 2
HG5 ....221 A6
St Margaret's Gdns 1
HG5 ....221 A6
St Margaret's Rd
Knaresborough HG5 ....221 A6
Mickletown LS26 ....200 B6
St Margaret's Terr
1 Ilkley LS29 ....218 B3
York YO1 ....228 E4
St Margarets Cl DL2 ....4 C3
St Mark's Ave HG2 ....222 D7
St Mark's Cl 1 YO12 ....212 C8
St Mark's Gr YO30 ....224 E2
St Martin's Ave YO11 ....213 A4
St Martin's La YO1 ....233 A2
St Martin's Pl 10 YO11 ....213 A4
St Martin's Sch 9 YO11 ....213 A4
St Martin's Sch 2 ....93 D8
St Martins Ave 2 LS25 ....176 F1
St Martins Way 11 TS15 ....24 E8
St Martins YO11 ....213 C1
St Martins 15 DL9 ....40 E4
St Mary's Ave
Barnoldswick BB18 ....171 E2
Harrogate HG2 ....219 C2
12 Hemingbrough YO8 ....198 F1
14 Swillington LS26 ....194 A1
Thirsk YO7 ....211 C4
St Mary's CE Prim Sch
8 Boston Spa LS23 ....188 E8
Longnewton TS21 ....5 A7
St Mary's Cl
Barton DL10 ....21 D7
13 Haxby YO32 ....166 E5
Ilkley LS29 ....218 C4
South Cowton DL7 ....22 E2
Strensall YO32 ....167 A7
Thirsk YO7 ....211 C4
St Mary's Coll TS4 ....6 F7
St Mary's Cres YO22 ....208 E6
St Mary's Dr YO7 ....211 C4
St Mary's Gdns BD23 ....173 B4
St Mary's La YO11 ....229 C4
St Mary's La YO30 ....233 A3
St Mary's Mus* 233 B2
St Mary's RC Prim Sch
Malton YO17 ....215 C3
Selby YO8 ....232 B2
St Mary's St 6 YO11 ....213 B6
St Mary's Terr YO30 ....233 A3
St Mary's Way YO7 ....211 C4
St Mary's Wlk
Harrogate HG2 ....219 C1
Mickletown LS25 ....194 F4
Middlesbrough TS5 ....6 E8
Scarborough YO12 ....213 A4
Thirsk YO7 ....211 C4
St Marys Cath TS8 ....7 B5
St Marys CE Prim Sch
DL10 ....209 E7
St Marys CE Prim Sch
YO23 ....182 D3
St Marys Cl
Cottingwith YO42 ....193 C5
14 Stokesley TS9 ....26 C7
St Marys Ct YO7 ....90 C3
St Marys Gate HG4 ....214 D5
St Marys Hospl YO12 ....212 F6
St Marys RC Prim Sch
HG5 ....221 A7
St Marys Terr YO30 ....233 A3
St Matthew's Cl
20 Leyburn DL8 ....60 D5
4 Naburn YO19 ....191 D8
St Maurice's Rd YO31 ....233 C3
St Michael St 6 YO17 ....215 C4
St Michael's La YO11 ....213 C1
St Michael's Mead
HG4 ....138 E6
St Michaels Cl 1 DL8 ....210 D2
St Michaels Gn 18 WF6 ....200 A1
St Michaels Way 20
LS29 ....174 F4
St Monica Hospl YO61 ....143 C8
St Monicas Ct 4 YO61 ....143 D8
St Monicas Garth 17
YO61 ....143 D8
St Nicholas Ave YO10 ....231 D4
St Nicholas CE Prim Sch
HG4 ....87 A1
St Nicholas Cl
Copmanthorpe YO23 ....230 A3
Richmond DL10 ....209 F8
St Nicholas Cliff 5
YO11 ....213 A5
St Nicholas Cres
YO23 ....230 A3
St Nicholas Croft
YO23 ....182 E3
St Nicholas Dr DL10 ....209 F7
St Nicholas Fields Nature
Reserve* YO10 ....228 F4
St Nicholas Gdns TS15 ....5 E4
St Nicholas Pl 1 YO10 ....228 F3

St Nicholas Rd
Copmanthorpe YO23 ....230 A3
Harrogate HG2 ....220 B2
Ilkley LS29 ....218 A5
St Nicholas St
Norton YO17 ....215 D3
Scarborough YO11 ....213 A6
St Nicholas Way 22
YO32 ....166 E5
St Nicholas Wlk HG2 ....220 B2
St Olave's Cl HG4 ....214 A3
St Olave's Rd YO30 ....233 A4
St Olave's Sch YO30 ....233 A3
St Oswald's CE Prim Sch
YO10 ....231 D7
St Oswald's Cl
Catton YO41 ....185 F6
Oswaldkirk YO62 ....93 A1
St Oswald's Rd YO10 ....231 D8
St Oswalds Cl
14 Catterick Garrison DL8 ....40 E4
Sowerby YO7 ....89 D3
St Oswalds Ct
6 Filey YO14 ....101 B3
York YO10 ....231 E7
St Oswalds Rd DL8 ....40 E4
St Patrick's Way HG2 ....220 B2
St Patricks RC Comp Sch
TS17 ....6 C7
St Paul's Terr
Darlington DL3 ....3 C7
YO24 ....228 A3
St Paul's Dr DL10 ....41 B6
St Paul's Dr DL10 ....41 B6
St Paul's Gr LS29 ....218 C4
St Paul's Rd YO17 ....6 B8
St Paul's Sq YO24 ....228 A3
St Paul's Terr
Darlington DL3 ....3 C7
York YO24 ....228 A4
St Paulinas RC VA Prim Sch
TS14 ....8 D6
St Paulinus Cl 4 DL7 ....210 B3
St Paulinus Dr 1 DL7 ....210 B3
St Pauls Mews YO24 ....228 A3
St Pauls Rise LS29 ....174 F4
St Peter & St Paul RC Prim
Sch DL8 ....60 D5
St Peter St YO17 ....215 D3
St Peter's Brafferton CE VA
Prim Sch YO61 ....115 F1
YO12 ....212 D8
St Peter's Cl 2 YO30 ....41 A5
St Peter's Cres YO17 ....215 D3
St Peter's Ct YO7 ....208 F4
St Peter's Garth LS14 ....188 A3
St Peter's Gr YO30 ....233 A4
St Peter's Rd DL10 ....204 F5
St Peter's Rd Drax YO8 ....204 F5
St Peter's Sch YO30 ....233 A4
St Peter's Sq 7 HG2 ....219 C2
St Peters CE Prim Sch
HG2 ....219 D1
St Peters Ct YO23 ....227 A5
St Peters Ct
31 Addingham LS29 ....174 F4
York YO30 ....233 A4
St Philip's Gr YO30 ....228 A8
St Philip's Way 28 LS29 ....174 F4
St Princes Sq 16 HG1 ....219 D2
St Princes St 15 HG1 ....219 D2
St Richards Rd 3 LS21 ....176 F1
St Robert's Cave* 221 D4
St Robert's Gdns HG5 ....221 B4
HG1 ....219 F4
St Robert's Rd HG5 ....221 B4
St Roberts Mews 4
HG1 ....219 F4
St Ronan's Cl 3 HG2 ....220 A1
St Ronan's Rd 2 HG2 ....220 A1
St Sampsons Sq YO1 ....233 B2
St Saviour's Pl YO1 ....233 C2
St Saviourgate YO1 ....233 C2
St Sepulchre St 7
YO11 ....213 B6
St Simon's Chapel (rems
of)* YO8 ....84 A7
St Stephen's Cl BD23 ....216 F4
St Stephen's Rd YO24 ....227 C2
St Stephen's Sq YO24 ....227 C1
St Stephens Cath Prim Sch
10 BD23 ....216 F4
St Stephens Gdns 1
DL7 ....210 D2
St Stephens Mews
YO30 ....225 A1
St Swithin's Wlk YO26 ....227 E4
St Teresa's RC Prim Sch
DL1 ....3 E4
St Thomas' Pl YO31 ....233 B4
St Thomas St YO11 ....213 A6
St Thomas's Cl 3 YO8 ....232 A5
St Thomas's Way
YO26 ....164 C3
St Trinians Cl DL10 ....209 F8
St Trinians Dr DL10 ....209 F8
St Wilfred Dr DL7 ....210 B3
St Wilfred's Gdns*
HG4 ....214 C6
St Wilfrid's RC Prim Sch
YO31 ....233 C3
St Wilfrid's Cath High Sch
WF7 ....200 E1
St Wilfrid's Cres 9 YO8 ....197 D1

St Wilfrid's Ct YO31 ....233 C3
St Wilfrid's Gdns ⁴ HG4 ...214 C6
St Wilfrid's Pl ⁴ HG4 ...214 C5
St Wilfrid's Rd
 1 Ripon HG4 ....214 C5
 3 Strensall YO32 ....167 B6
St Wilfrids RC Prim Sch
 HG4 ....214 B5
St Williams LS17 ....233 B3
St Winifred's Ave HG2 ...219 F1
St Winifred's Cl HG2 ...219 F1
St Winifred's Rd HG2 ...219 F1
St Wulstan Cl YO31 .....228 E2
Saithes Seaton Cty Prim Sch
 TS13 ....13 K2
Salents Cl
Birdsall YO17 ....148 C4
Duggleby YO17 ....149 B6
Salerno Cl ⁸ DL9 ....209 C1
Salisbury Cl ⁱ⁷ WF6 ...200 C2
Salisbury Dr ⁹ HG1 .....161 B3
Salisbury Rd YO26 .....227 F5
Salisbury St
Scarborough YO12 ......212 E3
Skipton BD23 ....216 E5
Salisbury Terr YO26 .....227 F5
Sallow Heath ¹⁶ HG3 ...161 B3
Salmon La DL8 ....87 B6
Salmond Rd ⁵ YO24 .....227 B1
Salt Pan Well Stps ¹¹
 YO22 ....208 E6
Salt Pans Rd YO13 ......54 D2
Saltburn Rd TS17 ....6 B8
Salter Rd YO11 ....99 F6
Salterforth Rd BB18 ....171 E1
Salterforth Rd BB18 ....172 A1
Saltergate Bank YO18 ...72 F8
Saltergate Com Jun & Inf Sch
 HG3 ....219 A5
Saltergate Dr HG3 ....161 B3
Saltergill La TS15 ....24 C8
Saltergill Sch TS15 ......5 D1
Salters Ave DL1 ....3 E6
Salters La DL1 ....3 F4
Salters La N DL1 ....3 D8
Salters La S DL1 ....3 E7
Saltersgill Ave TS4 ......6 F8
Saltersgill Cl ⁴ TS4 ...6 F8
Salton La YO62 ....94 B1
Salutation Rd DL3 ....3 A4
Sam La YO61 ....142 D8
Samuel Smith Old Brewery*
 LS24 ....189 E6
San Carlos St ⁷ DL9 ...40 E3
Sand Hutton CE VC Prim Sch
 YO41 ....168 B5
Sand Hutton Ct YO41 ...168 B5
Sand La
Barlby with Osgodby
 YO8 ....198 B4
Bubwith YO8 ....199 D5
Heslerton YO17 ....123 F1
Huby YO61 ....144 A5
Oldstead YO61 ....91 D3
Sherburn YO17 ....124 D7
South Milford LS25 ......195 F2
Stillington YO61 ....144 A6
Wistow YO8 ....197 E6
Sandacre Ct YO26 ......227 D5
Sandbeck DL10 ....209 C5
Sandbeck Ind Est
 LS22 ....180 C4
Sandbeck La LS22 ....180 D4
Sandbeck Way LS22 ....180 C4
Sandcroft Cl ⁴ YO24 ...230 D8
Sandcroft Rd YO24 .....230 D8
Sandens Ways DL10 ....197 D2
Sanderson Ave WF6 ....200 A1
Sanderson Rd DL2 ......3 F1
Sandfield La YO7 ....88 D4
Sandfield Terr ⁴ LS24 ...189 F6
Sandgate ⁷ YO12 ....208 D7
Sandgate Dr LS25 ....194 D1
Sandgate La LS25 ....194 E1
Sandgate Rise LS25 ....194 E1
Sandgate Terr LS25 ....194 E1
Sandhill Bank YO21 .....9 E1
Sandhill Cl
Harrogate HG1 ....219 F6
Pontefract WF8 ....201 B2
Sandhill Dr HG1 ....219 F6
Sandhill La ⁷ Bedale DL8 ..63 B3
Brayton YO8 ....197 D2
Sutton upon Derwent
 YO41 ....185 E2
Sandhill Rise WF8 ....201 B2
Sandhill Way HG1 ....219 F6
Sandholme ⁴ YO32 .....166 F5
Sandholmes La YO7 .....89 E3
Sandholme Cl
 ⁱ⁶ Easingwold YO61 ...143 D8
 ²² Settle BD24 ....131 D2
Sandhurst Gdns ⁴
 YO12 ....212 B7
Sandiacres ⁵ YO18 .....197 D1
Sandmartin Ct YO24 ...230 D8
Sandmoor Cl ⁵ YO11 ...208 B5
Sandown Cl Bagby YO7 ...90 B3
York YO24 ....227 E2
Sandpiper Cl
 ⁶ Eastfield YO12 ....99 E6
 ⁴ Filey YO14 ....101 A3
Sandpit La YO62 ....69 B1
Sandriggs DL3 ....3 B7
Sandringham Cl YO32 ...225 C2
Sandringham Rd
Byram cum Sutton WF11 ...201 E4

Sandringham Rd continued
Lockwood TS12 ....9 F6
Middlesbrough TS3 ....7 B8
 2 Ripon HG4 ....214 C3
 6 Wetherby LS22 ......180 C3
Sandringham St
Scarborough YO12 ......212 F7
York YO10 ....228 D2
Sandrock Rd ⁸ WF8 ....201 C1
Sands Cl YO14 ....127 D7
Sands La
Hunmanby YO14 ....127 A8
Rillington YO17 ....122 F5
Sands Rd YO14 ....127 B7
Sandsend Rd
Newholm-cum-Dunsley
 YO21 ....13 A3
Whitby YO21 ....208 A8
Sandside
Scarborough YO11 ......213 B6
Whitby YO22 ....208 D7
Sandsprunt La YO13 ....97 E6
Sandstock Rd YO31 .....229 B7
Sandwath La LS24 ....196 A8
Sandway Ave ⁸ YO8 ...197 B1
Sandway Cl ⁱ¹ YO8 ...197 B1
Sandway Dr
Camblesforth YO8 ....204 D4
 1 Thorpe Willoughby YO8 ..197 B1
Sandwith La YO8 ....204 B4
Sandwood Pk TS14 .....8 D5
Sandy Bank
Farnham HG5 ....162 D7
Northallerton DL6 ....210 F3
Romanby DL6 ....65 A7
Sandy Flatts La TS5 .....6 F6
Sandy Gap YO32 ....225 C7
Sandy Gate HG3 ....196 A4
Sandy La Alne YO61 ...143 A4
Dalton YO7 ....116 A8
 5 Embsay BD23 ....217 C7
Harton YO60 ....168 B8
 ⁱ⁰ Haxby YO32 ....166 E5
High & Low Bishopside
 HG3 ....137 D3
Humberton YO61 ....141 D8
North Duffield YO8 ......198 F8
Ripon HG4 ....214 B2
Scampston YO17 ....123 B5
Stockton on the Forest
 YO32 ....167 E4
Sandy La Bsns Ctr
 BD23 ....216 E3
Sandy Leas La TS21 ...5 A8
Sandy Rise YO8 ....232 C3
Sandybed Cres YO12 ...212 C4
Sandybed La
Scarborough YO12 ......212 C4
Wykeham YO13 ....98 F6
Sandyforth La BD22 ....186 E5
Sandyland ²² YO32 .....166 E5
Sandyridge YO26 ....224 A1
Sarah's Croft BD23 .....155 A1
Saunters Way YO23 ....230 F4
Savile Gr YO26 ....224 A1
Savile Rd
Castleford WF10 ....200 E4
Micklefield LS25 ....200 B6
Saville Gr YO30 ....228 A8
Saville St YO17 ....215 C4
Saw Wells La LS24 ......195 F6
Sawley Cl BD23 ....217 C7
Sawley Moor La HG4 ...138 D6
Sawley St ⁱ BD23 ......216 D3
Sawmill La YO17 ....92 F6
Sawyer's Cres YO23 ....230 C2
Sawyers Garth ⁸ LS29 ..175 A4
Sawyers Wlk ⁸ YO19 ...184 F7
Saxford Way ⁸ YO32 ...166 D5
Saxon Cl Shipton YO30 ..165 F5
 6 Thorpe Willoughby YO8 ..197 B1
Saxon Dr YO17 ....122 F5
Saxon Pl YO31 ....228 E7
Saxon Rd
Catterick Garrison DL9 ...209 F1
Ripon HG4 ....214 D5
Stamford Bridge YO41 ...168 D2
Whitby YO21 ....208 B7
Saxon Vale YO30 ....165 F5
Saxonfield TS8 ....7 A6
Saxton CE VC Prim Sch
 LS24 ....195 D7
Saxton Cl LS24 ....195 D8
Saxton La LS24 ....195 E8
Saxty Way YO7 ....211 A1
Scabbate Gate BD23 ...108 B3
Scackleton Bank
 YO62 ....119 C4
Scackleton La YO62 ....119 C4
Scafell Cl ⁴ YO30 ......224 E1
Scagglethorpe La
 YO17 ....122 C4
Scaife Gdns YO31 ....228 C7
Scaife Shay La YO7 ....116 A7
Scaife St YO31 ....228 C7
Scalby Ave YO12 ....212 C8
Scalby Beck Rd ²⁷ YO13 ..75 D5
Scalby Rd YO12 ....212 D5
Scalby Sch YO12 ....212 B8
Scaldhill La YO5 ....141 C7
Scale Hill LS22 ....177 D2
Scale The BD23 ....217 C5
Scallow Bank La DL8 ...59 B6
Scalm La
Hambleton YO8 ....196 F2
Selby YO8 ....197 A4

Scampston Hall*
 YO17 ....123 A6
Scampton Cl TS17 ......6 A6
Scar Field ⁹ BD23 ......134 E2
Scar Hos DL11 ....35 F5
Scar Rd BD23 ....171 E6
Scar St BD23 ....134 E2
Scarah Bank HG3 ....161 B8
Scarah La HG3 ....140 A2
Scarbeck Bank DL11 ...19 D7
Scarborough Art Gall*
 YO11 ....213 A5
Scarborough Bsns Pk
 YO11 ....99 F6
Scarborough Castle*
 YO11 ....213 C7
Scarborough Coll
 YO11 ....213 A2
Scarborough General Hospl
 YO12 ....212 B6
Scarborough Indoor Pool*
 YO12 ....212 E8
Scarborough Rd
Gristhorpe YO14 ....101 A4
Heslerton YO17 ....123 F6
Langtoft YO25 ....151 C7
Norton-on-Derwent
 YO17 ....215 F4
Norton-on-Derwent
 YO17 ....122 A3
Seamer YO12 ....99 D6
Stainton Dale YO13 .....53 F8
Scarborough Sixth Form Coll
 YO12 ....212 C4
Scarborough Sports Ctr
 YO11 ....213 A2
Scarborough Sta
 YO11 ....212 F5
Scarborough Terr
 YO30 ....233 B4
Scarcroft Hill YO24 .....228 B2
Scarcroft La YO23 ......233 A1
Scarcroft Prim Sch
 YO23 ....233 A1
Scarcroft Rd YO24 .....233 A1
Scarcroft View YO23 ...233 A1
Scardale Cres YO12 ....212 E8
Scardale Ct YO8 ....232 A2
Scargill Rd HG1 ....219 B4
Scarer's La YO26 ....142 B2
Scarfield Balk La DL11 ..17 E2
Scarlet Balk La YO12 ...122 C1
Scarth Cl ⁸ TS12 ....9 F7
Scarth Nick
Preston-under-Scar DL8 ..59 E6
Whorlton DL6 ....45 D6
Scarthingwell Cres
 LS24 ....195 D8
Scarthingwell La LS24 ..195 E8
Scate Moor La YO26 ...163 F3
Scaudercroft ¹⁰ YO19 ..184 F7
Scawling End Rd YO61 ..91 C3
Scawthorpe Cl WF8 ....201 C1
Scawton Ave ⁱ YO31 ...225 E2
Scholars Gate TS14 .....8 F5
Scholes Pk DL3 ....3 B5
Scholes La BD22 ....187 F1
Scholes Pk Ave ⁸ YO12 ..75 F5
Scholes Pk Cliff ⁱ YO12 ..75 F5
Scholes Pk Dr ⁸ YO12 ..75 F5
Scholes Pk Rd YO12 ....75 F5
Scholla La DL6 ....210 F5
Scholla Wlk DL6 ....210 F5
Scholes Rd WF10 ....201 B8
School Cl Huby YO61 ...144 A4
Selby YO8 ....232 B3
 ⁱ⁰ Stamford Bridge YO41 ..168 D2
School Croft WF11 .....201 E4
School Fields BB18 .....172 A2
School Garth YO7 ....89 E3
School Hill
Bainbridge DL8 ....57 D5
 8 Settle BD24 ....131 E2
School House Dr YO12 ..99 D6
School La
Addingham LS29 ....174 F5
Askham Bryan YO23 ....182 D3
Bellerby DL8 ....60 D7
Bishopthorpe YO23 .....231 A4
Burton Fleming YO25 ...126 E3
Collingham LS22 ....188 A8
Copmanthorpe YO23 ...230 A2
Darby Dale YO13 ....159 F8
Easby DL8 ....172 A1
Easington BB7 ....152 B3
Eppleby DL11 ....1 D4
Great Ayton TS9 ....8 A1
Heslington YO10 ....229 B1
Lealholm Bridge BB8 ...186 C3
Lawkland LA2 ....130 C3
Lotherton cum Aberford
 LS25 ....194 F8
Malton YO17 ....215 C4
 4 Nawton YO62 ....93 D7
Newton-le-Willows DL8 ..62 B4
Osmotherley DL6 ....45 B4
 ²⁶ Scagglethorpe YO17 ..165 F1
South Milford LS25 .....195 F2
 8 Spofforth HG3 ....179 E6
Thornton-le-Beans DL6 ..65 B5
Walton LS23 ....188 F8
Wray-with-Botton LA2 ..128 A6
York YO10 ....231 E7
School Rd
Hemingbrough YO8 .....198 F1
Wetherby LS22 ....180 C3
School St
Castleford WF10 ....200 F5
 2 Earby BB18 ....186 A7

School St continued
York YO24 ....227 D3
Schoolgate LS15 ....194 C8
Score Ray La YO26 ......164 A5
Scoreby La YO41 ....168 B1
Scoresby Terr ⁷ YO21 ..208 D5
Scoska Wood National
 Nature Reserve*
 BD23 ....107 B3
Scosthrop La BD23 .....154 E6
Scotch Cnr
Middleton Tyas DL10 ...21 B4
Oldstead YO61 ....91 C4
Scotch George La
 HG5 ....221 A7
Scotchman La YO60 ....168 A8
Scotpit La DL6 ....43 E4
Scots Dike Terr DL10 ...209 D6
Scots Dyke Cl DL10 ....20 F7
Scott Cl
 ⁱ⁶ Glusburn BD20 ....187 E7
 ⁱ⁸ Swillington LS26 ...194 A1
Scott Moncrieff Rd
 YO32 ....167 B6
Scott Rd YO8 ....232 C6
Scott St YO23 ....228 B2
Scotton Bank DL8 ....40 D2
Scotton Ct HG5 ....162 A6
Scotton Dr HG5 ....220 C8
Scotton Gdns ⁸ DL9 ...40 E3
Scotton Gr
Knaresborough HG5 ...220 C8
Scotton HG5 ....162 A5
Scotton Lingerfield Com
 Prim Sch HG5 ....162 B7
Scotton Moor HG5 ......220 C8
Scotton Pk DL9 ....40 E3
Scotton Rd DL9 ....40 E3
Scrifrain La LS22 ....180 C5
Scriven Gr ⁸ HG5 ......166 F5
Scriven Rd HG5 ....221 A7
Scroggs La DL8 ....86 E7
Scrogs La DL8 ....59 B6
Scrope Ave ⁴ YO31 ....228 E5
Scupdale Rd DL6 ....45 E8
Scurragh House La
 DL10 ....21 C2
Scurragh La DL10 ......21 B2
Sea App YO14 ....100 F6
Sea Cliff Cres YO11 ....213 B2
Sea Cliff Rd YO11 ......213 B2
Sea Life & Marine
 Sanctuary* YO12 ......75 F5
Sea View YO14 ....101 C1
Sea View Cl
 5 Scarborough YO11 ..100 B8
Whitby YO21 ....208 A6
Sea View Cl YO11 ......100 B8
Sea View Dr ⁸ YO11 ...100 B8
Sea View Gdns ⁸ YO11 ..100 B8
Sea View Gr ⁴ YO11 ...100 B8
Seafield Ave ⁱ YO11 ...100 B7
Seafire Cl YO30 ....225 A3
Seagram Cres DL10 ....209 C8
Seal Bank YO12 ....81 D1
Seamer & Irton Com Prim
 Sch YO12 ....99 D6
Seamer Moor Hill
 YO12 ....212 B1
Seamer Moor La YO12 ..212 B1
Seamer Rd
East Ayton YO13 ....99 B7
Eastfield YO12 ....99 F8
Hilton TS15 ....6 C2
Maltby TS8 ....6 E3
Scarborough YO12 ......212 E3
Thornton TS8 ....6 D4
Seamer Rd Cnr YO12 ...212 E4
Seamer Rd Ret Pk
 YO12 ....212 E1
Seamer St 2 YO12 ....212 E3
Seamer Sta YO12 ....99 F6
Seaton Cl YO10 ....229 C4
Seaton Cres TS13 ......13 K2
Seaton Garth TS13 .....13 K2
Seave Cl La YO60 ......164 D2
Seavegate ⁴ YO13 .....99 B8
Seavegate Cl ⁸ YO13 ..99 B8
Seaview Ave ⁵ YO12 ...75 E5
Second Ave
Menwith with Darley
 HG3 ....160 A4
 8 Pickering YO18 ......95 F7
Wetherby LS22 ....180 C3
York YO31 ....228 F6
Second Comm La YO8 ..197 C4
Sedber La BD23 ....216 B4
Sedbergh Dr LS29 ......218 B3
Sedbergh Pk LS29 ......218 B3
Sedbusk La DL8 ....56 D6
Sedge Rise LS24 ....189 D5
Sedgefield Rd TS5 ......6 E6
Sedley Cl HG1 ....219 E2
Seebohm Mews ⁴ DL6 ..210 E3
Seed La YO8 ....203 C6
Sefton Ave YO31 ....228 F8
Sefton Dr LS29 ....218 B3
Sefton Way TS15 ....5 D2
Seg La YO8 ....204 F3
Seggans Rd YO26 ......142 A1
Segrave Rd DL9 ....40 E4
Segrave Wlk ⁸ YO26 ...227 E4
Selbourne ⁸ BB18 .....172 A1
Selby Abbey YO8 ....232 D5
Selby Abbey CE Prim Sch
 YO8 ....232 C5
Selby Coll Selby YO8 ...232 D1
Selby Coll YO8 ....232 F3

Selby Coll continued
Selby YO8 ....232 C5
Selby CP Sch YO8 ......232 B5
Selby Cres DL3 ....3 A7
Selby Sch YO8 ....232 B4
Selby Ironworks Bsns Ctr
 YO8 ....232 D5
Selby Rd
Eggborough DN14 ......202 F1
Fulford YO19 ....231 E6
Garforth LS25 ....194 B3
Ledston LS25 ....195 A2
Riccall YO19 ....198 A8
Snaith DN14 ....204 C1
Swillington LS15 ....194 A3
Wistow YO8 ....197 D6
Womersley DN14 ....207 A4
Selby Rly Sports Club
 YO8 ....232 D5
Selby Sta YO8 ....232 D5
Seldon Rd YO26 ....227 C5
Self Gdns YO62 ....70 F3
Selley Pk Dr YO12 ......212 B4
Selside Shaw BD24 ....105 A7
Selstone Cres ⁷ YO22 ..32 A6
Semer Wr Nature Reserve*
 DL8 ....57 B1
Senhouse Rd DL1 ......3 F5
Seph Way YO17 ....215 A2
Sergeant Bank HG4 ....86 B8
Sessay CE VC Prim Sch
 YO7 ....116 C5
Sessions House Yd ¹⁰
 WF8 ....201 B1
Settle CE VC Prim Sch
 BD24 ....131 E2
Settle Coll BD24 ....131 D2
Settle Mid Sch BD24 ...131 D3
Settle Rd BD24 ....155 A6
Settle Sta BD24 ....131 D2
Settle Swimming Pool
 BD24 ....131 D3
Settrington All Saint's CE
 Prim Sch YO17 ....122 D1
Settrington Rd YO12 ...212 B5
Seven St YO17 ....121 C1
Seven Wells YO17 ......121 A4
Seventh Ave YO31 ......228 F5
Severfield Cl YO7 ....211 D2
Severn Dr
Garforth LS25 ....194 D3
Guisborough TS14 ....8 E6
Severn Gr YO26 ....227 C8
Severn Way DL1 ....3 D3
Severus St YO24 ....227 D4
Sewell's Cave* LA2 ....131 A5
Sexhow La TS9 ....25 F4
Seymour Cres TS16 ....5 D4
Seymour Gr
Eaglescliffe TS16 ....5 D4
York YO31 ....228 F6
Shackleton Cl YO21 ...208 C5
Shady La BD20 ....173 C2
Shaftesbury Ave DN14 ..202 C3
Shaker Stile Rd YO18 ...96 B7
Shakespeare Ave 2
 DN6 ....206 E1
Shakespeare Cl 8 DL10 ..41 C7
Shakespeare Cres
 WF10 ....201 B3
Shallowdale Gr ⁱ YO10 ..229 C3
Shambles YO1 ....233 B2
Shambles La YO7 ......114 C5
Shambles The 8 YO17 ..215 B4
Shandon Pk TS8 ....7 C5
Shandy Hall* YO61 .....117 C8
Shannon St ²⁰ LS29 ...175 C2
Shannon Lea DL2 ....4 C4
Sharow CE Prim Sch
 HG4 ....214 F7
Sharow La HG4 ....214 E6
Sharp Hill La YO8 ....204 F6
Sharpe Howe* YO11 ...126 A8
Sharphaw Ave BD23 ...217 A2
Sharphaw View BD23 ...155 D1
Shaw Ave WF6 ....200 B1
Shaw Barn La LS22 ....180 B3
Shaw Cl WF6 ....200 B1
Shaw Cres YO61 ....144 A5
Shaw Dr YO62 ....70 B1
Shaw La Farnham HG5 ..162 C7
Fenwick DN6 ....207 D2
North Rigton HG3 ....178 B6
Thirsk with Stockeld
 HG3 ....179 D7
Shaw Rise WF8 ....200 B1
Shawclose La YO62 ....67 A4
Shawcroft Ct DL10 .....209 E8
Shawl Terr ⁱ¹ DL8 ......60 D5
Shaws La
Barwick in Elmet & Scholes
 LS15 ....194 B7
Hawes DL8 ....56 E4
Shaw's Terr YO24 ......233 A1
Sheep Rake La YO25 ...151 F4
Sheep St ¹¹ BD23 ......216 F4
Sheepcote La HG3 ......159 F5
Sheepdyke La YO14 ...127 A8
Sheepfoot Hill YO17 ...215 D4
Sheepwalk La
Castleford WF10 ....200 B3
Kirby Grindalythe YO17 ..150 B7
Sheephill Bank YO7 ....66 D5
Sheepwash La DN14 ...207 A4

Sheldrake Cl 9 YO14 ....101 A4
Sheldrake Rd WF10 ....200 E3
Shelley Cl YO11 ....100 B6
Shelley Ct HG1 ....219 E2
Shelley Dr WF11 ....201 D2
Shelley Gr YO30 ....224 F1
Shelton Ave 2 YO13 ....99 B8
Shepherd Ct TS12 ....9 E7
Shepherd Gate LA2 ....130 F5
Shepherd Hill DL6 ....45 D8
Shepherd's Rd YO62 ....70 B4
Shepherdfields La
  YO60 ....146 E5
Shepherdies The HG4 ....113 C8
Shepherds Dr 18 YO11 ....100 B7
Sherbrooke Cl 18 YO62 ....70 B1
Sherburn CE VC Prim Sch
  YO17 ....124 D7
Sherburn Enterprise Pk
  LS25 ....196 B4
Sherburn High Sch
  LS25 ....195 F3
Sherburn in Elmet Sta
  LS25 ....196 A4
Sherburn Rd DL6 ....232 A8
Sherburn St 1 YO8 ....197 B8
Sherburn Willows Nature
  Reserve* LS25 ....195 E3
Sheridan Rd BB8 ....186 B3
Sheriff Hutton Castle (rems
  of)* YO60 ....145 D5
Sheriff Hutton Prim Sch
  YO60 ....145 C5
Sherriff Hutton House*
  ....145 D4
Sherringham Dr YO24 ....230 D8
Sherwood Brow BD24 ....131 D7
Sherwood Cl
  Hunton DL8 ....61 E7
  10 Norton DL6 ....206 E1
Sherwood Dr HG2 ....220 D2
Sherwood Gr
  Huntington YO32 ....225 F1
  York YO26 ....227 B6
Sherwood Rd 5 YO12 ....212 F5
Shetland Cl TS5 ....6 E6
Shilton Garth Cl 8
  YO32 ....225 F7
Shipton Low Rd YO30 ....165 E5
Shipton Rd
  Clifton YO30 ....227 F8
  Rawcliffe YO30 ....224 D2
  York YO30 ....228 A7
Shipton St 3 YO30 ....228 B7
Shipton St Inf Sch
  YO30 ....228 B7
Shipyard Ind Est YO8 ....232 E5
Shipyard Rd YO8 ....232 E5
Shirbutt La YO26 ....182 C8
Shire Cl 11 YO11 ....100 B7
Shire Croft 11 YO11 ....100 B7
Shire Fold YO11 ....100 B6
Shire Garth DL6 ....24 B1
Shire Gr YO17 ....95 D2
Shire Rd YO7 ....211 B4
Shires Croft BD23 ....217 E8
Shires La BD23 ....217 D8
Shirley Ave Ripon HG4 ....214 B4
  York YO26 ....227 C6
Shoebridge Ave BD20 ....187 F7
Shop Hill YO22 ....33 B4
Shop La Cowling BD22 ....187 A6
  Danby YO21 ....29 B3
  Middleton YO18 ....95 D8
Short Cl TS18 ....5 F7
Short La
  Farndale East YO62 ....48 F4
  West Haddlesey YO8 ....202 F6
Short Lee La BD23 ....216 F6
Short Rd YO7 ....115 B2
Shortacre La YO42 ....193 E2
Shortbank Cl BD23 ....217 B3
Shortbank Rd BD23 ....217 B3
Shorthorn La 2 DL3 ....3 A7
Shortsill La HG5 ....163 B5
Shotel Cl YO30 ....227 F8
Showfield Cl LS25 ....195 F4
Showfield Dr 17 YO61 ....143 C8
Showfield La YO17 ....215 C6
Shrubberies The YO8 ....198 E2
Shute Rd DL9 ....209 E1
Shutt La DL8 ....56 E6
Shuttleworth St 58
  BB18 ....172 A1
Shuttocks Fold LS25 ....194 D2
Sicklinghall Com Prim Sch
  LS22 ....179 D3
Sicklinghall Rd LS22 ....179 F3
Side Gate YO12 ....99 D1
Sidegate La BD20 ....186 F8
Sidgwick Ct 7 BD23 ....217 A3
Siding La YO8 ....198 B5
Sidings La YO11 ....143 B4
Sidings The
  12 Bridgehouse Gate HG3 ....137 B4
  Gristhorpe YO14 ....131 D2
  Skipton BD23 ....216 E3
Sidmouth Cl TS8 ....7 D6
Sidmouth Sq 9 DL9 ....40 E4
Signals Ct 7 YO12 ....75 F5
Sigston Castle* DL6 ....44 D2
Sike La YO7 ....115 B6
Sikelands La DL11 ....38 F4

Silicar La HG4 ....88 B1
Sills La YO30 ....165 B6
Silly La LA2 ....129 A2
Silsden Rd
  Addingham LS29 ....174 D4
  Low Bradley BD20 ....173 E3
Silver Garth DL10 ....21 C7
Silver Hill DL2 ....22 C2
Silver Mdws DL11 ....21 C7
Silver St Askrigg DL8 ....57 E5
  Barton DL10 ....21 C7
  Fairburn WF11 ....201 D6
  Hackforth DL8 ....62 E8
  4 Knaresborough HG5 ....221 B5
  Masham HG4 ....86 C3
  Reeth, Fremington & Healaugh
  DL11 ....38 B6
  3 Riccall YO19 ....198 A8
  17 Scarborough YO11 ....213 A6
  Thirsk YO7 ....211 C1
  Whitby YO21 ....208 D7
  Whitley DN14 ....207 A7
  York YO1 ....233 B2
Silverdale Cl 5 HG3 ....160 A6
Silverdale Ct YO24 ....230 D7
Silverdale Rd BD24 ....131 F8
Silverfields Rd HG1 ....220 A3
Silverton Rd TS14 ....8 F5
Silverwood Ave 5
  YO14 ....101 A3
Sim Balk La YO24 ....230 E5
Simbach Cl BD23 ....217 B3
Simon Howe
  Gaston YO32 ....125 A5
  Sherburn YO12 ....124 F6
Simpson Ave 6 YO14 ....126 F8
Simpson Cl BB18 ....171 E2
Simpson's La Jun & Inf Sch
  WF11 ....201 E2
Simpson's Yd 3 YO8 ....232 C6
Simpsons La WF11 ....201 E2
Sinclair Ct YO12 ....212 E5
Sinderby La YO7 ....88 B4
Sinks La DL8 ....62 C4
Sinnington Cl TS14 ....8 F6
Sinnington Cliff Rd
  YO62 ....95 A8
Sinnington Com Prim Sch
  YO62 ....94 F8
Sinnington Rd TS17 ....6 B6
Sir Douglas Pk TS17 ....6 A7
Sir John's La LS25 ....195 E4
Sirocco Ct YO31 ....228 D8
Sissy Bank DL8 ....59 D6
Sitwell Gr YO26 ....227 C5
Sitwell St YO12 ....212 E5
Siward St YO10 ....229 A3
Siward's Way YO10 ....229 A2
Siwards How* YO10 ....229 B1
Sixth Ave YO31 ....228 E5
Skates La YO61 ....144 B3
Sked Dale YO17 ....124 E6
Skeeby Cl 3 TS18 ....5 D8
Skegmer La YO60 ....145 F4
Skelda Rise LS29 ....218 B3
Skelder Rd YO21 ....31 E8
Skeldergate YO1 ....233 B2
Skelf St LS24 ....190 C1
Skelgate La DL11 ....38 B6
Skellbank HG4 ....214 B4
Skellbank Cl HG4 ....214 E4
Skelldale Cl HG4 ....214 E4
Skelldale View HG4 ....214 E4
Skellfield Terr HG4 ....214 D4
Skellgarth HG4 ....214 D4
Skellgill La DL8 ....57 C6
Skelton Cl 3 YO30 ....228 A6
Skelton Ellers TS14 ....9 A8
Skelton La
  Givendale HG4 ....140 C8
  Marske DL11 ....39 B7
  Skelton YO32 ....224 D8
Skelton Prim Sch
  YO30 ....224 C5
Skelton Rd
  Skelton YO51 ....140 E6
  Thornaby TS17 ....6 B8
Skelton Windmill*
  YO51 ....140 F8
Skerne Pk Prim Sch DL1 ....3 C4
Skerningham Ave 8 DL3 ....3 A7
Skeugh Head La DL11 ....35 E6
Skeugh La YO61 ....144 D6
Skewsby Gr YO31 ....225 F1
Skibeden BD23 ....217 E6
Skibeden Ct 4 BD23 ....217 B5
Skiddaw YO24 ....230 C7
Skiddaw Ct TS7 ....7 C6
Skinner La 17 WF8 ....201 B1
Skinner St YO21 ....208 D7
Skiplam Cl YO12 ....212 B5
Skiplam Rd YO62 ....69 D2
Skipper La YO25 ....125 E3
Skipton Castle* 217 A5
Skipton Girls' High Sch
  BD23 ....216 E5
Skipton Hospl BD23 ....216 E3
Skipton Little Theatre*
  BD23 ....216 F3
Skipton Old Rd BB8 ....186 A3
Skipton Parish Church Sch
  BD23 ....217 A3
Skipton Rd
  Addingham LS29 ....174 E5
  Barnoldswick BB18 ....171 E2
  Bradleys Both BD20 ....173 D4

Skipton Rd continued
  Colne BB8 ....186 A2
  Cononley BD20 ....173 C2
  Earby BB18 ....172 A2
  Embsay with Eastby
  BD23 ....217 C7
  Farnhill BD20 ....187 E8
  Fellistcliffe HG3 ....160 E3
  Fewston LS21 ....159 D2
  Gargrave BD23 ....155 D1
  Glusburn BD20 ....187 F8
  Harrogate HG3 ....219 A5
  Hellifield BD23 ....154 B3
  Ilkley LS29 ....218 A4
  Silsden BD20 ....174 B1
  Skipton BD23 ....217 B6
Skipton Sta HG1 ....219 D4
Skipton Sta BD23 ....216 E3
Skipwith Comm Nature
  Reserve* YO8 ....198 E8
Skipwith Rd YO19 ....192 B6
Skirt Bank YO7 ....66 C7
Skottowe Cres TS9 ....7 F2
Skottowe Dr TS9 ....7 F2
Skurkhill La YO62 ....92 E7
Skyreholme Bank
  BD23 ....157 F7
Skyreholme La BD23 ....157 F7
Slack La HG3 ....160 B4
Slackgap La CA17 ....14 A8
Slaidburn Cl 2 DL6 ....210 E3
Slaidburn Rd LA2 ....129 B4
Slate Hill YO21 ....29 D4
Slates La LS29 ....218 B7
Slayde The TS15 ....5 E2
Sled Gates YO22 ....33 B3
Sled La DL10 ....41 F4
Sledgate YO17 ....122 F5
Sledgate Garth YO17 ....122 F5
Sledmere CE VC Prim Sch
  YO25 ....150 B3
Sledmere House*
  YO25 ....150 B3
Sledmere Rd YO25 ....151 B6
Sleegill DL10 ....209 B6
Sleigh La YO60 ....120 A1
Sleightholme Dale Rd
  YO62 ....69 D5
Sleightholme Moor Rd
  YO62 ....16 D7
Sleights CE VC Prim Sch
  YO22 ....32 A6
Sleights La
  Acklam YO17 ....169 E7
  Amotherby YO17 ....121 A6
  Birstwith HG3 ....160 C4
  Rainton with Newby YO7 ....114 E5
Sleights Rd YO62 ....69 D6
Sleights Sta YO22 ....32 A7
Sleights The LS17 ....178 A2
Slessor Rd
  6 Catterick DL10 ....41 E4
  York YO24 ....227 B1
Slice La LS24 ....190 A6
Slim Rd DL9 ....209 C2
Slingsby Ave HG5 ....221 A4
Slingsby Bank YO62 ....120 C4
Slingsby Cl YO62 ....120 B5
Slingsby Com Prim Sch
  YO62 ....120 B5
Slingsby Cres HG1 ....219 F4
Slingsby Gdns 19 YO62 ....70 B1
Slingsby Gdns DL7 ....210 B3
Slingsby Gr YO24 ....230 E8
Slingsby Wlk HG2 ....219 F1
Slip Inn Bank DL11 ....19 E6
Slippery Ford La BD22 ....187 E3
Smales' St YO1 ....233 B1
Smary La YO19 ....184 D7
Smawthorne Ave
  WF10 ....200 E4
Smawthorne Gr WF10 ....200 E4
Smawthorne Henry Moore
  Prim Sch WF10 ....200 E4
Smawthorne La WF10 ....200 E4
Smay La YO22 ....33 D5
Smearbottoms La
  BD23 ....133 C3
Smeathorns Rd TS12 ....9 F4
Smeatley's La DN6 ....206 C4
Smeaton Gr
  5 Swillington LS26 ....194 A1
  York YO26 ....227 C5
Smeaton Rd YO41 ....185 D7
Smiddy Hill
  18 Pickering YO18 ....95 F6
  Walton LS23 ....181 A2
Smiddyfields 5 YO22 ....32 A6
Smirthwaite View 14
  WF6 ....200 A1
Smith Cl YO10 ....231 F8
Smith La HG4 ....114 A4
Smith St 18 BB18 ....171 D1
Smith's La Egton YO22 ....30 E3
  Flaxton YO60 ....145 D1
Smithfield Cl 7 HG4 ....214 B2
Smithfield Rd DL1 ....3 D4
Smithgutter La DL10 ....21 D2
Smithie Cl YO32 ....225 D5
Smithson Ave WF10 ....201 B3
Smithson Cl DL10 ....21 D2
Smithson Ct YO17 ....215 B5
Smithson's La YO21 ....141 B4
Smithson's La HG3 ....177 A8
Smithsons Ct HG4 ....214 C5
Smithy Croft Rd BD23 ....155 D1

Smithy La Denton LS29 ....176 A4
  Scotton HG5 ....162 A6
  Thornton in Lonsdale
  LA6 ....103 A4
  Ulleskelf LS24 ....190 C2
Smithy Rd DL9 ....209 D1
Smithy La YO25 ....125 D4
Snainton CE VC Prim Sch
  YO13 ....98 A5
Snainton La YO13 ....97 F7
Snaith Rd
  Pollington DN14 ....207 F7
  Rawcliffe DN14 ....205 A1
Snaith Sta DN14 ....204 C1
Snaizeholme Rd DL8 ....55 E1
Snape Castle* BT 87 A7
Snape Com Prim Sch
  DL8 ....87 A7
Snape Hill YO62 ....93 E7
Snargate Hill YO62 ....118 E3
Sneaton La YO22 ....208 B1
Sneaton Thorpe La
  YO22 ....32 E5
Sneck Gate La TS8 ....7 B2
Sneck Yate Bank YO7 ....67 A2
Snipe Cl YO24 ....101 A4
Snipe La Hurworth DL2 ....3 C3
  Loftus TS13 ....11 A6
Snowden Carr Rd
  LS21 ....176 E5
Snowden Cl 14 HG4 ....214 B2
Snowden Ct YO23 ....182 D3
Snowdon Gr 18 TS17 ....5 F4
Snowfield Ind Est
  YO17 ....215 C6
Snowfield La YO61 ....142 F5
Snydale Ave 4 WF6 ....200 B1
Snydale Cl WF6 ....200 B1
Snydale Ct 18 WF6 ....200 B1
Snydale Gr WF6 ....200 B1
Snydale Rd WF6 ....200 A1
Sober Hall Ave TS17 ....6 A4
Socarrs La YO62 ....119 F7
Sod House Gn DL2 ....23 B8
Somerset Cl 6 YO30 ....224 E3
Somerset Dr HG2 ....220 D3
Somerset Rd HG2 ....228 D8
Somerset Terr YO11 ....213 A5
Somme Barracks DL9 ....40 F3
Sommerset Pastures
  YO61 ....116 F2
Sopwith Cl TS18 ....5 F8
Sorrel Gr 22 HG3 ....161 B3
Sorrell Gr TS14 ....8 D6
Sough La BB18 ....186 A8
Sour La BD23 ....216 B6
Sourby La LS21 ....176 D7
Soursikes Field Rd
  YO51 ....141 D5
South App
  Aberford LS25 ....188 F1
  Bramham cum Oglethorpe
  LS23 ....188 C5
  Shutton with Hazlewood
  LS24 ....189 A2
South Ave
  Castleford WF10 ....200 C4
  20 Scalby YO13 ....75 D5
South Back La
  Stillington YO61 ....144 C6
  Terrington YO60 ....119 E1
  Tollerton YO61 ....143 B2
South Baileygate WF8 ....201 C1
South Bank Ave BD23 ....228 B1
South Beech Ave HG2 ....220 C3
South Cleveland Hospl
  TS4 ....7 B8
South Cliff Dr YO14 ....101 B1
South Craven Sch 38
  BD20 ....187 E7
South Cres Ripon HG4 ....214 C4
  Thirsk YO7 ....211 C2
South Cres Ave 24 YO14 ....101 B3
South Cres Cl 51 YO14 ....101 B3
South Cres Rd YO14 ....101 B3
South Dowber La YO7 ....211 D4
South Down Rd 3 YO32 ....225 F5
South Dr HG2 ....222 E8
South Duffield Rd
  YO8 ....198 C4
South End Bedale DL8 ....63 A3
  Burniston YO13 ....75 D7
  Osmotherley DL6 ....45 B3
South End Ave 6 DL8 ....63 A3
South End Cl YO13 ....75 D7
South End La DN14 ....207 B4
South Esp YO1 ....233 B1
South Field La YO26 ....181 B6
South Gate 18 YO62 ....92 F6
South Grange Rd HG4 ....214 B2
South Hawksworth St 2
  LS29 ....218 B4
South House Pavement
  Nature Reserve*
  BD24 ....104 F3
South Ings La YO62 ....70 F3
South Kilvington CE VC Prim
  Sch YO7 ....211 B4
South La
  Bishop Wilton YO42 ....169 F1
  Cawood YO8 ....197 B7
  Thornton Dale YO18 ....96 D6
South Milford Com Prim Sch
  13 LS25 ....195 F2
South Milford Sta
  LS25 ....195 F2

South Moor La
  Garriston DL8 ....61 A7
  Sowerby YO7 ....89 F3
South Otterington CE VC
  Prim Sch DL7 ....64 F2
South Parade
  Hurworth-on-Tees DL2 ....22 C8
  Ilkley LS29 ....218 A4
  Northallerton DL7 ....210 D3
  Norton YO17 ....215 E3
  8 Selby YO8 ....232 C5
South Pk Ave YO24 ....233 A1
South Pk Ave TS6 ....7 F8
South Pk La LS22 ....180 A8
South Pk Rd HG1 ....219 E1
South Ridge LS29 ....194 D1
South Ruddings La
  YO19 ....192 F7
South Side TS15 ....25 C5
South St
  Barmby on the Marsh
  DN14 ....205 A7
  Burton Fleming YO25 ....126 F3
  Scalby YO13 ....75 D5
South Terr YO7 ....211 B2
South Town La TS13 ....10 E8
South Vale DL6 ....210 E2
South View
  Burniston YO13 ....75 D7
  Castleford WF10 ....201 B5
  2 Egglescliffe TS16 ....5 D4
  3 Glusburn BD20 ....173 E1
  Healaugh LS24 ....182 A2
  Hunton DL8 ....61 E7
  Ilkley LS29 ....218 B3
  11 Leyburn DL8 ....60 D5
  Northallerton DL6 ....210 F6
  Ripon HG4 ....214 D2
  2 Rudby TS15 ....25 D5
  6 Whitby YO21 ....208 D5
South View Terr BD20 ....174 B1
South Wood La 11 BD23 ....134 E3
Southdean Dr TS8 ....6 F6
Southdene TS14 ....101 B3
Southend Ave DL3 ....3 C4
Southend Gdns 8 YO21 ....208 D5
Southerscales Nature
  Reserve* LA6 ....104 C7
Southey St 1 BD23 ....217 A3
Southfield YO17 ....122 D3
Southfield Ave HG4 ....214 B2
Southfield Cl
  6 Hurworth-on-Tees DL2 ....3 E1
  Rufforth YO23 ....182 D6
Southfield Cres 2
  YO24 ....230 E8
Southfield La
  28 Addingham LS29 ....174 F4
  Kellington DN14 ....202 E2
Southfield Rd
  28 Addingham LS29 ....174 F4
  Burley in Warfedale
  LS29 ....176 C1
  Littlethorpe HG4 ....214 B2
Southfield Terr
  22 Addingham LS29 ....174 F4
  7 Skipton BD23 ....216 F3
Southfields Rd YO32 ....167 B7
Southgate
  Eastfield YO12 ....99 E6
  Pickering YO18 ....95 F7
  Ripon HG4 ....214 C4
Southgate Ave HG4 ....214 C4
Southgate Cl 7 HG4 ....214 C4
Southlands
  18 Haxby YO32 ....166 E5
  16 Hemsley YO62 ....92 F6
  18 Hemingbrough YO8 ....198 F1
  2 High & Low Bishopside
  HG3 ....137 B4
Southlands Ave 5
  YO21 ....208 C7
Southlands Cl
  Escrick YO19 ....192 B6
  6 South Milford LS25 ....195 F2
Southlands Gr YO12 ....212 B7
Southlands Rd YO23 ....228 B2
Southlea YO17 ....122 D3
Southmoor La WF11 ....202 B1
Southmoor Rd YO19 ....192 F5
Southolme Cl 22 YO51 ....141 B5
Southolme Dr 7 YO30 ....224 F1
Southolme Wlk 25 YO51 ....141 B5
Southville Terr HG1 ....219 B5
Southway
  Harrogate HG2 ....222 C8
  Ilkley LS29 ....218 D3
Southwold Cl 11 YO11 ....100 B7
Southwold Cl 5 YO11 ....100 B7
Southwold Rise 6
  YO11 ....100 B7
Southwood Rd TS16 ....5 D7
Southwood Rd YO11 ....100 B7
Sovereign Gdns 2 WF6 ....200 A1
Sovereign Pk HG1 ....219 B2
Sowarth Field 21 BD24 ....131 D2
Sowerby Cres TS9 ....26 B7
Sowerby Prim Sch
  YO7 ....211 B1
Sowerby Rd Thirsk YO7 ....211 B2
  York YO26 ....227 D4
Sowerby Terr YO7 ....211 B2
Sowerby Way TS16 ....5 D5
Sowgate La WF8 ....201 E8
Spa Complex The*
  ....213 B4
Spa La Harrogate HG2 ....220 C3

Spa La continued
Middleton YO18 ....95 B6
Spa Mews HG2 ....220 D3
Spa Pk Maze* HG4 ...214 B5
Spa Rd Gainford DL2 ......1 C7
Harrogate HG2 ....220 C3
Spa St HG2 ....220 C3
Spa Terr 3 HG2 ....220 C3
Spa The YO11 ....213 A4
Spalding Ave YO30 ...228 B7
Sparrington La YO61 ..144 B5
Sparrow Hall Dr DL1 ...3 E8
Spartal La LS25 ....200 F8
Spaunton Bank YO62 ...70 E5
Spaunton La YO62 .....70 E4
Spawd Bone La WF11 .201 F2
Speculation St YO1 ...228 E4
Speedwell Rd WF10 ..200 C3
Speeton Ave TS5 ....6 F7
Spellow Cres HG5 ....140 E1
Spellow Gr HG5 ......140 E1
Spen Brow LA2 ....128 E6
Spen Comon La LS24 .188 F3
Spen La YO1 ....233 C3
Spencer Ct 4 TS9 ......8 A2
Spenceley Pl DL11 .....2 A2
Spencer Cl 5 BD20 ...287 F8
Spencer St
  22 Glusburn BD20 ...187 E7
  3 York YO23 ....233 B1
Spencer Wlk BD23 ....217 C3
Spencer's Holt HG1 ..219 D7
Spencer's Way YO1 ..219 D7
Speng La YO26 ....182 B4
Spennithorne CE Prim Sch
  DL8 ....60 F4
Spey Bank YO24 .....230 C6
Spiker's Hill La YO13 ..74 F2
Spindle Cl YO24 .....230 C8
Spindle Mill BD23 ...216 F4
Spink La WF8 ....201 B1
Spinksburn La HG3 ..159 F1
Spinner La HG3 ....161 A8
Spinner Ct BD23 .....216 F4
Spinney The
  Darlington DL3 ....3 B4
  Draughton BD23 .....174 B7
  6 Easingwold YO61 .143 C8
  Knaresborough HG5 .221 C6
  1 Scarborough YO12 .212 B3
  Tees-side Airport DL2 ..4 D4
  York YO24 ....230 F7
Spinniker Dr 4 YO21 .208 C5
Spital Bridge YO22 ..208 E5
Spital Field Ct 1 YO17 .215 C4
Spital Rd YO12 ....99 E7
Spital St YO17 ....215 B4
Spital The TS15 ....5 D3
Spitalcroft HG5 ......221 B4
Spitalfields TS15 ......5 D2
Spitfire Cl DL10 ......41 F6
Spitfire Way LS25 ...196 B4
Spitlands La HG5 ....163 B7
Spital Hardwick La
  WF10 ....201 B3
Spittlerush La DN6 ..206 D2
Spofforth Castle*
  HG3 ....179 D6
Spofforth CE Contolled Prim
  Sch HG3 ....179 E5
Spofforth Hill LS22 ..180 B3
Spofforth La
  Follifoot HG3 ....223 F4
  North Deighton LS22 .180 A6
Spofforth Rd HG3 ....223 F4
Spofforth La LS22 ....180 A7
Spout La LA2 ....102 B8
Spreight La Stps YO11 .213 B7
Spring Bank YO12 ...212 E3
Spring Bank Cl HG4 ..214 C7
Spring Bank Mdw
  HG4 ....214 C7
Spring Bank Rd HG4 .214 C7
Spring Cl
  Garforth LS25 ....194 D4
  Middlesbrough TS18 ...6 B8
  12 Sleights YO22 .....32 A6
Spring Ct HG3 ....160 E6
Spring Gdns 10 YO11 .100 B6
Spring Gr
  Harrogate HG1 ......219 C3
  Laneshaw Bridge BB8 .186 B3
Spring Hall Garth
  YO17 ....215 A3
Spring Hill
  Stonegrave YO62 .....93 C1
  Welbury DL6 ....24 B1
  Whitby YO21 ....208 D6
Spring Hill Sch HG4 .113 E4
Spring Hill Terr 10
  YO21 ....208 D6
Spring La Birdforth YO7 .116 F8
  Kirkby Overblow HG3 .179 A2
  Long Marston YO26 ..182 A5
  Pannal HG3 ....222 C3
  Wetherby LS22 ......180 E3
  York YO10 ....229 A1
Spring Mount HG1 ...219 C3
Spring Rise BD23 ....174 B8
Spring St 3 YO61 ....143 C8
Spring Terr DL7 ......210 C4
Spring Vale YO21 ....208 C6
Spring Way TS18 ......5 F8
Spring Wlk YO8 ......232 A1
Springbank
  Marton cum Grafton
  YO51 ....141 E2
  Swillington LS25 ....194 B3

Springbank Ave YO19 .184 E7
Springfield
  Bentham LA2 ....129 B8
  Clifford LS23 ....188 E7
  4 Scarborough YO11 .213 B6
  Skeeby DL10 ....21 A1
  Stokesley TS9 ....26 C7
Springfield Ave
  4 Earby BB18 ....172 B1
  Harrogate HG1 ......219 C3
  Ilkley LS29 ....218 C4
  11 Pontefract WF8 ..201 C1
Springfield Ct
  Barlby with Osgodby
  YO8 ....198 B5
  20 Boroughbridge YO51 .141 B5
  Heworth YO31 ....229 C7
  1 Leyburn DL8 ....60 D5
  5 Pateley Bridge HG3 .137 C4
  Ripon HG4 ....214 B7
  Thirsk YO7 ....211 B4
Springfield Cres
  Bentham LA2 ....129 B8
  3 Kirk Smeaton WF8 .206 C3
Springfield Dr
  9 Barlby YO8 ....198 B5
  19 Boroughbridge YO51 .141 B5
Springfield Garth
  YO17 ....215 D3
Springfield Gdns 1 TS9 .26 C7
Springfield Gr
  21 Boroughbridge YO51 .141 B5
  Kirklevington TS15 .....5 F1
Springfield La
  4 Kirkbymoorside YO62 ..70 C1
  Tockwith YO26 ......181 C7
Springfield Mews
  HG1 ....219 C3
Springfield Mount
  LS29 ....174 F5
Springfield Pl LS25 ..194 B3
Springfield Prim Sch
  DL1 ....3 E7
Springfield Rd
  18 Boroughbridge YO51 .141 B5
  Darlington DL1 ....3 C4
  12 Gerassington BD23 ..134 E2
  8 Poppleton YO26 ....165 F1
  Sherburn in Elmet LS25 .195 F5
Springfield Rise 1
  YO26 ....164 A8
Springfield Terr YO17 .124 D7
Springfield Way
  7 Pateley Bridge HG3 .137 C4
  York YO31 ....229 B7
Springfields
  18 Knottingley WF11 .202 A2
  5 Skipton BD23 .....217 B4
Springfields Ave 17
  WF11 ....202 A2
Springhead Specl Sch
  YO12 ....212 E2
Springhill Cl YO12 ...212 E4
Springhill Ct 7 LS24 .189 E6
Springhill La YO12 ...212 D3
Springhill Rd YO12 ..212 E4
Springmead Dr LS25 .194 C3
Springmount 3 BB18 .172 B1
Springs La
  Ellerton-on-Swale DL10 ..41 F4
  Ilkley LS29 ....218 C4
  Walton LS23 ....180 F3
  Whashton DL11 ....20 B4
Springs Leisure Ctr TS9 .26 C7
Springs Terr LS29 ...218 B4
Springs The 4 DL8 ...60 E2
Springwater Sch HG2 .220 D4
Springwell Ave 11 LS26 .194 A1
Springwell Cl BD20 ..187 B6
Springwell Gdns 3
  DL7 ....210 D4
Springwell La 7 DL7 .210 B4
Springwell Rd 10 LS26 .194 A1
Springwell Terr E 1
  DL7 ....210 D4
Springwell Terr W 2
  DL7 ....210 D4
Springwood YO22 ....225 D2
Spruce Cl YO12 ......225 D2
Spruce Gill Ave 4 DL8 .63 B3
Spruce Gill Dr 5 DL8 ..63 B3
Spruisty Rd HG1 .....219 C4
Spurr Ct YO24 ....230 C8
Spurriergate YO1 ....233 B2
Square The
  Boston Spa LS23 ....188 F8
  Castleford WF10 ....201 B4
  Ingleton LA6 ....103 D4
  Kippax LS25 ....194 D1
  Knottingley WF11 ...200 E1
  Leeming DL7 ....63 F3
  1 Tadcaster LS24 ...189 F6
Stable Rd YO8 ......204 D7
Stabler Cl 15 YO32 .166 D5
Stablers Wlk
  Earswick YO32 ......225 F7
  18 Pontefract WF6 ..200 A2
Stables La LS23 .....188 F8
Stackhouse La
  Giggleswick BD24 ..131 D4
  Lawkland BD24 .....130 F2
Stags Way YO10 ......41 F7
Stainburn Ave WF10 ..201 A3
Stainburn La LS21 ...177 E2
Staindale TS14 ....8 D6

Staindale Cl YO30 ....224 E2
Staindrop Dr TS5 ......6 F7
Staindrop Rd DL3 ......3 A6
Stained Glass Ctr*
  YO11 ....100 C5
Stainforth Gdns YO12 ..6 B5
Stainforth La BD24 ...131 D5
Stainforth Rd BD24 ..131 E4
Stainsacre La
  Hawsker-cum-Stainsacre
  YO22 ....32 F6
  Whitby YO22 ....208 F3
Stainsby Rd TS5 ....6 D8
Stainton Rd TS9 ....6 F1
Stainton Way
  Coulby Newham TS8 ...7 A5
  Stainton & Thornton TS8 ..6 E5
Staintondale Shire Horse
  Farm* YO13 ....54 C5
Staithe St 3 YO8 ....199 D7
Staithes Cl 2 YO26 ..227 B4
Staithes La TS13 ......13 K2
Stake Rd DL8 ....57 C1
Stakesby Com Prim Sch
  YO21 ....208 B6
Stakesby Rd YO21 ...208 B6
Stakesby Vale YO21 .208 C6
Stakesby Vale Ct
  YO21 ....208 B5
Stamford Bridge Inf Sch
  YO41 ....168 D2
Stamford Bridge Rd
  YO19 ....184 E7
Stamford Bridge W
  YO41 ....168 C2
Stamford St E 10 YO26 .227 F5
Stamford St W YO26 .227 F5
Stammergate YO7 ...211 C3
Stammergate La LS22 .180 A1
Stamp Hill Cl 7 LS29 .174 E4
Stan Valley 2 WF8 ..206 C3
Standard Ct DL7 .....210 B6
Standard Way DL6 ...210 B6
Standard Way Ind Est
  DL6 ....210 C6
Standridge Clough La
  BB18 ....172 B1
Standroyd Dr BB8 ...186 A3
Standroyd Rd BB8 ...186 A3
Stang La
  Arkengarthdale DL11 ..17 E3
  Farnham HG5 ....162 C7
  Hope DL11 ....18 A8
Stang Top
  Arkengarthdale DL11 ..17 F5
  Hope DL11 ....18 A6
Stanghow Rd TS12 ....9 F8
Stangs La BD23 .....157 D6
Stanhope Dr HG2 ...220 B2
Stanhope Gr TS5 ......6 E8
Stanhope Rd N DL3 ...3 C5
Staniland Dr YO8 ...232 A5
Stanley Ave YO32 ...225 D7
Stanley Cl
  4 Catterick Garrison DL9 .40 E3
  22 Eastfield YO11 ...100 B6
  Great Ayton TS9 ......7 F1
  Richmond DL10 ....209 D8
Stanley St
  Castleford WF10 ....200 F4
  4 Scarborough YO12 .213 A7
  York YO31 ....233 C4
Stansfield Brow BD20 .187 A8
Stansfield Dr WF10 ..201 B4
Stansfield Rd WF10 ..201 A4
Stanstead Way TS17 ...6 C7
Stansted Gr DL2 ....4 D4
Stanyforth Cres YO26 .164 C2
Stape Rd YO18 ....71 F7
Stapleton Bank DL2 ...3 A2
Stapleton Cl
  3 Bedale DL8 ....63 B2
  18 Seamer YO12 ......99 D6
Stapley La DL8 ....87 F4
Star Carr La YO12 .....99 E4
Starbeck Cl YO21 ...208 B5
Starbeck Com Prim Sch
  HG2 ....220 D4
Starbeck Sta YO12 ..220 C4
Starbeck Swimming Baths
  HG2 ....220 D3
Starfits La
  Fadmoor YO62 ....69 F3
  Welburn YO62 ....94 A8
Starkey Cres YO31 ..229 A5
Starkey La BD20 .....173 F1
Starmire BD22 ....187 A6
Starra Field La YO26 .163 F5
Station Ave
  20 Filey YO14 ....101 B3
  2 Haxby YO32 ......166 E5
  Harrogate HG2 ......219 E2
  New Earswick YO32 .225 D3
  Whitby YO22 ....208 B7
  York YO1 ....233 A2
Station Bridge HG1 ..219 D2
Station Cl Dacre HG3 .159 F8
  6 East Ayton/West Ayton
  YO13 ....99 A7
  Hambleton YO8 .....196 F2
  Sharow HG4 ....214 D7
Station Dr HG4 ......214 D7
Station Fields LS25 ..194 C4
Station Gr 19 BD20 ..187 F8
Station La
  Barmby on the Marsh
  DN14 ....205 B7

Station La continued
  Burton Leonard HG3 ..139 F3
Cliffe YO8 ....198 E3
Cloughton YO13 ......54 D1
Gristhorpe YO14 ....100 E4
Morton-on-Swale DL7 ..64 A7
Shipton YO30 ....165 E5
Station Par HG1 .....219 D2
Station Plaza* LS29 ..218 B3
Station Rd
  Ampleforth YO62 .....92 C1
  Beadlam YO62 ....93 D7
  Brompton DL6 ....43 F4
  Brompton-on-Swale DL10 ..41 B6
  Burley in Wharfedale
  LS29 ....176 C1
  Carlton DN14 ....204 C3
  Castleford WF10 ....200 E4
  Cayton YO11 ....100 B5
  Church Fenton LS24 .196 B7
  Clapham LA2 ....130 C7
  Copmanthorpe YO23 .230 B2
  Danby YO21 ....29 A7
  Fylingdales YO22 ....33 C8
  Gainford DL2 ....1 C8
  Gilling East YO62 ...118 F8
  Glusburn BD20 .....187 E8
  Goldsborough HG5 ..163 A3
  Great Ayton TS9 ......8 A1
  Great Preston WF10 .200 D8
  Hambleton YO8 .....196 F1
  Haxby YO32 ....166 F5
  Hellifield BD23 .....154 B4
  Helmsley YO62 ....92 F6
  Hensall DN14 ....203 C1
  Heslerton YO17 ......97 D1
  High Bentham LA2 ..129 A8
  Hinderwell TS13 .....11 F7
  Horton in Ribblesdale
  BD24 ....105 C3
  Ilkley LS29 ....218 B4
  Kildale YO21 ....27 E8
  Kippax LS25 ....200 C8
  Kirk Hammerton YO26 ..164 C2
  9 Knaresborough HG5 .221 A6
  Long Preston BD23 .153 F4
  Menwith with Darley
  HG3 ....160 A6
  Mickletown LS26 ....200 B6
  Middleton St George DL2 ..4 C5
  Normanton WF6 ....200 A2
  Norton DN6 ....206 F2
  Nunnington YO62 .....93 E2
  Pannal HG3 ....222 E2
  24 Poppleton YO26 .165 A1
  Rawcliffe DN14 .....205 A1
  Riccall YO19 ....198 A8
  Richmond DL10 ....209 C7
  Scalby YO13 ....75 D5
  Scruton DL7 ....63 E6
  Selby YO8 ....232 D5
  Settle BD24 ....131 D3
  Sleights YO22 ....32 A6
  Snainton YO13 ....97 F4
  South Otterington DL7 ..64 F2
  Sowerby YO7 ....211 A2
  Stainton Dale YO13 ..54 A8
  Stokesley TS9 ....26 C7
  Thirsk YO7 ....89 D4
  Threshfield BD23 ...134 D2
  Tollerton YO61 .....143 B3
  Wharram YO17 ......148 F4
  Whixley YO26 ....164 A3
  Wistow YO8 ....197 C6
  Womersley DN6 ....206 F6
  York YO1 ....233 A2
Station Rise YO1 ....233 A2
Station Sq
  4 Strensall YO32 ...167 B7
  4 Whitby YO21 .....208 D6
Station Terr
  Ampleforth YO51 ...141 B6
  Great Preston WF10 .200 E6
Station View
  Cliffe YO8 ....198 D3
  2 Harrogate HG1 ...220 C3
  Seamer YO12 ....99 E7
  8 Skipton BD23 ....216 D3
Station Way YO17 ...215 C3
Staupes Rd HG3 .....159 B3
Staveley Com Prim Sch
  HG5 ....140 E1
Staveley Nature Reserve*
  HG5 ....140 E2
Staxton Carr La YO12 ..99 D3
Staxton Hill YO12 ...125 C8
Staynor Ave YO8 ....232 E3
Stead La LS14 ....188 A3
Stean La HG3 ....110 A4
Steelmoor La YO60 .146 C2
Steeple Cl 4 YO32 ..166 D5
Steeton La YO26 ....182 A8
Steeton Way LS25 ..195 E2
Steincroft Rd 7 LS25 .195 F2
Stella Gdns 10 WF8 .201 C1
Stelling Rd DL8 ......38 E7
Stephen Bank DL11 ..18 H8
Stephen Joseph Theatre*
  YO11 ....212 F5
Stephen's Wlk YO8 ..232 B1
Stephenson Cl
  Knaresborough HG5 .221 B4
  York YO31 ....225 E1
Stephenson Way 2
  DL10 ....41 C7
Stephenson Way
  YO26 ....227 F5
Stephenson's La YO26 .164 A2

Stephensons Way
  LS29 ....218 C4
Stephenwath La YO41 .169 C5
Stepin Turn YO62 .....49 B1
Stepney Dr YO12 ....212 D4
Stepney Gr YO12 ....212 C5
Stepney Hill YO12 ...212 B3
Stepney Rd YO12 ....212 D4
Stepney Rise YO12 ..212 D5
Sterling Pk YO23 ....225 A3
Sterne Ave YO31 ....229 A5
Sterne Way YO61 ...144 C3
Sterne Way HG4 ....214 B6
Stevenson Pl HG5 ...220 F5
Steward Cl YO8 .....197 D1
Stewart La YO19 ....191 C4
Stillington Prim Sch
  YO61 ....144 C7
Stillington Rd
  Easingwold HG4 ...143 D8
  Huby YO61 ....144 A4
Stinton La
  Boroughbridge YO51 .141 C4
  Helperby YO61 .....142 A8
Stirling Gr YO10 ....231 F8
Stirling Rd
  Burley in Wharfedale
  LS29 ....176 B1
  York YO30 ....224 F3
Stirling Way TS17 .....6 B6
Stirrup Cl 7 Norton YO17 .215 E2
  York YO24 ....230 B8
Stirton La BD23 .....216 C5
Stirtonber BD23 .....216 E5
Stittenham Hill YO60 .146 A6
Stobarts La TS15 ......5 B1
Stock Stile La HG3 ..160 D5
Stockdale Cl 8 HG5 .221 B5
Stockdale Ct DL6 ...210 F3
Stockdale La LS24 ..131 F2
Stockdale Wlk HG5 .221 B5
Stockeld La LS22 ...179 E3
Stockeld Pk YO13* ..179 E3
Stockeld Rd LS29 ...218 A4
Stockfield La HG5 ..141 D2
Stockfield Pk House*
  LS22 ....179 F4
Stockholm Cl 1 YO19 .184 E7
Stocking Hill TS9 .....25 E1
Stocking La
  Hambleton YO8 .....196 E1
  Hillam LS25 ....202 B2
  Knottingley WF11 ..202 B2
  Lotherton cum Aberford
  LS25 ....195 A7
Stockinger La LS29 .174 F4
Stocks La 1 HG3 ....160 A6
Stockshill 7 YO8 ......99 D6
Stockshott La BD20 .173 C2
Stockton Hall YO32 .167 D3
Stockton La
  Heworth YO32 ......226 D1
  York YO31 ....229 A7
Stockton on the Forest Prim
  Sch YO32 ....167 D3
Stockton Rd
  Darlington DL1 ....3 F7
  Sadberge DL2 ....4 C7
  South Kilvington YO7 .211 B6
Stockwell Ave
  Ingleby TS17 ....6 B5
  Knaresborough HG5 .221 B6
Stockwell Cres 6 HG5 .221 B5
Stockwell Ct 9 HG5 .221 B5
Stockwell Dr HG5 ...221 B7
Stockwell Gr HG5 ...221 B7
Stockwell La HG5 ...221 B6
Stockwell Pl HG5 ...221 B6
Stockwell View HG5 .221 B7
Stockwith La YO8 ..204 A4
Stokelake Rd 5 HG1 .219 E3
Stokesley Com Prim Sch
  TS9 ....26 C7
Stokesley Ind Pk TS9 ..26 C6
Stokesley Leisure Ctr
  TS9 ....26 D7
Stokesley Rd
  Brompton DL6 ....44 A3
  Coulby Newham TS7 ...7 B7
  Guisborough TS14 .....8 C6
  Middlesbrough TS7 ....7 B6
  Northallerton DL6 ..210 C4
Stokesley Sch TS9 ...26 C7
Stone Bramble 22 HG3 .161 B3
Stone Bridge Dr YO41 .185 F5
Stone Ct 8 YO13 ......75 D5
Stone Dale YO42 ...193 D3
Stone Garth 3 YO62 ..92 F6
Stone Gate YO26 ...164 A4
Stone Head La BD22 .186 E6
Stone Man La DL11 ...19 C5
Stone Riggs YO23 ...167 D2
Stone Rings Cl HG2 .222 E6
Stone Rings Grange
  HG2 ....222 E5
Stone Rings La HG2 .222 E5
Stone Stoup Hill TS9 ..27 C5
Stonebeck Ave HG1 .219 B4

Stonebeck Gate La
YO21 .... 29 D4
Stonebow The
Thornton-le-Beans DL6 ... 65 B5
York YO1 .... 233 C2
Stonebridge Cres 2 TS17 .. 6 D6
Stonebridgegate HG4 ... 214 D5
Stonecrop Ave 5 HG3 ... 161 B3
Stonecrop Dr 1 HG3 ... 161 B3
Stonecross Rd YO21 ... 208 A6
Stoned Horse La
YO26 .... 164 C4
Stonefall Ave HG2 ... 220 C3
Stonefall Dr HG2 ... 220 B2
Stonefall Mews HG2 ... 220 C3
Stonefall Pl 2 HG2 ... 220 C3
Stonefield Ave YO61 ... 143 C8
Stonefield Garth 5
YO61 .... 143 C8
Stonefield La 4 YO61 ... 143 C8
Stonegate
Hunmanby YO14 ... 126 F8
York YO1 .... 233 B3
Stonehaven Way DL1 ... 3 F8
Stonelands Ct 2 YO30 ... 225 A1
Stoneleigh Gate YO26 ... 164 B3
Stonepit Balk YO17 ... 149 C5
Stonepit Hill YO17 ... 149 C6
Stonepit La
Birdsall YO17 ... 148 D6
Gristhorpe YO14 ... 100 E5
Stonesdale La 3 HG5 ... 221 D5
Stonesdale La DL11 ... 35 E8
Stonethwaite 5 YO24 ... 230 C7
Stoney Bank Rd BB18 ... 172 B1
Stoney Haggs Rd YO12 ... 99 E7
Stoneyborough Cl
YO7 .... 211 C4
Stoneyborough La YO7 ... 211 C4
Stony Cross YO62 ... 93 E7
Stony Ct 5 YO11 ... 213 C1
Stony La
East Scalby DL6 ... 44 F5
2 Scalby YO13 ... 75 D5
Storgsgate Bank DL11 ... 20 A5
Stoop Cl YO32 ... 225 C8
Stooperdale Ave DL3 ... 3 B7
Stoopes Hill 3 BB18 ... 172 B1
Storey Cl 3 YO62 ... 92 F6
Storiths La BD23 ... 175 A8
Storking La YO61 ... 185 F6
Stor La YO13 ... 74 E5
Storth Gill La BD24 ... 131 A1
Stourton Rd LS29 ... 175 C3
Stow Ct YO32 ... 225 E3
Stps The LS22 ... 180 C2
Strafford Rd 4 DL10 ... 41 E4
Straight La
Addingham LS29 ... 174 E3
Aldwark YO61 ... 142 C3
Burton Leonard HG3 ... 140 A3
Holtby YO19 ... 184 F8
Middleham DL8 ... 60 F2
Straights The DL8 ... 58 C4
Strait La
Copt Hewick HG4 ... 114 B2
Danby YO21 ... 29 C6
Hurworth DL2 ... 3 F1
Stainton & Thornton TS8 ... 6 D5
Weeton LS17 ... 178 B2
Well DL8 ... 87 A3
Straits La YO13 ... 99 A3
Stranglands La WF11 ... 201 C3
Stratford Way YO32 ... 225 E3
Strathmore Dr 9 TS15 ... 24 E8
Strathmore Rd LS29 ... 218 C5
Straw Gate DL2 ... 3 A2
Strawberry Fileds Prim Sch
LS25 .... 194 C3
Strawberry Ct YO12 ... 212 D4
Strawberry Dale HG1 ... 219 D3
Strawberry Dale Ave 3
HG1 .... 219 D3
Strawberry Dale Sq 1
HG1 .... 219 D3
Strawberry Dale Terr 2
HG1 .... 219 D3
Strawgate Gr DL2 ... 3 A3
Stray Garth YO31 ... 228 F7
Stray Rd
Harrogate HG2 ... 222 D8
York YO31 ... 229 B6
Stray Rein HG2 ... 219 E1
Stray The Darlington DL1 ... 3 E5
Henderskelfe YO60 ... 146 D8
Longnewton TS21 ... 5 A7
Stray Wlk HG2 ... 222 E8
Straylands Gr YO31 ... 228 F8
Street 1 LS23 ... 189 A8
Street 2
Thorp Arch LS23 ... 181 A3
Walton LS23 ... 189 A8
Street 3 LS23 ... 181 A1
Street 4 LS23 ... 181 A1
Street 5 LS23 ... 181 A2
Street 6 LS23 ... 181 A1
Street 7 LS23 ... 181 B1
Street 8 LS23 ... 181 B1
Street Head La BD22 ... 187 F1
Street The Bewerley HG3 ... 137 B4
Bubwith YO8 ... 199 F5
Colton LS24 ... 190 D7
Glaisdale YO21 ... 29 E3
Middleton YO18 ... 95 E7
Pickhill with Roxby YO7 ... 88 B6

Street The 8 LS29 ... 174 E4
Strensall Comm Nature
Reserve* YO60 ... 167 D8
Strensall Dr 1 YO12 ... 75 F5
Strensall Pk YO32 ... 167 A5
Strensall Rd
Earswick YO32 ... 226 A7
York YO32 ... 225 F6
Stretton Cl WF7 ... 200 D1
Strickland Rd 12 YO14 ... 127 A8
Strikes La BD20 ... 187 F6
Stripe La
Hartwith cum Winsley
HG3 .... 140 B8
Skelton YO30 ... 224 B5
Stripe The 11 TS9 ... 26 C7
Stuart Ave DL10 ... 209 C8
Stuart Cl
4 Scarborough YO11 ... 100 B7
2 Strensall YO32 ... 167 B7
Stuart Gr
Eggborough DN14 ... 203 A2
1 Pontefract WF6 ... 200 A2
8 Thorpe Willoughby YO8 ... 197 B1
Stuart Rd YO24 ... 227 D1
Stuart St
10 Barnoldswick BB18 ... 171 E1
Pontefract WF8 ... 201 B1
Stubbing La BD23 ... 81 B1
Stubbing Nook La DL8 ... 62 B2
Stubbs La
Cridling Stubbs WF11 ... 206 A8
Norton DN6 ... 206 E2
Stainton Dale YO13 ... 53 F5
Stubbs Rd DN6 ... 206 D3
Stubden Gr YO30 ... 224 F2
Stubham Rise LS29 ... 218 A5
Stud Fold Bank HG3 ... 110 B3
Studford Ring* YO62 ... 92 C2
Studley Cl DL7 ... 210 B2
Studley La HG4 ... 113 C1
Studley Rd
Harrogate HG1 ... 219 D3
Ripon HG4 ... 214 A4
Studley Roger HG4 ... 113 D3
Studley Terr 15 YO22 ... 208 E6
Stump Cross Caverns*
HG3 .... 136 A2
Stumpcross Cl 14 WF8 ... 201 C2
Stumpcross La WF8 ... 201 C2
Stumpcross Mdws
WF8 .... 201 D1
Stumpcross Way 15
WF8 .... 201 C2
Stumps La HG3 ... 160 A5
Stunstead Rd BB8 ... 186 B2
Sturdee Gr YO31 ... 228 D7
Sturdy House La
Marske DL11 ... 19 E2
Whashton DL11 ... 20 A4
Sturton Grange La
LS25 .... 194 D4
Sturton La LS25 ... 194 D4
Stuteville Cl 4 YO62 ... 70 C1
Stutton Rd LS24 ... 189 D4
Stygate La DN6 ... 206 E1
Sudforth La DN14 ... 202 C3
Suffield Hill YO13 ... 75 A5
Sugar Hill 4 LS29 ... 174 F4
Sugar Loaf Ct 16 TS17 ... 5 F4
Summer Hill Rd LS26 ... 200 B6
Summerbridge Com Prim
Sch HG3 ... 138 A1
Summerfield BD23 ... 172 A3
Summerfield Cl 1
WF11 .... 201 F4
Summerfield Dr WF11 ... 201 F4
Summerfield La YO22 ... 33 A7
Summerfield Rd YO24 ... 230 C7
Summerscales St 2
YO26 .... 227 B2
Sun Ct 2 YO26 ... 227 B2
Sun La LS29 ... 176 C1
Sun Lounge Theatre
YO14 .... 101 B3
Sun St Cononley BD20 ... 173 C1
6 Cowling BD22 ... 187 B6
Thornaby TS17 ... 6 A8
Sunderland Rd BD20 ... 173 E3
Sundew Heath 24 HG3 ... 161 B3
Sundial Ct BD23 ... 217 A4
Sunningdale LS25 ... 194 F4
Sunningdale Cl 1 YO26 ... 227 B5
Sunningdale Dr TS16 ... 5 E5
Sunningdale Gr 1
YO21 .... 208 B5
Sunningdales 27 WF6 ... 200 B1
Sunny Bank 8 WF11 ... 202 A2
Sunny Bank Rd 6 BD20 ... 187 E7
Sunnybank Rd LS25 ... 195 A3
Sunnycrest Ave DL10 ... 209 D8
Sunnydale 3 YO32 ... 225 D7
Sunnyfield TS9 ... 7 F1
Sunnyside Prim Sch TS8 ... 7 A6
Sunset Dr LS29 ... 218 D5
Sunset Terr LS29 ... 218 E5
Sunstar Gr TS7 ... 7 B6
Sur Gate
Harwood Dale YO13 ... 53 F1
Suffield-cum-Everley
YO13 .... 74 F8
Surrey Way YO30 ... 227 F8
Surtees St 3 Darlington DL3 ... 3 C6
York YO30 ... 228 B7
Sussex Cl Bedale DL8 ... 63 A2
York YO10 ... 229 C2
Sussex Rd YO10 ... 229 C2
Sussex St 4 Bedale DL8 ... 63 A2
14 Scarborough YO11 ... 213 A4

Sussex Way 14 YO32 ... 167 A7
Sutcliffe Cl 6 YO21 ... 208 B6
Sutcliffe Gall* YO21 ... 208 D7
Sutherland Rd YO18 ... 71 C6
Sutherland St YO23 ... 228 B1
Sutor Cl YO23 ... 230 B3
Sutton Ave 7 DL9 ... 41 A5
Sutton Bank YO7 ... 91 A5
Sutton Bank Visitor Ctr*
YO7 .... 91 B6
Sutton Bridge* YO41 ... 185 C2
Sutton Cl 5 YO7 ... 211 C3
Sutton Dr DL7 ... 210 C2
Sutton Grange Cl YO7 ... 211 C3
Sutton in Craven CE VC Prim
Sch 5 BD20 ... 187 E7
Sutton in Craven Com Prim
Sch BD20 ... 187 E7
Sutton La Byram WF11 ... 201 E4
Byram cum Sutton
WF11 .... 202 A4
Ellington High & Low HG4 ... 86 A5
Fearby HG4 ... 85 F4
Steeton with Eastburn
BD20 .... 187 F7
Sutton Pk* YO7 ... 114 C3
Sutton St YO7 ... 211 E3
Sutton St YO7 ... 215 D3
Sutton upon Derwent CE VC
Prim Sch YO41 ... 185 C2
Sutton Way
Middlesbrough TS4 ... 6 F8
York YO30 ... 228 B8
Sutton-on-the-Forest CE
Prim Sch YO61 ... 144 C3
Sutton-under-Whitestonecliffe
CE VC Prim Sch YO7 ... 90 E5
Swadford St BD23 ... 216 F4
Swain Ct DL6 ... 210 D5
Swainby Abbey* DL8 ... 88 B8
Swainby Ellers DL6 ... 25 D1
Swainby La DL8 ... 87 F7
Swainsea Dr 3 YO18 ... 95 F7
Swainsea La YO18 ... 95 F8
Swainstead Raike
BD24 .... 153 B8
Swainston Cl TS5 ... 6 E7
Swale App 22 WF6 ... 200 B1
Swale Ave YO26 ... 230 E8
Swale Hall La DL11 ... 38 B5
Swale La Catterick DL10 ... 41 E5
Pickhill with Roxby YO7 ... 88 C7
Swale Pasture La DL10 ... 41 E5
Swale View YO7 ... 115 B6
Swaledale Ave DL8 ... 3 B6
Swaledale Folk Mus*
DL11 .... 38 C6
Swaledale Rd 22 DL9 ... 40 E4
Swaledale Sch DL8 ... 63 A3
Swallow Cl TS14 ... 8 D6
Swallows The 3 YO32 ... 167 B8
Swan Cl YO19 ... 192 A7
Swan Farm Ct YO19 ... 192 A7
Swan Hill Rd YO11 ... 213 A6
Swan La YO7 ... 65 F2
Swan Rd HG1 ... 219 C2
Swan St BD23 ... 173 B4
Swan Syke Dr 8 DN6 ... 206 F2
Swang Rd YO13 ... 75 A6
Swanhills La YO13 ... 98 F3
Swanland Rd YO62 ... 92 F7
Swann St YO23 ... 233 A1
Swarcliffe Rd HG1 ... 220 B4
Swartha La BD20 ... 174 D2
Swarthlands La YO13 ... 75 D7
Sweeming La LS25 ... 196 C5
Sweet Bits La HG5 ... 221 C8
Sweet Briar HG3 ... 161 B3
Sweetbecks Cl 12 YO11 ... 100 A6
Swillington La LS26 ... 194 A2
Swillington Prim Sch
LS26 .... 194 A1
Swinburn Ct 12 HG4 ... 86 C3
Swinburn Rd 11 HG4 ... 86 C3
Swinburne Cl HG1 ... 219 E7
Swinburne Rd TS16 ... 5 E6
Swincliffe La HG3 ... 160 D5
Swindale La TS12 ... 9 F5
Swindon La YO13 ... 178 E4
Swinegate YO1 ... 233 B2
Swinegate St E YO1 ... 233 B3
Swineherd La YO62 ... 70 F1
Swinneybeck Bank
HG4 .... 85 E5
Swinsty Ct YO30 ... 224 F1
Swinton Ct HG2 ... 222 B8
Swinton La YO17 ... 121 B3
Swinton Rd HG4 ... 86 C3
Swinton Terr HG4 ... 86 C3
Swire Way DL10 ... 209 D7
Swires La BD20 ... 173 C3
Swordfish Way LS25 ... 196 B4
Sycamore Ave
4 Catton YO7 ... 89 A1
Filey YO14 ... 101 A4
Kippax LS25 ... 194 C1
Knottingley WF11 ... 201 E1
Malton YO17 ... 215 D5
Richmond DL10 ... 209 C8
York YO32 ... 225 D4
Sycamore Cl continued

Selby YO8 ... 232 A4
Skelton YO30 ... 224 C5
Slingsby YO62 ... 120 B5
Spennithorne DL8 ... 60 F4
Sycamore Ct
2 Catterick DL10 ... 41 D5
Hellifield BD23 ... 154 B3
2 Pontefract WF8 ... 201 C1
Sycamore Dr
11 Addingham LS29 ... 175 A4
8 Bedale DL8 ... 63 A2
Harrogate HG2 ... 220 C3
Norton-le-Clay YO7 ... 115 B1
Sycamore Gr
Sherburn YO17 ... 124 E7
Steeton with Eastburn
BD20 .... 187 F7
Sycamore La DL7 ... 63 D4
Sycamore Pl
New Earswick YO32 ... 225 D4
York YO30 ... 233 A3
Sycamore Rd
Barlby with Osgodby
HG4 .... 198 B5
Ripon HG4 ... 214 B2
Sycamore Terr YO30 ... 233 A3
Sycamore View 17 YO26 ... 165 F1
Sycamore Way 18 BB18 ... 171 D1
Sydall's Way 1 DL10 ... 41 E4
Sydney Ave DL6 ... 210 E4
Sydney St 8 YO7 ... 212 F7
Sykehead La YO62 ... 93 D6
Sykes Barrel 3 BD24 ... 131 D3
Sykes Cl HG1 ... 219 C5
Sykes La YO61 ... 143 B3

T

Tabard Hamlet 5 DN14 ... 202 F2
Tabard Rd 6 DN14 ... 202 F2
Tabards The 7 DN14 ... 202 F2
Tadcaster C Com Prim Sch 8
LS24 .... 189 F6
Tadcaster Gram Sch
LS24 .... 189 B5
Tadcaster Leisure Ctr
LS24 .... 189 E6
Tadcaster Rd YO24 ... 227 F1
Tadcaster Rd Dringhouses
YO23 .... 230 E5
Tadcaster Sports & Leisure
Ctr LS24 ... 189 E6
Talbenny Gr 32 TS17 ... 5 F4
Talbot Ct YO22 ... 208 E5
Talbot St YO26 ... 200 A1
Talisman Cl 17 TS16 ... 5 D5
Tally Hill YO61 ... 144 A4
Talybont Dr 19 TS17 ... 5 F4
Tameside TS9 ... 26 C8
Tamworth Rd 8 YO30 ... 224 F1
Tanfield Dr 6 LS29 ... 176 C1
Tanfield La HG4 ... 114 A8
Tang Hall La YO31 ... 229 A5
Tang Hall Prim Sch
YO31 .... 228 F5
Tang Rd HG3 ... 160 D4
Tanner La YO7 ... 233 A2
Tanner's Moat YO1 ... 233 A2
Tannery Ct 10 HG5 ... 221 B5
Tannery La DL7 ... 210 D5
Tanpit La
Easingwold YO61 ... 143 C8
Walden Stubbs DN6 ... 206 E3
Tanshelf Sta WF8 ... 201 A1
Tansy Cl 1 HG3 ... 161 B3
Tansy Rd 3 HG3 ... 161 B3
Tanton Rd TS9 ... 7 B1
Tarbard Ave 14 HG4 ... 113 D2
Tarbert Cres 2 YO24 ... 230 B7
Tarn Ct YO24 ... 218 C3
Tarn Moor Cres BD23 ... 216 E6
Tarr Stps TS17 ... 6 A3
Tasmania Sq TS7 ... 7 C6
Tate Cl YO8 ... 197 D6
Tate Hill YO22 ... 208 D7
Tate Rd DL10 ... 209 C8
Tatefield Pl 1 LS25 ... 194 D1
Tatham Fells Sch LA2 ... 128 F3
Tatton Cl YO30 ... 224 E1
Taurus Ct YO23 ... 233 A1
Taylor Gr 12 LS26 ... 200 C6
Taylor Hill YO18 ... 71 F7
Taylor St 8 BB18 ... 171 D1
Taylorsons Terr 2
YO22 .... 208 E7
Teal Cl Castleford WF10 ... 200 E3
2 Filey YO14 ... 101 A3
Teal Dr YO24 ... 230 C8
Teal La 6 YO18 ... 95 F7
Teal Rd DL1 ... 3 F5
Teapottery The* DL8 ... 60 E5
Teasel Gr 51 HG3 ... 161 B3
Tebay Cl 7 YO7 ... 211 B1
Tedder Ave TS17 ... 6 B6
Tedder Prim Sch TS17 ... 6 C6
Tedder Rd YO24 ... 230 E8
Tedworth Cl TS14 ... 8 F5
Tees Bank Ave TS18 ... 5 E8
Tees Cottage Pumping Sta &
Mus* DL2 ... 2 B5
Tees Grange Ave DL3 ... 3 A5
Tees View Gainford DL2 ... 1 D7
Hurworth-on-Tees DL2 ... 22 C8
Teesdale Ave DL3 ... 3 A4
Teesdale Rd DL9 ... 40 E4

Teesgate TS17 ... 6 C8
Teeside Tertiary Coll
TS4 .... 7 B8
Teeside High Sch TS16 ... 5 E5
Teeside Ind Est TS17 ... 6 C2
Teeswater Dr 12 DL3 ... 3 A7
Teesway DL2 ... 4 A1
Telford Cl WF10 ... 200 F3
Telford Terr 1 YO24 ... 228 B2
Templar Cl DN14 ... 202 F1
Templar Gdns LS22 ... 180 C4
Templar Way YO8 ... 232 C2
Temple Ave YO10 ... 229 B4
Temple Bank DL8 ... 59 A3
Temple Cl DL10 ... 209 B6
Temple Garth YO23 ... 230 C1
Temple La
Burton cum Walden DL8 ... 82 D3
Copmanthorpe YO23 ... 230 C1
Temple Manor* YO8 ... 203 D4
Temple Rd YO23 ... 230 F4
Temple Sq DL10 ... 209 B6
Temple St WF10 ... 200 F4
Templeforest Half Acres Jun &
Inf Sch WF10 ... 200 F3
Templemead YO31 ... 228 E8
Tems Side 3 BD24 ... 131 D2
Tems St 2 BD24 ... 131 D2
Ten Thorn La YO26 ... 227 A4
Tennant St YO8 ... 232 B6
Tennent Rd YO24 ... 227 B2
Tennis Ct La YO11 ... 143 A3
Tennyson Ave
1 Campsall DN6 ... 206 E1
Harrogate HG1 ... 219 E7
Scarborough YO12 ... 212 D7
York YO30 ... 228 C7
Tennyson Way 3 WF8 ... 201 B1
Tenter Fields YO7 ... 88 D1
Tenter Hill LS23 ... 188 D5
Tentergate Ave 4 HG5 ... 221 A7
Tentergate Cl 3 HG5 ... 221 A7
Tentergate Gdns 2
HG5 .... 221 A7
Tentergate La HG5 ... 221 A7
Tentergate Rd 5 HG5 ... 221 A7
Tenters Cl WF11 ... 201 E3
Tern Pk 6 LS22 ... 180 A1
Terrington Bank YO60 ... 119 C2
Terrington CE VA Prim Sch
YO60 .... 119 E1
Terrington Cl YO12 ... 167 B8
Terrington Hall Sch
YO60 .... 119 F1
Terrington S Bank
YO60 .... 119 D1
Terrington View YO60 ... 145 C5
Terror Twr* YO11 ... 213 B6
Terry Ave YO1 ... 233 B1
Terry St YO23 ... 228 C1
Tetherings La YO13 ... 98 F5
Tewit Well Ave HG2 ... 222 E7
Tewit Well Rd HG2 ... 222 F7
Thackadale La YO17 ... 121 A1
Thackeray Gr TS5 ... 6 E8
Thacking La LA6 ... 103 D4
Thames Ave
Guisborough TS14 ... 8 E6
Thornaby TS17 ... 6 B7
Thanet Rd YO24 ... 227 D1
Thanets Ct 8 BD23 ... 216 F3
Thatch Cl YO8 ... 232 C4
Thatchers Croft YO23 ... 230 C3
Theakston Hargill DL8 ... 87 E8
Theakston La DL10 ... 209 C6
Theresa Cl 8 YO31 ... 225 F1
Thickrash Brow LA2 ... 129 A7
Thief La Barlow YO8 ... 232 F1
York YO10 ... 228 F3
Thiefgate La HG4 ... 86 E3
Thiefhole La DL7 ... 65 B3
Third Ave
10 Wetherby LS22 ... 180 C3
York YO31 ... 228 F5
Thirkleby Way YO10 ... 229 C4
Thirlby Way 8 TS14 ... 8 F7
Thirlmere Cl 3 YO7 ... 89 C4
Thirlmere Dr YO31 ... 229 A6
Thirlway Dr HG4 ... 214 B6
Thirsk Bank
Angram Grange YO61 ... 117 B8
Thornton-le-Moor DL7 ... 65 B3
Thirsk Bsns Pk YO7 ... 211 B2
Thirsk Com Prim Sch
YO7 .... 211 C4
Thirsk Ind PK* YO7 ... 211 C3
Thirsk Mus* YO7 ... 211 B3
Thirsk Racecourse*
YO7 .... 211 A3
Thirsk Rd
Eaglescliffe TS15 ... 5 E2
Easingwold YO61 ... 117 B1
Kirkby TS9 ... 26 C6
Romanby DL6 ... 210 F1
Thirsk Sch & Sixth Form Coll
YO7 .... 211 B1
Thirsk Sta YO7 ... 89 D4
Thirsk Swimming Pool
YO7 .... 211 C4
Thirty Acre La YO51 ... 163 A6
Thirwall Dr TS17 ... 6 A4
Thistle Cl
Northallerton DL7 ... 210 D1
Selby YO8 ... 232 C2
Thistle Hill HG5 ... 221 B3
Thistle Rise TS8 ... 6 F6
Thistlebar Rd YO51 ... 141 D2

Thomas Chippendale Prim
Sch LS21 ....176 F1
Thomas Gill Rd **7** HG3 ..137 F1
Thomas St **6** Selby YO8 ..232 D6
2 York YO10 ....228 B3
Thomason Foss (Waterfall)*
YO22 ....31 C1
Thompson Cl
9 Barlby YO8 ....198 B4
28 Scalby YO12 ....75 D5
Thompson Dr **6** YO21 ..167 B8
Thompson Pl **6** YO26 ..227 E5
Thompson St E DL1 .....3 D7
Thompson St W DL1 ....3 C7
Thoresby La DL8 ....59 B5
Thoresby Rd YO24 ....227 B1
Thorington Gdns TS17 ..6 B4
Thorn Nook YO31 ....6 B8
Thorn Tree Ave **3** YO14 ..101 B4
Thorn Wath La YO62 ....48 E4
Thornaby Com Sch TS17 ..6 B7
Thornaby Rd TS17 ......6 B7
Thornaby Swimming Baths
TS17 ....6 A8
Thornaby Village Prim Sch
TS17 ....6 B7
Thornborough Cres **4**
DL8 ....60 D5
Thornbrough Rd DL6 ..210 E3
Thornburgh Rd YO11 ..99 F6
Thorncroft **8** YO19 ..184 F7
Thorndale St BD23 ....154 B3
Thornden Bldgs YO8 ..232 D5
Thorndikes La HG5 ....141 A2
Thorne Cl **18** WF6 ....200 B1
Thorner CE Prim Sch
LS14 ....188 A3
Thorner Gr BD20 ......174 C2
Thorner La LS23 ......188 B5
Thorner Rd LS23 ......188 B4
Thornfield Ave
Dishforth YO7 ....115 A4
3 York YO31 ....228 F8
Thornfield Bsns Pk
DL7 ....210 B6
Thornfield Dr **7** YO31 ..225 E2
Thornfield Gr TS5 ......6 E8
Thornfield Rd DL8 ....87 C3
Thornhill
6 Eastfield YO11 ....100 A6
Northallerton DL6 ....210 E3
Richmond DL10 ....209 B6
Thornhill Rd WF10 ....200 F3
Thornhills **19** YO32 ..166 F5
Thornlands **9** YO61 ..117 D1
Thornley Ave DL7 ....210 D3
Thorns La YO51 ....140 F4
Thornthwaite Brow
HG3 ....159 E5
Thornton Cl
18 Easingwold YO61 ..143 D8
Stainton & Thornton TS8 ..6 D4
Thornton Dale CE VC Prim
Sch YO18 ....96 C5
Thornton Hts BD23 ..172 A3
Thornton La Dent LA10 ..78 A4
Marishes YO17 ....96 B1
Thornton in Lonsdale
LA6 ....103 C4
Thornton-on-the-Hill
YO61 ....117 D4
Thornton Moor Cl
YO30 ....224 F2
Thornton Rd
Coulby Newham TS8 ....6 D4
Pickering YO18 ....96 A6
Thornton St
14 Burley in Wharfedale
LS29 ....176 C1
Darlington DL1 ....3 C5
3 Skipton BD23 ......216 D3
Thornton Vale TS8 ......6 E4
Thornton Watlass CE Prim
Sch HG4 ....86 D8
Thornton-in-Craven Com
Prim Sch BD23 ......172 A3
Thorntree Gdns DL2 ....4 C4
Thorntree Gr YO30 ....225 B2
Thorntree La DN14 ....207 C6
Thorntree Rd
Northallerton DL6 ....210 F6
Thornaby TS17 ....6 C7
Thornview Rd BD23 ..154 B3
Thornwood Ave TS15 ..5 A4
Thornwood Covert **1**
YO24 ....227 C1
Thorny Hill La YO51 ..141 E2
Thorny La YO42 ......169 F2
Thorp Arch Pk LS23 ..180 F1
Thorp Arch Trad Est
LS23 ....189 A8
Thorp Perrow Arboretum &
Falconry Ctr* DL8 ....87 A8
Thorpe Bassett La
YO17 ....122 E1
Thorpe Chase HG4 ....214 E3
Thorpe Gn Bank **1** YO22 ..33 C3
Thorpe Gn La YO26 ..164 B7
Thorpe La
Ampleforth YO62 ......118 B8
Cawood YO8 ....197 B8
Cracoe BD23 ....156 C7
Fylingdales YO22 ......33 C4
Thorpe BD23 ....156 D8
Thorpe Prebend House
Heritage Ctr* HG4 ..214 E5
Thorpe Rd HG4 ....86 C2
Thorpe St YO23 ......228 B2

Thorpe Willoughby CP Sch
YO8 ....197 B2
Threapland BD23 ......156 C7
Three Lakes Ind Est
YO8 ....232 D2
Three Lakes Ret Pk
YO8 ....232 D3
Three Tuns Wynd **7** TS9 ..26 C7
Threshfield Prim Sch
BD23 ....134 D2
Thrintoft La DL7 ....64 A4
Thrintoft Moor La DL7 ..64 A8
Thrope La HG3 ....110 C4
Throstle Farm Sch
WF11 ....201 F1
Throstle Nest Cl LS21 ..176 E1
Throstle Nest Dr HG2 ..222 D6
Thornexby Gr **3** YO22 ..12 F7
Thornexby La YO12 ..212 B7
Thruscross La HG3 ....159 B5
Thrussendale Rd
YO17 ....169 E8
Thunderhead Ridge
WF10 ....200 F3
Thurland Castle* LA6 ..102 B3
Thurston Rd DL6 ......210 C7
Thwaite Holme La DL8 ..57 F5
Thwaite La LA2 ....128 E5
Thwaites Ave LS29 ....218 C4
Thwaites La
Markington with Wallerthwaite
HG3 ....139 D5
Nether Silton YO7 ......66 C7
Thirkleby High & Low with
Osgodby YO7 ....90 E1
Thweng Way TS14 ......8 E6
Thwing Rd YO25 ......126 E2
Tib Garth LS22 ....180 A2
Tibby Butts **26** YO13 ..75 D5
Tickergate La DL7 ......63 A8
Tidkin La TS14 ....8 E6
Tile Cl BD23 ....217 B3
Tillman Cl **8** BD24 ..131 D2
Tilmire Cl **7** YO10 ..231 F8
Timble Gr HG1 ....219 B5
Timmys La DL2 ....3 F1
Tindall St YO12 ......212 F5
Tinker La YO23 ....182 D6
Tinkers' La HG3 ......139 A1
Tinkingfield La LS22 ..181 A5
Tinkler La Milby YO51 ..141 C6
Winsley HG3 ....160 E8
Tinkler's La WF11 ....202 D6
Tinley Garth YO62 ......70 B1
Tinley Gdns **14** YO62 ..70 B1
Tintagel Ct WF6 ......200 A2
Tiplady Cl **10** YO61 ..143 C8
Tippaty La WF11 ......202 A4
Tirril Way TS7 ....7 C5
Tithe Barn Fold LS15 ..194 B8
Tithe Barn Rd **2** WF11 ..202 A2
Tithe Barn Way DN14 ..202 F3
Tithe Cl YO24 ....230 D8
Tithe Way HG4 ....114 F1
Tivoli Pl LS29 ....218 C3
Toadham La DN14 ....207 C5
Toby Ct YO32 ....167 A7
Toc La YO18 ....97 C5
Tockwith CE VC Prim Sch
YO26 ....181 C7
Tockwith La YO26 ....181 D6
Tockwith Rd
Long Marston YO26 ..181 F6
Tockwith LS22 ....180 F7
Tod Holes La BD23 ..153 B4
Todd La DL7 ....63 B8
Todds Ct BD23 ....211 C3
Todley Hall Rd BD22 ..187 F3
Todmanhaw La BD23 ..153 E3
Toft Gn YO1 ....233 A2
Toft Ings La YO61 ....143 B8
Tofta Rd YO23 ....54 A5
Tofting La YO17 ......148 B5
Tofts Cl TS15 ....24 B8
Tofts Fort The* DL11 ..1 E2
Tofts La Danby YO21 ..29 B5
Follifoot HG3 ....223 F4
Humberton YO61 ....141 F8
Pickering YO18 ....95 F3
Tholthorpe YO61 ......141 F3
Welbury DL6 ....24 B1
Tofts Rd YO18 ....95 F3
Toll Bar Cl **3** YO8 ..196 E1
Toll Bar Rd WF10 ....200 C4
Toll Bar Way LS24 ....189 F7
Tollergate YO11 ......213 A7
Tollerton Rd YO30 ....165 B7
Tollesby La TS7 ....7 B6
Tollesby Rd TS5 ....6 F8
Tom Cat La
Bilton-in-Ainsty with Bickerton
LS22 ....181 A2
Birdsall YO17 ....148 B4
Tom Dando Cl WF6 ..200 C1
Tom Hall Ct **12** DL8 ..63 A2
Tom La Cowling BD22 ..186 E7
Dunsforths YO61 ......141 F3
Tom Smith's Cross
DL6 ....25 D1
Tomahawk Trail WF10 ..200 F3
Tomgill Bank DL8 ......58 E2
Tomlinson Way LS25 ..195 E4
Top Fold WF11 ....201 D6
Top House Farm Mews **2**
WF11 ....201 D6
Top La Colne BB8 ....186 B2
Copmanthorpe YO23 ..230 B3
Norwood LS21 ....177 A6

Top Stone Cl LS25 ....201 F6
Topcliff Ct YO8 ......232 B7
Topcliffe CE VC Prim Sch
YO7 ....115 C2
Topcliffe Rd
Sowerby YO7 ....89 E3
Thirsk YO7 ....211 B1
Thornaby TS17 ....6 C7
Toremill Cl YO32 ....225 D4
Torrance Dr DL1 ....3 F8
Torridon Pl YO24 ....230 B7
Torrs Rd HG1 ....220 A3
Tostig Ave YO26 ....227 C5
Tostig Cl **14** YO41 ..168 D2
Toulston La LS23 ....188 F5
Tout Hill YO60 ....146 E5
Tow Scar Rd LA6 ....103 C5
Tower Cl HG2 ....222 D6
Tower Cres LS24 ......189 D6
Tower Croft **7** YO61 ..117 D1
Tower Pl YO1 ....233 B2
Tower Rd Darlington DL3 ..3 B6
Ripon HG4 ....214 C6
Tower St
Harrogate HG1 ......219 D1
10 Richmond DL10 ..209 C6
York YO1 ....233 B1
Tower St Castle W **4**
DL10 ....209 C6
Tower The* HG4 ......139 B6
Tower View DN14 ....204 C2
Towers Paddock
WF10 ....201 A4
Town End YO7 ....211 B2
Town End Ave DN14 ..204 C3
Town End Cl
5 Glusburn BD20 ....187 E7
9 Monk Fryston YO8 ..96 A6
Town End Gdns **3**
YO32 ....166 D5
Town Farm Cl **18** YO42 ..70 B1
Town Head **2** YO7 ..115 A6
Town Hall & Craven Mus*
BD23 ....217 A4
Town Head Ave **1**
BD24 ....131 E2
Town Head Way **14**
BD24 ....131 D2
Town Hill LS23 ......188 E5
Town St
Bishop Thornton HG3 ..138 F1
Brandsby-cum-Stearsby
YO61 ....118 D3
Malton YO17 ....215 E6
Nidd HG3 ....161 E7
Scampston YO17 ....123 A6
Settrington YO17 ....122 C1
Towncliose View LS25 ..200 C8
Townend Ct **3** YO26 ..164 A8
Townend Pl **3** BD20 ..187 E7
Townend St YO10 ....233 B4
Townhead **2** BD24 ..131 E2
Townhead Fold **18** LS29 ..174 F4
Townhead La LA2 ....130 E8
Towthorpe Moor La
YO32 ....167 C5
Towthorpe Rd YO32 ..166 F5
Towton Ave **6** YO24 ..227 F2
Trafalgar Cl **6** HG2 ..219 D1
Trafalgar Ct
11 Harrogate HG1 ..219 D1
Ilkley LS29 ....218 B4
Scarborough YO12 ..212 F7
Trafalgar Sq YO12 ..212 F7
Trafalgar St YO23 ....228 B1
Trafalgar St W YO12 ..212 F6
Trafalgar Terr YO12 ..212 F7
Trafford Ct **19** DL1 ....3 F6
Trafford Rd DN6 ......206 E2
Train La **14** YO18 ......95 F7
Tranby Ave YO10 ....229 A4
Tranmire Cl YO7 ......211 D4
Tranmore La DN14 ....203 B3
Trans Wlk LS24 ......190 B1
Tranter Rd TS4 ....6 F8
Trapping Hill HG3 ....110 C4
Trattles Hill YO13 ......54 D2
Travellers Garth YO17 ..121 C1
Trawden Forest Prim Sch
BB8 ....186 A1
Trawden Rd BB8 ......186 A3
Treasurer's House*
YO31 ....233 B3
Trecastell **28** TS17 ....6 B8
Treesdale Rd **4** HG2 ..219 C1
Trefoil Cl **3** YO24 ....18 A6
Trefoil Dr **8** HG3 ....161 B3
Trefoil Wood TS7 ......7 A5
Trencar La YO61 ....91 A2
Trenchard Ave TS17 ....6 B6
Trenchard Rd YO26 ..227 B6
Trenfield Ct YO24 ....227 F3
Trenholme Cl **7** TS17 ..6 B6
Trenholme La TS15 ....25 B3
Trent Ave
Garforth LS25 ....194 D3
3 Pontefract WF6 ....200 A2
4 York YO32 ....225 F6
Trent Way YO24 ......230 D7
Trentholme Dr **2** YO24 ..228 A2
Trevine Gdns TS17 ......5 F4
Trevino Ct TS16 ....5 E5
Trevithick Cl **7** TS16 ..5 D5
Trevor Gr **3** YO24 ..227 F2
Tribune Way YO30 ....225 A3
Trimdon Ave TS5 ......6 D7

Trinity Church Sq **9**
DL10 ....209 C6
Trinity Cl **1** YO11 ..212 F3
Trinity Gdns **2** YO11 ..212 F3
Trinity La Ripon HG4 ..214 B5
York YO1 ....233 A2
Trinity Mews DL3 ......3 C5
Trinity Pk HG4 ....214 B6
Trinity Rd Darlington DL3 ..3 C5
Harrogate HG2 ......219 D1
Scarborough YO11 ..212 F3
Trinket La LA2 ....128 B6
Trip Garth LS22 ......180 A1
Trip La Collingham LS22 ..180 A1
Sicklinghall LS22 ....179 F1
Triplins La HG4 ......113 B6
Tristram Ave DL3 ......3 C7
Troon Cl **3** YO26 ....227 B5
Trousdale Hill YO60 ..147 A7
Troutbeck **7** YO24 ..230 C7
Troutbeck Cl **11** YO18 ..95 F6
Troutbeck Dr YO30 ..224 E2
Trumfleet La DN6 ....207 D1
Trumbles La **1** WF11 ..202 A2
Truro Cres **8** HG3 ..161 B3
Truro Dr **10** WF6 ....200 A2
Truro Rd **7** HG3 ....161 B3
Truro Wlk **8** WF6 ..200 A2
Trust Fold LS25 ......201 E6
Tudor Cl DL6 ....210 E5
Tudor Dr **1** YO8 ....197 B1
Tudor Rd
Richmond DL10 ......209 D7
York YO24 ....227 C2
Tudor Way YO32 ....167 B8
Tufton Pl BD23 ......216 F3
Tuke Ave YO10 ......229 C4
Tumbledown Cl **5** DL9 ..40 E3
Tune St YO8 ....198 B4
Tunstall Rd
Catterick DL10 ....41 D4
Harrogate HG2 ......220 B3
Turbary La YO32 ....226 E6
Turbary Rd LA6 ......103 B7
Turfy Hill DL8 ....56 C4
Turker Cl DL6 ....210 E5
Turker La Baldersby YO7 ..88 D1
Catton YO7 ....114 F8
Turks Head Ct YO1 ..233 C3
Turnberry Ave TS16 ....5 E4
Turnberry Dr YO26 ..227 B4
Turnberry Way TS8 ....7 C5
Turner Cl DL9 ....209 C2
Turner Cres **6** LS21 ..177 A1
Turner La LS29 ......174 E4
Turner St **18** BB18 ..171 E1
Turners' Croft YO10 ..229 A1
Turners Sq **9** YO7 ..232 C5
Turnham La YO8 ......198 C2
Turnhead Cres YO8 ..198 B5
Turnhead Ct YO8 ....198 B5
Turnmire Rd **1** YO22 ..230 E8
Turnpike La LS22 ....181 B5
Turnpike Rd LA2 ......189 F7
Turnshaw Rd BD22 ..187 F1
Turpin Ct YO1 ....233 C1
Turpin La LS25 ......196 A2
Turton Rd TS15 ....5 D2
Turver's La WF11 ....202 C2
Tuscany Way WF6 ..200 A3
Tuthill LS29 ....213 B6
Tutin Rd DL7 ....63 C5
Twelve Acre Bank DL8 ..40 E1
Twin Pike Way **12** YO32 ..166 D5
Twine Wlk **7** LA6 ..102 F3
Twizzie Gill View **6**
TS13 ....11 A8
Two Laws Rd BB8 ....187 B1
Tyler Cl WF6 ....200 C1
Tyn Garth YO19 ......191 D8
Tyne Cres DL1 ....3 D3
Typhoon Cl DL10 ......41 F6
Tyseley Gr **4** BB18 ..172 A1
Tyson Pl HG2 ....220 B2

Uldale Cl **6** HG5 ....221 D5
Uldale Dr TS16 ....5 E4
Ulla Gn LS24 ....190 B1
Ulleskelf Sta LS24 ....190 B2
Ullswater YO24 ......230 D7
Ullswater Ave TS5 ....6 E8
Ullswater Dr LS22 ....180 B3
Ullswater Rise **5** LS22 ..180 B3
Ulnaby La DL2 ....2 C7
Undercliffe Rise YO11 ..99 F7
Undercroft **8** YO19 ..184 F7
Underlands La HG4 ..114 C7
Underwit Rd YO8 ....204 C4
Union House BD23 ..216 F4
Union La YO8 ....232 C4
Union St **28** Filey YO14 ..101 B3
Harrogate HG1 ......219 D3
Skipton BD23 ....216 F3
York YO1 ....233 B4
Unity Cl HG1 ....219 C5
Unity Gr HG1 ....219 C5
Unity St **8** BB18 ..186 A7

Vale Ave WF11 ......201 E2
Vale Cres
Bishop Wilton YO42 ..169 F2
Knottingley WF11 ....201 E2
Vale Crest WF11 ......201 E2
Vale Ct HG5 ....221 A6
Vale Sch WF11 ....201 E2
Vale The
10 Collingham LS22 ..188 A8
Middlesbrough TS5 ....6 F8
Skipton YO30 ....224 B5
Vale View HG4 ....114 B2
Valley Bride Rd **8** YO11 ..213 F5
Valley Bridge Par
YO11 ....213 A5
Valley Dr
Barnoldswick BB18 ..171 E2
Eaglescliffe TS15 ......5 E3
Great Preston LS26 ..200 C8
Harrogate HG2 ......219 C1
Ilkley LS29 ....218 D4
Valley Gdns* HG2 ..219 C2
Valley Mount HG2 ..219 C2
Valley Rd
Barnoldswick BB18 ..171 E1
Darlby HG3 ....160 A6
32 Earby BB18 ......172 A1
Harrogate HG2 ......219 C2
Ilkley LS29 ....218 D5
Kippax LS25 ....194 C2
Northallerton DL6 ..210 F3
Scarborough YO12 ..212 E4
Whitby YO21 ....208 A6
Valley Ridge LS25 ..194 C2
Valley View
3 Ampleforth YO62 ..92 C1
Clint HG3 ....160 A8
Danby YO21 ....29 C6
3 Glusburn BD20 ..187 E8
Wheldrake YO19 ....192 F7
Valuation La **1** YO11 ..141 B5
Van Mildert Way TS18 ..5 F8
Vanbrugh Dr YO10 ..229 C4
Vanbrugh Way YO10 ..229 A2
Vane Ct TS21 ....4 F7
Vane St DL3 ....3 C5
Vasey Cl **3** DL8 ......63 B2
Vaughan Rd **10** DN6 ..206 E1
Vavasour Ct YO23 ..230 B2
Vaynor Dr **17** TS17 ....5 F4
Venables Rd TS14 ......8 E6

Village The continued
Haxby YO32 .....166 E5
Skelton YO30 .....224 B5
Stockton on the Forest
  YO32 .....167 D3
Strensall YO32 .....167 B7
York YO10 .....229 C4
Village Wy DL7 .....42 B1
Villiers Ct 8 YO62 .....92 F6
Vimy Rd DL9 .....40 E3
Vincent St 12 YO12 .....213 A7
Vincent Way YO24 .....230 C8
Vine Cl TS14 .....8 F6
Vine Farm Cl YO26 .....164 A4
Vine Gdns YO8 .....199 D7
Vine St 1 YO11 .....215 E4
Vine St Darlington DL3 .....3 B6
  Norton YO17 .....215 E4
  6 Scarborough YO12 .....212 F6
  York YO23 .....228 C2
Vinstra Cl DL10 .....209 D8
Virginia Gdns TS5 .....6 E6
Vivers Way YO8 .....232 D5
Vivers Pl 1 YO62 .....70 C1
Vivis La YO18 .....95 F6
Volta St YO8 .....232 E4
Vulcan Way TS17 .....6 B6
Vyner St Ripon HG4 .....214 D4
  York YO31 .....228 C7

W

Waddington St 37 BB18 .....172 A1
Wade House La YO8 .....204 F4
Waggoners Dr 3 YO23 .....230 B3
Wain Cl
  15 Eastfield YO11 .....100 B7
  South Milford LS25 .....195 E2
Wain Gap LS25 .....195 F2
Wain's Gr YO24 .....230 D7
Wain's La YO12 .....99 D2
Wain's Rd YO24 .....230 D8
Waincroft 8 YO32 .....167 A6
Wainleigh Way WF6 .....200 B1
Wainers Cl 3 YO23 .....230 B3
Wainfleet Rd HG1 .....219 D6
Wainman's La YO51 .....140 F4
Wainstones Cl 4 BD22 .....187 B6
Wainstones Ct TS9 .....7 F1
Wainstones Dr TS9 .....7 F1
Waite La YO13 .....53 F2
Waithwith Rd DL9 .....209 B1
Waitlands La DL1 .....20 A7
Wakefield Coll WF10 .....200 D3
Wakefield Rd
  Garforth LS25 .....194 B3
  10 Normanton South WF6 .....200 A1
  Swillington LS25 .....194 A2
Wakeman Rd HG4 .....214 C3
Walburn Head DL11 .....39 D3
Walburn Stubbs Rd
  DN6 .....206 E2
Walker Cl St DL3 .....3 C7
Walker Cl YO8 .....187 D7
Walker Dr YO24 .....230 C8
Walker La
  Menwith with Darley
    HG3 .....160 A6
  Wheldrake YO19 .....192 F7
Walker St YO21 .....208 D6
Walker Terr 8 BD23 .....223 F4
Walker's La BD20 .....174 B4
Walkers Fold HG5 .....221 B5
Walkerville Ave 7 DL9 .....41 A5
Walkerville Ind Est DL9 .....41 B5
Walkington La 7 YO30 .....165 B8
Walled Gdn The*
  YO17 .....123 A6
Wallgates La YO17 .....215 D4
Wallingham YO1 .....233 C2
Walmsley Gdns YO12 .....212 C5
Walney Rd YO31 .....229 A5
Walnut Cl
  Saxton with Scarthingwell
    LS24 .....195 D8
  York YO10 .....229 A1
Walnut Gr YO12 .....212 A5
Walnut Gr HG1 .....219 E6
Walpole St YO31 .....228 D7
Walton Ave
  Gargrave BD23 .....155 C1
  Middlesbrough TS5 .....6 E8
  Pannal HG3 .....222 F2
Walton Chase LS23 .....180 F2
Walton Cl
  Gargrave BD23 .....172 C8
  Huby YO61 .....144 A4
Walton Head La HG3 .....178 F4
Walton Pk HG3 .....222 E2
Walton Pl Pannal HG3 .....222 E2
  York YO26 .....227 B3
Walton Rd
  Walton LS23 .....181 A2
  Wetherby LS22 .....180 E2
Walton St
  6 Cowling BD22 .....187 B6
  Skipton BD23 .....216 F1
Walworth Ave BD20 .....203 B8
Walworth St N 4 YO26 .....227 F5
Walworth St S 5 YO26 .....227 F5
Wand Hill TS12 .....9 E8
Wand La DN14 .....203 C3
Wandale La YO17 .....95 A2
Wandales Cl YO17 .....215 F3
Wandales Ct YO13 .....75 D8
Wandales Dr YO13 .....75 D8

Wandales La YO60 .....146 B6
Wandales Rd YO13 .....75 D8
Wandel Balk YO61 .....144 B6
Wandels La YO21 .....29 B6
Wandesford Gr DL9 .....209 F1
Wandhill 3 YO32 .....166 E5
Wandhill Gdns TS12 .....9 E8
Wandle The YO26 .....227 A2
Wansbeck 3 YO24 .....230 B7
Wapping La YO40 .....94 C7
War Dale La YO13 .....54 C5
War Field La LS22 .....180 F6
Warbler Cl TS17 .....6 A5
Ward Ct YO23 .....233 B1
Ward St BD23 .....217 A4
Wardale Ave TS5 .....6 E6
Wardrop Rd DL9 .....209 C1
Wareham Rd YO11 .....99 F6
Warehill La YO61 .....143 C2
Warlbeck 22 LS29 .....175 C2
Warley Wise La BB8 .....186 D6
Warren Ave YO11 .....201 E2
Warren La
  Bramham cum Oglethorpe
    LS24 .....189 A5
  Brearton HG3 .....162 A8
  Kirkby Malzeard HG4 .....112 D4
Warren Pl YO21 .....219 D5
Warren Rd La DL10 .....20 C6
Warth La LA6 .....103 C3
Warthill CE VC Prim Sch
  YO19 .....167 F2
Warwick Cl YO60 .....145 D5
Warwick Cres HG2 .....222 E8
Warwick Dr 2 BB18 .....172 A1
Warwick Pl YO12 .....92 F7
Warwick St YO31 .....228 D7
Wasdale Cl 2 YO30 .....224 E1
Wash Beck La YO62 .....93 F6
Washbeck Cl YO12 .....212 E4
Washbrook Dr DL1 .....3 E4
Washburn Cl 8 YO14 .....101 A3
Washburn Cotts LS21 .....159 F1
Washburn Courts HG3 .....159 F1
Washburn Dr 4 BD20 .....187 E8
Washfold La DL8 .....60 A6
Washford Cl TS17 .....6 A3
Washington Ave 4 DL1 .....3 D4
Washington Cl HG4 .....214 C2
Wass Bank Rd YO61 .....91 F2
Wass Way TS16 .....5 D5
Waste La YO62 .....48 F2
Watchet Rd 11 DL9 .....40 E4
Water Bag Bank 8 HG5 .....221 A6
Water End YO26 .....227 E5
Water Gap YO18 .....97 B5
Water Garth DN14 .....202 F4
Water Hill La YO8 .....232 D6
Water Houses BD24 .....132 E6
Water La
  Camblesforth YO8 .....204 D5
  8 Clifton YO30 .....225 A1
  Dalton YO7 .....115 E7
  Dunnington YO19 .....184 F7
  Eggborough DN14 .....203 A2
  Exelby, Leeming & Newton
    DL7 .....63 D4
  Hemingbrough YO8 .....198 F1
  Huttons Ambo YO60 .....147 C6
  Kirby Grindalythe YO17 .....149 B8
  Kirby Underdale YO41 .....170 A5
  Kirk Smeaton WF8 .....206 C3
  Knaresborough HG5 .....221 C8
  Loftus TS13 .....10 E8
  North Stainley with Sleningford
    HG4 .....113 C6
  7 Pontefract WF8 .....201 C1
  Selby YO8 .....232 C6
  South Stainley with Cayton
    HG3 .....139 D2
  Thorpe Bassett YO17 .....123 A3
  Welburn YO60 .....146 E7
  Whitby YO21 .....208 B3
  York YO30 .....228 A7
Water Skellgate HG4 .....214 C5
Water Slack La YO26 .....164 C4
Water St 5 Earby BB18 .....172 A1
  Gargrave BD23 .....155 D1
  Malton YO17 .....215 C4
  Skipton BD23 .....216 F4
Water St Com Prim Sch
  BD23 .....216 F4
Water Way Garth
  DN14 .....207 F6
Waterdale Pk YO31 .....225 E1
Waterfall Fold 1 WF8 .....201 C2
Watergate
  Mickletown LS26 .....200 A5
  12 Pontefract WF8 .....201 B1
Watergate Rd HG3 .....139 A4
Waterhouse La 22 YO11 .....213 A6
Waterings 19 YO12 .....166 D5
Waterloo
  Grosmont YO22 .....31 C4
  12 Richmond DL10 .....209 C6
Waterloo Cl WF10 .....200 E3
Waterloo Rd BB18 .....186 A7
Waterloo St
  Harrogate HG1 .....219 E4
  2 Richmond DL10 .....209 C6
Waterloo Terr 3 YO21 .....208 D6
Waterman Ct 3 YO7 .....211 C1
Watermill Cl HG4 .....113 C7
Watermill Croft HG4 .....113 C7
Watermill La HG4 .....113 C7
Waters End 1 .....1 D7
Waters La DL10 .....20 E1

Watershed Mill Bsns Ctr
  BD24 .....131 D3
Watershed Mill Visitor Ctr*
  BD24 .....131 D3
Waterside
  3 Boroughbridge YO51 .....141 B6
  Knaresborough HG5 .....221 A5
  4 Ripon HG4 .....214 C4
  Skipton BD23 .....216 F2
  7 Thirsk YO7 .....211 C3
Waterside Rd 4 TS17 .....6 A3
Waterside La LS22 .....180 D2
Waterstead Cres 1
  YO21 .....208 D5
Waterstead La YO21 .....208 C5
Watery La Airton BD23 .....155 A5
  Giggleswick BD24 .....131 C1
  Stapleton with Thorp DL8 .....86 F7
Wath La Catton YO41 .....185 C8
  Copgrove HG3 .....140 D1
  High & Low Bishopside
    HG3 .....137 B6
  Humberton YO61 .....141 E8
  Norwood YO61 .....190 B2
Wath Rd HG3 .....137 B5
Wathcote Cl DL10 .....209 F8
Wathcote Pl DL10 .....209 F8
Wathgill Camp DL11 .....39 C3
Watlass La DL8 .....86 E8
Watlass Moor La HG4 .....86 D7
Watling Cl DL11 .....19 E6
Watling Rd WF10 .....201 C5
Watson Cl 9 YO14 .....127 A8
Watson St
  4 Normanton South WF6 .....200 A1
  York YO24 .....228 A3
Watson's Houses 7
  BD23 .....216 F4
Watson's La
  Newton Kyme cum Toulston
  LS24 .....189 B7
  Norwood HG3 .....177 B8
  Reighton YO14 .....127 D6
Wattle Syke LS22 .....180 B1
Wattlers Cl YO23 .....230 C3
Wattlesyke LS22 .....188 C8
Wavell Com Inf & Jun Sch
  DL9 .....209 D1
Wavell Rd DL9 .....209 D1
Wavell St YO8 .....232 A6
Waveney Gr YO30 .....228 B8
Waver La DL6 .....43 F8
Waverley Cl DN14 .....204 C2
Waverley Cres YO31 .....229 A5
Waverley St YO31 .....233 C3
Waydale Cl YO62 .....70 A2
Wayfaring Cl YO17 .....215 F2
Wayne Tarbard Cl 12
  HG4 .....113 D2
Waynefleet Gr 3 YO10 .....229 A3
Wayside Ave 1 HG2 .....220 B1
Wayside Cl 4 HG2 .....220 B1
Wayside Cres HG2 .....220 A1
Wayside Gr HG2 .....220 A1
Wayside Terr LS17 .....178 B2
Wayside The DL2 .....3 E1
Wayside Wlk 5 HG2 .....220 B1
Weaponness Dr YO11 .....213 A2
Weaponness La
  Eastfield YO11 .....99 F8
  Scarborough YO11 .....212 F1
Weaponness Pk YO11 .....213 A2
Weaponness Valley Cl 5
  YO11 .....212 F3
Weaponness Valley Rd
  YO11 .....212 F3
Weardale YO11 .....99 F8
Weardale Rd 20 DL9 .....40 E4
Weary Bank TS15 .....25 B8
Weavers Cl YO23 .....230 B3
Weavers Ct
  5 Stokesley TS9 .....26 C7
  Trawden BB8 .....186 A1
Weavers Gn DL7 .....210 C3
Weavers Pk YO23 .....230 B3
Weaverthorpe CE VC Prim
  YO17 .....124 E2
Webster Pl 1 WF10 .....200 D3
Weddall Cl YO24 .....227 F1
Wedderburn Ave HG2 .....220 C3
Wedderburn Cl HG2 .....220 C3
Wedderburn Cty Inf Sch
  HG2 .....220 B2
Wedderburn Dr HG2 .....220 C2
Wedderburn Lodge 2
  HG2 .....220 C3
Wedderburn Rd HG2 .....220 B2
Wedgewood Ct LS24 .....189 D4
Weeland Ct 16 WF11 .....202 A2
Weeland Rd Beal DN14 .....202 E3
  Hensall DN14 .....203 E2
Weeton La LS17 .....178 B2
Weeton Sta LS17 .....178 B2
Weets View BB18 .....171 E2
Welbeck Ave DL1 .....3 F7
Welborn Cl YO10 .....229 A4
Welborn Ct YO10 .....229 A4
Welbury Dr YO11 .....99 D6
Welburn Com Prim Sch
  YO60 .....146 D6
Welburn Gr TS7 .....7 D7
Welburn Hall Sch YO62 .....94 A7
Welburn La YO60 .....147 A8
Welfare Ave LS15 .....194 C8
Welford Rd 5 YO14 .....101 B3
Welham Hill YO17 .....147 E7

Welham Rd YO17 .....215 D3
Well Bank DL8 .....87 A4
Well Cl
  Great & Little Preston
    LS25 .....200 C8
  3 Whitby YO21 .....208 B7
Well Cl Terr 4 YO21 .....208 B7
Well La Kippax LS25 .....194 D1
  Redmire DL8 .....59 C5
  Seamer TS9 .....6 F2
  Stape with Thorp DL8 .....87 A6
  South Milford LS25 .....195 F2
  Yearsley YO61 .....118 C5
Welland Dr LS25 .....194 D3
Welland Rise YO26 .....227 D5
Wellbrook Cl TS17 .....6 B4
Wellesley Cl YO30 .....225 A2
Wellesleys Mews
  DL10 .....209 B7
Wellfield Ct HG2 .....222 B6
Wellfield La 18 LS29 .....176 C1
Wellhouse St 5 BB18 .....171 E1
Wellington Ct 9 HG2 .....219 C2
Wellington Gdns HG4 .....214 C4
Wellington Lodge Llamas*
  YO13 .....54 B5
Wellington Mews 9
  HG4 .....214 C5
Wellington Pl DL10 .....209 B7
Wellington Rd
  Ilkley LS29 .....218 B4
  2 Whitby YO21 .....208 D6
Wellington Row YO1 .....233 A2
Wellington Sq 6 HG2 .....219 C2
Wellington St
  1 Knaresborough HG5 .....221 B5
  16 Ripon HG4 .....214 C5
  12 Skipton BD23 .....217 A3
  York YO10 .....228 E3
Wellington Terr YO21 .....208 E6
Wellington Way 4 DL10 .....41 C7
Wellingtonia Dr 5 DN6 .....206 F1
Wells Cl YO8 .....232 A5
Wells La Barton DL10 .....21 D7
  Kellington DN14 .....202 E3
  Malton YO17 .....215 C4
Wells Mews YO26 .....218 B3
Wells Prom YO26 .....218 B4
Wells Wlk YO26 .....218 B3
Wells Wlk The LS29 .....95 F7
Wellspring Cl TS17 .....6 D7
Welton Ave YO26 .....227 D5
Welton Ct YO21 .....208 C7
Welwyn Dr YO10 .....231 E8
Wemyss Rd 11 HG4 .....113 D2
Wendel Ave LS15 .....194 B8
Wendy Ave HG4 .....214 B3
Wenham Rd YO24 .....230 E8
Wenlock Dr YO19 .....192 B6
Wenlock Terr YO10 .....228 D1
Wenning Ave LA2 .....129 A7
Wenning Bank LA2 .....129 A7
Wennington Hall Sch
  LA2 .....102 B1
Wennington Rd LA2 .....128 A6
Wennington Sta LA2 .....128 A4
Wensley Gr HG2 .....222 D7
Wensley Rd
  Harrogate HG2 .....222 D7
  15 Leyburn DL8 .....60 D5
  Northallerton DL7 .....210 B2
Wensleydale Ave 2
  BD23 .....217 B4
Wensleydale Creamery*
  DL8 .....56 C4
Wensleydale Dr YO10 .....229 C4
Wensleydale Pottery*
  DL8 .....56 D4
Wensleydale Rd 11 DL9 .....40 E4
Wensleydale Sch The
  DL8 .....60 D5
Wentcliffe Br BB18 .....172 A1
Wentdale 1 WF8 .....206 C3
Wentworth Ave YO61 .....116 F5
Wentworth Cl
  Camblesforth YO8 .....204 D4
  Harrogate HG2 .....220 D4
  Eggborough DN14 .....203 A2
Wentworth Cres
  Harrogate HG2 .....220 D3
  Scarborough YO11 .....208 B5
Wentworth Dr HG2 .....220 D4
Wentworth Gate LS22 .....180 A3
Wentworth Rd YO24 .....228 B3
Wentworth St YO17 .....215 B5
Wentworth Way
  Eaglescliffe TS16 .....5 E4
  5 Hunmanby YO14 .....126 F8
  York YO10 .....228 F2
Werkdyke The YO1 .....233 C3
Wescoe Hill La LS17 .....178 A5
Wesley Pl YO1 .....233 C2
Wesley Sq 2 TS13 .....13 K2
Wesson Cl 8 DL9 .....40 E4
West Acres 2 WF11 .....201 E4
West Acres Cl 7 YO13 .....99 A7
West Auckland Rd DL3 .....3 A7
West Bank
  Scarborough YO12 .....212 E4

274 Ver - Wes

Vernon Cl YO23 .....231 A3
Vernon Gr 4 YO12 .....212 D8
Vernon Pl 3 YO11 .....213 A5
Vernon Rd
  2 Harrogate HG2 .....222 E7
  11 Scarborough YO11 .....213 A5
  Trawden Forest BB8 .....186 B3
  York YO30 .....224 E2
Vesper Dr YO24 .....227 B3
Vesper Wlk YO32 .....225 F6
Vicar Hill La YO7 .....116 D8
Vicarage Cl
  2 Bubwith YO8 .....199 D7
  10 Hunmanby YO14 .....126 F8
  Seamer YO12 .....99 D6
Vicarage Gdns 11 YO10 .....229 C4
Vicarage La
  Bishop Wilton YO42 .....169 F2
  Bramham LS23 .....188 E5
  16 Knaresborough HG5 .....221 A6
  Naburn YO19 .....191 E8
  Sherburn YO17 .....124 D8
Vicarage Rd
  Barnoldswick BB18 .....171 E2
  16 Catterick Garrison DL9 .....40 A4
  3 Kelbrook & Sough
    BB18 .....186 A7
Vicar's La YO61 .....144 C6
Vicars Cl YO23 .....230 B2
Vicars Croft DL6 .....210 E5
Vicars Terr WF10 .....200 D6
Vickers Cl TS18 .....5 F7
Vickers Rd 2 DL9 .....40 E4
Vickers St 1 WF10 .....200 E4
Victor St YO11 .....233 B1
Victoria Ave
  11 Filey YO14 .....101 B3
  Harrogate HG1 .....219 D2
  Ilkley LS29 .....175 C2
  Knaresborough HG5 .....221 B8
  Ripon HG4 .....214 D5
  Thirsk YO7 .....211 B2
Victoria Cave* BD24 .....131 F4
Victoria Cl
  Great Preston WF10 .....200 E6
  Ilkley LS29 .....218 A4
Victoria Ct 15 YO30 .....227 F5
Victoria Dr 9 LS29 .....175 C2
Victoria Emb DL1 .....3 C4
Victoria Farm Cl YO23 .....182 C6
Victoria Gdns 17 LS29 .....175 C2
Victoria Gr
  8 Ilkley LS29 .....175 C2
  Ripon HG4 .....214 C5
Victoria Par 18 YO11 .....212 F5
Victoria Pk 1 YO12 .....212 F7
Victoria Pk Ave 2 YO12 .....212 F7
Victoria Pk Mount
  YO12 .....212 E7
Victoria Pl 3 YO21 .....208 D6
Victoria St
  1 Barnoldswick BB18 .....171 E1
  2B Burley in Warfedale
    LS29 .....176 C1
  Cowling BD22 .....187 B6
  Darlington DL1 .....3 C5
  Earby BB18 .....172 A1
  Glusburn BD20 .....187 E7
  Harrogate HG2 .....219 C1
  17 Ilkley LS29 .....175 C2
  1 Malton YO17 .....215 B4
  Richmond DL10 .....209 D7
  Scarborough YO11 .....212 F5
  Thornaby TS17 .....6 B8
Victoria Sh Ctr HG1 .....219 D2
Victoria Sq BD23 .....216 F4
Victoria St
  2A Earby BB18 .....172 A1
  Glusburn BD20 .....187 E7
  Great Preston WF10 .....200 D6
  Pontefract WF8 .....201 B2
  Scarborough YO12 .....212 F6
  Settle BD24 .....131 E2
  16 Skipton BD23 .....216 F4
  York YO31 .....233 B1
Victoria Terr
  11 Harrogate HG1 .....220 C4
  Northallerton DL7 .....210 D4
  3 Skipton BD23 .....216 F4
Victoria Way 2 YO32 .....228 F8
Victoria Works Ind Est
  BD20 .....187 F8
Victory Rd LS29 .....218 B4
Viewley Hill Ave TS8 .....6 F5
Viewley Hill Prim Sch
  TS8 .....6 F5
Viking Cl 20 YO41 .....168 D2
Viking Dr 5 YO19 .....197 F8
Viking Rd
  Stamford Bridge YO41 .....168 D2
  York YO26 .....227 C5
Vikings Ct 6 DL6 .....43 F3
Villa Cl YO8 .....198 F1
Villa Ct YO26 .....227 B7
Villa Fields 4 DN14 .....204 C1
Village Cl 3 YO32 .....228 E6
Village Farm Cl 7
  DN14 .....202 D4
Village Fold DL7 .....42 B1
Village Garth 1 YO32 .....166 E5
Village Paddock TS18 .....5 E8
Village Rd TS15 .....24 B8
Village St YO30 .....224 E3
Village The
  Boston Spa LS23 .....180 F1

West Bank *continued*
York YO24 ....227 E3
West Bank Rd BD23 ...216 E4
West Barnby La YO21 ...12 B3
West Beck Way TS8 ......7 B6
West Burton CE Prim Sch
DL8 ....58 F1
West Cam Rd BD23 .....79 E6
West Cl Carthorpe DL8 ...87 E6
   Normanton WF6 ....200 A1
   Swinton YO17 ....121 B4
West Cl DL8 [18] 171 D2
West Cliff Ave [5] YO21 .208 B7
West Cliff Prim Sch
YO21 ....208 C7
West Cliffe Cre [9] HG2 ...219 C1
West Cliffe Ct HG2 .....219 B1
West Cliffe Mews [5]
HG2 ....219 C1
West Cliffe Mount
HG2 ....219 B1
West Cliffe Terr HG2 ...219 B1
West Craven High Tech Coll
BB18 ....171 E1
West Craven Swimming Pool
BB18 ....171 E1
West Croft
   [18] Addingham LS29 ...174 F4
   [5] Glusburn BD20 .....187 E6
West Ct [3] YO19 ......197 F8
West Dale LS23 ....180 E1
West Dene BD20 ....174 B2
West Dike Rd YO18 .....71 F5
West Edge Rd WF8 ....206 A3
West End
   Boston Spa LS23 ......180 E1
   Guisborough TS14 ....8 E6
   Hurworth-on-Tees DL2 ...3 E1
   Hutton Rudby TS15 ....25 C5
   Kirkbymoorside YO62 ...70 B1
   Muston YO14 ....100 F2
   Osmotherley DL6 ......45 B4
   Pollington DN14 ......207 F6
   Rawcliffe DN14 ....205 A2
   Sheriff Hutton YO60 ...145 C5
   Stokesley TS9 ....26 C7
   Strensall YO32 ....167 A7
West End App LS24 ....190 B3
West End Ave
   Appleton Roebuck YO23 .190 F5
   Harrogate HG2 ....222 B8
   Richmond DL10 ....209 A7
West End Cl
   North Duffield YO8 ....199 A8
   [3] Strensall YO32 ....167 B7
West End Ct [5] YO11 ..100 B5
West End Gdns
   Egglescliffe TS16 ....5 D4
   Pollington DN14 ......207 F6
West End Rd DN6 .....206 E2
West End View [4] YO11 .100 B6
West End Way TS18 .....5 F8
West Field La
   Arkendale HG5 ....163 A8
   East Witton Town DL8 ...60 F1
   Upper Poppleton YO26 .165 E1
West Field Rd [2] BB18 .171 D2
West Fields YO62 ....70 B1
West Garforth Jun Sch
LS25 ....194 C3
West Garth
   Cayton YO11 ....100 B6
   Sherburn YO17 ....124 D8
   Ulleskelf LS24 ....190 B3
West Garth Gdns [23]
YO11 ....100 B6
West Gate
   Thornton-le-Dale YO18 ...96 C5
   Wetherby LS22 ....180 B3
   Wykeham YO13 ....98 D6
West Gr
   Bishop Thornton HG3 ...139 A2
   Swinton YO17 ....121 B4
West Gr Rd HG1 ....219 D4
West Hall La LS29 .....175 A5
West Heslerton CE VC Prim
Sch YO17 ....123 F6
West Ing La BD23 ......171 A5
West Ings Cl [4] WF11 ..202 A3
West Ings Cres [5]
WF11 ....202 A3
West Ings Ct [1] WF11 ..202 A3
West Ings La [2] WF11 ..202 A3
West Ings Mews [8]
WF11 ....202 A3
West Ings Way [3] WF11 .202 A3
West La
   Appleton Wiske DL6 ....24 A3
   Askwith LS21 ....176 C3
   Azerley HG4 ....112 F3
   Beverley HG3 ....136 E4
   Boston Spa LS23 .....180 E1
   Burn YO8 ....203 C6
   Burniston YO13 ....54 C1
   Burton Fleming YO25 ...126 E3
   Caldwell DL11 ....1 B4
   Cononley BD20 ....173 C2
   Dalton-on-Tees DL2 ....22 D8
   Danby YO21 ....29 C8
   East Layton DL11 .....20 A8
   Embsay BD23 ....217 D8
   Hampsthwaite HG3 ....161 A4
   Hornby DL6 ....24 A2
   [2] Low Bradley BD20 ..173 E3
   Melsonby DL10 ....20 E7
   Mickleby TS13 ....12 A4
   Nether Silton YO7 .....66 B7

West La *continued*
   North Deighton LS22 ...179 F6
   Snainton YO13 ....97 F5
   Stillington YO61 ......143 F7
   Sutton BD20 ....187 E6
   Sykehouse DN14 ......207 F2
   Whixley YO26 ....163 F5
West Lea Ave HG2 .....222 B7
West Lodge Gdns
   YO17 ....215 A4
West Lund [17] YO62 ....70 B1
West Lund La YO62 .....94 B8
West Mead WF10 ......201 A4
West Moor La DL8 ......61 E4
West Moor Rd
   Darlington DL2 ....3 E3
   Raskelf YO61 ....116 E2
West Mount LS24 ......189 E5
West Oaks Sch LS23 ....188 E8
West Par Rd [11] YO12 ..212 F5
West Parade LS29 .....218 C4
West Pasture
   Kirkbymoorside YO62 ...70 B1
   [7] Pickering YO18 .....95 F6
West Pier YO11 ....213 B6
West Pk
   Harrogate HG2 ....219 D1
   Selby YO8 ....232 A4
West Pk Cl HG2 ....212 C8
West Pk Cres YO12 ....212 C7
West Pk Hosp DL3 ....3 A7
West Pk Rd [13] YO13 ...75 D5
   [12] Filey YO14 ....101 B3
   Melsonby DL10 ....20 E7
West Row DL2 ....4 C7
West Sandgate Terr [19]
YO11 ....213 B6
West Side Rd YO13 .....53 A1
West Sq [7] YO11 ......212 F5
West St
   Castleford WF10 ......200 E4
   Egglescliffe TS15 ....5 D4
   Gargrave BD23 ....155 D1
   Gayles DL11 ....19 E6
   Harrogate HG1 ....219 C5
   Ilkley LS29 ....218 B4
   Muston YO14 ....100 A1
   Normanton South WF6 .200 A1
   Scarborough YO11 ....213 A4
   Swinton YO17 ....121 B4
West Terr
   Richmond DL10 ....209 B7
   Scarborough YO11 ....212 F4
   [10] Whitby YO21 ......208 D7
West Thorpe YO24 .....230 D8
West Vale [37] YO14 ...101 B3
West View
   Carleton BD23 ....173 B4
   Darlington DL3 ....3 A5
   Draughton BD23 ......174 B7
   Ilkley LS29 ....218 B3
   Kippax LS25 ....194 D1
   Micklefield LS25 ......195 A3
   North Deighton LS22 ...180 A6
   Ripon HG4 ....214 D2
   Sherburn in Elmet LS25 .195 E3
West View Ave [25] LS29 .176 C1
West View [26] LS29 ...176 C1
West View Terr
   Egglescliffe TS16 ....5 D4
   [16] Knaresborough HG5 .221 A6
West Villa YO61 ....144 A4
West Way YO61 ....118 A3
West Wood La YO23 ...182 E4
Westacres [5] DL2 ....4 C4
Westbeck Gdns TS5 ......6 F8
Westborough [1] YO11 ..213 A5
Westbourne Ave
   Harrogate HG2 ....222 D8
   Whitby YO21 ....208 A6
Westbourne Cl YO21 ...208 A6
Westbourne Cres
   LS25 ....194 B3
Westbourne Gdns
   YO8 ....232 C4
Westbourne Gr
   [8] Pickering YO18 .....95 F7
   [1] Ripon HG4 ....214 C5
   [11] Scarborough YO11 ..213 A4
   Selby YO8 ....232 C4
   Whitby YO21 ....208 A6
Westbourne Pk YO12 ...212 E4
Westbourne Rd
   Scarborough YO11 ....212 F3
   Selby YO8 ....232 C4
   Whitby YO21 ....208 A6
Westbourne Terr
   Selby YO8 ....232 C4
   Thirsk YO7 ....211 A2
Westbury St TS17 ....6 B8
Westcroft La YO18 .....196 E1
Westdene HG2 ....222 B7
Westend La DN14 ......207 B6
Westerdale [4] YO18 ....95 F6
Westerdale Ct [2] YO30 .228 A6
Western Ave WF8 ......201 C1
Western Ct [6] WF8 ....201 C1
Western Gales Way [33]
WF6 ....200 B1
Western Prim Sch
YO24 ....227 C1
Western Rd BD23 ......217 B3
Western Terr YO12 .....212 F7
Western Way [4] YO18 ...95 E7
Westerns La HG3 ......139 C4
Westfield YO8 ....232 B4

Westfield Ave
   Castleford WF10 ......200 E2
   Castleford LS25 ......200 D7
   [3] Eggborough DN14 ..202 F2
   Rawcliffe DN14 ....205 A1
   [6] Scalby YO12 ....75 D5
   Selby YO8 ....232 B4
Westfield Cl
   [2] Eggborough DN14 ..202 F2
   [3] Haxby YO32 ....166 E5
   South Milford LS25 ...195 E2
Westfield Cres [12] LS24 .189 E6
Westfield Ct
   Copmanthorpe YO23 ...230 A2
   [1] South Milford LS25 .195 F2
Westfield Dr
   Hurworth-on-Tees DL2 ...3 E1
   York YO10 ....231 D8
Westfield Gn YO26 .....181 C7
Westfield Gr
   Allerton Bywater WF10 .200 D7
   [4] Eggborough DN14 ..202 F2
   [2] Haxby YO32 ....166 D5
Westfield La
   Exelby, Leeming & Newton
   DL8 ....63 C2
   Kippax LS25 ....194 C1
   Ledsham LS25 ....195 C1
   Lockton YO18 ....72 E4
   Normanby YO62 ....94 F4
   North Wf8 ....206 C2
   South Milford LS25 ...195 F2
   Thirsk YO7 ....211 A3
   Thoralby DL8 ....59 C6
   Thorganby YO19 ......193 A5
   Thornton-le-Dale YO18 ..96 C5
   Wigginton YO32 ......166 D5
Westfield Pl
   [10] Haxby YO32 ......166 E5
   York YO24 ....227 A1
Westfield Rd
   [1] Eggborough DN14 ..202 F2
   [20] Haxby YO32 ......166 E5
   [3] North Duffield YO8 .199 A7
   Rawcliffe DN14 ....205 A1
   Selby YO8 ....232 B4
   [2] Stokesley TS9 ......26 C7
   Tockwith YO26 ....181 C7
Westfield Sq [8] LS24 ..189 E6
Westfield Terr
   [2] Great Preston WF10 .200 D7
   Castleford LS25 ......189 E6
   [1] Thornton Dale YO18 .96 D5
Westfield Way YO17 ...215 F4
Westfields
   Castleford WF10 ......200 E3
   Richmond DL10 ....209 A7
   Scorton DL10 ....41 E6
Westfields Ct DL10 ....209 B7
Westfield YO17 ....215 E6
Westgarth
   Collingham LS22 ......180 A2
   Northallerton DL7 .....210 D4
Westgate
   [2] Barnoldswick BB18 .171 D1
   Egglescliffe TS15 ....5 D3
   Guisborough TS14 ....8 F6
   Malton YO17 ....215 E6
   Pickering YO18 ....95 F7
   Rillington YO17 ......122 F5
   Ripon HG4 ....214 C5
   Tadcaster LS24 ......189 E6
   Thirsk YO7 ....211 B2
Westgate Carr Rd
   YO18 ....95 D5
Westgate La
   Malton YO17 ....215 D6
Westgate Rd
   Thornton in Lonsdale
   LA6 ....103 C5
Westgate Rd DL3 ....3 B7
Westholme [10] TS5 ......6 F8
Westholme Bank DL8 ...58 F2
Westholme Cres [3] HG4 ..86 C3
Westholme Ct [3] HG4 ...86 C3
Westholme Rd [1] HG4 ...86 C3
Westland Cl [3] BD20 ...187 F7
Westlands
   Bilton-in-Ainsty with Bickerton
   YO26 ....181 D5
   [6] Kirklevington TS15 ..24 E8
   Pickering YO18 ....96 A7
   Stokesley TS9 ....26 C7
Westlands Ave [1] YO21 .208 C7
Westlands Gr YO31 .....228 F7
Westlands La YO7 ......211 A4
Westlands Rd DL3 ....3 B6
Westlands Way TS18 .....5 F8
Westlands Bsns Ctr
YO26 ....181 C6
Westminster Cl HG3 ...222 C3
Westminster Cres
   HG3 ....222 D2
Westminster Dr HG3 ...222 D3
Westminster Gate
   HG3 ....222 C3
Westminster Gr HG3 ...222 C3
Westminster Pl YO26 ..224 B1
Westminster Rd
   Pannal HG3 ....222 C3
   York YO30 ....228 A6
Westminster Rise
   HG3 ....222 D2
Westmoreland St
   Darlington DL3 ....3 C7
   [1] Harrogate HG1 .....219 E3

Westmoreland St *continued*
   [16] Skipton BD23 .....217 A3
Westmount Cl HG4 .....214 B6
Weston Cres [7] LS21 ..176 F1
Weston Dr LS21 ....176 E1
Weston La LS21 ....176 F1
Weston Moor Rd LS21 .176 E4
Weston Pk View LS21 ..176 E1
Weston Rd LS29 ....218 B4
Weston Ridge LS21 ....176 F1
Westover Rd YO12 .....212 F4
Westpit La YO32 ......167 A7
Westridge Cres [1] DL9 ..40 F5
Westside Cl YO17 .....215 B4
Westside Rd
   Bransdale YO62 ....48 B5
   Fadmoor YO62 ....69 E7
Westview Cl
   [3] Low Bradley BD20 ..173 E3
   York YO26 ....227 B7
Westville Ave LS29 ....218 A4
Westville Cl [6] LS29 ...218 A4
Westville House Prep Sch
LS29 ....218 B7
Westville Oval LS29 ...219 C6
Westville Rd LS29 .....218 A4
Westway Eastfield YO11 ..99 F7
   Harrogate HG2 ....222 B8
Westwood
   Carleton BD23 ....173 B4
   Scarborough YO11 ....212 F5
Westwood Cl [2] YO11 ..212 F4
Westwood Dr LS29 .....218 A2
Westwood Gdns [3]
YO11 ....212 F4
Westwood La
   Ampleforth YO62 ......92 A2
   West Tanfield HG4 .....86 E1
Westwood Mews
   Carleton BD23 ....173 B4
   [1] Dunnington YO19 ..184 F7
Westwood Rd
   Ripon HG4 ....214 A2
   Scarborough YO11 ....212 F4
Westwood Terr YO23 ...228 B1
Westwood Way LS23 ..188 E8
Wetherby Bsns Pk
LS22 ....180 B3
Wetherby Bsns Pk
LS22 ....180 C3
Wetherby High Sch
LS22 ....180 C3
Wetherby Leisure Ctr
LS22 ....180 C2
Wetherby Racecourse
LS22 ....180 E3
Wetherby Rd
   [8] Boroughbridge YO51 .141 B4
   Bramham cum Oglethorpe
   LS23 ....188 E6
   Harrogate HG2 ....220 B1
   Kirk Deighton LS22 ...180 B3
   Knaresborough HG5 ...221 D4
   Sicklinghall LS22 .....179 E3
   Tadcaster LS24 ......189 D6
   Walton LS23 ....180 B2
   York YO26 ....227 B3
Wethercote La YO7 .....67 C1
Wetlands La DL11 ......18 G7
Weydale Ave YO12 .....212 E8
Weymouth Ave TS8 ......7 A4
Weymouth Rd [1] HG1 ..219 E4
Whaddon Chase TS14 ...8 E6
Whaites La YO7 ....211 A4
Whales La DN14 ....202 E3
Wham La BD24 ....130 F1
Wharf Dr YO24 ....230 D8
Wharf Gr [8] LS22 .....180 B3
Wharfe Dr
   Grassington BD23 .....134 D3
   Kearby with Netherby
   LS22 ....179 B1
Wharfe La LS29 ....175 A4
Wharfe View
   Grassington BD23 .....134 D3
   Kirkby Overblow HG3 ..179 A6
West View Rd LS29 ....218 B4
Wharfedale Ave YO24 ..227 A1
Wharfedale Cl [2] BD23 .217 B4
Wharfedale Cres
   Harrogate HG2 ....222 B7
   Tadcaster LS24 ......189 E6
Wharfedale Dr
   Ilkley LS29 ....218 C4
   Normanton WF6 ......200 A3
Wharfedale General Hospl
LS29 ....176 F1
Wharfedale Pl HG2 ....222 C7
Wharfedale View [5]
LS29 ....174 F4
Wharfeside Ave LS29 ..218 C5
Wharfeside La LS29 ...218 C5
Wharncliffe Pl [14] YO10 .231 A3
Wharncliffe Dr YO30 ..224 F2
Wharram Quarry Nature
Reserve YO17 ....148 F4
Wharton Ave YO30 ....228 B2
Wharton Rd WF11 .....168 D2
Whartons Prim Sch The
LS21 ....177 A1
Whartons The LS21 ....177 A1
Whashton Rd DL11 ....208 C8
   Richmond DL10 ....209 C3
Wheatcroft [6] YO32 ...167 A6
Wheatcroft Ave YO11 ..213 B1

Wheatcroft Com Prim Sch
YO11 ....213 B1
Wheatdale Rd LS24 ....190 B2
Wheatear La TS17 ....6 A5
Wheatfield La YO32 ....225 C8
Wheatlands
   Great Ayton TS9 ......8 A2
   Ilkley LS29 ....218 C4
Wheatlands Ave [8]
BD20 ....187 E8
Wheatlands Dr [4] TS13 ..11 A8
Wheatlands Gr
   Harrogate HG2 ....222 E8
   York YO26 ....227 C6
Wheatlands La
   [7] Glusburn BD20 ....187 E8
   Roecliffe YO51 ....140 E4
Wheatlands Rd HG2 ...222 E7
Wheatlands Rd E HG2 ..222 E8
Wheatlands Way HG2 ..222 E7
Wheatley Ave
   Ilkley LS29 ....218 A5
   Normanton South WF6 .200 A1
Wheatley Dr YO32 .....225 C8
Wheatley Gdns [2] LS29 .218 A5
Wheatley La [3] LS29 ..218 A5
Wheatley Rd LS29 .....218 A5
Wheatley Rise LS29 ...218 A5
Wheeldale Cres TS17 ...6 B7
Wheeldale Ct [1] YO32 ..225 C8
Wheeldale Cl [8] TS14 ...8 F7
Wheelgate YO17 ......215 C4
Wheelgate Sq [7] YO17 .215 C4
Wheelhouse Sq YO12 ..212 F6
Wheelhouse The [4]
YO30 ....224 B5
Wheels La YO8 ....204 F3
Wheelwright Cl
Copmanthorpe YO23 ...230 B2
   Sutton upon Derwent
   YO41 ....185 C1
Wheelwrights Courts
BD23 ....154 B3
Wheldale La WF10 ....201 B5
Wheldon Rd WF10 ....201 A5
Wheldrake CE Prim Sch
YO19 ....193 A8
Wheldrake Ings Nature
Reserve YO19 ....193 C7
Wheldrake La
   Deighton YO19 ......184 B1
   Escrick YO19 ....192 B5
Whenby Gr YO31 .....225 F1
Whenby La YO60 .....145 C6
Whernside TS7 ....7 C5
Whernside Ave YO31 ..229 A5
Whessoe Rd DL3 ....3 C8
Whin Bank YO12 ......212 D5
Whin Cl
   [3] Strensall YO32 ....167 B6
   York YO24 ....230 F7
Whin Garth YO24 .....230 F6
Whin Gn YO22 ....32 A6
Whin Hill YO17 ....147 E1
Whin La
   South Milford LS25 ...195 D2
   Warlaby DL7 ....64 C5
Whin Rd YO24 ....230 F6
Whinbeck Ave WF6 ....200 B1
Whinbush Way DL1 ......3 F8
Whinchat Tail TS14 .....8 D6
Whincup Ave HG5 .....221 B6
Whincup Cl [6] HG5 ...221 B6
Whincup Gr [7] HG5 ...221 B6
Whinfield [34] LS29 ...175 C2
Whinfield Ave BD23 ...216 F3
Whinfield Rd DL1 ....3 E7
Whinfield Rd Jun & Inf Sch
DL1 ....3 F7
Whinfields The [1] HG3 .138 A1
Whingroves TS17 ......16 C8
Whinmoor Hill YO7 .....66 C2
Whinney Ave HG3 .....222 B8
Whinney Mire La LA2 ..103 E1
Whinny Bank YO61 ....117 C8
Whinny Gill Rd BD23 ..217 B3
Whinny Hagg La YO8 ..197 A2
Whinny Hill DL9 ....40 E3
Whinny La YO60 ......168 A7
Whinnythwaite La
   YO26 ....181 C8
Whins La
   Spofforth with Stockeld
   HG3 ....179 E4
   Thorp Arch LS23 .....180 F1
Whins The YO12 ......212 A7
Whinstone View [18] TS9 .8 A5
Whinwath La DL8 ......87 F4
Whipley Bank HG3 ....161 A8
Whipley La HG3 ......161 B8
Whip-ma-whop-ma-gate
YO1 ....233 C2
Whipperdale Bank
   Leyburn DL8 ....60 A8
   Redmire DL8 ....38 F1
Whistler Cl YO23 .....230 C3
Whistler Dr WF10 .....200 F4
Whiston Dr [18] YO14 ..101 B3
Whitby Ave
   Guisborough TS14 .....8 F6
   York YO31 ....229 A4

Whitby Benedictine Abbey
(rems of)* YO22 ....208 E7
Whitby Bsns Pk YO22 ....32 F8
Whitby Com Coll
YO21 ....208 C5
Whitby Dr YO21 ....229 A7
Whitby Gate YO18 ......96 D6
Whitby Hospl YO21 ....208 D6
Whitby Jet Heritage Ctr*
YO22 ....208 A7
Whitby Leisure Ctr
YO21 ....208 C7
Whitby Mus & Art Gall*
YO21 ....208 C6
Whitby Pavilion & Theatre
YO21 ....208 C8
Whitby Rd
Guisborough TS14 ......9 A7
Pickering YO18 ....96 B8
Staithes TS13 ....13 K2
Whitby Sta YO21 ......208 D6
Whitby Way DL3 ....3 A7
Whitcliffe Ave HG4 ..214 B4
Whitcliffe Cres HG4 ..214 B3
Whitcliffe Dr HG4 ....214 B3
Whitcliffe Dr HG4 ....214 B3
Whitcliffe Grange
DL10 ....209 A7
Whitcliffe La
Littlethorpe HG4 ......139 D8
Ripon HG4 ....214 A2
Whitcliffe Pl DL10 ..209 A7
Whitcliffe Terr DL10 ..209 A7
White Bridge Rd YO21 ..208 B8
White Canons Ct 4
DL10 ....209 E8
White Canons Wlk 3
DL10 ....209 E8
White Cross Rd YO31 ..228 D7
White Cross Way
YO41 ....169 A2
White Friars Cl DL10 ..209 E8
White Friars Gdns 6
DL10 ....209 E8
White Friars Wlk 5
DL10 ....209 E8
White Gate
Heslerton YO17 ......123 E6
Sherburn WF17 ......124 C6
White Gate Hill YO21 ..100 B2
White Hart Cres 4 DL1 ..3 F6
White Hill La BD20 ..172 E1
White Hills Croft
BD23 ....216 E6
White Hills La BD23 ..216 E6
White Horse Cl YO32 ..225 F5
White Horse Fold
WF10 ....200 F7
White Horse La YO12 ..99 D6
White Horse Mews 3
HG3 ....179 C5
White Horse of Kilburn*
YO61 ....91 B4
White House Croft TS21 ..5 A7
White House Dale
YO24 ....227 F1
White House Dr YO24 ..227 F1
White House Gdns 4
YO24 ....228 A2
White House Gr 1
YO41 ....185 B2
White House Rise
YO24 ....227 F1
White House Wynd
DL6 ....24 D2
White La BD22 ....187 F1
White Lands DL10 ....209 E7
White Lee Ave BB7 ....186 B1
White Ley Rd DN6 ....206 C1
White Leys Cl BB18 ..171 F1
White Leys Rd YO21 ..208 A7
White Lilac Cl DL10 ..209 E7
White Lodge YO8 ....232 B4
White Pastures DL10 ..209 E7
White Point Ave 1
YO21 ....208 B7
White Point Rd YO21 ..208 B8
White Point Rd YO21 ..208 B8
White Rose Ave 3
YO32 ....225 D3
White Rose Candles*
HG4 ....60 C5
White Rose Cl
Huby YO61 ....144 A5
8 Linton-on-Ouse YO30 ..164 F7
Nether Poppleton YO26 ..224 C1
White Rose Cres DL10 ..209 E7
White Rose Gr YO32 ..225 D3
White Rose Way
Nether Poppleton YO26 ..227 C8
Thirsk YO7 ....211 C4
White Scar Cave*
LA6 ....104 A4
White Sprunt Hill
YO17 ....125 A1
White Wall La HG3 ..232 B6
White Wall La HG3 ..160 D4
White Way YO13 ......94 F1
White Way Heads YO18 ..51 F4
Whitebridge Dr DL1 ....3 D6
Whitecarr La YO62 ....95 A5
Whitecliffe Cres LS26 ..194 A1
Whitecliffe Dr LS26 ..194 A1
Whitecliffe Rise LS26 ..194 A1
Whitecote La LS25 ....195 D2

Whitecross Gdns
YO31 ....228 D7
Whitecross Hill DL8 ..87 F3
Whitefield Bglws
DN14 ....206 F8
Whitefield La DN14 ..202 E1
Whitefields Dr DL10 ..209 E7
Whitefields Gate 1
DL10 ....209 E8
Whitefields Wlk 2
DL10 ....209 E8
Whitefriars Ct 9 BD24 ..131 D2
Whitegate Cl 7 TS13 ..13 K2
Whitegate La HG4 ....114 F1
Whitehall Landing
YO22 ....208 D5
Whitehead Hill 1 YO11 ..213 B6
Whitehill Rd BD22 ....187 E3
Whitehouse Ave LS26 ..200 B8
Whitehouse Cres
LS26 ....200 B8
Whitehouse Dr LS26 ..200 B8
Whitehouse La
Great & Little Preston
LS26 ....200 B8
Swillington LS26 ......194 B2
Whitelass Cl YO7 ....211 B4
Whitemoor La YO8 ....198 C6
Whiteoak Ave YO61 ..143 C8
Whitepits La LA2 ....129 A5
Whiterose Dr YO41 ..168 D2
Whiterow Rd DL8 ......82 F7
Whitestone Ct YO7 ..211 D3
Whitestone Dr YO31 ..225 E2
Whitestone Gr YO31 ..225 E2
Whitewall YO17 ......215 D1
Whitewall Cnr Hill
YO17 ....147 E8
Whiteway Head HG5 ..221 A4
Whitewood Ctr WF10 ..200 D3
Whitfield Ave YO18 ....96 A6
Whitkirk Pl YO12 ....101 A4
Whitley & Eggborough CP
Sch DN14 ....202 F1
Whitley Bridge Sta
DN14 ....202 F1
Whitley Cl YO30 ......225 A1
Whitley Pl WF10 ......200 E6
Whitley Rd
Elvington YO41 ......185 A3
Norton-le-Clay YO7 ..115 B1
Thornaby TS17 ....6 B6
Whitley Thorpe La
DN14 ....202 F1
Whitsundale Cl 4 HG5 ..221 D5
Whittle St 6 YO7 ......89 B1
Whitton Croft Rd 9
LS29 ....218 B4
Whitton Pl YO10 ......229 C4
Whitwell Dr HG4 ....114 B8
Whitwell Rd YO60 ..146 E5
Whitwood Comm La
WF10 ....200 C3
Whitwood La WF10 ..200 C3
Whixley Field La YO26 ..164 B4
Whixley La YO26 ....163 E2
Whorlton Castle (rems of)*
DL6 ....25 D1
Whorlton La DL6 ......45 E8
Whyett Bank YO21 ....28 F6
Wickets The
8 Hutton Rudby TS15 ..25 C5
Middlesbrough TS7 ....7 B6
Widdale Rd HG5 ......221 D5
Widdowfield St DL3 ....3 C6
Wide Howe La YO7 ..114 E8
Wide La YO10 ....127 E5
Widgeon Cl 4 YO14 ..101 A4
Wigginton Prim Sch
YO32 ....166 D5
Wigginton Rd YO31 ..233 B4
Wigginton Terr YO31 ..228 C8
Wighill Garth LS24 ..189 E6
Wighill La LS24 ......181 F3
Wighill La LS24 ......189 E8
Wilberforce Ave YO30 ..228 B7
Wilberfoss CE VC Prim Sch
YO41 ....185 E6
Wilcock La BD20 ....173 F2
Wild Rd DL1 ....4 A4
Wildair Cl 2 DL3 ......3 A7
Wilfreds Gr 6 YO8 ..198 B4
Wilfreds Rd 5 YO8 ..198 B4
Wilken Cres TS14 ......8 F7
Wilkinson Ct HG4 ....214 B6
Wilkinson St TS12 ......9 E7
Wilkinson Way
6 Otley LS21 ....176 F1
3 Strensall YO32 ....167 A7
Wilkinsons Ct 22 YO61 ..143 C8
Willance Gr DL10 ....209 A7
Willans Gr YO26 ......227 E4
Willaston Cres HG2 ..220 A4
Willaston Rd 1 HG1 ..220 A3
Willerby Carr La YO12 ..99 C3
Willgutter La BD22 ..187 F1
William Crosthwaite
TS17 ....6 B4
William Jacques Dr
YO8 ....198 E2
William Plows Ave
YO10 ....228 E2
William Rd YO8 ......198 B4
William St 18 BD20 ..172 A1
William's Hill Ring & Bailey*
DL8 ....60 E2

Williamson Cl 14 HG4 ..214 C5
Williamson Dr 11 HG4 ..214 C5
Williamson Gdns HG4 ..214 A4
Willins Cl 10 TS15 ....25 C5
Willis St YO10 ....228 E3
Willitoft Rd YO8 ....199 F6
Willoughby Way YO24 ..230 B8
Willow Ave
Catterick Garrison DL9 ..209 B1
Clifford LS23 ....188 E7
Willow Bank
14 Brayton YO8 ......197 D1
York YO32 ....225 E4
Willow Bank Dr 1 WF8 ..201 C1
Willow Beck Rd DL6 ..210 D6
Willow Bridge La YO7 ..115 F8
Willow Brook Cl YO17 ..215 F4
Willow Chase The TS21 ..4 F7
Willow Cl
20 Burley in Warfedale
LS29 ....176 C1
2 Filey YO14 ....101 B4
Willow Cres
Clifford LS23 ....188 E7
Richmond DL10 ......209 D8
Willow Ct Kexby YO41 ..168 C2
2 North Featherstone
WF7 ....200 E1
18 Pickering YO18 ....95 F6
Willow Dr 8 Bedale DL8 ..63 B3
Eston & South Bank TS6 ..7 E8
1 North Duffield YO8 ..199 A7
Willow Garth
Ferrensby HG5 ......162 F7
Scalby YO12 ....212 A7
16 Thornton Dale YO18 ..96 D5
Willow Garth Ave
BD20 ....187 E8
Willow Garth La DN6 ..207 A1
Willow Glade
5 Boston Spa LS23 ..188 E7
York YO32 ....225 E4
Willow Gr
4 Boston Spa LS23 ..188 E7
Earswick YO32 ......226 A7
Harrogate HG1 ......219 E5
York YO31 ....228 F7
Willow La
Boston Spa LS23 ......188 E7
North Featherstone
WF7 ....200 E1
Willow La E 4 WF7 ..200 E1
Willow Pk Rd YO41 ..185 F5
Willow Rd
8 Campsall DN6 ....206 F1
Darlington DL3 ......3 B6
10 Knottingley WF11 ..202 A3
Tadcaster LS24 ......210 D2
Willow Rise
Kirkbymoorside YO62 ..70 B1
Tadcaster LS24 ......189 D5
Thorpe Willoughby YO8 ..197 B1
Willow Tree Gdns 9
LS29 ....176 C1
Willow View
1 Catterick DL10 ......41 D5
Cliffe YO8 ....198 E3
Willow Way 8 BD20 ..187 E6
Willow Wlk 1 HG4 ..214 B2
Willowbank TS8 ....7 A5
Willowbridge Cl 8
WF10 ....200 D3
Willowbridge La
WF10 ....200 D3
Willowbridge Rd WF8 ..206 C2
Willowbridge Way
WF10 ....200 D3
Willowdene La WF8 ..201 E2
Willowgarth LS9 ....225 C1
Willowgate 24 YO18 ..95 F7
Willows Ave TS8 ......6 C4
Willows The
1 Hambleton YO8 ....196 E1
Middlesbrough TS7 ....7 C6
8 Strensall YO32 ....167 B7
Willy Howe* YO25 ..126 C3
Wilmath Cl YO13 ....75 D7
Wilmot Rd LS29 ....218 C4
Wilson St
Castleford WF10 ....200 E4
Guisborough TS14 ....8 E6
Lockwood TS12 ......9 F7
18 Pontefract WF8 ..201 B1
Wilson's La 5 YO13 ..54 F4
Wilstrope Gr 1 YO10 ..231 F8
Wilstrop Farm Rd
YO23 ....230 A2
Wilton Carr La YO18 ..97 A4
Wilton Ings La YO18 ..97 A4
Wilton La TS14 ......8 F7
Wilton Rd LS29 ......218 A3
Wilton Rise YO24 ....227 F3
Wimbledon Cl 2 DL1 ..3 F6
Wimpole Cl 6 YO30 ..225 A1
Winchester Ave 3
YO26 ....227 E4
Winchester Gr 1 YO26 ..227 E4
Winchester Way DL1 ..3 F6
Windermere YO24 ....230 D7
Windermere Dr WF11 ..201 F1
Windgate Hill La YO8 ..197 B6
Windle La BD20 ......173 D1
Windleston Dr TS3 ....7 B8
Windmill Gdns YO8 ..232 B7
Windmill La LS24 ....189 D5
Windmill La
Norton DN6 ....206 D1

Windmill La continued
York YO10 ....229 B2
Windmill Mdw 16 DN6 ..206 F1
Windmill Mdws WF10 ..185 E6
Windmill Rd LS23 ....188 F6
Windmill Rise
Aberford LS25 ......194 F7
Tadcaster LS24 ......189 D5
York YO26 ....227 E3
Windrose Cl 8 WF6 ..200 A2
Windross Sq 11 YO61 ..143 C8
Windsor Ave
Richmond DL10 ......209 D8
Skipton BD23 ....217 A4
Windsor Cl 17 WF6 ..200 B1
Windsor Cres
Middlesbrough TS7 ....7 D6
7 Whitby YO21 ....208 D6
Windsor Dr
2 Haxby YO32 ......166 D5
Lockwood TS12 ......9 F7
Windsor Garth YO24 ..227 D1
Windsor Gr HG2 ....220 A1
Windsor Mews HG2 ..221 B5
Windsor Pl BB18 ....171 E2
Windsor Rd
24 Catterick Garrison DL9 ..40 E4
4 Harrogate HG2 ....220 A1
Ripon HG4 ....214 C3
Middlesbrough TS7 ....7 B7
Windsor St 1 YO23 ..228 B1
Windsor Terr YO21 ..208 D6
Windy Hill LA2 ......129 B8
Winewall La BD8 ....186 A3
Winewall Rd 11 BB8 ..186 A3
Winksley Banks Rd
HG4 ....112 E2
Winksley Gr HG3 ....219 A4
Winn La YO7 ....115 C6
Winnow La LS23 ....188 D8
Winscar Gr 9 YO30 ..224 E3
Winston Ave BD20 ..187 F8
Winston Ct
Northallerton DL6 ..210 E6
Norton YO17 ....215 E3
Winterburn La BD23 ..155 D5
Winterscale Ct TS10 ..128 D2
Winterscale St YO10 ..228 D1
Winthrop Cl YO17 ..215 C5
Winton Rd DL6 ......210 E6
Wise House La YO17 ..215 F7
Wisker La YO32 ....226 C7
Wistow Gn 3 YO32 ..134 E3
Wistow Parochial CE VC Prim
Sch YO8 ....197 D6
Wistow Rd YO8 ......232 A8
Wistowgate YO8 ....197 B8
Witch La YO25 ......127 B2
Witham Dr 4 YO62 ..226 A4
Witton Cres DL3 ......3 A5
Witton Steeps DL8 ..59 E2
Wizards Workshop*
YO7 ....208 C8
Wobeck La HG4 ......114 B7
Woburn Cl YO30 ....167 B8
Woburn Way WF6 ..200 A1
Wold La YO10 ....99 D1
Wold Newton Foundation
LS25 ....126 A4
Wold Newton Rd
YO25 ....126 E3
Wold Rd YO17 ......149 E8
Wold St YO17 ......215 D3
Wold View YO14 ....100 F2
Wold View Gr 5 YO12 ..99 E6
Woldcroft YO17 ......215 C2
Wolds Way Lavender*
YO25 ....123 B5
Woldview Rd YO41 ..185 E5
Wolfe Ave YO31 ....228 F5
Wolsey Ave YO8 ....197 B8
Wolsey Croft LS25 ..195 F4
Wolsey Dr YO23 ....231 A3
Wolsey Gdns 12 LS25 ..195 F4
Wolsingham Dr TS5 ....6 D7
Wolsley St YO10 ....228 D1
Wolviston Ave YO10 ..229 C3
Womersley CE VC Jun & Inf
Sch DN6 ....206 C6
Womersley Pk Gdns
DN6 ....206 D5
Womersley Rd WF11 ..202 A2
Wood Acre Cl BD23 ..134 C3
Wood Aven Cl 38 HG3 ..161 B3
Wood Cl
Bradleys Both BD20 ..173 D3
Skipton BD23 ....216 E5
4 Strensall YO32 ....167 A7
Wood End Dir
YO8 ....197 B1
Wood End La DL8 ....59 D5
Wood Gate YO13 ......74 A1
Wood Hill Cl YO51 ..141 D1
Wood La
Acaster Selby YO23 ..191 B2
Austwick LA2 ......131 A8
Birkin WF11 ....202 D6
Gainford DL2 ....4 A1
10 Grassington BD23 ..134 E2
Great Preston LS26 ..200 C7
Low Coniscliffe & Merrybent
DL2 ....2 E4

Wood La continued
Spennithorne DL8 ....61 A3
Thorp Arch LS23 ....180 F2
9 Thorpe Willoughby
YO8 ....197 B1
Threshfield BD23 ....134 B3
Whitwood WF10 ......200 C3
Wood Lea 1 WF11 ..201 E4
Wood Rd HG2 ....220 B1
Wood Row LS26 ......200 A6
Wood St
Castleford WF10 ....200 E4
Norton YO17 ....215 D3
York YO31 ....228 E6
Wood View
Airton LS14 ....205 E3
Embsay BD23 ....217 C7
Harrogate HG1 ......219 C3
Wood View Ave WF10 ..200 D4
Wood Way YO32 ....226 A4
Woodall Ave YO12 ..212 F7
Woodall Ct 9 YO8 ..197 D6
Wood's Cl YO13 ......75 C8
Wood's Gr YO13 ......75 C8
Woodbine Cl 12 TS9 ....8 A2
Woodbine Terr 6 HG1 ..219 C3
Woodbridge Ave LS25 ..194 E5
Woodburn Dr 3 DL8 ..60 D5
Woodcock Dr
Eston & South Bank TS6 ..7 F8
9 Haxby YO32 ......166 F5
Woodcock Dr 8 DL9 ..40 F2
Woodcrest Rd DL3 ....3 B4
Wooden Hill La DL7 ..210 B2
Woodend Ave WF10 ..200 C7
Woodend Cres WF10 ..200 C7
Woodfield Ave HG1 ..219 E4
Woodfield Cl HG1 ..219 E4
Woodfield Com Prim Sch
HG1 ....219 F5
Woodfield Dr
Harrogate HG1 ......219 F6
6 Low Bradley BD20 ..173 E3
Woodfield Gdns 5 HG1 ..219 E4
Woodfield Gr HG1 ..219 E4
Woodfield Pl 6 HG1 ..219 E4
Woodfield Rd HG1 ..219 F7
Woodfield Sq 1 HG1 ..219 E4
Woodfield View HG1 ..219 E4
Woodfield Wlk HG1 ..219 E4
Woodford Pl 1 YO24 ..227 D1
Woodgate YO12 ......212 D5
Woodgate La LS17 ..178 B2
Woodhall Dr HG1 ..219 F6
Woodhall Gr
Harrogate HG1 ......219 F6
Mickletown LS26 ....200 B6
3 Stockton-on-Tees TS18 ..5 D8
Woodhall La
Hemingbrough YO8 ..199 B3
Kexby YO41 ....206 D6
Woodhead Fld La
YO62 ....70 A4
Woodhill View WF8 ..201 B1
Woodhouse Gr 4 YO31 ..229 A5
Woodhouse Rd BD23 ..157 B7
Woodhouse Rd
8 Guisborough TS14 ..8 E6
Thornaby YO19 ....193 A3
Woodland Ave YO12 ..212 D6
Woodland Chase
YO30 ....225 B1
Woodland Cl YO12 ..212 D6
Woodland Cres LS26 ..194 A1
Woodland Dr DL7 ....63 F3
Woodland Gr YO12 ..212 C6
Woodland Pl
New Earswick YO32 ..225 E4
Scarborough YO12 ..212 C6
Woodland Ravine
YO12 ....212 D6
Woodland Rd 3 DL3 ..3 B6
Woodland Rise YO12 ..212 D6
Woodland St 3 BD22 ..187 B6
Woodland Terr DL3 ....3 B5
Woodland View YO7 ..89 A1
Woodland Way
4 Airmyn DN14 ....205 E4
Longnewton TS21 ....4 F7
York YO32 ....225 F4
Woodlands
Escrick YO19 ......192 B5
Ilkley LS29 ....218 D4
Woodlands Ave
Harrogate HG2 ......220 B1
Norton YO17 ....215 E3
Rillington YO17 ....122 F5
Tadcaster LS24 ....189 D5
Woodlands Cl
4 Barlby with Osgodby
YO8 ....198 B4
Goldsborough HG5 ..163 A3
Harrogate HG2 ......220 C2
18 Ilkley LS29 ......175 C2
Sherburn in Elmet LS25 ..195 F2
Woodlands Com Jun Sch
HG2 ....220 B2
Woodlands Cres HG2 ..220 C2
Woodlands Croft
LS25 ....200 D8
Woodlands Ct
18 Barlby with Osgodby
YO8 ....198 B4
3 Harrogate HG2 ....220 B1
Woodlands Dr
14 Barlby with Osgodby
YO8 ....198 B4

Woodlands Dr *continued*
Egglescliffe TS15 ....5 E3
Garforth LS25 ....194 D3
Harrogate HG2 ....220 C1
Middlesbrough TS6 ....7 F8
Scarborough YO12 ....212 B5
Skipton BD23 ....216 E5
Woodlands Gdns 8 HG2 ....4 C5
Woodlands Gn 8 HG2 ....220 B1
Woodlands Gr
Harrogate HG2 ....220 C2
8 Ilkley LS29 ....175 C2
Kippax LS25 ....200 E8
Rillington YO17 ....122 F5
York YO31 ....229 A7
Woodlands La LS25 ....202 B7
Woodlands Rd
Harrogate HG2 ....220 C2
Rillington YO17 ....122 F5
Woodlands Rise
1 Harrogate HG2 ....220 C2
14 Ilkley LS29 ....175 C2
Norton DN6 ....206 E1
Woodlands Sch The
YO12 ....212 B5
Woodlands The TS7 ....7 D5
Woodlands View
11 Barlby with Osgodby
YO8 ....198 B4
Kippax LS25 ....200 E8
3 Tadcaster LS24 ....189 D5
2 Thornton Dale YO18 ....96 D5
Woodlands Way
Hurworth DL2 ....3 D1
7 Hurworth-on-Tees DL2 ..22 D8
Woodlands Wlk
Harrogate HG2 ....220 C2
Scarborough YO12 ....212 D6
Skipton BD23 ....216 E5
Stokesley TS9 ....26 C8
Woodlea Ave YO26 ....227 C4
Woodlea Bank YO26 ....227 D4
Woodlea Cres YO26 ....227 D4
Woodlea Gr YO26 ....227 D5
Woodleigh Ave LS25 ....194 C4
Woodleigh Cl 2 YO32 ..167 A6
Woodleigh Sch YO17 ....148 A6
Woodley Gr TS7 ....7 D7
Woodman La LA6 ....102 B6
Woodman Terr BD23 ..216 F4
Woodmanwray La
HG3 ....159 C8
Woodpark Ave HG5 ....221 A7
Woodpark Dr HG5 ....221 A7
Woodpecker Rd 12
LS29 ....176 C1
Woodrow Ave TS7 ....7 B6
Woodrow Cres LS26 ....200 A6
Woodroyd Gdns LS29 ..218 F3
Woodruff Cl 27 HG3 ....161 B3
Woodrush TS8 ....7 B4
Woods Ct HG2 ....222 C6
Woods La YO26 ....142 B2
Woods Pl LS29 ....218 C4
Woodside
Castleford WF10 ....201 B4
Harrogate HG1 ....219 E2
Hutton Rudby TS15 ....25 C6
5 Leyburn DL8 ....60 D5
Woodside Ave YO31 ....229 A6
Woodside Cl 3 YO61 ..117 D1
Woodside Gr
Allerton Bywater WF10 ..200 C7
3 Stockton-on-Tees TS18 ..5 E8
Woodside La BD20 ....173 C2

Woodside Rd
Ganton YO12 ....125 A8
Silsden BD20 ....174 B1
Woodside St WF10 ....200 C7
Woodsmill Quay YO1 ..233 B2
Woodstock Cl DL6 ....210 B6
Woodstock Way YO7 ..211 D3
Woodthorpe Prim Sch
YO24 ....230 C7
Woodvale TS8 ....7 B5
Woodvale Rd DL3 ....3 B4
Woodview Cl DN14 ....207 A7
Woodville Ave
Middlesbrough TS4 ....6 F8
3 Stalby YO12 ....212 D8
Woodville Terr YO8 ....232 E3
Woolcotts Cl 1 TS17 ....6 A3
Wooldale Dr YO14 ....101 B4
Wooler St YO12 ....212 E5
Woolmoor Cl YO7 ....211 D4
Woolnough Ave YO10 ..229 B3
Woolpots La YO61 ....117 B4
Woolsington Dr DL2 ....4 C4
Worcester Dr YO31 ....229 B5
Wordsworth App 2
WF8 ....201 B1
Wordsworth Ave 4
DN6 ....206 E1
Wordsworth Cl YO13 ..75 C5
Wordsworth Cres
Harrogate HG2 ....222 C8
York YO24 ....230 D7
Wordsworth Dr WF11 ..201 D3
Workhouse Mus of Poor
Law* HG4 ....214 C6
Worsall Rd TS15 ....5 D2
Worsall Toll Bar TS15 ..24 B7
Worsendale Rd YO42 ..169 F2
Worsley Cl TS16 ....5 E7
Worsley Cres TS7 ....7 B5
Worsley Ct YO17 ......215 A3
Woundales La
Knayton with Brawith YO7 ..65 F4
Upsall YO7 ....66 A2
Wrangham Dr 1 YO14 ..127 A8
Wray with Botton Endowed
Sch LA2 ....128 A6
Wray's Ave YO31 ......225 E1
Wrea Head Cl 2 YO13 ..75 D5
Wrea La 1 YO12 ......212 F6
Wreaks La HG4 ....111 E6
Wreaks Rd
Birstwith HG3 ....160 E6
Harrogate HG1 ....220 B3
Wrelton Cliff Rd YO18 ..95 B8
Wrelton Hall Gdns
YO18 ....71 C1
Wren Croft 5 WF8 ....201 B2
Wren Hall La YO8 ....204 E6
Wren La 2 YO8 ....232 D5
Wrenbeck Cl 1 LS21 ..177 A1
Wrenbeck Cl 2 LS21 ..177 A1
Wrenbeck Dr LS21 ....177 A1
Wressle Sta YO8 ......199 D2
Wrexham Rd LS29 ....176 B1
Wreyfield Dr YO12 ....212 C7
Wright St 30 BD20 ....187 E7
Wrights La WF11 ....206 B8
Wycar 1 DL8 ....63 A2
Wycliffe Ave
Northallerton DL7 ....210 C2
York YO10 ....229 B3
Wycliffe Rd DL7 ....22 E1
Wycoller Ctry Pk*
BB8 ....186 D2

Wydale La YO13 ....98 B6
Wydale Rd YO10 ......229 D4
Wydale Rise YO13 ......98 A5
Wydra La HG3 ....159 F1
Wykeham Abbey*
YO13 ....98 E5
Wykeham Ave TS14 ....8 E5
Wykeham Carr Rd
YO13 ....98 E3
Wykeham CE VC Prim Sch
YO13 ....98 E6
Wykeham Dale YO13 ....93 B8
Wykeham La YO13 ......98 E7
Wykeham Rd YO17 ....122 A5
Wykeham St YO12 ....212 E5
Wykeham Way TS8 ......7 A6
Wylam Ave DL1 ....3 D7
Wynam La YO41 ......185 C1
Wynbrook Ct YO13 ......75 C5
Wynd Cl 2 TS15 ....25 C5
Wynd The 3 Bedale DL8 ..63 A3
Hawes DL8 ....56 D4
Hutton Rudby TS15 ......25 D5
Skeeby DL10 ....20 F1
Wytherstone Gdn*
YO62 ....69 B1
Wyvil Cres LS29 ......218 E4
Wyvil Rd LS29 ....218 E5
Wyville Gr DL8 ....61 E7

X

Xscape* WF10 ....200 F2

Y

Yafforth Rd DL7 ......210 B6
Yall Flat La YO21 ......29 B6
Yan Brow YO62 ....70 C3
Yarborough Cl DL10 ....41 B2
Yarburgh Cl 4 DN14 ..204 B1
Yarburgh Gr 2 YO26 ..227 E5
Yarburgh Way YO10 ..229 C3
Yarde Ave DL10 ....41 E4
Yarker Bank La DL8 ....60 C6
Yarlside La BD23 ......171 B4
Yarm Back La TS18 ......5 D8
Yarm La TS9 ....7 D1
Yarm Prim Sch TS15 ......5 E2
Yarm Rd Darlington DL1 ..3 E5
Egglescliffe TS16 ....5 E5
Hilton TS15 ....6 C2
Middleton St George DL2 ..4 C4
Yarm Rd Ind Est DL1 ......3 F5
Yarm Sta TS15 ....5 E2
Yarrow Dr HG3 ....161 B3
Yatts Rd YO18 ....96 A8
Yaud Sike La YO18 ......95 E5
Yeadon Wlk 12 DL2 ......4 C4
Yealand Ave BD24 ....131 D3
Yearby Cl TS5 ....6 D7
Yearsley Cres YO31 ..228 D7
Yearsley Gr YO31 ....225 E1
Yearsley Gr From Prim Sch
YO32 ....225 F1
Yearsley Moor Bank
YO62 ....118 B7
Yearsley Swimming Pool
YO31 ....228 D8
Yederick Rd YO13 ......98 B8
Yedingham Priory (site of)*
YO17 ....97 D2

Yedmandale Rd
2 East Ayton/West Ayton
YO13 ....99 A7
Hutton Buscel YO13 ......98 F7
Yeomans Mount 11 HG3 ..137 B4
Yew Tree Cl
Acaster Malbis YO23 ....191 C8
Harrogate HG2 ....222 C4
18 Low Bradley BD20 ..173 E3
Rufforth YO23 ....182 C6
Selby YO8 ....232 C6
18 Sleights YO22 ....32 A6
Yew Tree Gdns HG2 ..222 B5
Yew Tree La HG2 ......222 C5
Yew Tree Mews YO19 ..229 C5
Yew Tree Pk DN14 ....207 A7
Yew Tree Wlk HG2 ....222 B6
Yew Wlk The TS21 ......4 F7
Yewbank Cl 3 LS29 ..218 A4
Yewbank Terr LS29 ..218 A4
Yewcroft LS29 ....218 A4
Yewdale Rd HG2 ......220 A1
Yiewsley Dr DL3 ....3 A5
YMCA Leisure Ctr
YO11 ....213 A6
YMCA Theatre & L Ctr*
YO11 ....213 A7
Yoadwath Bank YO62 ..70 C3
Yoredale Ave
Darlington DL3 ....3 B6
17 Leyburn DL8 ....60 D5
York Abbey* YO30 ......233 A3
York Art Gall* YO30 ....233 B3
York Barbican Leisure Ctr
YO10 ....233 C1
York Bridge Rd YO61 ..143 B2
York Castle Mus*
YO1 ....233 C1
York City Football Club
YO30 ....233 A4
York Cl 2 HG5 ....221 C5
York Coll YO24 ....230 E6
York District Hospl
YO30 ....233 B4
York Dungeon* YO1 ..233 B2
York Garth 1 HG5 ....221 C5
York Ind Pk YO17 ....121 C1
York La Flaxton YO60 ..167 E8
Knaresborough HG5 ......221 B5
York Minster* YO1 ..233 B3
York Model Rly*
YO24 ....233 A2
York Pl Harrogate HG2 ..219 E1
Knaresborough HG5 ......221 B5
Scarborough YO11 ......213 A5
York Racecourse (The
Knavesmire)* YO24 ..228 A1
Barlby YO8 ....198 B5
Bilbrough YO23 ....182 B2
Bilton-in-Ainsty with Bickerton
LS22 ....181 A4
Boroughbridge YO51 ....141 B5
37 Burley in Warfedale
LS29 ....176 C1
Cliffe YO8 ....198 E3
Colburn DL9 ....40 E4
Cottam YO25 ....151 B2
Dunnington YO19 ......184 D6
Easingwold YO61 ......143 C7
Flaxby HG5 ....163 B5
Green Hammerton YO26 ..164 B3
Harrogate HG1 ....219 C2
Haxby YO32 ....225 D7
Kilham YO25 ....151 F3

York Rd *continued*
Kirk Hammerton YO26 ..164 C3
Knaresborough HG5 ....221 D5
Leavening YO17 ....147 E2
Long Marston YO26 ....182 A6
Malton YO17 ....215 A3
Middlesbrough TS7 ....7 D6
Naburn YO19 ....191 D8
North Duffield YO8 ....199 A8
Riccall YO19 ....192 A1
Sledmere YO25 ....150 E1
Sowerby YO7 ....211 E1
Stillingfleet YO19 ......191 D4
Strensall YO32 ....167 A6
Sutton-on-the-Forest
YO61 ....144 C2
Tadcaster LS24 ....189 F6
Wetherby LS22 ....180 C3
York YO26 ....227 C3
York Rd Ind Est LS22 ..180 C3
York Rise BD23 ......154 B3
York St
Barnoldswick BB18 ....171 D1
Castleford WF10 ......200 E4
Crathorne TS15 ....24 E6
5 Dunnington YO19 ..184 E7
12 Glusburn BD20 ......187 E8
1 Selby YO8 ....232 C5
York St John, Coll of the Univ
of Leeds YO10 ....229 B3
York Sta YO24 ....233 A2
York Steiner Sch
YO10 ....228 D1
York View DL10 ......209 E8
York Villas WF6 ......200 A1
Yorkdale Cl 4 YO8 ....196 F1
Yorkdale Dr 3 YO8 ..196 F1
Yorkersgate YO17 ....215 B4
Yorkshire Air Mus*
YO41 ....184 F3
Yorkshire Carriage Mus*
DL8 ....58 F3
Yorkshire Coast Coll of F & H
Ed YO12 ....212 B6
Yorkshire Dales Falconry &
Wildlife Conservation Ctr*
LA2 ....131 A5
Yorkshire Dales National Pk
Ctr* BD24 ....131 D3
Yorkshire Lavender*
YO60 ....119 E1
Yorkshire Mus* YO30 ..233 A3
Yorkshire Mus of Farming*
YO19 ....184 D7
Young Bank La YO62 ..70 C2
Young's Ct LS25 ......194 F7
Young's Dr 3 HG3 ....161 B2
Youngs Way 10 DL10 ..41 E4
Ypres Rd DL9 ....209 D1
Yule La YO26 ....164 C3

Z

Zetland Dr DL10 ......209 F8
Zetland St DL6 ......210 D4